AAT Tutorial Text

Unit 18 Auditing

First edition June 1994

ISBN 0 7517 6035 8

British Library Cataloguing-in-Publication Data
A catalogue record for this book
is available from the British Library

Published by

BPP Publishing Limited
Aldine House, Aldine Place
London W12 8AW

Printed in Great Britain by
Ashford Colour Press, Gosport, Hampshire

We are grateful to the Auditing Practices Board for permission to reproduce the draft glossary of auditing terms.

We are also grateful to the Lead Body for Accounting for permission to reproduce extracts from the Standards of Competence for Accounting, and to the Association of Accounting Technicians, the Chartered Association of Certified Accountants, the Chartered Institute of Management Accountants, the Institute of Chartered Secretaries and Administrators and the Institute of Chartered Accountants in England and Wales for permission to reproduce past examination questions in exercises. The suggested solutions to the exercises and test your knowledge questions have been prepared by BPP Publishing Limited.

PREFACE

For years the market leader in targeted study texts and practice and revision material for the AAT qualification, BPP has built on its extensive experience in the field of publishing for professional qualifications by producing material specifically for the AAT's new Education and Training Scheme. The new scheme has accreditation from the National Council for Vocational Qualifications (NCVQ) and it aims to ensure that aspiring accounting technicians at different levels (NVQ/SVQ levels 2, 3 and 4) can demonstrate that they are qualified to do the tasks they perform by the achievement of certain recognised standards of competence.

BPP's Tutorial Text for Unit 18 of the Technician stage *Implementing Auditing Procedures* covers what the student needs to know and how tasks need to be performed, based on the standards of competence for Unit 18, which are set out on Pages (viii) to (xi). Each chapter contains a set of comprehensive exercises to aid the learning process.

BPP's study material has the following features.

- It takes a practical, active approach to teaching, centred on what the student needs to be able to do at the end of the learning and practice process.
- It emphasises the importance of understanding the practical nature of assessment and provides students with plenty of opportunity to practise for such assessments.
- It can be linked into a college course by being used as course material.

BPP Publishing
June 1994

For details of the other BPP titles relevant to your studies for this Unit and for a full list of books in the BPP AAT range, please turn to pages 403 and 404. If you wish to send us your comments on this Tutorial Text, please turn to page 405.

HOW TO USE THIS TUTORIAL TEXT

This Tutorial Text has been designed to help students and lecturers to get to grips as effectively as possible with the standards of competence for Unit 18 *Implementing Auditing Procedures.*

Coverage of the units and elements of competence in the text is indicated on pages (viii) to (xi) by chapter references set against each performance criterion.

As a further guide - and a convenient means of monitoring your progress - we have included a *study checklist* on page (xiii) on which to chart your completion of chapters.

Each chapter of the Tutorial Text is divided into sections and contains:

- learning objectives
- an introduction, indicating how the subject area relates to others in the Unit
- clear, concise topic-by-topic coverage
- exercises to reinforce learning, confirm understanding and stimulate thought
- a 'roundup' of the key points in the chapter
- a test your knowledge quiz.

Exercises

Exercises are provided throughout the text to enable you to check your progress as you work through the text. These come in a large variety of forms: some test your ability to do a calculation just described, others see whether you have taken in the full significance of a piece of information. Some are meant to be discussed with colleagues, friends or fellow students.

A suggested solution is usually given, but sometimes in an abbreviated form to help you avoid the temptation of merely reading the exercise rather than actively engaging your brain. We think it is preferable on the whole to give the solution immediately after the exercise rather than making you hunt for it at the end of the chapter, losing your place and your concentration. Cover up the solution with a piece of paper if you find the temptation to cheat too great!

Chapter roundup and Test your knowledge quiz

At the end of each chapter you will find two boxes. The first is the *Chapter roundup* which summarises key points and arguments and sets out what you should know or be able to do having studied the chapter. The second box is a quiz that serves a number of purposes.

(a) It is an essential part of the chapter roundup and can be glanced over quickly to remind yourself of key issues covered by the chapter.

(b) It is a quiz pure and simple. Try doing it in your head on the train in the morning to revise what you read the night before.

(c) It is a revision tool. When you have finished the last chapter of the Tutorial Text, sit down with pen and paper and try to answer all the questions fully.

As well as the quiz at the end of each chapter, we have include a full length quiz after the last chapter which you can use to give yourself an overall test on auditing, or which you may choose to use for revision purposes.

The test your knowledge quizzes, as well as the exercises in the chapters, are there to help you to *learn* the auditing practices and principles given, before you embark on your portfolio.

Appendix

The appendix to this Tutorial Text discusses some of the skills required for the devolved assessment units at the Technician Level. You will find that only some of it applies to Unit 18, but you should find it useful and illuminating.

Glossary

The Auditing Practices Board draft glossary of auditing terms has been reprinted in this Tutorial Text for your information.

List of cases and Index

The Tutorial Text ends with a comprehensive list of relevant cases and a useful index to help you locate key topics.

Health and safety

You may well have studied Health and Safety at Foundation or Intermediate level. It is covered in the Units 24 - 28 Business Knowledge combined text produced by BPP. However, if you do not have that text but you need to study Health and Safety, we can supply a separate booklet for £2.00 including postage. An order form is included at the end of this Tutorial Text.

A note on pronouns

On occasions in this Study Text, 'he' is used for 'he or she', 'him' for 'him or her' and so forth. Whilst we try to avoid this practice it is sometimes necessary for reasons of style. No prejudice or stereotyping according to sex is intended or assumed.

STANDARDS OF COMPETENCE

The new competence-based Education and Training Scheme of the Association of Accounting Technicians (AAT) is based on an analysis of the work of accounting staff in a wide range of industries and types of organisations. The Standards of Competence for Accounting which students are expected to meet are based on this analysis.

The Standards identify the *key purpose* of the accounting occupation, which is to 'operate, maintain and improve systems to record, plan, monitor and report on the financial activities of an organisation', and a number of *key roles* of the occupation. Each key role is subdivided into *units of competence*. By successfully completing assessments in specified units of competence, students can gain qualifications at NVQ/SVQ levels 2, 3 and 4, which correspond to the AAT Foundation, Intermediate and Technician stages of competence respectively.

Technician stage key roles and units of competence

The key roles and unit titles for the AAT Technician stage (NVQ/SVQ level 4) are set out below.

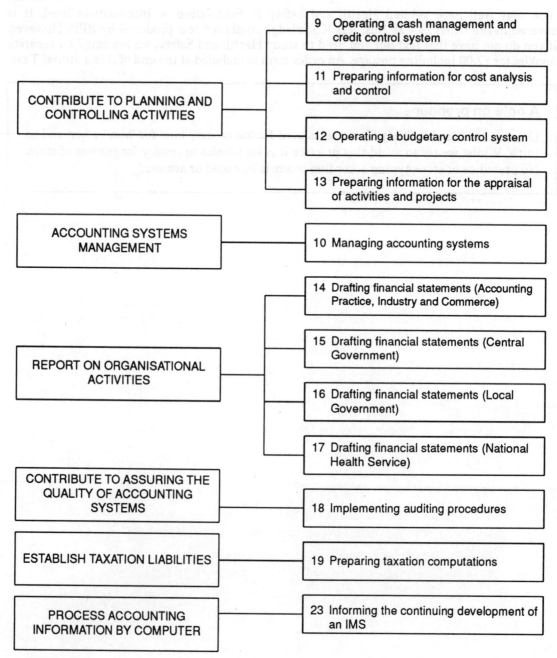

CONTRIBUTE TO PLANNING AND CONTROLLING ACTIVITIES	9 Operating a cash management and credit control system
	11 Preparing information for cost analysis and control
	12 Operating a budgetary control system
	13 Preparing information for the appraisal of activities and projects
ACCOUNTING SYSTEMS MANAGEMENT	10 Managing accounting systems
REPORT ON ORGANISATIONAL ACTIVITIES	14 Drafting financial statements (Accounting Practice, Industry and Commerce)
	15 Drafting financial statements (Central Government)
	16 Drafting financial statements (Local Government)
	17 Drafting financial statements (National Health Service)
CONTRIBUTE TO ASSURING THE QUALITY OF ACCOUNTING SYSTEMS	18 Implementing auditing procedures
ESTABLISH TAXATION LIABILITIES	19 Preparing taxation computations
PROCESS ACCOUNTING INFORMATION BY COMPUTER	23 Informing the continuing development of an IMS

Units and elements of competence

Units of competence are divided into elements of competence describing activities which the individual should be able to perform.

Each element includes a set of *performance criteria* which define what constitutes competent performance. Each element also includes a range statement which defines the situations, contexts, methods etc in which the competence should be displayed.

Supplementing the standards of competence are statements of knowledge and understanding which underpin competent performance of the standards.

The elements of competence for Unit 18 *Implementing Auditing Procedures* are set out below. The performance criteria and range statements for each element are listed first, followed by the knowledge and understanding required for the unit. Performance criteria and areas of knowledge and understanding are cross-referenced below to chapters in the *Tutorial Text.*

Unit 18: Implementing audit procedures

18.1 Contribute to the planning of an audit assignment

Performance criteria		*Chapter(s) in this Text*
1	The proposed audit plan is formulated clearly in consultation with appropriate personnel and submitted for approval by the audit manager	5 - 7
2	Systems under review are ascertained and clearly recorded on appropriate working papers, control objectives are correctly identified, risks assessed, and significant weaknesses in control recorded	5 - 7
3	Appropriate tests are devised in accordance with defined procedures	5 - 7
4	Account balances to be verified and the associated risks are identified	5 - 7
5	Confidentiality and security procedures are followed	2, 6

Range statement

1 Recording and evaluation of systems for routine cash and credit transactions including capital transactions

2 Devising of compliance tests (for evidence of performance of controls) and substantive tests (for verification of account balances and transactions related to cash, bank, debtors, creditors, fixed assets and stock)

18.2 Contribute to the conduct of an audit assignment

Performance criteria		*Chapter(s) in this Text*
1	Tests as specified in the audit plan are correctly conducted and the results properly recorded	8, 10
2	The existence, completeness, ownership and valuation of assets and liabilities is established and supported by appropriate evidence	11 - 14
3	Any matters of an exceptional and/or unusual nature are identified and promptly referred to the audit supervisor	11 - 14
4	Material and significant errors, deficiencies or other variations from standard are identified, recorded and brought to the attention of the audit supervisor	11 - 14
5	Where relevant, the IT environment is examined and assessed	15

6	Discussions with staff operating the system to be audited are conducted in a manner which maintains good relationships between auditing and operational staff	Appendix
7	Confidentiality and security procedures are followed	2

Range statement

1 Type of test:
- Compliance testing for evidence of performance controls
- Substantive testing of account balances and routine cash and credit transactions including capital transactions

2 Assets and liabilities to be verified: cash, bank, stock, debtors, creditors, fixed assets

18.3 Prepare related draft reports

Performance criteria		*Chapter(s) in this Text*
1	Clear, concise draft reports are promptly prepared, and submitted for review and approval	16, 17
2	Conclusions are valid and supported by evidence	16, 17
3	Recommendations are constructive and practicable	16, 17
4	Preliminary conclusions and recommendations are discussed and agreed with the audit supervisor	16, 17
5	Confidentiality and security procedures are follows	2

Range statement

1 Draft reports relating to assignments are prepared for editing and presentation by a responsible authority

2 Systems to be audited: manual and computerised

Note. Competence in this Unit may be displayed in the context of either internal or external audit

Knowledge and understanding

The business environment	*Chapter(s) in this Text*
• A general understanding of the legal duties of auditors: the content of reports, the definition of proper records	1, 4, 17, 18
• A general understanding of the liability of auditors under contract and negligence including liability to third parties. Relevant legislation, relevant auditing standards and guidelines	1,2, 3
Auditing techniques	
• Types of audit: relationship between internal and external audit	1
• Recording and evaluating systems: conventional symbols, flowcharts, ICQs, checklists etc	7
• Testing techniques: physical examination, reperformance, third party confirmation, vouching, documentary evidence, identification of unusual items	8, 9
• Basic sampling techniques in auditing: confidence levels, selection techniques (random numbers, interval sampling, stratified sampling)	9

• The use of audit files and working papers	6
• Auditing techniques in an IT environment	15

Auditing principles and theory

• Principles of control: separation of functions, need for authorisation, recording custody, vouching and verification	7

The organisation

• Background understanding that the accounting system of an organisation are affected by its organisational structure, its administrative systems and procedures and the nature of its business transactions	All
• An understanding of the organisation's systems and knowledge of specific auditing procedures will be required where the competence is assessed in the workplace	All

ASSESSMENT STRUCTURE

Devolved and central assessment

The units of competence in the AAT Education and Training Scheme are assessed by a combination of devolved assessment and central assessment.

Devolved assessment tests students' ability to apply the skills detailed in the various units of competence. Devolved assessment may be carried out by means of:

(a) simulations of workplace activities set by AAT-approved assessors; or
(b) observation in the workplace by AAT-approved assessors.

Central assessments are set and marked by the AAT, and concentrate on testing students' grasp of the knowledge and understanding which underpins units of competence.

The Technician stage

The assessment structure for the Technician stage is as follows.

Central assessment

Units 9, 11, 12, 13, 14, 15, 16, 17, 19.

Each unit can be 'signed off' on completion of the relevant central assessment.

Devolved assessment

Units 10, 18, 23, 25.

Students will prepare an 'accounting portfolio' to evidence their competence in these units. The portfolios will be assessed by assessment centres against certain standards.

Unit 18 Implementing auditing procedures

You will submit a portfolio of work which will include documentary evidence of each of the three elements of the standard. Wherever possible this should be in the form of original documents (for example, the audit programme, ICQs, draft audit report etc). If there are confidentiality issues then it would probably be acceptable for you to write an extended commentary to describe the work undertaken. It is possible that you will face oral questioning, to test your understanding of some areas, such as legal issues and aspects of auditing work which you may not have met in practice. It is likely that you will be asked to expand on or explain certain parts of your portfolio to the assessor.

STUDY CHECKLIST

This page is designed to help you chart your progress through the Tutorial Text. You can tick off each topic as you study. Insert the dates you complete the chapters in the relevant boxes. You will thus ensure that you are on track to complete your study before the final assessment.

		Text chapters *Date completed*
	PART A: THE PLANNING OF AN AUDIT ASSIGNMENT	
1	The nature, purpose and scope of auditing	
2	The regulatory framework of auditing	
3	Auditing requirements of the Companies Act 1985	
4	The audit appointment process	
5	Audit objectives	
6	Audit evidence and documentation	
7	Internal control evaluation	
	PART B: THE CONDUCT OF AN AUDIT ASSIGNMENT	
8	Compliance and substantive testing	
9	Audit sampling	
10	Compliance testing	
11	The balance sheet audit	
12	Stocks and work in progress	
13	Other balance sheet assets	
14	Share capital, reserves and liabilities	
15	Auditing in a computer environment	
	PART C: PREPARATION OF DRAFT REPORTS	
16	Forming an audit judgement	
17	The standard external audit report	
18	Auditors' responsibilities and legal liabilities	
	TEST YOUR KNOWLEDGE QUIZ	

Part A

The planning of an audit assignment

Chapter 1

THE NATURE, PURPOSE AND SCOPE OF AUDITING

This chapter covers the following topics.

1 The purpose of external audit

2 The scope of an external audit

3 The chronology of an audit

Introduction

Part A of the Tutorial Text, as well as covering the planning aspects of the audit, looks at the general structure of the audit and various legalistic aspects of auditing. These areas of knowledge and understanding are fundamental to your ability to carry out an audit in a proper manner. Since the more general theoretical and legal aspects of auditing are unlikely to arise in a practical situation, you may find yourself answering oral questions about such matters.

Throughout this text, however, your main aim should be to consider the application of the theory in this text to *practical auditing.*

1 THE PURPOSE OF EXTERNAL AUDIT

Definition of an audit

1.1 'An "audit" is the independent examination of, and expression of an opinion on, the financial statements of an enterprise.' *(Explanatory foreword, auditing standards and guidelines)*

This succinct definition of the audit is worth some closer examination.

1.2 The auditor is an *independent* person. The external auditor is from outside the enterprise, and certain statutory and professional rules which we shall consider later seek to ensure his independence. As well as following such rules, the auditor should approach his task with an independence of mind. He should not just *be* independent; he should also be *seen to be* independent.

1.3 The audit is an *examination* of the financial statements. The responsibility for preparing the statements lies with the directors, who may delegate the work involved to employees. You may well know that many enterprises, particularly smaller businesses, engage the firm which acts as their auditor to assist with preparing the accounts. The preparation of the accounts and their subsequent audit are two separate functions; ideally, these two tasks should not be carried out by the same staff in the accountancy firm.

1.4 The end product of the auditor's examination is the *expression of an opinion* by the auditor. In most cases, the auditor is required to state whether, in his opinion, the accounts show a 'true and fair view'. The meaning of 'true and fair' will be discussed later.

The role of the auditor

1.5 In the modern commercial environment, it is desirable that businesses which are operated as companies with limited liability should produce accounts which will indicate how successfully they are performing. But the owners of a business require something more than accounts because the managers responsible for preparing them may, either unintentionally or by deliberate manipulation, produce accounts which are misleading. An independent examination of the accounts is needed so that the owners of the business can assess how well management have discharged their stewardship.

1.6 The role of the auditor today has parallels with earlier forms of auditing. The need for an independent 'auditor' was apparent when businesses developed in which there was a division of interests between those who carried out the day-to-day management of the undertaking and those who provided necessary finance but did not participate in management. The auditor can be seen as a mediator between such parties, who have potentially conflicting interests.

1.7 The work of the auditor today is regulated mainly from two sources:

(a) statutes, of which the Companies Act 1985 is the most important;
(b) professional pronouncements on auditing.

Professional pronouncements include the rules of professional conduct issued by the professional bodies to which auditors belong. The most important professional pronouncements on the practice of auditing in the UK are the auditing standards and guidelines which were issued by the Auditing Practices Committee (APC). (The APC was the precursor of the new Auditing Practices Board (APB) which was set up on 1 April 1991.)

1.8 The statutory framework of auditing is discussed in Chapter 2.

2 THE SCOPE OF EXTERNAL AUDIT

Statutory and non-statutory audits

2.1 Audits are required under statute in the case of a large number of undertakings, including the following.

Undertaking	*Principal Act*
Limited companies	Companies Act 1985
Building societies	Building Societies Act 1965
Trade unions and employer associations	Trade Union and Labour Relations Act 1974
Housing Associations	Various acts depending on the legal constitution of the housing association, including: Industrial and Provident Societies Act 1965; Friendly and Industrial and Provident Societies Act 1968; Housing Act 1980; Companies Act 1985; Housing Association Act 1985.
Certain charities	Various acts depending on the status of the charity, including special Acts of Parliament.
Unincorporated investment businesses	Regulations made under the Financial Services Act 1986.

2.2 Non-statutory audits are performed by independent auditors because the owners, proprietors, members, trustees, professional and governing bodies or other interested parties want them, rather than because the law requires them. In consequence, auditing may extend to every type of undertaking which produces accounts, including:

(a) clubs;
(b) charities (assuming that an audit is not in any event statutory);
(c) sole traders; and
(d) partnerships.

2.3 There are also forms of financial statement other than the annual reported figures where those responsible for the statement, or those to whom the statement is made, wish an independent opinion to be expressed as to whether it gives a *true and fair view*. Examples would include:

(a) summaries of sales in support of a statement of royalties payable where goods are sold under licence;

(b) statements of expenditure in support of applications for regional development or other government grants; and

(c) the circulation figures of a newspaper or magazine, used when soliciting advertising.

2.4 In all such audits the auditor must take into account any regulations contained in the internal rules or constitution of the undertaking. Examples of the regulations which the auditor would need to refer to in such assignments would include:

(a) the rules of clubs, societies and charities;

(b) partnership agreements. The audit of a partnership is not normally required by statute and so the auditor must agree with the client what his rights and duties are going to be.

Advantages of the non-statutory audit

2.5 In addition to the advantages common to all forms of audit, including the verification of accounts, recommendations on accounting and control systems and the possible detection of errors and fraud, the audit of the accounts of a partnership may be seen to have the following advantages.

(a) It can provide a means of settling accounts between the partners.

(b) Where audited accounts are available this may make the accounts more acceptable to the Inland Revenue when it comes to agreeing an individual partner's liability to tax. The partners may well wish to take advantage of the auditor's services in the additional role of tax adviser.

(c) The sale of the business or the negotiation of loan or overdraft facilities may be facilitated if the firm is able to produce audited accounts.

(d) An audit on behalf of a 'sleeping partner' is useful since generally such a person will have little other means of checking the accounts of the business, or confirming the share of profits due to him.

2.6 Some of the advantages above will also apply in the audit of the accounts of a sole trader, club or charity.

Do small companies need audits?

2.7 There has been a long-running debate in the UK as to whether small companies need a statutory audit, for the following reasons.

(a) Where the shareholders and managers of a company are the same people the independent audit becomes superfluous and an unnecessary expense.

(b) The close involvement of the manager/owner in the day to day business means that he or she will have a better idea of the state of the company (and not just in historical terms) than an auditor.

2.8 Such arguments, however, fail to recognise the following points.

(a) The accuracy and honesty of the financial statements used as the basis for tax returns is relied upon heavily by the Inland Revenue and Customs and Excise authorities, and the credibility of such statements is supported by the opinion of the independent auditor.

(b) There are other interested parties who may place reliance on financial information. Trade and loan creditors, bankers and potential investors, for example, may be approached by both the large and small company to provide considerable credit or finance. Such users gain assurance from the independent opinion of auditors.

This question is discussed in more detail in Chapter 8.

2.9 The 1975 discussion paper *The Corporate Report* identified seven categories of users of accounts:

(a) the equity investor group, namely existing shareholders and potential investors;

(b) the loan creditor group, for example debenture holders;

(c) the employee group, including both employees and their trade union or staff association representatives;

(d) the analyst-adviser group, such as merchant banks and stockbrokers;

(e) the business contact group, for example customers and trade creditors;

(f) the government, such as the Inland Revenue and Customs and Excise;

(g) the public.

External and internal audit

2.10 We have discussed auditing in particular in the context of the APC definition quoted at the start of Section 1 of this chapter. The definition relates to the work of an *external* auditor, an independent person brought in from outside an organisation to review the accounts prepared by management. It is worthwhile at this stage to mention the different work performed by an *internal auditor* (we will discuss the internal auditor in more detail later).

2.11 The management of an organisation will wish to establish systems to ensure that business activities are carried out efficiently. They will institute clerical, administrative and financial controls. Even in very small businesses with informal accounting systems it will be found that some limited checks and controls are present.

2.12 Larger organisations may appoint full-time staff whose function is to monitor and report on the running of the company's operations. Such internal audit staff would constitute an example of the kind of control mentioned in the previous paragraph. Although some of the work carried out by internal auditors is similar to that performed by external auditors, there are important distinctions between the nature of the two functions.

(a) The external auditor is independent of the organisation, whereas the internal auditor (as an employee) is responsible to the management.

(b) The responsibility of the external auditor is fixed by statute, but the internal auditor's responsibilities are decided by management.

(c) The external auditor reports to the members, not to the management (directors), as in the case of the internal auditor.

(d) The external auditor performs work to enable him to express an opinion on the truth and fairness of the accounts (see Chapter 17). The internal auditor's work may range over many areas and activities, both operational and financial, as determined by management.

2.13 Some external audits will be carried out by sole practitioners who hold a valid practising certificate. More often, on all but the smallest audits, a partnership will be appointed. The reporting partner will take overall responsibility for the conduct of the audit assignment, and will sign the audit report. Although overall responsibility rests with the reporting partner, he may delegate aspects of the audit work to staff of the firm.

2.14 The usual hierarchy of staff on a typical company audit assignment is illustrated in the diagram below.

Reporting partner
|
Audit manager
|
Supervisors/audit seniors
|
Audit assistants.

The expectation gap

2.15 In this text, we are primarily concerned with the role of the external auditor as defined by the auditing profession, and as determined by regulation and by statute law. While studying this, it is worth considering how this role compares with the public's perception of what the auditor's job is.

2.16 There are some common misconceptions in relation to the role of the auditor, even among 'financially aware' people, including the following examples.

(a) Many people think that the auditor reports to the directors of a company, rather than the members.

(b) Some think that a qualified audit report is more favourable than an unqualified audit report, whereas the converse is true (see Chapter 17).

(c) There is a perception that it is the auditor's duty to detect fraud, when in fact the detection of fraud is the responsibility of the directors (see Chapter 18).

2.17 These findings highlight the 'expectation gap' between what auditors do and what people in general think that they do. Add the fact that many 'financially aware' people do not look at the report and accounts of a company they are considering investing in, and you have some sobering facts for the auditor to contemplate!

2.18 Some of the recent large company collapses have emphasised the need to reduce the expectation gap. For this reason, reports such as that of the Cadbury Committee *The financial aspects of corporate governance* have been published. The Cadbury report aims to reduce the expectation gap (at least in relation to quoted companies) by laying out a (voluntary or Stock Exchange imposed) 19 point code of conduct for directors, as well as making suggestions for the content of company reports (and in particular the directors' and auditor's reports). The report is only concerned with public companies, although the principles should be applied to smaller or private companies. The suggestions in the Cadbury Committee report will be mentioned in this text where applicable and, for examination purposes, you should note how topical this area is at present.

Audit firms

2.19 The external auditing market in the UK is dominated by the larger firms of chartered accountants. The vast majority of Stock Exchange listed companies use one of the 'top twenty' chartered firms as their auditors. The market for the audit of small and unlisted companies is spread more widely around smaller firms of accountants as well as the large chartered firms.

2.20 The huge 'Big Five' accountancy partnerships of today, with hundreds of partners each and annual fee income of hundreds of millions of pounds, were created as the result of a series of mergers as well as through organic growth.

Auditing remains a core business of these firms, but there is an increasing tendency to diversify into areas such as management consultancy, special acquisitions and investigations work and corporate finance advice.

3 THE CHRONOLOGY OF AN AUDIT

3.1 The chart on the next page outlines the main stages of an audit that are *normally* followed.

3.2 Before examining each stage in detail it is worth stating the more important duties of the auditor of a limited company. He must satisfy himself that:

(a) proper accounting records have been kept;

(b) the accounts are in agreement with the accounting records;

(c) the accounts have been prepared in accordance with the Act, and relevant SSAPs and FRSs;

(d) the balance sheet shows a true and fair view of the state of the company's affairs and the profit and loss account shows a true and fair view of the results for the period.

The objects of most other audits will be broadly similar.

3.3 It follows that a major part of the auditor's work will involve;

(a) making such tests and enquiries as he considers necessary to form an opinion as to the reliability of the accounting records as a basis for the preparation of accounts;

(b) checking the accounts against the underlying records; and

(c) reviewing the accounts for compliance with the Companies Act and accounting standards.

3.4 We will now look at the various stage identified in the diagram above.

Stage 1

3.5 The first stage in any audit should be to determine its scope and the auditor's general approach. For statutory audits the scope is clearly laid down in the Companies Act as expanded by the standards of current best practice. A letter of engagement will be submitted or confirmed before the start of each annual audit.

3.6 In addition to the letter of engagement it is common for auditors to prepare an audit planning memorandum to be placed on the audit file. The purpose of this memorandum is to provide a record of the major areas to which the auditors attach special significance and to highlight any particular difficulties or points of concern peculiar to the audit client.

3.7 The detailed audit planning which arises from the determination of the scope of work is discussed further in Chapter 5.

Stages 2 - 4

3.8 The objectives of these stages are as follows.

(a) *Stage 2*. To determine the flow of documents and extent of controls in existence. This is very much a fact finding exercise, achieved by discussing the accounting system and document flow with all the relevant departments, including typically, sales, purchases, cash, stock and accounts personnel. It is good practice to make a rough record of the system during this fact finding stage, which will be converted to a formal record at Stage 3 below.

A DIAGRAMMATIC REPRESENTATION OF THE SYSTEMS AUDIT

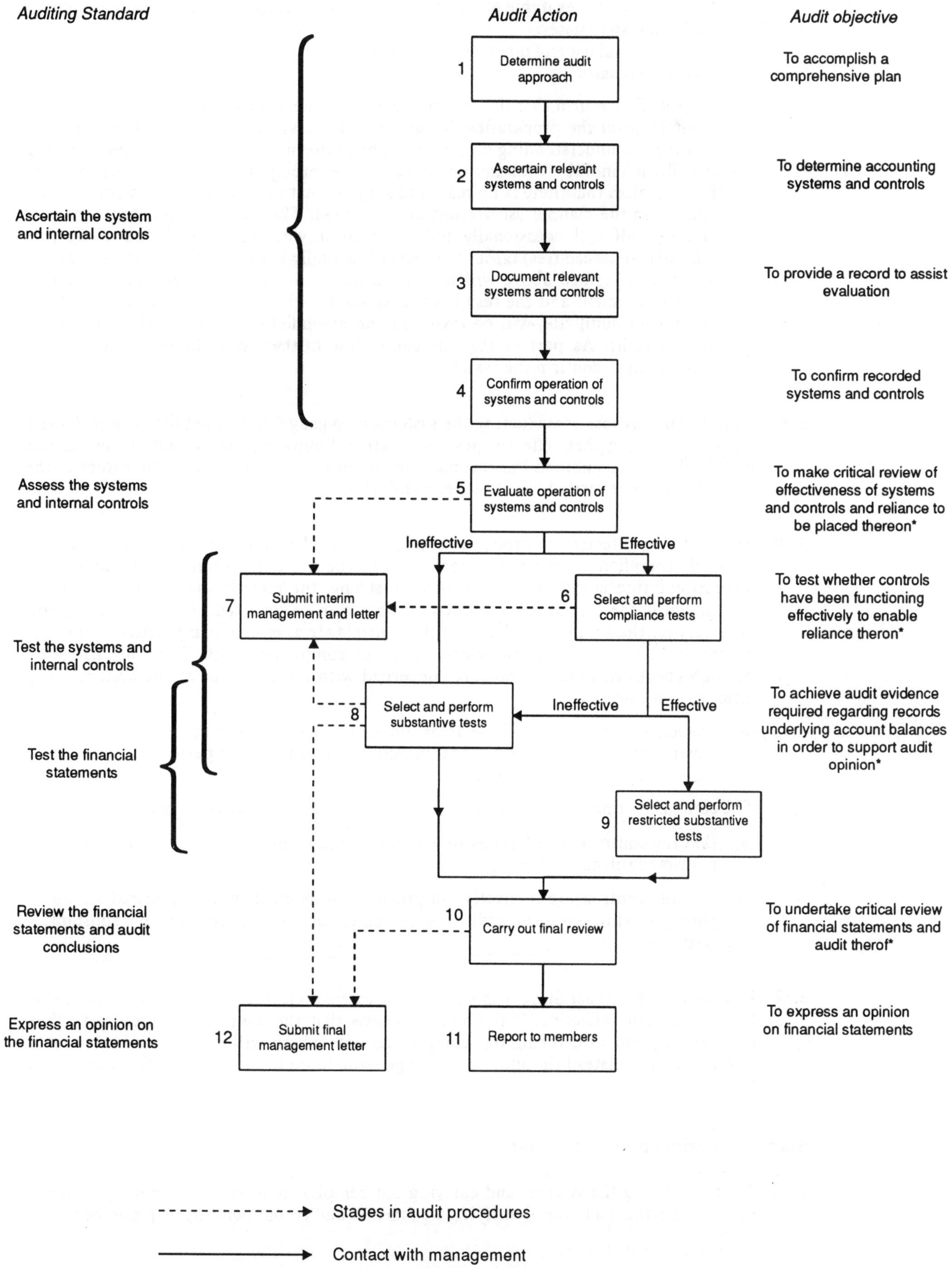

* A secondary objective of this audit action is to recommend to management improvements in systems controls and in accounting procedures and practices

(b) *Stage 3.* To prepare a comprehensive record to facilitate evaluation of the systems. Such a record may include:

(i) charts; for example organisation charts and records of the books of account;
(ii) narrative notes;
(iii) internal control questionnaires (ICQs);
(iv) flowcharts.

(c) *Stage 4.* To confirm that the system recorded is the same as that in operation. After completion of the preparation (or update) of the systems records the auditor will confirm his understanding of the system by performing 'walk-through' tests, tracing literally a handful of transactions of each type through the system. This procedure will establish that there is no reason to suppose that the accounting system does not operate in the manner ascertained and recorded. The need for this check arises as client's staff will occasionally tell the auditor what they should be doing (the established procedures) rather than what is actually being done in practice. Stages 2 and 3 as described above will be carried out in detail at the beginning of a new audit assignment and the results of these stages, which will be incorporated in the permanent audit file, will be reviewed and amended each year at the start of the annual audit. As part of this annual review further walk-through tests will be carried out to confirm the system.

3.9 *Stage 5.* The purpose of evaluating the systems is to gauge their reliability and formulate a basis for testing their effectiveness in practice. Following the evaluation the auditor will be able to recommend improvement to the system and determine the extent of the further tests to be carried out at Stages 6 and 8 below.

3.10 *Stage 6.* Given effective controls, the objective is to select and perform tests designed to establish compliance with the system. One of the most important points underlying modern auditing is that, if the controls are strong, the records should be reliable and consequently the amount of detailed testing can be reduced. It is, however, still necessary for the auditor to check that the controls are as effective in practice as they are on paper. The auditor will, therefore, carry out compliance tests. These are like walk through checks in so far as they are concerned with the workings of the system. They differ in that they:

(a) are concerned only with those areas subject to effective control;
(b) cover a representative sample of transactions throughout the period.

3.11 The conclusion drawn from the results of a compliance test may be either:

(a) that the controls are effective, in which case the auditor will only need to carry out restricted substantive tests; or

(b) that the controls are ineffective in practice, although they had appeared strong on paper, in which case the auditor will need to carry out more extensive substantive tests.

3.12 It should be noted that Stage 6 should only be carried out if the controls are evaluated at Stage 5 as being effective. If the auditor knows that the controls are ineffective then there is no point in carrying out compliance tests which will merely confirm what is already known. Instead the auditor should go straight on to carry out his full substantive tests.

Stage 7. Interim comments letter

3.13 After evaluating the systems and carrying out compliance tests, it is normal practice to send management a letter identifying weaknesses and recommending improvements.

Stages 8 and 9. Substantive tests

3.14 These are not concerned with the workings of the system, but with substantiating the figures in the books of account, and eventually, in the final accounts themselves. The tests are designed for two purposes:

(a) to support the figures in the accounts; and
(b) where errors exist, to assess their effect in monetary terms.

Before designing a substantive test it is essential to consider whether any errors produced by weak systems could lead to material differences. If the answer is 'NO' there is no point in performing a test.

Stages 10 - 12

3.15 (a) *Stage 10.* The aim of the overall review (including an analytical review) is to determine the overall reliability of the accounts by making a critical analysis of content and presentation.

(b) *Stage 11.* The report to the members is the end product of the audit in which the auditors express their opinion of the accounts.

(c) *Stage 12.* The final letter to management is an important non-statutory end product of the audit. Its purpose is to make further suggestions for improvements in the systems and to place on record specific points in connection with the audit and accounts.

3.16 It is worth giving a practical example of the different types of tests discussed above to remove any confusion. If we were considering a material purchases system then the tests might include the following.

(a) *Walk through tests:* taking a few transactions and following them through every stage of the system from material requisition to settlement of the supplier's invoice. This would take place at Stage 4 in the chart.

(b) *Compliance tests:* taking a representative sample of transactions spread over the year, perhaps chosen using random numbers, and testing certain significant controls only. For a purchases system, compliance tests might be applied to the purchase payments routine by checking that purchase invoices have been authorised before payment and checking control account reconciliations to verify the completeness of postings to the purchase ledger.

(c) *Substantive tests:* taking a relatively large sample of transactions, perhaps biased to include high value items, and testing for completeness and accuracy, for example testing calculations of purchase invoices and postings, via the day book, to the purchases account and purchase ledger to confirm validity of purchases figure.

The nature of the systems-based audit

3.17 The chart that we have used to demonstrate the principal stages in the audit process is headed 'A diagrammatic representation of the systems audit'. The phrase 'systems audit' is not to be found in the auditing standards and guidelines, yet it is a well established term. The phrase refers to an audit approach used for many medium and large companies and is based on the assumption that such companies have internal control systems which will constitute a reliable base for the preparation of the accounts. In other words, the characteristic of a systems audit is an examination of internal control.

3.18 Many small companies cannot achieve satisfactory internal control and it is clearly futile for the auditor to seek to rely on controls if they are non-existent or unreliable. For such enterprises the auditor has no alternative but to carry out a so called 'substantive audit' involving extensive verification of transactions, followed by a detailed examination of the balance sheet (verification of assets and liabilities and review of the financial statements).

3.19 The contemporary audit approach to reasonably sophisticated companies is to carry out system-based audit work during the course of the accounting year, followed by balance sheet audit work at the year end. If the systems audit work is successful, and the controls prove reliable, the auditor can use his judgement to reduce the extent of the balance sheet work. In no circumstances will the balance sheet work be eliminated entirely.

Risk-based audits

3.20 In recent years there has been a shift away from the systems-based auditing towards risk-based auditing.

3.21 Risk-based auditing refers to the development of auditing techniques which are responsive to risk factors in an audit. The auditor applies judgement to determine what level of risk pertains to different areas of a client's system and devises appropriate audit tests. This approach should ensure that the greatest audit effort is directed at the riskiest areas, so that the chance of detected errors is improved and time is not spent on unnecessary testing of 'safe' areas.

3.22 The increased use of risk-based auditing reflects two factors.

(a) The growing complexity of the business environment increases the danger of fraud or misstatement; factors such as the developing use of computerised systems and the growing internationalisation of business are relevant here.

(b) Pressures are increasingly exerted by audit clients for the auditor to keep fee levels down while providing an improved level of service.

Risk-based auditing is responsive to both factors. It allows risk areas to be identified, so that the audit can concentrate on the areas presenting the greatest danger of fraud or misstatement. Audit work can be kept to a minimum on low risk areas, making the best use of audit staff time and effort. You should realise that a risk-based audit is merely an extension of the systems-based audit. The stages of the audit shown in the diagram on Page 9 will still be followed in a risk-based audit.

Interim and final audits

3.23 Whereas the split between the systems and balance sheet audits is concerned with the type of work covered, that between the interim and final audits is concerned with timing. The interim audit will normally take place approximately three-quarters of the way through the financial year.

3.24 There is an element of similarity between systems/balance sheet work and interim/final audits in as much as the majority of the systems work will be carried out during the interim audit and the majority of the balance-sheet work during the final audit. However, it will be necessary to complete some systems work during the final audit so that transactions between the time of the interim and final audits do not escape the auditor's attention. Similarly, some substantive testing is very likely to be carried out during the interim (for example verifying fixed assets additions to date).

3.25 With very small audits, it is sometimes considered unnecessary to carry out an interim audit. This means that, as a matter of convenience, all the audit work will be carried out in a single phase, commencing typically a short time before the year-end and continuing into the post balance sheet period.

3.26 At the other extreme, with large companies it is sometimes necessary to carry out more than one interim audit or to adopt a continuous auditing approach. In the case of a continuous audit the auditor's staff will either make several visits to the client spread throughout the year or, as in the case of very large companies, some of the audit staff will be present at the client's premises virtually all the time.

3.27 There are advantages and disadvantages of a continuous audit approach.

(a) *Advantages*

(i) The continual or regular attendance of the auditor may act as a deterrent to fraud.

(ii) Weaknesses in the client's systems are noticed earlier and, if they exist, errors and fraud may be discovered more quickly.

(iii) It is sometimes possible to start the balance sheet work before the year end. This will lead to swifter financial reporting.

(iv) The auditor's work is spread more evenly throughout the year. This will help to relieve the pressures on staff that arise for many audit firms during the first few months of each year.

(b) *Disadvantages*

(i) Audit staff who spend much of their time working on one client may find their independence adversely affected.

(ii) The auditor's frequent (and sometimes unexpected) visits may cause inconvenience to the client.

(iii) It is possible that figures may be altered (innocently or fraudulently) after they have been checked.

(iv) It may be found that outstanding points and queries raised at one visit are forgotten and not followed up at a later stage. Strict control is needed to ensure that this does not happen particularly where the staff assigned to the audit have changed.

Exercise

James Johnson is a sole trader. His business has grown rapidly over the last few years and he has asked John Jameson to become a partner in his firm. Jameson has agreed, but he has said that he will only become a partner if the books are properly audited every year. James asks you why John might want an audit and what advantages it could bring to the business.

Required

Answer the queries raised by James Johnson.

Solution

(a) John might decide that an audit is desirable because James has been in charge alone for a long time. James needs someone who is objective and can understand the accounting records to reassure him that the business is producing the results claimed by James. The other reasons for such a request are reflected in part (b).

(b) The advantages of an audit for a partnership include the following.

(i) Any weaknesses in the accounting system of the business would be highlighted and improvements to the system would be suggested by the auditor. These could save both time and money.

(ii) Arguments between the partners would be avoided if the accounts are checked by an independent auditor. This will be the case particularly in the calculation of the partners' profit shares.

(iii) Third parties who have an interest in the accounts will find them more convincing if they are audited. Examples of such third parties will include Customs & Excise, the Inland Revenue and bankers and other potential sources of finance or credit.

Chapter roundup

- In this chapter, we have:
  - defined the purpose of an audit and set this in the context of the development of auditing;
  - identified statute and professional pronouncements as the two main regulating influences on the external auditor;
  - discussed the use of audited financial statements by various categories of users;
  - outlined briefly the function of internal audit as compared with external audit;
  - discussed the gap in expectations between what auditor do and what others think that auditors do.
- You should memorise the definition of an audit and bear it in mind when studying the remaining chapters of this text: 'An audit is the independent examination of, and expression of an opinion on, the financial statements of an enterprise'.
- We have identified the stages of a typical audit, which should give you an overview of the audit process.

Test your knowledge

1 Define an audit. (see para 1.1)

2 What is the main reason why an audit is considered to be necessary? (1.5)

3 Who is responsible for issuing auditing standards and guidelines? (1.7)

4 List four types of undertaking for which audits are a statutory obligation. (2.1)

5 What advantages is a partnership likely to gain from an audit? (2.5)

6 List the seven categories of people identified in *The Corporate Report* as users of audited information. (2.9)

7 Briefly sketch the typical stages of an audit defined in terms of the audit action required. (Audit diagram, 3.3)

8 What is a 'walk through test'? (3.8(c))

9 Distinguish a compliance test and a walk through test. (3.10)

10 What is a 'systems audit'? (3.17)

11 Distinguish 'interim' and 'final' audits. (3.23)

Chapter 2

THE REGULATORY FRAMEWORK OF AUDITING

This chapter covers the following topics.

1 The structure of the UK accounting and auditing profession

2 Auditing standards and guidelines

3 Setting accounting standards

4 The role of government

5 The EC and international auditing bodies

6 Professional ethics

7 Independence

Introduction

This chapter describes the main bodies and the major factors which govern auditing. The Companies Act 1985 is mentioned in Section 1 as it relates to the eligibility of the auditor. This topic is included here (rather than in Chapter 3 which covers other Companies Act auditing provisions) because of the direct impact of the accountancy bodies on eligibility. Note that, as AAT members cannot become Registered Auditors, all our examples in this Tutorial Text will assume that you are working for a firm of Certified or Chartered Accountants.

You should already be familiar with the accounting standard-setting process from your studies for Unit 14 *Financial Statements*. Of more importance here is the auditing standard-setting process, described in Section 2. This has changed relatively recently, with a new body, the Auditing Practices Board (APB), about to produce a new set of standards.

The more secondary role of the government and European influences are discussed briefly in Sections 4 and 5.

The rest of the chapter deals with ethical issues, the most important of which are independence and confidentiality.

1 THE STRUCTURE OF THE UK ACCOUNTING AND AUDITING PROFESSION

1.1 In the UK there are quite a large number of different accountancy, or accountancy-related, institutes and associations. Here are just a few of them.

The Association of Accounting Technicians (AAT)
The Chartered Association of Certified Accountants (ACCA)
The Institute of Chartered Accountants in England and Wales (ICAEW)
The Chartered Institute of Management Accountants (CIMA)
The Chartered Institute of Public Finance and Accounting (CIPFA).

1.2 All these bodies vary from each other, either moderately or radically, depending on the nature of their aims and the specialisms their members wish to attain. They are all, however, characterised by various attributes common across the accounting profession.

(a) Entrance requirements are stringent, normally involving several years of examinations, often combined with practical experience.

(b) Each body requires its members to follow a strict code of ethics and behaviour and any breach of the code is disciplined.

(c) The accountancy bodies all aim to maintain standards by keeping their members up to date with relevant technical developments.

1.3 The membership of all these bodies is scattered through practice, industry, government and public bodies.

The external auditing profession

1.4 The Companies Act 1985 (as amended by CA 1989) requires an auditor to hold an 'appropriate qualification'. A person holds an 'appropriate qualification' if he or she:

(a) has satisfied existing criteria for appointment as an auditor under CA 1985; or
(b) holds a recognised qualification obtained in the UK; or
(c) holds an approved overseas qualification.

1.5 Those attempting the qualification must attain university entrance level or have at least seven years' professional experience. Recognition is only given once examinations are passed, testing theoretical knowledge which must be applied in practice.

Three years' practical training must be undertaken and at least two years of this must be with a fully qualified auditor. In addition, a 'substantial part' of the training must be in company or similar audit work.

1.6 The EC Eighth Directive forced reciprocity on EC member states, which means that each EC member must recognise nationals of other member states holding the required certificate. Reciprocity with non-member states is at the discretion of the Secretary of State. The Recognised Qualifying Bodies (RQBs) offering the qualification should set up rules to ensure compliance with the Act (see below).

1.7 CA 1989 brought UK legislation into line with the EC Eighth Directive on company law. This Directive requires that persons carrying out statutory audits must be approved by the authorities of EC member states. The authority to give this approval in the UK is delegated to Recognised Supervisory Bodies (RSBs). The new legislation introduced certain rules and procedures which RSBs must embody in their own rules. Under the new Act, an auditor must be a member of an RSB and be eligible under its own rules: special authorisation from the Secretary of State is no longer an option. Registers of individuals and firms eligible to act as auditors have also been set up.

1.8 The four recognised bodies which were given immediately approval when the rules came into force on 1 October 1991, are as follows.

(a) The Chartered Association of Certified Accountants (ACCA).
(b) The Institute of Chartered Accountants in England and Wales (ICAEW).
(c) The Institute of Chartered Accountants of Scotland (ICAS).
(d) The Institute of Chartered Accountants in Ireland (ICAI).

These bodies had been recognised under the previous legislation. Another auditing body, the Association of Authorised Public Accountants (AAPA), was also recognised recently, the first new auditing body in 43 years.

1.9 The RSBs are required to have rules to ensure that persons eligible for appointment as a company auditor are either (4(1), Sch 11, CA 1989):

(a) individuals holding an appropriate qualification; or
(b) firms controlled by qualified persons.

1.10 A number of other requirements concern the procedures which RSBs must follow to maintain the competence of members. Under CA 1989, the RSB's rules must:

(a) ensure that only 'fit and proper' persons are appointed as company auditors (6, Sch 11);

(b) ensure that company audit work is conducted properly and with 'professional integrity' (7, Sch 11);

(c) include rules as to the technical standards of company audit work (8, Sch 11) (presumably this means auditing standards and guidelines, although the Act does not state this);

(d) ensure that eligible persons maintain an 'appropriate level of competence' (9, Sch 11);

(e) ensure that all firms eligible under its rules have arrangements to prevent:

  (i) individuals not holding an appropriate qualification; and

  (ii) persons who are not members of the firm from being able to exert influence over an audit which would be likely to affect the independence or integrity of the audit (7, Sch 11).

1.11 The RSB's rules must provide for adequate monitoring and enforcement of compliance with its rules and must (10-13, Sch 11) include provisions relating to:

(a) admission and expulsion of members;
(b) investigation of complaints against members;
(c) compulsory professional indemnity insurance.

1.12 Professional qualifications, which will be prerequisites for membership of an RSB, will be offered by Recognised Qualifying Bodies (RQBs) approved by the Secretary of State.

1.13 Up-to-date lists of approved auditors and their names and addresses are maintained by the RSBs. This register of auditors must be made available to the public.

1.14 The RSBs and their officers, are exempt from damages in respect of any action arising out of the exercise of their statutory duties, unless they have acted in bad faith.

1.15 Membership of an RSB is the main prerequisite for eligibility as an auditor. CA 1989 allows a 'firm' to be appointed as a company auditor. A firm may be either a body corporate (such as a company) or a partnership. The eligibility of companies to act as auditors is new for the UK, although in some other EC countries, companies may already act as auditors. Under the old 1985 Act, technically only individuals could act as auditors. Although in practice auditors generally signed audit reports in the name of their partnership, the partnership as such was not eligible to act as auditor. The 1989 Act removed this anomaly by allowing partnerships to act as auditors.

1.16 Under the Companies Act 1985, a person is ineligible for appointment as a company auditor if he or she is:

(a) an officer or employee of the company;

(b) a partner or employee of such a person;

(c) a partnership in which such a person is a partner;

(d) ineligible by virtue of (a), (b) or (c) for appointment as auditor of any parent or subsidiary undertaking or a subsidiary undertaking of any parent undertaking of the company; or

(e) there exists between him or her or any associate (or his or hers) and the company (or company as referred to in (d) above) a connection of any description as may be specified in regulations laid down by Secretary of State.

1.17 The legislation does not disqualify the following from being an auditor of a limited company:

(a) a shareholder of the company;

(b) a debtor or creditor of the company;

(c) a close relative (such as a husband, wife, son or daughter) of an officer or employee of the company.

1.18 However, the regulations of the accountancy bodies applying to their own members are stricter than statute in this respect.

1.19 Under the Companies Act 1985, a person may also be ineligible on the grounds of 'lack of independence'; the definition of lack of independence is to be determined by statutory instrument following consultation with the professional bodies.

1.20 Under s 389 CA 1985, if during their term of office a company auditor becomes ineligible for appointment to the office, he must vacate office and give notice in writing to the company. A person who acts as company auditor when he is ineligible is guilty of an offence and is liable to a fine which can be imposed in respect of each day on which continued contravention occurs. If an audit is carried out by an auditor who was ineligible, the DTI may require a second audit, or a review of the first audit, to be conducted by an eligible person. The company must comply with such a requirement within 21 days. In such a case, the company may recover the costs of complying from the ineligible auditor.

Exercise 1

Outline the role of the Recognised Supervisory Bodies (RSBs).

Solution

See Paragraphs 1.7 - 1.15.

Supervisory and monitoring roles

1.21 The requirement mentioned in Paragraph 1.10 that RSB's should ensure that company audit work is conducted properly and so on, has proved most onerous. To visit each registered auditor for monitoring purposes will take some considerable time, even to complete one cycle (ie visit all of them once). These monitoring visits are time-consuming and expensive, but they are required by law.

1.22 To satisfy the requirements of the DTI for effective monitoring, RSBs must implement procedures for inspecting their registered auditors on a regular basis. The Joint Monitoring Unit (JMU) was set up for this purpose by the Institute of Chartered Accountants in England and Wales, the Institute of Chartered Accountants in Scotland and the Irish Institute.

1.23 All registered auditing firms will be inspected. The frequency of inspection will depend on the number of partners, number of offices and number of listed company audits (these factors are also reflected in the size of annual registration fees payable). The length of JMU inspections depends on the size of the firm and may be combined with Financial Services Act 1986 based inspections where necessary.

1.24 The inspection is usually preceded by a pre-visit questionnaire (PVQ), received eight to twelve weeks before the visit, and required to be returned within 21 days of receipt. This helps with the planning for the visit and allows the inspectors to ask for further information in advance. The PVQ will require a great deal of supplementary material to be returned along with the PVQ form, including:

(a) organisation charts for the firm and for the audit section;

(b) the firm's audit manual or, for small firms, standard procedures and forms in use;

(c) the firm's quality control procedures and its specimen forms;

(d) schedules detailing the firm's internal monitoring over the previous 12 months;

(e) written procedures covering recruitment, training, dissemination of technical information and consultation arrangements on technical and ethical matters;

(f) qualifications and experience of personnel with computer expertise;

(g) analysis of clients in special categories which might create high audit risk (to be reconciled to the firm's initial application form);

(h) analysis of audit fee income per partner, indicating for each partner, *inter alia*, the amount of his/her highest audit fee and lowest audit cost, and any non-audit services also provided to the clients in question;

(i) reconciliation of the firm's total fee income and total audit fee income respectively to its initial application form;

(j) for small firms, details of external consultation and review arrangements in force.

1.25 The approach during the visit is either substantive or compliance based, depending on the JMU's assessment of the firm's internal monitoring systems, which is itself based on the initial application and the PVQ information. Both types of inspection involve examination of audit files selected at random, and also files from categories known to the high risk. The substantive approach obviously entails a larger sample size and in each case it seeks to verify:

(a) that planning, recording, supervision and review work have been satisfactorily carried out; and

(b) that the work recorded, including appropriate consultation, provides a sound basis for the audit opinion.

1.26 The compliance approach is designed to test the efficiency of the firm's partners and staff. Inspectors also attend an internal peer review, assess the critical criteria against which the audit in question is judged, and the effectiveness with which the necessary remedial steps are pursued.

1.27 Each inspection ends with an interview at which detailed findings are discussed and any necessary recommendations are issued. Notes are taken and subsequently copied to the JMU who, once satisfied that they adequately reflect what was agreed, will retain them as its record. If necessary, these notes can be passed to the registration authorities for consideration of any further action.

1.28 The problems with such monitoring include the fact that the number of registered auditors which need to be visited is far too great in comparison with the resources available to the JMU. This means that some auditors may not be inspected for many years. It may be that the moves to abandon the audit of small companies will relieve this situation as some sole practitioners give up their registration as their clients no longer need an audit.

2 AUDITING STANDARDS AND GUIDELINES

2.1 It is generally accepted that the statutory audit in the UK, as we know it today, effectively came into being with the Companies Act 1948. From that date the UK profession, led by the large international chartered firms, has been steadily developing sophisticated and increasingly cost-effective audit techniques. It is fair to say that the inspiration for many of these UK techniques was US methodology; their codification of auditing standards was achieved much earlier than ours.

2.2 There have been recent changes in the means by which auditing standards are set. Until recently, developing auditing standards and guidelines were the work of the Auditing Practices Committee (APC) which was essentially made up of auditors, although it also drew some members from other backgrounds such as the legal profession, government and from industry and commerce.

2.3 One of the criticisms of this system was that it is not satisfactory for auditing standards and guidelines to be produced by a committee made up almost solely of representatives of the main professional accounting bodies. Another problem was the APC's lack of authority, stemming from the fact that auditing standards and guidelines required the approval of all the professional accounting bodies before they could be issued. The change also follows intense debate about the responsibility of auditors following a number of major company collapses.

The APB and Statements of Auditing Standards (SASs)

2.4 On 1 April 1991, a new Auditing Practices Board (APB) was set up to replace the APC. This new body:

(a) is empowered to issue auditing standards in its own right;

(b) has strong representation from outside the accounting profession;

(c) has a larger budget than the APC which it replaces;

(d) has a commitment to openness, with agenda papers being circulated to interested parties, and an annual report being published.

2.5 The APB issued a document in May 1993 entitled *The scope and authority of APB pronouncements*. The APB will make three categories of pronouncement:

(a) Statements of Auditing Standards (SASs);
(b) Practice Notes; and
(c) Bulletins.

2.6 The scope of SASs is given as follows.

> 'SASs contain basic principles and essential procedures ('Auditing Standards') which are indicated by bold type and with which auditors are required to comply, except where otherwise stated in the SAS concerned, in the conduct of any audit of financial statements. SASs are also published containing Auditing Standards which apply, as stated therein, to other audits and related services, provided by auditors.
>
> In addition to SASs of general application the APB issues SASs containing additional Auditing Standards applicable to the conduct of audits of certain types of entities, such as those within specialised industries.
>
> SASs also include explanatory and other material which, rather than being prescriptive, is designed to assist auditors in interpreting and applying Auditing Standards. Auditing Standards need not be applied to matters whose effect is in the auditors' judgement not material.'

2.7 The authority of SASs is given in the document.

> 'Auditors who do not comply with Auditing Standards when performing company or other audits in Great Britain make themselves liable to regulatory action by the RSB with whom they are registered and which may include the withdrawal of registration and hence of eligibility to perform company audits.'

2.8 Practice Notes will be issued 'to assist auditors in applying Auditing Standards of general application to particular circumstances and industries'.

2.9 Bulletins will be issued 'to provide auditors with timely guidance on new or emerging issues'.

2.10 Practice Notes and Bulletins are persuasive rather than prescriptive, but they indicate good practice and have a similar status to the explanatory material in SASs. Both Practice Notes and Bulletins may be included in later SASs.

2.11 In April 1993 the APB published the planned structure of its proposed revision of auditing standards and guidelines. The proposed structure is reproduced here, and the intention is gradually to phase out the old standards and guidelines as new Statements of Auditing Standards are produced.

PROPOSED STRUCTURE OF STATEMENTS OF AUDITING STANDARDS

		Existing equivalent pronouncement [2]
Series 001/099	*Introductory matters*	
010	Scope and authority of APB pronouncements**[1]	3.0/ED
Series 100/199	*Responsibility*	
100	Objective and basic principles*	3.101
110	Fraud and error*	3.418
120	Compliance of law and regulations [1]	ED
130	Going concern*	3.410
140	Engagement letters	3.406
150	Subsequent events*	3.402
160	Other information in documents containing audited financial statements*	3.411
170	Comparative figures	3.403
Series 200/299	*Planning, controlling and recording*	
200	Planning*	3.201
210	Knowledge of the business	-
220	Materiality and audit risk*	-
230	Documentation*	3.201
240	Quality control for audit work*	3.201/3.409
Series 300/399	*Accounting systems and internal control*	
300	Audit risk assessment*	3.202/3.204
310	Auditing in an information system environment	3.407
Series 400/499	*Evidence*	
400	Audit evidence*	3.203
410	Analytical procedures*	3.417
420	Audit of accounting estimates*	-
430	Audit sampling*	ED
440	Management representations*	3.404
450	Opening balances and comparatives	3.403
460	Related parties	-
470	Overall review of financial statements*	3.205
Series 500/599	*Using the work of others*	
500	Considering the work of internal audit*	3.408
510	The relationship between principle auditors and other auditors*	3.415
520	Using the work of an expert*	3.413

		Existing equivalent pronouncement [2]
Series 600/699	*Reporting*	
600	The auditors' report on financial statements [1**]	3.102/ED
610	Reports to management	3.414
620	The auditors' right and duty to report to regulators in the financial sector	
Series 700/799	*Engagements other than audits of financial statements*	
Series 800/899	*Particular industries and sectors*	
-	*Glossary of terms* [3]	

Notes

1 Development of these pronouncements is being undertaken by separate APB task forces, rather than as part of the revision project.

2 Some existing pronouncements will be replaced by more than one SAS; conversely, others will be dealt with as part of a different topic.

Where the existing equivalent pronouncement is listed as ED, this indicates the existence of an exposure draft issued by the APB (or by its predecessor body, the Auditing Practices Committee) which has not yet been finalised.

In cases where there is no existing equivalent pronouncement, the subject matter may be referred to in other pronouncements (for example, by the IAPC).

3 A glossary of terms is being developed for publication in conjunction with the final batch of SASs to be prepared as part of this revisions project (see Appendix at the end of this Tutorial Text).

* Produced in exposure draft (at June 1994).

** Produced as a full standard (at June 1994).

2.12 The APB stated that priority would be given to auditing standards and guidelines of 'general application'. Specialised industry guidelines will be reviewed and updated separately. The APB published exposure drafts relating to all SASs of general application by 31 October 1993.

2.13 When the current exposure drafts of SASs marked above become full standards, many of the existing guidelines will be withdrawn.

2.14 You are not required to be familiar with exposure drafts of SASs, but you should be aware of these potential standards. For Unit 18, you should be more concerned with existing guidelines (discussed below) rather than these exposure drafts.

2.15 The APB has excluded certain guidelines from the revision project. These will be reviewed and updated separately:

(a) 3.401 Bank reports for audit purposes;
(b) 3.405 Attendance at stocktaking;
(c) 3.412 Prospectuses and the reporting accountant;
(d) 3.503 Reports by auditors under company legislation in the United Kingdom;
(e) 3.506 The auditors' statement on the summary financial statement.

2.16 In relation to (d) and (e) above, the new SAS *Auditors' report on financial statements* includes references to some of the legal requirements relating to reports by auditors under company legislation in the UK. However, it does not cover all the reports considered in the guideline dealing with reports by auditors under company legislation.

2.17 The APB has also decided to withdraw these auditing guidelines, effective 31 March 1993:

(a) 3.505 Audit reports and information on the effects of changing prices; and
(b) 3.416 Applicability to the public sector of auditing standards and guidelines.

The APC and auditing standards and guidelines

2.18 We should also clarify the scope and authority of the current auditing standards and guidelines as determined by the APC, because they have been adopted by the APB until such time as they are amended or superseded.

> '*Auditing Standards*
>
> Auditing Standards prescribe the basic principles and practices which members of the Accountancy Bodies are expected to follow in the conduct of an audit. Auditing Standards apply whenever an audit is carried out by them.
>
> Members of the Accountancy Bodies who assume responsibility as auditors are expected to observe Auditing Standards. Apparent failures by members to observe Auditing Standards may be enquired into by the appropriate committees established by the Councils of the Accountancy Bodies, and disciplinary action may result.
>
> It would be impracticable to establish a code of rules sufficiently elaborate to cater for all situations and circumstances which an auditor might encounter. Such a code could not provide for innovations in business and financial practice and might hinder necessary development and experiment in auditing practice. In the observance of Auditing Standards, therefore, the auditor must exercise his judgement in determining both the auditing procedures necessary in the circumstances to afford a reasonable basis for his opinion and the wording of his report.
>
> Explanatory notes added to the text of Auditing Standards have the same scope and authority as Auditing Guidelines.'
>
> '*Auditing Guidelines*
>
> Auditing Guidelines are intended to assist the auditor by giving guidance on:
>
> (a) procedures by which Auditing Standards may be applied;
>
> (b) the application of Auditing Standards to specific items appearing in the financial statements of enterprises;
>
> (c) the application of Auditing Standards to particular sectors, industries and service organisations;
>
> (d) specific types of reporting engagement other than audits; and
>
> (e) other matters relating to the proper performance of audit work.
>
> Auditing Guidelines are intended to be persuasive. They are not prescriptive and there may be occasions when the auditor considers it appropriate to depart from the guidance given. However, they should normally be followed, and the auditor should be prepared to explain departures if called upon to do so.'
>
> '*Auditing Standards and Guidelines and the law*
>
> Members are advised that a court of law may, when considering the adequacy of the work of an auditor, take into account any pronouncements or publications which it thinks may be indicative of good practice. Auditing Standards and Guidelines are likely to be so regarded.'

Exercise 2

Auditors frequently refer to the terms 'standards' and 'procedures'. The term 'standards' deals with the quality of the auditors' work, whilst 'procedures' relates to the techniques of audit testing used in trying to gather audit evidence.

Required

Explain the scope and purpose of the auditing standards and auditing guidelines.

Solution

Auditing standards

These prescribe the basic principles and practices which members are expected to follow in the conduct of an audit. Auditing standards will apply whenever an audit is carried out.

The APC acknowledged that it would be impractical to establish a code of rules sufficiently elaborate to cater for all situations and circumstances which an auditor might encounter. Such a code could not provide for innovations in business and financial practice and might hinder necessary development and experiment in auditing practice. In the observance of auditing standards it is therefore necessary for an auditor to exercise his judgement in determining both the auditing procedures necessary in the circumstances to afford a reasonable basis for his opinion and the wording of his report.

Auditing guidelines

These are intended to give guidance on:

(a) procedures by which auditing standards may be applied;

(b) the application of the auditing standards to specific items appearing in the financial statements of enterprises;

(c) the application of auditing standards to particular sectors, industries and organisations;

(d) special types of reporting engagement; and

(e) other matters relating to the proper performance of all audit work.

Auditing guidelines do not prescribe basic principles and practices. They are intended to be persuasive rather than prescriptive.

The APC advised members that a court of law may, when considering the adequacy of the work of an auditor, take into account any pronouncements or publications which it thinks may be indicative of good practice and that auditing standards and guidelines are likely to be so regarded.

The new APB document on the scope and authority of auditing standards and related documents gives approximately the same authority to the new Statements of Auditing Standards (SASs). The SASs must be complied with during any company or other audit. Practice Notes and Bulletins give explanatory up to date information, but they are not prescriptive.

2.19 Until recently there were two APC auditing standards in issue, *The auditor's operational standard* and *The audit report* standard. The audit report is, to a large extent, the 'end product' of the auditor's work and this standard has now been replaced by a new APB SAS. We shall postpone further discussion of the reporting standard until we have thoroughly covered the audit in operation.

2.20 The matters dealt with in *The auditor's operational standard* are the cornerstones of auditing. Here is the full text.

'The auditor's operational standard (Issued April 1980)

This Auditing Standard should be read in conjunction with the Explanatory Foreword to Auditing Standards and Guidelines. General guidance on procedures by which this auditing standard may be complied with are given in auditing guidelines:

Planning, controlling and recording
Accounting systems
Audit evidence
Internal controls
Review of financial statements

1 This auditing standard applies whenever an audit is carried out.

Planning, controlling and recording

2 The auditor should adequately plan, control and record his work.

Accounting systems

3 The auditor should ascertain the enterprise's system of recording and processing transactions and assess its adequacy as a basis for the preparation of financial statements.

Audit evidence

4 The auditor should obtain relevant and reliable audit evidence sufficient to enable him to draw reasonable conclusions therefrom.

Internal controls

5 If the auditor wishes to place reliance on any internal controls, he should ascertain and evaluate those controls and perform compliance tests on their operation.

Review of financial statements

6 The auditor should carry out such a review of the financial statements as is sufficient, in conjunction with the conclusions drawn from the other audit evidence obtained, to give him a reasonable basis for his opinion on the financial statements.

Effective date

7 This auditing standard is effective for the audit of financial statements relating to accounting periods starting on or after 1 April 1980.'

2.21 Each of the key paragraphs 2 to 6 has an associated guideline, as indicated in the introduction to the standard. We will look at each of these guidelines in detail in the following chapters.

2.22 Auditing standards and guidelines in issue at the time of writing (June 1994) are summarised below.

AUDITING STANDARDS AND GUIDELINES

Number	*Title*	*Date of issue/revision*
	Explanatory foreword	January 1989
	Auditing standards	
3.101	The auditor's operational standard	April 1980
3.102	The audit report (now superseded)	March 1989
	Operational guidelines	
3.201	Planning, controlling and recording	April 1980
3.202	Accounting systems	"
3.203	Audit evidence	"
3.204	Internal controls	"
3.205	Review of financial statements	"
	Detailed operational guidelines	
3.401	Bank reports for audit purposes	June 1982
3.402	Events after the balance sheet date	November 1982
3.403	Amounts derived from the preceding financial statements	November 1982
3.404	Representations by management	July 1983
3.405	Attendance at stocktaking	October 1983
3.406	Engagement letters	May 1984
3.407	Auditing in a computer environment	June 1984
3.408	Reliance on internal audit	November 1984
3.409	Quality control	January 1985
3.410	The auditor's considerations in respect of going concern	August 1985
3.411	Financial information issued with audited financial statements	September 1985
3.412	Prospectuses and the reporting accountant	February 1986
3.413	Reliance on other specialists	May 1986
3.414	Reports to management	May 1986
3.415	Group financial statements - reliance on the work of other auditors	December 1986

Number	Title	Date of issue/revision
	Detailed operational guidelines (cont'd)	
3.416	Applicability to the public sector of auditing standards and guidelines (withdrawn 31.3.93)	July 1987
3.417	Analytical review	April 1988
3.418	The auditor's responsibility in relation to fraud, other irregularities and errors	April 1990
	Reporting guidelines	
3.503	Reports by auditors under company legislation in the UK	February 1991
3.505	Audit reports and information on the effects of changing prices (withdrawn 31.3.93)	October 1989
3.506	The auditor's statement on the summary financial statement	May 1991
	Industry guidelines	
3.301	Charities	October 1981
3.302	Building societies	March 1989
3.303	Trade unions and employers' associations	August 1984
3.304	Housing associations	November 1984
3.305	Impact of regulations on public sector audits	March 1988
3.306	Pension schemes in the United Kingdom	November 1988
3.307	Banks in the United Kingdom	March 1989
3.308	Guidance for internal auditors	June 1990
3.309	Communication between auditors and regulators under Section 109 and 108(1)(q) of FSA 1986	July 1990
3.310	General business insurers in the United Kingdom	March 1991
3.311	Life insurers in the United Kingdom	October 1991

3 SETTING ACCOUNTING STANDARDS

3.1 Some accounting principles (such as valuation of assets) are embodied in legislation, while others (for example current cost accounting, accounting for contingencies) are regulated by accounting standards. An accounting standard is a rule or set of rules which prescribes the method (or methods) by which accounts should be prepared and presented. These 'working regulations' are issued by a national or international body of the accountancy profession. In the UK, such standards were called Statements of Standard Accounting Practice (SSAPs) and were, until 31 July 1990, formulated by the Accounting Standards Committee (ASC). From now on, SSAPs will be replaced by Financial Reporting Standards (FRSs), the first five of which have already come into force.

3.2 The ASC (originally the Accounting Standards Steering Committee) was set up in 1970 as a joint committee of members of the six major accountancy bodies in Britain, the constituent members of the Consultative Committee of Accountancy Bodies (CCAB).

3.3 The ASC's terms of reference were:

(a) to review the standard of financial accounting and reporting;

(b) to publish consultative documents with a view to developing accounting standards;

(c) to propose accounting standards to the Councils of the six governing bodies of the ASC;

(d) to consult with representatives of industry, commerce, government, finance and other interested parties about such standards.

Consultation with these interest groups was not always satisfactory and some SSAPs have been criticised for being unrealistic or 'unfair'.

3.4 Once issued, SSAPs are intended to apply to all financial accounts which are 'intended to give a true and fair view of the financial position and profit and loss'. This includes overseas subsidiaries and associated companies incorporated in UK group accounts. A standard may, however, specify the 'scope' of its application. For example, SSAP 3 applies only to the audited accounts of listed companies (companies whose shares are listed on the Stock Exchange).

3.5 Although there are some areas where the contents of SSAPs overlap with provisions of company law, standard are detailed working regulations within the framework of government legislation, and they cover areas in which the law is silent. The accountancy profession prefers to make its own rules for self-regulation, rather than to have rules imposed by law. In addition, standards are not intended to override exemptions from disclosure which are allowed to special cases of companies by law.

3.6 The procedure used by the ASC was simply to issue the standards as Exposure Drafts (EDs) before gaining consensus for implementation of the standard.

3.7 In 1987 the CCAB established a review committee under the chairmanship of Sir Ronald Dearing, former chairman and chief executive of the Post Office and its report *The making of accounting standards* was published in September 1988. Its conclusions were, in essence, that the arrangements then in operation, where 21 unpaid ASC members met for a half-day once a month to discuss new standards, were no longer adequate to produce timely and authoritative pronouncements.

3.8 The Dearing committee proposed the following new arrangements, which were put into effect on 1 August 1990.

(a) The ASC was disbanded.

(b) A Financial Reporting Council (FRC) has been created to cover a wide constituency of interest at a high level. It will guide the standard setting body on policy and see that its work is properly financed. It will also fund and oversee the Review Panel. It has about 25 members drawn from users, preparers and auditors of accounts.

(c) The task of devising accounting standards is now carried out by a newly constituted Accounting Standards Board (ASB), with a full-time chairman and technical director. A majority of two thirds of the Board is required to approve a new standard. Until now, each new standard has had to be approved by the Councils of each of the six CCAB bodies separately before it could be published. The new ASB now issues standards itself on its own authority. The ASB will have to work hard to secure widespread support for its proposals and so it will liaise with the CCAB bodies and industrial groupings like the CBI. However, it will be able to produce standards more quickly than the ASC and it has the great advantage of legal backing.

(d) An offshoot of the ASB is the Urgent Issues Task Force (UITF), whose function is 'to tackle urgent matters not covered by existing standards, and for which, given the urgency, the normal standard-setting process would not be practicable' (Sir Ron Dearing).

(e) The Review Panel, chaired by a barrister, 'will be concerned with the examination and questioning of departures from accounting standards by large companies.' It has about 15 members from which smaller panels will be formed to tackle cases as they arise. The Review Panel is alerted to most cases for investigation by the results of the new CA 1985 requirement that companies must include in the notes to the accounts a statement that they have been prepared in accordance with applicable accounting standards or alternatively, giving details of material departures from those standards, with reasons. Although it is expected that most such referrals would be resolved by discussion, the Panel (and the Secretary of State for Trade and Industry) have the power to apply to the court for revision of the accounts, with all costs potentially payable (if the court action is successful) by the company's directors. The auditors may also be disciplined if the audit report on the defective accounts was not qualified with respect to the departure from standards. Revised accounts, whether prepared voluntarily or under duress, will have to be circulated to all persons likely to rely on the previous accounts.

3.9 The ASB's consultative process leads to the setting of Financial Reporting Standards (FRSs). To produce an FRS, first a working Draft for Discussion (DD) is published to get feedback from people closely involved with or with a direct interest in the standard setting process. The DD, as a result of this process, is converted into a Financial Reporting Exposure Draft (FRED), which has the same status as an ED had when the ASC was in existence. Candidates should be aware of the contents of FRSs and FREDs published by the ASB publishes other documents as Exposure Drafts, for example, chapters of the *Statement of Principles*.

Exercise 3

Outline the role of:

(a) the Accounting Standards Board;
(b) the Review Panel; and
(c) the Urgent Issues Task Force.

Solution

See Paragraph 3.8.

The relationship between auditing and accounting

3.10 Auditing and accounting are closely connected at many levels. In particular, there are some formal connections which arise between accounting (in a financial reporting sense) and auditing.

(a) The auditor of a company must report if a company has not followed an accounting standard in preparing its accounts.

(b) As we will see in a later chapter, when accounting standards are implemented in company accounts, it will give comfort that the accounts show a true and fair view. This will be very important to the auditor.

3.11 There are occasions where one person will act as both accountant and auditor. Many small or sole practitioners will prepare their clients accounts at the same time as auditing them. Care must be taken to document all the audit work, so it is not lost in the mechanics of accounting.

4 THE ROLE OF GOVERNMENT

4.1 As we have already seen, auditing is a self-regulating profession. The current regime was, however, instituted by statute (CA 1989), and in such instances the government has most effect on the auditing profession.

4.2 The CA 1989 was an instance where the UK government was choosing the best way to implement EC policy, in this case the Eighth Directive. Such EC pronouncements cannot simply appear as part of UK legislation; it is necessary for the government to find the right way of fitting it into the current UK statutory system.

4.3 The government will also introduce legislation on its own behalf, for example the legislation that requires external auditors to report to an external regulator (such as the Securities and Investments Board) under certain circumstances. Legislation was required in this kind of situation to give the auditor protection for his breach of confidentiality. The government has been involved in other aspects of auditing.

4.4 It is not unusual to find government officials sitting as observers at meetings, such as those of the APB.

4.5 The DTI will appoint inspectors to investigate company collapses or frauds and the auditors have often been criticised after such investigations, although never prosecuted.

4.6 The government has canvassed opinion from a wide range of bodies as to whether the 'small company' statutory audit should be abolished. Until recently nothing had came of the debate on this topic, which has been going on for about 20 years. In the last Budget, however, it was announced that some small companies could be exempted from the statutory audit (limits to be decided).

4.7 The Office of Fair Trading (OFT) has investigated the auditing and accounting professions for restrictive practices.

4.8 The DTI published a consultation document in 1986 called *Regulation of the auditing profession*. This was intended to spark a discussion about controversial aspects of auditing. It included a proposed ban on auditing firms offering non-audit services to clients. These proposals were not accepted, but the debate continues.

5 THE EC AND INTERNATIONAL AUDITING BODIES

5.1 We have already discussed the role of the EC itself on auditing. This has mainly been through the Eighth Directive, the provisions of which were implemented through the CA 1989 in the UK.

5.2 The European Commission has some impact on European auditing. For example, it recently adopted a proposal for a regulation for a voluntary Community environmental auditing scheme (known as the eco-audit scheme). The proposal is that the environmental auditor or auditors authorised for this purpose by a body recognised by the relevant members state. Environmental statements must be validated by authorised environmental auditors.

International Auditing Practices Committee (IAPC)

5.3 Similar in nature to the International Accounting Standards Committee (IASC),the IAPC issues International Standards on Auditing (ISAs). In general terms these standards have not been as detailed or stringent as UK auditing standards and guidelines.

5.4 Recently, however, the International Organisation of Securities Commissions (IOSCO) approved ISAs, so that multi-national accounts which are audited in compliance with ISAs are now acceptable to securities regulatory authorities around the world. It will also make transactions, such as cross border offerings, much easier and less costly than before. The ISA project took IOSCO five years to complete. It involved examining basic auditing principles and essential procedures. A joint task force identified a number of areas in which changes were needed and most of the resulting recommendations have been incorporated into the ISAs.

5.5 This development has been seen as important as it will provide an incentive for countries to bring their standards into line with international ones. The APB will be paying great attention to ISAs in its review of existing UK auditing pronouncements, to ensure that these reflect all the basic precepts of the international standards.

6 PROFESSIONAL ETHICS

6.1 There are a number of ethical issues which are of great importance to the client-auditor relationship. The onus is always on the auditor, not only to be ethical, but also to be *seen* to be ethical.

6.2 As is the case with the other accountancy bodies, the AAT does not leave its members adrift with no guidance on ethical matters. Although it is true that every situation involving ethical decisions is different, there is a strong case for laying down basic guidelines on fundamental issues. In this way, members have a measure by which to gauge their behaviour.

Guidelines on professional ethics

6.3 Consequently, the AAT publishes, in its annual handbook, *Guidelines on professional ethics*. These guidelines are structured as follows.

1 Introduction

2 Definitions

3 The public interest

4 Objectives

5 Fundamental principles

6 Detailed guidance

7 Guidance applicable to all accounting technicians

- 7.1 Objectivity
- 7.2 Resolution of ethical conflicts
- 7.3 Professional competence
- 7.4 Confidentiality
- 7.5 Tax practice
- 7.6 Cross border activities

8 Guidance applicable to self-employed accounting technicians

- 8.1 Independence in reporting
- 8.2 Fees and commissions
- 8.3 Activities incompatible with the practice of public accountancy
- 8.4 Clients' monies
- 8.5 Relations with other self-employed accounting technicians and other professional accountants in public practice
- 8.6 Advertising and solicitation

6.4 Establishing the *Guidelines* brought the AAT into line with the other accountancy bodies. Where a member of the AAT is also a member of one of the AAT's sponsoring bodies (ICAEW, ACCA etc), then he or she should first follow the statutory requirements of the country and secondly 'interpret these *Guidelines* in a manner that leads to best ethical practice'.

6.5 The *Guidelines* make the following points about the characteristics of accountants.

> 'The accounting profession, and this includes the accounting technician part of it, is distinguished by the following characteristics:
>
> (i) mastering of particular skills and techniques acquired by training and education;
>
> (ii) development of an ethical approach to the work and to clients acquired by experience and professional supervision under training and safeguarded by a strict disciplinary code;

(iii) acceptance of duties to society as a whole in addition to duties to the employer or the client;

(iv) an outlook which is essentially objective;

(v) rendering personal services to a high standard of conduct and performance.'

This paragraph places ethics at the centre of the *raison d'être* of an accountant.

6.6 The *Guidelines* also emphasise the public interest aspects of accountancy and the way accountants recognise and accept their responsibility to the public. Many people, not just clients, rely on the accountant's work.

6.7 The *objectives* of the accountancy profession can only be obtained if four basic needs are met.

(a) Credibility
(b) Professionalism
(c) Quality of service
(d) Confidence

Fundamental principles

6.8 These fundamental principles are very important indeed. The *Guidelines* state that:

> 'In order to achieve the objectives of the accountancy profession, members have to observe a number of prerequisites or fundamental principles.'

6.9 These fundamental principles are quoted in full here as you should *learn them.*

'(i) *Integrity*

An accounting technician should be straightforward and honest in performing professional work.

(ii) *Objectivity and independence*

An accounting technician should be fair and should not allow prejudice or bias or the influence of others to override objectivity.

(iii) *Professional competence and due care*

(a) An accounting technician in accepting a professional engagement or occupation implies that there is a level of competence necessary to carry out the work and that the knowledge, skill and experience of the accounting technician will be applied with reasonable care and diligence. They should therefore refrain from undertaking or continuing any assignments which they are not competent to carry out unless advice and assistance is obtained to ensure that the assignment is carried out satisfactorily.

(b) Having accepted an assignment the accounting technician should carry it out with due care, and by discharging professional responsibilities with competence and diligence.

(c) An accounting technician also has a continuing duty to maintain professional knowledge and skill at a level required to ensure that a client or employer receives the advantage of competent professional service based on up-to-date developments in practice, legislation and techniques.

(iv) *Confidentiality*

An accounting technician should respect the confidentiality of information acquired during the course of performing professional work and should not use or disclose any such information without proper and specific authority or unless there is a legal or professional right or duty to disclose.

(v) *Professional behaviour*

An accounting technician should act in a manner consistent with the good reputation of the profession and refrain from any conduct which might bring discredit to the profession.

(vi) *Technical standards*

Accounting technicians should ensure that they maintain their technical standards in areas relevant to their work through continuing professional development. They have a duty to carry out with care and skill, and in conformity with the professional and technical standard promulgated by the AAT and in the legislation of their country, the instructions of the client in so far as they are not incompatible with the requirements of integrity, objectivity and independence.'

6.10 As we saw above, the *Guidelines* then expand these fundamental principles into detailed guidance, split into two sections:

(a) guidance applicable to all accounting technicians; and
(b) guidance applications to self-employed accounting technicians.

6.11 In the case of the auditing units of competence, we need only look at *confidentiality* in the first section, and those aspects relating to *independence* (a very important auditing attribute) in the second.

Confidentiality

6.12 Confidentiality procedures are mentioned specifically in the units of competence and so it is important to look at what the AAT says on the subject. All the points made are valid and so the whole section is reproduced here.

'1 Accounting technicians have an obligation to respect the confidentiality of information about a client's or employer's affairs acquired in the course of professional work. The duty of confidentiality continues even after the end of the relationship between the accounting technician and the employer or client.

2 Confidentiality should always be observed by an accounting technician unless specific authority has been given to disclose information or there is a legal or professional duty to disclose.

3 Accounting technicians have an obligation to ensure that staff under their control and persons from whom advice and assistance is obtained respect the principle of confidentiality.

4 Confidentiality is a matter of usage of information and not just non-disclosure or disclosure. An accounting technician acquiring information in the course of professional work shall neither use nor appear to use that information for personal advantage or for the advantage of a third party.

5 An accounting technician has access to much confidential information about an employer's or client's affairs not otherwise disclosed to the public. Therefore he should be relied upon not to make unauthorised disclosure to other persons. This does not apply to disclosure of such information in order properly to discharge the accounting technician's responsibility according to the profession's standards.

6 The following are examples of the points which should be considered in determining the extent of which confidential information may be disclosed:

(i) When disclosure is authorised. When authorisation to disclose is given by the client or the employer the interests of all the parties including those third parties whose interests might be affected should be considered.

(ii) When disclosure is specifically required by law. This could lead to an accounting technician:

(a) producing documents or giving evidence in the course of legal proceedings; and

(b) disclosing to the appropriate public authorities infringements of the law which might have come to light.

(iii) Relationships should be avoided which allow prejudice, bias or influences of others to override objectivity. Equally, when reporting on financial information which comes under an accounting technician's review, relationships which undermine an impartial attitude should be avoided.

(iv) Members of the AAT have an obligation to ensure that personnel engaged on professional work adhere to the principles of objectivity and independence.'

6.13 Notice that this last paragraph gives more specific guidance than the previous five points.

Security procedures

6.14 It is worth mentioning here a matter closely related to confidentiality: security. Security procedures help to maintain the confidentiality of the client. They tend to be a combination of very practical measures and detailed rules governing the technician's right to impart information about a client. A typical list of security procedures is as follows.

(a) Do not discuss client matters with any third party, including family and friends, even in a general way.

(b) Do not use client information to your own gain, nor carry on insider dealing by passing price-sensitive information to others.

(c) Do not leave audit files unattended at a client's premises. Lock them up at night.

(d) Do not leave audit files (or computer equipment) in cars, even in the boot, or in unsecured private residences.

(e) Do not take working papers away from the office or the client unless strictly necessary.

7 INDEPENDENCE

7.1 The independence of the auditor is central to his or her ability to perform an audit properly; as such it has been given a section of its own for discussion. After looking at the AAT's guidance on this matter, we will move on to consider the broader aspects of independence and how the auditing profession as a whole has tried to improve auditor independence.

Independence in reporting

7.2 The AAT states the following.

'1 When undertaking a reporting assignment the accounting technician who is self-employed should be independent in fact and appearance.

2 The following paragraphs indicate some of those situations which, because of the actual or apparent lack of independence, would give a reasonable observer grounds for doubting the independence of a self-employed accounting technician.'

These 'following paragraphs' are discussed below. Remember that these apply to *all* self-employed accounting technicians, not just those acting as auditors.

Financial involvement with, or in the affairs of, clients

7.3 The *Guidelines* state the following.

'Financial involvement with a client will affect independence and may lead a reasonable observer to conclude that it has been impaired. Such involvement can arise in a number of ways.

(a) By direct or indirect financial interest.

(b) By loans to or from the client or any officer, director or principal shareholders of a client company.

(c) By holding a financial interest in a joint venture with a client or employee(s) of a client.

(d) When the receipt of fees from a client, or group of connected clients represents a large proportion of the total gross fees of an accounting technician, or of the practice as a whole, the dependence on that client or group of clients should inevitably come under scrutiny and could raise doubts as to independence.'

7.4 **The last point about fees is very important. There is no hard-and-fast rule about what constitutes an unacceptable proportion of total gross fees (although the ICAEW, dealing with Registered Auditors, gives guidance of 10-15%). However, if the fees are all or a large part of fee income then the accounting technician should 'carefully consider whether independence has been impaired'.**

Appointment in companies

7.5 'When an accounting technician who is self-employed is or was, within the period under current view or immediately proceeding an assignment:

(i) a member of the Board, an officer or employee of a company;

(ii) a partner of, or in the employment of, a member of the Board or an officer or employee of a company,

then he would be regarded as having an interest which could detract from independence when reporting on that company.'

Provision of other services to audit clients

7.6 The *Guidelines* state:

> 'When an accounting technician, in addition to carrying out an audit or other reporting function, provides other services to a client, care should be taken to render advice and not to be placed in the position of reporting on management decisions which they have recommended.'

7.7 **The commentary goes on to make the crucial point that, when providing advisory services (such as taxation and management consultancy), the accounting technician should be careful not to usurp the management function (ie make management decisions for the company). This would impair the independence of the auditor.**

Personal and family relationships

7.8 While not prescribing ethical requirements in detail, the *Guidelines* states the following.

> 'Personal and family relationships can affect independence. There is a particular need to ensure that an independent approach to any assignment is not endangered as a consequence of any personal or family relationship.'

Contingency fees

7.9 **In common with the rest of the profession, accounting technicians may not offer work on a contingency fee basis.**

> 'Professional services should not be offered or rendered to a client under an arrangement whereby no fee will be charged unless a specified finding or result is obtained or when the fee is otherwise contingent upon the findings or results of such services.
>
> (a) Fees should not be regarded as being contingent if fixed by a court or other public authority.
>
> (b) Fees charged on a percentage or similar basis should be regarded as contingent fees.

(c) Fees may be waived in certain circumstances; this does not mean that they are on a contingency fee basis provided they are not reinstated at a future date.'

Goods and services

7.10 The *Guidelines* state:

'Acceptance of goods and services from a client may be a threat to independence. Acceptance of undue hospitality poses a similar threat.

Goods and services should not be accepted by accounting technicians, their spouses or dependent children except on business terms no more favourable than those generally available to others. Hospitality and gifts on a scale which is not commensurate with the normal courtesies of social life should not be accepted.'

Ownership of the capital

7.11 The *Guidelines* state:

'Ideally, the capital of a practice should be owned entirely by the accounting technicians and/or the accountants in the practice. However, ownership of capital by others is permitted provided that the majority of both the ownership of the capital and the voting rights lies only with the accounting technicians and/or the accountants in the practice.'

7.12 This principle is extended to 'borrowings from others ... that might constitute an evasion of the rule concerning ownership of the capital'.

Letters of engagement

7.13 We will look at letters of engagement in detail in Chapter 4. In the meantime, the *Guidelines* make the following points.

'Self-employed accounting technicians should ensure that they receive an engagement letter from each client at the commencement of services to that client.

The purpose of the engagement letter is to provide written confirmation of the work to be undertaken and the extent of the responsibilities of the accounting technician. The content to be agreed with the client should cover the scope of work to be undertaken, the various services to be provided, the responsibilities of the client and accounting technician and the basis of fees to be charged.

Once agreed and accepted by the client in writing, the engagement letter should remain effective from year to year, but also be reviewed annually to ensure that it continues to reflect the client's circumstances.'

Exercise 4

Southern Engineering Ltd has undergone a period of substantial growth following its establishment five years ago by two engineers. Because of a lack of accounting expertise within the company it has traditionally looked to its auditors, Smith and Jones, for accounting services in the preparation of annual financial statements as well as for the statutory audit function. Smith and Jones have also provided advice in connection with the company's accounting and internal control systems.

Smith and Jones is a two partner firm of certified accountants whose clients are mainly sole traders, partnerships and small limited companies. Although Southern Engineering Ltd was originally a typical small company client, its growth over the last five years has meant that it now accounts for approximately 20% of Smith and Jones' gross fee income and the company has indicated that it may wish to issue shares on the unlisted securities market in the near future.

Required

(a) Discuss the extent to which it is acceptable and desirable that Smith and Jones have in the past provided the three services of statutory audit, advice in connection with systems, and accountancy services in the preparation of annual financial statements to Southern Engineering Ltd.

(b) Discuss the acceptability and desirability of Smith and Jones continuing to act in the future as auditors to Southern Engineering Ltd while continuing to provide the other services.

Solution

(a) It is frequently the case that auditors, especially of small companies, provide other, non-audit services. The risk arises that, in such cases, the auditor's objectivity may be impaired. This is particularly possible where the auditor is involved in advising the client on systems, as it becomes difficult for the auditor to remain sufficiently detached to comment critically on any weaknesses or shortcomings which appear when systems are implemented. A clear distinction must be drawn between the auditor's advisory capacity - in systems or accountancy work - and the executive responsibility, which is still that of the company's management. Undue involvement with non-audit services must be avoided, lest it detracts from the auditor's essential independence and objectivity.

(b) The ethical guidance of the accounting bodies recommends that fee income from a single client should not exceed 15% of a practice's total gross fees. As Southern Engineering's fees now represent 20% of fee income (and would, presumably, increase when the company makes an issue on the USM) it seems Smith and Jones have to consider ways of reducing their dependence on this one client. This might well be done by continuing as auditors but ceasing to provide accounting services and systems advice. (In any case, the ethical guidelines suggest that the auditors of a public company should not assist with accountancy save in exceptional circumstances).

Smith and Jones should keep the situation under review, even after they have moved to a pure audit role, to ensure that they are not again becoming unduly dependent on Southern Engineering as it expands.

Improving auditor independence

7.14 Many proposals have been put forward to help safeguard the independence of auditors and these are discussed in the following paragraphs.

Rotation of auditor appointments

7.15 It has been argued that the long-term nature of the company audit engagement tends to create a loss of auditor independence, due to an increasing familiarity with the company's management and staff, which works against the shareholders' and the public's interest. For this reason, it has been argued that there should be a rotation of the audit appointment every few years, allowing several firms of professional accountants periodically to conduct the engagement, and thereby preventing any unnecessary loss of physical independence which the present situation is thought to cause.

7.16 However, rotation of auditors may not be very popular in practice, owing mainly to the attendant disadvantages of upsetting the client company with continual changes of audit staff, the high costs of recurring first audits, and the present ability of auditors to retain a fresh approach to the audit by rotating members of the audit staff internally so that no member is permanently assigned to it, including the reporting partner. The Cadbury report on *The financial aspects of corporate governance* does not recommend compulsory rotation of audit firms, due to the loss of trust and experience built up over time and the risk to audit effectiveness it would entail. The report does suggest, however, that the accounting profession should draw up guidelines on the rotation of audit *partners*.

An audit court

7.17 It has been suggested that auditor independence has been eroded beyond repair in many cases, mainly because of the lack of apparent independence in his position when he is permitted to own shares in a client company, conduct management services on its behalf and be effectively employed by the company directors. Because of these factors, it is argued that the task of independent audit judgement should be removed from the auditor and given to a judicial court where eminent professional accountants would be appointed to judge the suitability of the accounting practices utilised by the company in producing its annual financial statements. The auditor in this situation would act as an evidence gatherer, responsible only for presenting the accounting facts to the court for its judgement and opinion.

Appointment by government or a government agency

7.18 It has been suggested that the auditor's appointment by the shareholders implies a certain lack of independence, firstly because it tends to ignore the interests of other important users of company financial statements; and secondly, because it tends to cause company directors to be the employers of the auditor, with the shareholders merely endorsing prior recommendations. It therefore has been proposed that the auditor should be appointed by a government agency such as the Department of Trade and Industry. The audit fees would be paid by this body out of levies on the companies based on their past fee record. The main argument for this suggestion is that it would give the auditor security of employment and leave him free to give a totally objective opinion on the accounting information in the company's financial statements. The main arguments against it are that it would be difficult to administer, could cause the costs of audits to rise substantially, and might well be the first step towards nationalising the accountancy profession.

A state auditing board

7.19 Commentators argue that the approach of the Sandilands Committee a few years back has proved that a government sponsored body has a useful role in shaping accountancy thinking and far from leading to increased party political interference has created an important contribution to the wider understanding of accountancy reports. It has therefore been argued that a state auditing board will become necessary. Its role might include:

(a) influencing new company legislation;
(b) formulating national accounting and auditing policy;
(c) enforcing Accounting Standards and International Accounting Standards (IASs);
(d) overseeing the appointment of auditors.

Any form of 'nationalisation' is likely to be opposed by the accountancy profession.

Audit committees

7.20 One American innovation which is gathering momentum slowly in this country is the audit committee. In the US already 80% of large companies have such committees and the Security and Exchange Commission have made it compulsory for all listed companies. One of the main reasons for audit committees arises from the difficulty auditors have in combating instances where the executive directors of a company are determined to mislead them. As a result it is felt that an audit committee preferably drawn from 'non-executive' directors of a client company would provide an invaluable independent liaison between the board and the auditors, thus strengthening the auditors' position and improving communication. Other advantages that are claimed to arise from the existence of an audit committee include:

(a) it will lead to increased confidence in the credibility and objectivity of financial reports;

(b) by specialising in the problems of financial reporting and thus, to some extent, fulfilling the directors' responsibility in this area, it will allow the executive directors to devote their attention to management; and

(c) in cases where the interests of the company, the executive directors and the employees conflict, the audit committee might provide an impartial body for the auditors to consult.

7.21 Opponents of audit committees argue that:

(a) there may be difficulty selecting sufficient non-executive directors with the necessary competence in auditing matters for the committee to be really effective; and

(b) the establishment of such a formalised reporting procedure may dissuade the auditors from raising matters of judgement and limit them to reporting only on matters of fact.

7.22 *The Cadbury Report* recommends that audit committees should be made compulsory under Stock Exchange rules in the UK and that the committee should consist entirely of non-executive directors, the majority of whom are independent of the company. The audit committee should have explicit authority and the resources to investigate any matters within their terms of reference. These requirements have been adopted for listed companies by the Stock Exchange.

Peer reviews

7.23 Some people have suggested that a system of 'auditing the auditors' should be established and indeed there have already been examples of such reviews being carried out on a mandatory basis in the USA. It would involve either:

(a) the profession as a whole establishing panels of experts to review and report on the practices and procedures of a firm of auditors; or simply,

(b) another independent firm of auditors carrying out the review.

The main object of such an exercise is to improve the quality and performance of audit work generally, but undoubtedly an important part of the 'brief' of the reviewer would be to consider whether the firm under review was sufficiently independent of its clients.

Independence and the EC Eighth Directive

7.24 The Eighth Directive (implemented by CA 1989) requires approval by the authorities in the member states of all persons who carry out statutory audits. In the UK, authority for such approval is delegated to Recognised Supervisory Bodies (RSBs) approved by the Secretary of State.

7.25 The Companies Act 1989 provides for the possibility of incorporated firms being appointed as company auditors. Such firms are required to have rules preventing individuals who do not hold an appropriate qualification from exerting an influence over the conduct of an audit in such a way as to affect the independence or integrity of the auditor.

7.26 The Act does not address shareholdings directly. It is likely that the rules of the RSBs will address this issue. Discussion on this issue has focused mainly on the extent to which shares in an incorporated audit firm may be held by persons outside the firm. The Directive allows up to 49% of the shares to be owned by outsiders, although many UK commentators have felt that the auditor's independence may be prejudiced if more than 25% of the shares are held externally. It may be that persons outside the firms will be prohibited from holding shares having voting rights. It is also likely that a company acting as auditor will be prohibited from acting as auditor to a company whose shares it holds, or to a company which is a shareholder of it.

Exercise 5

An auditor must ensure that his independence is not being compromised by providing other services to audit clients, and by other actions.

The additional services an auditor may provide include:

(a) taxation, preparing the company's corporation tax computation and negotiating with the Inland Revenue; dealing with the tax affairs of the company's directors;

(b) preparing periodic management accounts of the company, quarterly and annual accounts;

(c) advising the directors on legal and accounting matters in relation to the company, for example, preparing submissions to the bank to obtain additional finance, advising on changes in share ownership and capital structure of the company and valuation of the company's shares;

(d) attending meetings of the board of directors.

Required

In relation to a private company, of which you are auditor, consider:

(i) the benefits which may arise to the auditor and client in providing *each* of the above services;

(ii) the extent to which providing *each* of these services may compromise your independence, and the action you would take to minimise the risk to your independence of providing these services.

Solution

In all cases, the auditor will of course enjoy income additional to the audit fee. The client will probably benefit from a saving in using the same professional for all these types of work, because information gained on one assignment can be used on others, and the client will not be paying for the learning time of a new advisor. The client's staff and management should also save time, as they should not need to explain the business repeatedly to different people. (It has to be admitted, however, that changes in audit and other staff do often result in the client's needing to explain the same point in successive years.) The following individual comments may be made.

(a) *Taxation.* It is customary for the company's taxation liability to be at least checked, and often computed, as part of routine audit work. It is unlikely that independence would be impaired by this, or by routine correspondence with the Inland Revenue. Similarly, it is normal for an auditor to deal with directors' tax affairs. A problem would, however, arise here if there were any dispute between the company and its directors, as the auditor would suffer a conflict of interests and would probably be best advised to relinquish either the audit or the tax advisory role.

(b) *Accounts preparation.* This clearly gives the auditor a very good opportunity to keep in touch with the company's performance during the year and to take note of any possible audit problems as soon as they arise. There is, however, a risk that the auditor will not be as detached in carrying out the audit of accounts he or she has prepared as would be the case if the client had produced the accounts.

(c) *Advice to directors.* Clearly, the auditor will be able to draw on knowledge of the company in giving advice. There is a significant risk, however, that independence will be compromised, particularly if the advice turns out to have been mistaken. If the auditor has prepared a profit forecast for submission to the bank which subsequently proves over-optimistic, he or she may find it difficult to required the client to reflect the actual result in the year end accounts.

(d) *Board meetings.* There is a risk here that the auditor may completely forfeit independence by becoming too closely involved in the running of the company. The Companies Act regards as a director anyone who carries out the functions of a director, and an auditor would be exposed to this presumption if he or she attended meetings regularly. It would therefore be advisable for the auditor to attend only the board meetings at which the annual accounts are approved by the board.

The Cadbury Report

7.27 *The Cadbury Report* made various recommendations, some of which will improve auditor independence. Setting up an audit committee will put a wedge between the auditors and the executive directors, preventing the directors putting pressure on the auditors, threatening to replace them.

7.28 The confidentiality question has also been addressed by *The Cadbury Report* (discussed later). It is suggested that the protection given to auditors in regulated financial services industries to disclose certain matters should be extended to all auditors. This would allow auditors to report irregularities and frauds without breaking confidentially.

Chapter roundup

- In this chapter, we have looked at the whole of the regulatory framework which has a direct effect on auditing, as well as some of the other more indirect influences.
- The CA 1985 requirements for the eligibility, registration and training of auditors are extremely important as they are designed to maintain standards in the auditing profession.
- You must be able to discuss the scope and authority of Statements of Auditing Standards, Practice Notes and Bulletins.
- It will be useful to learn the scope and authority of the APC's standards and guidelines, particularly as they will remain in existence until replaced by the APB.
- Auditors must be aware of the accounting standard setting regime and the scope and authority of accounting standards as they have a direct impact on the audit work and the audit opinion.
- The effect of Government and international bodies on auditing is often only indirect, except EC directives.
- Rules on ethical conduct are laid down in the AAT's *Guidelines on Professional Ethics.*
- Confidentiality is important. Auditors are very limited as to when they can disclose client information without permission.
- Independence is perhaps the most important characteristic of the auditor. Current discussion is focused on the other services auditors sell to audit clients, and the recommendations of *The Cadbury Report*.

Test your knowledge

1 How is an auditor's 'appropriate qualification' defined? (see paras 1.4, 1.5)

2 What are the duties of RSBs under CA 1989? (1.10)

3 When is a person ineligible for appointment under CA 1985? (1.16, 1.19)

4 What were some of the criticisms of the APC? (2.3)

5 What type of documents will the APB produce? (2.5)

6 State the scope of Statements of Auditing Standards. (2.6)

7 What is the scope of the old auditing guidelines? (2.18)

8 What are the five measures outlined as necessary in an audit by *The auditor's operational standard*? (2.20)

9 Name the bodies set up as a result of the Dearing report. (3.8)

10 Under what circumstances is the auditor permitted to breach client confidentiality? (6.12)

11 What guidance is given by the AAT on the level of fee income which is appropriate from one client? (7.3, 7.4)

12 Are contingency fees allowed by the AAT? (7.9)

13 What are the advantages and disadvantages of audit committees in terms of auditor independence? (7.20, 7.21)

Chapter 3

AUDITING REQUIREMENTS OF THE COMPANIES ACT 1985

This chapter covers the following topics.

1 Introduction: the Companies Act

2 Appointment of auditors

3 Resignation and removal

4 Duties and rights of the auditor

Introduction

The Companies Act provisions relating to the auditor are extremely important. They enforce the regulatory framework discussed in the last chapter.

As mentioned at the beginning of Part A, these matters are unlikely to arise directly in practical auditing. The provisions relating to the appointment of auditors, however, have a practical impact on the audit appointment process which is discussed in Chapter 4.

These Companies Act provisions may be 'tested' through oral questioning after submission of your portfolio, so don't feel that you can simply read through this and then forget about it.

1 INTRODUCTION: THE COMPANIES ACT

1.1 Most audit work is concerned with companies incorporated under the Companies Act 1985, which has been amended in various respects by the Companies Act 1989.

1.2 The Companies Act legislation serves a number of purposes.

(a) It seeks to ensure the competence of auditors by requiring appropriate professional qualifications.

(b) It promotes the independence of the auditor by disqualifying certain persons for appointment as auditor and by means of rules regarding the removal and resignation of the auditor.

(c) It sets out the duties of the auditor.

(d) It gives the auditor certain rights to help him to carry out his duties.

2 APPOINTMENT OF AUDITORS

2.1 The 1985 Act requires that the auditor should be appointed by (and he will therefore be ultimately answerable to) the shareholders. The basic rule is that every company shall at each general meeting at which accounts are laid, appoint an auditor. He will hold office from the conclusion of that meeting until the conclusion of the next general meeting at which accounts are laid (s 385). The retiring auditor may be reappointed at the general meeting, but by positive resolution only. Re-appointment is not automatic.

2.2 The following are exceptions to the basic rule.

(a) The directors may appoint the auditor:

  (i) at any time before the first general meeting at which accounts are presented, such auditor to hold office until the conclusion of that meeting (s 385(3) CA 1985);

  (ii) to fill any casual vacancy in the office of auditor (s 388 CA 1985).

(b) If the directors fail to appoint the first auditor, these powers may be exercised by the members in general meeting.

The surviving or continuing auditor will continue to act while a casual vacancy continues.

2.3 Where no auditors are appointed or re-appointed at any general meeting of a company at which accounts are laid before the members, the Secretary of State may appoint a person to fill the vacancy (s 387 CA 1985). The company must inform the Secretary of State within one week of his power under this subsection becoming exercisable. Failure to give such notice makes the company and its officers who are in default liable to a daily fine.

2.4 In certain cases relating to appointment of an auditor special notice (28 days) is required for the appropriate resolutions at a general meeting (ss 388(3) and 391 A(1)(b) CA 1985). Such resolutions are those proposing:

(a) to appoint as auditor a person other than the retiring auditor;

(b) to fill a casual vacancy in the office of auditor; or

(c) to re-appoint as auditor a retiring auditor who was appointed by the directors to fill a casual vacancy.

2.5 On receipt of notice of one of these resolutions the company must immediately send a copy thereof (ss 388(4) and 391 A(2) CA 1985) to:

(a) the person whom it is intended to appoint;

(b) the retiring auditor, if applicable;

(c) the auditor who resigned, if applicable, where a casual vacancy was caused by a resignation.

Elective regime for private companies

2.6 The Companies Act 1989 introduced a regime whereby a private company may:

(a) substitute unanimous written agreement of its shareholders for resolutions of shareholders passed at a general meeting; and

(b) elect not to comply with some of the statutory requirements of the Companies Act. Such an election is called an elective resolution.

2.7 An elective resolution is only effective if:

(a) at least 21 days' notice in writing is given of the meeting stating that an elective resolution is to be proposed and stating the terms of the resolution; and

(b) the resolution is agreed at the meeting (or by written resolution) by all members entitled to vote or attend the meeting.

2.8 A provision is included whereby a private company may elect not to be required to appoint auditors annually (s 386 CA 1985). In such a case, the auditors in office will be deemed to be re-appointed annually. While the election is in force, any member may give notice in writing proposing that the auditor be removed, and the directors must convene a general meeting to decide the issue within 28 days of the notice.

2.9 A private company may also elect not to lay accounts before the members in general meeting (although under s 253 members and auditors may require a general meeting to be held for the laying of accounts). If the company makes such an election without making an election not to reappoint auditors annually (see the previous paragraph), it must hold a general meeting annually to re-elect the auditors (s 385A CA 1985). This meeting must be held within 28 days of dispatching the accounts to members, and an auditor so appointed will hold office until the corresponding time for appointing auditors for the next financial year.

2.10 The elective regime is likely to result in many private companies not holding annual general meetings, but instead dealing with AGM business in written resolutions which are signed by the directors.

Remuneration

2.11 The remuneration of the auditor, which will include any sums paid by the company in respect of the auditor's expenses, will be fixed (s 390A CA 1985) either by:

(a) whoever made his appointment which could be:

(i) the members;
(ii) the directors;
(iii) the Secretary of State; or

(b) in such manner as the company in general meeting may determine.

2.12 In practice the most common method is (b), with the members authorising the directors to fix the remuneration. Regardless of the manner in which the auditor's remuneration is fixed, it must be disclosed in the annual accounts of the company (s 390A(3) CA 1985).

2.13 S 390A(5) CA 1985 requires the disclosure in the company's accounts to include the value and nature of benefits in kind provided to the auditor. The Act also gives the Secretary of State the right to introduce regulations to require the disclosure of the remuneration of auditors and their associates in other capacities.

3 RESIGNATION AND REMOVAL

Resignation

3.1 Certain provisions of the Companies Act 1985 are designed to ensure that auditors do not resign without an explanation of their action. If an auditor wishes to resign part-way through his term of office he must carry out the following procedures.

(a) The auditor must deposit written notice of his resignation at the registered office of the company. Resignation is effective on the day the notice is received, unless the auditor has specified some later date.

(b) The auditor must accompany such notice with a statement (s 394 CA 1985) that either:

(i) there were no circumstances connected with this resignation which he considers should be brought to the notice of the members or creditors of the company; or

(ii) a statement detailing any such 'surrounding circumstances'.

Note. Unless there is a statement as required by s 394, the auditor's resignation will not be effective.

3.2 On receiving notice of the auditor's resignation, the company must send a copy of it to the Registrar of Companies within 14 days. Should the statement of circumstances so dictate, then further copies must be sent to all members and all debenture holders of the company. However, if aggrieved, the company or any other person may apply to the court within 14 days for it to rescind this requirement.

3.3 Where the court is satisfied that the auditor is using the notice to obtain needless publicity for defamatory matters, it will remove this obligation and direct that the applicant's costs be wholly or partly paid by the auditor. In this case the company will merely need to circulate a copy of the court's order. If the court rules in favour of the auditor, the company must send out the notice within 14 days of the date of this ruling.

3.4 In addition to depositing the explanatory statement at the company's registered office, the auditor may attach a signed requisition for the directors to convene an extraordinary general meeting, in order that the circumstances surrounding his resignation can be brought to the attention of the members. S 392A(5) requires that this meeting takes place within 28 days of the notice convening the meeting.

3.5 Before the general meeting is convened, the auditor may request the company to circulate to its members a written statement of circumstances. This prerogative exists whether the auditor himself requested the meeting or a meeting is to be held anyway. The company must circulate this statement to all members to whom notice of the meeting is being sent. If for any reason this fails to happen, the statement can be read out at the meeting. S 392A(7) provides the same safeguard as mentioned in the previous paragraph above against abuse of the auditor's right to do this. On application to the Court by the company or any aggrieved person, circulation and reading out of the statement may be dispensed with if the Court agrees that the auditor is abusing his rights to secure needless publicity for defamatory matters. Again, the court may require the auditor to pay costs.

3.6 An auditor who has resigned may exercise his right to attend and to receive relevant communications about any forthcoming meeting at which either his vacant office is to be filled or at which his term of office would have finished (s 392A(8)). He may also be heard at any such meeting which he attends on any part of the business which concerns him as former auditor of the company.

3.7 An anomaly in the CA 1985 rules was that auditors can apparently avoid giving the required reasons for relinquishing their office merely by not seeking re-appointment at the next AGM rather than by formally resigning. A few years ago, a leading firm of accountants gave up an audit by not seeking re-appointment after issuing a four page audit report with nineteen qualifications. They avoided having to make a statement giving reasons for their action, claiming that the audit report was comprehensive enough. The 1989 Act removed this anomaly by extending the requirement for a written statement to be made when an auditor ceases to hold office for whatever reason (s 394 CA 1985): this will include circumstances of removal by the members and failure to be reappointed by the members in general meeting.

Removal of an auditor

3.8 The auditor should not be susceptible to pressure from directors or groups of shareholders or others. The detailed provisions relating to the removal of the auditor, set out in ss 391 to 393 CA 1985, place the authority for removal of the auditor with the members in general meeting.

3.9 The objects of these provisions are:

(a) to preserve the right of the members to appoint the auditor of their choice; and

(b) to preserve the auditor's independence of the directors by not permitting directors, who may be in disagreement with the auditor, to dismiss him.

3.10 As already noted, under the 'elective regime' whereby a private company can dispense with annual appointment of the auditor, any member may deposit a written notice at the company's registered office proposing that the auditor's appointment be terminated. The directors must convene a general meeting at which the matter must be discussed within 28 days of such a notice (s 393 CA 1985).

3.11 Removal of the auditor before the expiration of his term of office requires the passing of an ordinary resolution of which special notice (28 days) has been given, the auditor being entitled to receive a copy of this resolution. If the resolution is passed then the company must notify the Registrar within 14 days of the date of the meeting (s 391(2) CA 1985).

3.12 Where an attempt is being made to remove an auditor during his term of office or where notice of a resolution to appoint another person in his place has been received by the company, the auditor may make representations as to why he thinks he ought to stay in office. Provided they are not received too late and are of reasonable length, he may require the company (s 391A(4)):

(a) to state in any notice of the resolution given to the members that representations have been made; and

(b) to send a copy of the representations to the members.

3.13 If the representations are not sent out either because they were received too late or because of the company's default, the auditor may require that they are read out at the meeting. This will not prejudice his normal right to speak at the meeting (s 391A(5)).

3.14 As with statements made on resignation, the representations need neither be sent out nor read at the meeting if, on the application either of the company or any other person who claims to be aggrieved, the court is satisfied that the auditor's right is being abused to obtain needless publicity for defamatory matter (s 391A(6)).

3.15 As noted earlier, under s 394 CA 1985, a statement must be made of any circumstances connected with the auditor ceasing to hold office which the auditor considers should be brought to the attention of members or creditors, and this provision applies in the case of removal as well as other circumstances of ceasing office.

3.16 An auditor who is being removed is given two further rights by the 1985 Act (s 391(4)).

(a) He is entitled to receive all notices relating to:

 (i) the general meeting at which his term of office would have expired;

 (ii) any general meeting at which it is proposed to fill the casual vacancy caused by his removal.

(b) He is entitled to attend such meetings and to speak at them on any part of the business which concerns him as former auditor.

But note that he may not requisition an extraordinary general meeting.

3.17 It should be appreciated that the directors as such cannot remove the auditor from office. Only if the directors are also members can they move a resolution to remove him (subject to their having the minimum specified voting rights).

4 DUTIES AND RIGHTS OF THE AUDITOR

Duties

4.1 The principal statutory duties of an auditor in respect of the audit of a limited company are set out in ss 235 and 237 CA 1985. The auditor is required to report on every balance sheet and profit and loss account laid before the company in general meeting.

4.2 The auditor must consider the following provisions.

s 235(2)	*Compliance with legislation*	**Whether the accounts have been prepared in accordance with the Act.**
s 235(2)	*Truth and fairness of accounts*	**Whether the balance sheet shows a true and fair view of the company's (c the group's) affairs at the end of the period and the profit and loss accoun shows a true and fair view of the results for the period.**
s 237(2)	*Proper records and returns*	**Whether proper accounting records have been kept and proper returns adequate for the audit received from branches not visited by the auditor.**
s 237(2)	*Agreement of accounts to records*	**Whether the accounts are in agreement with the accounting records.**
s 235(3)	*Consistency of directors' report*	**Whether the directors' report is consistent with the accounts.**

4.3 **Where the findings of the auditor are satisfactory, only compliance with legislation and truth and fairness of accounts need to be explicitly referred to in the audit report; the other matters can be reported by exception only.**

Rights

4.4 **The Companies Act provides statutory rights of the auditor to enable him to carry out his duties.**

4.5 **The principal rights, excepting those dealing with resignation or removal, are set out in the table opposite, and the following are notes on more detailed points.**

Rights on resignation or removal

4.6 **As we have already seen, an auditor has additional rights relating to resignation and removal. These may be summarised as follows:**

(a) **a right to make certain written representations in the event of the company proposing to appoint an auditor other than himself (s 391);**

(b) **a right to resign at any time by giving written notice which states whether or not there are any circumstances which the members or creditors ought to know about in connection with his resignation (s 392);**

(c) **a right to requisition an extraordinary general meeting to consider any such circumstances.**

s 389A(1)	*Access to records*	A right of access at all times to the books, accounts and vouchers of the company.
s 389A(1)	*Information and explanations*	A right to require from the company's officers such information and explanations as he thinks necessary for the performance of his duties as auditor.
s 390(1)(a) and (b)	*Attendance at/notices of general meetings*	A right to attend any general meetings of the company and to receive all notices of and communications relating to such meetings which any member of the company is entitled to receive.
s 390(1)(c)	*Right to speak at general meetings*	A right to be heard at general meetings which he attends on any part of the business that concerns him as auditor.
s 381B(2)-(4)	*Rights in relation to written resolutions*	A right to receive a copy of any written resolution proposed, and where a written resolution concerning him is proposed, to requisition, attend and be heard at any general meeting.
s 253	*Right to require laying of accounts*	A right to give notice in writing requiring that a general meeting be held for the purpose of laying the accounts and reports before the company.

Rights to information

4.7 Ss 389A and 390 CA 1985 states the auditors' rights to information as indicated above, and also provide specifically for a holding company auditor's right of access to information regarding and subsidiaries companies whether incorporated in the United Kingdom or not. For a UK subsidiary, the subsidiary company or its auditors must provide information; for a non-UK subsidiary, the parent company must take all reasonable steps to obtain the information.

4.8 The Act makes it an offence for a company's officer knowingly or recklessly to make a statement in any form to an auditor which:

(a) purports to convey any information or explanation required by the auditor; and
(b) is materially misleading, false or deceptive.

The penalty is a maximum of two years' imprisonment, a fine or both (s 389A(2)).

Rights in relation to written resolutions

4.9 The elective regime for private companies introduced in the Companies Act 1989 was mentioned earlier in the chapter. One of the elements of the new regime is to permit written resolutions in place of resolutions which would previously have required to be proposed at a general meeting.

4.10 The auditor has rights regarding such written resolutions. When a company wants to pass a written resolution without holding a meeting, it must send a copy to the auditor, who must advise the company, within seven days of receipt of the notice, if it concerns him as auditor and, if it does, whether it should be considered by a meeting.

If the auditor does not reply within seven days the company may assume that he has no objection to the matter being dealt with in writing and the resolution will be effective.

4.11 The company is entitled to take silence as indicating assent. Problems could arise if the auditor does not actually receive a copy of the resolution. An early reply will possibly bring forward the effective date of the resolution and could therefore enable the company to act more quickly. It is for these reasons considered to be good practice for the auditor to reply in writing in all cases even where he considers the matter does not concern him as auditor.

Rights to require laying of accounts

4.12 The right to require a general meeting for the laying of accounts applies where, under the elective regime for private companies, an election to dispense with the laying of accounts is in force. The same right is extended to members of the company.

4.13 The following comprehensive exercise covers all the topics in this chapter.

Exercise

You are a partner in Messrs Borg Connors & Co, Certified Accountants. You are approached by Mr Nastase, the managing director of Navratilova Enterprises Ltd, who asks your firm to become auditors of his company. In return for giving you this appointment Mr Nastase says that he will expect your firm to waive fifty per cent of your normal fee for the first year's audit. The existing auditors, Messrs Wade Austin & Co have not resigned but Mr Nastase informs you that they will not be re-appointed in the future.

Required

(a) What action should Messrs Borg Connors & Co take in response to the request from Mr Nastase to reduce their first year's fee by fifty per cent?

(b) Explain the procedure a company must go through to remove its auditors and appoint another firm of auditors in their place.

(c) Are Messrs Wade Austin & Co within their rights in not resigning when they know Mr Nastase wishes to replace them? Give reasons for your answer.

Solution

(a) The request by Mr Nastase that half of the first year's audit fee should be waived is quite improper. If this proposal were to be accepted it could be held that Borg Connors & Co had sought to procure work through the quoting of lower fees. This would be unethical and would result in disciplinary proceedings being taken against the firm.

It should be pointed out to Mr Nastase that the audit fee will be determined, in accordance with normal practice, by reference to the work involved in completion of a satisfactory audit taking into consideration the nature of the audit tasks involved and the level of staff required to carry out those tasks in an efficient manner. Mr Nastase should further be informed that if he is not prepared to accept an audit fee arrived at in this way and insists on there being a reduction then regrettably the nomination to act as auditor will have to be declined.

(b) Under the provisions of ss 391 to 393 Companies Act 1985 there are certain statutory procedures which must be followed by a company if it wishes to remove its existing auditors and appoint another firm of auditors in their place. The main rules relevant to this situation are summarised below.

(i) The general rule is that every company shall at each annual general meeting (AGM) appoint an auditor to hold office from the conclusion of that meeting until the conclusion of the next AGM.

(ii) Removal of the auditor requires the passing of an ordinary resolution of which special notice (28 days) has been given, the auditor being entitled to receive a copy of this resolution. If the resolution is passed then the company must notify the Registrar within 14 days of the date of the meeting.

(iii) Where an attempt has been made to remove an auditor during his term of office, or where notice of a resolution to appoint another person in his place has been received by the company, the auditor may make representations as to why he thinks he ought to stay in office.

Provided they are not received too late and are of reasonable length he may require the company:

(1) to state in any notice of the resolution given to the members that representations have been made, and

(2) to send a copy of the representations to the members.

(iv) If the representations are not sent out, either because they were received too late or because of the company's default, the auditor may require that they are read at the meeting. This will not prejudice his normal right to speak at the meeting.

(v) The auditor's representations need neither be sent out nor read at the meeting if, on the application of the company or any other person who claims to be aggrieved, the court is satisfied that the auditor's right is being abused to obtain needless publicity for defamatory matter.

(vi) The removed auditor has two further rights which are:

(1) he is entitled to receive all notices relating to the general meeting at which his term of office would have expired and of any general meeting at which it is proposed to fill the casual vacancy caused by his removal; and

(2) he is entitled to attend such meetings and to speak at them on any part of the business which concerns him as former auditor.

Finally it should be emphasised that the power to remove an auditor rests with the members and not with the directors.

Note. Under the 'elective regime', any member may deposit a written notice at the company's registered office proposing that the auditor's appointment be terminated.

(c) Wade Austin & Co have every right not to resign even though they may be aware that Mr Nastase, the managing director of the company, wishes to replace them. The auditors of a company are appointed by, and report to, the members of a company and the directors are not empowered, as directors, to remove the auditors.

If the reason for the proposed change arises out of a dispute between management and the auditors then the auditors have a right to put forward their views as seen above and to insist that any decision should be made by the members, but only once they have been made aware of all pertinent facts concerning the directors' wishes to have them removed from office as auditors.

Chapter roundup

- In this chapter, we have examined the statutory provisions on the audit of companies incorporated under the Companies Act. These provisions seek to ensure the competence and independence of the company auditor, and set out the auditor's duties and rights.
- You should learn the statutory requirements surrounding the auditor's:
  - appointment;
  - remuneration;
  - resignation;
  - removal;
  - duties; and
  - rights.
- The elective regime allows certain private companies to drop the requirement for an audit.

Test your knowledge

1. For what period does an auditor hold office? (see paras 2.1, 2.2)
2. In what circumstances is 'special notice' required in the context of an auditor's appointment? (2.4)
3. How may an auditor resign part way through his term of office? (3.1)
4. Where an attempt is made to remove an auditor during his term of office, what rights does the auditor have? (3.12 - 3.16)
5. What are the main statutory duties of an auditor? (4.1, 4.2)
6. What are the statutory rights of an auditor? (4.4 - 4.12)

Chapter 4

THE AUDIT APPOINTMENT PROCESS

This chapter covers the following topics.

1 Client screening

2 The engagement letter

3 Clearance procedures

Introduction

In the current economic climate, the acceptance of a new client can entail the undertaking of a significant amount of risk. Audit firms, particularly larger firms, now tend towards fairly stringent client acceptance procedures. This client screening helps to establish good 'high level' controls in a (potential) client, ie management/owner probity etc.

The engagement letter is an audit document of fundamental importance as it lays out the scope of the auditor's work *and* it highlights the respective responsibilities of directors and auditor. We will see these responsibilities reflected in the audit report in Chapter 17.

The procedures to be carried out both before and after the acceptance of a new client are straightforward and easy to learn.

1 CLIENT SCREENING

1.1 It has become common practice among large audit firms to carry out stringent checks on potential audit (and other) client companies and their management. There are a number of reasons for this, as we will see shortly. Smaller audit firms and sole practitioners may carry out some checks, but they will be on a much less formal basis and more reliance will be placed on face to face meetings with the potential client.

1.2 The procedures laid out here are tailored to the extreme case of a large audit firm and a large (probably public) company audit, but the procedures may be adapted for smaller audit firms and smaller audits. Some of the steps may seem excessive, and indeed the most stringent of them are more likely to be applied in the USA. At least part of the screening process will overlap with the clearance procedures laid out in Section 3 of this chapter.

1.3 Auditors are likely to be concerned with the following matters in relation to client screening:

(a) the basic factors to consider in determining whether to accept a prospective audit client;

(b) client acceptance procedures;

(c) the approvals required before accepting a prospective client;

(d) additional procedures for special cases, for example financial services companies;

(e) acceptance procedures for audit and how these will be adjusted for acceptance of clients for other types of work;

(f) the documentation of client acceptance.

Basic factors for consideration

1.4 Considerations of whether to accept a client will fall under these or similar headings:

(a) management integrity;
(b) risk;
(c) economics of the engagement;
(d) mutual satisfaction from the professional relationships;
(e) ability to perform the work.

Management integrity

1.5 The integrity of those managing a company will be of great importance. One has only to mention 'Maxwell' to see why!

Risk

1.6 In this context, 'risk' means the danger of damaging the audit firm's reputation. A low risk client is one which:

(a) has a viable business with good long-range prospects;

(b) is well financed with strong internal controls;

(c) applies conservative, prudent accounting principles, rather than those which are aggressive or dubious;

(d) has competent, honest management, particularly a good finance director, well qualified with a close relationship to the rest of the board.

1.7 Audit firms may have standard forms for analysing potential risk, particularly in specialist areas (banking, pensions, and so on) which will highlight industry-specific risk factors which must be addressed. Other factors to be addressed would include such matters as whether the potential client intends to apply for a full listing on the Stock Exchange in the near future, in which case the client should be treated as if it was already fully listed.

Engagement economics

1.8 Generally, the expected fees from a new client should reflect the level of risk expected. They should also offer the same sort of return expected of clients of this nature and the overall financial strategy of the audit firm. Occasionally, the audit firm will want the work to gain entry into the client's particular industry, or to establish better contacts within that industry. These factors will all contribute to a total expected economic return.

Relationship

1.9 It will be the case almost all the time that the audit firm will want the relationship with a client to be long term. This is not only to enjoy receiving fees year after year; it is also to allow the audit work to be enhanced by better knowledge of the client and thereby offer a better service.

1.10 Conflict of interest problems will be considered under this heading and it will be important to establish that no existing clients will cause difficulties as competitors of the new client. Other services to other clients may have an impact here, not just audit. For example, the litigation department may have agreed to act for a competitor of your potential client, or the litigation might even be against your potential client.

Ability to perform the work

1.11 The audit firm must have the resources to perform the work properly, as well as any relevant specialist knowledge or skills. The impact on existing engagements must be estimated, in terms of staff time and the timing of the audit.

Client acceptance procedures

1.12 When an opportunity arises to obtain a new client, either through the approach of the client or by an opportunity to tender, a partner (or very occasionally a senior manager) will be allocated to the 'client'. Should the work be obtained and accepted, this partner should then become the audit partner (or engagement partner). This partner will perform the client acceptance procedures as quickly and as early as possible, reducing the risk of spending too much time on a client which is ultimately rejected or not obtained in competition.

Investigations

1.13 There will probably be certain types of client which require a thorough investigation before acceptance. Each audit firm will have different criteria for deciding which clients should be investigated using an external agency, but examples would be:

(a) financial services companies (for example banks, brokers, insurance, credit or leasing companies);

(b) businesses whose receipts are mainly in cash, for example turf accountants, casinos, bingo halls and parking lots);

(c) other industries perceived as high risk for a variety of reasons, such as builders, contractors, waste management services and so on.

1.14 An investigation might be standard anyway for any potential client, unless the firm had knowledge gained over time of the company's reputation and the reputation of its managers and directors. This may seem excessive, particularly where such investigations are carried out by an external agency and are therefore costly, but many audit firms believe that they are cost effective in avoiding embarrassing or damaging situations.

1.15 Where it is decided that an investigation is not necessary, this fact must be documented, along with the relevant reasons. Authorisation will be requested from the partner responsible for relationships with audit clients as well as the regional managing partner before an audit client is accepted without an investigation.

1.16 An investigation request should be documented and a standard form may be available, similar to the one shown on the next page.

1.17 Where an investigation uncovers suspicious, unresolved allegations and questions or concerns about the reputation, ethics or business practices of a prospective client, it will be usual to consult the managing partner, and possibly the opinion of Counsel will be sought. Any such procedures must be fully documented.

1.18 The investigative report must be timely. If it is received too long before the client is accepted, then an update might be necessary. On the other hand, delay of acceptance of a client because the investigative report was still awaited would be extremely bad practice.

Request for Prospective Client Investigation

Regular Service ☐
Urgent service ☐

To : ______________________

____

____

Name and address of investigative agency

Legal form of prospective client

☐ Private company
☐ Public company
☐ Partnership
☐ Association
☐ Proprietorship
☐ Individual
☐ Government or Government Agency

1 Name and address of prospective client (attach current Dun & Bradstreet Report.)

2 Type of service to be provided. Audit ☐ Tax ☐ Consultancy ☐

Other ☐ ______________________
(Describe)

3 Identify prospective client's bankers and/or solicitors.

4 Information regarding key individuals to be investigated (list key owners and members of management; directors, officers, shareholders, partners, managers).

		If known		
Name and title	Approximate age	Home address	National Insurance number	Other business interests

5 Add any additional information that may reduce investigative time and expense (eg other names used and locations for this business; current or known litigation; identity of suppliers, customers, and current auditors/accountants).

______________ Date

______________ Signature of Partner or Senior Manager

______________ Office

Copy 1 - Send to investigative agency
Copy 2 - Attach to Client Acceptance Form
Copy 3 - Send to security partner, National Office

Inquiries of other sources

1.19 Confidential enquiries might be made of the prospective client's bankers, solicitors, underwriters or other relevant connection. If the prospective client already uses the firm for other services, such as tax and consultancy, then the relevant partner can be applied to for information. These enquiries should be timely. Any potential conflicts of interest due to litigation should be discussed with the partner in charge of litigation services.

Review of documents

1.20 The prospective client's most recent annual financial statements should be examined, along with any interim statements. Other similar documents worth examination might include the company's original 'placing' documents when it obtained a listing. For private companies it may be advisable to obtain a Dun & Bradstreet (credit rating) or similar report.

Previous accountants/auditors

1.21 The prospective client will be asked for permission for the firm to contact the outgoing auditors, to enquire whether there are any reasons why the firm should not take up the appointment. A refusal or limitation by the company will normally lead to a refusal as an audit client.

1.22 The firm should ask both the company and its former auditors whether there have been any fundamental disagreements or any events which have led to a report to the Stock Exchange or the relevant regulatory authority (for example the Bank of England). Where such a disagreement did arise, the matter should be referred to the regional managing partner. He or she should also be consulted if a prospective audit client expects the firm to accept an accounting policy that the previous auditors did not accept.

Internal controls

1.23 Discussions with the management of the company and with its former auditors should give an indication of the strength of the company's system of internal control. If possible, the most recent reports on the company's internal controls, by the external *or* internal auditors, should be examined to determine whether any material weakness exists. Any such weakness would need to be closely monitored if such a client was accepted.

1.24 The strength of the internal control system will be a major factor in the risk analysis of the company.

Level of risk

1.25 Where the risk level of a company's audit is determined as anything other than low, then the specific risks should be identified and documented. It might be necessary to assign specialists in response to these risks, particularly industry specialists, as independent reviewers. Some audit firms have procedures for closely monitoring audits which have been accepted, but which are considered high risk.

1.26 It is assumed that higher risk will be indicated by the following factors or events.

(a) prospective litigation about the company's reporting practices;

(b) qualification of its previous audit report;

(c) significant related party transactions with a sister company which has a different auditor;

(d) significant weaknesses in the internal control structure;

(e) they are unable to prepare financial statements;

(f) they follow aggressive, rather than prudent or conservative accounting policies.

Approval

1.27 Once all the relevant procedures and information gathering has taken place, the company can be put forward for approval. The engagement partner will have completed a client acceptance from and this, along with any other relevant documentations, will be submitted to the managing partner, or whichever partner is in overall charge of accepting clients. There may be formal procedures in place for collaboration to reach a decision over approval for certain situations:

(a) companies about to go public;
(b) derogatory information in the investigative report;
(c) financial services companies;
(d) companies with perceived problems requiring close monitoring;
(e) disagreements with previous auditors over accounting policies.

1.28 No audit work whatsoever should take place before the approval is given and documented, and probable not until the change of auditors has been notified to the Registrar (see Section 3).

Additional procedures

1.29 Additional procedures may be necessary for:

(a) financial services companies;
(b) banks;
(c) insurance companies;

and so on. These additional procedures are usually required because of the extra legislation and monitoring requirements surrounding such companies.

Documentation

1.30 The managing partner will maintain files relating to the consideration of prospective clients. When a decision is made not to accept a prospective client based on the results of an investigation or other information that raises questions about the prospective client's integrity, then a brief summary memorandum should be prepared. This should summarise the procedures undertaken, the problems which arose, and the reasons for refusal.

1.31 An example of a client acceptance form is given on the next few pages. These will obviously vary from firm to firm and many firms will not have a standard form.

Exercise 1

Take photocopies of all the forms in this section of the chapter. Obtain a set of published financial statements (through the *Financial Times* or at work).

Required

Fill in the forms as if the company in question was about to become a client. Invent any missing information.

Client Acceptance Form - Audit clients   Form A1.1

We perform our client acceptance procedures, and in particular the investigation procedures, as early in the proposal process as possible to avoid incurring significant time and effort on a prospective client that we might later decide not to accept.

Background Information

Prospective client__________ Accounting period __________

Address__________

Nature of business (eg industry, products or services, major customers, major suppliers)__________

If the business was started within the past 5 years, indicate the year: 19 ___ Company reg. no. __________

Type of service(s) to be rendered__________

Does the prospective client meet the definition of a "Stock Exchange engagement"? Yes _____ No_____

Is the prospective client considering "going public" in the next year? Yes _____ No_____ N/A _____

Anticipated person in charge__________

Anticipated independent reviewer, if identified __________

Total estimated fee (if available):

Year 1 £______ recurring £______ non-recurring

Year 2 £______ recurring £______ non-recurring

Billing and payment agreement and any special fee arrangements__________

Financial information (for last two years):

Year end	Total assets	Total debt	Shareholders' funds	Total turnover	Profit/(loss)

Has the prospectice client been investigated? Yes _____ No_____ If not, document in an attached memorandum the reasons for not requesting an investigation.

Was there any information in the investigative agency's (oral or attached written) report that indicates we should question whether to accept the prospective client? Yes _____ No_____ If yes, discuss in an attached memorandum along with any mitigating factors.

Key officers, directors, and major shareholders	Officer	Director	Own%	Other businesses/comments

Client Acceptance Form - Audit clients Form A1.2

List the principal solicitors, commercial bankers, and investment bankers with whom the prospective client has a relationship (indicate with an asterisk those individuals who are contacted as part of our client acceptance procedures) and other individuals contacted:

Individual	Firm or Bank
______	______
______	______
______	______
______	______
______	______

Did any matters arise in our contacts with the solicitors, commercial bankers, investment bankers, or others that need further consideration in deciding whether to accept the prospective client? **Yes ____ No ____**
If yes, describe the matters in an attached memorandum.

Predecessor Auditors/Accountants

Inquiries of prospective client regarding predecessor auditors/accountants:
Firm name and office ______
Length of firm's relationship with the prospective client ______
Services rendered to the prospective client ______

Type of opinion issued last year ______
Prospective client's reason(s) for changing auditors/accountants ______

Were there any disagreements with the predecessor auditors/accountants over accounting principles, audit, review, or compilation procedures, or other significant matters during the entity's two most recent fiscal years and any other subsequent interim period? Yes ____ No ____ If yes, describe the disagreements in an attached memorandum.

Any reportable conditions/material weaknesses in the internal control structure? Yes ____ No ____
If yes, describe the conditions/weaknesses in an attached memorandum.

Enquiries of predecessor auditors/accountants:
Date of inquiries ______
Names and titles of individuals who responded to our enquiries (should include the partner in charge) ______

Predecessor's understanding of the reason(s) for changing auditors/accountants ______

Any facts that might bear on the integrity of management ______

Have the predecessor's fees been paid in full? Yes ____ No ____ If not, indicate the reasons ______

Were there any disparities between the prospective client's replies and the preceding auditor's replies?
Yes ____ No ____ If yes, describe the differences in an attached memorandum.

Client Acceptance Form - Audit clients Form A1.3

Other significant considerations (Explain answers with an asterisk in an attached memorandum)

	Yes	No
1 Are there possible conflicts of interest with concerns of existing clients (eg conflicts with litigation services engagements)?	__*	__
2 Are there any independence issues, including family relationships, that need to be considered before we could accept the prospective client?	__*	__
3 Will the engagement require specialised (eg industry specific) knowledge and experience not now available in the local or area office?	__	__
If yes describe in an attached memorandum the plan to obtain the neccessary expertise from other offices and/or to develop it within the office and obtain the concurrence of the national regional director of industry services.		
Will the addition of the client adversely affect the ability of the office to staff any of its other engagements requiring similar expertise?	__*	__
4 Have any significant accounting or auditing issues been identified?	__*	__
5 Does the prospective client expect the firm to accept an accounting policy the predecessor auditors did not accept?	__*	__
6 Will we be auditing all entities under common control?	__	__
7 Are there significant related party transactions with consolidated or other entities that we will not be auditing?	__*	__
8 Does management have a proven track record in this or other businesses?	__	__
9 Does the prospective client have a high likelihood of (continued) business success?	__	__
10 Are there any conditions or events that indicate there could be substantial doubt about the prospective client's ability to continue as a going concern?	__*	__
11 For non-public entities, are there third parties (eg lenders or investors) whom we know would be receiving copies of our reports on the client's financial statements?	__*	__
12 Will the firm be assuming more than a low level of risk if this prospective client is accepted?	__*	__
13 Are there any other factors that should be considered in evaluating the prospective client?	__*	__

Other procedures

1 Seek information and advice from others in the firm who are likely to have significant information bearing on a decision to accept the prospective client, including other partners in the office, in other offices in the area, and where applicable, in other offices in cities where the entity has significant operations or where we have performed other services.

2 For a prospective client in a specialised industry, consult with the partner of industry services with regard to industry specific factors that should be addressed in considering the prospective client for acceptance.

3 For public and significant non-public prospective audit clients, contact the partner in charge of litigation services to determine if there are any conflicts or potential conflicts that need to be evaluated.

4 In the space below, list any head office personnel consulted when performing the client acceptance proceedures. If there are any unresolved issues remaining from those consultations, describe them in an attached memorandum.

Client Acceptance Form - Audit clients Form A1.4

Attachments (attach the following, where applicable, to this form)

- Memoranda, as required, to document considerations described elsewhere on this form
- Investigation report or memorandum documenting the reasons for not requesting an investigation

Accompanying information

- Public companies - the most recent annual shareholders' report, the form reporting the change in auditors and the predecessor auditors' letter. Any recent placing or other documents.
- Private companies - the most recent annual financial statements, and if available, the latest interim financial statements.

Conclusions

I have considered the professional, business, and economic factors regarding this engagement and recommend the acceptance of this prospective client.

Client will be ___ /will not be ___ designated for close-monitoring.

Evaluating Person______________________ Date ______________

Approvals

I am satisfied that this recommendation is in compliance with our policy on client acceptance of this prospective client. Acceptance of this client does ___ /does not ___ require the concurrence of the National Managing Partner.

Office Managing Partner ______________________ Date ______________

I concur with the acceptance of this prospective client.

National Managing Partner______________________ Date ______________

2 THE ENGAGEMENT LETTER

2.1 It is the purpose of an engagement letter to define clearly the extent of the auditor's responsibilities and so minimise the possibility of any misunderstanding between the client and the auditor. Further, the engagement letter provides written confirmation of the auditor's acceptance of the appointment, the scope of the audit, the form of his report and the scope of any non-audit services. If an engagement letter is not sent to clients, both new and existing, there is scope for argument about the precise extent of the respective obligations of the client and its directors and the auditor. The contents of an engagement letter should be discussed and agreed with management before it is sent and preferably prior to the audit appointment.

2.2 Guidance is available in the form of the detailed operational guideline *Engagement letters* from which the following comments are derived.

Timing

2.3 The auditor should send an engagement letter to all new clients soon after his appointment as auditor and, in any event, before the commencement of the first audit assignment. He should also consider sending an engagement letter to existing clients to whom no letter has previously been sent as soon as a suitable opportunity presents itself.

2.4 Once it has been agreed by the client, an engagement letter will, if it so provides, remain effective from one audit appointment to another until it is replaced. However, the engagement letter should be reviewed annually to ensure that it continues to reflect the client's circumstances. If a change has taken place, including a significant change in management, which materially affects the scope or understanding of the audit, the auditor should discuss the matter with management and where appropriate send a revised engagement letter.

Responsibility and scope of the audit

2.5 The letter should explain the principal statutory responsibilities of the client and the statutory and professional responsibilities of the auditor.

2.6 In the case of a company, it should be indicated that it is the statutory responsibility of the client to maintain proper accounting records, and to prepare financial statements which give a true and fair view and have been properly prepared in accordance with the Companies Act 1985 and other relevant legislation. It should also be indicated that the auditor's statutory responsibilities include making a report to the members stating whether in his opinion the financial statements give a true and fair view and whether they have been properly prepared in accordance with the Companies Act

2.7 It should be explained that the auditor has an obligation to satisfy himself whether or not the directors' report contains any matters which are inconsistent with the audited financial statements. Furthermore, it should be indicated that the auditor has a professional responsibility to report if the financial statements do not comply in any material respect with statements of standard accounting practice, unless in his opinion the non-compliance is justified in the circumstances.

2.8 The scope of the audit should be explained. In this connection, it should be pointed out that the audit will be conducted in accordance with approved auditing standards and having regard to relevant auditing guidelines. It should be indicated that:

(a) the auditor will obtain an understanding of the accounting system in order to assess its adequacy as a basis for the preparation of the financial statements;

(b) the auditor will expect to obtain relevant and reliable evidence sufficient to enable him to draw reasonable conclusions therefrom;

(c) the nature and extent of the tests will vary according to the auditor's assessment of the accounting system and, where he wishes to place reliance upon it, the system of internal control;

(d) the auditor will report to management any significant weaknesses in, or observations on, the client's systems which come to his notice and which he thinks should be brought to management's attention.

2.9 Where appropriate, reference should be made to recurring special arrangements concerning the audit. These could include arrangements in respect of internal auditors, divisions, overseas subsidiaries, other auditors and (in the case of a small business managed by directors who are the major shareholders) significant reliance on supervision by the directors.

Representations by management

2.10 Where appropriate it should be indicated that, prior to the completion of the audit, the auditor may seek written representations from management on matters having a material effect on the financial statements.

Irregularities and fraud

2.11 The responsibility for the prevention and detection of irregularity and fraud rests with management and this responsibility is fulfilled mainly through the implementation and continued operation of an adequate system of internal control. The engagement letter should make this clear. It should explain that the auditor will endeavour to plan his audit so that he has a reasonable expectation of detecting material misstatements in the financial statements resulting from irregularities or fraud, but that the examination should not be relied upon to disclose irregularities and frauds which may exist. If a special examination for irregularities or fraud is required by the client, then this should be specified separately in the engagement letter.

Accounting and taxation services

2.12 The auditor may undertake services in addition to carrying out his responsibilities as auditor. An engagement letter should adequately describe the nature and scope of those services. In the case of accounting services, the letter should distinguish the accountant's and the client's responsibilities in relation to them and to the day-to-day bookkeeping, the maintenance of all accounting records and the preparation of financial statements. Preferably this should be done in a separate letter but such services may form the subject of a section in the audit engagement letter.

2.13 In the case of the provision of taxation services, the responsibilities for the various procedures such as the preparation of tax computations and the submission of returns to the relevant authorities should be clearly set out, either in a section of the main letter or in a separate letter.

2.14 Where accounting, taxation or other services are undertaken on behalf of an audit client, information may be provided to members of the audit firm other than those engaged on the audit. If this is the case, it may be appropriate for the audit engagement letter to indicate that the auditor is not to be treated as having notice, for the purposes of his audit responsibilities, of the information given to such people.

Fees

2.15 Mention should normally be made of fees and of the basis on which they are computed, rendered and paid.

Agreement of terms

2.16 The engagement letter should include a request to management that they confirm in writing their agreement to the terms of the engagement. When agreed the letter will give rise to contractual obligations, and its precise content must therefore be carefully considered. In the case of a company, the auditor should request that the letter of acknowledgement be signed on behalf of the board.

Non-audit engagements

2.17 The principles contained in the guideline should also be followed in the case of non-audit engagements. In such a case, if purely accounting services are being provided to a client such as a sole trader or partnership, the engagement letter should make it clear that these services will be performed without any audit work being carried out.

2.18 A form of wording is set out below appropriate for a limited company audit. It is not a 'standard' wording; it must be tailored to specific circumstances. It could also be used as the basis of an engagement letter for unincorporated clients.

SPECIMEN ENGAGEMENT LETTER

To the directors of...

The purpose of this letter is to set out the basis on which we (are to) act as auditors of the company (and its subsidiaries) and the respective areas of responsibility of the company and of ourselves.

Audit

1 As directors of the above company, you are responsible for maintaining proper accounting records and preparing financial statements which give a true and fair view and have been properly prepared in accordance with the Companies Act 1985. You are also responsible for making available to us, as and when required, all the company's accounting records and all other records and related information, including minutes of all management and shareholders' meetings.

2 We have a statutory responsibility to report to the members whether in our opinion the financial statements give a true and fair view of the state of the company's affairs and of the profit or loss for the year and whether they have been properly prepared in accordance with the Companies Act 1985 (or other relevant legislation). In arriving at our opinion, we are required to consider the following matters, and to report on any in respect of which we are not satisfied:

(a) whether proper accounting records have been kept by the company and proper returns adequate for our audit have been received from branches not visited by us;

(b) whether the company's balance sheet and profit and loss account are in agreement with the accounting records and returns;

(c) whether we have obtained all the information and explanations which we think necessary for the purpose of our audit; and

(d) whether the information in the directors' report is consistent with that in the audited financial statements.

In addition, there are certain other matters which, according to the circumstances, may need to be dealt with in our report. For example, where the financial statements do not give full details of directors' remuneration or of transactions with the company, the Companies Act requires us to disclose such matters in our report.

3 We have a professional responsibility to report if the financial statements do not comply in any material respect with statements of standard accounting practice, unless in our opinion the non-compliance is justified in the circumstances.

4 Our audit will be conducted in accordance with the auditing standards issued by the accountancy bodies and will have regard to relevant auditing guidelines. Furthermore, it will be conducted in such a manner as we consider necessary to fulfil our responsibilities and will include such tests of transactions and of the existence, ownership and valuation of assets and liabilities as we consider necessary. We shall obtain an understanding of the accounting system in order to assess its adequacy as a basis for the preparation of the financial statements and to establish whether proper accounting records have been maintained. We shall expect to obtain such relevant and reliable evidence as we consider sufficient to enable us to draw reasonable conclusions therefrom. The nature and extent of our tests will vary according to our assessment of the company's accounting system, and where we wish to place reliance on it the system of internal control, and may cover any aspect of the business operations. We shall report to you any significant weaknesses in, or observations on, the company's systems which come to our notice and which we think should be brought to your attention.

5 As part of our normal audit procedures, we may request you to provide written confirmation of oral representations which we have received from you during the course of the audit.

6 In order to assist us with the examination of your financial statements, we shall request sight of all documents or statements, including the chairman's statement and the directors' report, which are due to be issued with the financial statements. We are also entitled to attend all general meetings of the company and to receive notice of all such meetings.

7 (Where appropriate). We appreciate that the present size of your business renders it uneconomic to create a system of internal control based on the segregation of duties for different functions within each area of the business. In the running of your company we understand that the directors are closely involved with the control of the company's transactions. In planning and performing our audit work we shall take account of this supervision. Further we may ask additionally for confirmation in writing that all the transactions undertaken by the company have been properly reflected and recorded in the accounting records, and our audit report on your company's financial statements may refer to this confirmation.

8 The responsibility for the prevention and detection of irregularities and fraud rests with yourselves. However we shall endeavour to plan our audit so that we have a reasonable expectation of detecting material misstatements in the financial statements or accounting records resulting from irregularities or fraud, but our examination should not be relied upon to disclose irregularities and frauds which may exist.

9 (Where appropriate). We shall not be treated as having notice, for the purposes of our audit responsibilities, of information provided to members of our firm other than those engaged on the audit (eg information provided in connection with accounting, taxation and other services).

Accounting and other services, and taxation services (either included here or set out in a separate letter.)

10 It was agreed that we should carry out the following services as your agents and on the basis that you will make full disclosure to us of all relevant information.

Accounting and other services

11 We shall:

(a) prepare the financial statements based on accounting records maintained by yourselves;

(b) provide assistance to the company secretary by preparing and lodging returns with the Registrar of Companies; and

(c) investigate irregularities and fraud upon receiving specific instructions.

Taxation services

12 We shall in respect of each accounting period prepare a computation of profits, adjusted in accordance with the provisions of the Taxes Acts, for the purpose of assessment to corporation tax. Subject to your approval, this will then be submitted to the Inspector of Taxes as being the company's formal return. We shall lodge formal notice of appeal against excessive or incorrect assessments to corporation tax where notice of such assessments is received by us. Where appropriate we shall also make formal application for postponement of tax in dispute and shall advise as to appropriate payments on account.

13 You will be responsible, unless otherwise agreed, for all other returns, more particularly: the returns of advance corporation tax and income tax deducted at source as required on Forms CT61, returns relating to employee taxes under PAYE and returns of employee expenses and benefits on form P11D. Your staff will deal with all returns and other requirements in relation to value added tax.

14 We shall be pleased to advise you on matters relating to the company's corporation tax liability, the implications of particular business transactions and on other taxation matters which you refer to us, such as national insurance, income tax deducted at source, employee benefits, value added tax and inheritance tax.

Fees

15 Our fees are computed on the basis of the time spent on your affairs by the partners and our staff, and on the levels of skill and responsibility involved. Unless otherwise agreed, our fees will be charged separately for each of the main classes of work described above, will be billed at appropriate intervals during the course of the year and will be due on presentation.

Agreement of terms

16 Once it has been agreed, this letter will remain effective, from one audit appointment to another, until it is replaced. We shall be grateful if you could confirm in writing your agreement to the terms of this letter, or let us know if they are not in accordance with your understanding of our terms of appointment.

Yours faithfully

Certified Accountants

Exercise 2

Explain why a letter of engagement is desirable for the auditor.

Solution

Reasons why it is desirable for the auditor to send a letter of engagement include the following.

(a) It defines the extent of the auditor's responsibilities and so minimises the possibility of any misunderstanding between the management of the enterprise and the auditor.

(b) It documents and confirms the auditor's acceptance of the appointment, the objective and scope of the audit, the extent of his responsibilities, and the form of his reports.

3 CLEARANCE PROCEDURES

3.1 We have already looked at the legal requirements when an auditor is appointed (see Chapter 3). This section covers the procedures that the auditor must undertake to ensure that his appointment is valid and that he is clear to act.

Before accepting nomination

3.2 Before a new audit client is accepted, the auditor concerned must ensure that there are no independence or other ethical problems likely to cause conflict with the ethical code. Furthermore, it is important for the new auditor to ensure that he has been appointed in a proper and legal manner, especially since one auditor's appointment is normally another auditor's removal or resignation.

3.3 The nominee auditor must take the following steps.

(a) Ensure that he is professionally qualified to act, not disqualified on any of the legal or ethical grounds set out in earlier chapters.

(b) Ensure that the firm's existing resources are adequate to service the needs of the new client: this will raise questions of staff and time availability and the firm's technical expertise.

(c) Seek references in respect of the new client company: it may be, as is often the case, that the directors of the company are already personally known to the firm; if not, independent enquiries should be made concerning the status of the company and its directors (agencies such as Dun & Bradstreet might be of assistance together with a formal search at Companies House).

(d) Communicate with the present auditor.

(i) The auditing bodies have laid down strict rules of conduct in their ethical statement entitled *Changes in professional appointments*, regarding the purpose and the nature of such a communication. The purpose is primarily to protect the shareholders. The proposed auditor should not accept nomination without first enquiring from the existing auditor whether there is any reason for or circumstances behind the proposed change of which he should be aware. A secondary reason for the communication is as matter of professional courtesy.

(ii) The statement requires the following actions on the part of the nominee.

(1) He should request the prospective client's permission to communicate with the auditor last appointed. If such permission is refused he should decline nomination.

(2) On receipt of permission, he should request in writing of the auditor last appointed all information which ought to be made available to him to enable him to decide whether he is prepared to accept nomination. (*Note*. If no reply is received, a further letter may be sent which states that if no answer is received by a specified date, it will be assumed that there are no reasons not to accept nomination.)

(iii) The incumbent auditor receiving the request in (ii)(2) above should perform the following.

(1) He should request permission of the client to discuss the client's affairs freely with the proposed nominee. If this request is not granted the member should report that fact to the proposed nominee, who, if a member, should not accept nomination.

(2) He should discuss freely with the proposed nominee all matters relevant to the appointment of which the latter should be aware, and disclose fully all information which appears to him to be relevant to the client's affairs or which may be reasonably requested of him by the proposed nominee.

3.4 The following draft indicates the contents of the initial communication.

> To: Retiring & Co
> Certified Accountants
>
> Dear Sirs
>
> Re: New Client Co Ltd
>
> We have been asked to allow our name to go forward for nomination as auditors of the above company, and we should therefore be grateful if you would please let us know whether there are any professional reasons why we should not accept nomination...... .
>
> Acquiring & Co
>
> Certified Accountants

3.5 The following letter would be sent if the nominee has not received a reply to the letter above within a reasonable time.

> To: Retiring & Co
> Certified Accountants
>
> Dear Sirs
>
> Re: New Client Co Ltd
>
> As we have been unable to obtain a reply to our letters of the 1 and 14 September we would inform you that, unless we hear from you by 30 September, we shall assume that there are no professional reasons preventing our acceptance of nomination as auditors of the above company and we shall allow our name to go forward. We ourselves are not aware of any reasons why we should not consent to act for this company.... .
>
> Acquiring & Co
>
> Certified Accountants.

3.6 Having negotiated these steps the auditor will be in a position to accept the nomination, or not, as the case may be.

3.7 These procedures can be demonstrated most easily in a decision chart, as shown below.

Procedures after accepting nomination

3.8 The following procedures should be carried out after accepting nomination.

(a) Ensure that the outgoing auditor's removal or resignation has been properly conducted in accordance with the Companies Act 1985.

The new auditor should see a valid notice of the outgoing auditor's resignation (under s392 CA 1985), or confirm that the outgoing auditor was properly removed (under s 391 CA 1985).

(b) Ensure that the new auditor's appointment is valid. The new auditor should obtain a copy of the resolution passed at the general meeting appointing him as the company's auditor.

(c) Set up and submit a letter of engagement to the directors of the company (see Section 2).

Appointment decision chart

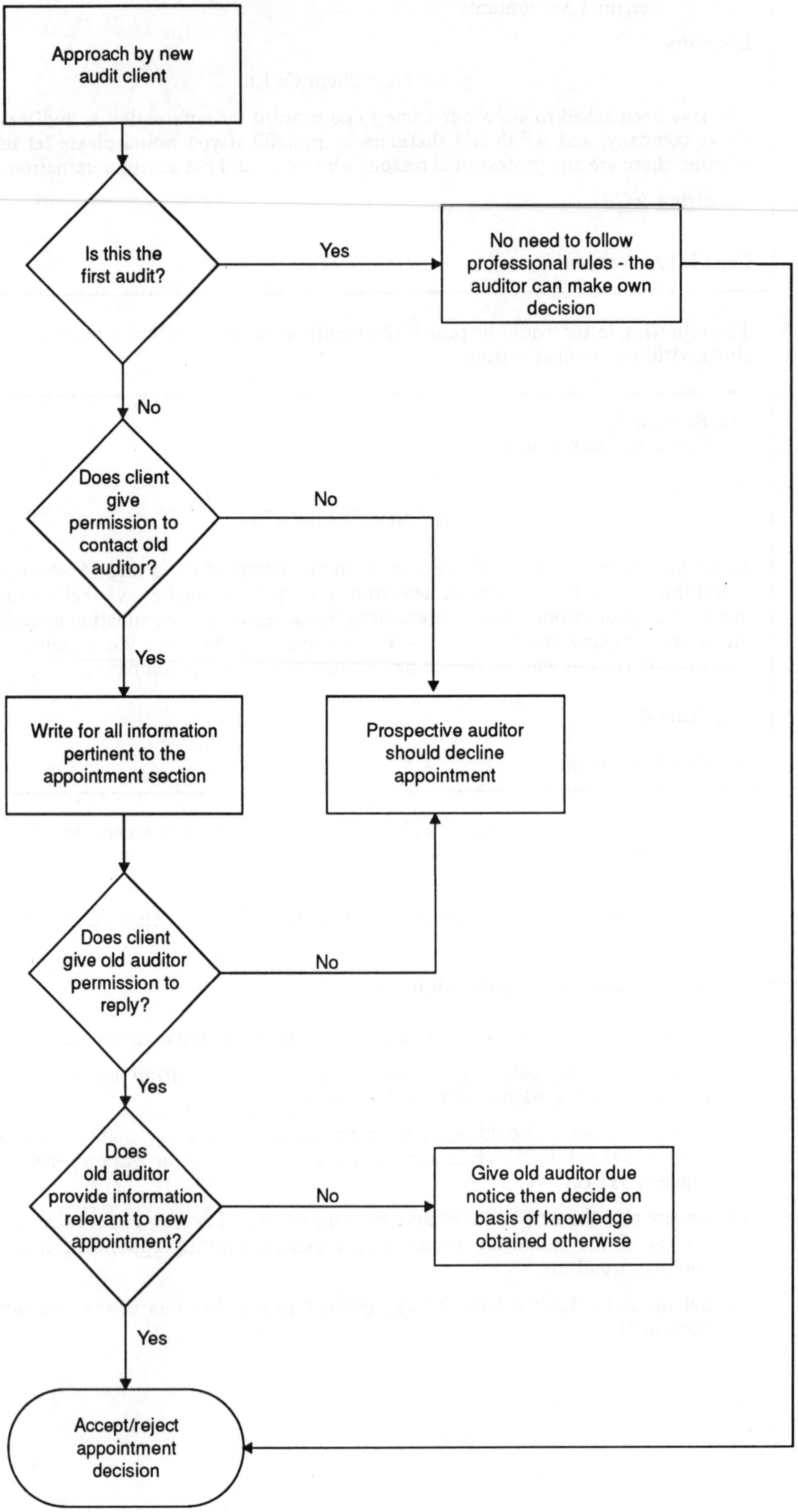

Other matters

3.9 Where the previous auditor has fees still owing by the client, the new auditor need not decline appointment solely for this reason. He should decide how far he may go in aiding the former auditor to obtain his fees, as well as whether he should accept the appointment. A suggestion to the client to pay the fees might be appropriate, but the new or prospective auditor should avoid entanglement in such a situation, otherwise he may be asked to give an opinion on whether the fees are reasonable or the work was 'up to standard'.

3.10 Once a new appointment has taken place, the new auditor should obtain all books and papers which belong to the client from the old auditor. The former accountant should ensure that all such documents are transferred, ***unless*** he has a lien over the books because of unpaid fees. The old auditor should also pass any useful information to the new auditor if it will be of help, without charge, unless a lot of work is involved.

3.11 Where an accountant is appointed to a non audit engagement at a client which has a different auditor or accountant performing work, the new accountant should inform the existing auditor/ accountant of his appointment as a matter of courtesy. This requirement may be waived in certain circumstances.

Chapter roundup

- Client screening can be very important in avoiding embarrassing or damaging situations after an audit has been carried out.
- A variety of screening procedures may be carried out, depending on the relative size of audit firm and company.
- Whatever the size or importance of the engagement, some documentation should be retained on client screening, no matter how rudimentary.
- The engagement letter is important for *all* types of engagement, not just audit. The contents will be tailored to specific circumstances.
- The outgoing and incoming auditor must communicate in relation to their mutual client. Care must be taken as to how the old auditor lays out any problems: it is necessary to avoid libel!

Test your knowledge

1 What matters are auditors likely to consider when screening a potential new client? (see para 1.3)

2 What are the basic factors to be looked into in client screening? (1.4)

3 What types of client are likely to be investigated before acceptance? (1.13)

4 When should an engagement letter be sent to audit clients? (2.3, 2.4)

5 Is it normal to include fee information in an engagement letter? (2.15)

6 What formal steps should the auditor take before accepting a new client? (3.3)

7 What procedures should the auditor undertake after accepting nomination? (3.8)

Chapter 5

AUDIT OBJECTIVES

This chapter covers the following topics.

Introduction

This chapter covers the aspects of the audit which will be considered at the earliest stages, during planning. It is unlikely that you will have direct experience of planning an audit, but you should acquaint yourself with all the planning documentation on every audit you carry out.

The evaluation of audit risk has become a very important part of the audit process as audit firms have shifted to a risk-based approach. Students often have difficulty understanding this topic, so you should pay careful attention to it, particularly as it affects audit sampling in a later chapter.

1 THE AUDITOR'S OPERATIONAL STANDARD

1.1 We have already reproduced the full text of this standard and you should refer back to Chapter 2 to refresh your memory. Remember that the standard lays out standards on:

(a) planning, controlling and recording;
(b) accounting systems;
(c) audit evidence;
(d) internal controls;
(e) review of financial statements.

1.2 Each of these standards has an accompanying audit guideline. The standard and each relevant guideline are introduced into this text where relevant.

1.3 The point to understand about *The auditor's operational standard* is that it brings together each part of the audit, providing an overview of the auditing process.

1.4 Remember what was said earlier about the legal status of the auditing standards and guidelines.

> 'A court of law may, when considering the adequacy of the work of an auditor, take into account any pronouncements or publications which it thinks may be indicative of good practice. Auditing standards and guidelines are likely to be so regarded.'

1.5 It is therefore in the auditor's best interest to follow this standard: if not, he may be liable.

2 PLANNING THE AUDIT

Acquiring knowledge of the business

2.1 In the first audit of any client, there is setting-up work necessary that will not be required in such depth in subsequent years. Sufficient work must be carried out to enable the auditor to gain a sound knowledge of the client's background, operations, accounting procedures and internal controls to allow him properly to plan the strategy and scope of his audit work. The following are some of the factors relating to the client environment that might need to be investigated and recorded.

(a) The historical background of the company.

(b) The characteristics of the company's business, including:

- (i) the economic climate of the industry;
- (ii) the factors affecting the industry;
- (iii) the position of the company in the industry;
- (iv) the main competitors;
- (v) the marketing methods;
- (vi) the methods of distribution;
- (vii) the production functions;
- (viii) labour relations.

(c) The structure of the organisation including the following:

- (i) the organisation chart of the company showing the names, responsibilities and authority of the officials;
- (ii) the location of the main operating accounting and custodian centres;
- (iii) whether an internal audit department exists;
- (iv) the flow of documentation including budgets and reports;
- (v) the books of account and ancillary records (in summary, not necessarily detailed form at this stage).

(d) Statutory information including:

- (i) unusual clauses in the Memorandum and Articles of Association;
- (ii) directors' interests in other businesses;
- (iii) charges on assets of the company;
- (iv) extent of distributable reserves.

(e) Accounts, accounting policies including:

- (i) copies of last five years' (say) statutory accounts, management accounts and forecasts;
- (ii) review for consistency of accounting policies including dates and effects of recent changes.

(f) Previous auditors:

- (i) weaknesses in controls noted by previous auditors (if available);
- (ii) reports of irregular transactions (if any).

(g) Taxation:

- (i) bases of computations and agreements with HMIT;
- (ii) letter of authority to Inland Revenue.

(h) Bankers: letter of authority to bankers to provide information concerning the client.

2.2 Once sufficient background information has been accumulated, and all the procedural niceties described in the earlier paragraphs have been satisfied then the auditor will be in a position to determine the audit approach and establish his comprehensive plan. There is, however, one particular problem associated with the first year audit that warrants consideration before we look at planning in detail: this is the problem of figures derived from the previous year's accounts.

Amounts derived from the preceding financial statements

2.3 In expressing an opinion on the accounts of a new client the auditor accepts responsibility not only for the accounts of the year being reported on, but also:

(a) the consistency of the application of accounting policies;

(b) the reliability of the opening balances (which have an effect on the profit or loss for the current year;

(c) the appropriateness of the comparative figures included in the accounts, in as much as they may render the current year's figures misleading.

2.4 Clarification of the auditor's responsibility for amounts taken from the preceding period's financial statements is provided in the detailed operational guideline *Amounts derived from the preceding financial statements* issued in November 1982. The following selected comments are extracted from this guideline.

2.5 Financial statements of companies incorporated under the provisions of the Companies Act 1985 are required to disclose corresponding amounts for all items in a company's balance sheet and profit and loss account. In other cases, financial statements usually contain corresponding amounts as a matter of law, regulation or good practice. Their purpose, unless stated otherwise, is to complement the amounts relating to the current period and not to re-present the complete financial statements for the preceding period. The auditor is not required to express an opinion on the corresponding amounts as such. His responsibility is to ensure that they are the amounts which appeared in the preceding period's financial statements or, where appropriate, have either been properly restated to achieve consistency and comparability with the current period's amounts, or have been restated due to a change of accounting policy or a correction of a fundamental error as required by FRS 3.

2.6 In these special circumstances the new auditor will have to satisfy himself as to the matters identified in Paragraph 2.3, but his lack of prior knowledge of the preceding period's financial statement will require him to apply additional procedures in order to obtain the necessary assurance.

2.7 The additional procedures that should be performed by the auditor may include any of the following:

(a) consultations with the client's management;

(b) review of the client's records, working papers and accounting and control procedures for the preceding period, particularly in so far as they affect the opening position;

(c) audit work on the current period, which will usually provide some evidence regarding opening balances; and

(d) in exceptional circumstances, substantive testing of the opening balances, if he does not consider the results of procedures (a) to (c) to be satisfactory.

2.8 In addition, the auditor may be able to hold consultations with the previous auditor. Whilst outgoing auditors can normally be expected to afford reasonable co-operation to their successors, neither ethical statements nor the law place them under a specific obligation to make working papers or other information available to their successors. Consultations would normally be limited to seeking information concerning the previous auditor's examination of particular areas which are important to his successor, and to obtaining clarification of any significant accounting matters which are not adequately dealt with in the client's records. If, however, such consultations are not possible or alternatively, if the preceding period's financial statements were unaudited, the only evidence about the opening position available to the auditor will be that generated by procedures such as those set out in Paragraph 2.7 above.

2.9 Under normal circumstances the auditor will be able to satisfy himself as to the opening position by performing the work set out in Paragraphs 2.7 and 2.8. If he is not able to satisfy himself in any material respect he will need to qualify his report for the possible effect on the financial statements.

Audit planning

2.10 *The auditor's operational standard* requires that 'the auditor should adequately plan, control and record his work'. The associated guideline stresses that audits, irrespective of their size, must be properly planned, controlled and recorded at each stage of their progress if they are to be efficiently and effectively carried out. It is convenient to consider planning, controlling and recording separately although, as already stated, they are not mutually exclusive.

2.11 The auditing guideline *Planning, controlling and recording* under the heading 'planning' makes the following broad observations regarding the scope and objectives of audit planning.

> 'The form and nature of the planning required for an audit will be affected by the size and complexity of the enterprise, the commercial environment in which it operates, the method of processing transactions and the reporting requirements to which it is subject. In this context the auditor should aim to provide an effective and economic service within an appropriate time-scale.
>
> Adequate audit planning:
>
> (a) establishes the intended means of achieving the objectives of the audit;
> (b) assists in the direction and control of the work;
> (c) helps to ensure that attention is devoted to critical aspects of the audit; and
> (d) helps to ensure that the work is completed expeditiously.
>
> In order to plan his work adequately the auditor needs to understand the nature of the business of the enterprise, its organisation, its method of operating and the industry in which it is involved, so that he is able to appreciate which events and transactions are likely to have a significant effect on the financial statements.'

2.12 With regard to specific planning procedures and decisions the guideline states the following.

> 'The auditor should consider the outline audit approach he proposes to adopt, including the extent to which he may wish to rely on internal controls and any aspects of the audit which need particular attention. He should also take into account in his planning any additional work which he has agreed to undertake.
>
> Preparatory procedures which the auditor should consider include the following:
>
> (a) reviewing matters raised in the audit of the previous year which may have continuing relevance in the current year;
>
> (b) assessing the effects of any changes in legislation or accounting practice affecting the financial statements of the enterprise;
>
> (c) reviewing interim or management accounts where these are available and consulting with the management and staff of the enterprise. Matters which should be considered include current trading circumstances, and significant changes in:
>
> (i) the business carried on;
> (ii) the enterprise's management;
>
> (d) identifying any significant changes in the enterprise's accounting procedures, such as a new computer based system.
>
> The auditor should also consider:
>
> (a) the timing of significant phases of the preparation of the financial statements;
>
> (b) the extent to which analyses and summaries can be prepared by the enterprise's employees;

(c) the relevance of any work to be carried out by the enterprise's internal auditors.

The auditor will need to determine the number of audit staff required, the experience and special skills they need to possess and the timing of their audit visits. He will need to ensure that all audit staff are briefed regarding the enterprise's affairs and the nature and scope of the work they are required to carry out. The preparation of a memorandum setting out the outline audit approach may be helpful.'

It should be noted that the guideline is written in the context of the established audit engagement rather than the first time audit. As we have seen earlier, planning the first audit raises special problems due to the auditor's relative lack of knowledge and precedent.

2.13 To appreciate better the significance of certain of the comments above it is useful to establish some prerequisites for effective organisation of an accounting office. Efficient organisation is necessary so that a firm can provide a competent service to clients in compliance with auditing standards, and of course, be profitable.

2.14 Efficient organisation may be achieved by ensuring that the following procedures are used.

(a) Efficient time recording and costing methods.

(b) Preparation of time and cost budgets for audit (and other work); audits being performed by an efficient staff team working under the supervision of competent managers who are responsible to their partners.

(c) Experience and knowledge used to the maximum advantage of clients when providing audit, accounting, taxation and other services. This may lead to the creation of separate departments, for instance, a taxation department, management consultancy department, secretarial services department. Not all firms adopt this approach, however, some preferring to retain a 'general practice' approach. Whatever the organisation structure, there must be adequate numbers of staff who are knowledgeable and experienced in the areas of professional expertise provided by the firm.

(d) Consistent practices within the firm including provision of an audit procedures manual, system for preparation and retention of audit working papers and a degree of standardisation regarding check-lists, standard forms and certain audit procedures, for example sampling techniques.

2.15 The objectives and preparatory procedures outlined in Paragraphs 2.11 and 2.12 provide an overview of the planning function. To appreciate a little more fully how the planning objectives in Paragraph 2.11 are achieved it is helpful to look at three practical aspects of planning in greater detail:

(a) audit risk evaluation;
(b) materiality;
(c) use of analytical review.

The concept of audit risk and materiality were introduced in Chapter 4. We now consider them in a little more detail.

The planning memorandum

2.16 We have established that audit planning is a vital stage in the audit process. It is one thing to make intelligent planning decisions, but another to ensure that they are satisfactorily recorded. The preparation of a planning memorandum is therefore established best practice.

Exercise 1

An auditing guideline has been issued on *Amounts derived from preceding financial statements*, and one of the matters it considers is where one firm of auditors takes over from another firm. You have recently been appointed auditor of Lowdham Castings Ltd, a company which has been trading for about thirty years, and are carrying out the audit for the year ended 30 September 19X6. The company's turnover is about £500,000 and its normal profit before tax is about £30,000.

Required

Discuss your responsibilities in relation to the corresponding amounts included in the accounts for the year ended 30 September 19X6. You should also consider the information you would require from the retiring auditor.

Solution

Consideration of the financial statements of the preceding period is necessary in the audit of the current period's financial statements in relation to three main aspects.

(a) *Opening position.* Obtaining satisfaction that those amounts which have a direct effect on the current period's results or closing position have been properly brought forward.

(b) *Accounting policies.* Determining whether the accounting policies adopted for the current period are consistent with those of the previous period.

(c) *Corresponding amounts.* Determining that the corresponding amounts are properly shown in the current period's financial statements.

The auditor's main concern will therefore be to satisfy himself that there were no material misstatements in the previous year's financial statements which may have a bearing upon his work in the current year.

The new auditor does not have to 're-audit' the previous year's financial statements, but he will have to pay more attention to them than would normally be the case where he had himself been the auditor in the earlier period. A useful source of audit evidence will clearly be the previous auditor, and, with the client's permission, he should be contacted to see if he is prepared to co-operate. Certainly, any known areas of weakness should be discussed with the previous auditors and it is also possible that they might be prepared to provide copies of their working papers (although there is no legal or ethical provision which requires the previous auditor to co-operate in this way).

3 AUDIT RISK

3.1 *Audit risk* (or ultimate risk) is the risk that the auditor will issue an inappropriate opinion on the accounts. Put another way, audit risk is the risk that the auditor gives an unqualified opinion on the accounts when he should have given a qualified opinion; *or* he gives an opinion qualified for a particular reason where that reason was not justified.

3.2 Audit risk can never be completely eliminated. This means that auditors will always be exposed to the damaging consequences of a negligence action, including costs of legal action and through adverse publicity. The auditor is called upon the make subjective judgements in the course of forming an opinion and so fraud or error may possibly go undetected.

3.3 The preferred method of minimising audit risk has been to systemise the audit approach, so that all aspects have been standardised. This standardised solution has been achieved through *The operational standard*, auditing guidelines and audit firms' own manuals.

Systems v risk-based approach

3.4 The systems approach to auditing is based on the principle that, by studying and evaluating the internal control system, the auditor can form an opinion as to the quality of the accounting system (completeness, susceptibility to error). This opinion then determines the level of substantive testing undertaken on the items in the financial statements. This approach was described briefly in Chapter 1.

3.5 More recently, auditors have realised that the systems approach, although it gives a useful framework, does not deal directly with audit risk. The approach does not provide a rational means of linking all the different sources of audit evidence used to form an opinion (analytical review, knowledge of the company and the industry, assessment of the control system and so on).

3.6 The systems approach has also been accused of inflexibility, because it may cause the auditor to perform compliance testing which is actually not necessary. If it is perfectly clear from a review (control environment, past history etc) that no assurance will be gained from compliance testing, the auditor should just move straight on to the detailed substantive testing. This saves time and audit resources are concentrated where they are most required.

3.7 A *risk-centred methodology* has now taken over from the established systems approach. This methodology gives the auditor an overall measure of risk, but as the same time it provides a quantification of each stage of the audit. The extent of detailed testing required is determined by a purely risk-based perspective. A diagrammatic view of the risk-based approach is given below.

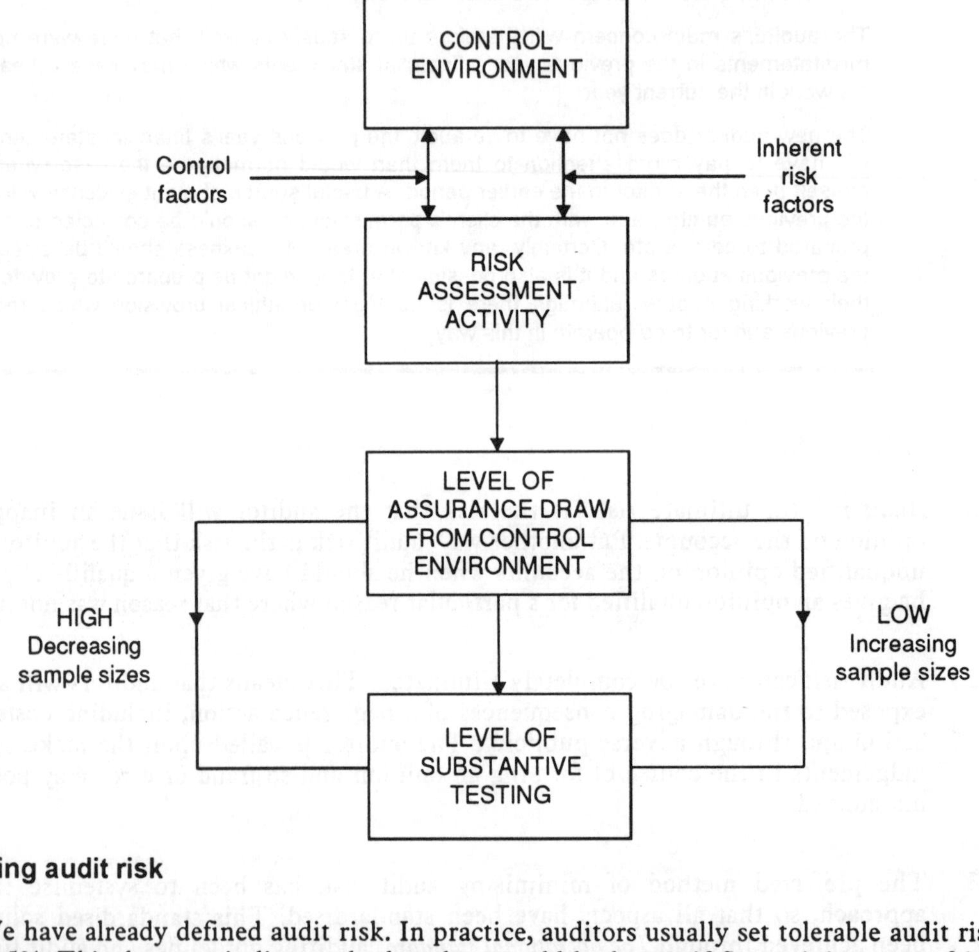

Assessing audit risk

3.8 We have already defined audit risk. In practice, auditors usually set tolerable audit risk at 5%. This does not indicate whether they would be happy if five opinions out of 100 were wrong, nor is it based on any mathematical theory. The 5% is just a magic number.

3.9 *Audit risk* (AR) is seen as dividing into at least three categories as shown on the diagram overleaf. We will describe each one of these underlying categories, before looking at how they make up audit risk.

3.10 *Inherent risk* (IR) arises from factors which may cause errors or irregularities to be present. The level of inherent risk will depend on various conditions existing *within the enterprise* as well as on conditions *outside the enterprise*. Examples of conditions existing outside the enterprise include:

(a) macroeconomic factors such as general recession (this might, for example, threaten the collectability of debtors), or impending government legislation; and

(b) factors from within the industry, such as consumer demand conditions which might jeopardise future viability of the enterprise, technological changes rendering stocks obsolete.

3.11 Example of inherent risk conditions within the enterprise which could affect the auditor's assessment of audit risk include:

(a) poor management, which could be affecting the business overall;

(b) key personnel with a motive for attempting to distort the financial statements (for instance, if managers are on a performance-related bonus scheme, or subsidiary company managers are pressurised by group management;

(c) susceptibility of account balances to be misstated as the result of fraud;

(d) poor quality control, potentially leading to production of defective goods (which might therefore subsequently be returned by customers).

3.12 The *control risk* (CR) perceived by the auditor (the risk that material errors will not be prevented or detected by internal controls) depends upon his assessment of the system of internal control. Even in the best system, some control risk will remain, for example because it will always be possible for management to override controls, or for fraudulent collusion between two or more employees to occur. In an audit based wholly on substantive tests, detection risk assumes more importance.

3.13 The assessment of the risk of material misstatements (inherent risk coupled with control risk) may be expressed 'as normal' or 'high' depending on the risk factors identified. It may be that an internal control is itself designed to minimise an inherent risk of the enterprise. In such a case, it will not be worthwhile to try to evaluate separately the inherent risk and control risk elements of the overall risk that material misstatements may occur.

3.14 After making his assessment of inherent risk and control risks, including any assessment which he decides to make of the system of internal controls, the auditor is in a position to design appropriate tests whose overall objective is to *detect* any misstatements in the accounting records or financial statements. The design, extent and performance of these tests carry the risk that any misstatements which have occurred may fail to be detected and this is *detection risk* (DR).

3.15 Unlike the levels of control risk and inherent risk, the level of detection risk can be directly controlled by the auditor, since he can modify his programme of testing to alter the level of detection risk. The risk that material misstatements may occur, control risk and inherent risk, cannot be *altered* by the auditor, although it can be *assessed* by him in his audit planning.

3.16 *Sampling risk* (SR) is the risk that the conclusion drawn by the auditor from the results of testing a particular characteristic of a sample of items differs from the conclusion he or she would have drawn had the entire population been tested in like fashion.

3.17 *Non-sampling risk* (NSR) represents all those risks of drawing an incorrect conclusion from an audit test that are not due specifically to sampling. This includes, for example, the risk that an auditor will draw an incorrect conclusion about an individual item in the sample tested.

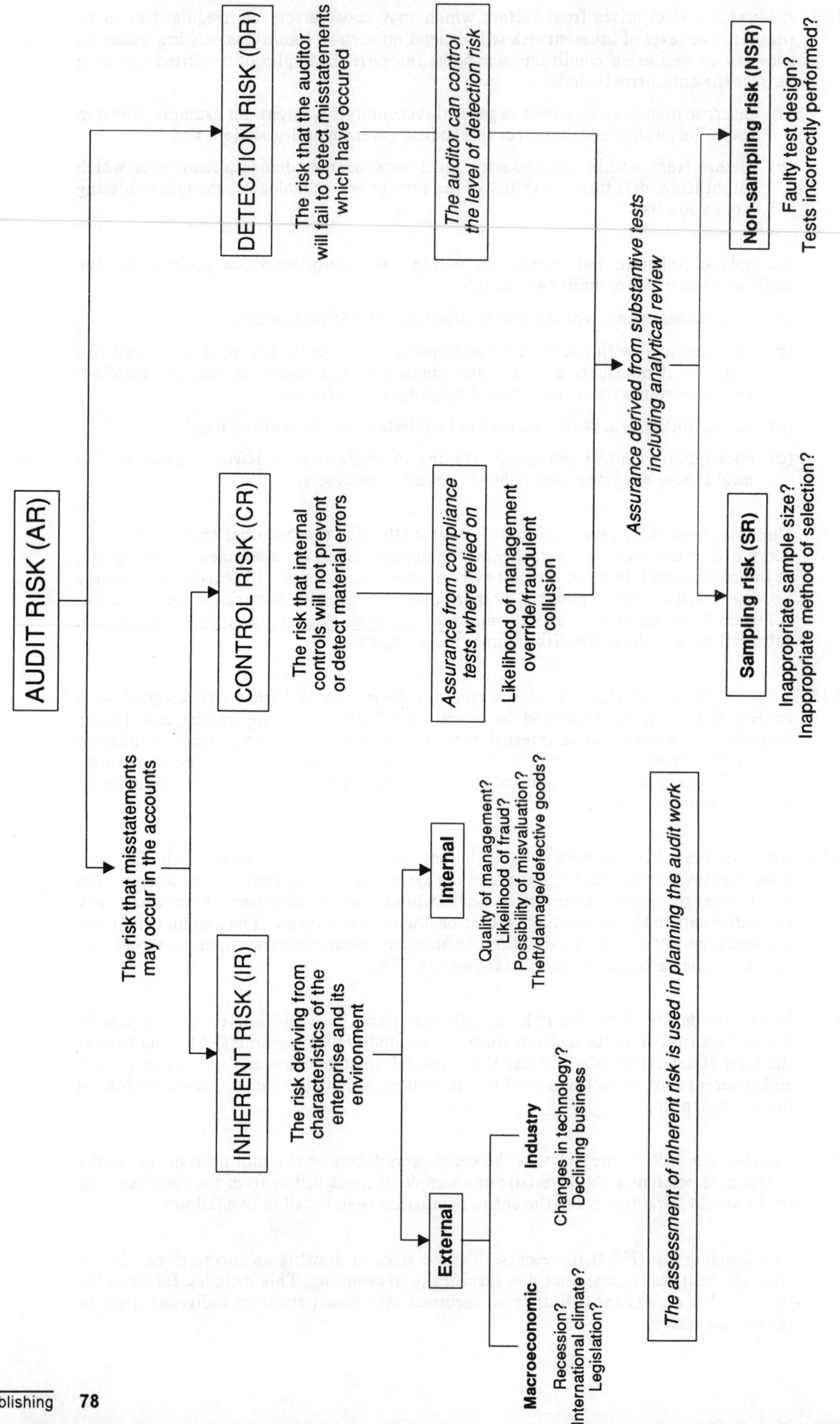
AUDIT RISK (AR)
The risk that misstatements may occur in the accounts
INHERENT RISK (IR)
The risk deriving from characteristics of the enterprise and its environment
External
Macroeconomic
Recession? International climate? Legislation?
Industry
Changes in technology? Declining business
Internal
Quality of management? Likelihood of fraud? Possibility of misvaluation? Theft/damage/defective goods?
The assessment of inherent risk is used in planning the audit work
CONTROL RISK (CR)
The risk that internal controls will not prevent or detect material errors
Assurance from compliance tests where relied on
Likelihood of management override/fraudulent collusion
DETECTION RISK (DR)
The risk that the auditor will fail to detect misstatements which have occured
The auditor can control the level of detection risk
Assurance derived from substantive tests including analytical review
Sampling risk (SR)
Inappropriate sample size? Inappropriate method of selection?
Non-sampling risk (NSR)
Faulty test design? Tests incorrectly performed?

3.18 Two subsets of detection risk which are also used to define audit risk are as follows.

(a) *Substantive test risk* (STR) is the risk that material errors will not be detected through the use of detailed substantive testing procedures.

(b) *Analytical review risk* (ARR) is the risk that analytical review procedures will not detect material errors.

3.19 Audit risk is defined as the product of certain of these types of underlying risk. The usual definition is:

$AR = IR \times CR \times DR$

or, breaking detection risk down:

$AR = IR \times CR \times ARR \times STR$

and an alternative to the last formula was given by the APC:

$AR = IR \times CR \times DR \times SR$

3.20 In order to apply a value to the risk categories, the auditor must decide on the level of assurance required from the detailed substantive tests, given that assurances have been gained from other sources.

Establishing detection risk

3.21 An example of how risk percentages are subjectively attached to some of these risk categories is shown here.

Qualitative assurance	*Inherent risk (IR)*	*Control risk (CR)*	*Analytical review risk (ARR))*
	%	%	%
None	100	100	100
Low	100	80	90
Moderate	90	60	70
High	80	30	50

3.22 The following examples show how detection risk can be found using the above figures.

Example: detection risk (1)

3.23 The client company is considered low risk. Audit risk is the maximum tolerated: 5%. Inherent risk is 80% as the client is well established in a stable industry. The company has a strong internal control system with no recent changes, so control risk is 30%.

What is the detection risk?

Solution

3.24 $AR = IR \times CR \times DR$

$$DR = \frac{AR}{IR \times CR}$$

$$DR = \frac{0.05}{0.8 \times 0.3} = 0.2083$$

The level of audit assurance required from substantive testing is:

100 – 20.83 = 79.16%

This is a relatively low figure and the sample size will be relatively small.

Example: detection risk (2)

3.25 The client company is considered high risk. The audit risk is the maximum tolerated: 2%. The client has only been in business for two years and the industry is high-tech so the inherent risk is set at 100%. The company has a weak internal control system, with easy management override so control risk is set at 70%.

What is the detection risk?

Solution

3.26 $DR = \frac{0.02}{1.0 \times 0.7} = 0.0286$

The minimum confidence level (or the level of audit assurance) is:

100 – 2.86 = 97.14%

which would indicate a larger sample size.

3.27 These examples indicate that the more the auditor can rely on the system of internal control and the more assurance he can gain from other sources, then the lower the amount of substantive testing required (and vice versa).

3.28 As a summary, the diagram given opposite shows the relationship between inherent risk, control risk and detection risk.

Exercise 2

Define the following terms:

(a) audit risk;
(b) inherent risk;
(c) control risk;
(d) detection risk;
(e) sampling risk.

Solution

(a) See Paragraph 3.1.
(b) See Paragraph 3.10.
(c) See Paragraph 3.12.
(d) See Paragraph 3.14.
(e) See Paragraph 3.16.

---

4 PLANNING MATERIALITY

4.1 The main purpose of an audit is to express an opinion on the truth and fairness of the results and financial position shown by the accounts. The first way in which the concept of materiality affects the audit is that it is one of the factors which influences the nature and size of audit tests; the auditor needs to design audit procedures to verify only those items which could be materially wrong and he need only do sufficient work to satisfy himself that balances and transactions do not contain material errors. Hence, if an auditor sets a materiality level of £50,000, he may direct little audit work towards verifying prepayments totalling £10,000. The second way in which the concept of materiality affects audit work is when deciding whether to seek adjustment for errors found. The auditor is concerned that adjustments are made for material errors, not for immaterial errors.

4.2 It is becoming increasingly common practice for the auditor to set a materiality level at the initial planning stage of the audit to act as a guideline for determining the extent of audit testing and for deciding whether to seek adjustment for errors or whether to qualify his audit report.

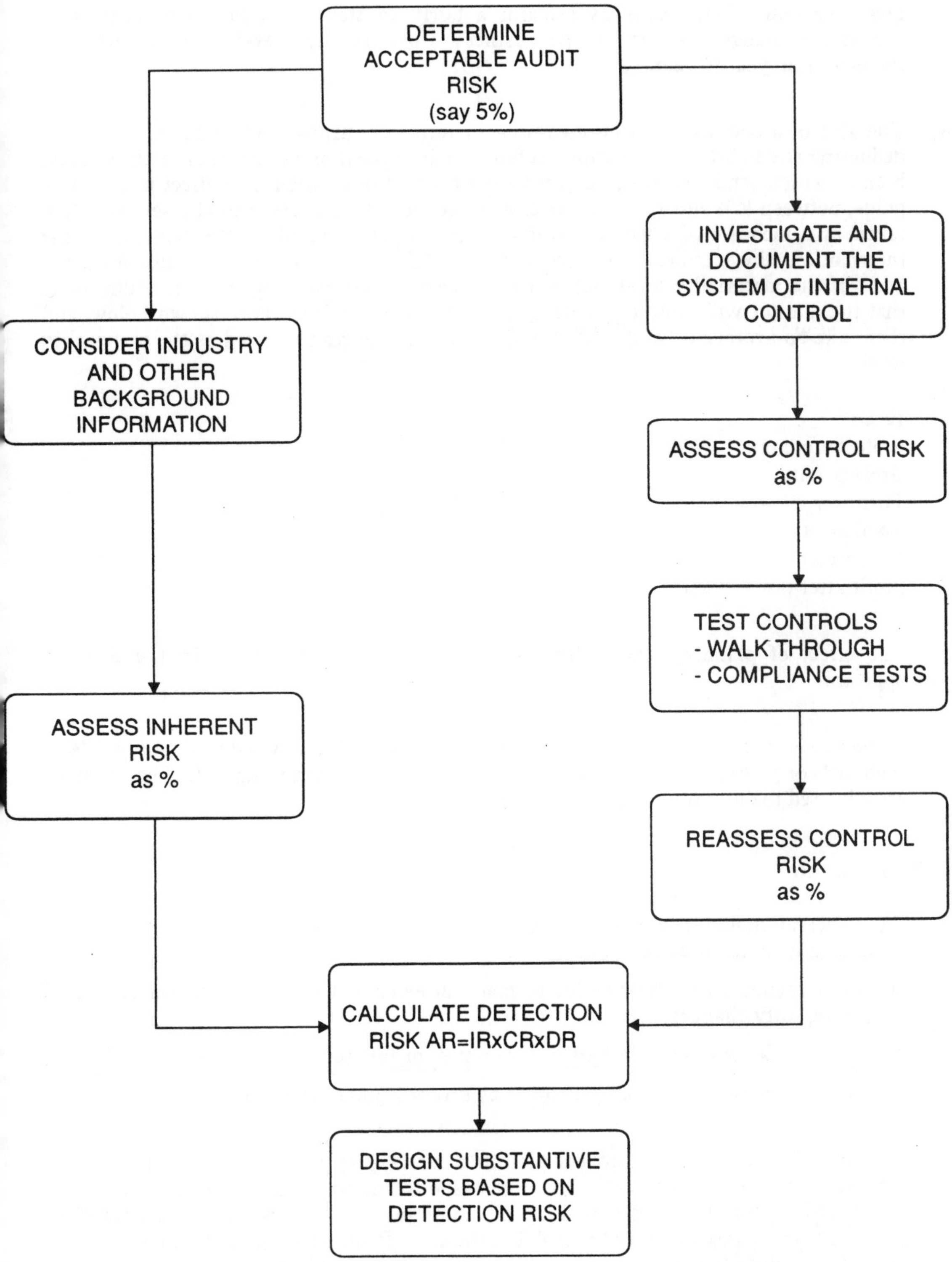

Note. At any point in the procedure the auditor may determine that he does not wish to rely on the internal control system (ie control risk is set at 100%). He can then jump immediately to calculating detection risk based on CR=100% and subsequently plan substantive testing on that basis.

4.3 To set the materiality level the auditor needs to decide the level of errors which would distort the view given by the accounts. Because many users of accounts are primarily interested in the profitability of the company, the level is often expressed as a proportion of its profits (typically 5% of profit before tax). Some argue, however, that it is more sound to think of materiality in terms of the size of the business and hence recognise that, if the company remains a fairly constant size, the materiality level should not change; similarly if the business is growing, the level of materiality will increase from year to year.

4.4 The size of a company can be measured in terms of turnover and total assets before deducting any liabilities (sometimes referred to in legislation as 'the balance sheet total') both of which tend not to be subject to the fluctuations which may affect profit. As a guide, between ½% and 1% of turnover and between 1% and 2% of total assets are often taken as a measure of what is material. These figures, based on the latest available information (the previous year's accounts if nothing else is available) hence form the basis of the materiality levels set and evidenced in the planning memorandum. Note that the auditor will often calculate a range of values, such as those shown below, and then take an average or weighted average of all the figures produced as the materiality level.

Value	%
Profit before tax	5
Gross profit	½ - 1
Turnover	½ - 1
Total assets	1 - 2
Net assets	2 - 5
Profit after tax	5 - 10

4.5 The effect of planning materiality on the audit process is shown in the diagram opposite.

4.6 *Tolerable error* may be set at planning materiality, but it is usually reduced to, say 75% or even 50% of planning materiality so as to take account of sampling risk. The tolerable error is used to determine the sample size.

Audit evaluation

4.7 The level of materiality must be reviewed constantly as the audit progresses and changes may be required because:

(a) draft accounts are altered (due to material error and so on) and therefore overall materiality changes;

(b) external factors cause changes in the control or inherent risk estimates;

(c) such changes as are in (b) are caused by errors found during testing.

4.8 At the end of the testing process planning materiality will once again be used to determine whether adjustments should be made to the financial statements. All errors discovered during the audit which are not material on their own are added together. Projected errors are calculated by applying the error found in a sample to the population as a whole. (Note that a projected error greater than tolerable error in any one account will probably lead to further testing.)

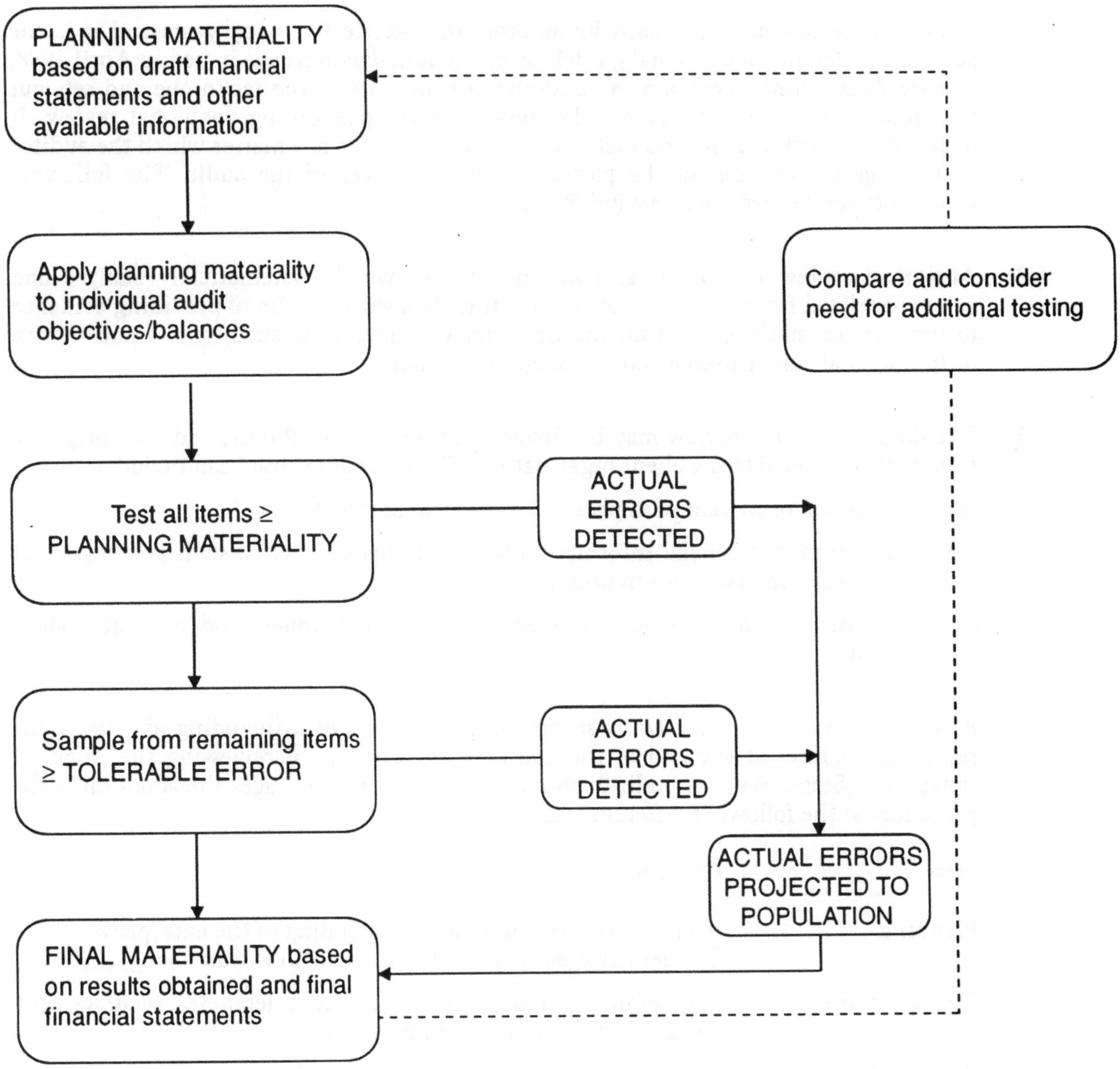

4.9 Once all such errors have been totalled, the auditors will approach the managers of the company with certain attitudes, often determined by this or similar estimates. (*Note*. PBT = Profit Before Tax).

Total error	*Action*
≥ 10% PBT	Ask for adjustment and qualify if not made.
≤ 5% PBT	Ask for adjustment but no further action if not made.
10% ≥ 5% PBT	Ask for adjustment. If not made, consider each error and combination in terms of true and fair view.

Accounting estimates

4.10 Accounting estimates rely on management judgement and are therefore subjective. They include depreciation, bad debt provisions, stock provisions and so on. It is not possible to determine overall error without examining each individual estimate for possible error. As such, the auditor must determine each individual estimation error and then decide whether there is an overall trend into error.

5 ANALYTICAL REVIEW

5.1 Analytical review has been used by auditors in practice for many years and it is the subject of a detailed operational guideline entitled *Analytical review* issued in April 1988. The guideline aims to explain the underlying principles of the technique and sets out the factors which the auditor should consider when performing analytical review. It does not deal with the specific methods to be applied; this is a matter which the auditor must judge in the light of the particular circumstances of the audit. The following comments are derived from this guideline.

5.2 Analytical review is defined as audit procedures which systematically analyse and compare related figures, trends, ratios and other data with the aim of providing evidence to support the audit opinion on the financial statements. As such, it is a substantive technique that can be used at various stages in the audit.

5.3 The data used in the review may be financial or non-financial data, and may originate from within or outside the client organisation. The procedures used can include:

(a) comparison of current with prior year's figures, or ratios;

(b) comparison of financial information with anticipated results, such as budgets, or with similar industry information;

(c) comparison of data using advanced statistical techniques, and computer audit software.

5.4 Analytical review can be used at several stages in the audit, including as part of the review procedures at the end of the audit, in the context of reviewing the financial statements (Stage 10 of our audit diagram). The guideline envisages the adoption of the procedure at the following different stages.

Stage	*Objectives*
Planning	To improve the auditor's understanding of the enterprise. To identify areas of potential risk or significant change.
Detailed testing	To obtain assurance as to the completeness, accuracy and validity of transactions and balances.
Review of financial statements and formulation of the opinion	To support conclusions from other audit work. To assess the overall reasonableness of the financial statements.

5.5 In determining the extent of the auditor's use of analytical review, consideration should be given to:

(a) the nature of the enterprise and its operations;

(b) knowledge of the client, problems which have arisen in the past and the inherent risk;

(c) the availability of financial and non-financial information;

(d) the reliability, relevance, comparability and independence of available information; and

(e) cost effectiveness.

5.6 The audit staff who perform analytical review should possess experience, judgement and a thorough knowledge of the enterprise, and the factors that might affect it. In addition, the risk of relying on analytical review is heightened in areas of the audit which are subject to a high degree of management discretion.

5.7 Analytical review can be used to evaluate:

(a) financial information of individual enterprises or particular activities; and
(b) individual account areas (for example debtors, stock or depreciation charges).

5.8 The application of analytical review is basically a four stage process as follows:

(a) identify the factors likely to have a material effect on the items in the financial statements;

(b) ascertain the probable relationships between these factors and such items;

(c) predict the likely range of values of individual items; and

(d) compare the prediction with the actual recorded amounts. This will indicate the extent to which any further audit work may be required.

5.9 The auditor should consider the implications of any significant fluctuations, unusual items or those which are inconsistent with audit evidence obtained from other sources. Management should be requested to provide explanations for these significant fluctuations. However, before placing full reliance on such explanations, the auditor should try and corroborate them by independent evidence, or examine them critically in the light of other audit evidence.

5.10 Obviously, the auditor's reaction to significant fluctuations will depend upon the stage in the audit that has been reached, and the explanations so far received.

(a) At the planning stage, the auditor will react by deciding the extent, nature and direction of other audit tests. Where explanations reveal changes in the enterprise or its activities, the auditor will need to ensure that the audit approach takes these changes into account.

(b) At the detailed testing stage, where the explanations received cannot be substantiated, the auditor will need to obtain sufficient evidence using alternative methods.

(c) At the final review stage, the auditor would not expect to find any unexpected material fluctuations.

5.11 The extent of the auditor's reliance on analytical review will be based on his assessment of the risk of failing to detect material error. Where certain items are not individually significant to the financial statements, the auditor may rely largely or even entirely on analytical review.

5.12 In assessing the risk of failure to detect material error, the following factors should be considered:

(a) the relevance, reliability, comparability and independence of the data being used;

(b) for internally generated data, the adequacy of controls over the preparation of financial and non-financial information;

(c) the accuracy with which the figures being examined by analytical review procedures can be predicted; and

(d) the materiality of the items.

5.13 Analytical review, like other audit procedures, needs to be properly recorded. The documentation should show:

(a) the information examined, its sources and reliability;
(b) the extent and type of fluctuations found;
(c) explanations for significant fluctuations;
(d) the verification of those explanations;
(e) the conclusions drawn by the auditor; and
(f) any further action taken.

In addition, a client profile may be built up in the permanent file detailing key ratios and trends from year to year, for use in subsequent years.

6 AUDIT PROGRAMMES

6.1 The result of the audit planning process will be an *audit programme*. This lays out the procedures to be carried out during the audit. It is usual to combine the interim and final audit programmes, but this is not always the case.

6.2 The objectives of preparing audit programmes are:

(a) to assist in planning the audit, so that efficient and effective procedures are applied in accordance with the audit strategy and where prepared, the substantive testing plan;

(b) to provide clear instructions to staff as to the nature, extent and timing of procedures;

(c) to provide a record of the work done and the conclusions drawn, as a basis for effective quality control and to meet audit evidence requirements.

6.3 For the purposes of efficiency and quality control each firm will wish to consider specifying procedures in relation to the form and content of audit programmes. The following may be considered appropriate.

(a) Programmes should describe the nature of procedures in sufficient detail to provide adequate instruction to members of the audit team carrying out the work.

(b) Programmes should indicate the extent of testing and the intended timing of the work.

(c) Programmes should show against each procedure the following:

(i) a cross-reference to the related working papers recording the evidence obtained;

(ii) the initials of the member of the audit team carrying out the work;

(iii) the date on which the work was completed;

(iv) whether any exceptions were found in carrying out the test and whether they were satisfactorily cleared. Any matters for partner attention should be clearly identified.

6.4 An audit programme should be prepared for each account balance or class of transaction where significant substantive procedures are to be carried out. The procedures specified in the programme should be designed to provide the requisite degree of substantive assurance in relation to each audit objective.

6.5 The audit senior should ensure that audit programmes are prepared or updated. The engagement manager should review and approve each audit programme, ensuring that the nature, extent and timing of procedures are appropriate to the audit strategy and where prepared the substantive testing plan. It is preferable for the engagement manager's approval to be given before procedures are carried out, as well as on completion of work.

Standardised audit programmes

6.6 Audit programmes can be prepared individually, as suggested above, for each audit. Alternatively, some firms give their staff standardised audit programmes. One of the main aims of such standardised programmes is to ensure completeness in the performance of audit testing. Such audit programmes would normally cover the following areas:

(a) investments;
(b) tangible fixed assets;
(c) stocks and work in progress;
(d) debtors;
(e) bank and cash balances;
(f) creditors;
(g) taxation;
(h) debentures and loans;
(i) inter-company balances;
(j) commitments and contingencies;
(k) reserves;
(l) share capital and statutory books;
(m) minutes of directors' meetings;
(n) profit and loss account items;
(o) analytical review.

6.7 Standardised audit programmes are seen as a small help towards avoiding liability. The liability issue is more of a problem when every audit programme consists of the audit senior's or manager's personal view of what should be tested.

6.8 There is a trade-off between laying down exactly what should be done, without exception or deviation, and giving freedom to each auditor to decide what to do using his or her own personal judgement. Since both extremes increase risk, a middle way is often used: audit manuals produced by audit firms will *suggest* what should be included in the audit programme. This is much better than dictating what is in the programme or giving no guidance whatsoever.

6.9 Auditors are trained to use their professional judgement and using a standardised audit programme prevents that happening. The standardised audit programme becomes a crutch rather than a tool as the auditor stops thinking about what he is doing and why he is doing it.

6.10 Firms which use standardised audit forms do not intend them to be used as a crutch, but rather as a tool. The programme suggests actions which the auditor should take but the auditor can reject or expand on the ideas. Such audit programmes are usually seen as the bare minimum of the work expected on an audit. Auditors must remember this and took to expand the work requested in complicated or important areas.

7 STAFFING AND TRAINING

7.1 Professional audit staff are highly trained and educated. They are not only trained through examination but through a long period of work experience.

7.2 We have already mentioned the usual hierarchy of audit staff. The audit juniors will be training and therefore unqualified. The audit senior will usually be qualified, perhaps only recently. The manager and in particular the audit partner will have a great many years' post qualification experience.

7.3 As you will know by now, the examinations for accountants are extremely hard and cover a wide range of related topics in great depth. Upon qualification the auditor should be completely up to date, both technically and practically.

Continuing professional education

7.4 After qualifying, accountants are not allowed to stop learning. Most of the major accountancy bodies require their members in public practice (and often all their members) to undertake *continuing professional education*. This usually consists of a certain number of hours of private study or reading supplemented by formal courses, making up a minimum number of hours per year.

7.5 Members in practice are required to fill in forms annually stating the number of hours of study they have undertaken.

7.6 As well as continuing professional education, many large audit firms run frequent internal courses for staff to update them on technical issues. In the case of small firms, there are private companies which offer the same type of course for a fee.

Staffing audits

7.7 When planning the audit the partner or manager must decide how many staff are to be allocated to the assignment, how experienced (which grade) and whether any of them will require special knowledge, skills or experience. For example, the client may undertake complicated leasing transactions, so an auditor with some experience of leasing would be required.

7.8 The partner will look at the staffing of the audit in previous years and he will need to decide whether that level of staffing was acceptable. He might judge this by looking at the amount of overtime worked last year and whether the budgeted cost was over or under run. This must be gauged with reference to any unexpected problems which arose in the previous year and whether they are likely to recur.

Reliance on other specialists

7.9 In some instances it may be that the auditor recognises the need for an expert opinion. Where such consultations take place, it must be clear that the auditor is not and can not delegate any of his duties to the 'expert'. *Reliance on other specialists* is an APC detailed operational guideline issued in May 1986. Many of the circumstances likely to give rise to the requirement for expert evidence crystallise during the balance sheet audit. The comments that follow are derived from the guideline.

7.10 For the purpose of the guideline, a specialist is a person or firm possessing special skills, knowledge and experience in a discipline other than accounting or auditing.

7.11 The guideline does not, however, apply to specialists in the employment of the auditor as, under the *Explanatory foreword to the auditing standards and guidelines*, they fall within the definition of the auditor himself. Reliance on the work of other auditors, both external and internal, is dealt with in separate guidelines. Additional detailed guidance on the relationship of auditors and actuaries of long-term insurance funds is also given separately and, because of their specialist nature separate guidance has also been developed on the audit of pension schemes.

Examples of specialist evidence

7.12 During the course of an audit, the auditor may need to consider evidence in the form of statistical data, reports, opinions, valuations or statements from specialists such as valuers, architects, engineers, actuaries, geologists, lawyers, stockbrokers and quantity surveyors. Examples include:

(a) valuations of fixed assets, including freehold and leasehold property, plant and machinery, works of art and antiques;

(b) the measurement of work done on long-term contracts;

(c) valuations of certain types of stocks and consumable materials, including the determination of their quantity and composition;

(d) geological determination of mineral reserves and characteristics;

(e) the legal interpretation of agreements, statutes or regulations;

(f) legal opinions on the outcomes of disputes and litigation; and

(g) actuarial advice for the purpose of assessing the cost of pension provision and its disclosure in the employer's financial statements.

7.13 The guideline is presented in the context of reliance on the work of a particular specialist. Where the nature of the business of an enterprise is such that a number of specialists produce reports routinely for management purposes, (for example, regular site valuation reports by quantity surveyors in a contracting company) the scope of the work performed by the auditor will need to take account of the frequent and systematic way that reports are produced and his previous experience of the reliability and objectivity of such information.

Considerations for the auditor

7.14 When planning the audit, the auditor should consider whether specialist evidence may be necessary in order to form his opinion.

When determining the need for specialist evidence regarding information in, or relevant to, the financial statements, the auditor should consider:

(a) the materiality of, and the likelihood of significant error in, the information being examined;

(b) the complexity of the information, together with his knowledge and understanding of it and of any specialism relating to it; and

(c) whether there are any alternative sources of audit evidence.

7.15 Requests for specialist evidence should be made either by the management of the client, or by the auditor, after obtaining the consent of management.

7.16 Where management is unable or unwilling to obtain specialist evidence, the auditor does not have a responsibility to seek that evidence independently by engaging his own specialist. If there is insufficient alternative audit evidence to enable the auditor to draw reasonable conclusions, then he can properly discharge his responsibilities by qualifying his audit report.

7.17 The auditor should satisfy himself that the specialist is competent to provide the audit evidence he requires. Normally this will be indicated by technical qualifications or membership of an appropriate professional body. Exceptionally, in the absence of any such indications of his competence, the specialist's experience and established reputation may be taken into account.

7.18 The auditor should consider the relationship between the specialist and the client; whether, for example, the specialist or any of his partners or co-directors are closely related to the client, or are directors or employees of the client or its associates. In particular, the auditor should consider whether the specialist's objectivity is likely to be impaired by such a relationship. This may be the case if the specialist has a significant financial interest in the client. He should also consider the extent to which the specialist is bound by the disciplines of his professional body or by statutory requirements to act responsibly, notwithstanding his relationship to the client.

7.19 The auditor's assessment of the specialist's competence and objectivity will influence his evaluation of the evidence provided by the specialist, and his decision on the extent to which he can place reliance on that evidence. If the auditor believes that the specialist may not be sufficiently competent or objective to provide the audit evidence which is needed, he should discuss his reservations with the management of the client.

7.20 Where the evidence of a specialist is to be provided, there should preferably be consultation between the auditor, the client and the specialist, in order to establish the specialist's terms of reference. This should take place as soon as is practicable after the specialist has been appointed. The terms of reference should be documented, reviewed annually where applicable, and preferably confirmed in writing, and should include the following:

(a) the objectives, scope and subject matter of the specialist's work;

(b) the sources of information to be provided to the specialist;

(c) the identification of any relationship which may affect the specialist's objectivity;

(d) the assumptions upon which the specialist's report depends, and the bases to be used, and their compatibility with the assumptions and bases used in preparing the financial statements;

(e) where appropriate, a comparison of the assumptions and bases to be used with those used in preceding periods, together with explanations for any changes;

(f) the use to be made of the specialist's findings in relation to the financial statements or other financial information on which the auditor is required to report;

(g) the form and content of the specialist's report or opinion that would enable the auditor to determine whether or not the findings of the specialist constitute acceptable audit evidence.

7.21 Where it is not practicable for consultation to take place before the specialist carries out his work, the auditor will nevertheless need to obtain an understanding of the specialist's terms of reference and of the work he has been instructed to carry out.

7.22 The auditor will need to evaluate the audit evidence provided by the specialist to determine whether it is sufficient, relevant and reliable enough for him to draw reasonable conclusions from it. The procedures which the auditor will apply will depend upon the nature of the evidence, the circumstances necessitating its preparation, the materiality of the items to which it relates and the auditor's assessment of the specialist's competence and objectivity.

7.23 The auditor should make a detailed examination of the specialist's evidence including ascertaining whether:

(a) the data provided by management to the specialist is compatible with that used for the preparation of the financial statements;

(b) the assumptions and bases used by the specialist are compatible with those used in preparing the financial statements, and consistent with earlier years;

(c) the information supplied by the specialist has been prepared and presented in accordance with his terms of reference;

(d) the specialist has qualified his opinion, or expressed any reservations;

(e) the effective date of the specialist's findings is acceptable;

(f) the details of the specialist's findings are fairly reflected in the financial statements.

7.24 The specialist is responsible for ensuring that he uses assumptions and bases which are appropriate and reasonable. Where the skills applied by the specialist involve highly complex, technical considerations, then it may be that the level of the auditor's understanding of them can be no higher than that of the informed layman. However, the auditor should obtain a general understanding of the assumptions and bases used by the specialist, and consider whether they appear reasonable, given his knowledge of the client's business, and consistent with other audit evidence.

7.25 Where specialist evidence is obtained on a recurring basis, comparison of the key features of the findings with those of prior years may indicate to the auditor whether there are any grounds for doubting the reasonableness of the evidence.

7.26 If the auditor considers that the specialist's evidence is not relevant or reliable enough to assist him in forming an opinion on the financial statements, or that the specialist may not have acted within his terms of reference, the auditor should endeavour to resolve the matter by discussion with the management of the client and with the specialist and by further examination of the specialist's findings. In rare circumstances it may be necessary to obtain the opinion of another specialist. However, a second opinion might only relate to part of the original specialist's evidence, for example, the appropriateness of the bases used.

7.27 The auditor should not ordinarily refer in his report to any specialist on whose evidence he has relied. Such a reference might be misunderstood as either a qualification of his opinion or a division of responsibility, when neither of these is intended.

7.28 Where the auditor is unable to satisfy himself regarding the specialist's evidence, or where no such evidence is available, and there is no satisfactory alternative source of audit evidence, he should consider qualifying his audit report. The situations in which this may be necessary include:

(a) where management is unable or unwilling to obtain specialist evidence;

(b) where the relevance and reliability of the specialist's evidence remains uncertain;

(c) where management refuses to accept and make use of specialist evidence which is relevant, reliable and material to the financial statements; and

(d) where management refuses to agree to the appointment of another specialist when the auditor considers that a second opinion is needed.

Exercise 3

You are the manager in charge of the audit of Ruddington Furniture plc for the year ended 31 July 19X2, and you have been asked to describe the work which should be carried out in planning the audit and in monitoring its progress.

Ruddington Furniture plc buys domestic furniture from manufacturers and sells it to the general public. The company's head office and main warehouse are on the same site, and there are sales branches with associated warehouses in different parts of the country.

Your firm has been auditor of the company for a number of years. All the company's accounting records are maintained on the computer at head office. When a sale takes place at the branch, the salesman checks that the furniture the customer requires is in stock, and if it is, the customer pays for the items by cash, cheque or credit card (or charge card) and collects them from the warehouse. Where the items are not in stock, it is possible to find whether they are available at another local branch, or an order can be placed for the stock.

In previous years' audits there have been problems at branches of the actual stock being less than the computer book stock quantities. Also, problems have been experienced in identifying and valuing damaged stock and goods returned by customers. The company has a small internal audit department and their work includes periodic visits to branches.

The company was subject to a management buy-out in February 19X0 which resulted in high gearing. You understand that because of a recession in the furniture trade the company has liquidity problems and that currently it is negotiating with the bank to obtain additional finance.

Required

List and describe the matters you will consider and the work you will carry out in planning the audit.

Solution

In planning the audit the following matters should be taken into consideration.

(a) The audit files for the previous year should be examined in detail and any important matters should be considered which arise therefrom which might have a bearing on the current year's audit.

(b) Any recent changes in legislation or accounting standards which might affect the financial statements of Ruddington Furniture plc should be considered.

(c) If possible, the management accounts for the year should be obtained from the company. These should be examined to gain information about the trading performance of the company, perhaps in comparison with any budget which is available. Any significant changes in the management or key employees of the company, as well as in the accounting system and procedures, should be noted.

(d) The management of the company should be consulted in advance and the timing of the audit should be agreed. In particular:

  (i) the timing of the stocktake and the level of attendance by the auditors;

  (ii) the timing of significant phases of the preparation of the financial statements;

  (iii) the extent to which analyses and summaries can be prepared by the company's employees;

  (iv) the relevance of any work to be carried out by the enterprise's internal auditors.

(e) In terms of the stocktaking procedures, these should be reviewed in detail. In addition, it would be useful to obtain the results of any stock counts during the year, to consider whether problems still exist in the comparison between book and actual stock levels.

(f) In the light of the known liquidity problems of the company, it would be prudent to obtain any forecasts and budgets for the following year or years. This may be useful in performing any post balance sheet review, particularly if there is any considerable period between the end of the audit and the date the directors plan to sign the accounts (and the AGM).

(g) The internal auditors may be of use in the performance of the external audit. Their work should be examined to determine whether it is reliable and relevant, and some of the tests they have performed should be reperformed for this purpose. If it is decided that their work can be relied upon, this may reduce some of the testing the external auditors can perform. The internal audit work should highlight problem areas within the company and reduce the risks of the external auditor missing any fraud or errors.

(h) It should be possible at this stage to decide what the general audit approach is to be. It should be the case that a company of the size of Ruddington Furniture will have a strong system of internal control, as is indicated to some extent by the presence of the internal audit department. A risk-based audit approach is therefore most likely.

(i) It will be necessary to determine which audit staff are to be used. The staff chosen should be suitably qualified and experienced. The number of staff needs to be determined, particularly in relation to the number of stocktake visits the auditors will undertake. Larger branches should be visited and smaller branches in rotation over a few years.

(j) A timetable should be prepared for the audit, including the items for the principal phases of the audit, the date the audit report will be signed and an estimate of fees, costs and profit.

Chapter roundup

- This chapter has covered some very important areas of the planning process.
- When a new client is acquired the auditor must obtain knowledge of the business from various sources. Particular procedures must be applied to preceding financial statements at a new audit client.
- The auditor must plan all aspects of the audit very carefully.
- Audit risk or inherent risk can be broken down into many components. A risk-based audit will make use of the risk model to determine the amount and extent of audit testing.
- The calculation or estimation of planning materiality is not based on any scientific exercise, but on experience and judgement.
- Analytical review procedures are most useful at the planning stage, allowing risk areas to be identified.
- The auditor may only rely on other specialists once specific audit procedures have taken place.

Test your knowledge

1 List the factors to be investigated when acquiring knowledge of a new client's business. (see para 2.1)

2 For what does a new auditor accept responsibility apart from the current year accounts? (2.3)

3 What preparatory procedures should the auditor undertake in his planning? (2.12)

4 How does a risk-centred methodology differ from a systems audit approach? (3.7)

5 Give some examples of inherent risk conditions within the enterprise. (3.11)

6 At what level is planning materiality often estimated? (4.3, 4.4)

7 What areas would a standardised audit programme cover? (6.6)

8 What should be included in the terms of reference for an outside specialist? (7.20)

Chapter 6

AUDIT EVIDENCE AND DOCUMENTATION

This chapter covers the following topics.

1 The nature of audit evidence
2 Documenting the audit process
3 Quality control procedures

Introduction

Before we can start the audit, we must determine what kind of evidence we are looking for; particularly what kinds of evidence would satisfy an auditor and what kinds would not.

We will then look at how audit evidence is documented and the kinds of working papers which should be kept on file.

Quality control is mentioned here as it is closely allied to the proper documentation of the audit; this is particularly the case in the review process. Quality control will be mentioned again in Chapter 18, when we look at the auditor's liability.

1 THE NATURE OF AUDIT EVIDENCE

1.1 We have established that the auditor must have the appropriate personal qualities. In order to reach a position in which he can express a professional opinion, the auditor needs to gather evidence from various sources. The auditing standards and guidelines, whose scope and authority were discussed in Chapter 2, provide guidance on how to obtain this evidence.

1.2 The auditing standards state that 'the auditor should obtain relevant and reliable audit evidence, sufficient to enable him to draw reasonable conclusions therefrom'.

1.3 The ways in which the auditor uses his professional judgement to assess the relevance, reliability and sufficiency of audit evidence is considered in the auditing guideline *Audit evidence*.

(a) *Sufficiency*. The auditor can rarely be certain of the validity of the financial statements. However, he needs to obtain sufficient, relevant and reliable evidence to form a reasonable basis for his opinion thereon. The auditor's judgement as to what constitutes sufficient, relevant and reliable audit evidence is influenced by such factors as:

(i) his knowledge of the business of the enterprise and the industry in which it operates;

(ii) the degree of risk of misstatement through errors or irregularities; this risk may be affected by such factors as:

(1) the nature and materiality of the items in the financial statements;

(2) the auditor's experience as to the reliability of the management and staff of the enterprise and of its records;

(3) the financial position of its records;

(4) possible management bias;

(iii) the persuasiveness of the evidence.

(b) *Relevance*. The relevance of the audit evidence should be considered in relation to the overall audit objective of forming an opinion and reporting on the financial statements. To achieve this objective the auditor needs to obtain evidence to enable him to draw reasonable conclusions in answer to the following questions.

Balance sheet items

(i) Have all of the assets and liabilities been recorded?

(ii) Do the recorded assets and liabilities exist?

(iii) Are the assets owned by the enterprise and are the liabilities properly those of the enterprise?

(iv) Have the amounts attributed to the assets and liabilities been arrived at in accordance with the stated accounting policies, on an acceptable and consistent basis?

(v) Have the assets, liabilities and capital and reserves been properly disclosed?

Profit and loss account items

(vi) Have all income and expenses been recorded?

(vii) Did the recorded income and expense transactions in fact occur?

(viii) Have the income and expenses been measured in accordance with the stated accounting policies, on an acceptable and consistent basis?

(ix) Have income and expenses been properly disclosed where appropriate?

(c) *Reliability*. Although the reliability of audit evidence is dependent upon the particular circumstances, the following general presumptions may be stated:

(i) documentary evidence is more reliable than oral evidence;

(ii) evidence obtained from independent sources outside the enterprise is more reliable than that secured solely from within the enterprise;

(iii) evidence originated by the auditor by such means as analysis and physical inspection is more reliable than evidence obtained from others.

The auditor should consider whether the conclusions drawn from differing types of evidence are consistent with one another. When audit evidence obtained from one source appears inconsistent with that obtained from another, the reliability of each remains in doubt until further work has been done to resolve the inconsistency. However, when the individual items of evidence relating to a particular matter are all consistent, then the auditor may obtain a cumulative degree of assurance higher than that which he obtains from the individual items.

Exercise 1

The examination of evidence is fundamental to the audit process. *The auditor's operational standard* states that 'the auditor should obtain relevant and reliable audit evidence sufficient to enable him to draw reasonable conclusions therefrom'. Evidence is available to the auditor from sources under his own control., from the management of the company and from third parties. Each of these sources presents the auditor with differing considerations as to the quality of the evidence so produced.

Required

(a) Discuss the quality of the following types of audit evidence, giving two examples of each form of evidence.

(i) Evidence originated by the auditor.
(ii) Evidence created by third parties.
(iii) Evidence created by the management of the client.

(b) Describe the general considerations which the auditor must bear in mind when evaluating audit evidence.

Solution

(a) (i) Evidence originated by the auditor is particularly reliable, as there is little risk of its manipulation by management. The auditor knows this because he has prepared it himself. It is therefore, in general, the most reliable type of audit evidence. Examples include the following.

(1) Analytical review procedures, such as the calculation of ratios and trends in order to examine unusual variations.

(2) Physical inspection or observation, such as attendance at physical stocktakes or inspection of a fixed asset.

(3) Re-performance of calculations making up figures in the accounts, such as the computation of total stock values.

(ii) Third party evidence is more reliable than client-produced evidence to the extent that it is obtained from sources independent of the client. Its reliability will be reduced if it is obtained from sources which are not independent, or if there is a risk that client personnel may be able to and have reason to suppress or manipulate it. This, for instance, is an argument against having replies to circularisations sent to the client instead of the auditor. Examples of third-party evidence include the following.

(1) Circularisation of debtors or creditors and other requests from the auditor for confirming evidence, such as requests for confirmation of bank balances.

(2) Reports produced by other specialists, such as property valuations, actuarial valuations, legal opinions. In evaluating such evidence, the auditor needs to take into account the qualifications of the specialist, his or her independence of the client and the terms of reference under which the work was carried out.

(3) Documents held by the client which were issued by third parties, such as invoices, price lists and statements. These may sometimes be manipulated by the client, to the extent that items may be suppressed or altered, and to this extent they are less reliable than confirmations received direct.

(iii) The auditor cannot place the same degree of reliance on evidence produced by client management as on that produced outside the client organisation. It will, however, often be necessary to place some reliance on the client's evidence. The auditor will need to apply judgement in doing so, taking into account previous experience of the client's reliability and the extent to which the client's representations appear compatible with other audit findings, as well as the materiality of the item under discussion. Examples of evidence originating from client management include the following.

(1) The company's accounting records and supporting schedules. Although these are prepared by management, the auditor has a statutory right to examine such records in full: this right enhances the quality of this information.

(2) The client's explanations of, for instance, apparently unusual fluctuations in results. Such evidence requires interpretation by the auditor, and being oral evidence, only limited reliance can be placed upon it.

(3) Information provided to the auditor about the internal control system. The auditor needs to check that this information is accurate and up-to-date, and that it does not simply describe an idealised system which is not adhered to in practice.

(b) Audit evidence will often not be wholly conclusive. The auditor must obtain evidence which is sufficient to form the basis for his audit conclusions. The evidence gathered should also be relevant to those conclusions, and sufficiently reliable ultimately to form the basis for the audit opinion. The auditor must exercise skill and judgement to ensure that evidence is correctly interpreted and that only valid inferences are drawn from it.

Factors influencing this judgement of whether evidence supporting a particular item is sufficient, relevant and reliable will include the auditor's knowledge of the business, including its financial position, the auditor's assessment of any possible management bias, the nature and materiality of the items involved and the reliability of management and of the accounting records on previous occasions. Certain general principles can be stated. Written evidence is preferable to oral evidence; independent evidence obtained from outside the organisation is more reliable than that obtained internally; and that evidence generated by the auditor is more reliable than that obtained from others.

2 DOCUMENTING THE AUDIT PROCESS

2.1 It is essential that all audit work is documented: the working papers are the tangible evidence of the work done in support of the audit opinion.

2.2 The guideline *Planning, controlling and recording* identifies the reasons for preparing audit working papers as follows.

(a) The reporting partner needs to be able to satisfy himself that work delegated by him has been properly performed. The reporting partner can generally only do this by having available to him detailed working papers prepared by the audit staff who performed the work.

(b) Working papers provide for future reference, details of problems encountered, together with evidence of work performed and conclusions drawn therefrom in arriving at the audit opinion.

(c) The preparation of working papers encourages the auditor to adopt a methodical approach.

2.3 The exact form that working papers should take cannot be prescribed: each firm will have its own disciplines. Whatever form the papers take, however, they must achieve the main objectives set out above.

2.4 The guideline stresses that 'audit working papers should always be sufficiently complete and detailed to enable an experienced auditor with no previous connection with the audit subsequently to ascertain from them what work was performed and to support the conclusions reached'. It also emphasises the special care needed to record difficult questions of principle or of judgement. The auditor should record all relevant information known to him at the time, the conclusions to be reached based on that information and the views of management.

2.5 Although the guideline does not attempt to define precisely the form of working papers it does indicate what might typically be contained therein as follows.

(a) Information which will be of continuing importance to the audit (for example the Memorandum and Articles of Association).

(b) Audit planning information.

(c) The auditor's assessment of the enterprise's accounting system and, if appropriate, his review and evaluation of its internal controls.

(d) Details of the audit work carried out, notes of errors or exceptions found and action taken thereon, together with the conclusions drawn by the audit staff who performed the various sections of the work.

(e) Evidence that the work of the audit staff has been properly reviewed.

(f) Records of relevant balances and other financial information, including analysis and summaries supporting the financial statements.

(g) A summary of significant points affecting the financial statements and the audit report, showing how these points were dealt with.

2.6 Working papers are conventionally subdivided into current audit files and permanent audit files for convenience and control. The characteristic of current working papers is that they relate specifically to the audit of a particular set of accounts whereas permanent papers comprise matters of continuing importance affecting the client. Hence items (a) and (c) above are typically retained on the permanent file.

2.7 The guideline does not use the terms permanent and current working papers, but these terms do appear in UEC Statement 3 *The auditor's working papers*. This statement not only contains a more comprehensive list than above of typical working papers but also classifies them into permanent and current. This listing is reproduced here in full.

2.8 The permanent audit file might include, *inter alia:*

(a) a copy of the enterprise's statutes and other legal or statutory documents governing the enterprise's existence;

(b) other important legal documents and agreements;

(c) a description of the business, its operations, together with the address of its locations and this section might also include details of specific matters relating to the industry or activity in which the enterprise is involved and which might affect the audit;

(d) an organisation chart showing the (top) management functions and the division of responsibilities;

*(e) details of the system of accounting, including, where applicable, details of computer applications;

(f) an internal control questionnaire, memorandum or other means of assessing the adequacy of the internal control system, including those areas where information is processed by means of a computer;

(g) a letter of engagement defining the auditor's understanding of the work to be performed and his responsibilities, together with confirmation from the client that the letter sets out the position as the client also understands it;

(h) correspondence, or notes of discussions with the client on internal control matters;

(i) in the case of group companies details of all companies in the group including names and addresses of the auditors of the subsidiaries; this section might also contain a record of all information concerning other auditors on whose work reliance is placed for the purpose of the audit of group accounts;

(j) the principal accounting policies followed, key ratios, history of capital, profits and reserves;

(k) a reasoned description of the audit approach adopted;

(l) details of important matters arising from each audit, and a record of what decisions were taken and how they were arrived at.

2.9 The current audit file might include, *inter alia:*

(a) a copy of the audited financial statements and any report prepared as a result of the audit work carried out;

(b) an annual audit programme detailing the audit steps to be taken and recording the audit steps carried out;

(c) details of the audit plan, including time budgets, staffing and statement of the scope and level of tests;

(d) schedules showing an analysis of the individual items in the financial statements, the notes thereto and the management's report; the schedules should also show comparative figures and state how the auditor has verified the existence, ownership and the amounts at which they are stated in the financial statements; there should also be evidence that the fairness of the presentation of items in the financial statements has been considered; these schedules should contain the auditor's conclusions, and should be cross-referenced to supporting schedules and external documentary evidence, as appropriate;

(e) notes of meetings and all correspondence relating to the audit, including all certificates and other third party audit confirmations;

(f) extracts from meetings of shareholders, management, directors and other relevant bodies;

(g) records of detailed audit tests carried out, the reasons for the timing and level of the tests, together with the conclusions drawn from those tests;

(h) the information received from the other auditors regarding the financial statements audited by them;

(i) records of queries raised by the auditors and how such queries have been dealt with;

(j) a letter or a statement from the management representing that they have supplied the auditors with all the information and explanations relevant to the audit and disclosed in the financial statements all matters required by statute and accounting standards;

(k) a review of post balance sheet date events up to the date of signing the audit report;

(l) names and initials of the audit staff.

2.10 The APC guideline states:

> 'The use of standardised working papers may improve the efficiency with which they are prepared and reviewed. Used properly they help to instruct audit staff and facilitate the delegation off work while providing a means to control its quality.
>
> However, despite the advantages of standardising the routine documentation of the audit (eg checklists, specimen letters, standard organisation of the working papers) it is never appropriate to follow mechanically a 'standard' approach to the conduct and documentation of the audit without regard to the need to exercise professional judgement.'

2.11 There should be a degree of standardisation of working papers and practically all firms recognise this need.

2.12 Finally, it should be noted that working papers are the property of the auditor and he should adopt procedures to ensure their safe custody and confidentiality.

2.13 In certain cases in the public sector, working papers are the property of the Secretary of State, and the terms of an audit appointment require that such papers must be surrendered to him by the auditor upon resignation or termination of that appointment (auditing guideline *Applicability to the public sector of auditing standards and guidelines*).

Exercise 2

The auditing guideline *Planning, controlling and recording* contains the following statement with regard to working papers: 'Audit working papers should always be sufficiently complete and detailed to enable an experienced auditor with no previous connection with the audit subsequently to ascertain from them what work was performed and to support the conclusions reached.'

Required

(a) Describe four benefits that the auditor will obtain from working papers that meet the above requirement.

(b) In the case of a significant item requiring exercise of judgement (for instance, a material claim for damages) show what types of matter should be recorded in the current file in respect of it and give reasons for inclusion. You should use a material claim for damages to illustrate your answer.

(c) List three types of information typically retained in the audit permanent file and state why they should be available for easy reference.

(d) Comment on the desirability of using standardised working papers and give an example of such a working paper and its use.

Solution

(a) Four benefits that the auditor will obtain from working papers that meet the requirement stated in the question are as follows.

(i) The reporting partner needs to be able to satisfy himself that work delegated by him has been properly performed. The reporting partner can generally only do this by having available to him detailed working papers prepared by the audit staff who performed the work.

(ii) Working papers will provide, for future reference, details of audit problems encountered, together with evidence of work performed and conclusions drawn therefrom in arriving at the audit opinion. This can be invaluable if, at some future date, the adequacy of the auditor's work is called into question in the event of litigation against him by either the client or some third party.

(iii) Good working papers will not only assist in the control of the current audit, but will also be invaluable in the planning and control of future audits.

(iv) The preparation of working papers encourages the auditor to adopt a methodical approach to his audit work, which in turn is likely to improve the quality of that work.

(b) Audit working papers should include a summary of all significant matters identified which may require the exercise of judgement, together with the auditor's conclusions thereon. If difficult questions arise, the auditor should record the relevant information received and summarise both the management's and his conclusions. It is in such areas as these that the auditor's judgement may be subsequently questioned, particularly by a third party who has the benefit of hindsight.

It is important to be able to tell what facts were known at the time the auditor reached his conclusion and to be able to demonstrate that, based on those facts, the conclusion was reasonable.

With the above general principles in mind, the specific matters which should be recorded in the current file in respect of a material claim for damages would include:

(i) who made the claim and on what grounds, the amount of the claim, the date when the grounds arose and the possible effect of the claim on other possible claimants;

(ii) full details of management's estimates, with reasons, of the probable outcome of the claim;

(iii) full details of the specific audit work carried out in relation to the claim (for example details of correspondence with the company's legal advisers) together with the conclusions reached as a result of such work.

(c) Three types of information typically retained in the audit permanent file, and the reasons for so retaining them, are:

(i) a brief history of the organisation in that this will assist the auditor in understanding how the organisation came to be what it is today;

(ii) an organisation chart which will show who is who within the organisation and thus help the auditor to appreciate the division of duties and responsibilities within the organisation;

(iii) copies of all important documents relating to the organisation such as a copy of its constitution (for example memorandum and articles of association or partnership agreement, and so on) these will be used as a reference point for the various 'authorities' in relation to the client to which the auditor will have to give regard during the course of his audit work.

(d) The use of standardised working papers may improve the efficiency with which they are prepared and reviewed. Used properly, they help to instruct audit staff and facilitate the delegation of work while providing a means to control its quality.

However, despite the advantages of standardising the routine documentation of the audit (for example checklists for compliance of the financial statements with statutory disclosure requirements), it is never appropriate to follow mechanically a standard approach to the conduct and documentation of the audit without regard to the need to exercise professional judgement.

3 QUALITY CONTROL PROCEDURES

3.1 **Having established that it is essential to the effectiveness and efficiency of an audit for an appropriate degree of planning to be carried out prior to the commencement of the work, the guideline *Planning, controlling and recording* outlines the various procedures needed in controlling an audit.**

Controlling the audit

3.2 The guideline identifies three key elements of control: the direction of audit staff, their supervision and a review of the work they have done. The degree of supervision required will depend on the complexity of the assignment and the experience and proficiency of the audit staff. It is important to appreciate that, as it is the reporting partner who forms the audit opinion, he above all needs to be satisfied that the audit work is being performed to an acceptable standard.

3.3 The guideline notes that management structures vary between firms of auditors. It is also true that audits vary in size and complexity: some will require a small audit team, while others will require considerable manpower resources.

3.4 Control procedures should be designed and applied to ensure the following:

(a) that work is allocated to audit staff who have appropriate training, experience and proficiency;

(b) that audit staff of all levels clearly understand their responsibilities, the objective of the procedures which they are required to perform, and the channels of communication should any significant problems be encountered during the audit;

(c) that working papers provide adequate evidence of the work that has been carried out; and

(d) that the work performed by each member of the audit staff is reviewed by more senior persons in the audit firm to ensure that it was adequately performed and to enable a proper assessment to be made of the results of the work and the audit conclusions drawn therefrom.

3.5 During the final stages of an audit special care needs to be taken as pressures are greatest. Hence control is particularly important to ensure that mistakes and omissions do not occur. The use of an audit completion checklist, with sections to be filled in by the reporting partner and his staff, in particular the audit manager, helps to provide such control. The use of such a checklist is discussed further in Chapter 16.

3.6 One further technique that aids control is consultation. Where matters of principle or contentious matters arise which may affect the audit opinion the partner should consider consulting another experienced accountant. Such an accountant may be a fellow partner or senior colleague, or another practitioner. If an independent practitioner is consulted, care must be taken to ensure confidentiality of the client's affairs.

3.7 Finally, it should be appreciated that the guideline is concerned only with control of specific audits. The closing line of the guideline states that:

> 'The auditor should also consider how the overall quality of the work carried out within the firm can best be monitored and maintained.'

This is control in a broader sense, or quality control, which is the subject of a detailed operational guideline discussed in Chapter 18. Briefly, the scope of such quality control procedures will include:

(a) communication;
(b) acceptance of appointment and re-appointment as auditor;
(c) professional ethics;
(d) skills and competence;
(e) consultation;
(f) monitoring the firm's procedures.

3.8 The aspect of quality control we need to concentrate as here is the review procedures which are initiated over working papers.

Review of audit working papers

3.9 **Throughout the audit, a system of review of all working papers will be used. In the case of a large audit, the work of junior audit staff will be reviewed by the audit senior(s). In turn, the audit manager will review the work of the audit senior and at least some, if not all, of the work performed by the audit juniors. The overall and final review will be undertaken by the partner responsible for the audit opinion.**

3.10 The importance of the review of audit working papers cannot be overestimated.

3.11 Each working paper should be initialled (or signed) and dated by the person who prepared it.

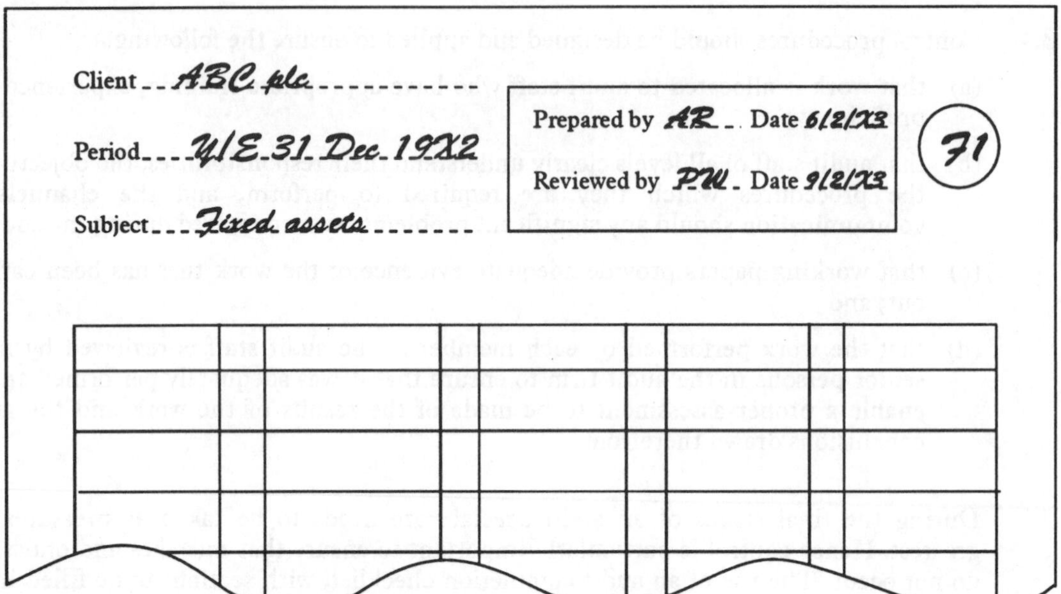

3.12 When a review takes place, the reviewer will often use a separate working paper to record queries *and* their answer.

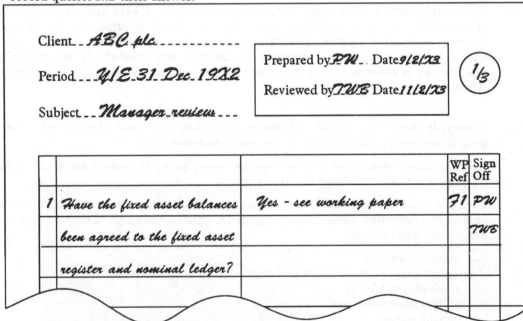

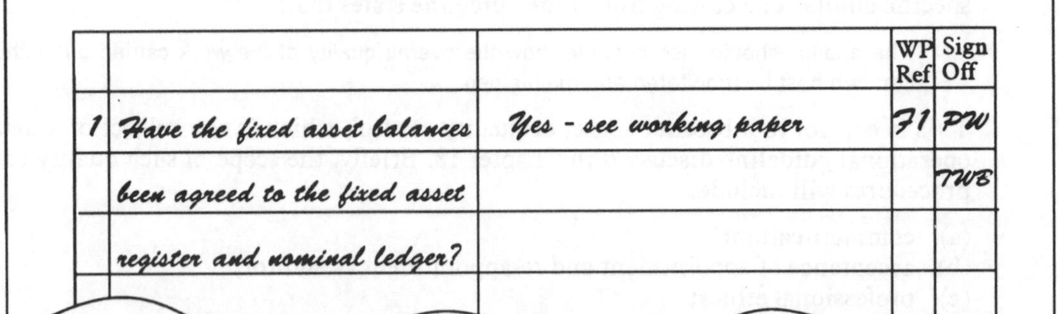

3.13 The need to sign off all working papers and queries acts as an extra check, helping to ensure that all work has been carried out and completed.

3.14 In summary the final review should enable the auditor:

(a) to ensure that the figures in the draft accounts make sense in the light of the audit evidence;

(b) to assess the impact of any unadjusted errors and decide whether to press for adjustments;

(c) to check that all appropriate disclosure and other requirements have been complied with in the financial statements;

(d) to check that there is sufficient relevant reliable audit evidence to support the audit opinion;

(e) to consider what recommendations can be made to client in the management letter(s);

(f) to prepare the way for the following year's audit by summarising any points which will be relevant to that audit and by ensuring that the permanent file is up-to-date.

3.15 In addition, where there is a separate interim audit, the review of the interim work provides a link between that visit and the final audit. In order better to appreciate the nature of the review process the following paragraphs define typical manager and partner responsibilities - they should be seen merely as a guide as it is difficult, and undesirable, to lay down hard and fast rules.

Manager review

3.16 The manager may be responsible for:

(a) review of detailed working papers prepared by the senior and assistants, which will include an examination of the permanent file, the detailed audit programme, supporting working papers and conclusions drawn;

(b) consideration of analytical review evidence;

(c) review of the financial statements, supplementing the review performed by the senior in charge evidenced by completion of an accounting requirements checklist;

(d) consideration and editing of the 'points for partner' schedule: this schedule is normally prepared by the senior in charge and typically contains the following elements to aid the partner in his review:

   (i) a brief explanation of the results and financial position as shown by the draft accounts and of any changes from prior years, budget and expectations;

   (ii) an explanation of any audit problems including areas where major judgements have been exercised;

   (iii) a brief explanation of any outstanding work which it has proved impossible to complete;

   (iv) a summary of the costs of the audit to date (plus an estimate to complete) together with an explanation of any variances from budget; and

   (v) a schedule of unadjusted errors, showing cycle by cycle the effect on the profit and loss account and the balance sheet.

(e) review and editing of management letter, letter of representation, audit time summary and fee note;

(f) review of corporation tax computations and supporting schedules.

Reporting partner review

3.17 The reporting partner may be responsible for:

(a) examination and review of the audit files in sufficient detail to be satisfied that the audit staff, including the manager, have performed their work satisfactorily;

(b) review of 'points for partner' schedule with manager and formulation of decisions;

(c) approval of the management letter for submission to the client (this may be a second letter, following up one sent after completion of the interim audit, or a letter covering the whole audit);

(d) approval of the financial statements having reviewed analytical review evidence and the subsequent events programme;

(e) ensuring that all material points are cleared (at his discretion he might decide to consult with his colleagues to obtain a second opinion in respect of any contentious matters);

(f) review and approval of representation letter and fee note;

(g) approval of the final typed financial statements.

3.18 It will be appreciated from the above summary that the partner is primarily a reviewer and decision maker. Having satisfactorily completed his final review he will be in a position to form his audit opinion, qualified or unqualified, and subsequently sign and date the audit report (after formal approval of the financial statements by the directors).

3.19 In a practical world it should be appreciated that the final review stage is not only a check on the quality and effectiveness of the audit. It is also the opportunity to assess the service given to the client and determine improvements that can be made in future years.

De-briefing meeting

3.20 It is becoming common practice to introduce a further review stage in the audit process, referred to as the debriefing meeting. This meeting is timed to take place as soon as practicable after completion of the audit. Its purpose is to review the conduct of the audit as a whole with the objective of improving performance of individuals and conduct of future audits and more specifically to develop the initial plan for the following year's audit. The debriefing meeting for the audit just completed could hence alternatively be considered as the first stage of the following year's audit. It is usually considered expedient to hold the meeting no more than a few weeks after the audit report has been signed and dated so that the audit is still relatively fresh in the minds of the audit team. The meeting is normally chaired by the reporting partner and in attendance will be the assignment manager, senior in charge and other support staff at the discretion of the partner.

Chapter roundup

- The auditor must be able to evaluate all types of audit evidence in terms of its sufficiency, relevance and reliability.
- The proper completion of working papers is fundamental to the recording of the audit.
- You should be able to state what kind of information is retained in the current and permanent files.
- Review procedures are a major component in the quality control of individual audits.

Test your knowledge

1 What are the three essential characteristics of the evidence required by an auditor? (see para 1.2)

2 Differentiate between the reliability of evidence from third parties, evidence created by the auditor and oral evidence. (1.3)

3 What are the reasons for preparing audit working papers? (2.2)

4 What are the typical contents of working papers? (2.5)

5 What are the different characteristics of working papers contained in the current file from those in the permanent file? (2.6)

6 What are the advantages and disadvantages of using standardised working papers? (2.10, 2.11)

7 How should control procedures affect the audit? (3.4)

8 State the functions of the final review. (3.14)

Chapter 7

INTERNAL CONTROL EVALUATION

This chapter covers the following topics.

Introduction

The modern audit encompasses reliance on internal controls in order to reduce the amount of testing of final balances.

The evaluation of a client's system will generally take place at the planning stage, when it will also be recorded and assessed. If the auditor wishes to rely on the internal controls within the system, then these controls must be tested and control testing, along with all other forms of audit testing and verification, will be covered in the next part of this Tutorial Text.

The use of flowcharts is also studied in Unit 23 in relation to computers and computer systems.

Competence in Unit 18 can be displayed in the context of either external or internal audit. In Section 4 we look at internal audit and its relationship with external audit. Remember, however, that most of the rest of the text applies equally to external and internal audit.

Reports to management, covered in Section 5, are also applicable to both external and internal audit. Reports by external audit tend to take a specific form and an auditing guideline governs this type of 'management letter'.

1 INTERNAL CONTROLS

1.1 All companies should have a satisfactory accounting system and, as regards accounting records, must comply with the requirements of the Companies Act 1985. The guideline *Accounting systems* reads as follows.

> 'Depending upon the size and nature of the business concerned an accounting system will frequently need to incorporate internal controls to provide assurance that:
>
> (a) all the transactions and other accounting information which should be recorded have in fact been recorded;
>
> (b) errors or irregularities in processing accounting information will become apparent;
>
> (c) assets and liabilities recorded in the accounting system exist and are recorded at the correct amounts.'

1.2 *Internal controls* supplement the accounting system, providing management with greater assurance regarding the integrity of the accounting environment. We can now turn to the auditing guideline *Internal controls* which in its initial paragraphs emphasises management's responsibility for internal control.

1.3 First, an internal control system is defined as being:

'...the whole system of controls, financial and otherwise, established by the management in order to carry on the business of the enterprise in an orderly and efficient manner, ensure adherence to management policies, safeguard the assets and secure as far as possible the completeness and accuracy of the records. The individual components of an internal control system are known as "controls" or "internal controls".'

1.4 **Second, management's responsibility is defined in the following terms.**

'It is a responsibility of management to decide the extent of the internal control system which is appropriate to the enterprise. The nature and extent of controls will vary between enterprises and also from one part of an enterprise to another. The controls used will depend on the nature, size and volume of the transactions, the degree of control which members of management are able to exercise personally, the geographical distribution of the enterprise and many other factors. The choice of controls may reflect a comparison of the cost of operating individual controls against the benefits expected to be derived from them.

The operating procedures and methods of recording and processing transactions used by small enterprises often differ significantly from those of large enterprises. Many of the internal controls which would be relevant to the larger enterprise are not practical, appropriate or necessary in the small enterprise. Managements of small enterprises have less need to depend on formal internal controls for the reliability of the records and other information, because of their personal contact with, or involvement in, the operation of enterprise staff.'

1.5 **An appendix to the guideline describes the main types of internal controls which may be found. You could use 'SOAP SPAM' as a mnemonic to help you remember the different types.**

S egregation of duties
O rganisation
A uthorisation and approval
P hysical
S upervisory
P ersonnel
A rithmetical and accounting
M anagement

TYPES OF INTERNAL CONTROLS

'The following is a description of some of the types of controls which the auditor may find in many enterprises and on some or a combination of which he may seek to place some degree of reliance.

1 *Organisation.* Enterprises should have a plan of their organisation, defining and allocating responsibilities and identifying lines of reporting for all aspects of the enterprise's operations, including the controls. The delegation of authority and responsibility should be clearly specified.

2 *Segregation of duties.* One of the prime means of control is the separation of those responsibilities or duties which would, if combined, enable one individual to record and process a complete transaction. Segregation of duties reduces the risk of intentional manipulation or error and increases the element of checking. Functions which should be separated include those of authorisation, execution, custody, recording and, in the case of a computer-based accounting system, systems development and daily operations.

3 *Physical.* These are concerned mainly with the custody of assets and involve procedures and security measures designed to ensure that access to assets is limited to authorised personnel. This includes both direct access and indirect access via documentation. These controls assume importance in the case of valuable, portable, exchangeable or desirable assets.

4 *Authorisation and approval.* All transactions should require authorisation or approval by an appropriate responsible person. The limits for these authorisations should be specified.

5 *Arithmetical and accounting.* These are the controls within the recording function which check that the transactions to be recorded and processed have been authorised, that they are all included and that they are correctly recorded and accurately processed. Such controls include checking the arithmetical accuracy of the records, the maintenance and checking of totals, reconciliations, control accounts and trial balances, and accounting for documents.

6 *Personnel.* There should be procedures to ensure that personnel have capabilities commensurate with their responsibilities. Inevitably, the proper functioning of any system depends on the competence and integrity of those operating it. The qualifications, selection and training as well as the innate personal characteristics of the personnel involved are important features to be considered in setting up any control system.

7 *Supervision.* Any system of internal control should include the supervision by responsible officials of day-to-day transactions and the recording thereof.

8 *Management.* These are the controls exercised by management outside the day-to-day routine of the system. They include the overall supervisory controls exercised by management, the review of management accounts and comparison thereof with budgets, the internal audit function and any other special review procedures.'

1.6 Management should introduce appropriate controls to prevent or substantially reduce intentional and unintentional errors in the accounting system. The possibility of intentional errors (or fraud) is restricted by ensuring an effective segregation of duties. There are three elements to most transactions.

(a) Authority to initiate the transaction, committing the company to carry out the contract (authorisation).

(b) Control over recording the transaction in the company's records.

(c) Custody of assets and determination of their release.

Each of these elements should therefore ideally be carried out by separate individuals within each area of accounting. It is worth noting that, in *The financial aspects of corporate governance*, the Cadbury Committee recommends segregation of duties at board level, with clear division of responsibilities such that no one individual has unfettered powers of decision making.

Limitations on the effectiveness of internal controls

1.7 The guideline warns that no internal control system is foolproof.

'No internal control system, however elaborate, can by itself guarantee efficient administration and the completeness and accuracy of the records, nor can it be proof against fraudulent collusion, especially on the part of those holding positions of authority or trust. Internal controls depending on segregation of duties can be avoided by collusion. Authorisation controls can be abused by the person in whom the authority is vested. Whilst the competence and integrity of the personnel operating the controls may be ensured by selection and training, these qualities may alter due to pressure exerted both within and without the enterprise. Human error due to errors of judgement or interpretation, to misunderstanding, carelessness, fatigue or distraction may undermine the effective operation of internal controls.'

1.8 The auditor will need to be aware of the possibility that even the best looking system can break down; hence, as we have established, his reliance on internal controls (confirmed by compliance testing) is only part of his audit evidence, some substantive work will always be carried out.

Why internal control interests the auditor

1.9 Paragraph 5 of *The auditor's operational standard* states:

'If the auditor wishes to place reliance on any internal controls, he should ascertain and evaluate those controls and perform compliance tests on their operation.'

1.10 Returning to the guideline *Internal controls* we can re-state why the auditor may wish to place reliance on internal controls. Paragraph 7 states:

'The auditor's objective in evaluating and testing internal controls is to determine the degree of reliance which he may place on the information contained in the accounting records. If he obtains reasonable assurance by means of compliance test that the internal controls are effective in ensuring the completeness and accuracy of the accounting records and the validity of entries therein, he may limit the extent of his substantive testing.'

1.11 The auditor needs to ascertain and record the internal control system in order to make a preliminary evaluation of the effectiveness of its component controls and to determine the extent of his reliance on these controls. This recording will normally be carried out concurrently with the recording of the accounting system; the use of flowcharting techniques is a simple yet effective way of achieving this dual objective.

Exercise 1

Internal control is defined in the auditing standards and guidelines as:

'The whole system of controls, financial and otherwise, established by the management in order to:

(a) carry on the business of the enterprise in an orderly and efficient manner;
(b) ensure adherence to management policies;
(c) safeguard the assets; and
(d) secure as far as possible the completeness and accuracy of the records.'

Explain the meaning and relevance to the auditor giving an opinion on financial statements of each of the management objectives (a) to (d) above.

Solution

The auditor's objective in evaluating and testing internal controls is to determine the degree of reliance which he may place on the information contained in the accounting records. If he obtains reasonable assurance by means of compliance tests that the internal controls are effective in ensuring the completeness and accuracy of the accounting records and the validity of the entries therein, he may limit the extent of his substantive testing.

(a) *'carry on the business of the enterprise in an orderly and efficient manner'*

An organisation which is efficient and conducts its affairs in an orderly manner is much more likely to be able to supply the auditor with sufficient and reliable audit evidence on which to base his audit opinion, and more importantly, the level of inherent and control risk will be lower, giving extra assurance that the financial statements do not contain material errors.

(b) *'ensure adherence to management policies'*

It is management's responsibility to set up an effective system of internal control and management policy provides the broad framework within which internal controls have to operate. Unless management does have a pre-determined set of policies, then it is very difficult to imagine how the company could be expected to operate efficiently. Management policy will cover all aspects of the company's activities and will range from broad corporate objectives to specific areas such as determining selling prices and wage rates.

Given that the auditor must have a sound understanding of the company's affairs generally, and of specific areas of control in particular, then the fact that management policies are followed will make the task of the auditor easier in that he will be able to rely more readily on the information produced by the systems established by management.

(c) *'safeguard the assets'*

This objective may relate to the physical protection of assets (for example locking monies in a safe at night) or to less direct safeguarding (for example ensuring that there is adequate insurance cover for all assets). It can also be seen as relating to the maintenance of proper records in respect of all assets.

The auditor will be concerned to ensure that the company has properly safeguarded its assets so that he can form an opinion on the existence of specific assets and, more generally, on whether the company's records can be taken as a reliable basis for the preparation of financial statements. Reliance on the underlying records will be particularly significant where the figures in the financial statements are derived from such records rather than as the result of physical inspection.

(d) *'secure as far as possible the completeness and accuracy of the records'*

This objective is most clearly related to statutory requirements relating to both management and auditor. The company has an obligation under the Companies Act 1985 to maintain proper accounting records. The auditor must form an opinion on whether the company has fulfilled this obligation and also conclude whether the financial statements are in agreement with the underlying records.

2 ASCERTAINING THE SYSTEM

2.1 As part of his audit planning, particularly in determining the nature and timing of his audit tests, the auditor needs to consider the effectiveness of the accounting system in providing a timely and methodical 'capture' of accounting information. The auditor will make a record of the accounting system in order:

(a) to provide evidence of the system upon which the subsequent audit tests were based; and
(b) to act as a base for the planning of future audits.

2.2 Paragraph 3 of *The auditor's operational standard* states:

'The auditor should ascertain the enterprise's system of recording and processing transactions and assess its adequacy as a basis for the preparation of financial statements.'

Paragraph 3 applies *irrespective of whether the auditor seeks to rely on internal controls*. In the case of a limited company audit, the auditor has a concurrent but distinct responsibility to form an opinion as to whether proper accounting records have been kept in compliance with the Companies Act 1985. We look at the nature of an accounting system and the techniques for ascertaining, recording and confirming in this chapter.

2.3 The accounting system will incorporate internal controls. The evaluation of internal controls is dealt with in the separate guideline *Internal controls*. In practice the auditor carries out his work of recording and evaluating controls at the same time as his assessment of the accounting system.

2.4 Later in the chapter we will examine the nature of internal controls, their significance to management and the auditor, and the auditor's evaluation techniques. Two particular aspects of internal controls and the auditor are the subject of detailed operational guidelines: the external auditor's reliance on the internal audit function and the technique of the management letter. These guidelines are discussed in later chapters.

The requirements of an accounting system

2.5 Before any audit tests can be designed and performed, it is necessary to understand the accounting records kept and the manner in which transactions are processed through the accounting system. As mentioned, this is necessary whether or not internal controls are likely to be relied on.

2.6 The management of a company requires complete and accurate accounting and other records to assist it in:

(a) controlling the business;
(b) safeguarding the assets;
(c) preparing financial statements; and
(d) complying with statutory requirements.

2.7 Clearly accounting systems vary enormously in their sophistication. To quote from the auditing guideline *Accounting systems:*

> 'What constitutes an adequate accounting system will depend on the size, nature and complexity of the enterprise. In its simplest form for a small business dealing primarily with cash sales and with only a few suppliers the accounting system may only need to consist of an analysed cash book and a list of unpaid invoices. In contrast, a company manufacturing several different products and operating through a number of dispersed locations may need a complex accounting system to enable information required for financial statements to be assembled.'

2.8 Many accounting systems are of course computerised. This does not alter the audit principles and approach. It may mean, however, that specialist assistance is required to record and assess the system and this is a requirement that should be identified at the initial planning stage of the audit.

2.9 It is important to appreciate that an accounting system embraces not merely the recording function but all the stages leading up to recording for each type of transaction. Unless the source documents of all authentic transactions are completely and accurately captured and recorded for processing, the account balance to which the transaction stream is posted is unlikely to be materially correct. By way of illustration let us look at the purchases cycle (we will assume that the purchases are of goods and not services). When ascertaining the purchases accounting system the auditor will typically need to concern himself with the following functions, departments and documents.

Function	*Department*	*Document raised internally (I) or received from outside (O)*
Initiation	Warehouse	Requisition (I)
Authorisation/execution	Buying or ordering	Purchase order (I)
Custody	Goods inwards	Goods inwards or received note (GIN or GRN) (I) Delivery note (O)
Invoice approval	Purchase ledger	Purchase invoice (O)
Recording	Computer/accounting machine etc (accounting records)	Purchase invoice in form suitable for posting (I or O)
Cash settlement	Cashier	Cheque/giro (I) Remittance advice (I) Statement (O)

2.10 When ascertaining a system, the auditor will need to determine the flow of documents within and between the appropriate departments from initiation of the transaction through to recording. The term 'from cradle to grave' is sometimes used to describe the life cycle of a transaction.

Accounting records: statutory requirements

2.11 The responsibility for installing and maintaining a satisfactory accounting system rests, in the case of a company, with the directors. Four objectives have been defined in Paragraph 2.6 emphasising why management require an accurate accounting system. We must now look at objective (d) a little more closely for it directly affects the auditor as well as the directors.

2.12 S 221 and 222(1) and (5) of the Companies Act 1985 require the following.

S 221: (1) Every company shall keep accounting records which are sufficient to show and explain the company's transactions and are such that they:

(a) disclose with reasonable accuracy, at any time, the financial position of the company at that time; and

(b) enable the directors to ensure that any balance sheet and profit and loss account prepared under this Part complies with the requirements of this Act.

(2) The accounting records shall in particular contain:

(a) entries from day to day of all sums of money received and expended by the company, and the matters in respect of which the receipt and expenditure takes place; and

(b) a record of the assets and liabilities of the company.

(3) If the company's business involves dealing in goods, the accounting records shall contain:

(a) statements of stock held by the company at the end of each financial year of the company;

(b) all statements of stocktakings from which any such statement of stock as is mentioned in paragraph (a) has been or is to be prepared; and

(c) except in the case of goods sold by way of ordinary retail trade, statements of all goods sold and purchased, showing the goods and the buyers and sellers in sufficient detail to enable all these to be identified.

(4) A parent company which has a subsidiary undertaking in relation to which the above requirements do not apply shall take reasonable steps to secure that the undertaking keeps such accounting records as to enable the directors of the parent company to ensure that any balance sheet and profit and loss account prepared under this Part complies with the requirements of this Act.

(5) If a company fails to comply with any provision of this section, every officer of the company who is in default is guilty of an offence unless he shows that he acted honestly and that in the circumstances in which the company's business was carried on the default was excusable.

(6) A person guilty of an offence under this section is liable to imprisonment or a fine, or both.

S 222: (1) A company's accounting records shall be kept at its registered office or such other place as the directors think fit, and shall at all times be open to inspection by the company's officers .... .

(5) Accounting records which a company is required by s 221 to keep shall be preserved by it:

(a) in the case of a private company, for three years from the date on which they are made; and

(b) in the case of a public company, for six years from the date on which they are made.

2.13 **Officers of a company are liable to imprisonment or a fine (or both) if found guilty of knowingly failing to comply with the above sections.**

2.14 **The Companies Act does not require a company to implement a system of internal controls. Some types of enterprise, such as banks and building societies, are required by statute to maintain internal control systems. (Some commentators argue that corporate legislation should impose similar disciplines on companies of a certain size or upon particular classes of company).**

Ascertaining, recording and confirming the accounting system

2.15 The auditing guideline *Accounting systems* states:

> 'The auditor will need to obtain an understanding of the enterprise as a whole and how the accounting system reflects assets and liabilities and transactions.
>
> The auditor will need to ascertain and record the accounting system in order to assess its adequacy as a basis for the preparation of financial statements. The extent to which the auditor should record the enterprise's accounting system and the method used will depend on the complexity and nature of the system and on the degree of reliance he plans to place on internal controls. Where the auditor plans to rely on internal controls, the accounting system needs to be recorded in considerable detail so as to facilitate the evaluation of the controls and the preparation of a programme of compliance and substantive tests. The record may take the form of narrative notes, flowcharts or checklists or a combination of them.'

2.16 The final sentence above identifies the three principal recording techniques:

(a) narrative notes;
(b) flowcharts;
(c) checklists (internal control questionnaires or ICQs).

2.17 The main purpose of the internal control questionnaire is to evaluate a system and not to describe it. We will hence therefore consider the ICQ later. Occasionally it may be found that in answering the questions in an ICQ the auditor will discover more detail about the system than is already recorded in the flowcharts and/or narrative notes, and this will help him in ascertaining and recording the system.

2.18 *Flowcharts* are the best way of recording any system which involves the movement of documents from one person to another, and are particularly important when the auditor wishes to rely on any controls in the system. *Narrative notes* are preferable for very simple systems where all the paperwork is handled by only one or two people. They are also helpful to amplify particular procedures on flowcharts. Really complex systems may only be adequately documented by a combination of all three techniques in Paragraph 2.16.

2.19 Whatever method of recording the system is used, the record will be retained on the permanent file. With established clients, it is of course only necessary for the auditor to update the records on the permanent file year by year. For a new client, or a client whose systems have changed substantially, the auditor will be required to set up a comprehensive record from scratch. Occasionally, clients may have their own in-house procedural manuals. In such circumstances the auditor may be able to save time by obtaining copies of these manuals. Care must be taken however to ensure that such manuals achieve the auditor's objective; often clients use them more as a means of instructing their staff in a particular area rather than to give a complete description of the system. Let us now examine the techniques of narrative notes and flowcharts in more detail.

Narrative notes

2.20 Narrative notes have the advantage of being simple to record but they are awkward to change. The purpose of the notes is to describe and explain the system, at the same time making any comments or criticisms which will help to demonstrate an intelligent understanding of the system. For each system they need to deal with the following questions.

(a) What functions are performed and by whom?
(b) What documents are used?
(c) Where do the documents originate and what is their destination?
(d) What sequence are retained documents filed in?
(e) What books are kept and where?

2.21 Narrative notes can be used to support flow charts. They can effectively explain error procedures or uncomplicated alternatives to standard procedures and may also be used to provide additional information on operations or checks.

Flowcharts

2.22 There are two methods of flowcharting in regular use:

(a) document flowcharts; and
(b) information flowcharts.

2.23 Document flowcharts are more commonly used because they are relatively easy to prepare. All documents are followed through from 'cradle to grave' and *all* operations and controls are shown.

2.24 Information flowcharts are prepared in the reverse direction from the flow: they start with the entry in the general/nominal ledger and work back to the actual transaction. They concentrate on significant information flows and ignore any unimportant documents or copies of documents. They are subsequently more compact than document flowcharts and are intended to highlight key controls. They are easy to understand but require skill and experience to compile them. We shall concentrate on document flowcharts in the remainder of this chapter.

2.25 Note the following rules of flowcharting.

(a) A flowchart should only be used when the system being reviewed cannot be readily understood in words. The purpose of a flowchart is to help the understanding of a complex system, but the price is that the complexity of the system is replaced by using a 'foreign' diagrammatic language in preference to English. It follows that where a system is readily understood in narrative English, it need not be charted.

(b) Flowcharts should be kept simple, so that the overall structure or flow is clear at first sight. In keeping a flowchart simple the following points should be noted.

   (i) There must be conformity of symbols, with each symbol representing one and only one thing.

   (ii) The direction of the flowchart should be from top to bottom and from left to right. There must be no loose ends and the main flow should finish at the bottom right hand corner, not in the middle of the page.

   (iii) Connecting lines should cross only where absolutely necessary to preserve the chart's simplicity.

2.26 *Advantages* of using flowcharts include the following.

(a) After a little experience they can be prepared quickly. It is often found that an auditor can draw a draft chart as the client describes the system.

(b) As the information is presented in a standard form, they are fairly easy to follow and to review.

(c) They generally ensure that the system is recorded in its entirety, as all document flows have to be traced from beginning to end and any 'loose ends' will be apparent from a cursory examination.

(d) They eliminate the need for extensive narrative and can be of considerable help in highlighting the salient points of control and any weaknesses in the system.

Disadvantages of flowcharts include the following.

(a) They are only really suitable for describing standard systems. Procedures for dealing with unusual transactions will normally have to be recorded using narrative notes.

(b) They are useful for recording the flow of documents, but once the records or the assets to which they relate have become static they can no longer be used for describing the controls (for example over fixed assets).

(c) Major amendment is difficult without redrawing.

(d) Time can be wasted by charting areas that are of no audit significance (a criticism of *document* not information flowcharts).

2.27 The following notes are intended to (re)familiarise students with basic flowcharting conventions for manual systems.

2.28 Basic symbols will be used for the charting of all systems, but where the client's system involves mechanised or computerised processing, then further symbols may be required to supplement the basic ones. The basic symbols used are shown below.

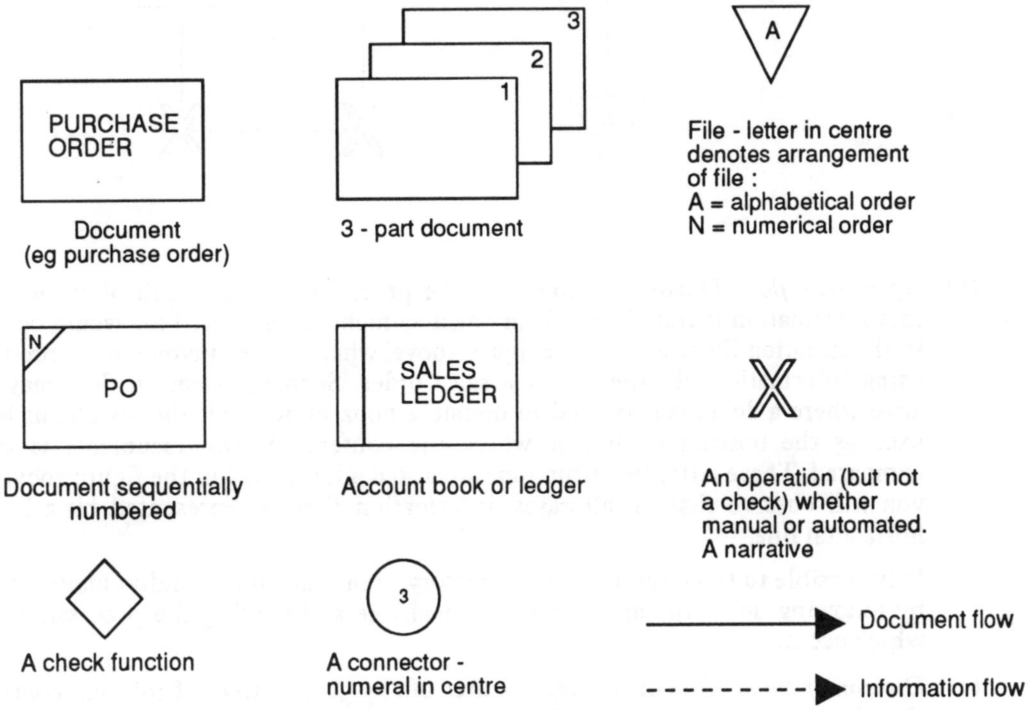

2.29 Preparation of a basic flowchart will involve the following.

(a) *Document flows*. The document flow is basically from top to bottom of the chart, the basic symbols being used to represent the various operations applied to a document during the processing cycle. Those symbols showing the sequence of operations taking place within the one department are joined by a vertical line as illustrated in the figure below.

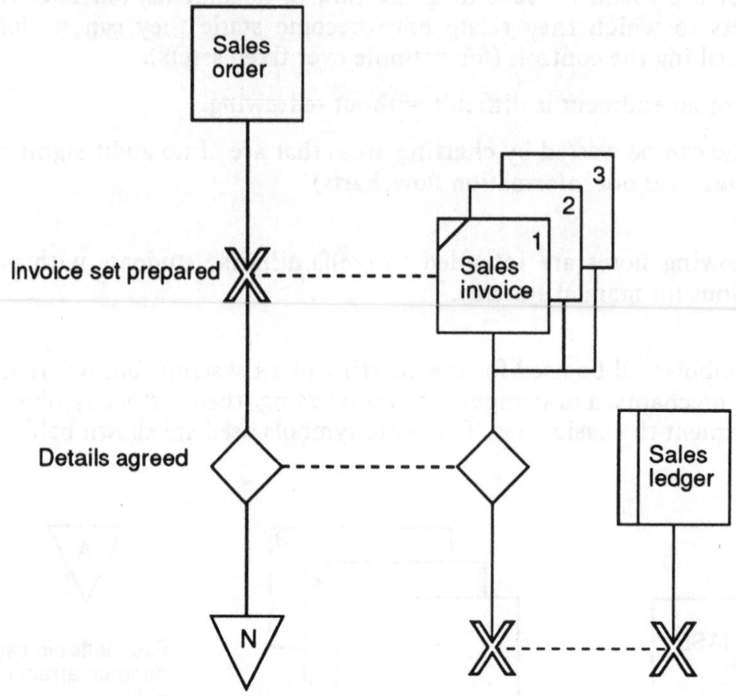

(b) *Information flow.* During the course of the processing cycle it will often be found that information is transferred from one document to another. This would occur as in the situation illustrated in the figure above, where a sales invoice set is produced using information obtained from a sales order. Such information flow may also arise where a document is used to update a book of account, the document being used as the posting media, or where the content of two documents is being compared. These latter two situations are also demonstrated in the figure above and you will observe that, in all cases, information flow is represented by a broken horizontal line.

It is possible to trace the processing history of any document individually, simply by following down the appropriate vertical line and reading the processing steps which occur.

(c) *Division of duties.* One of the key features of any good system of internal control is that there should be a system of 'internal check'. Internal check is the requirement for a division of duties amongst the available staff so that one person's work is independently reviewed by another, no one person having complete responsibility for all aspects of a transaction.

Since the main purpose of a flow chart is to record the controls operating within a company's system, it would clearly be advantageous if the structure of the chart itself could indicate the division of duties. With this method of flow charting this is achieved by dividing the chart into vertical columns. In a smaller enterprise there would be one column to show the duties of each individual, whereas in a large company the vertical columns would show the division of duties amongst the various departments.

The figure below shows, in a small company, the division of duties between Mr Major and Mr Minor.

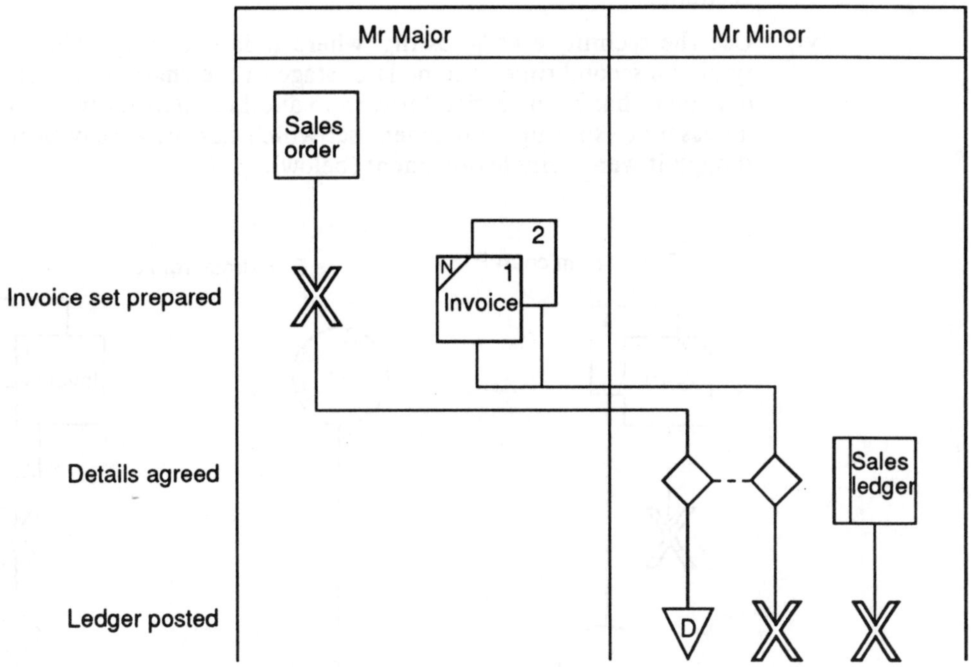

(d) *Sequence and description of operations.* To facilitate ease of reference each operation shown on the chart is numbered in sequence on the chart, a separate column being used for this purpose, as shown below. Note carefully that the operation number is set on the same horizontal plane as the symbols representing the process being described and that every operation, including check functions and filing must be given a number. It is essential that care is taken when drawing the chart to ensure that no two unconnected operations appear on the same horizontal plane.

Finally, the chart will be completed by the inclusion of a narrative column which will describe significant operations. Narrative should be kept to a minimum and only included where in fact it is required, for example filing of documents would frequently not need any narrative. Where the chart indicates a check function, some narrative will however always be required.

(e) *Chart organisation.* Any flowchart will basically comprise the symbols described but a critical factor in good flowcharting is chart organisation. The following may provide some useful hints.

(i) On the whole you should aim to chart the flow of documents etc from top left down, in stages, towards bottom right. Reversal of flow from right to left may be necessary at times. However, if reverse flow occurs too frequently the chart will be that much more difficult to read.

(ii) Do not use diagonal lines: all document flow lines should be either horizontal or vertical. There is a convention that a vertical document flow line represents a 'movement in time', whereas a horizontal document line represents a 'movement in space'.

(iii) Where an intersection of flow lines on the chart is unavoidable, there being no intention to suggest a merge. The continual direction of flow is most clearly shown by having a 'bridge' on the crossing line.

(iv) Do not try to get too much detail onto one chart. It is much better to split a system into logical sections, and then chart each section separately. Where several charts are used each chart should be given an identifying number. Continuation between charts is achieved by use of the connector symbol.

(v) Make sure that the flow line showing the life of a document is complete, for example do not end a document flow line in a temporary file or at an operation symbol, unless of course the operation involves sending the document out of the business, as where an invoice copy is mailed to a customer.

(vi) Use the technique of 'ghosting' where it is necessary to show a document symbol a second time at some later stage in the chart. This will arise where a document has been carried forward to another chart, or when it is eventually necessary to split up a document set which has previously been processed as though it were a single document (below).

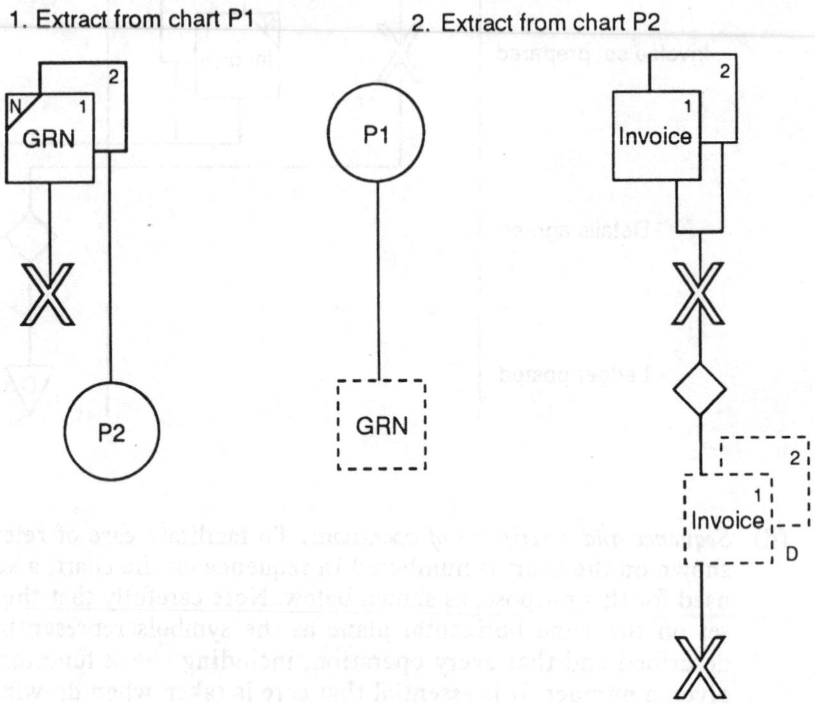

2.30 On the following pages you will find two charts which illustrate typical procedures in a company's purchasing system.

(a) Ordering and receiving of goods.
(b) Approval of invoices.

Confirming the system: the walk through check

2.31 Whatever method of recording the system is used, its accuracy must be confirmed. This is achieved by means of 'walk through tests (or checks).' The nature and purpose of such tests are explained in of the auditing guideline *Accounting systems.*

> 'As an aid to recording the accounting system, the auditor should consider tracing a small number of transactions (possibly one or two of each type) through the system. This procedure (often known as 'walk-through checks') will confirm that there is no reason to suppose that the accounting system does not operate in the manner recorded. The procedure is particularly appropriate where the enterprise has itself prepared the record of the system which the auditor is to use.'

2.32 Any error may indicate that the system has not been recorded correctly, and clearly the systems records must be amended before detailed audit tests are designed and conducted. The walk through test, being confined to so few items, does not provide any significant audit reliance on the operation of the accounting system or the internal controls. Walk through tests should be performed at the commencement of each annual audit. Even if the client has confirmed that there have been no changes since the previous audit, the auditor must nevertheless confirm that his record of the system still represents the actual system in operation.

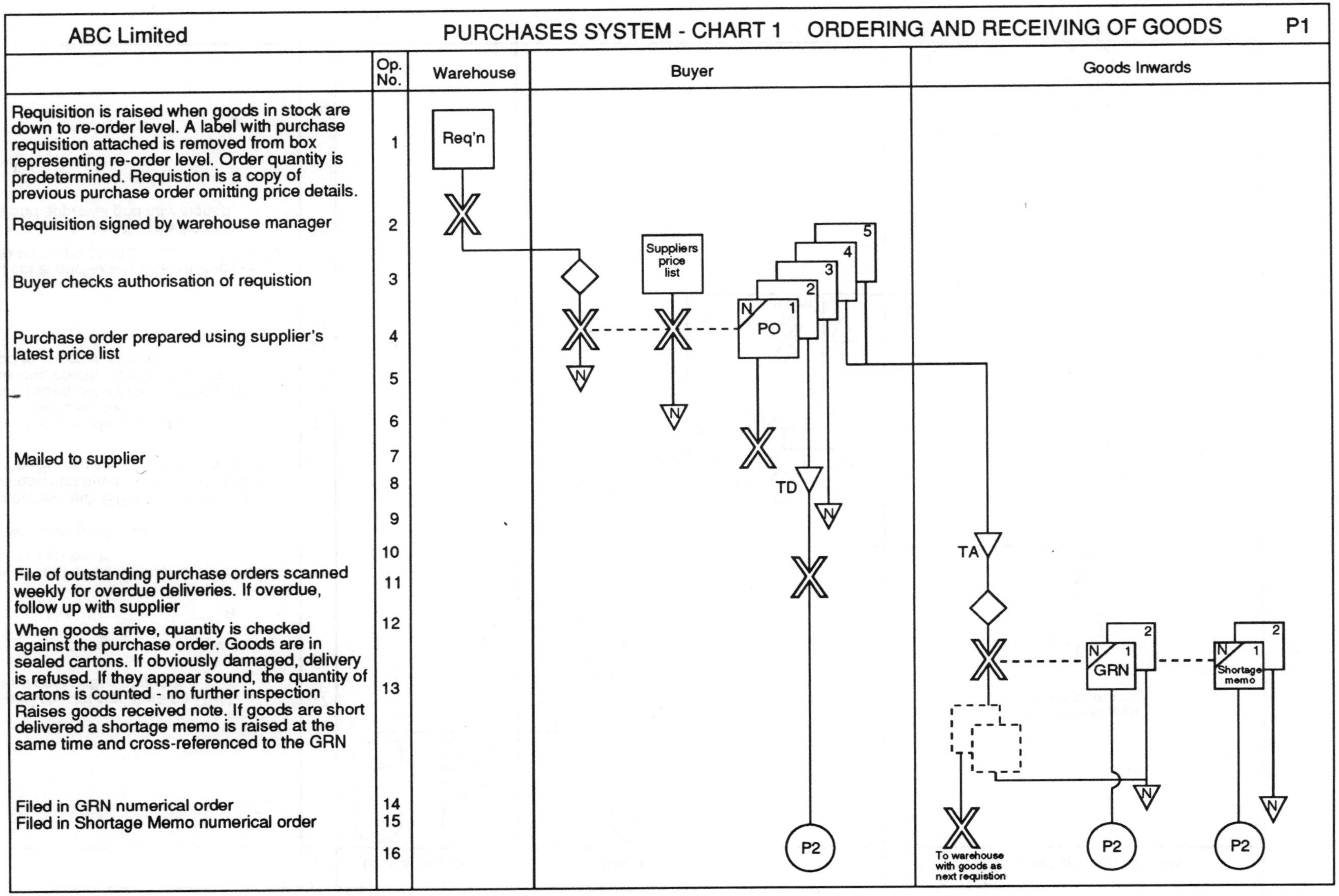
ABC Limited
PURCHASES SYSTEM - CHART 1 ORDERING AND RECEIVING OF GOODS
P1
Op. No.
Warehouse
Buyer
Goods Inwards
Requisition is raised when goods in stock are down to re-order level. A label with purchase requisition attached is removed from box representing re-order level. Order quantity is predetermined. Requistion is a copy of previous purchase order omitting price details.
1
Requisition signed by warehouse manager
2
Buyer checks authorisation of requistion
3
Purchase order prepared using supplier's latest price list
4
5
6
Mailed to supplier
7
8
9
10
File of outstanding purchase orders scanned weekly for overdue deliveries. If overdue, follow up with supplier
11
When goods arrive, quantity is checked against the purchase order. Goods are in sealed cartons. If obviously damaged, delivery is refused. If they appear sound, the quantity of cartons is counted - no further inspection
12
Raises goods received note. If goods are short delivered a shortage memo is raised at the same time and cross-referenced to the GRN
13
Filed in GRN numerical order
14
Filed in Shortage Memo numerical order
15
16
Req'n
N
Suppliers price list
N
PO
1
2
3
4
5
TD
N
P2
TA
GRN
1
2
N
P2
Shortage memo
1
2
N
P2
To warehouse with goods as next requistion

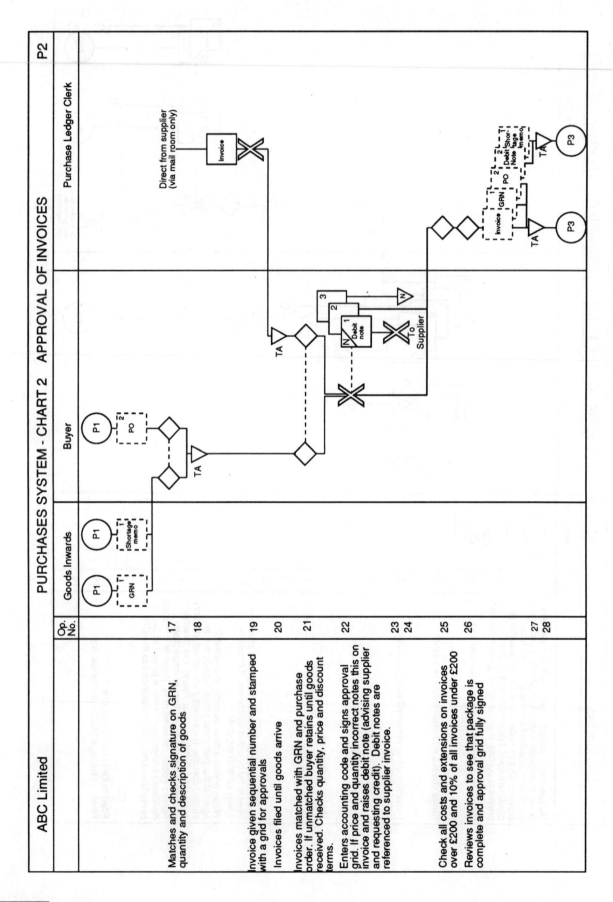

ABC Limited | **PURCHASES SYSTEM - CHART 2 APPROVAL OF INVOICES** | **P2**

	Op. No.
Matches and checks signature on GRN, quantity and description of goods	17
	18
Invoice given sequential number and stamped with a grid for approvals	19
Invoices filed until goods arrive	20
Invoices matched with GRN and purchase order. If unmatched buyer retains until goods received. Checks quantity, price and discount terms.	21
Enters accounting code and signs approval grid. If price and quantity incorrect notes this on invoice and raises debit note (advising supplier and requesting credit). Debit notes are referenced to supplier invoice.	22
	23
	24
Check all costs and extensions on invoices over £200 and 10% of all invoices under £200	25
Reviews invoices to see that package is complete and approval grid fully signed	26
	27
	28

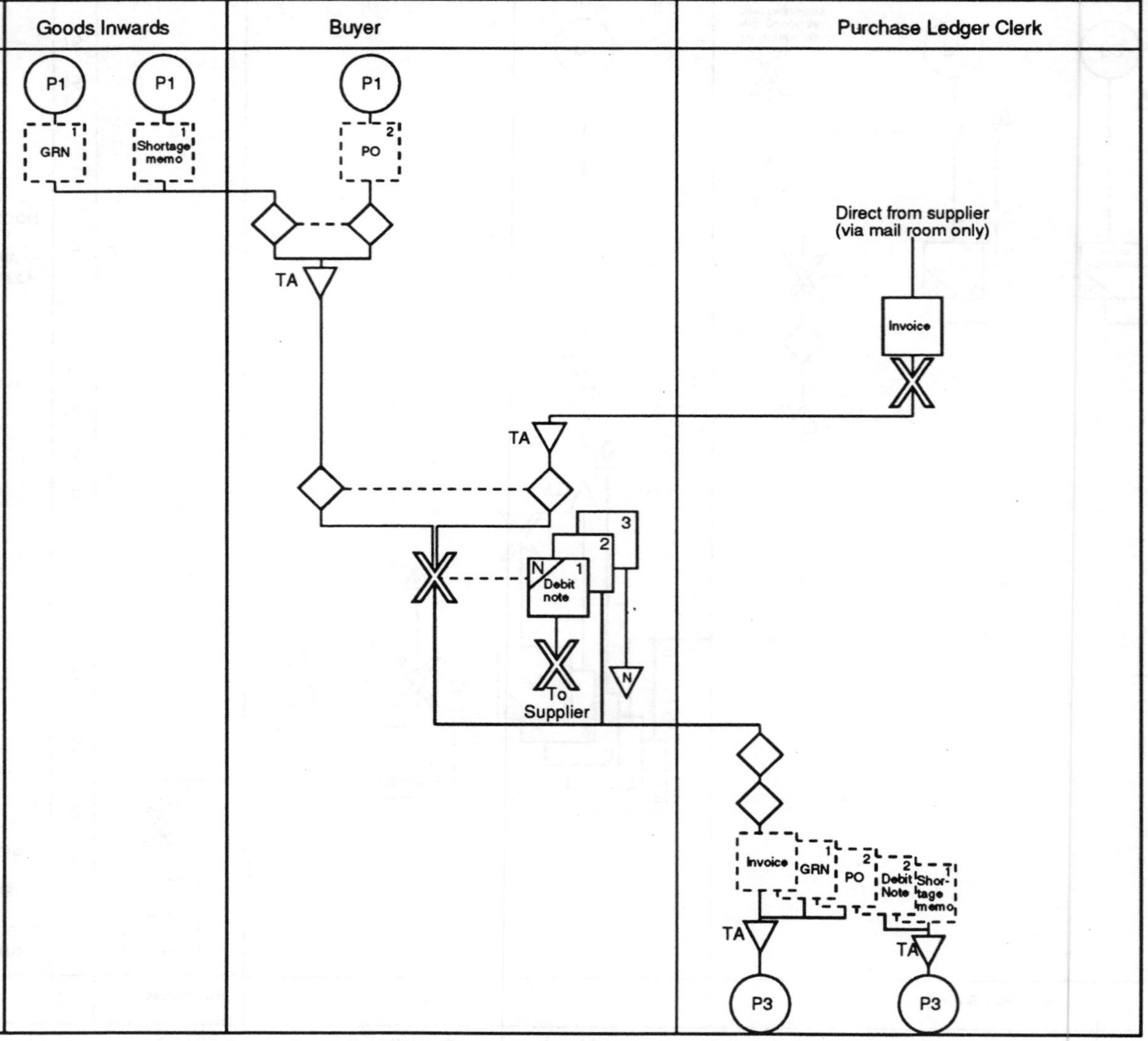

2.33 The following specimen working paper demonstrates the nature of the walk through test.

Anyco Ltd	Prepared by: AB	
Year ended: 30 September 19X0		Date: 1 August 19X0
	Reviewed by: BC	
Title Sales walk through test		Date: 8 August 19X0
Customer order		
	Date:	4.6.X0
	No:	16450
	Goods description:	widget type 6
	Quantity:	600 (2 boxes)
	Agreed price:	£25
Despatch note		
	Date:	7.6.X0
	No:	15943
Goods description agreed to order		✓
Quantity agreed to order		✓
Evidence of check by goods outwards		✓
Invoice	Date:	8.6.X0
	No:	15468
Goods agreed to order and despatch note		✓
Quantity agreed to order and despatch note		✓
Price agreed to order price		✓
Posting	Invoice correctly entered in:	
	sales day book	✓
	sales ledger	✓
Conclusion		
	The credit sales system is correctly recorded on our flowchart	

3 EVALUATING THE INTERNAL CONTROL SYSTEM

3.1 Having documented the system, including internal controls, and confirmed its operation by means of walk through tests, the auditor will then commence his evaluation. We can return to the auditing guideline *Internal controls* to establish the two principal techniques available to him.

> 'The evaluation of internal controls will be assisted by the use of documentation designed to help identify the internal controls on which the auditor may wish to place reliance. Such documentation can take a variety of forms but might be based on questions asking either:
>
> (a) whether controls exist which meet specified control objectives; or
>
> (b) whether they are controls which prevent or detect particular specified errors or omissions.'

3.2 The two documents referred to in terms of their objectives in (a) and (b) are more recognisable to the auditor as the Internal Control Questionnaire (ICQ) and Internal Control Evaluation Questionnaire (ICEQ) respectively.

Internal Control Questionnaires (ICQs)

3.3 The major question which internal control questionnaires are designed to answer is 'How good is the system of controls?' Where strengths are identified, the auditor will perform work in the relevant areas. If, however, weaknesses are discovered he should then ask:

(a) what errors or irregularities could be made possible by these weaknesses;

(b) could such errors or irregularities be material to the accounts; and hence

(c) what substantive audit tests will enable such errors or irregularities to be discovered and quantified?

3.4 Although there are many different forms of ICQ in practice, they all conform to the following basic principles:

(a) they comprise a list of questions designed to determine whether desirable controls are present; and

(b) they are formulated so that there is one to cover each of the major transaction cycles.

3.5 Since it is the primary purpose of an ICQ to evaluate the system rather than describe it, one of the most effective ways of designing the questionnaire is to phrase the questions so that all the answers can be given as 'YES' or 'NO' and a 'NO' answer indicates a weakness in the system. An example would be:

Are purchase invoices checked to goods received notes before being passed for payment?	YES/NO/Comments

A 'NO' answer to that question clearly indicates a weakness in the company's payment procedures.

3.6 The ICQ questions below dealing with goods inward provide additional illustrations of the ICQ approach.

Goods inward

(a) Are supplies examined on arrival as to quantity and quality?

(b) Is such an examination evidenced in some way?

(c) Is the receipt of supplies recorded, perhaps by means of goods inwards notes?

(d) Are receipt records prepared by a person independent of those responsible for:

(i) ordering functions;
(ii) the processing and recording of invoices.

(e) Are goods inwards records controlled to ensure that invoices are obtained for all goods received and to enable the liability for unbilled goods to be determined (by pre-numbering the records and accounting for all serial numbers)?

(f) (i) Are goods inward records regularly reviewed for items for which no invoices have been received?

(ii) Are any such items investigated?

(g) Are these records reviewed by a person independent of those responsible for the receipt and control of goods?

3.7 One of the strengths of ICQs is that they facilitate the orderly evaluation of controls present in a system. They also provide evidence of the basis of the audit approach for the benefit of the manager and partner.

3.8 A weakness of ICQs is that they can promote a somewhat standardised approach to evaluation. The answering of the questions becomes an end in itself, rather than the means to an end. The auditor is concerned whether the controls do or do not prevent the possibility of material errors occurring. This is not always easy to determine with an ICQ where the questions are notionally of equal weight. In many systems a particular 'No' answer (say, referring to a lack of segregation of duties) may cancel the apparent value of a string of 'Yes' answers. Each situation must be judged on its own merits and hence, although the ICQs are a standard pre-printed pack, they should be used with imagination. As using ICQs is a skilled and responsible task, the evaluation should be performed by a senior member of the audit team.

Internal Control Evaluation Questionnaires (ICEQs)

3.9 In recent years many auditing firms have developed and implemented an evaluation technique more concerned with assessing whether specific errors (or frauds) are possible rather than establishing whether certain desirable controls are present. This is achieved by reducing the control criteria for each transaction stream down to a handful of key questions (or control questions) whose characteristic is that they concentrate on the significant errors or omissions that could occur at each phase of the appropriate cycle if controls are weak.

3.10 The nature of the key questions may best be understood by reference to the examples on the following pages.

Internal control evaluation questionnaire: control questions

The sales (revenue) cycle

Is there reasonable assurance:

(a) that sales are properly authorised?
(b) that all goods despatched are invoiced?
(c) that all invoices are properly prepared?
(d) that all invoices are recorded?
(e) that invoices are properly supported?
(f) that all credits to customers' accounts are valid?
(g) that cash and cheques received are properly recorded and deposited?
(h) that slow payers will be chased and that bad and doubtful debts will be provided against?
(i) that all transactions are properly accounted for?
(j) that cash sales are properly dealt with?
(k) that sundry sales are controlled?
(l) that at the period end the system will neither overstate nor understate debtors?

The purchases (expenditure) cycle

Is there reasonable assurance:

(a) that goods or services could not be received without a liability being recorded?

(b) that receipt of goods or services is required in order to establish a liability?

(c) that a liability will be recorded:

 (i) only for authorised items; and
 (ii) at the proper amount?

(d) that all payments are properly authorised?

(e) that all credits due from suppliers are received?

(f) that all transactions are properly accounted for?

(g) that at the period end liabilities are neither overstated nor understated by the system?

(h) that the balance at the bank is properly recorded at all times?

(i) that unauthorised cash payments could not be made and that the balance of petty cash is correctly stated at all times?

Wages and salaries

Is there reasonable assurance:

(a) that employees are only paid for work done?
(b) that employees are paid the correct amount (gross and net)?
(c) that the right employees actually receive the right amount?
(d) that accounting for payroll costs and deductions is accurate?

Stock

Is there reasonable assurance:

(a) that stock is safeguarded from physical loss (eg fire, theft, deterioration)?
(b) that stock records are accurate and up to date?
(c) that the recorded stock exists?
(d) that the cut off is reliable?
(e) that the costing system is reliable?
(f) that the stock sheets are accurately compiled?
(g) that the stock valuation is fair?

Fixed tangible assets

Is there reasonable assurance:

(a) that recorded assets actually exist and belong to the company?
(b) that capital expenditure is authorised and reported?
(c) that disposals of fixed assets are authorised and reported?
(d) that depreciation is realistic?
(e) that fixed assets are correctly accounted for?

Investments

Is there reasonable assurance:

(a) that recorded investments belong to the company and are safeguarded from loss?

(b) that all income, rights or bonus issues are properly received and accounted for?

(c) that investment transactions are made only in accordance with company policy and are appropriately authorised and documented?

(d) that the carrying values of investments are reasonably stated?

Management information and general controls

Is the nominal ledger satisfactorily controlled?

Are journal entries adequately controlled?

Does the organisation structure provide a clear definition of the extent and limitation of authority?

Are the systems operated by competent employees, who are adequately supported?

If there is an internal audit function, is it adequate?

Are financial planning procedures adequate?

Are periodic internal reporting procedures adequate?

3.11 Each key control question is supported by detailed control points to be considered. For example, the detailed control points to be considered in relation to key control question (b) for the expenditure cycle (Is there reasonable assurance that receipt of goods or services is required to establish a liability?) are as follows.

(1) Is segregation of duties satisfactory?

(2) Are controls over relevant master files satisfactory?

(3) Is there a record that all goods received have been checked for:

- weight or number?
- quality and damage?

(4) Are all goods received taken on charge in the detailed stock ledgers:

- by means of the goods received note?
- or by means of purchase invoices?
- are there, in a computerised system, sensible control totals (hash totals, money values and so on) to reconcile the stock system input with the creditors system?

(5) Are all invoices initialled to show that:

- receipt of goods has been checked against the goods received records?
- receipt of services has been verified by the person using it?
- quality of goods has been checked against the inspection?

(6) In a computerised invoice approval system are there print-outs (examined by a responsible person) of:

- cases where order, GRN and invoice are present but they are not equal ('equal' within predetermined tolerances of minor discrepancies)?
- cases where invoices have been input but there is no corresponding GRN?

(7) Is there adequate control over direct purchases?

(8) Are receiving documents effectively cancelled (for example cross-referenced) to prevent their supporting two invoices?

Audit risk and internal controls

3.12 We explained earlier how, at the planning stage, the auditor will need to assess audit risk, including the possibility that material errors could give arise due to irregularities or to fraud. We have also seen that an auditor who wishes to place reliance upon the internal control system must always evaluate and test individual controls in order to assess the extent to which errors can be prevented. Both the ICQs and ICEQs can help the auditor to identify areas where material irregularities are most likely to occur.

3.13 The auditing guideline covering fraud, other irregularities and errors identifies the following six key areas where special emphasis might be required in considering the risk of material misstatements:

(a) segregation of duties;

(b) authorisation (particularly of expense items and new ledger accounts);

(c) completeness and accuracy of accounting data (for example reconciliation procedures);

(d) procedures to safeguard assets;

(e) comprehensiveness of controls (for example including all relevant sub-systems);

(f) adequacy of internal audit (where applicable).

3.14 The auditor needs to be aware that management can override controls, and that this possibly may facilitate fraud by senior management.

3.15 Where accounting procedures are computerised, the auditor must ensure that a lack of data processing controls cannot be used either to suppress evidence of irregularity or to allow errors to arise in the first place.

4 INTERNAL AUDIT

4.1 Remember what we said earlier about internal audit: large organisations may appoint full time staff whose function is to monitor and report on the running of the company's operations.

4.2 We now look in more detail at internal audit, which is an aspect of internal control. The auditing guideline *Guidance for internal auditors* defines internal audit as:

> 'an independent appraisal function established by the management of an organisation for the review of the internal control system as a service to the organisation. It objectively examines, evaluates and reports on the adequacy of internal control as a contribution to the proper, economic, efficient and effective use of resources.'

4.3 The scope and objectives of internal audit vary widely. Normally, however, internal audit operates in one or more of the following broad areas.

(a) Review of accounting systems and related internal controls.

(b) Examination of financial and operating information for management, including detailed testing of transactions and balances.

(c) Review of the economy, efficiency and effectiveness of operations and of the functioning of non-financial controls.

(d) Review of the implementation of corporate policies, plans and procedures.

(e) Special investigations.

4.4 The essentials for effective internal auditing are as follows.

(a) *Independence*. The internal auditor should have the independence in terms of organisational status and personal objectivity which permits the proper performance of his duties.

(b) *Staffing and training*. Like external audit teams, the internal audit unit should be appropriately staffed in terms of numbers, grades, qualifications and experience, having regard to its responsibilities and objectives. Training should be a planned and continuing process at all levels.

(c) *Relationships*. The internal auditor should seek to foster constructive working relationships and mutual understanding with management, with external auditors, with any other review agencies and, where one exists, with the audit committee.

(d) *Due care*. The internal auditor cannot be expected to give total assurance that control weaknesses or irregularities do not exist, but he should exercise due care in fulfilling his responsibilities.

(e) *Planning, controlling and recording*. Like the external auditor, the internal auditor should adequately plan, control and record his work. As part of the planning process the internal auditor should identify the whole range of systems within the organisation.

(f) *Evaluation of the internal control system*. The internal auditor should identify and evaluate the organisation's internal control system as a basis for reporting upon its adequacy and effectiveness.

(g) *Evidence*. The internal auditor should obtain sufficient, relevant and reliable evidence on which to base reasonable conclusions and recommendations.

(h) *Reporting and follow-up*. The internal auditor should ensure that findings, conclusions and recommendations arising from each internal audit assignment are communicated promptly to the appropriate level of management and he should actively seek a response.

The external auditor and reliance on internal audit

4.5 Internal audit is an example of a management control exercised outside the day-to-day routine of the accounting system.

4.6 Where an enterprise's internal control system includes internal audit the external auditor may be able to place reliance on that internal audit function. In order to establish in what circumstances such reliance may be justified and to determine the procedures that need to be followed by the external auditor we can turn to the detailed operational guideline *Reliance on internal audit*.

4.7 Certain of the objectives of internal audit may be similar to those of external audit, and procedures similar to those carried out during an external audit may be followed. Accordingly, the external auditor should make an assessment of the internal audit function in order to be able to determine whether or not he wishes to place reliance on the work of internal audit. An external auditor may be able to place reliance on internal audit as a means of reducing the work he performs himself in:

(a) the documentation and evaluation of accounting systems and internal controls;
(b) compliance and substantive testing.

4.8 The scope of internal audit's work will generally be determined in advance and a programme of work will be prepared. Where reliance is placed on the work of internal audit, the external auditor will need to take into account this programme of work and amend the planned extent of his own audit work accordingly. In addition, the external auditor may agree with management that internal audit may render him direct assistance by performing certain of the procedures necessary to accomplish the objectives of the external audit but under the control of the chief internal auditor, who would then have to consider the effect on his department's programme of work.

Scope and objectives of internal audit

4.9 The scope and objectives of internal audit vary widely and are dependent upon the responsibilities assigned to it by management, the size and structure of the enterprise and the skills and experience of the internal auditors.

4.10 Where internal audit staff carry out routine tasks such as authorisation and approval or day-to-day arithmetical and accounting controls, they are not functioning as internal auditors and these tasks are not dealt with in this guideline: this is because these tasks are recognised as other types of internal controls by the Appendix to the auditing guideline *Internal controls*. Moreover, objectivity may be impaired when internal auditors audit any activity which they themselves carried out or over which they had authority. The possibility of impairment should be considered when deciding whether to place reliance on internal audit.

The relationship between external and internal audit

4.11 Unlike the internal auditor who is normally an employee of the enterprise or a related enterprise, the external auditor is required to be independent of the enterprise, usually having a statutory responsibility to report on the financial statements giving an account of management's stewardship.

4.12 Although the extent of the work of the external auditor may be reduced by placing reliance on the work of internal audit, the responsibility to report is that of the external auditor alone, and therefore is indivisible and is not reduced by this reliance.

Procedures

4.13 Before any decision is taken to place reliance on internal audit, it is necessary for the external auditor to make an assessment of the likely effectiveness and the relevance of the internal audit function. The criteria for making this assessment should include the following.

(a) *The degree of independence.* The external auditor should evaluate the organisational status and reporting responsibilities of the internal auditor and consider any constraints or restrictions placed upon him.

(b) *The scope and objectives of the internal audit function.* The external auditor should examine the internal auditor's formal terms of reference and should ascertain the scope and objectives of internal audit assignments.

(c) *Due professional care.* The external auditor should consider whether the work of internal audit generally appears to be properly planned, controlled, recorded and reviewed.

(d) *Technical competence.* The external auditor should ascertain whether the work of internal audit is performed by persons having adequate training and proficiency as auditors. Indications of technical competence may be membership of an appropriate professional body or the possession of relevant practical experience, such as computer auditing skills.

(e) *Internal audit reports.* The external auditor should consider the quality of reports issued by internal audit and ascertain whether management considers, responds to and, where appropriate, acts upon internal audit reports, and whether this is evidenced.

(f) *Level of resources available.* The external auditor should consider whether internal audit has adequate resources, for example in terms of staff and of computer facilities.

4.14 Where the external auditor decides that he may be able to place reliance on internal audit, he should consider in determining the extent of that reliance:

(a) the materiality of the areas or the items to be tested or of the information to be obtained;

(b) the level of audit risk inherent in the areas or items to be tested or in the information to be obtained;

(c) the level of judgement required;

(d) the sufficiency of complementary audit evidence;

(e) specialist skills possessed by internal audit staff.

4.15 The external auditor should be involved in the audit of all material matters in the financial statements particularly in those areas where there is significant risk of misstatement. High audit risk does not preclude placing some reliance on internal audit, but the external auditor should ensure that the extent of his involvement is sufficient to enable him to form his own conclusions.

4.16 Having decided that he may be able to place reliance on the work of internal audit, the external auditor should agree with the chief internal auditor the timing of internal audit work, test levels, sample selection and the form of documentation to be used.

4.17 Where the external auditor places reliance on the work of internal audit, he should review that work and satisfy himself that it is being properly controlled. In this connection the external auditor should:

(a) consider whether the work has been appropriately staffed and properly planned, supervised and reviewed;

(b) compare the results of the work with those of the external auditor's staff on similar audit areas or items, if any;

(c) satisfy himself that any exceptions or unusual matters that have come to light as a result of the work have been properly resolved;

(d) examine reports relating to the work produced by internal audit and management's response to those reports.

4.18 In addition, the external auditor should determine whether internal audit will be able to complete, on a timely basis, the programme that it has agreed to undertake and, if it will not, he should make appropriate alternative arrangements.

4.19 Where the external auditor places reliance on internal audit, whether by means of direct assistance or otherwise, he should satisfy himself that sufficient evidence is obtained to afford a reasonable basis for the conclusions reached by internal audit, and that those conclusions are appropriate to the circumstances and are consistent with the results of the work performed. This may involve him in performing supplementary work to satisfy himself.

Exercise 2

The growing recognition by management of the benefits of good internal control, and the complexities of an adequate system of internal control have led to the development of internal auditing as a form of control over all other internal controls. The emergence of the internal auditor as a specialist in internal control is the result of an evolutionary process similar in many ways to the evolution of independent auditing.

Required

(a) Explain why the internal and independent auditors' review of internal control procedures differ in purpose.

(b) Explain the reasons why an internal auditor should or should not report his findings on internal control to the following selection of company officials:

(i) the chief accountant;

(ii) the board of directors.

(c) Explain whether the independent auditor can place any reliance upon the internal auditor's work when the latter's main role is to be of service and assistance to management.

Solution

(a) The internal auditor reviews and tests the system of internal control and reports to management in order to improve the information received by managers and to help in their task of running the company. The internal auditor will recommend changes to the system to make sure that the management receives objective information which is efficiently produced. The internal auditor will also have a duty to search for and discover fraud.

The external auditor reviews the system of internal control in order to determine the extent of the substantive work required on the year end accounts. The external auditor reports to the shareholders rather than the managers or directors. It is usual, however, for the external auditors to issue a letter of weakness to the managers, laying out any areas of weakness and recommendations for improvement in the system of internal control. The external auditor reports on the truth and fairness of the financial statements, not directly on the system of internal control. The auditor does not have a specific duty to detect fraud, although he should plan the audit procedures so as to detect any material misstatement in the accounts on which he gives an opinion.

(b) (i) *Board of directors*

A high level of independence is achieved by the internal auditors if they report directly to the Board. There may be problems with this approach.

(1) The members of the Board may not understand all the implications of the internal audit reports when accounting or technical information is required.

(2) The Board may not have enough time to spend considering the reports in sufficient depth. Important recommendations might therefore remain unimplemented.

A way around these problems might be to delegate the review of internal audit reports to an audit committee, which would act as a kind of sub-committee to the main board. The audit committee might be made up largely of non-executive directors who have more time and more independence from the day-to-day running of the company.

(ii) *Chief accountant*

It would be inappropriate for internal audit to report to the chief accountant, who is largely in charge of running the system of internal control. It may be feasible for him to receive the report as well as the Board. Otherwise, the internal audit function cannot be effectively independent as the chief accountant could suppress unfavourable reports or he could just not act on the recommendations of such reports.

(c) The internal audit function is itself part of the system of internal control: it is an internal control over internal controls. As such, the external auditor should be able to test it and, if it is found to be reliable, he can rely on it.

To check the reliability of the work of the internal auditor, I would consider the following matters.

(i) *The degree of independence of the internal auditor.* I would assess the organisational status and reporting responsibilities of the internal auditor and consider any restrictions placed upon him. Although an internal auditor is an employee of the enterprise and cannot therefore be independent of it, he should be able to plan and carry out his work as he wishes and have access to senior management. He should be free of any responsibility which may create a conflict of interest, and of a situation where those staff on whom he is reporting are responsible for his or his staff's appointment, promotion or pay.

(ii) *The scope and objectives of the internal audit function.* I would examine the internal auditor's formal terms of reference and ascertain the scope and objectives of internal audit assignments.

(iii) *Quality of work.* I would consider whether the work of internal audit is properly planned, controlled, recorded and reviewed. Examples of good practice include the existence of an adequate audit manual, plans and procedures for supervision individual assignments, and satisfactory arrangements for ensuring adequate quality control, reporting and follow-up.

(iv) *Technical competence.* Internal audit should be performed by persons having adequate training and competence as auditors. Indications of technical competence may be membership of an appropriate professional body or attendance at regular training courses.

(v) *Reports.* I would consider the quality of reports issued by internal audit and find out whether management considers and acts upon such reports.

If I find that where the internal auditor's work is reliable, I will be able to place reliance on that work when appropriate. This may mean that I will need to carry out less audit work. However, it should be emphasised that I cannot rely totally on the internal auditor's work in relation to any particular audit objective: internal audit work provides only one form of evidence, and the internal auditor is not independent of company management. I may be able to reduce the number of items which I test, but I will not be able to leave a particular type of test (for example, a debtors' circularisation) entirely to internal audit. I remain responsible for the opinion which I form on the accounts.

5 REPORTING TO MANAGEMENT

5.1 We mentioned in previous chapters that the auditor would report any weaknesses discovered in the system of internal control to the management of the company. This report takes the form of an *interim management letter.* After the end of the audit, the auditor might send a further letter (or both types will be combined in one letter after the end of the audit). The final management letter will be of a different nature and it is discussed later in this section.

The interim management letter

5.2 The auditor performs compliance tests to obtain reasonable assurance that the controls on which he wishes to rely have been functioning properly; where the preliminary evaluation has disclosed weaknesses in, or the absence of controls, such that material errors or omissions could arise he will move directly to designing and carrying out substantive tests.

5.3 Paragraphs 21 and 22 of the auditing guideline *Internal controls* state:

'It is important that the auditor should report, as soon as practicable, significant weaknesses in internal controls which come to his attention during the course of an audit to an appropriately senior level of management of the enterprise. Any such report should indicate that the weaknesses notified are only those which have come to the attention of the auditor during the course of his normal audit work and are not necessarily, therefore, all the weaknesses which may exist.

The fact that the auditor reports weaknesses in internal controls to management does not absolve:

(a) management from its responsibility for the maintenance of an adequate internal control system;

(b) the auditor from the need to consider the effect of such weaknesses on the extent of his audit work and on his audit opinion.'

5.4 The technique of the management letter is well-established in practice but it is only relatively recently that formal guidance has been provided by the APC in the form of a detailed operational guideline entitled *Reports to management*. The following comments are derived from this guideline.

5.5 Reports to management are known by various names, for example management letters, post audit letters and letters of weaknesses. The report should preferably take the form of a letter. Occasionally, the volume or nature of the auditor's comments may be such that this form of report is either unnecessary or inappropriate. In these circumstances the report will consist of a record of a discussion with management forming part of the auditor's working papers. The principles outlined in the guideline should be followed whatever method is used to report to management on matters which have arisen during the audit.

5.6 The auditor's primary duty is to express an opinion on the financial statements and this responsibility is not reduced by any reports made to management.

Purpose

5.7 The principal purpose of a report to management is to enable the auditor to give his comments on the accounting records, systems and controls that he has examined during the course of his audit. Significant areas of weakness in systems and controls that might lead to material errors should be highlighted and brought to management's attention.

5.8 There is usually no requirement for the auditor to make a report to management where no significant weaknesses have come to his attention. However, the auditor should be aware that in certain cases, for example in local authority, Stock Exchange firm and housing association audits, there is a specific requirement to make a report to management.

5.9 As a secondary purpose, a report to management may also be used to provide management with other constructive advice. The auditor might, for example, be able to suggest areas where economies could be made or where resources could be used more efficiently. A report to management is also a useful means of communicating matters that have come to the auditor's attention during the audit that might have an impact on future audits.

Timing

5.10 A report to management will normally be a natural by-product of the audit, and the auditor should incorporate the need to report in the planning of the audit.

5.11 To be effective, the report should be made as soon as possible after completion of the audit procedures giving rise to comment. Where the audit work is performed on more than one visit, it will often be appropriate to report to management after interim audit work has been completed as well as after the final visit. If there are procedures that need to be improved before the financial year end the auditor should raise them in a letter or in discussion at an interim stage. As soon as an accounting breakdown is identified or serious weaknesses are apparent senior management should be informed without delay.

Contents

5.12 Generally the following matters, arising out of the audit, will be included in a report to management:

(a) weaknesses in the structure of accounting systems and internal controls;
(b) deficiencies in the operation of accounting systems and internal controls;
(c) unsuitable accounting policies and practices;
(d) non-compliance with accounting standards or legislation.

5.13 An auditor may have a specific duty to form an opinion as to whether proper accounting records have been kept. For example, this duty is laid upon the auditor of a company by the Companies Act 1985. In such a case, if a qualified audit report is necessary because of (b) above, a report to management is no substitute for a qualified audit report.

5.14 In the public sector the auditor may have an additional responsibility, where required by statute or the terms of engagement, to report certain matters arising from the audit, including such weaknesses, to a third party such as a sponsoring department or audit supervisory body or the public (auditing guideline *Applicability to the public sector of auditing standards and guidelines).*

5.15 Reports to management should explain clearly the risks arising from internal control weaknesses. The use of specific examples discovered in the audit to illustrate the potential effects of weaknesses helps readers to understand the nature of the problems which require rectification. It is normally helpful for the auditor to make recommendations for improvements so that weaknesses can be eliminated. This should not however delay the issuing of any report. It should be borne in mind that determination of appropriate improvements in systems and the assessment of the cost-effectiveness of additional controls may be complex issues that in any event are management's responsibility.

Format and presentation

5.16 The report should be clear, constructive and concise. Careful presentation will help the recipient to understand the significance of the comments and devise corrective actions. The following factors should therefore be borne in mind.

5.17 It is important that matters of concern should be discussed and recorded as they arise to ensure that the auditor has properly understood the situation. These discussions may take place with members of staff at an operating level as well as with executives concerned solely with finance and accounting. When the points in the report are drafted they should be cleared for factual accuracy with the client staff concerned.

5.18 The auditor should explain in his report to management that it only includes those matters which came to his attention as a result of the audit procedures, and that it should not be regarded as a comprehensive statement of all weaknesses that exist or all improvements that might be made.

5.19 The report may contain matters of varying levels of significance and thus make it difficult for senior management to identify points of significance. The auditor can deal with this by giving the report a 'tiered' structure so that major points are dealt with by the directors and minor points are considered by less senior personnel. Alternatively, by agreement with the client, this objective might best be achieved by preparing separate reports for different levels of management, and reporting that this has been done.

5.20 When submitting his report the auditor should use his best endeavours to ensure that its contents reach those members of management who have the power to act on the findings. It is usually appropriate to address the report, or that part of the report containing the major points, to the Board of Directors or equivalent body even if the receipt of a report of less important points is delegated by the Board.

5.21 If the auditor chooses not to send a formal letter or report but considers it preferable to discuss any weaknesses with management, the discussion should be minuted or otherwise recorded in writing. Management should be provided with a copy of the note to ensure the discussion has been fairly reflected. The written record of any such discussions should be filed with the audit working papers.

Management response

5.22 The auditor should request a reply to all the points raised, indicating what action management intends to take as a result of the comments made in the report. It should be made clear in the report that the auditor expects at least an acknowledgement of the report or, where he considers it appropriate, the directors' discussion of the report to be recorded in the board minutes.

5.23 Where weaknesses have been discussed with client staff as and when they arise, the responses made by staff should be embodied where possible in the final form of a report. This will be particularly useful where, say, senior management receive the report and need to be informed of the action taken by their staff.

Third parties interested in reports to management

5.24 Any report made to management should be regarded as confidential communication. The auditor should therefore not normally reveal the contents of the report to any third party without the prior written consent of the management of the company.

5.25 In practice, the auditor has little control over what happens to the report once it has been despatched. Occasionally management may provide third parties with copies of the report, for example, their bankers or certain regulatory authorities. Therefore care should be taken to protect the auditor's position from exposure to liability in negligence to any third parties who may seek to rely on the report. Accordingly, the auditor should state clearly in his report that it has been prepared for the private use of his client. However, the auditor should recognise that the report may be disclosed by management to third parties, and in certain cases it may be appropriate for the auditor to request that the report is not circulated to any third parties without his prior consent.

5.26 Reports to management may contain comments which are critical of members of the client's management or staff, and could lay the auditor open to a charge of defamation. The auditor should therefore ensure that his comments are factually accurate, and do not include any gratuitous remarks of a personal nature.

Specimen management letter

5.27 A specimen letter is provided below which demonstrates how the principles described in the previous paragraphs are put into practice. The following points should be noted.

(a) *Timing*. This particular letter is submitted after the conclusion of the interim audit. This is the conventional approach where a separate interim audit has been performed. A further letter may be submitted at the conclusion of the audit. If no separate interim audit is carried out, one letter will be sent after all audit work has been completed.

(b) *Format*. The letter contains a *caveat*, advising the directors that it only contains those matters which have come to the auditor's attention as a result of his audit procedures and is hence not to be regarded as a comprehensive statement of all the weaknesses that may exist.

(c) *Contents*. The letter identifies specific weaknesses but also the risk arising from those weaknesses and practical recommendations for improvements.

(d) *Response*. In the penultimate paragraph the auditor emphasises that he requires a response to the points made in the letter, preferably in the form of management's action programme.

SPECIMEN MANAGEMENT LETTER

AB & Co
Certified Accountants
29 High Street
London, N10 4KB

The Board of Directors,
Manufacturing Co Limited,
15 South Street
London, S20 1CX

1 April 198X

Members of the board,

Financial statements for the year ended 31 May 198X

In accordance with our normal practice we set out in this letter certain matters which arose as a result of our review of the accounting systems and procedures operated by your company during our recent interim audit.

We would point out that the matters dealt with in this letter came to our notice during the conduct of our normal audit procedures which are designed primarily for the purpose of expressing our opinion on the financial statements of your company. In consequence our work did not encompass a detailed review of all aspects of the system and cannot be relied on necessarily to disclose defalcations or other irregularities or to include all possible improvements in internal control.

1 *Purchases: ordering procedures*

Present system

During the course of our work we discovered that it was the practice of the stores to order certain goods from X Ltd orally without preparing either a purchase requisition or purchase order.

Implications

There is therefore the possibility of liabilities being set up for unauthorised items and at a non-competitive price.

Recommendations

We recommend that the buying department should be responsible for such orders and, if they are placed orally, an official order should be raised as confirmation.

2 *Purchase ledger reconciliation*

Present system

Although your procedures require that the purchase ledger is reconciled against the control account on the nominal ledger at the end of every month, this was not done in December or January.

Implications

The balance on the purchase ledger was short by some £2,120 of the nominal ledger control account at 31 January 198X for which no explanation could be offered. This implies a serious breakdown in the purchase invoice and/or cash payment batching and posting procedures.

Recommendations

It is important in future that this reconciliation is performed regularly by a responsible official independent of the day to day purchase ledger, cashier and nominal ledger functions.

3 *Sales ledger: credit control*

Present system

As at 28 February 198X debtors account for approximately 12 weeks' sales, although your standard credit terms are cash within 30 days of statement, equivalent to an average of about 40 days (6 weeks) of sales.

Implications

This has resulted in increased overdraft usage and difficulty in settling some key suppliers accounts on time.

Recommendations

We recommend that a more structured system of debt collection be considered using standard letters and that statements should be sent out a week earlier if possible.

4 *Preparation of payroll and maintenance of personnel records*

Present system
Under your present system, just two members of staff are entirely and equally responsible for the maintenance of personnel records and preparation of the payroll. Furthermore, the only independent check of any nature on the payroll is that the chief accountant confirms that the amount of the wages cheque presented to him for signature agrees with the total of the net wages column in the payroll. This latter check does not involve any consideration of the reasonableness of the amount of the total net wages cheque or the monies being shown as due to individual employees.

Implications
It is a serious weakness of your present system, that so much responsibility is vested in the hands of just two people. This situation is made worse by the fact that there is no clearly defined division of duties as between the two of them. In our opinion, it would be far too easy for fraud to take place in this area (eg by inserting the names of 'dummy workmen' into the personnel records and hence on to the payroll) and/or for clerical errors to go undetected.

Recommendations

(i) Some person other than the two wages clerks be made responsible for maintaining the personnel records and for periodically (but on a surprise basis) checking them against the details on the payroll;

(ii) The two wages clerks be allocated specific duties in relation to the preparation of the payroll, with each clerk independently reviewing the work of the other;

(iii) When the payroll is presented in support of the cheque for signature to the chief accountant, that he should be responsible for assessing the reasonableness of the overall charge for wages that week.

Our comments have been discussed with your finance director and the chief accountant and these matters will be considered by us again during future audits. We look forward to receiving your comments on the points made. Should you require any further information or explanations do not hesitate to contact us.

We should like to take this opportunity of thanking your staff for their co-operation and assistance during the course of our audit.

Yours faithfully

ABC & Co

Exercise 3

List the most important reasons for an auditor giving a management letter to a client.

Solution

The principal purposes of a management letter are as follows.

(a) To enable the auditor to highlight weaknesses in the accounting records, systems and controls which he has identified during the course of his audit, and which may lead to material errors.

(b) To provide management with constructive advice on various aspects of the business which the auditor may have identified during the course of the audit.

(c) To highlight matters that may have an effect on future audits.

(d) To comply with specific requirements as laid down by, for example, local authorities, housing associations.

Chapter roundup

- **Note the distinction between the accounting system, which must be ascertained, recorded and assessed, and an internal control system which is desirable but not normally mandatory.**
- **Remember the mnemonic SOAPSPAM for the different types of internal controls.**
- **Learn the CA 1985 requirements relating to the accounting records.**
- **Appreciate that the walk through test is an aid to recording the system and not an evaluation tool.**
- **You must learn the flowchart symbols as you may be asked to interpret a flowchart or even draw one.**
- **You should appreciate the difference between an ICQ and an ICEQ.**
- **The work of the internal auditor is to some extent complimentary with that of the external auditor, but there are several important differences, which you should be able to distinguish.**
- **The external auditor may rely on the work of the internal audit department after it has been assessed as a reliable internal control.**
- **A management letter may be sent after both the interim and final audits, or combined in one letter at the end. The primary purpose of a management letter is to inform the management of weaknesses in the system of internal controls, but the letter can be used for a variety of other purposes.**

Test your knowledge

1 Define the internal control system. (see para 1.3)

2 What are the eight main types of internal control? (1.5)

3 Why should an auditor wish to place reliance on internal controls? (1.10)

4 Why does management require a complete and accurate accounting system? (2.6)

5 What are the principal statutory requirements regarding a company's accounting records? (2.12)

6 What are the principal advantages and disadvantages of flowcharts? (2.26)

7 What is a walk through test? (2.31)

8 What is the distinction between an ICQ and an ICEQ? (3.1, 3.2)

9 What are the inherent weaknesses of ICQs? (3.8)

10 What are the possible key control questions relevant to the purchases cycle? (3.10)

11 What procedures must the external auditor undertake before he can place reliance on the internal audit function? (4.13)

12 What audit matters may be included in a report to management? (5.12)

13 How may the auditor protect himself from exposure to liability to third parties who may seek to rely on his management letter? (5.25)

Part B

The conduct of an audit assignment

Chapter 8

COMPLIANCE AND SUBSTANTIVE TESTING

This chapter covers the following topics.

Introduction

This chapter lays out the basis for testing the financial records of a company as part of the audit process.

The main categories of types of audit tests are *compliance tests* and *substantive tests*, both of which are described here. The next chapter looks at specific sampling techniques in the testing process.

Small company audits are discussed here at this 'middle point' because all auditing techniques tend to be rolled together to audit a small company. The validity of control assessment is examined here, but sampling tests are usually not necessary in the small company situation.

1 AUDIT TESTING TECHNIQUES

1.1 After the system of internal controls has been evaluated the next stage is to design a programme of audit tests. If the controls have been assessed as effective, the auditor will design compliance tests to check how well they operate in practice; if the controls are considered to be weak, he will move directly to substantive testing to obtain direct assurance that transactions have been recorded completely and correctly.

The range of techniques

1.2 The types of audit evidence can be divided on the basis of the way in which they are obtained. The guideline identifies the following techniques of audit testing.

(a) *Inspection*

(i) In reviewing documents or records, thought should be given to their reliability.

(ii) Inspection of tangible assets reveals existence but not ownership, cost or value.

(b) *Observation* to judge performance of operations, but only at the time of observation.

(c) *Enquiry*, oral or written, from within or without the organisation. The auditor must judge reliability, depending on the knowledge, competence, experience and independence of the respondent.

(d) *Computation*. Arithmetical checking and independent calculation.

(e) *Analytical review*. This is examined in detail in Chapter 16.

1.3 In conducting his tests, the auditor should inspect original documents wherever possible. When it appears that the original document is not readily available, the auditor should consider the following points in deciding whether he may rely on a copy as evidence of the document's contents.

(a) The reason why the original is not available (the auditor might, for example, consider it suspicious that the original of one document is not available when those of other similar documents are present).

(b) The controls over the process of making the copy.

(c) The extent to which other evidence supports the contents of the copy.

(d) Whether the document was internally generated or derived from an external source.

1.4 It is generally considered that, provided there are adequate controls over the copying process, copies of internally generated documents are satisfactory evidence for audit purposes. Indeed, the original may well be in the hands of third parties (for example sales invoices). The auditor will normally, however, seek additional evidence to support that obtained from the copies (for example in the case of sales, direct confirmation from the debtors).

1.5 In the case of external documents, it is agreed that, no matter how good the control procedures are, internally produced copies are not satisfactory as audit evidence. The reasons for this include the following.

(a) The original may have been altered in a way that is not apparent from the copy.

(b) The copy may not contain all relevant information, for example the information on the back of the original.

2 COMPLIANCE VS SUBSTANTIVE TESTING

2.1 To obtain audit evidence the auditor will carry out his audit tests classified as 'substantive' or 'compliance' according to their primary purpose, applying a combination of the techniques identified in Paragraph 1.2. Both such purposes are sometimes achieved concurrently. Let us refresh our memories as to the formal definitions of compliance and substantive tests.

(a) *Compliance tests* are those tests which seek to provide audit evidence that internal control procedures are being applied as prescribed.

(b) *Substantive tests* are those tests of transactions and balances, and other procedures such as analytical review, which seek to provide audit evidence as to the completeness, accuracy and validity of the information contained in the accounting records or in the financial statements.

Compliance tests

2.2 Where the preliminary evaluation described previously, using ICQs or ICEQs as the case may be, indicates that there are key controls which meet the objective which the auditor has identified he should design and carry out compliance tests if he wishes to rely on them. Where the evaluation discloses weaknesses, or the absence of internal controls, such that material error or omission could arise in the accounting records or the financial statements, the auditor will move directly to designing and carrying out substantive tests.

2.3 It should be noted that it is the control which is being tested by a compliance test, and not the transaction which may be the medium used for the test. For this reason the auditor should record and investigate all exceptions revealed by his compliance testing, regardless of the amount involved in the particular transaction. (An 'exception' in this context is where a control has not been operated correctly whether or not a quantitative error has occurred.)

2.4 If compliance tests disclose no exceptions the auditor may reasonably place reliance on the effective functioning of the internal controls tested. He can, therefore, limit his substantive tests on the relevant information in the accounting records.

2.5 If the compliance tests have disclosed exceptions which indicate that the control being tested was not operating properly in practice, the auditor should determine the reasons for this. He needs to assess whether each exception is only an isolated departure or is representative of others, and whether it indicates the possible existence of errors in the accounting records. If the explanation he receives suggests that the exception is only an isolated departure, then he must confirm the validity of the explanation, for example by carrying out further tests. If the explanation or the further tests confirm that the control being tested was not operating properly throughout the period, then he cannot rely on that control. In these circumstances the auditor is unable to restrict his substantive testing unless he can identify an alternative control on which to rely. Before relying on that alternative control he must carry out suitable compliance tests on it.

2.6 If reliance is to be placed on the operation of controls, the auditor should ensure that there is evidence of the effectiveness of those controls throughout the whole period under review. The compliance tests carried out at the interim stage will therefore need to be supplemented by further tests for the remainder of the financial year. These additional tests will be carried out during the final audit.

2.7 Alternatively, the auditor will need to carry out other procedures to enable him to gain adequate assurance as to the reliability of the accounting records during the period which has not been subject to compliance tests. In determining the alternative procedures which are necessary he should consider:

(a) the results of earlier compliance tests;

(b) whether, according to enquiries made, controls have remained the same for the remaining period;

(c) the length of the remaining period;

(d) the nature and size of the transactions and account items involved; and

(e) the substantive tests which he will carry out irrespective of the adequacy of controls.

2.8 Where the internal control system has changed during the accounting period under review, the auditor will have to evaluate and test the internal controls on which he wishes to rely, both before and after the change.

2.9 The main aim of any compliance test is to discover whether there are any deviations from the prescribed system which may have a material effect on the reliability of the records as a basis for the accounts. The auditor is hence only concerned with those controls ('key controls') whose failure could lead to material misstatement and are not compensated for by other controls. Controls which are not key should not be tested nor should they be relied on as they cannot give any audit assurance. Also the auditor will only seek to rely on internal controls where it is cost effective:

(a) the reliance on internal controls enables the auditor to reduce specific substantive tests; and

(b) the time costs of identifying key controls and carrying out the compliance testing is less than the time costs saved by reducing the substantive testing.

2.10 The types of key control that the auditor will be looking out for during his evaluation and testing will, of course, be derived from those classified in the Appendix to the guideline *Internal controls*. It should be appreciated, however, that the nature of the compliance test will vary with the type of control.

2.11 The normal compliance philosophy is to test only for evidence of the control being performed; for example, completion of an invoice grid stamp on a purchase invoice. Strictly a control can only be tested, and subsequently relied upon, if there is some evidence of its performance. This evidence might typically be a signature or initials on a document indicating authorisation or checking of computation. The testing technique being applied here is clearly 'inspection' (see Paragraph 1.2(a)).

2.12 However, there is a problem where a control does not leave permanent evidence of its performance. It may be possible to test it by observing its performance (see Paragraph 1.2 (b)) or by attempting to defeat it. For example, controls over the opening of post and the distribution of wages may be observed on a surprise basis. Password controls on computer terminals may be tested by attempting to defeat this control and by examining the record of passwords issued and password changes.

2.13 Where a compliance test is carried out on a sample basis the auditor should consider whether the same sample can be used for any substantive tests on the same documents: clearly, where practicable, compliance and substantive tests should be carried out simultaneously. Some compliance tests can be achieved by perusing the whole of the population rather than by sampling, for example if purchase invoices are being tested for proper completion and initialling of a grid stamp, the test may be effectively and simply achieved by flicking through invoice files or batches to ensure that all invoices appear to carry the completed stamp.

2.14 The auditor's compliance programme will embrace all material transaction types where key controls have been identified at the evaluation stage. The tests, results of the tests and conclusions must be recorded in the audit working papers. Normally such information is retained on the current file, but some firms prefer to record the compliance tests on schedules which are effectively extensions of the ICEQs, in which case they may be considered part of the permanent file information.

Compliance testing and the audit risk model

2.15 We examined the audit risk model in Chapter 5. We saw there that control risk is defined as:

> 'the risk that material errors will not be prevented or detected by internal controls.'

2.16 The auditor will therefore use compliance tests to check the estimate of control risk. Where compliance tests are successful, then control risk can be set low, at say 30%. The risk-based approach we examined in Chapter 5 would then reduce the necessary sample size for any substantive procedures in the same area.

2.17 Obviously, the lower the *assessed* level of control risk, the more persuasive the evidence should be that the controls are effective. The extent of compliance testing will depend on how much the auditor plans to rely on the control and the availability and interrelationships of other evidence. So where two independent controls produce the same control objective, the extent of testing on each control can be reduced.

Substantive tests

2.18 The principal objectives of transaction work are to determine:

(a) whether all income and expenses have been recorded; and
(b) whether the recorded income and expense transactions did in fact occur.

In short, we are concerned with completeness, accuracy and validity.

2.19 Some audit comfort in terms of satisfying this objective will be gained from successful compliance testing, but it will always be necessary to perform substantive work. Broadly speaking the tests will fall into two categories:

(a) tests to discover errors (resulting in over or under statement); and
(b) tests to discover omissions (resulting in under statement).

2.20 Tests designed to discover errors will start with the records in which the transactions are recorded and check from the entries to supporting documents or other evidence. Such tests should detect any over statement and also any under statement through causes other than omission.

2.21 Tests designed to discover omissions must start from outside the accounting records and then check back to those records. For example, if the test is designed to discover whether all raw material purchases have been properly processed the test would start, say, with goods received notes and check them to the stock records or purchase ledger. Understatements through omission will never be revealed by starting with the account itself as there is clearly no chance of selecting items that have been omitted from the account.

2.22 For most systems it is desirable to include tests designed to discover both errors and omissions and it is important that the type of test, and direction of the test, is recognised before selecting the test sample. If the sample which tested the accuracy and validity of the sales ledger were chosen from a file of sales invoices then it would not substantiate the fact that there were no errors in the sales ledger. The approach known as 'directional testing' which is discussed below, applies this testing discipline.

2.23 When designing his programme the auditor will invoke the techniques described in Paragraph 1.2 as he thinks fit; many transaction tests are likely to fall within categories (a) and (d), inspection and computation.

Directional testing

2.24 Audit objectives can be related to five attributes, which you might like to remember using the acronym COVED.

C ompleteness
O wnership
V aluation
E xistence
D isclosure

The technique that a number of the larger accounting practices use to test the first four of these attributes is referred to as 'directional testing'. The fifth attribute, disclosure, is tested as part of the review of financial statements.

2.25 The concept of directional testing derives from the principle of double-entry bookkeeping, in that for every debit there is a corresponding credit. (This of course presupposes that the double entry is complete and that the accounting records balance.) Therefore, any misstatement of a debit entry will result in either a corresponding misstatement of a credit entry or a misstatement in the opposite direction, of another debit entry. By designing audit tests carefully the auditor is able to use this principle in drawing audit conclusions, not only about the debit or credit entries that he has directly tested, but also about the corresponding credit or debit entries that are necessary to balance the books.

2.26 Tests are therefore designed in the following way.

(a) *Debit items* (expenditure or assets) are tested for overstatement. This is done by selecting debit entries recorded in the nominal ledger and ensuring that they represent valid entries in terms of value, existence and ownership.

For example, if a fixed asset entry in the nominal ledger of £1,000 is selected, it would be overstated if it should have been recorded at anything less than £1,000 or if the company did not own it, or indeed if it did not exist (for example it had been sold or the amount of £1,000 in fact represented a revenue expense).

(b) *Credit items* (income or liabilities) are tested for understatement. This is done by selecting items from appropriate sources independent of the nominal ledger and ensuring that they result in the correct nominal ledger entry.

For example, the auditor might select a goods despatched note and ensure that the resultant sale has been recorded in the nominal ledger sales account. Sales would be understated if the nominal ledger did not reflect the transaction at all (completeness) or reflected it at less than full value (say if goods valued at £1,000 were recorded in the sales account at £900, there would be an understatement of £100).

2.27 The matrix set out below demonstrates how directional testing is applied to give assurance on all account areas in the financial statements.

Type of account	*Purpose of primary test*	*Primary test also gives comfort on*			
		Assets	*Liabilities*	*Income*	*Expenses*
Assets	Overstatement (O)	U	O	O	U
Liabilities	Understatement (U)	U	O	O	U
Income	Understatement (U)	U	O	O	U
Expense	Overstatement (O)	U	O	O	U

2.28 Thus, a test for the overstatement of an asset simultaneously gives comfort on understatement of other assets, overstatement of liabilities, overstatement of income and understatement of expenses.

2.29 It can be seen from the matrix that assets can only be understated by virtue of:

(a) other assets being overstated; or
(b) liabilities being understated; or
(c) income being understated; or
(d) expenses being overstated.

2.30 Similarly, liabilities can only be overstated by virtue of:

(a) assets being overstated; or
(b) other liabilities being understated; or
(c) income being understated; or
(d) expenses being overstated.

2.31 So, by performing the primary tests shown in the matrix, the auditor obtains audit assurance in other audit areas. Successful completion of the primary tests will therefore result in his having tested all account areas both for overstatement and understatement.

2.32 The major advantage of the directional audit approach, testing assets and expense for overstatement only, and liabilities and income for understatement only, is its cost-effectiveness. This arises because items are not tested for both overstatement and understatement. It also audits directly the more likely types of transactional misstatement, namely unrecorded income and improper expense (whether arising intentionally or unintentionally).

2.33 The conclusions drawn from the interim audit tests will form the basis for amendments to the balance sheet audit programme. Interim notes should be prepared linking the interim and final visits. Such notes should identify the following matters.

(a) Work outstanding from the interim audit.

(b) Proposals for reduction in work at final visit (where parts of the system have been evaluated and tested as strong).

(c) Problems identified during the interim audit and effect on final audit work.

(d) Advance planning matters, for example, date for setting up debtors' circularisation, date of stocktake.

In addition, the interim management letter will be drafted, approved and submitted.

2.34 Finally, a few points on audit terminology which you may come across.

(a) *Procedural tests*: these are basically the same as compliance tests.

(b) *Weakness tests*: these are basically the same as substantive tests of transactions.

(c) *Depth tests*: these are compliance tests but conducted rather like a walk-through test. Tests on different control features are strung together so they become in effect a walk-through test. Unlike a walk-through test, however, the sample must be representative of the population to achieve the compliance objectives.

(d) *Vouching tests*: vouching may be defined as the examination by the auditor of all the documentary evidence which is available to support the authenticity of transactions entered in the client's records. It is therefore a substantive test involving inspection.

Exercise 1

Explain what you understand by the following terms as applied to audit tests, indicating the circumstances in which their use would be appropriate, and giving in each case an illustration of their use in practice.

(a) Rotational.
(b) Walk-through.
(c) Depth.

Solution

(a) *Rotational tests*

An auditor often cannot practicably visit all the locations of a client's business every year, and may find it difficult to test all aspects of a large and complex organisation within the time and fee constraints of the audit. Where the auditor is satisfied that the client has good systems of internal control, it may be possible to rotate the audit work. A rotational audit of locations would involve audit visits to a number of branches each year, so that all were covered in the course of two or more years. Under a rotational systems audit, a full systems audit would be carried out on certain areas (for example the sales system) whilst others (for example purchases, cash) were covered by, for instance, walkthrough tests and analytical review. Care should always be taken that all areas do receive a full audit every 2-3 years.

(b) *Walk-through tests*

A walk-through test involves the test of very small numbers of transactions. It does not provide audit information, but allows the auditor to check that he fully understands a system and has recorded it correctly. A walk-through test of the sales system, for instance, would involve the auditor in tracing the stages in a sales transaction from receipt of the order via despatch of the goods, delivery note and invoice to the record in the sales ledger.

(c) *Depth tests*

A depth test covers all aspects of a transaction, using a much larger sample than the walk- through test. (Sample size will depend on the auditor's assessment of the level of risk involved and the confidence level required.) A depth test on sales debtor receipts, for instance, would involve checking the posting of a sample of receipts from the client's list to sales ledger accounts, sales ledger control accounts and via paying-in books and so forth to the bank account.

---

3 SMALL COMPANY AUDITS

The small business environment

3.1 As has already been pointed out, all limited companies are required by statute to have their accounts audited, with the exception of dormant companies, whose shareholders have the powers to dispense with an audit.

Note. The Companies Act 1985 does not differentiate in any way between the scope of an audit for large and small companies; nor does it make any difference whether they are public or private. The auditor's rights and duties remain the same.

3.2 The debate on whether or not small companies ought to continue to have an audit must not detract from the fact that the auditor is currently required not only to comply with the Companies Act 1985 but also to apply auditing standards in all cases.

3.3 In March 1985 the Department of Trade and Industry issued a report entitled *Burdens on Business*. It gave a useful insight into how businesses see the administrative and legislative burdens imposed on them by government. Company law, which encompasses the statutory audit, was ranked thirteenth as a burden, behind such matters as VAT, PAYE and employment protection.

3.4 As a result of the *Burdens on Business* report, a working group of the Institute of Directors was set up. The recommendations of this group have led to the inclusion in the Companies Act 1989 of various deregulatory measures designed to simplify procedures for private companies. The most important of these measures are those which allow private companies to substitute unanimous written agreement of the shareholders for resolutions passed in general meeting, and the so-called 'elective regime', which allows a private company to opt out of certain requirements of company law including the requirement to hold AGMs and the laying of accounts and reports before a general meeting. Some small changes have also been made to the 'abbreviated accounts' rules. But the requirement for an audit of all non-dormant companies remains.

The problem of control

3.5 It might seem convenient if we could, at the outset, define small enterprises in absolute terms, perhaps by reference to those companies defined as small for the purpose of abbreviated accounts eligibility. But the auditing standards and guidelines do not attempt to be so precise. Size alone will inevitably be a rather arbitrary criterion for distinguishing those companies which present special audit problems. A more useful distinguishing feature is the extent of internal control, because of the relative lack of formal controls in smaller enterprises.

3.6 Many of the controls which would be relevant to a large enterprise are neither practical nor appropriate for the small enterprise. For these the most important form of internal control is generally the close involvement of the directors or proprietors. However, that very involvement will enable them to override controls and, if they wish, to exclude transactions from the records. This possibility can lead to difficulties for the auditor not because there is a general lack of controls but because the evidence available as to their operation and the completeness of the records is insufficient.

3.7 Segregation of duties will often appear inadequate in enterprises having a small number of staff. Similarly, because of the scale of the operation, organisation and management controls are likely to be rudimentary at best. The onus is therefore on the proprietor, by virtue of his day-to-day involvement, to compensate for this lack. This involvement should encompass physical, authorisation, arithmetical and accounting checks as well as supervision.

3.8 But it is important to stress that in a well run small company there is a system of internal control. In any case, all companies must comply with the provisions of the Companies Act concerning the maintenance of a proper accounting system.

3.9 Where the manager of a small business is not himself the owner, he may not possess the same degree of commitment to the running of it as an owner-manager would. In such cases, the auditor will have to consider the adequacy of controls exercised by the shareholders over the manager in assessing internal control.

Minimum business controls

3.10 Having established that proprietor involvement is the key to internal control in the small enterprise, we need next to be rather more precise and identify the types of control relevant to each principal accounting area. These controls can be referred to as 'minimum business controls'. It is important to appreciate that such controls will not, and cannot, be evaluated and relied on by the auditor as in a 'systems' audit approach, but they do provide overall comfort to the auditor, particularly when determining whether to seek to rely on management assurances as to the completeness of the accounting records.

3.11 The following checklist provides illustrative examples of such minimum standards of internal control.

Mail

(a) Is all mail received and opened by the proprietor?

(b) If the proprietor does not himself open the mail, is it opened by a person not connected with the accounts (for example the proprietor's secretary) and read by him before it is distributed to the staff?

Receipts

(a) Are all cheques and postal orders received by post counted by the proprietor before they are passed to the cashier?

(b) Are all cheques and postal orders crossed to the company's branch of its bankers 'Not negotiable - account payee only'.

(c) Are cash sales and credit sale receipts over the counter controlled by locked cash register tapes which only the proprietor can open?

(d) Does the proprietor reconcile the cash register totals with the cash sales receipts daily?

(e) Is the person performing the duties of cashier barred any responsibility concerning the sales, purchase or nominal ledgers?

Banking

(a) Is all cash received banked intact at intervals of not more than three days?

(b) Does the proprietor reconcile all monies received with the copy paying-in slips at regular intervals?

Payments

(a) Are all payments except sundry expenses made by cheques?

(b) Does the proprietor sign all cheques?

(c) Are cheques signed by the proprietor only after he has satisfied himself that:

 (i) he has approved and cancelled all vouchers supporting the payment;
 (ii) all cheques are crossed:

  (1) not negotiable?
  (2) account payee only?

 (iii) all cheque numbers are accounted for?

(d) Are petty cash expenses controlled by the imprest system?

(e) **Does the proprietor review all expenses and initial the petty cash book before reimbursing the cashier?**

Bank statements

(a) **Are bank statements and paid cheques sent direct to the proprietor and opened only by him?**

(b) **Does the proprietor scrutinise all paid cheques to ensure that he has signed them all before he passes them to the cashier?**

(c) **Does the proprietor:**

(i) **prepare a bank reconciliation each month? or**
(ii) **review in detail a reconciliation produced by the cashier?**

Orders

(a) Are all purchase orders issued:

(i) serially numbered by the printer;
(ii) pre-printed duplicate order forms?

(b) Does the proprietor approve all orders?

Receipt of goods

Are delivery notes:

(a) checked with goods;
(b) compared with the copy order;
(c) compared with the invoice?

Wages

(a) Is a separate cheque drawn for the exact amount to pay wages and PAYE/National Insurance?

(b) Does the proprietor either prepare or examine the wages records before signing the cheque?

(c) Does the proprietor initial the wages records after his examination?

(d) Does the proprietor oversee the distribution of the wages packets or does he distribute them himself?

Debtors

(a) If credit is granted to customers does the proprietor:

(i) authorise every extension of credit to a customer; or
(ii) approve credit limits for each customer?

(b) Does the proprietor authorise all:

(i) write offs of bad debts?
(ii) sales returns and allowances?
(iii) discounts other than routine cash discounts?

(c) Does the proprietor receive a monthly list of debtors, showing the age of the debts?

(d) Are all authorisations by the proprietor evidenced by his initials?

Goods outwards

(a) Are pre-numbered despatch notes prepared for all goods leaving the premises?

(b) Are all despatch notes:

(i) accounted for?
(ii) cross referenced with invoices and credit notes?

(c) Is the proprietor satisfied that all goods leaving the premises have been accounted for?

Stock

Does the proprietor scrutinise the stocks regularly:

(a) to keep abreast of what is in stock?

(b) to discover obsolete items?
(c) to discover damaged articles?
(d) to ensure that stock levels are kept under control?

3.12 Although the above types of control are desirable and feasible, they are nevertheless relatively informal. Consequently evidence of their performance tends to be lacking and they may indeed be overridden as there is no check on the proprietor himself.

Application of auditing standards to small businesses

3.13 Can the auditing standards be applied to small companies? Yes. The following paragraphs identify the particular points that affect the auditor's approach to such businesses.

3.14 *Planning, controlling and recording*. Planning may not be a major task in the case of a small client, but some planning is clearly necessary. Control over work delegated to staff is just as important in the case of a small client as it is in a large one, as is the need to record the audit work done and evidence obtained.

3.15 *Accounting systems*. If there is not some kind of organised system for gathering together the basic accounting data (details of purchases, sales, cash received and paid and so on), no amount of auditing will provide assurance that the accounts show a true and fair view. The guideline does not suggest that such a system of data collection need be anything other than simple, but it must be comprehensive and must also comply with the accounting records requirements of s 221 Companies Act 1985.

3.16 *Audit evidence*. The auditor needs to obtain the same degree of assurance in order to give an unqualified opinion on the financial statements of both small and large enterprises, and the collection of appropriate audit evidence is of course the key to this. In many situations it may be possible to reach a conclusion that will support an unqualified opinion on the financial statements by combining the evidence obtained from extensive substantive testing of transactions with a full review of costs and margins. However, in some businesses such as those where most transactions are for cash and there is no regular pattern of costs and margins, the available evidence may be inadequate to support an opinion on the financial statements.

The auditor needs to satisfy himself both about the system and about the management assurances he receives. The use of a minimum business controls checklist, incorporating the types of question identified above, may provide the auditor with comfort as regards the first requirement. When assessing the possibility that management assurances might be inaccurate, the auditor must consider whether his examination of the records, the audit evidence available to him and his knowledge of all the circumstances affecting the company are consistent with and support the assurances. He must also form an opinion as to the honesty and reliability of management, based on previous experience and having due regard to the prevailing circumstances. Reliance on management assurances must be justified, and should be supported by written representation where appropriate.

3.17 *Internal controls*. There is no requirement in the auditing standards for the auditor to seek to rely on a system of internal control. We have seen that, although the need for internal controls may be fulfilled largely by the proprietor himself, that means that the auditor may find little evidence that controls have been properly exercised. It is only where there is evidence of the operation of internal control that the auditor can rely on it.

3.18 *Review of financial statements*. The need to review financial statements, including the use of analytical review techniques, is well established in respect of clients of all sizes. Because the shareholder accounts of small companies must comply with the requirements of the Companies Act 1985 and SSAPs like those of large companies, the financial statements must be reviewed by the auditor to ensure that compliance is achieved.

3.19 To reiterate, the duties and responsibilities of the auditors in respect of the individual small company client are the same as in larger audits, and the satisfactory accomplishment of the work requires the application of the principles of auditing to the individual case. Because the relationship with the directors is frequently less formal and because other professional services including accountancy work are often provided, it is particularly important that the arrangement and scope of the work should be clearly defined and confirmed in the engagement letter.

The need for the small company audit

3.20 Is the statutory audit of small companies of sufficient value to anyone to justify the administrative and financial burden imposed on the company?

3.21 The DTI consultative document *Accounting and audit requirements for small firms* sought to elicit the views of interested parties regarding both the abolition of the audit requirement and the relaxation of accounting rules for small companies. In examining the arguments for and against exempting small companies from the statutory audit requirement, it suggested that the protection afforded by an audit is not essential where all shareholders are directors, who should normally be in a position to get a view of the company's affairs without being required to commission an independent audit. Nevertheless, it was acknowledged that the interests of other investors such as banks and trade creditors require protection and that such persons could require their own independent audits in the absence of any statutory requirement.

3.22 The options for change identified by the paper were as follows.

(a) Abolish the audit requirement for small companies where all the members are directors.

(b) Abolish the audit requirement for all small companies below a certain size, though not for all small companies as presently defined.

(c) Abolish the audit requirement for all small companies and allow members to decide the company's policy on auditing of accounts in the light of its particular circumstances.

3.23 The consultative document then proceeded to discuss the form and content of accounts. It explained that when the Fourth Directive was implemented there was a choice. Small companies could be allowed to do no more than prepare and file a modified balance sheet with supporting notes. Alternatively full accounts might be circulated to shareholders but at the same time the publication of modified accounts could be permitted. In view of the lack of any consensus at the time, the latter alternative was adopted as a compromise solution, which protected shareholders' interests and still afforded the company a measure of privacy from the outside world. In exploring the possibility of any further relaxation from the current requirements, the DTI put forward the following options.

(a) Allow small owner-managed companies to produce modified accounts only.

(b) Allow all small companies to produce modified accounts only, subject to shareholder approval.

(c) Allow a sub-category, which is not defined in the consultative document, of small companies to produce modified accounts only, again subject to shareholder approval.

3.24 Finally, the consultative document asked for comments on whether the present size criteria for small and medium sized companies should be raised in order to take account of inflation. This followed the earlier adoption by the EC of a short directive increasing the original financial thresholds contained in the Fourth Directive.

3.25 To examine in greater detail the pros and cons it is useful to refer to the audit brief *Small companies: the need for audit*, which was issued as a consultative document back in 1979, prior to the implementation of the Fourth Directive in the Companies Act 1981.

The small companies audit brief

3.26 The case for retaining the present system rests on the value of the statutory audit to those who have an interest in audited accounts, ie the users of accounts. The audit brief defines these interested parties as:

(a) shareholders;
(b) banks and other institutional creditors;
(c) trade creditors;
(d) taxing authorities;
(e) employees;
(f) management.

This list is very similar to the list of users given in *The Corporate Report*.

3.27 The brief proceeds to put forward arguments for and against change from the viewpoint of each type of user.

(a) *Shareholders*

Against change	Shareholders not involved in management need the reassurance given by audited accounts. Furthermore, the existence of the audit deters the directors from treating the company's assets as their own to the detriment of minority shareholders. Audited financial statements are invaluable in arriving at a fair valuation of the shares in an unquoted company either for taxation or other purposes.
For change	Where all the shareholders are also executive directors or closely related to them, the benefit gained from an audit may not be worth its cost.

(b) *Banks and other institutional creditors*

Against change	Banks rely on accounts for the purposes of making loans and reviewing the value of security.
For change	There is doubt whether banks rely on the audited accounts of companies to a greater extent than those of unincorporated associations of a similar size which have not been audited. A review of the way in which the bank accounts of the company have been conducted and of forecasts and management accounts are at least as important to the banks as the appraisal of the audited accounts. There is no reason why a bank should not make an audit a precondition of granting a loan.

(c) *Trade creditors*

Against change	Creditors and potential creditors should have the opportunity to assess the strength of their customers by examining audited financial statements either themselves or through a credit company.
For change	In practice, only limited reliance is placed on the accounts available from the Registrar of Companies as they are usually filed so late as to be of little significance in granting short term credit.

(d) *Tax authorities*

Against change	The Inland Revenue and Customs and Excise rely on accounts for computing corporation tax and checking VAT returns.
For change	There is little evidence to suggest that the tax authorities rely on audited accounts to a significantly greater extent than those, which, whilst being unaudited have been prepared by an independent accountant.

(e) *Employees*

Against change	Employees are entitled to be able to assess audited accounts when entering wage negotiations and considering the future viability of their employer.
For change	There is little evidence to suggest that, in the case of small companies, such assessments are made.

(f) *Management*

Against change	The audit provides management with a useful independent check on the accuracy of the accounting systems and the auditor is frequently able to recommend improvements in those systems.
For change	If the law were changed, the management of a company could, if they so desired, still elect to have an independent audit. It is likely, however, that a review accompanied by a management consultancy report would represent a greater benefit for a similar cost.

Finance Act 1993: Compilation reports

3.28 Arising from measures announced in the Finance Act 1993, the audit burden is likely to be reduced for small companies in the very near future. The DTI has produced draft proposals in this respect, and the APB has already produced a draft response entitled *Small company compilation reports.*

3.29 The draft DTI regulations propose that a small company with turnover of not more than £90,000 (and balance sheet totals not more than £1.4m) should be entirely exempt from a statutory audit of its annual accounts; companies with a turnover of between £90,000 and £350,000 (and subject to the same limit on balance sheet totals) will also be exempt, provided that the directors ensure a *compilation report* is prepared by a suitably qualified accountant. In either case, there are provisions designed to allow shareholders to request an audit. There are also a number of categories of company which are not eligible for the exemption.

3.30 It is estimated by Government that approximately 500,000 companies could be effected by these new exemptions.

3.31 The compilation report is a new form of statutory report. It is to be made by a suitably qualified reporting accountant, who must be independent of the company, but who need not be a registered auditor.

3.32 The draft DTI regulations specify that the compilation report should be addressed to the members of the company (its shareholders), and that it should include the reporting accountant's opinion on a number of matters, namely:

(a) whether the accounts agree with the accounting records;

(b) whether the accounts have been drawn up in a manner consistent with certain statutory accounting provisions specified by the draft regulations; and

(c) the company's entitlement to exemption from an audit.

3.33 The reporting accountant is not required to perform an audit of the accounts, and does not need to carry out an audit in order to give this report: the procedures to be applied in this engagement, and the assurance provided by the compilation report, are therefore much less than in an audit.

Exercise 2

Describe the audit procedures you would employ, in addition to the routine vouching of sales and cash, to verify that all income due to the company has been recorded and included in the accounts, and in addition, the problems you may experience in so doing, in the following two specific cases:

(a) a small manufacturing company which purchases and sells goods on credit; and
(b) a small retail store which purchases goods on credit and sells them for cash.

You may assume in each case that the company keeps good records of its transactions.

Solution

The audit procedures required, in addition to the routine vouching of sales and cash, to verify that all income due to the company has been recorded and included in the accounts, in the two specific cases referred to in the question, would be as follows.

(a) *Small manufacturing company*

Given that the company sells goods on credit, considerable satisfaction may be gained as to the accuracy of the sales income figure by confirming that the year end debtors figure is reasonable. The audit work required to do this would include:

(i) test checking that sales ledger balances have been correctly extracted;

(ii) verifying that the sales ledger control account agrees with the list of sales ledger balances;

(iii) test checking that the year end cut-off is correct in particular ensuring that invoices have been charged in the correct period and that adequate provision has been made for credit notes issued in the post balance sheet period which relate to sales made before the balance sheet date;

(iv) seeking direct confirmation of debtor balances by circularisation, with careful enquiry being made into any balances where the customer does not agree with the client's balance;

In addition to the above, the auditor should consider the use of analytical review techniques to assess the reasonableness of the sales figure. Significant ratios to be considered would include:

(i) the gross profit rate;
(ii) the average number of days sales in debtors.

The auditor should consider the above, and the general level of turnover, in the light of the previous year's figures for the client and also in comparison with the results of any similar sized clients within the same industry.

The main problems likely to face the auditor with this client are:

(i) poor response to the debtor circularisation; and

(ii) the lack of similar sized clients within the same industry, resulting in an inability to make meaningful comparisons of the manufacturing company's ratios with those of other companies.

(b) *Small retail store*

Since the sales of this client are all for cash, then the various tests detailed above relating to debtors are clearly not applicable. Instead, the auditor will need to concentrate on assessing the reasonableness of the figure for sales income by means of analytical review techniques. In particular he should consider:

(i) the consistency of the gross profit rate as compared with previous years;

(ii) whether the reported income appears reasonable given the gross profit rate and the recorded purchases and opening and closing stocks.

Specific confirmation should be sought from the proprietors that no goods have been sold on credit and also that any goods taken for the proprietors' own consumption have been fully recorded.

The main problem with this client is likely to be that a detailed analysis of sales of goods with a different mark-up is unlikely to be available. This could mean that significant inaccuracies could result from placing undue reliance on an overall gross profit rate.

Since no third party evidence is directly available in relation to sales, the auditor will be much more dependent upon management representations than is the case with the small manufacturing company. As the closing stock is likely to be the key figure in the accounts the auditor should satisfy himself as to the reasonableness of this amount by attending the stocktaking in order to assess the efficiency of the client's stocktaking procedures.

In both cases the auditor may be forced to conclude that he has not been able to obtain sufficient, relevant and reliable audit evidence on which to base his audit opinion. This is likely to result in a qualification of the audit report on the grounds of uncertainty.

Chapter roundup

- The auditor's techniques of obtaining evidence are:
  - inspection;
  - observation;
  - enquiry;
  - computation;
  - analytical review.
- You should try to understand the *objectives* of compliance and substantive tests as this will help you to design individual tests.
- Compliance testing is closely associated with the estimation of control risk in the audit risk model.
- You should appreciate the operational *and* reporting problems confronting the auditor of small companies. The auditor will normally adopt a broadly substantive approach.

Test your knowledge

1. What are the five principal techniques for obtaining audit evidence available to the auditor? (see para 1.2)
2. How are compliance and substantive tests defined? (2.1)
3. What should the auditor do when a control does not leave permanent evidence of its performance? (2.12)
4. What effect does a successful compliance test have on control risk? (2.16, 2.17)
5. What are procedural tests and weakness tests? (2.34)
6. What minimum business controls would be appropriate to mail opening and receipts in a small company? (3.11)
7. What arguments would each user of accounts have for and against small company audits? (3.27)

Chapter 9

AUDIT SAMPLING

This chapter covers the following topics.

1 Audit sampling

2 Compliance tests: attribute sampling

3 Substantive tests: variables sampling

Introduction

We have looked at different types of audit tests in the last chapter. Once the type of test has been determined, the auditor needs to decide how he or she will select the items to be tested from the whole population.

This is not as simple as it sounds. The auditor will want to select a sample which reflects, as closely as possible, the characteristics of the population from which the same has been selected. If this is *not* the case, then the auditor cannot draw valid conclusion from the tests carried out on the sample.

These problems have produced suggested solutions ranging from the very simple to the very complex. The more sophisticated sampling techniques involve the use of probabilities and statistics. We will explain these as simply as possible as you are not expected to understand the more complicated aspects of sampling theory.

Sampling theory is closely associated with the definition of auditing risk and you should refer back to Chapter 5 to remind yourself of the relevant definitions.

1 AUDIT SAMPLING

1.1 The APC have recognised the need for guidance on the important topic of audit sampling, and a draft guideline and draft audit brief *Audit sampling* were published in April 1987. The following comments are taken from these documents.

1.2 Audit tests may be carried out using various techniques which fall into the broad categories of inspection, observation, enquiry or computation. The auditor may apply such tests to an entire set of data (100% testing) or he may choose to draw conclusions about the entire set of data ('the population') by testing a representative sample of items selected from it; this latter procedure is 'audit sampling'.

1.3 Audit sampling is defined as the application of a compliance or substantive test to less than 100% of the items within an account balance, class of transactions or other population, as representative of that population, to enable the auditor to obtain and evaluate evidence of some characteristic of that population and to assist in forming a conclusion concerning that characteristic.

1.4 Audit sampling does not include audit procedures where the auditor tests only those individual items within a population which have a particular significance (for example all items individually over a certain amount or those which the auditor believes are particularly prone to error); in such cases the auditor is simply testing part of the population in its entirety and cannot use the results to draw conclusions about the rest of the population.

1.5 Because the auditor does not examine all the items in the population when applying audit sampling, there is a risk that the conclusion that he draws will be different from that which he would have drawn had he examined the entire population; this is 'sampling risk'. The auditor should use a rational basis for planning, selecting and testing the sample and for evaluating the results so that he has adequate assurance that the sample is representative of the population, and that sampling risk is reduced to an acceptable level.

Stages of audit sampling

1.6 Audit sampling can be divided into four basic stages.

(1) Planning the sample
(2) Selecting the items to be tested
(3) Testing the items
(4) Evaluating the results of the tests

Stage 1: Planning the sample

1.7 Having decided to use audit sampling the auditor needs to plan the sample properly. The factors to consider include:

(a) the audit objectives;

(b) the population and sampling unit;

(c) the definition of error (in substantive tests) or deviation (in compliance tests);

(d) the sample size, which will be influenced by:

(i) the assurance required (or risk accepted) having regard to other sources of evidence available;

(ii) the tolerable error/deviation rate;

(iii) the expected error/deviation rate;

(iv) the stratification.

1.8 The sampling unit is any of the individual items that constitute the population. For example, in substantive tests the sampling unit may be the individual balances making up an account balance, the underlying transactions or monetary units. In compliance tests the sampling unit depends on the way in which the control is exercised; for example if a control is performed on each sales invoice then the sales invoice is the sampling unit.

1.9 Before performing tests on the sample the auditor should define clearly those test results and conditions that will be considered errors or deviations by reference to the audit objective.

1.10 The sample size may be affected by the following four related factors, which all require the auditor's judgement.

(a) *Assurance required* (or *risk accepted*). As we have seen, 'audit risk' (or 'ultimate risk') is the risk accepted by the auditor that an invalid conclusion will be drawn after completion of all audit procedures. The risk that the auditor may draw an invalid conclusion that no material errors exist when in fact they do, is composed of:

(i) the risk that material errors may occur ('inherent risk');

(ii) the risk that the internal controls may fail to prevent or correct such material errors ('control risk'); and

(iii) the risk that the auditor's substantive tests may fail to detect any remaining material errors ('detection risk').

Sampling risk, which is one component of audit risk, is the converse of assurance required by the auditor. Absolute assurance that the sample is representative of the population is never possible from a sampling procedure. The auditor therefore has to accept a risk ('sampling risk') that he may reach a different conclusion by sampling than he would if he examined the entire population. The degree of assurance the auditor plans to obtain from the results of the sample has a direct effect on the sample size. The greater the degree of assurance required the larger will be the required sample size.

(b) *Tolerable error/deviation* rate is the maximum error or deviation rate the auditor is prepared to accept in the population and still conclude that his audit objective has been achieved. Tolerable error is not the same as materiality relating to the financial statements: tolerable error is an audit planning measure and is used at the level of individual audit procedures whereas materiality relates to the financial statements and can only be finally determined when complete financial statements are available.

The larger the tolerable error or deviation rate, the smaller need be the sample size.

(c) *Expected error/deviation rate*. If the auditor expects errors or deviations to be present before performing tests, for example, because of the results of a previous year's tests or his evaluation of internal controls, he will need to take this into account in selecting an efficient sampling method and determining the sample size.

(d) *Stratification* is the process of dividing a population into sub-populations (or 'strata') so that items within each sub-population are expected to have similar characteristics in certain respects, such as monetary value. This reduces the degree of variation between items. By stratifying, the auditor can devote more of his attention to those items considered most vulnerable to material error.

Stage 2: Selecting the items to be tested

1.11 The purpose of audit sampling is to draw a conclusion about the entire population from which the sample was selected. Thus it is necessary that the sample items should be selected in such a way that they can be expected to be representative of the population as a whole. A sample cannot be relied on to be representative unless it is drawn from the whole of the population. The aim is to ensure that within each stratum all sampling units should have a quantifiable (often an equal) chance of being selected.

1.12 Representative selection methods commonly in use include random, value weighted, systematic or haphazard selection. Sampling one or a few blocks of items in sequence will not generally be representative.

Stage 3: Testing the items

1.13 Having selected the sample items the auditor should carry out the pre-determined audit tests for each item. If this is not possible for particular sample items, alternative procedures which provide equivalent evidence should be carried out on the same selected items. If it is not possible to carry out alternative procedures on those items the auditor should consider the effect on his conclusions of assuming the items to be in error. The auditor may eventually have to accept that the test was inconclusive if sufficient evidence cannot be found, in which case he will seek alternative audit evidence from other tests.

Stage 4: Evaluating the results of the tests

1.14 Having tested the items in the sample, the auditor should perform the following steps to evaluate the results of his tests.

(a) *Analysis of errors or deviations*. In assessing any errors or deviations discovered, the auditor may conclude that many have a common and potentially significant feature, in which case he may decide to identify all items in the population which possess that common feature, thereby producing a sub-population on which he may carry out further tests. He should then perform separate evaluations for each sub-population.

(b) *Projection of errors*. The auditor should estimate the expected error or deviation rate in the whole population by projecting the results of the sample to the population from which it was selected. This is undertaken to obtain a broad view of the scale of the possible error or deviation rate for comparison with tolerable error and is not meant to imply that the precise amount or rate of error in the whole population is known. Accordingly projected errors should be used with great caution.

(c) *Assessing the risk of an incorrect conclusion*. The auditor cannot in general expect the projected error or deviation rate to be a precise measure of the actual error or deviation rate present in the population. Actual error may be greater or smaller than projected error. The auditor must therefore consider, on the basis of his sample results and relevant evidence obtained from other audit procedures, the possible level(s) which the actual error or deviation rate might take and in particular the likelihood that the actual error or deviation rate may exceed tolerable error or deviation rate.

Summary of results

1.15 The auditor should consider, by reference to the amount which is ultimately considered to be material to the financial statements, the results from all audit procedures, both sampling and other, and the total estimated unadjusted error, to determine whether he has obtained sufficient appropriate audit evidence for each account balance or class of transactions. He should then aggregate these results to consider whether he has obtained sufficient evidence for the financial statements as a whole.

Statistical and non-statistical (judgemental) sampling

1.16 Both non-statistical and statistical sampling require the use of professional judgement in planning, testing and evaluating the sample. Statistical sampling, however, requires the use of random selection and uses probability theory to determine the sample size, evaluate quantitatively the sample results and measure the sampling risk. Non-statistical sampling may use non-random sample selection methods, does not rely on probability theory and requires more subjectivity in making sampling decisions. Statistical sampling provides a measure of sampling risk to assist the auditor in drawing his conclusion regarding the total population; the auditor using non-statistical sampling will also need to consider whether the sample provides a reasonable basis for making an inference about the total population.

1.17 The audit brief on audit sampling takes the discussion of certain topics further. The following points are made about statistical and non-statistical sampling.

1.18 Statistical sampling differs from non-statistical sampling, in that it uses probability theory to measure sampling risk and to evaluate the sample results. In making the choice between a statistical and a non-statistical sampling procedure, the auditor weighs up the benefits against the costs of the two methods for the particular circumstances.

1.19 The more obvious benefits of statistical sampling are as follows.

(a) It imposes on the auditor a more formal discipline as regards planning the audit of a population in that he cannot perform the mechanics of selecting a statistical sample until he has decided on the tolerable error in respect of the population and the amount of audit assurance that he wishes to obtain from the sample.

(b) The required sample size is determined objectively. Once the auditor has used his judgement to decide subjectively on the tolerable error and the level of assurance required, the statistical method determines the sample size required to satisfy his objectives.

(c) The evaluation of test results is made more precisely and the sampling risk is quantified.

1.20 The main types of statistical sampling approaches used in auditing can be categorised either as attribute sampling or as variables sampling and we will examine these two approaches in the next two sections.

When to sample (and when not)

1.21 Sampling is necessary in most audit environments, but there are situations where sampling is inappropriate. Moreover, for sampling to be useful and successful in auditing, certain conditions should prevail.

1.22 Sampling is *not* appropriate in the following situations and circumstances.

(a) Where populations are too small, statistical theory cannot be applied without creating unacceptable margins of error.

(b) Earlier tests or information might have put the auditor on enquiry.

(c) Populations might not be suitable either because:

(i) they are not kept in a suitable format for sampling in that the client has to rearrange the data for further processing; or

(ii) they are non-homogeneous which means that sorting is required before sampling can take place.

(d) Balances or transactions which are of great significance in terms of size, but few in number.

(e) Statutory disclosure items where a full check is required, for example directors' transactions.

1.23 The following conditions must prevail for audit sampling to be successful.

(a) Every item in the population must stand an equal chance of selection. All statistical sampling methods depend for their effectiveness on the randomness with which the sample is chosen. Random sampling involves the use of random or systematic selection procedures and the complete elimination of the auditor's own judgement in the selection process, otherwise *selection bias* undermines the validity of the sample.

(b) The population should cover the whole of the time period under review, not just say six months of a full year period.

(c) The population must be of a sufficient size to allow the statistical methods normally used to apply (see next two sections).

(d) The sample population chosen should relate directly to the objective and relevant direction (see below) of the audit test.

(e) The anticipated rate of error must be low. If many systems errors are expected compliance testing should be abandoned and the auditor should go straight to the substantive testing programme. Where a lot of errors are expected to be found by the substantive tests, then these may have to be carried out by detailed vouching, not by sampling.

(f) The population to be sampled should represent all the major types of transaction covered by the test objective if the auditor intends to use the sample to assess the value or error rate of the whole population.

(g) For a sample to be selected, each sampling unit in the population must be clearly identifiable. This identification can be achieved, for example, by every £1 in a population.

(h) As stated above, a reasonably homogeneous population should be tested in the type of balance and in origin. It may be in order to *stratify* the population into sub-populations which are more homogeneous.

Materiality in testing

1.24 **We have already looked at materiality in planning and in general terms. During testing, materiality must be considered not just in terms of size (in money), but also frequency of occurrence. The auditor will determine the materiality of substantive errors in terms of overall materiality as based on the draft financial statements. Errors or exceptions in compliance tests must be judged as 'material' or otherwise in the context of the frequency of exceptions, the importance of the control tested and whether there are any compensating (independent) controls.**

Exercise 1

You are required to present the arguments for and against the use of statistical sampling in auditing and reach a conclusion on the subject.

Solution

An inevitable characteristic of audit testing is that a sample only of transactions or items can be examined. The auditor examines a sample of items and thereby seeks to obtain assurance that the whole group is acceptable.

Provided that conditions are appropriate for its use, a statistical approach to sampling is likely to have many advantages over the alternative of judgement sampling.

Conditions favouring the use of statistical sampling are:

(a) existence of large and homogeneous groups of items;
(b) low expected error rate and clear definition of error;
(c) reasonable ease of identifying and obtaining access to items selected.

If these conditions are present, statistical sampling is likely to have the following advantages.

(a) At the conclusion of a test the auditor is able to state a definite level of confidence he may have that the whole population conforms to the sample result, within a stated precision limit.

(b) Sample size is objectively determined, having regard to the degree of risk the auditor is prepared to accept for each application.

(c) It may be possible to use smaller sample sizes, thus saving time and money.

(d) The process of fixing required precision and confidence levels compels the auditor to consider and clarify his audit objectives.

(e) The results of tests can be expressed in precise mathematical terms.

(f) Bias is eliminated.

Statistical sampling is not without disadvantages.

(a) The technique may be applied blindly without prior consideration of the suitability of the statistical sampling for the audit task to be performed. This disadvantage may be overcome by establishing soundly-based procedures for use in the firm, incorporating guidelines on sampling in the firm's audit manual, instituting training programmes for audit staff and proper supervision.

(b) Unsuspected patterns or bias in sample selection may invalidate the conclusions. The probability of these factors arising must be carefully judged by the auditor before he decides to adopt statistical sampling.

(c) It frequently needs back-up by further tests within the population reviewed: large items, non-routine items, sensitive items like directors' transactions.

(d) At the conclusion of a statistical sampling-based test the auditor may fail to appreciate the further action necessary based on the results obtained. This potential disadvantage may be overcome by adequate training and supervision, and by requiring careful evaluation of all statistical sampling tests.

(e) Statistical sampling may be applied carelessly, without due confirmation that the sample selected is acceptably random.

(f) The selection exercise can be time consuming.

(g) The degree of tolerance of acceptable error must be predetermined.

The disadvantages listed above can all be overcome if the technique is applied sensibly and competently.

Provided that the conditions favouring its use are present, statistical sampling is a useful technique for several auditing tasks.

(a) Compliance testing.
(b) Substantive testing.
(c) Debtor and creditor circularisation.
(d) Fraud investigation using discovery sampling.

Statistical techniques should be used when they are convenient and of positive use to the auditor in achieving a level of reliability in his results. If they are used selectively, in cases where their advantages are conspicuous and their disadvantages can be reduced to a minimum, they can make a significant contribution towards greater quality control on an audit. But it is hard to resist the argument that properly devised and controlled 'judgemental methods' can achieve the same high standards with fewer administrative or technical problems.

2 COMPLIANCE TESTS: ATTRIBUTE SAMPLING

2.1 *Attribute sampling* is concerned with sampling units which can only take one of two possible values (say 0 or 1) and is generally used to provide information about either the rate of occurrence of an event or of certain characteristics in a population. It can thus be used to measure what proportion of items in a population have a particular property and what proportion of items do not have that property. It deals only with rates of occurrence of events not monetary amounts and it is now primarily used in compliance testing. Each occurrence of, or deviation from, a prescribed control procedure is given equal weight in the evaluation of the results, regardless of the monetary amount of the transaction. However, one statistical sampling approach, *monetary unit sampling*, uses attribute sampling theory to express a conclusion in monetary amounts.

2.2 In attribute sampling the sample size is calculated as:

$$\text{Sample size} = \frac{\text{Reliability factor}}{\text{Precision}}$$

where the *reliability factor*, taken from tables, is associated with the level of assurance the auditor wants or needs to obtain from the test. Such a table is given below and it shows the relationship between risk levels, and the reliability factor.

Risk level	*Reliability factor*	
	No of errors	*One error*
1%	4.6	6.61
5%	3.0	4.75
10%	2.3	3.89
15%	1.9	3.38
20%	1.6	3.00
30%	1.2	2.44

2.3 The precision level is the number of errors the auditor is willing to accept in a population to be assured that the population is correct. For example, if the auditor decided that the population could be accepted as correct with no more than a 10% (say) risk that two or more out of every 100 items was incorrect, then the precision level would be 0.03 (in other words, less than three are incorrect).

Exercise 2

Calculate the sample sizes which should be used in compliance tests in the following circumstances.

(a) No errors anticipated in the sample; accept 5% risk that four or more items in 100 are incorrect in the population.

(b) One error anticipated in the sample; accept 1% risk that three or more items in 100 are incorrect in the population.

Solution

(a) Sample size = $\frac{3.0}{0.05}$ = 60 items

(b) Sample size = $\frac{6.61}{0.04}$ = 165 items

2.4 **It is frequently the case that auditing firms (particularly large firms) will standardise their approach to attribute sampling by giving set sample sizes for given planned levels of reliance. This standard approach is based on the assumption that the recommended sample sizes approximate to the sizes which would be obtained if the above reliability formula were applied.**

2.5 **Given below is a table which demonstrates this approach. The number of deviations allowed does not rise over two on the assumption that more than two deviations will automatically lead to the conclusion that compliance testing should not take place as the control(s) cannot be relied on.**

Planned reliance (degree)	*Deviations expected*	*Sample size*
Low	0	15
	1	25
	2	40
Moderate	0	30
	1	50
	2	75
High	0	45
	1	80
	2	110

2.6 **The test is then started. If it becomes apparent that the anticipated error rate of two or less has in fact been underestimated, the auditor may decide to abandon the half completed test and go straight away to substantive testing.**

2.7 **In order to interpret the results of the test and give an analysis of the degree of reliance warranted, a table such as the one shown below would be given.**

	Degree of reliance warranted for number of errors found in sample						
Sample size	*0*	*1*	*2*	*3*	*4-5*	*6-7*	*8+*
15	L	N	N	N	N	N	N
25	L	L	N	N	N	N	N
30	M	L	N	N	N	N	N
40	M	L	L	N	N	N	N
45/50	H	M	L	L	N	N	N
75/80	H	H	M	M	L	L	N
110	H	H	H	M	M	L	L

Key N = None M = Moderate
L = Low H = High

2.8 **Although the method of attribute sampling appears to be statistically acceptable, there is a perception problem which is at risk of being hidden by numbers. What does it really mean when an auditor states that he or she is 99% confident that a control will only fail once for every 100 times it is used?**

3 SUBSTANTIVE TESTS: VARIABLES SAMPLING

3.1 *Variables sampling* is concerned with sampling units which can take a value within a continuous range of possible values and is used to provide conclusions as to the monetary value of a population. The auditor can use it to estimate the value of a population by extrapolating statistically the value of a representative sample of items drawn from the population. He can also use it to determine the accuracy of a population that has already been ascribed a value (generally described as 'hypothesis testing'). Thus, he can use variables sampling both in an auditing context to test the amounts of populations such as debtors, payroll expense and fixed assets additions, and also in an accounting context to value populations such as stock by counting and pricing only a proportion of the items in the population.

3.2 The proper use of variables sampling involves the estimation of the number of units in a population *and* the calculation of the standard deviation of the population. This can be difficult and time consuming as test samples must be used to obtain the relevant information. To avoid these problems, a new testing technique was developed in the 1960s called *Monetary Unit Sampling (MUS)*.

Monetary unit sampling (MUS)

3.3 MUS has two main characteristics: items are selected for testing by weighting the items in proportion to their value and inferences are drawn based on 'attribute sampling' concepts.

3.4 MUS produces conclusions based on monetary amounts, *not* occurrence rates, by defining each £1 of a population as a separate sampling unit. Thus, a purchase ledger of £3.6m is described as a population of 3.6m sampling units of £1; an individual balance of £4,000 merely represents 4,000 £1 sampling units.

3.5 We saw in Section 2 above that the sample size under attribute sampling was calculated as:

$$\text{Sample size} = \frac{\text{Reliability factor}}{\text{Precision}}$$

3.6 This formula is restated in monetary terms for MUS.

$$\text{Precision (as above)} = \frac{\text{Tolerable error}}{\text{Population value}}$$

Thus:

$$\text{Sample size} = \frac{\text{Reliability factor} \times \text{Population value}}{\text{Tolerable error}}$$

3.7 Having calculated the sample size, the auditor can then select the sample items. Firstly, the sampling interval must be calculated using either:

$$\text{Sampling interval} = \frac{\text{Population value}}{\text{Sample size}}$$

or

$$\text{Sampling interval} = \frac{\text{Tolerable error}}{\text{Reliability factor}}$$

3.8 **Given a sample size of £X, the auditor will then select every X sampling unit in the population, starting from zero and added cumulatively (0, X, 2X etc), starting from a random point in the population.**

Exercise 3

Using the information in (a) in Exercise 2 in Section 2, show the selection of sample items, given that:

(a) tolerable error = £200,000;

(b) population value = £5m;

(c) random start at item 10,000;

(d) the first ten ledger balances on the ledger in question are: £25,000; £27,250; £75,100; £8,450; £9,900; £1,720; £98,210; £227,190; £3,590; £48,620.

Solution

$$\text{Sample size} = \frac{\text{Reliability factor} \times \text{population value}}{\text{Tolerable error}}$$

$$= \frac{3.0 \times 5{,}000{,}000}{200{,}000} = 75$$

$$\text{Sampling interval} = \frac{\text{Population value}}{\text{Sample size}}$$

$$= \frac{£5{,}000{,}000}{75} = £66{,}666$$

The sample will be selected as follows.

Ledger balance	*Value*	*Cumulative value*	*Select pound*
£	£	£	£
1	25,000	25,000	10,000
2	27,250	52,250	
3	75,100	127,350	76,666
4	8,450	135,800	
5	9,900	145,700	143,332
6	1,720	147,420	
7	98,210	245,630	209,998
8	227,190	472,820	276,664
			343,330
			409,996
9	3,590	476,410	
10	48,620	525,030	476,662
etc	etc	etc	etc

3.9 **The sample in the above exercise will not be as great as 75 because of item 8 on the ledger (and other balances of a similar value will have the same effect). This demonstrates one of the advantages of MUS in that all items larger than the sampling interval will be selected. This selection of larger items gives a weighting which makes the reduction in the sample size acceptable.**

Evaluation of MUS results

3.10 Where no errors are found in the sample, then the 'precision' achieved will be that predicted in terms of 'tolerable error' by the auditor before the test was carried out. The conclusion can then be drawn that the population from which the sample is drawn is not overstated by more than the monetary precision specified here (usually materiality).

3.11 This conclusion cannot be drawn when errors are found. It is then necessary to differentiate between two different types of error.

3.12 Where an error is in an item *larger* than the sampling interval, the auditor will be assured that the absolute amount of error in this top 'strata' of balances is known, because *all* such items have been examined in the test.

3.13 Where an error is found in an item which is *smaller* than the sampling interval, then it will be necessary to *project* the level of error on to the rest of the population. Using the information in Exercise 3 above, we will carry out an evaluation of 'results'.

Example: evaluating MUS

3.14 *Stage 1: Sort the errors*

The errors should be sorted into the two types mentioned above, into over- and under-statements and the errors in the smaller items should be 'grossed up'.

	Errors £	*Sampling interval* £	*Item value* £	*Expected value of error on sampling interval* £
Overstatements				
	1,300	66,666	75,400	1,300
	2,360	66,666	29,480	5,333 (8%)
	3,660			6,633
Understatements				
	400	66,666	82,500	400
	900	66,666	18,000	3,333 (4%)
	1,300			3,733

3.15 Where the error was found in an item lower than the sampling interval, then the interval is 'tainted' by the proportional error in the item applied to the interval value. Where the error is in a larger item, this is the exact amount of the error in the sample.

3.16 *Stage 2: Calculate the true reliability factor*

A true reliability factor can now be found and substituted for the assumed factor in the original calculation. The auditor can then examine the effect on the tolerable error rate. The APC audit brief calls this the 'precision gap widening factor'.

3.17 One approach is to rank the errors and multiply them by a 'precision adjustment factor'. This produces a new 'precision limit' (the old tolerable error adjusted for the errors found, which have themselves been adjusted by the precision adjustment factor).

3.18 If the revised monetary precision is greater than the tolerable error, the audit brief recommends the following actions.

(a) Ask the client to adjust for any specific errors identified.

(b) Reconsider such aspects of the process as risk levels, tolerable error and sample size. Great care should be taken before original audit judgements are revised.

(c) Consider the need for further adjustments of the account balances concerned, for example additional debt provision.

(d) Consider the eventual form of the audit report - is a qualification or a disclaimer required?

Monetary unit sampling vs variables sampling

3.19 *Advantages*

(a) MUS is generally easier to use than variables sampling. Because it is based on attribute sampling theory, the auditor can design and evaluate the sample manually with little difficulty. He can also select samples in a relatively straightforward way, either manually or by computer.

(b) MUS will stratify items by monetary value (so that the probability with which each item may be selected will be proportional to its monetary value). In addition, it will automatically stratify the population to ensure that the auditor selects all items over a certain size (the sampling interval), even though they do not form part of the sample but are separately evaluated.

(c) If the auditor expects to find few if any errors in his sample, he will generally obtain a lower sample size than he would if he used variables sampling.

Disadvantages

(a) MUS does not cope easily with errors of understatement or where there are negative-valued items in the population. Consequently, practical non mathematically based methods have been evolved.

(b) MUS sampling can be over-conservative in evaluating errors. This may cause the auditor to reject an acceptable population.

(c) Where the auditor cannot use computerised sample selection, adding cumulatively through the population (the most common means of sample selection for MUS) by hand can be time- consuming. This disadvantage will be offset where the auditor decides he wishes to check the addition of the population anyway.

(d) Where there are likely to be numerous errors, the sample size needed in order to obtain an acceptable result can become larger than the corresponding sample size using variables sampling.

(e) As sample selection is based on every nth £ in the population, the sample can only be extended by dividing the sampling interval by a whole number and using the same random start in order that the original sample items could all be selected again. This means the new sample will be at least twice the size of the original sample.

3.20 MUS will normally prove to be a useful procedure for the auditor where:

(a) he is primarily concerned with tests for overstatement and where significant understatements are not expected (debtors, fixed assets and some stock tests are common examples); and

(b) he will be able to select the sample relatively easily (where the records are held on computer or where there are relatively few items within the population).

3.21 *Variables sampling* has a number of advantages and disadvantages.

Advantages

(a) Variables sampling will generally be more efficient than MUS if there is likely to be a large number of differences between recorded value and audited value.

(b) The auditor can increase the sample size more easily if he uses variables sampling than if he uses MUS.

(c) He can more easily cope with zero and negative value items in the population when he uses variables sampling.

Disadvantages

(a) Variables sampling is far more complicated to use than MUS. The auditor generally needs to use a computer program to design an efficient application. He will also need to attain a reasonable level of mathematical sophistication to avoid potential misapplications.

(b) The size of the sample depends largely on the value of the standard deviation of the population. Because this value is unknown, the auditor can only estimate its value, at best. This makes it difficult for him to quantify in advance the sample size required and could lead either to an initial sample that is larger than is absolutely necessary or to a later requirement to increase the sample size further.

3.22 The auditor will generally use MUS only to test populations for overstatement. As with other sampling approaches, it is very difficult to use MUS to test populations directly for understatement. There are two reasons for this. Firstly, items that are omitted completely from the population will have no probability at all of being selected. Secondly, items whose monetary amount is understated will have too low a probability of being selected, so that the chances of selecting a £1,000 item recorded as £1 will be negligible.

3.23 There are also circumstances in which it is not practicable to use MUS because the population being audited does not contain monetary amounts. A common example is despatch notes. In this instance, the auditor may decide to take out a numerical statistical sample based on the number of items in the population. However, he can evaluate a numerical statistical sample only in terms of the rate of occurrence of errors, not in monetary terms. Therefore he may decide that a numerical statistical sample has few, if any, advantages over a non-statistical sample.

Chapter roundup

- There are four basic stages in audit sampling.
  - Planning the sample.
  - Selecting the items to be tested.
  - Testing the items.
  - Evaluating the results of the test.
- You should appreciate the effect risk analysis has on sampling, particularly from the material covered in Chapter 5.
- Sampling is not always possible or desirable and each set of circumstances must be judged for the appropriateness of testing procedures.
- Attribute sampling is suitable for compliance testing and it is based on calculation of a sample size in relation to a reliability factor and an acceptable precision level.
- Variables sampling is suitable for substantive testing but in its true form it is time consuming and difficult.
- Monetary unit sampling (MUS) makes it much easier to test populations substantively, by adopting many of the techniques in attribute sampling.

Test your knowledge

1 Define 'audit sampling'. (see para 1.3)

2 What factors will be taken into account when planning a sample? (1.7)

3 What is 'stratification'? (1.10(d))

4 What is the difference between statistical sampling and non-statistical sampling? (1.18)

5 When is sampling not appropriate? (1.22)

6 What conditions must exist if sampling is to be successful? (1.23)

7 Define the 'precision level'. (2.3)

Chapter 10

COMPLIANCE TESTING

This chapter covers the following topics.

Introduction

We have examined compliance testing in the last few chapters and considered its definition, methods of sample selection and evaluation. In this and the next chapter we will look at how compliance testing might be applied in practice. We will examine each major component of an average accounting system:

(a) sales;
(b) purchases;
(c) wages;
(d) cash;
(e) other systems: stock; fixed assets; investments; and management information and general controls.

You will recall from Chapter 5 that the auditor must ascertain the accounting system and the system of internal control. The auditor will then decide which controls, if any, he wishes to rely on and plan compliance tests to determine whether such reliance can be warranted. For each of the systems listed above we will look at the considerations the auditor will bear in mind while assessing the internal controls and then go on to look at a 'standard' compliance test programme.

The auditor will almost certainly use the ICEQ completed for each component part of the system to draw up the compliance controls to be tested and provide information as to their strength and importance. You should refer back to the ICEQ shown in Chapter 5.

1 THE SALES SYSTEM

1.1 The three separate elements into which accounting controls may be divided clearly appear in the consideration of sales procedures. They are selling (authorisation), goods outwards (custody) and accounting (recording).

Control considerations

1.2 *Selling*: considerations include the following.

(a) What arrangements are to be made to ensure that goods are sold at their correct price and to deal with and check exchanges, discounts and special reductions including those in connection with cash sales.

(b) Who is to be responsible for, and how control is to be maintained over, the granting of credit terms to customers.

(c) Who is to be responsible for accepting customer's orders and what procedure is to be adopted for issuing production orders and despatch notes.

(d) Who is to be responsible for the preparation of invoices and credit notes and what controls are to be instituted to prevent errors and irregularities (for instance, how selling prices are to be ascertained and authorised, how the issue of credit notes is to be controlled and checked, what checks there should be on prices, quantities, extensions and totals shown on invoices and credit notes, and how such documents in blank or completed form are to be protected against loss or misuse).

(e) What special controls are to be exercised over the despatch of goods free of charge or on special terms.

1.3 *Goods outwards*: factors to be considered include the following.

(a) Who may authorise the despatch of goods and how is such authority evidenced.

(b) What arrangements are to be made to examine and record goods outwards (preferably this should be done by a person who has no access to stocks and has no accounting or invoicing duties).

(c) The procedure to be instituted for agreeing goods outwards records with customers' orders, despatch notes and invoices.

1.4 *Accounting*: so far as possible sales ledger staff should have no access to cash, cash books or stocks, and should not be responsible for invoicing and other duties normally assigned to sales staff. The following are amongst matters which should be considered.

(a) The appointment of persons as far as possible separately responsible for:

(i) recording sales and sales returns;
(ii) maintaining customers' accounts;
(iii) preparing debtors' statements.

(b) The establishment of appropriate control procedures in connection with sales returns, price adjustments and similar matters.

(c) Arrangements to ensure that goods despatched but not invoiced (or vice versa) during an accounting period are properly dealt with in the accounts of the periods concerned (cut-off procedures).

(d) The establishment of arrangements to deal with sales to companies or branches forming part of the same group.

(e) What procedures are to be adopted for the preparation, checking and despatch of debtors' statements and for ensuring that they are not subject to interference before despatch.

(f) How discounts granted and special terms are to be authorised and evidenced.

(g) Who is to deal with customers' queries arising in connection with statements.

(h) What procedure is to be adopted for reviewing and following up overdue accounts.

(i) Who is to authorise the writing off of bad debts, and how such authority is to be evidenced.

(j) The institution of a sales control account and its regular checking preferably by an independent official against customers' balances on the sales ledger.

Compliance tests

1.5 The following compliance tests will often be relevant.

1 Select a sample of items from the goods despatched records and check as described below.

2 Non-routine sales (scrap, fixed assets etc);

(a) with appropriate supporting evidence;
(b) see approval by duly authorised officials;
(c) check entries in plant register etc.

3 Other sales:

(a) with customers' orders;

(b) with internal sales orders approved by duly authorised officials;

(c) with sales invoices:

(i) quantities;

(ii) prices charged with official price lists;

(iii) see that trade discounts have been properly dealt with;

(iv) check calculations and additions;

(v) check entries in sales day book and verify that they are correctly analysed. See that VAT, where chargeable, has been properly dealt with;

(vi) check postings to sales ledger. Generally scrutinise accounts arising in this text to see whether credit limits have been observed;

(d) check entries in stock records.

4 Select a sample of credit notes and check as follows:

(a) with correspondence or other supporting evidence;

(b) see approval by duly authorised officials;

(c) check entries in stock records;

(d) check entries in record of goods returned;

(e) check calculations and additions;

(f) check entries in day book and verify they are correctly analysed. See that VAT where chargeable, has been properly dealt with;

(g) check postings to sales ledger.

5 Test numerical sequence of despatch notes and enquire into missing numbers.

6 Test numerical sequence of invoices and credit notes, enquire into missing numbers and inspect copies of those cancelled.

Sales day book

7 (a) Test check entries with invoices and credit notes respectively.

(b) Test check additions and cross casts and test check postings to nominal ledger and control account.

(c) Test check postings to sales ledger.

Sales ledger

8 Select a sample of accounts and:

(a) test check entries back into books of prime entry;

(b) test check additions and balances carried down;

(c) note and enquire into contra entries.

9 See that control account balancing has been regularly carried on during the year.

Conclusions

10 Write conclusions covering any errors or weaknesses discovered during the above tests and noting any possible management letter points.

1.6 The following exercise should help you apply these 'standard' tests to a practical situation.

Exercise 1

Your firm has recently been appointed the auditor of Clifton Manufacturing plc, which sells all its products to other companies on credit. You have been asked to carry out the audit of the sales system, in order to assess its reliability, and its use as a basis for verification of the year end trade debtors.

Your initial investigations have revealed that the accounting system for sales is similar to those in other large companies, and generally there are sufficient staff for there to be a proper division of duties for internal control purposes. The company operates from a single site, and all goods are despatched from the same point in the factory. The company employs a credit controller who approves the creditworthiness of customers when the order is accepted, performs a further authorisation immediately before the goods are despatched and is responsible for collecting debts from customers. The selling price of the company's products are set by the sales director, and he authorises the list of these prices. The sales department uses this list to price customer orders.

The company has a computerised sales system in which details of the goods to be despatched are entered into the computer. The computer calculates the prices, using a standing data file of sales prices, and produces a sales invoice, which it posts to the sales ledger. Cash received is posted to the sales ledger by the accounts department. The chief accountant must authorise the addition of new customers to the sales ledger standing data file, and any adjustments to sales ledger balances.

Required

(a) List and briefly describe the principal aims in auditing the sales system (see note at the end of the question).

(b) In relation to the sales depth test:

(i) state the point in the system where you would select the items to check, and give reasons to justify your choice;

(ii) describe the basis you would use to select items to check, and describe the factors you would consider in determining the number of items to check.

(c) List and briefly describe the tests you would perform, excluding the sales depth test, in checking the reliability of the sales system of Clifton Manufacturing plc. You should describe the block tests you would perform, but you are not required to describe in detail how you would carry out a debtors' circularisation.

Solution

(a) The sales audit has two main purposes.

(i) The audit verifies that sales are being recorded correctly by the company, in that:

(1) sales are made to creditworthy customers;

(2) every despatch of goods results in a correctly priced sales invoice being raised;

(3) all sales invoices are posted to the sales ledger;

(4) the figure for sales in the accounts is supported by a series of legitimate transactions;

(ii) The audit also ensures that cash receipts are being correctly accounted for, in that:

(1) all sales result in cash being received;
(2) all cash received is properly safeguarded;
(3) all cash received results in the appropriate cashbook entries.

Internal control is important because it enables the auditor to place some degree of reliance upon the accounting system. Where internal control is good he may need to carry out fewer detailed tests in order to express an opinion on the accounts, with consequent cost savings for himself (and for the client).

(b) (i) *Understatement of sales*

Because all goods produced by Clifton Manufacturing plc should result in a sale, it would seem most appropriate either to select items for testing from the records of finished items entered into store (but this might only be feasible where there were identifiable serial numbers and we are not told what goods the company manufactures) or from goods despatched records. There would be serious disadvantages in selecting a sample from some other part of the system.

(1) A sample selected entirely from sales orders would not pick up those items where no order had been received.

(2) A sample selected from sales invoices would not identify those items where goods had been ordered and/or despatched but where no invoice had been

raised. Selecting a sample from cash received records would have similar disadvantages.

(ii) *Overstatement of sales*

Where directional testing is used, sales will be tested for overstatement in conjunction with testing assets and expenses for overstatement and liabilities for understatement. Where directional testing is not being used in any form, it may be necessary to select a sample from the sales balance recorded in the nominal ledger.

(iii) If the sample is selected from goods despatched notes, it will not be possible to give any weighting to the monetary amounts involved. However, the serial numbering of despatch records should allow the auditor to select a sample statistically, using random numbers or some similar means of generating an objective selection. The size of the selection will depend very much upon the adequacy of internal control, the maximum rate of error which the auditor would be prepared to accept and the confidence level required. Where a sample is being selected from the nominal ledger in order to test sales for overstatement, some form of monetary sampling could be used.

(c) A number of other tests would be appropriate, including the following.

(i) Block tests consist in checking one form of documentation against another or testing a single control via a particular transaction sequence. Preferably, they should be spread evenly through the accounting period. They are particularly useful where additional confidence is required and provide one way of testing any weaknesses which may have been highlighted either by the review of internal control or by the normal transactions audit. Block tests which could be applied in the case of Clifton Manufacturing include:

(1) checking goods despatched against stock records to ensure that all finished goods removed from store result in a despatch;

(2) checking despatch notes against sales invoices to ensure that all despatches are being invoiced;

(3) checking prices quoted on invoices against standing data to ensure that goods are being correctly priced;

(4) checking the posting of the sales ledger over a specified period by checking the opening balance against the previous period's total and checking all postings from the ledger back to the supporting documentation and from the supporting documentation into the ledger over the period;

(5) testing weak areas as identified by either the transactions audit or the review of internal control.

(ii) Sequence checks would include checking the sequence of numbered documents such as customer orders, despatch notes and sales invoices.

(iii) Credit control tests would include:

(1) reviewing the authorisation of new customers and the setting of credit limits for new and existing customers;

(2) checking the authorisation procedures prior to processing of customer orders and despatch of the goods;

(3) testing the procedures for collecting debts due from customers, including potential bad debts, plus the procedures for providing against or writing off bad debts incurred.

(iv) Checks on the computer system, which might involve using computer assisted audit techniques (CAATs), would include:

(1) checking the procedures for maintaining and updating standing data files, such as the customer file and the price file;

(2) inspecting error reports where these have been produced and reviewing in general the error and rejection procedures;

(3) checking the procedures for maintaining master files and back-up files.

In addition to the normal sales transactions tests, it will also be necessary to conduct detailed testing of credit notes issued where these are material. Credit notes which are not properly controlled could be used in the perpetration of a fraud by clearing a customer's account prior to the misappropriation of cash received. Where directional testing is used, the normal procedure would be to select a sample of credit notes issued from the sales ledger and trace these back to goods returned notes or other supporting documentation. Credit notes can be tested for understatement by taking a sample of goods returned notes or other documentation and checking whether credit notes have been raised and posted to the nominal ledger. All credit notes should be properly authorised and there should be good reasons for their issue.

2 THE PURCHASES SYSTEM

2.1 We will follow the same procedure for the purchases system.

Control considerations

2.2 The three separate elements into which accounting controls may be divided also clearly appear in the consideration of purchase procedures. They are buying (authorisation), receipt of goods (custody) and accounting (recording).

2.3 *Buying*: factors to be considered include the following.

(a) The procedure to be followed when issuing requisitions for additions to and replacement of stocks, and the persons to be responsible for such requisitions.

(b) The preparation and authorisation of purchase orders (including procedures for authorising acceptance where tenders have been submitted or prices quoted).

(c) The institution of checks for the safe-keeping of order forms and safeguarding their use.

(d) As regards capital items, any special arrangements as to authorisations required (for a fuller description of this aspect see the section dealing with fixed assets below).

2.4 *Goods inwards*: factors to be considered include the following.

(a) Arrangements for examining goods inwards as to quantity, quality and condition; and for evidencing such examination.

(b) The appointment of a person responsible for accepting goods, and the procedure for recording and evidencing their arrival and acceptance.

(c) The procedure to be instituted for checking goods inwards records against authorised purchase orders.

2.5 *Accounting*: factors to be considered include the following.

(a) The appointment of persons so far as possible separately responsible for:

(i) checking suppliers' invoices;
(ii) recording purchases and purchase returns;
(iii) maintaining suppliers' ledger accounts or similar records;
(iv) checking suppliers' statements;
(v) authorising payment.

(b) Arrangements to ensure that before accounts are paid:

(i) the goods concerned have been received, accord with the purchase order, are properly priced and correctly invoiced;

(ii) the expenditure has been properly allocated; and

(iii) payment has been duly authorised by the official responsible.

Compliance tests

2.6 The following compliance tests will usually be relevant.

1 Select a sample of invoices representative of all types of transactions and check as follows.

(a) Invoices for capital expenditure, services, office supplies, expenses:

(i) with appropriating supporting evidence;

(ii) see approval by duly authorised officials and verify that authority limits are being observed;

(iii) check entries in plant register etc.

(b) Invoices for goods, raw materials:

(i) with purchase requisitions and purchase orders signed by duly authorised officials;

(ii) with goods received notes and inspection notes;

(iii) check entries in stock records;

(iv) see that partial deliveries are properly accounted for to ensure there is no duplicate payment;

(v) with quotations, price lists to see the price is in order;

(vi) if an invoice has not been passed due to some defect in the goods, weight or price discrepancy, trace entry in record of goods returned etc and see credit note duly received from the supplier.

(c) Check calculations and additions.

(d) Check entries in purchase day book and verify that they are correctly analysed.

(e) Check posting to purchase ledger.

2 Select a sample of credit notes and verify the correctness of credit received with correspondence etc and:

(a) check entries in stock records;

(b) check entries in record of returns;

(c) check entries in purchase day book and verify that they are correctly analysed;

(d) check postings to purchase ledger.

3 Select a sample of items from record of returns and verify credit notes are duly received from the suppliers.

4 Test numerical sequence and enquire into missing numbers:

(a) purchase requisitions;
(b) purchase orders;
(c) goods received notes;
(d) return notes;
(e) suppliers' invoices.

5 Examine file of unmatched purchase requisitions, purchase orders, goods received notes (those for which invoices do not appear to have been received) and obtain satisfactory explanations for items outstanding for an unreasonable time.

6 Examine file of unprocessed invoices and obtain satisfactory explanations for items outstanding for an unreasonable time.

Purchase day book

7 (a) Select entries at random and examine invoices - verify that they are initialled for prices, calculations and extensions and cross-referenced to purchase orders, goods received notes etc. See that they have been duly authorised for payment.

(b) Make a similar test check of credit notes.

(c) Test check additions and cross-casts and check postings to nominal ledger accounts and control account.

(d) Test check postings of entries to purchase ledger.

Purchase ledger

8 (a) Select a sample of accounts and:

(i) test check entries back into books of prime entry;
(ii) test check additions and balances forward;
(iii) note and enquire into all contra entries.

(b) See that control account balancing has been regularly carried out during the year.

(c) Examine control account for unusual entries.

Conclusions

9 Write conclusions covering any errors or weaknesses discovered during the above tests and noting any possible management letter points.

2.7 Once again the following exercise should help you to apply these 'standard' tests to a question.

Exercise 2

You have recently been appointed auditor of Dryden Manufacturing Ltd and are commencing the audit of the purchases system for the year ended 31 December 19X6. The company has about 200 employees and generally has sufficient staff for there to be a proper division of duties for internal control purposes.

You are required, for the audit of the company's purchases system:

(a) to describe how you would evaluate the controls, and how your audit tests would be affected by the results of this evaluation;

(b) to list and describe the audit tests you would perform (your answer should include consideration of:

(i) the number of items you would select for testing;

(ii) the basis of selecting the items;

(iii) what action you would take if errors are found, and you should consider the effect of the size and frequency of errors);

(c) to describe the general form of your conclusions on the results of testing the purchase system and how these conclusions may influence your work at the final audit.

Solution

(a) Many large audit firms now use a standard method of internal control evaluation (ICE) based on the key control question. The characteristics of this system are usually as follows.

(i) It is concerned only with the primary or key controls.

(ii) The format of the questionnaires leads to a detailed assessment of each of the primary control areas.

(iii) The ICE schedules can normally be linked and cross-referenced to the flowcharts, ICQs or other systems records.

(iv) It encourages the audit staff to design their tests to suit the particular needs of each client's systems. In other words, it ensures that time is not wasted in performing 'standard' audit programme tests that are not relevant to the circumstances, and that there is a direct link between the evaluation of the system of internal control and the tests carried out.

One method of constructing an ICE could be by listing under each major control question the answers of the detailed questions relating to that control which appear in the ICQ and then answering the major question on the basis of the subsidiary questions.

It is also important that against each major control question in the ICE there should be space for the auditor to cross-reference his answer to the action he has taken (eg modifying the audit programme or advising the client of weaknesses). An ICE will be useless unless the appropriate action is taken as a result of the evaluation.

(b) The audit tests necessary in relation to the purchases system will depend very much upon the auditor's evaluation of the strengths of the system. Assuming there to be a sound system of internal control in operation, then it will be necessary to carry out a programme of both compliance and substantive tests and these will be spread over the interim and final audit visits. There are no prescribed rules as to the nature of the tests to be carried out nor of the sample sizes required. The auditor must exercise his professional judgement to determine what tests are required and the number of items which he will need to examine in order to provide a base from which he may form his audit opinion.

Typically the majority of compliance tests will be carried out on the occasion of the interim audit and should cover tests on the following.

(i) Sequence of purchase orders.

(ii) Approval of purchase orders.

(iii) Adherence to authority limits.

(iv) Sequence of goods received records.

(v) Sequence of goods returned records.

(vi) Authorisation of adjustments to purchase ledger balances.

(vii) Serial numbering of purchase orders.

(viii) Sequence of purchase invoices.

(ix) Correlation of purchase invoices with purchase orders and goods received records.

(x) Correlation of credit notes with goods returned records.

(xi) Checking of castings and extensions on purchase invoices.

(xii) Coding of purchase invoices for accounting classification purposes.

(xiii) Correct segregation of VAT.

(xiv) Initialling of purchase invoice 'grid' for work done.

(xv) Approval of purchase invoices for processing into accounting system.

Some substantive tests would also be carried out at interim audit in the area of purchases and creditors but these are not considered here.

Since the main aim of the testing at the interim stage is to ensure that the company's laid down procedures are being properly applied, it will be necessary to follow up an error on a transaction of £5 in the same way as an error in a transaction of £50,000. Where errors are found further testing will usually be necessary in the area of weakness. If the errors persist, then management should be informed of the facts and the matters should be noted in the interim comments letter sent by the auditor to the client.

(c) If the results of the auditor's tests on the purchases system are satisfactory he may conclude that it will produce reliable accounting records and this in turn will mean that he may keep substantive testing at the year end to a minimum. If, however, the compliance tests reveal weaknesses in the system then at the final audit, the auditor will have to carry out a more extensive programme of substantive tests.

3 THE WAGES SYSTEM

3.1 We will follow the same procedures as in Sections 1 and 2: control considerations, 'standard' compliance tests and then a practical exercise.

Control considerations

3.2 While in practice separate arrangements are generally made for dealing with wages and salaries, the considerations involved are broadly similar and for convenience the two aspects are here treated together.

3.3 *General arrangements*: responsibility for the preparation of pay sheets should be delegated to a suitable person, and adequate staff appointed to assist him. The extent to which the staff responsible for preparing wages and salaries may perform other duties should be clearly defined. In this connection full advantage should be taken where possible of the division of duties, and checks available where automatic wage-accounting systems are in use. *Inter alia* provision should be made as to:

(a) who may authorise the engagement and discharge of employees;

(b) who may authorise general and individual changes in rates of pay;

(c) how notification of changes in personnel and rates of pay are to be recorded and controlled to prevent irregularities and errors in the preparation and payment of wages and salaries;

(d) how deductions from employees' pay other than for income tax and national insurance are to be authorised;

(e) what arrangements are to be made for recording hours worked (in the case of hourly paid workers) or work done (in the case of piece workers) and for ensuring that the records are subject to scrutiny and approval by an appropriate official before being passed to the wages department; special supervision and control arrangements may be desirable where overtime working is material;

(f) whether advances of pay are to be permitted, if so, who may authorise them, what limitations are to be imposed, how they are to be notified to and dealt with by wages and salaries departments, and how they are to be recovered;

(g) how holiday pay is to be dealt with;

(h) who is to deal with pay queries.

3.4 *Preparation of payroll*: the procedure for preparing the payroll should be clearly established. Principal matters for consideration include the following.

(a) Matters such as: what records are to be used as bases for the compilation of the payroll and how they are to be authorised.

(b) Who is responsible:

  (i) for preparing pay sheets;

  (ii) for checking them; and

  (iii) for approving them (preferably separate persons) and by what means individual responsibility at each stage is to be indicated.

(c) What procedures are to be laid down for notifying and dealing with non-routine circumstances such as an employee's absence from work or employees leaving at short notice in the middle of a pay period.

3.5 *Payment of wages and salaries*: where employees are paid in cash the following matters are amongst those that require decisions.

(a) What arrangements are to be made to provide the requisite cash for paying out (for example by encashment of a cheque for the total amount of net wages) and what steps are to be taken to safeguard such monies during collection and transit and until distributed?

(b) What safeguards against irregularities are to be adopted (for example by arranging for pay packets to be filled by persons other than those responsible for preparing pay sheets, providing them with the exact amount of cash required and forbidding their access to other cash) and what particulars are to be given to payees?

(c) Who is to pay cash wages over to employees (preferably a person independent of those engaged in the preparation of pay sheets and pay packets), how payees' identities are to be verified; what officials are to be in attendance, and how distribution is to be recorded (for example by recipient's signature or by checking off names on the pay list)?

3.6 Where wages and salaries are paid by cheque or bank transfer the matters to be decided include:

(a) which persons are:

(i) to prepare; and

(ii) to sign cheques and bank transfer lists (preferably these persons should be independent of each other and of those responsible for preparing pay sheets);

(b) whether a separate wages and salaries bank account is to be maintained, what amounts are to be transferred to it from time to time (preferably on due dates the net amount required to meet pay cheques and transfers) and who is to be responsible for its regular reconciliation (preferably someone independent of those responsible for maintaining pay records).

3.7 *Deductions from pay*: appropriate arrangements should be made for dealing with statutory and other authorised deductions from pay, such as national insurance, PAYE, pension fund contributions, and savings held in trust. A primary consideration is the establishment of adequate controls over the records and authorising deductions.

3.8 Additional checks on pay arrangements: in addition to the routine arrangements and day-to-day checks referred to above, use may be made as judged desirable, of a number of independent overall checks on wages and salaries. Amongst those available may be listed the following.

(a) The maintenance, separate from wages and salaries departments, of employees' records, with which pay lists may be compared as necessary.

(b) The preparation of a reconciliation to explain changes in total pay and deductions between one pay day and the next.

(c) Surprise counts of cash (and any other valuables) held by wages and salaries departments.

(d) The comparison of actual pay totals with independently prepared figures such as budget estimates or standard costs and the investigation of variances.

(e) The agreement of gross earnings and total tax deducted for the year to 5 April with PAYE returns to the Inland Revenue.

Compliance tests

3.9 The following types of test would be applied.

Industrial wages and weekly salaries

1 Arrange to attend the pay-out of wages to confirm that the official procedures are being followed.

Industrial wages

2 In respect of a number of weeks select a sample of employees at random and check as follows.

(a) With personnel records; see that written authorities have been completed in respect of the engagement of new employees and discharges.

(b) Check calculation of gross pay with:

(i) authorised rates of pay;

(ii) production records. See that production bonuses have been authorised and properly calculated;

(iii) with clock cards, time sheets or other evidence of hours worked. Verify that overtime has been authorised.

(c) Examine receipts given by employees; trace unclaimed wages to unclaimed wages book.

(d) Trace gross wages earned to tax deduction cards and, where appropriate, to holiday pay records; check calculations of deductions for PAYE and national insurance.

(e) Check other deductions to appropriate records. In respect of voluntary deductions, see authority therefor completed by the employees concerned.

3 In respect of the weeks selected above:

(a) test check additions of payroll sheets;
(b) check totals of wages sheets selected in (a) to summary;
(c) check additions and cross-casts of summary;
(d) check postings of summary to nominal ledger (including control accounts);
(e) check total of net pay column to cash book;
(f) verify that the wages summary has been signed as approved for payment;
(g) verify that reconciliations have been made with:

(i) the previous week's payroll;
(ii) clock cards with time sheets/job cards (hours);
(iii) gross wages with costing analyses, production budgets;

Unclaimed wages

4 Test check entries in the unclaimed wages book with the entries on the wages sheets. Select any sample of entries in the unclaimed wages book and see that the payments have been authorised and receipts obtained from the employees.

5 See that unclaimed wages are banked regularly.

Holiday pay

6 Select a sample of payments in respect of holiday pay and verify with the underlying records and agreements the correctness of the amounts paid.

Salaries - weekly and monthly

7 In respect of a number of weeks/months select a sample of employees at random and check as follows.

(a) With personnel records. See that written authorities have been completed in respect of the engagement of new employees and discharges.

(b) Verify that gross salaries and bonuses are in accordance with personnel records, letters of engagement etc and that increases in pay have been properly authorised.

(c) Verify that overtime has been properly authorised.

(d) Trace gross salaries to tax deduction cards and check calculations of deductions for PAYE and national insurance.

(e) Verify that other deductions have been correctly made and accounted for.

(f) Check calculation of net pay.

(g) See receipts from employees paid in cash.

(h) Examine paid cheques or certified copy of bank list for employees paid by cheque or bank transfer.

8 In respect of a number of weeks/months:

(a) test check additions and cross-casts of payroll sheets;

(b) check totals of salaries sheets selected in (a) to summary;

(c) check additions and cross-casts of summary;

(d) check postings of summary to nominal ledger (including control accounts);

(e) check total of net pay column to cash book;

(f) verify that the summary has been signed as approved for payment;

(g) verify that the total salaries has been reconciled with the previous week/month or standard payroll.

Deductions

9 **Scrutinise the control accounts maintained for various deductions. Test check to see that the employer's contribution for national insurance has been correctly calculated. Test check to se that the payments to the Inland Revenue and other bodies are correct.**

Conclusions

10 **Write conclusions covering any errors or weaknesses discovered during the above tests and noting any possible management letter points.**

Exercise 3

You have been asked to carry out the audit of the wages system by the senior in charge of the audit of Bingham Manufacturing plc.

Most of the employees are paid their wages weekly in cash. However, directors, senior managers and some office staff have their salaries paid monthly by a direct payment into their bank account. Employees are paid a fixed rate per hour with supplements for overtime. The time employees work is recorded on clock cards, and overtime must be authorised by the works manager. Wage rates are authorised by the managing director, and the grade of an employee is decided by the works manager for all works employees, and the managing director for all other employees.

The personnel department keep a record of when employees start with the company and when they leave. The payroll is prepared by the wages department using a computer, which calculates the employee's gross pay from the hours worked (including overtime), determines the deductions for income tax, national insurance and other non-statutory deductions (pension contributions, savings, union deductions and so on), calculate the net pay and prints the payslip. The wage packets are prepared by the wages department. Employees sign for their pay when they receive their wage packet.

Required

(a) Briefly describe the principal aims in auditing a wages system.

(b) In relation to a starters and leavers test:

(i) briefly describe the purpose of this test;
(ii) describe how you would carry out the test.

(c) List and briefly describe:

(i) the principal audit objectives in carrying out a check of the pay-out of wages;
(ii) the checks you would perform in carrying out a wages pay-out test;
(iii) the tests you would perform in checking the unclaimed wages system.

Solution

(a) Audit of a wages system should seek to ensure that there is an effective system of internal control in operation in order to minimise the likelihood of error, fraud or other irregularity occurring. Division of duties should be present where practicable. One source of weakness in this case is the fact that staff in the wages department are responsible for both preparation of the wage packets and preparation of the payroll.

There are a number of other specific objectives in the audit of the wages system; these are to ensure that:

(i) no errors or irregularities have taken place which are material to the financial statements;

(ii) wages paid are at the authorised rates for the times actually worked;

(iii) wages payments are made only to valid employees;

(iv) deductions from employees' pay are calculated accurately and have been paid over to the appropriate third parties (for example the Inland Revenue, pension scheme or trade union) on time and in the correct amount;

(v) holiday pay is calculated correctly and paid in accordance with the terms and conditions of individuals' employment contracts.

(b) (i) The main purpose of a test of employees joining and leaving is to ensure that pay in respect of these employees does not extend to periods before they started employment (for joiners) or after they leave employment (for leavers).

(ii) Firstly, I would compile a list of starters and leavers between two dates (perhaps six months apart) from personnel records of staff starting and leaving dates, checking that these records have been authorised by a responsible official.

The payroll at each of these two dates can then be examined and it will be possible to check that for employees leaving between the two dates, there is no pay shown at the later date and that for employees joining there is no pay at the earlier date. If the examination of the payroll at the two dates revealed other apparent starters or leavers, these instances would be investigated.

The payroll would be scrutinised around the date of starting or leaving for a sample of starters and leavers in order to ensure that pay starts or ceases at the appropriate date. This test would need to take into account any special procedures which apply. For example, leavers may be paid final holiday pay early, on the date they cease work but prior to their date of officially ceasing employment. Similarly, special arrangements might apply to the pay of employees joining.

(c) (i) The principal objectives of the auditor in attending a wages payout are to ensure that:

(1) all wage packets are either collected by an apparently bona fide employee or are recorded as unclaimed wages;

(2) no person collects more than one wage packet;

(3) only wages claimed are signed for as collected;

(4) all unclaimed wages are accounted for by a responsible official;

(5) the wages payout is in general carried out in an orderly way.

(ii) Procedures to be carried out in performing a check on the wages payout include the following.

(1) Ensure that cash counted for wage packets is checked by a second employee and that the total cash is reconciled to the total net cash wages shown on the payroll.

(2) Ensure that names of employees are checked against the payroll before wage packages are removed from the wages department.

(3) Ensure that security measures are in evidence in taking wage packets to the location of the payout (at least two people should do this).

(4) Ensure that appropriate procedures take place when wages are handed out. One person should hand out the wage packets; another should obtain the employee's signature. Each employee should take only the packet bearing his or her name, and should sign as acknowledgement of receipt of the wages. A responsible official should be on hand to identify each employee receiving a wage packet.

(5) Ensure that unclaimed wages are returned to the wages department and that the names of the employees concerned are recorded in the unclaimed wages book. This procedure should be carried out by a responsible official other than the person who prepares the payroll or makes up the wage packets. Employees who are absent at the time of the wages payout should collect their wages from the wages department: other employees should not be permitted to claim the wages of missing employees on their behalf.

(6) Be put upon enquiry for any unusual or untoward occurrences or procedures.

(iii) The tests I would carry out on unclaimed wages would be as follows.

(1) Check that the unclaimed wages book has been regularly and properly written up.

(2) Check that signatures of employees claiming wages which were not collected at the payout are entered in the book.

(3) Test check a sample of employees' signatures to personnel files.

(4) Ensure that wages unclaimed for a certain period (say, two weeks) are banked. The cashier should sign and date the unclaimed wages book for each banking. Agree banking to cash book and general ledger account.

(5) Check that wage packets are present for all employees who have not claimed their wages as recorded in the unclaimed wages book. Consider test counting the contents of a sample of wage packets.

4 THE CASH SYSTEM

Control considerations

4.1 The following matters should be considered.

Cash at bank and in hand: receipts

4.2 *Receipts by post and cash sales*: considerations involved in dealing with cash and cheques received by post include the following.

(a) Institute safeguards to minimise the risk of interception of mail between its receipt and opening.

(b) Wherever possible, appoint a responsible person, independent of the cashier, to open, or supervise the opening of, mail.

(c) Ensure that cash and cheques received are:

(i) adequately protected (for instance, by the restrictive crossing of all cheques, money orders and the like on first handling); and

(ii) properly accounted for (for instance, by the preparation of post-lists of moneys received for independent comparison with subsequent records and book entries).

4.3 *Control over cash sales and collections*: it should be decided:

(a) who is to be authorised to receive cash and cash articles (whether such items are to be received only by cashiers or may be accepted by sales assistants, travellers, roundsmen, or others);

(b) how sales and the receipt of cash and cash articles are to be evidenced, and what checks may be usefully adopted as regards such transactions (for instance, by use of serially numbered receipt forms or counterfoils, or cash registers incorporating sealed till rolls).

4.4 Custody and control of money received: money received should be subject to adequate safeguards and controls at all stages up to lodgement in the bank. Amongst the matters which may require consideration are the following.

(a) The appointment of suitable persons to be responsible at different stages for the collection and handling of money received, with clearly defined responsibilities.

(b) How, by whom, and with what frequency cash offices and registers are to be cleared.

(c) What arrangements are to be made for agreeing cash collections with cash and sales records (preferably this should be carried out by a person independent of the receiving cashier or employee).

(d) According to the nature of the business, what arrangements are to be made for dealing with, recording and investigating any cash shortages or surpluses.

4.5 *Recording*: incoming cash and cheques should be recorded as soon as possible. Means of recording include, as appropriate, receipt forms and counterfoils, cash registers and post lists. Matters for consideration include the following.

(a) Who is to be responsible for maintaining records of money received?

(b) What practicable limitations may be put on the duties and responsibilities of the receiving cashier particularly as regards dealing with such matters as other books of account, other funds, securities and negotiable instruments, sales invoices, credit notes and cash payments?

(c) Who is to perform the receiving cashier's functions during his absence at lunch, on holiday, or through sickness?

(d) In what circumstances, if any, receipts are to be given, whether copies are to be retained; the serial numbering of receipt books and forms; how their issue and use are to be controlled; what arrangements are to be made, and who is to be responsible for checking receipt counterfoils against:

(i) cash records; and

(ii) bank paying-in slips and how alterations to receipts are to be authorised and evidenced?

4.6 *Paying into bank*: it is desirable that cash and cheques received should be lodged with the bank with the minimum of delay. Adequate control over bank lodgements will involve rules as to the following.

(a) How frequently payments are to be made into the bank (preferably daily).

(b) Who is to make up the bank paying-in slips (preferably this should be done by a person independent of the receiving and recording cashier) and whether there is to be any independent check of paying-in slips against post-lists, receipt counterfoils and cash book entries.

(c) Who is to make payments into the bank (preferably not the person responsible for preparing paying-in slips).

(d) Whether all receipts are to be banked intact; if not, how disbursements are to be controlled.

4.7 *Cash and bank balances*: questions to be decided in connection with the control of cash balances include the following.

(a) What amounts are to be retained as cash floats at cash desks and registers, whether payments out of cash received are to be permitted.

(b) What restrictions are to be imposed as to access to cash registers and offices.

(c) Rules regarding the size of cash floats to meet expenses, and their methods of reimbursement.

(d) The frequency with which cash floats are to be checked by independent officials.

(e) What arrangements are to be made for safeguarding cash left on the premises outside business hours.

(f) Whether any special insurance arrangements (such as fidelity guarantee and cash insurance) are judged desirable having regard to the nature of the business, the sums handled, and the length of time they are kept on the premises.

(g) What additional independent checks on cash may be usefully operated (for instance, by periodic surprise cash counts).

(h) What arrangements are to be made for the control of funds held in trust for employees, both those which are the legal responsibility of the company and, as necessary, those which are held by nominated employees independent of the company's authority (for instance, sick funds or holiday clubs).

4.8 Regular reconciliation of bank accounts by a responsible official is an essential element of control over bank balances. Considerations involve deciding to whom bank statements may be issued, how frequently reconciliations should be performed, by whom, and the detailed procedure to be followed. Special factors include the treatment of long-standing unpresented cheques, stop-payment notices, examination of the sequence of cheque numbers and comparison of cheque details with details recorded in the cash book. Where possible, the person responsible for carrying out the bank reconciliation should not be concerned with handling cash and cheques received or with arrangements for disbursements.

Cash at bank and in hand: payments

4.9 *Cheque and cash payments*: the arrangements for controlling payments will depend to a great extent on the nature of business transacted, the volume of payments involved and the size of the company.

4.10 *Cheque payments*: among the points to be decided in settling the system for payments by cheque are the following.

(a) What procedure is to be adopted for controlling the supply and issue of cheques for use, and who is to be responsible for their safe-keeping.

(b) Who is responsible for preparing cheques and traders' credit lists.

(c) What documents are to be used as authorisation for preparing cheques and traders' credit lists, rules as to their presentation to cheque signatories as evidence in support of payment, and the steps to be taken to ensure that payment cannot be made twice on the strength of the same document.

(d) The names, number and status of persons authorised to sign cheques, limitations as to their authority; the minimum number of signatories required for each cheque; if only one signatory is required, whether additional independent authorisation of payments is desirable; if more than one signatory is required, how it is to be ensured that those concerned will operate effective independent scrutiny (for instance, by prohibiting the signing by any signatory of blank cheques in advance); limitations, if any, as to the amount permissible to be drawn on one signature; whether cheques drawn in favour of persons signing are to be prohibited.

(e) Safeguards to be adopted if cheques are signed mechanically or carry printed signatures.

(f) The extent to which cheques issued should be restrictively crossed; and the circumstances, if any, in which blank or bearer cheques may be issued.

(g) Arrangements for the prompt despatch of signed cheques and precautions against interception.

(h) Arrangements for obtaining paid cheques; whether they are to be regarded as sufficient evidence of payment or whether receipts are to be required; and the procedure to be followed in dealing with paid cheques returned as regards examination and preservation.

(i) The arrangements to be made to ensure that payments are made within discount periods.

4.11 *Cash payments*: factors to be considered include the following.

(a) Nomination of a responsible person to authorise expenditure, the means of indicating such authorisation and the documentation to be presented and preserved as evidence.

(b) Arrangements to ensure that the vouchers supporting payments cannot be presented for payment twice.

(c) Whether any limit is to be imposed as regards amounts disbursed in respect of individual payments.

(d) Rules as to cash advances to employees and officials, IOUs and the cashing of cheques.

The 'imprest system' may be used whereby the expenditure incurred during the period of the imprest (ie fixed sum advance) is independently checked before refund of the amount expended.

4.12 *Cheque and cash payments generally*: arrangements should be such that so far as practicable the cashier is not concerned with keeping or writing-up books of account other than those recording disbursements nor should he have access to, or be responsible for the custody of, securities, title deeds or negotiable instruments belonging to the company.

Similarly, so far as possible the person responsible for preparing cheques or traders' credit lists should not himself be a cheque signatory, cheque signatories in turn should not be responsible for recording payments.

On the other hand, it must be recognised that in the circumstances of smaller companies, staff limitations often make it impossible to divide duties in this manner and in such cases considerable responsibility falls on the adequacy of managerial supervision.

Compliance tests

4.13 The following types of compliance test should be useful.

Cash receipts

1 *Remittances received by post*

(a) Confirm that the official procedures for opening the post are being followed.

(b) Confirm that cheques etc received by post are immediately crossed in favour of the company.

(c) Select items entered in the rough cash book (or other record of cash, cheques etc received by post), and trace entries to:

(i) cash book;
(ii) paying-in book;
(iii) counterfoil or carbon copy receipts;

verify amounts entered as received with remittance advices or other supporting evidence.

2 *Cash sales, branch takings*. Select a sample of cash sales summaries/branch from different locations and check as follows.

(a) With till rolls or copy cash sale notes.

(b) If branch takings are banked locally, check with paying-in slip date-stamped and initialled by the bank. Verify that takings are banked intact daily.

(c) If payments are made out of takings, vouch expenditure paid thereout.

3 *Collections* by travellers, salesmen etc. Select a sample of items from the original collection records and verify as follows.

(a) Trace amounts to cash book via collectors' cash sheets or other collection records.

(b) Check entries on cash sheets or collection records with collectors' receipt books.

(c) Verify that goods delivered to travellers/salesmen have been regularly reconciled with sales and stocks in hand.

4 *Receipts cash book*

(a) Select several days throughout the period and check in detail as follows.

(i) With entries in rough cash book, receipts, branch returns or other records.

(ii) Non-trade receipts with satisfactory documentary evidence.

(iii) With paying-in slips obtained direct from the bank, observing that there is no delay in banking monies received. Check additions of paying-in slips.

(iv) Check additions of cash book.

(v) Check postings to the sales ledger.

(vi) Check postings to the purchase ledger.

(vii) Check postings to the nominal ledger, including control accounts.

(b) Scrutinise periods not covered by the foregoing audit tests and examine items of a special or unusual nature.

Cash payments

5 Select a sample of payments and check in detail as follows.

(a) With paid cheques, noting that cheques are signed by the persons authorised to do so within their authority limits.

(b) If payments are effected by means of traders' credits, trace the selected items to the detailed lists of suppliers to be credited, duly stamped by the bank. Agree totals with paid cheques drawn in favour of the banks concerned.

(c) With suppliers' invoices for goods and services. Verify that supporting documents are signed as having been checked and passed for payment and have been stamped 'paid'.

(d) With suppliers' statements.

(e) With other documentary evidence, as appropriate - agreements, authorised expense vouchers, wages/salaries records, petty cash books etc.

6 *Payments cash book*

(a) Select a sample of weeks and check as follows.

(i) With paid cheques, noting that the cheques are signed only by duly authorised persons within their authority limits.

(ii) Check the sequence of the cheque numbers and enquire into missing numbers.

(iii) Trace transfers to other bank accounts, petty cash books or other records, as appropriate.

(iv) Check additions, including extensions, and balances forward at the beginning and end of the months covering the periods chosen.

(v) Check postings to the sales ledger.

(vi) Check postings to the purchase ledger.

(vii) Check postings to the nominal ledger, including the control accounts.

(b) Where practicable, scrutinise periods not covered by the preceding tests and examine items which appear to be of a special or unusual nature.

Bank reconciliations

7 Select a period which includes a reconciliation date and check as follows.

(a) Compare cash book(s) and bank statements in detail, clearing both records for the period chosen. Simultaneously check items outstanding at the reconciliation date to bank reconciliations concerned.

(b) Verify contra items appearing in the cash books or bank statements.

(c) Note and obtain satisfactory explanations for all items in the cash book for which there are no corresponding entries in the bank statement and vice versa.

(d) Examine all lodgements in respect of which payment has been refused by the bank and ensure that they are cleared on representation or that other appropriate steps have been taken to effect recovery of the amount due.

8 Verify that reconciliations have been prepared at regular intervals throughout the year.

Petty cash

9 Select a sample of payments, and check with supporting vouchers, noting that they are properly approved. See that vouchers and other supporting documents have been marked and initialled by the cashier to prevent their re-use.

10 Select a sample of week and check as follows.

(a) Trace amounts received to cash books.

(b) Additions and balances carried forward.

(c) Postings to the nominal ledger.

Conclusions

11 Write conclusions covering any errors or weaknesses discovered during the above tests and noting any possible management letter points.

5 OTHER IMPORTANT SYSTEMS

5.1 The systems we will look at here are:

(a) the stock system;
(b) the fixed asset system; and
(c) investments.

The stock system

Control considerations

5.2 Stocks may be as susceptible to irregularities as cash and, indeed, in some circumstances the risks of loss may be materially higher. Arrangements for the control of stocks should be framed with this in mind.

5.3 The stock control procedures should ensure that stocks held are adequately protected against loss or misuse, are properly applied in the operations of the business, and are duly accounted for. According to the nature of the business separate arrangements may be necessary for different categories of stocks, such as raw materials, components, work in progress, finished goods and consumable stores.

5.4 Amongst the main considerations may be listed the following.

(a) What arrangements are to be made for receiving, checking and recording goods inwards (see also purchases and trade creditors in Section 2 above).

(b) Who is to be responsible for the safeguarding of stocks and what precautions are to be taken against theft, misuse and deterioration.

(c) What arrangements are to be made for controlling (through maximum and minimum stock limits) and recording stocks (for example by stock ledgers, independent control accounts and continuous stock records such as bin cards), who is to be responsible for keeping stock records (preferably persons who have no access to stocks and are not responsible for sales and purchase records). and what procedure is to be followed as to the periodic reconciliation of stock records with the financial accounts.

(d) How movements of stock out of store (or from one process or department to another) are to be authorised, evidenced and recorded, and what steps are to be taken to guard against irregularities.

(e) What arrangements are to be made for dealing with and accounting for returnable containers (both suppliers' and own).

(f) What arrangements are to be made for dealing with and maintaining accounting control over company stocks held by others (for instance goods in warehouse, on consignment or in course of processing) and goods belonging to others held by the company (for example how withdrawals are to be authorised and evidenced, and how goods belonging to others are to be distinguished from own goods).

(g) What persons are to be responsible for physically checking stocks, at what intervals such checks are to be carried out, and what procedures are to be followed (for instance, if continuous stocktaking procedures are in use, arrangements should ensure that all categories of stock are counted at appropriate intervals, normally at least once a year. counts should preferably be conducted by persons independent of storekeepers. how stock counts are to be recorded and evidenced, and what cut-off procedures are to be operated to ensure that stocks are adjusted to take proper account of year-end sales and purchases invoiced).

(h) What bases are to be adopted for computing the amount at which stocks are to be stated in the accounts (these should be in accordance with SSAP 9 and should be applied consistently from year to year), and which persons are to perform and check the calculations.

(i) What arrangements are to be made for the periodic review of the condition of stocks, how damaged, slow-moving and obsolete stocks are to be dealt with and how write-offs are to be authorised.

(j) What steps are to be taken to control and account for scrap and waste, and receipts from the disposal of such items.

Compliance tests

5.5 Most of the testing relating to stock has been covered in the purchase and sales testing outlined in Sections 1 and 2 above. Other compliance tests which might be carried out in certain circumstances include the following.

1 Test check stock counts carried out from time to time (eg monthly) during the period and carry out these checks.

   (a) All discrepancies between book and actual figures have been fully investigated.

   (b) Check that all such discrepancies have been signed off by a senior manager.

   (c) Check that obsolete, damaged or slow-moving goods have been marked accordingly and written down to NRV.

2 Select a sample of goods movements on stock records and agree to goods received and goods despatched notes.

3 Select a sample of goods received and goods despatched notes and agree to stock records.

The fixed asset system

Control considerations

5.6 Some of the principal matters to be decided in connection with controls relating to fixed assets are as follows.

(a) Who is to authorise capital expenditure and how such authorisation is to be evidenced.

(b) Who is to authorise the sale, scrapping or transfer of fixed assets, how such authorisation is to be evidenced, and what arrangements are to be made for controlling and dealing with receipts and disposals.

(c) Who is to maintain accounting records in respect of fixed assets and how it is to be ensured that the proper accounting distinction is observed between capital and revenue expenditure.

(d) What arrangements are to be made for keeping plant and property registers and how frequently they are to be agreed with the relevant accounts and physically verified.

(e) What arrangements are to be made to ensure that fixed assets are properly maintained and applied in the service of the company (for example by periodic physical checks as to their location, operation and condition).

(f) Where fixed assets are transferred between branches or members of the same group, what arrangements in respect of pricing, depreciation and accounting are to be made.

(g) How depreciation rates are to be authorised and evidenced, and which persons are to be responsible for carrying out and checking the necessary calculations.

Compliance tests

5.7 The following tests should be carried out.

1 Select a sample of fixed asset purchases during the year.

(a) Check authorisation (and board approval if necessary).

(b) Vouch purchase price to invoice and recorded price in fixed asset register and nominal ledger.

(c) check correct depreciation rates applied.

2 Select a sample of fixed asset disposals from during the year.

(a) Check disposal authorised by senior official.
(b) Check proceeds to cash book.
(c) Check invoice issued for any proceeds.
(d) Agree recording of proceeds in the nominal ledger.
(e) Check calculations of profit or loss on disposal.

3 Select a sample of fixed assets from the monthly fixed asset registers.

(a) Check physical existence of asset.
(b) Ensure asset in good condition.
(c) Consider whether asset value should be written down.

4 Select a sample of actual fixed assets of all varieties:

(a) Agree existence to fixed asset register.
(b) Consider whether asset worth depreciated amount or if write down required.

The investments system

Control considerations

5.8 Arrangements for dealing with investments will involve, *inter alia*, determining the following.

(a) Who is to be responsible for authorising purchases and sales of investments, and how such authorisations are to be evidenced (those responsible should preferably have no concern with cash or the custody of documents of title).

(b) What arrangements should be made for maintaining a detailed investment register, and who should be responsible for agreeing it periodically with the investment control account and physically verifying the documents of title.

(c) What arrangements are to be made for checking contract notes against authorised purchase or sale instructions and for ensuring that charges are correctly calculated: for dealing with share transfers, and for ensuring that share certificates are duly received or delivered and that bonuses, rights, capital repayments and dividends or interest are received and properly accounted for.

Documents of title: adequate arrangements should be made for the scheduling and safe custody of property deeds, share certificates and other documents of title, with the object of protecting them against loss and irregularities. Preferably they should be deposited in a secure place under the authority and control of at least two responsible persons, and access to or withdrawal of such documents should be permissible only on the authority of such persons acting jointly.

Compliance tests

5.9 The following compliance test will be relevant.

1 Select a sample of purchases and sales of investments from during the period.

(a) Check that the transaction is authorised.

(b) Agree sales proceeds/purchase price to contract notes and cash book.

(c) For listed investments, check published share price, which should be close to the deal price.

(d) Check movements properly entered in investment register.

General procedures

5.10 As well as testing based on individual components of the accounting system, the auditor will also perform some general tests, including the following.

1 Test postings from books of prime entry to the nominal ledger.
2 Check that the nominal ledger is regularly balanced.
3 Test vouch a sample of journal entries to original documentation.

Chapter roundup

- The sales and purchases systems will be the most important components of most company accounting systems. The testing of these systems is therefore crucial.
- The compliance testing of the sales system will be centred round selling (authorisation), goods outwards (custody) and accounting (recording).
- Similarly, the purchases systems compliance tests will be based around buying (authorisation), goods inwards (custody) and accounting (recording).
- Note that all weaknesses discovered in these tests will be included in an *interim management letter* as a report to the management. Management letters were discussed in Chapter 7.
- The rest of these systems may or may not be of great importance within a company's accounting system; it will depend on the company's business and scale of operations. Obviously, most manufacturing companies will have a large payroll *and* fixed asset register.
- Wages and salaries are usually dealt with in very different ways, but they are often grouped together for audit testing purposes.
- The controls over cash receipts and payments are important as a prevention of fraud or pilfering. You may be asked to devise audit test for the particular purpose of testing security.
- Stock testing will usually be incorporated into the sales and purchases systems testing, but some separate tests may be instituted, in particular to test controls over regular stocktaking.
- Fixed asset testing will usually revolve around authorisation, existence and condition.

Test your knowledge

1 What factors should the auditor consider when looking at controls over selling? (see para 1.2)

2 How are 'goods outward' controlled? (1.3)

3 What are the main control considerations over accounting for sales? (1.4)

4 What are the control procedures over the buying element of purchasing which the auditor should consider? (2.3)

5 What procedures should be in place to control 'goods inwards'? (2.4)

6 Explain the control procedures over recording purchases. (2.5)

7 What factors should the auditor take into account when testing the preparation of payroll? (3.4)

8 What control procedures should be considered in relation to the payment of wages and salaries? (3.5, 3.6)

9 What procedures should be in place over custody and control over money received? (4.4) and cash payments? (4.11, 4.12)

10 List the principal matters to be considered in connection with controls over fixed assets. (5.6)

Chapter 11

THE BALANCE SHEET AUDIT

This chapter covers the following topics.

1 Financial review procedures

2 The financial statements

3 Accounting estimates

Introduction

This chapter serves as an introduction to the chapters on substantive testing which follow (Chapters 12 to 14). It is important to recognise the aims of the 'final' or substantive audit.

Remember that the level of substantive testing required will depend on the results of the previous compliance testing in each area and consequently the perceived level of risk attached to each balance.

The substantive areas of the audit will also require a significant amount of financial accounting knowledge, particularly of SSAPs and FRSs. It is suggested that you refer to your financial accounting study material (probably from Paper 1) where necessary as you read through this and the next three chapters.

1 FINANCIAL REVIEW PROCEDURES

1.1 The interim audit will have established whether the accounting and internal control systems provide reasonable assurance that the accounting records form a reliable base for the preparation of the financial statements for the period under review. Attention now turns to the financial statements themselves. From a company's viewpoint, relatively soon after the year end they will extract a trial balance from the accounting records and prepare the first draft of the accounts. For this draft to be meaningful it is of course important that the accounting records are substantially complete. Hence the debtors and creditors ledgers will have been closed off and generally all routine transactions will have been posted. Certain post-trial balance adjustments will normally be necessary to ensure completeness of the assets and liabilities. Typically, these will include adjustments to purchases and sales to ensure proper cut-off, provision for sundry accruals and prepayments and the incorporation of the closing stock figure.

1.2 The balance sheet audit work is motivated by the requirement of the operational standard for the auditor to 'obtain relevant and reliable evidence sufficient to enable him to draw reasonable conclusions therefrom'. More detailed objectives have already been highlighted, but they merit repeating here.

(a) Have all of the assets and liabilities been recorded?

(b) Do the recorded assets and liabilities exist?

(c) Are the assets owned by the enterprise and are the liabilities properly those of the enterprise?

(d) Have the amounts attributed to the assets and liabilities been arrived at in accordance with the stated accounting policies, on an acceptable and consistent basis?

(e) Have the assets, liabilities and capital and reserves been properly disclosed?

(f) Have the income and expenses been measured in accordance with the stated accounting policies, on an acceptable and consistent basis?

(g) Have income and expenses been properly disclosed where appropriate?

1.3 Much balance sheet audit work is expended in relation to objectives (a) to (d) above, or, to use our previously established shorthand, the completeness, existence, ownership and valuation of the assets and liabilities. Objectives (e) to (g) are principally concerned with disclosure and will be considered by the auditor as part of his review of the financial statements. The approach of this chapter and the next three is therefore to establish for each major balance sheet category how the auditor might obtain audit evidence to confirm its completeness, existence, ownership and valuation. Any special accounting or disclosure problems are also highlighted. It should be recalled, however, that as regards 'completeness', the auditor is heavily reliant on the effectiveness of the internal control system in ensuring that all data is satisfactorily captured in the accounting records. If internal control is very weak the auditor may not be able to obtain sufficient evidence as regards completeness, and hence may have to qualify his audit report.

Timing of balance sheet audit work

1.4 The work discussed in this chapter will commence at or very soon after the year-end of the client. Judicious planning will have determined in advance the precise timetable that the client is adopting for the preparation of the accounts and hence when the individual elements of accounting information will be available to the auditor. The auditor will also be concerned with the timing of any physical stocktaking and whether it will take place on the last day of the financial year.

1.5 The assets and liabilities verification work will proceed well into the 'post balance sheet period'. The auditor will take advantage of the fact that he has access to information arising subsequent to the year end when forming his opinion in respect of the assets and liabilities at the balance sheet date. This is an important accounting as well as auditing principle embraced by SSAPs 17 and 18. The accounting and auditing implications in general of the post balance sheet period are considered further later and, as we shall see, certain procedures are performed right up to the date of signing the audit report. Clearly, as the post balance sheet period progresses, the auditor will devote more time to his detailed review of the financial statements.

1.6 Nevertheless, it is the verification work that requires the major time and manpower resources in the post balance sheet period. Finally, it must be recalled that the auditor may also need to perform certain work outstanding from the interim audit. This is likely to include further compliance testing in respect of the period of the financial year not covered by his earlier transactions audit work.

2 THE FINANCIAL STATEMENTS

2.1 The content of the financial statements should be familiar to you now. They will consist of:

(a) the *primary statements:*

(i) balance sheet;
(ii) profit and loss account;
(iii) statement of total recognised gains and losses;
(iv) cash flow statement;

(b) the *notes to the accounts*, including the note of historical cost profits and losses and the notes to the cash flow statement (required by FRS 1 *Cash flow statements*);

(c) the *directors' report*, the contents of which are governed by statute to a certain extent;

(d) the *chairman's report*, which is a 'blurb' for the company about its performance and future intentions;

(e) the *auditor's report* on the financial statements, giving an opinion as to their truth and fairness.

Exercise

Obtain a copy of a set of recent financial statements.

Required

Examine the financial statements and list out the account balances you feel would be of primary importance in the audit of that company or group.

2.2 No matter how sophisticated a set of financial statements appear to be, it is worth remembering that *all* financial statements make the same basic assertions, the most important of which are based on the fundamental accounting concepts in SSAP 2.

Matching concept

2.3 There is a basic assumption that all costs have been matched to the revenues they helped to produce. From a balance sheet point of view this means that accruals an prepayments will be necessary to ensure that costs and revenues are matched correctly.

Going concern

2.4 The financial statements of the business should have been prepared on a going concern basis. This primarily affects the value of assets in the balance sheet. A valuation on a break up basis, where assets were sold individually for a quick return, would be much lower than their going concern valuation.

Prudence

2.5 The financial statements should have been prepared on a prudent basis, with all anticipated losses provided for but no profits anticipated. Where the prudence and matching concepts come into conflict then the prudence concept should prevail.

Consistency

2.6 Accounting policies and practices should be applied consistently from year to year and in relation to similar items within the financial statements. This means that it is expected that, say two similar fixed assets are accounted for in the same way in the financial statements.

True and fair

2.7 Another assertion, not included in SSAP 2, is the 'true and fair assertion'. The 'true and fair' assertion is clearly shown in the audit report. The issue of 'truth and fairness' has troubled auditors ever since the phrase was brought into common use. Legal opinion indicates that it is not capable of precise and enduring legal definition as an abstract concept. What constitutes 'truth and fairness' may change over time, particularly as corporate disclosure requirements expand and change.

Fundamental balance sheet assertions

2.8 Underlying all the concepts discussed above are some assertions about the balance sheet which are much more fundamental. You will recognise them, although you may not have thought of them in this context before.

Cost

2.9 Accounts are prepared under the historic cost convention. Assets, liabilities, expenses and revenues are usually shown in the accounts at actual or original cost and the law sometimes actually requires disclosure of cost. Cost is easy for the auditor to check.

Authority

2.10 This means authority to acquire assets, pay creditors, dispose of assets and so on. It is a common aspect of all control systems to ensure that *all* authorised and *only* authorised transactions are processed and the user of the accounts will surely assume that they represent only authorised transactions.

Value

2.11 Financial statements are primarily prepared under the historical cost convention, but still they contain an assortment of values with items stated at original purchase cost (raw materials, creditors), revalued amount (land and buildings), at net realisable value (trade debtors less the provision for bad and doubtful debts), at 'fair value' (usually replacement cost) (asset acquired by takeover) and market value (net realisable value) is occasionally stated along with the historical cost (quoted investments).

Ignoring the debate about value, the auditor should simply aim to apply the valuation rules of the Companies Act 1985 or SSAPs, or otherwise go by industry best practice and the prudence concept.

Existence

2.12 The underlying asset behind 'cost' or 'valuation' must exist, otherwise it has been misappropriated or lost or it has been badly maintained and is thus worthless.

Beneficial ownership

2.13 Legal ownership of assets and legal obligations to creditors can become very complex in some group accounting situations and auditors must take great care to ensure that beneficial ownership or the responsibility for debts is correctly attributed in a group accounting context.

Presentation

2.14 Presentation is generally specified in advance by the Companies Act 1985 and relevant SSAPs and FRSs, but it is still the auditor's duty to review the proposed disclosures and the form of their presentation in the light of what, in the circumstances, he or she considers to be a true and fair view.

2.15 You must bear all these assertions in mind during the balance sheet audit which is covered in the next four chapters.

3 ACCOUNTING ESTIMATES

3.1 'Accounting estimate' means an approximation of the amount of an item in the absence of a precise means of measurement. Examples are:

(a) allowances to reduce inventory and accounts receivable to their estimated realisable value;

(b) depreciation provision;

(c) provision for deferred taxation;

(d) provision for a loss from a lawsuit;

(e) profits or losses on construction contracts in progress; and

(f) provision to meet warranty claims.

3.2 Management is responsible for making accounting estimates included in the financial statements. These estimates are often made in conditions of uncertainty regarding the outcome of events and involve the use of judgement. As a result, the risk of a material misstatement generally increases when accounting estimates are involved.

3.3 In seeking sufficient appropriate audit evidence on which to base the audit opinion evidence supporting accounting estimates is generally more persuasive than conclusive. Consequently, in their consideration of accounting estimates auditors are more likely to need to exercise judgement than in other areas of an audit.

3.4 The following points are relevant.

(a) The auditor should obtain sufficient appropriate audit evidence regarding the accounting estimates material to the financial statements.

(b) The auditor should obtain sufficient appropriate audit evidence as to whether an accounting estimate is *reasonable* in the circumstances and, when required, is appropriately disclosed.

(c) The auditor should adopt one or a combination of the following approaches in the audit of an accounting estimate:

(i) review and test the process used by management to develop the estimate;

(ii) use an independent estimate for comparison with that prepared by management; or

(iii) review subsequent events which confirm the estimate made.

(d) The auditor should make a final assessment of the reasonableness of the accounting estimate based on the auditor's knowledge of the entity and its industry and whether it is consistent with other evidence obtained during the audit.

Chapter roundup

- The balance sheet audit work is concerned with the recording, existence, ownership, disclosure and treatment of assets and liabilities.
- The timing of balance sheet work is important because of the requirements of SSAPs 17 and 18 in the post balance sheet period.
- The fundamental accounting concepts and the true and fair view are underpinned by the balance sheet assertions relating to:

  Cost
  Authority
  Value
  Existence
  Beneficial **O**wnership
  Presentation

  Note the mnemonic: CAVEBOP.
- The audit of accounting estimates will usually be based around balance sheet work.

Test your knowledge

1 What are the objectives of the balance sheet (and final) audit work? (see para 1.2)

2 What do the financial statements consist of? (2.1)

3 List and describe the four fundamental accounting concepts in SSAP 2. (2.2 - 2.6)

4 Is there a precise, legal definition of 'truth and fairness'? (2.7)

5 List the fundamental balance sheet assertions. (2.9 - 2.14)

6 What should the auditor do about so many different values in the balance sheet? (2.11)

7 Give some examples of accounting estimates. (3.1)

Chapter 12

STOCKS AND WORK IN PROGRESS

This chapter covers the following topics.

Introduction

No balance sheet audit area creates more potential problems for the auditor than that of stocks. Stock is often a material figure in the context of the profit and loss account *and* the balance sheet and as regards bases of valuation it is one of the more subjective areas. Closing stock does not normally form an integrated part of the double entry bookkeeping system and hence a misstatement (under or overstatement) may not be detected from tests in other audit areas.

This is a summary of why stocks and work in progress is often the most difficult and time consuming part of the audit.

(a) Stock and work in progress often represent a significant asset on the balance sheet.

(b) The value of closing stock and work in progress has a direct impact on profit.

(c) Stock is often made up of a large number of diverse items with different unit values.

(d) The valuation of work in progress is often a subjective process as the decision as to the stage which work in progress has reached and the costs to be included is often subjective. This also applies to the allocation of overheads to stock.

(e) Verification of the existence of stock and work in progress involves attendance at the stock-take and extensive follow-up procedures.

(f) The provision for slow-moving and obsolete stock is another subjective area.

(g) The physical control of stock is often difficult because of multiple locations, stock held by third parties and so on.

(h) Different valuation methods are allowed under SSAP 9, although they must be applied consistently.

The four main elements of the audit of stocks (completeness, existence, ownership and valuation) require careful consideration. Typically, the auditor will adopt the following broad approach to the audit of the four elements.

(a) Existence and apparent ownership will be verified by observing the stocktake (whether year-end or continuous).

(b) Raw material costs and further comfort on ownership will be verified by checking invoice prices (cost ascertainment may require evaluation of a standard costing system). Cost in the case of work in progress and finished goods will involve consideration of overhead absorption bases.

(c) Completeness is checked by observing the stocktake, checking that stocktaking records are correctly processed, applying analytical review procedures and occasionally relying on stock records where internal control has been evaluated and tested as strong.

(d) Valuation is checked by comparing cost with net realisable value. A working knowledge of SSAP 9 *Stocks and long-term contracts* is necessary here.

1 REGULATORY ASPECTS OF STOCK

1.1 The rules surrounding the audit of stocks and the related reporting requirements come from three sources:

(a) CA 1985 (disclosure, basis of valuation);

(b) SSAP 9 *Stocks and long-term contracts* (departure, disclosure and valuation); and

(c) the auditing standards and guidelines relating to the audit of stock (audit approach, valuation).

Companies Act 1985

1.2 CA 1985 lays out the format of the balance sheet and under stock in current assets the following headings must be used.

1 Raw materials and consumables
2 Work in progress
3 Finished goods and goods for resale
4 Payments on account

1.3 In terms of valuation, CA 1985 states that all current assets should be stated at the lower of their purchase price and their net realisable value. 'Purchase price' can be interpreted as 'fair value'. 'Production cost' is determined according to the provision of SSAP 9.

1.4 CA 1985 allows certain methods of identifying cost, because it recognises that it is impossible to identify cost for each item individually. The methods allowed are:

(a) first in first out (FIFO)
(b) last in last out (LILO)
(c) weighted average cost;
(d) other similar methods, such as standard cost.

SSAP 9 does *not* allow LIFO as a method of valuation.

SSAP 9 Stocks and long-term contracts

1.5 SSAP 9 defines *net realisable value* as the estimated or actual selling price, net of trade discounts but before settlement discounts, less all further costs to completion and all cost to be incurred in marketing, selling and distributing the good or service.

1.6 *Cost* is defined by SSAP 9 as that expenditure which has been incurred in the normal course of business in bringing the product or service to its present location and condition. This includes the purchase price plus costs of conversion (production) appropriate to the location and condition of the stock.

1.7 Cost of conversion include:

(a) costs specifically attributable to units of production;

(b) production overheads; and

(c) other overheads attribute to bringing the product or service to its present location and condition.

Exercise 1

Give two main reasons why stock and work in progress is one of the most difficult areas of the audit.

Solution

The audit of stocks and work-in-progress is often the most difficult and time consuming part of the audit for the following reasons.

(a) Stock and work in progress often represent a significant asset on the balance sheet.

(b) The value of closing stock and work in progress has a direct impact on profit.

(c) Stock is often made up of a large number of diverse items with different unit values.

(d) The valuation of work in progress is often a subjective process as the decision as to the stage which work in progress has reached and the costs to be included is often subjective. This also applies to the allocation of overheads to stock.

(e) Verification of the existence of stock and work in progress involves attendance at the stock-take and extensive follow-up procedures.

(f) The provision for slow-moving and obsolete stock is another subjective area.

(g) The physical control of stock is often difficult because of multiple locations, stock held by third parties and so on.

(h) Different valuation methods are allowed under SSAP 9, although they must be applied consistently.

2 THE STOCKTAKE

2.1 The detailed operational guideline *Attendance at stocktaking* is primarily concerned with aspects of the verification of 'existence'. The following comments are derived from the guideline.

2.2 It is the responsibility of the management of an enterprise to ensure that the amount at which stocks are shown in the financial statements represents stocks physically in existence and includes all stocks owned by the enterprise. Management satisfies this responsibility by carrying out appropriate procedures which will normally involve ensuring that all stocks are subject to a count at least once in every financial year. Further, where the auditor attends any physical count of stocks in order to obtain audit evidence, this responsibility will not be reduced.

2.3 In the case of a company, management has responsibilities to maintain proper accounting records and to include all statements of stocktakings in those records.

2.4 It is the responsibility of the auditor to obtain audit evidence in order to enable him to draw conclusions about the validity of the quantities upon which are based the amount of stocks shown in the financial statements. The principal sources of this evidence are stock records, stock control systems, the results of any stocktaking and test-counts made by the auditor himself. By reviewing the enterprise's stock records and stock control systems, the auditor can decide to what extent he needs to rely upon attendance at stocktaking to obtain the necessary audit evidence.

2.5 Where stocks are material in the enterprise's financial statements, and the auditor is placing reliance upon management's stocktake in order to provide evidence of existence, then the auditor should attend the stocktaking. This is because attendance at stocktaking is normally the best way of providing evidence of the proper functioning of management's stocktaking procedures, and hence of the existence of stocks and their condition.

2.6 Evidence of the existence of work in progress will frequently be obtained by a stocktake. However, the nature of the work in progress may be such that it is impracticable to determine its existence by a count. Management may place substantial reliance on internal controls designed to ensure the completeness and accuracy of records of work in progress. In such circumstances there may not be a stocktake which could be attended by the auditor. Nevertheless, inspection of the work in progress will assist the auditor to plan his audit procedures, and it may also help on such matters as the determination of the stage of completion of construction or engineering work in progress.

2.7 Physical verification of stocks may be by means of a full count (or measurement in the case of bulk stocks) of all the stocks at the year end or at a selected date before or shortly after the year end, or by means of a count of part of the stocks in which case it may be possible to extrapolate the total statistically. Alternatively, verification may be by means of the counting or measurement of stocks during the course of the year using continuous stock-checking methods. Some business enterprises use continuous stock-checking methods for certain stocks and carry out a full count of other stocks at a selected date.

2.8 The evidence of the existence of stocks provided by the stocktake results is most effective when the stocktaking is carried out at the end of the financial year. Stocktaking carried out before or after the year end may also be acceptable for audit purposes provided records of stock movements in the intervening period are such that the movements can be examined and substantiated. The auditor should bear in mind that the greater the interval between the stocktaking and the year end the greater will be his difficulties in substantiating the amount of stocks at the balance sheet date. Such difficulties will, however, be lessened by the existence of a well developed system of internal control and satisfactory stock records.

2.9 Where continuous stock-checking methods are being used, the auditor should perform tests designed to confirm that management:

(a) maintains adequate stock records that are kept up-to-date;

(b) has satisfactory procedures for stocktaking and test-counting, so that in normal circumstances, the programme of counts will cover all stocks at least once during the year; and

(c) investigates and corrects all material differences between the book stock records and the physical counts.

2.10 The auditor needs to do this to gain assurance that the stock-checking system as a whole is effective in maintaining accurate stock records from which the amount of stocks in the financial statements can be derived. It is unlikely that he will be able to obtain such assurance if the three matters above are not confirmed satisfactorily, in which circumstances a full count at the year end may be necessary.

2.11 The following paragraphs set out the principal procedures which may be carried out by an auditor when attending a stocktake, but are not intended to provide a comprehensive list of the audit procedures which the auditor may find it necessary to perform during his attendance.

Before the stocktaking: planning

2.12 The auditor should plan his audit coverage of a stocktake by carrying out the following.

(a) Review the working papers for the previous year, where applicable, and discuss with management any significant changes in stocks over the year.

(b) Discuss stocktaking arrangements and instructions with management.

(c) Familiarise himself with the nature and volume of the stocks, the identification of high value items and the method of accounting for stocks.

(d) Consider the location of the stock and assessing the implications of this for stock control and recording.

(e) Review the systems of internal control and accounting relating to stocks, so as to identify potential areas of difficulty (for example cut-off).

(f) Consider any internal audit involvement, with a view to deciding the reliance which can be placed on it.

(g) Ensure that a representative selection of locations, stocks and procedures are covered, and particular attention is given to high value items where these form a significant proportion of the total stock value.

(h) Arrange to obtain from third parties confirmation of stocks held by them, but if the auditor considers that such stocks are a material part of the enterprise's total stock, or the third party is not considered to be independent or reliable, then the auditor should arrange either for him or for the third party's auditor to attend a stocktake at the third party's premises.

(i) Establish whether expert help needs to be obtained to substantiate quantities or to identify the nature and condition of the stocks, where they are very specialised.

2.13 The auditor should examine the way the stocktaking is organised and should evaluate the adequacy of the client's stocktaking instructions. Such instructions should preferably be in writing, cover all phases of the stocktaking procedures, be issued in good time and be discussed with those responsible for carrying out the stocktaking to ensure that procedures are understood and that potential difficulties are anticipated. If the instructions are found to be inadequate, the auditor should seek improvements to them.

2.14 The draft version of the guideline *Attendance at stocktaking* contained, as an appendix, a listing of matters that the auditor should have regard to when reviewing a client's stocktaking instructions. Although this appendix did not find its way into the authorised version of the guideline that we are reviewing, its contents are useful to the auditor in the light of his responsibilities in Paragraph 2.13, and are hence reproduced here in full.

(a) Supervision of the planning and execution of the stocktake by sufficient senior and qualified personnel drawn from various departments: at least some of the officials should not normally be involved with the custody of stocks.

(b) Tidying and marking stock to facilitate counting of items of stock. The whole of the stock-taking area should be divided into sections for control purposes.

(c) The serial numbering and control of the issue and return of all the rough count records, and their retention as required by the Companies Act.

(d) Systematic carrying out of counts to ensure coverage of the whole stock.

(e) Arrangements for the count to be conducted by at least two people, with one counting and the other primarily to check the count, or alternatively for two independent counts to be carried out; and for any differences arising to be investigated and resolved.

(f) Stock sheets being completed in ink and being signed by those who carried out and checked the count.

(g) Information to be recorded on the count records. (Normally this will include the location and identity of the stock items, the unit of count, the quantity counted, the condition of the items and the stage reached in the production process.)

(h) Restriction and control of the production process and stock movements during the count.

(i) Identification and segregation of damaged, obsolete, slow moving, third parties' stocks and returnable stocks, so that these can be properly accounted for and recorded.

(j) Recording the quantity, condition and stage of production of all the work in progress for subsequent checking with the costing and stock records.

(k) Co-ordination of the count with cut off procedures so that documentation concerned with the flow of goods can be reconciled with the financial records. For this purpose, last numbers of goods inwards and outward records and of internal transfer records should be noted.

(l) Reconciliation with the stock records, if any, and identification and correction of differences.

During the stocktaking

2.15 During the stocktaking, the auditor should ascertain whether the client's staff are carrying out their instructions properly so as to provide reasonable assurance that the stocktaking will be accurate. He should make test counts to satisfy himself that procedures and internal controls relating to the stocktaking are working properly. If the manner of carrying out the stocktaking or the results of the test-counts are not satisfactory, the auditor should immediately draw the matter to the attention of the management supervising the stocktaking and he may have to request a recount of part or all of the stocks.

2.16 When carrying out test-counts, the auditor should select items both from count records and from the physical stocks and check one to the other to gain assurance as to the completeness and accuracy of the count records. In this context, he should give particular consideration to those stocks which he believes, for example from the stock records or from his prior year working papers, to have a high value either individually or as a category of stock. The auditor should include in his working papers items for subsequent testing, such as photocopies of (or extracts from) rough stocksheets and details of the sequence of stocksheets.

2.17 The auditor should ensure that the procedures for identifying damaged, obsolete and slow moving stock operate properly. He should obtain (from his observations and by discussion with storekeepers or other staff) information about the stocks' condition, age, usage and in the case of work in progress, its stage of completion. Further, he should ascertain that stock held on behalf of third parties is separately identified and accounted for.

2.18 In addition, the auditor should:

(a) conclude whether the stocktaking has been properly carried out and is sufficiently reliable as a basis for determining the existence of stocks;

(b) consider where any amendment is necessary to his subsequent audit procedures; and

(c) try to gain from his observations an overall impression of the levels and values of stocks held so that he may, in due course, judge whether the figure for stocks appearing in the financial statements is reasonable.

2.19 The auditor's working papers should include details of his observations and tests, the manner in which points that are relevant and material to the stocks being counted or measured have been dealt with by the client, instances where the client's procedures have not been satisfactorily carried out and the auditor's conclusions.

After the stocktaking

2.20 After the stocktaking, the matters recorded in the auditor's working papers at the time of the count or measurement should be followed up. For example, details of the last serial numbers of goods inwards and outwards notes and of movements during the stocktaking should be used in order to check cut-off. Further, photocopies of (or extracts from) rough stocksheets and details of test-counts, and of the sequence of rough stocksheets, may be used to check that the final stocksheets are accurate and complete.

2.21 The auditor should ensure that continuous stock records have been adjusted to the amounts physically counted or measured and that differences have been investigated. Where appropriate, he should ensure also that management has instituted proper procedures to deal with transactions between stocktaking and the year end, and also test those procedures. In addition, he should check replies from third parties about stocks held by or for them, follow up all queries and notify senior management of serious problems encountered during the stocktaking.

2.22 After the three audit phases of the stocktake have been completed the auditor should have gained sufficient assurance regarding existence and some assurance as regards completeness and ownership. The auditor will now concern himself with valuation verification, which may also provide him with some further assurance in respect of completeness and ownership.

Exercise 2

In connection with your examination of the financial statements of Camry Products Ltd for the year ended 31 March 19X9, you are reviewing the plans for a physical stock count at the company's warehouse on 31 March 19X9. The company assembles domestic appliances, and stocks of finished appliances, unassembled parts and sundry stocks are stored in the warehouse which is adjacent to the company's assembly plant. The plant will continue to produce goods during the stock count until 5pm on 31 March 19X9. On 30 March 19X9, the warehouse staff will deliver the estimated quantities of unassembled parts and sundry stocks which will be required for production for 31 March 19X9; however, emergency requisitions by the factory will be filled on 31 March. During the stock count, the warehouse staff will continue to receive parts and sundry stocks, and to despatch finished appliances. Appliances which are completed on 31 March 19X9 will remain in the assembly plant until after the physical stock count has been completed.

Required

(a) List the principal procedures which the auditor should carry out when planning attendance at a company's stocktake.

(b) Describe the procedures which Camry Products Ltd should establish in order to ensure that all stock items are counted and that no item of stock is counted twice.

Solution

(a) In planning attendance at a stocktake the auditor should:

(i) review previous year's audit working papers and discuss any developments in the year with management;

(ii) obtain and review a copy of the company's stocktaking instructions;

(iii) arrange attendance at stockcount planning meetings, with the consent of management;

(iv) gain an understanding of the nature of the stock and of any special stocktaking problems this is likely to present, for example liquid in tanks, scrap in piles;

(v) consider whether specialist involvement is likely to be required as a result of any circumstances noted in (iv) above;

(vi) obtain a full list of all locations at which stock is held, including an estimate of the amount and value of stock held at different locations;

(vii) using the results of the above steps, plan for audit attendance by appropriately experienced audit staff at all locations where material stocks are held, subject to other factors (for example rotational auditing, reliance on internal controls);

(viii) consider the impact of internal controls upon the nature and timing of the stocktaking attendance;

(ix) ascertain whether stocks are held by third parties and if so make arrangements to obtain written confirmation of them or, if necessary, to attend the stocktake of them.

(b) Procedures to ensure a complete count and to prevent double-counting are particularly important in this case because stock movements will continue throughout the stocktake.

(i) Clear instructions should be given as to stocktaking procedures, and an official, preferably not someone normally responsible for stock, should be given responsibility for organising the count and dealing with queries.

(ii) Before the count, all locations should be tidied and stock should be laid out in an orderly manner.

(iii) All stock should be clearly identified and should be marked after being counted by a tag or indelible mark, so that it is evident that it has been counted.

(iv) Prenumbered stock sheets should be issued to counters and should be accounted for at the end of the stocktake.

(v) Counters should be given responsibility for specific areas of the warehouse. Each area should be subject to a recount.

(vi) A separate record should be kept of all goods received or issued during the day (for example by noting the GRN or despatch note numbers involved).

(vii) Goods received on the day should be physically segregated until the count has been completed.

(viii) Similarly, goods due to be despatched on the day should be identified in advance and moved to a special area or clearly marked so that they are not inadvertently counted in stock as well as being included in sales.

3 CUT-OFF

3.1 The auditor should consider whether management has instituted adequate cut-off procedures: procedures intended to ensure that movements into, within and out of stocks are properly identified and reflected in the accounting records. The auditor's procedures during the stocktaking will depend on the manner in which the year end stock value is to be determined. For example, where stocks are determined by a full count and evaluation at the year end, the auditor should test the arrangements made to segregate stocks owned by third parties and he should identify goods movement documents for reconciliation with financial records of purchases and sales. Alternatively, where the full count and evaluation is at an interim date and the year end stocks are determined by updating such valuation by the cost of purchases and sales, the auditor should perform those procedures during his attendance at the stocktaking and in addition should test the financial cut-off (involving the matching of costs with revenues) at the year end.

3.2 Cut-off is most critical to the accurate recording of transactions in a manufacturing enterprise at particular point in the accounting cycle as follows:

(a) the point of purchase and receipt of goods and service;
(b) the requisitioning of raw materials for production;
(c) the transfer of completed work-in-progress to finished goods stocks; and
(d) the sale and despatch of finished goods.

These points should be identified by management, and appropriate procedures instituted at the period end in order to ensure accurate cut-off. In the case of many businesses, a full stock count will be carried out at the period end.

3.3 There should ideally be no movement of stocks during the stock count. If movements are necessary, they should be carefully controlled. Preferably, receipts and despatches should be suspended for the full period of the count. It may not be practicable to suspend all deliveries, in which case any deliveries which are received during the count should be segregated from other stocks and carefully documented to ensure that they are accounted for accurately.

3.4 Appropriate systems of recording of receipts and despatches of goods should be in place, and also a system for documenting materials requisition. Goods received notes (GRNs) and goods despatched notes (GDNs) should be sequentially pre-numbered. Management should make note of the final GRN and GDN and materials requisition numbers before the commencement of the stock count. These numbers can then be used to check subsequently that purchases and sales have been recorded in the current period.

3.5 Purchase invoices should be recorded as liabilities only if the goods were received prior to the stock count. A schedule of 'goods received not invoiced' should be prepared, and items on the list should be accrued for in the accounts.

3.6 Sales cut-off is generally more straightforward to achieve correctly than purchases cut-off. Invoices for goods despatched after the stock count should not appear in the profit and loss accounts for the period.

3.7 Arrangements should be made to ensure that the cut-off arrangement for stock held by third parties are satisfactory.

3.8 At the stocktake, therefore, the auditor should carry out the following procedures.

(a) Make a record during the stocktaking attendance of all movement notes relating to the period, including:
   (i) all interdepartmental requisition numbers;
   (ii) the last goods received notes(s) and despatch note(s) prior to the count;
   (iii) the first goods received notes(s) and despatch note(s) after the count.

(b) Observe whether correct cut-off procedures are being followed in the despatch and receiving areas. Discuss procedures with company staff performing the count to ensure they are understood.

(c) Ensure that no goods finished on the day of the count are transferred to the warehouse.

3.9 During the final audit, the auditor will use the cut-off information from the stocktake to perform the following tests.

(a) Match up the goods received notes with purchase invoices (or stock accounts where goods had not been invoiced at the year end) and ensure the liability has been recorded in the correct period. Only goods received before the year end should be recorded as purchases.

(b) Match up the goods despatched note to sales invoices and ensure the income has been recorded in the correct period. Only stocks despatched before the year end should be recorded as sales.

(c) Match up the requisition notes to the work in progress figures for the receiving department to ensure correctly recorded.

Exercise 3

Using the information in Exercise 2 above, describe the audit procedures you would carry out at the time of the stocktake in order to ensure that cut-off is correct.

Solution

In order to ensure that cut-off stock is correct, the following procedures should be carried out.

(a) Make a record during the stocktaking attendance of all movement notes relating to the period, including:
   (i) all interdepartmental requisition numbers;
   (ii) the last goods received note and despatch note prior to the count;
   (iii) the first goods received note and despatch note after the count. This information can be used for subsequent cut-off tests.

(b) Observe whether correct cut-off procedures are being followed in the despatch and receiving areas. Discuss procedures with company staff performing the count to ensure they are understood.

(c) Ensure that no goods finished on the day of the count are transferred to the warehouse.

---

4 STOCK VALUATION PROCEDURES

Assessment of cost and net realisable value

4.1 The audit objective will be to determine that stocks have been properly and consistently valued at cost, or where stocks are excess, slow-moving, obsolete or defective, reduced to net realisable value. Different considerations will apply to raw materials and components, work in progress and finished goods.

4.2 It is important that the auditor understands how the company determines the cost of an item for stock valuation purposes. Cost, for this purpose, should include an appropriate proportion of overheads, in accordance with SSAP 9. There are several ways of determining cost (FIFO, actual invoice price, latest invoice price, average cost, selling price less the gross profit percentage). He must ensure that the company is applying the method consistently and that each year the method used gives a fair approximation to cost. He may need to support this by procedures such as reviewing price changes near the year end, ageing the stock held, and checking gross profit margins to reliable management accounts.

4.3 In the case of raw materials and bought in components, where valuation is derived from actual cost, the auditor should check that the correct prices have been used to value items by referring to suppliers' invoices. If any stock was purchased at varying prices he should ensure that the stock valuation reflects this fact. The stock valuation may include unrealised profit if stock is valued at the latest invoice price. Reference to suppliers' invoice will also provide the auditor with assurance as regards ownership.

Valuation of work in progress and finished goods (other than long-term contract work in progress)

4.4 As we saw in Paragraph 1.10, SSAP 9 defines 'cost' as comprising the cost of purchase plus the cost of conversion. The cost of conversion comprises:

(a) costs specifically attributable to units of production;

(b) production overheads; and

(c) other overheads attributable to bringing the product or service to its present location and condition.

4.5 The auditor should ensure that the client includes a proportion of overheads appropriate to bringing the stock to its present location and condition. The basis of overhead allocation should be consistent with prior years and should be calculated on the normal level of production activity. Thus, overheads arising from reduced levels of activity, idle time or inefficient production should be written off.

4.6 There are many methods of allocating overheads and consequently different audit approaches to reviewing the proportion of overheads added to cost. It is not practicable to discuss these in detail in this text. The auditor should ascertain the particular method used by the client and ensure that the overhead element included in stocks is reasonable and consistent.

4.7 Difficulty may be experienced if the client operates a system of total overhead absorption. It will be necessary for those overheads that are of a general, non productive nature to be identified and excluded from the stock valuation.

4.8 The value of work in progress comprises the value of the materials, expenses, direct labour and overheads that have brought the item to its present condition and location.

4.9 The audit procedures will depend on the methods used by the client to value work in progress and finished goods, and on the adequacy of the system of internal control.

4.10 With a valuation derived from actual costs, the auditor should ensure that the unit costs are properly prepared by checking to supporting documentation such as suppliers' invoices, payroll summaries (to ascertain direct labour rates), production reports and time summaries (to ascertain actual hours worked on specific projects). He can either test the system generally in this way, and then test the valuation of specific items by referring to cost records, or he can select individual items of work in progress and examine the documentation supporting their actual costs.

4.11 The auditor should consider what tests he can carry out to check the reasonableness of the valuation of stocks and work in progress. Ratio analysis techniques may assist comparisons being made with stock items and stock categories from the previous year's stock summaries. If the client has a computerised stock accounting system, the auditor may be able to request an exception report, listing, for example, all items whose value has changed by more than a specified amount. A reasonableness check will also provide the auditor with assurance regarding completeness.

4.12 Wherever possible cost and net realisable value should be compared for each item of stock. Where this is impracticable, the comparison may be done by stock group or category. Surpluses from one category should not be set off against deficits from another in making this comparison.

4.13 The auditor should review and test the client's system for identifying slow-moving, obsolete or damaged stock. This will necessitate following up any such items that were identified at the stocktaking and ensuring that the client has made adequate provision to write down the items to net realisable value (see Paragraph 2.17).

4.14 Where the company has stock records, these should be examined to identify slow-moving items. This kind of check can often be made easier if the company has a computerised stock system. It may be possible to incorporate into a computer audit program certain tests and checks such as listing items whose value or quantity has not moved over the previous year, and listing work in progress job numbers which have not had any significant value added over the previous six months.

4.15 An important procedure is to examine the prices at which finished goods have been sold after the year-end. This enables the auditor to ascertain whether any finished goods items need to be reduced below cost. When making this judgement, the auditor should ensure that the selling price takes account of any trade discounts that the client gives, and has been reduced by costs of disposal. This adjusted price is compared with the carrying value of the finished goods.

4.16 Quantities of goods sold after the year end should also be reviewed to determine that year end stock has, or will be, realised. If significant quantities of finished goods stock remain unsold for an unusual time after the year-end, the auditor should consider the need to make appropriate provision.

4.17 For work in progress, the ultimate selling price should be compared with the carrying value at the year end plus costs to be incurred after the year end to bring work in progress to a finished state.

4.18 If raw material costs have been reduced after the year-end, it may be necessary to consider the net realisable value of final products incorporating the relevant raw materials to determine if write-down is needed in respect of those raw materials. This is a possibility, albeit remote, in sectors such as food and confectionery. A dramatic decrease in costs of a volatile commodity such as coffee or cocoa could affect the retail price of products based on these commodities in the short term, justifying a write down in the raw material cost. Conversely, a fall in the realisable value of finished goods should not alone be considered a justification for writing down raw material costs.

Exercise 4

Your firm is the auditor of Arnold Electrical Ltd and you have been asked to audit the valuation of the company's stock at 31 May 19X1 in accordance with SSAP 9 *Stocks and long-term contracts*. Arnold Electrical Ltd operates from a single store and purchases domestic electrical equipment from wholesalers and manufacturers and sells them to the general public. These products include video and audio equipment, washing machines, refrigerators and freezers. In addition, it sells small items such as electrical plugs, magnetic tape for video and audio recorders, records and compact discs.

A full stocktake was carried out at the year end, and you are satisfied that the stock was counted accurately and there are no cut-off errors. Because of the limited time available between the year end and the completion of the audit, the company have valued the stock at cost by recording the selling price and deducting the normal gross profit margin. Stock which the company believes to be worth less than cost has been valued at net realisable value. The selling price used is that on the item in the store when it was counted.

The stock has been divided into three categories.

(a) Video and audio equipment: televisions, video recorders, video cameras and audio equipment.

(b) Domestic equipment: washing machines, refrigerators and freezers.

(c) Sundry stocks: electrical plugs, magnetic tapes and compact discs.

The normal gross profit margin for each of these categories has been determined and this figure has been used to calculate the cost of the stock (by deducting the gross profit margin from the selling price). In answering the question you should assume there are no sales taxes (for example, value added tax in the UK).

Required

(a) List and describe the audit work you will carry out to check that the stock has been correctly valued at cost.

(b) List and describe the audit work you will carry out:

(i) to find stock which should be valued at net realisable value; and
(ii) to check that net realisable value for this stock is correct.

(c) List and describe the other work you will perform to check that the stock value is accurate.

Note. In answering the question you are only required to check that the price per unit of the stock is correct. You should assume that the stock quantities are accurate and there are no purchases or sales cut-off errors.

Solution

(a) This method of valuation at cost is permitted by SSAP 9, but it is usually applied to large retail concerns which stock thousands of low value items, for example supermarket chains. This method is only permitted when it can be shown that it gives a reasonable approximation of the actual cost.

The following tests should be performed to ensure that the stock is correctly valued at cost.

(i) Obtain a schedule of the client calculations of the gross profit margins. Check the mathematical accuracy and consider the reliability of all sources of information used in the calculation.

(ii) Where the normal overall gross margin has been used, check the reasonableness of the figure by comparing it to the monthly management accounts for the year and last year's published accounts.

It will also be necessary to test a sample of items to make sure that gross profit does not vary too much across all items of stock (which is unlikely for Arnold Electrical). The test will compare selling price to purchase price.

(iii) If a weighted average gross margin has been used, check that the weighting is correct in terms of the proportion of each type of product in closing stock.

(iv) Select a sample of high value stock lines and check the reasonableness of the gross profit estimate by calculating the gross profit for each of those lines. Sales price will be compared to stock sheets and to sale prices in the shop at the year end. Cost will be checked by examining purchase invoices. The weighted average profit margin for the selected lines can then be calculated and compared to the gross margin applied to the whole stock. *(Note.* High value stock lines may consist of individual items with a high selling price, or a large number of low value items.)

(v) Overvaluation of slow moving stock is possible when the prices of those items are affected by inflation. To check this, examine the stock sheets for any slow moving items (or ask the management of the company or use my own observation). Compare the value of the stock at the end of the accounting period to cost according to purchase invoices. If an overvaluation has occurred it should be quantified.

(vi) Check whether any goods were being offered for sale at reduced prices at the year end. If the reduced price is greater than cost, the use of an average gross profit percentage will cause stock to be undervalued. This undervaluation must be quantified. If full selling price was used in the calculation then the problem will not arise. Check a sample of stock items to sales invoices issued around the year end to make sure that the correct price was used in the stock costing calculation.

(b) (i) Stock which may be worth less than cost will include:

(1) slow moving stock;
(2) obsolete or superseded stock;
(3) seconds stock and items that have been damaged;
(4) stock which is being, or is soon likely to be, sold at reduced prices;
(5) discontinued stock lines.

To identify stock which may be worth less than cost the following work will be carried out.

(1) Examine the computerised stock control system and list items showing an unacceptably low turnover rate. An unacceptable rate of turnover may be different for different items, but stock representing more than six months' sales is likely to qualify.

(2) Check the stock printout for items already described as seconds or recorded as damaged.

(3) Discuss with management the current position regarding slow moving stock and their plans and expectations in respect of products that may be discontinued. The standard system must be carefully considered and estimates obtained of the likely selling price of existing stock. The most likely outcome regarding the use and value of discontinued components must be decided. Finished goods where the selling price is less than cost will be valued at net realisable value. This is defined as the actual or estimated selling price less costs to completion and marketing, selling and distribution expenses.

(4) At the stocktake, look for stock which is dusty, inaccessible and in general not moving and mark on the stock sheets.

(5) Find out whether any lines are unreliable and therefore frequently returned for repairs as these may be unpopular.

(6) Check with the trade press or other sources to see whether any of the equipment is out of date.

(ii) Determining the net realisable value of stock is a difficult task and involves management in judging how much stock can be sold and at what price, together with deciding whether to sell off raw materials and components separately or to assemble them into finished products. This is a high risk audit area and care must be taken over making prudent provisions to write down stock from cost to net realisable value. Each separate type of stock item should be considered separately in deciding on the level of provision.

To determine whether the net realisable value of the stock the following tests should be carried out.

(1) Find the actual selling prices from the latest sales invoice. For items still selling, invoices will be very recent, but for slow moving and obsolete items the invoiced prices will be out of date and allowance will have to be made for this (probably a reduction in estimating the most likely sale price of the stock concerned).

(2) Estimate the value of marketing, selling and distributing expenses using past figures for the types of finished goods concerned as a base. I would update and check for reasonableness against the most recent accounting records.

(3) Discuss with management what selling prices are likely to be where there is little past evidence. Costs to completion will be questioned where these are difficult to estimate and where there are any unusual assembly, selling or distribution problems.

(c) The following procedures would also be performed to check the value of stock at the year end.

(i) Compare current results with prior year(s). This would include gross profit margins, sales and stock turnover. Marked variations from the current year's results should be investigated.

(ii) Consider the effects of new technology and new fashions. The electrical appliance business will be exposed to obsolescence problems. Quantify any necessary write down.

(iii) Compare selling prices to those charged elsewhere. If the prices elsewhere are lower, than the distortion in selling price might affect the value of the stock of Arnold Electrical. Alternatively, if prices elsewhere are higher, then the company's prices may occasionally fall below cost. Again, any adjustment discovered to be necessary must be quantified.

(iv) Compare the valuation of stock this year to that at the end of last year. This will be particularly useful for lines held at both dates. If the values are comparable, taking account of inflation, then the current valuation is more likely to be correct.

(v) Sale prices should be checked as long after the year end as possible, to make sure that prices were not kept artificially high over the year end and then reduced at a later date. Stock turnover should also be examined on this same basis.

Chapter roundup

- The audit of stocks and work in progress is difficult and time consuming, but it is of primary importance.
- The valuation and disclosure rules for stock are laid down in SSAP 9 and CA 1985. The relevant auditing standards and guidelines give guidance on the procedures for auditing stock.
- Stocktake procedures are vital as they provide evidence which cannot be obtained elsewhere or at any other time about the quantities and conditions of stocks and work in progress.
- Cut-off procedures will affect both the sales and purchases audits.
- Valuation of stocks and work in progress is not that easy. As well as comparing cost and net realisable value, the auditor must determine whether cost has been calculated correctly.

Test your knowledge

1 Why is the audit of stocks and work in progress so important? (see Introduction)

2 Define 'net realisable value' and 'cost' of stock. (1.5, 1.6)

3 In what circumstances should the auditor attend a client's stocktaking? (2.5)

4 Where continuous stock-checking methods are being used, what are the objectives of the auditor's tests? (2.9)

5 What are the principal procedures that should be carried out before the auditor attends a stocktaking? (2.12)

6 At which points in the accounting cycle is cut-off most critical? (3.2)

7 List the principal procedures the auditor should carry out at the stocktaking to ensure cut-off is carried out correctly. (3.8)

8 How will the auditor determine whether cost of finished goods exceeds net realisable value? (4.15, 4.16)

Chapter 13

OTHER BALANCE SHEET ASSETS

This chapter covers the following topics.

Introduction

The final audit will concentrate on the balance sheet to a great extent. The asset side of the balance sheet (other than stocks) is covered in this chapter; the liability side is covered in Chapter 14.

Although each audit client is different, most of these items will be present in the final accounts. The importance of each balance sheet component will also vary from client to client.

You should make sure that you are fully conversant with the 'standard' procedures, such as the debtors' circularisation and bank letter.

1 TANGIBLE FIXED ASSETS

1.1 The auditor's substantive work in respect of intangible and tangible fixed assets may involve two important techniques highlighted earlier in this text: third party confirmations and reliance on specialist. The former may be used in the context of verification of title (ownership) and the latter in circumstances where selective revaluation of tangible fixed assets has taken place in the year under review carried out by an internal or external professional valuer. It is, however, the subjective area of depreciation and amortisation that may cause the greatest audit headache.

The audit of tangible fixed assets

Internal control considerations

1.2 In order to ascertain whether the amounts of fixed assets are properly stated in the financial statements it is highly desirable that the client maintains proper fixed asset registers to facilitate identification of those assets. Where such registers are not maintained the auditor must record in his working papers the movements that have taken place in the fixed assets during the year. He should ensure that the company has proper controls over substantial expenditure on capital assets and over any disposals. Such controls may include capital expenditure proposals suitably authorised, disposal of asset forms, and authorisation in Board Minutes. Any lack of control should be referred to in the management letter.

Ownership and existence: freehold and leasehold properties

1.3 The verification of the client's title to property shown in the accounts is strictly a matter for a solicitor, although for normal audit purposes *prima facie* evidence of title is acceptable. If the deeds are held on the client's premises the auditor should inspect them at or near the balance sheet date; if held by an independent third party, and that third party is a bank, solicitor, insurance company or another recognised depository, it will normally be sufficient to obtain a certificate stating whether or not the deeds are held in safe custody or as security. Where there is doubt about the status of the third party, he should seek to inspect the deeds himself at the party's premises.

1.4 When deeds are inspected the auditor would normally expect to see the following.

(a) *Registered land*. The Land Registry Certificate should be available, ensuring that the land is registered in the client's name. Charges are also recorded on the certificate, together with subsequent discharges. This Certificate is conclusive evidence of title and where it is seen, there is normally no need to examine conveyances and other deeds; in cases of doubt or if the certificate is on deposit at the Land Registry because of current dealings a search may be carried out, preferably through the company's solicitors, at the Land Registry.

(b) *Unregistered land*. The latest conveyance should be examined, ensuring that the title is conveyed to client.

(c) *Leasehold property*. The assignment of a lease and/or the lease itself should be seen, ensuring that the lease is current and that the client is named as the lessee.

1.5 Where a certificate is obtained from a third party, the certificate should state in what capacity and on what terms the deeds are held, together with an adequate description. If the certificate is couched in unsatisfactory terms, such as '... an envelope purporting to contain...' the auditor should arrange physically to inspect the deeds. In future years he should request confirmation that the deeds examined have not been withdrawn from the depository during the year; if they have, a further inspection will be necessary.

1.6 The examination of title deeds does not itself verify the actual existence of buildings, even if the deeds refer to them. They may have been subsequently demolished (perish the thought), the auditor should consider a physical inspection of any buildings whose existence may be in doubt.

1.7 Occasionally in groups of companies, deeds may be in the name of one company, whereas the property is carried in the books of another company. In such cases written acknowledgement should be seen that the deeds are held by the first company in capacity as nominees; if necessary legal advice should be sought on this subject.

Ownership and existence: other tangible assets

1.8 Ownership of assets such as plant, machinery and motor vehicles is usually relatively easy for the auditor to verify by examining relevant purchase documents, such as invoices but care must be taken with assets purchased under hire purchase and finance lease arrangements (SSAP 21). Existence verification will be facilitated if the company maintains a plant register: assets can be selected at random from the register and physically inspected. The register should also help identify old assets which may no longer be in use.

Valuation: land and buildings

1.9 In a year in which property is revalued, a copy of the valuation should be obtained and placed on the permanent file. The auditor should ensure that the valuation has been prepared on an acceptable basis, which, in most cases, will be the open market value of the property reflecting its existing use. The auditor will also of course, be concerned with the competence and independence of the specialist performing the valuation. Such a specialist may be an employee of the client or a third party. The auditor will have regard to the considerations of the guideline *Reliance on other specialists* discussed in Chapter 8 earlier, when assessing the integrity of the valuation.

Future capital expenditure

1.10 Board minutes, capital expenditure proposals and any other relevant company documents should be scrutinised in order to verify or ascertain the extent of:

(a) capital expenditure for which the company has contracted and for which provision in the financial statements has not been made;

(b) capital expenditure authorised by the directors but for which no contracts have been placed.

The extent of authorised and contracted for capital expenditure may be confirmed in the letter of representation.

Depreciation

1.11 This is a somewhat subjective area. The auditor must have due regard to the accounting principles and disclosure requirements of SSAP 12 and the Companies Act 1985. It is worthwhile summarising the more important matters.

1.12 Special considerations apply in respect of investment properties (SSAP 19): see your financial accounting studies.

Summary of audit procedures

1.13 The following series of tests summarise the substantive procedures that the auditor may perform in respect of tangible fixed assets.

(a) *General*

(i) Obtain or prepare a summary of tangible fixed assets under categories, showing how the figures of gross book value, accumulated depreciation and net book value appearing in the trial balance/draft accounts reconcile with the opening position.

(ii) Obtain or prepare a list of additions during the year and verify by inspection of architects' certificates, solicitors' completion statements, suppliers' invoices etc. Make physical inspection of any item over £..... and random selection of others.

(iii) Where the client has used his own labour force to construct assets, ensure that materials, labour and overheads, if appropriate, have been correctly analysed and are properly charged to capital.

(iv) Enquire into the availability of regional development grants for any of the expenditure. Ensure that appropriate claims have been made and grants received and receivable properly accounted for in accordance with SSAP 4 (see your financial accounting studies).

(v) Obtain or prepare a list of disposals and scrappings from fixed assets during the year. Reconcile original cost with sale proceeds and verify book profits and losses.

(b) *Buildings*

(i) Verify title to land and buildings by inspection of title deeds, land registry certificates or leases. Check that all deeds link up with the draft balance sheet.

(ii) Obtain a certificate from solicitors temporarily holding deeds, stating the purpose for which they are being held and that they hold them free from any mortgage or lien. Where deeds are held by bankers, obtain a similar certificate stating also that the deeds are held for safe custody only.

(c) *Plant and equipment/motor vehicles*

(i) Examine the fixed asset register and ensure that all additions and disposals are entered therein. Confirm that the major items in the register are in existence, in use, and appear in good condition. Prepare a schedule of the items inspected and file on the current audit file.

(ii) Check the reconciliation of the fixed asset register to the trial balance/draft accounts.

(iii) Examine documents of title (for example invoices) for assets purchased during year including, if applicable, hire purchase agreements and operating lease agreements.

(iv) Confirm that the company physically inspects all the items in the fixed asset register each year.

(v) Inspect vehicle registration books or verify sale proceeds if sold since the balance sheet date and reconcile opening and closing vehicles by numbers as well as amounts. Confirm that all vehicles are used for the purposes of the company's business.

(vi) If a fixed asset register is not kept, obtain a schedule for the permanent file of the major items of fixed assets showing the original cost and estimated present depreciated value, or update the existing schedule. Reconcile both the total cost and total depreciated value with the figures appearing in the balance sheet. Confirm that the major items on the schedule are in existence, in use, and in good condition. Prepare a schedule of the items inspected and file on the current audit file.

(vii) Obtain confirmation from a responsible official that all movements on fixed assets have been included in the draft accounts (including scrappings).

(d) *Depreciation*

(i) Review depreciation rates applied in relation to:

(1) asset lives;
(2) replacement policy;
(3) past experience of gains and losses on disposal;
(4) consistency with prior years and accounting policy;

(ii) For revalued assets, ensure that the charge for depreciation is based on the revalued amount.

(iii) Compare ratios of depreciation to fixed assets (by category) with:

(1) previous years;
(2) depreciation policy rates.

(iv) Ensure no further depreciation provided on fully depreciated assets.

(e) *Charges and commitments*

(i) Review for evidence of charges in statutory books and by company search.

(ii) Review leases of leasehold properties to ensure that company has fulfilled covenants therein.

(iii) Examine invoices received after year-end, orders and minutes for evidence of capital commitments.

(f) *Insurance*

Review insurance policies in force for all categories of tangible fixed assets and consider the adequacy of their insured values and check expiry dates.

Exercise 1

You are the manager in charge of the audit of M plc, a building and construction company, and you are reviewing the fixed asset section of the current audit file for the year ended 30 September 19X5. You find the following five matters which the audit senior has identified as problem areas. He is reviewing the company's proposed treatment of the five transactions in the accounts and is not sure that he has yet carried out sufficient audit work.

The five matters are as follows.

(a) During the year M plc built a new canteen for its own staff at a cost of £450,000. This amount has been included in buildings as at 30 September 19X5.

(b) Loose tools included in the financial statements at a total cost of £166,000 are tools used on two of the construction sites on which M operates. They are classified as fixed assets and depreciated over two years.

(c) A dumper truck, previously written off in the company's accounting records has been refurbished at a cost of £46,000 and this amount included in plant and machinery as at 30 September 19X5.

(d) The company's main office block has been revalued from £216,000 to £266,000 and this amount included in the balance sheet as at 30 September 19X5.

(e) A deposit of £20,000 for new equipment has been included under the heading plant and machinery although the final instalment of £35,000 was not paid over until 31 October 19X5 which was the date of delivery of the plant.

You are required, for each of the above matters:

(a) to comment on the acceptability of the accounting treatment and disclosure as indicated above; and

(b) to outline the audit work and evidence required to substantiate the assets.

Solution

(a) Acceptability of accounting treatment and disclosure

(i) *New staff canteen.* The costs of building a new staff canteen can quite properly be capitalised and treated as part of buildings in the balance sheet. The company's normal depreciation policy should be applied, subject only to the canteen being completed and in use at the year end.

(ii) *Loose tools.* Loose tools tend to have a very limited life and individually not to be material in value. For these reasons any capitalisation policy must be extremely prudent. The acceptability of this accounting treatment would depend on the policy in previous years and normal practice within the industry.

(iii) *Dumper truck.* The refurbishment costs have obviously extended the useful life of this asset and it therefore seems reasonable to capitalise the expenditure. Depreciation should be charged on the refurbishment costs over the estimated remaining useful life.

(iv) *Revaluation of office block.* The revaluation of property is acceptable, but the auditor will need to ensure that the company complies with a number of disclosure requirements. A note to the accounts should give details of the revaluation and the name of the valuer. The surplus on revaluation should be transferred to a separate non-distributable reserve in the balance sheet as part of shareholders' funds. In addition, the audit report will make reference to this modification of the use of the historical cost convention used in the preparation of the financial statements.

(v) *Deposit for new equipment.* As the equipment was not actually in the company's possession and use at the year end, the deposit should not have been shown as plant and machinery, but rather as a payment on account. If the amount was considered to be material a note to the accounts should give details of this prepayment.

(b) The audit work and evidence required to substantiate each of the assets referred to in (a) above would be as follows.

(i) *New staff canteen*

(1) Physically confirm existence of the asset.

(2) Confirm title to building by reference to Land Registry Certificate.

(3) Ascertain and confirm the details of any security granted over the asset, ensuring that this is properly recorded and disclosed.

(4) The detailed costings of the building should be tested and reasonable explanations obtained for any material variances from the original budget. Particular care should be taken in assessing the reasonableness of any overheads included as an element of cost.

(5) The depreciation policy should be reviewed for adequacy and consistency.

(ii) *Loose tools*

(1) The two sites where the loose tools are used should be visited to physically confirm the existence and condition of a sample of them.

(2) Cost of the loose tools should be vouched to purchase invoices and the company's asset register.

(3) Evidence should be sought to substantiate the company's estimate of a two year life for these assets.

(4) The auditor should review control procedures for safe custody of the loose tools.

(5) The company's policy with regard to scrapping and/or sale of tools no longer required should be reviewed to ensure that any proceeds are properly recorded and the assets register appropriately updated.

(iii) *Dumper truck*

(1) The truck should be inspected to confirm its condition and the fact that it is still being used.

(2) If the vehicle is used at all on public roads then the vehicle registration document should be inspected as some evidence of title.

(3) The insurance policy for the truck should be inspected as some evidence of valuation.

(4) The expenditure on refurbishment should be vouched to suppliers' invoices or company's payroll records where any of the work has been done by the client's own staff.

(5) The depreciation policy should be carefully reviewed and assessed for its reasonableness by discussion with management and past experience of similar vehicles.

(iv) *Revaluation of office block*

(1) The building should be inspected to confirm its existence and state of repair.

(2) Documents of title should be examined.

(3) Enquiry should be made as to any charges on the building and confirmation obtained that these have been properly recorded and disclosed.

(4) The valuer's certificate should be reviewed and agreed to the amount used in the financial statements, with consideration also being given to his qualifications, experience and reputation.

(5) Consideration should be given to assessing the reasonableness of the valuation by comparison with any similar properties which may have recently changed hands on the open market.

(v) *Deposit for new equipment*

(1) The payment of the deposit should be agreed to the contract for purchase of the equipment.

(2) The existence of the plant should be confirmed following its delivery on 31 October 19X5 as it is unlikely that the audit work will have been completed by that date.

2 INTANGIBLE FIXED ASSETS

2.1 The types of asset we are likely to encounter under this heading include patents, licences, trade marks, development costs and goodwill. All intangibles have a finite economic life and should hence be amortised.

2.2 The following substantive procedures could be performed in respect of intangible assets.

(a) *General*. Prepare analyses of movements on both cost and amortisation accounts. Note the nature of the assets and the periods of amortisation.

(b) *Patents and trade marks*

(i) In respect of patents and trade-marks and similar items acquired during the period, inspect the purchase agreements, assignments and other supporting evidence. Where patents have been developed by the company, verify the amount capitalised with supporting costing records.

(ii) Where patents or trade-marks are maintained by a patent agent, obtain confirmation of all patents and trade-marks in force. Verify the payment of annual renewal fees.

(c) *Goodwill*

(i) Where goodwill has been purchased during the period ensure that it reflects the difference between the fair value of the consideration given and the aggregate of the fair values of the separable net assets acquired. Such goodwill should normally be eliminated from the accounts immediately on acquisition against reserves. It may however, be eliminated from the accounts by amortisation through the profit and loss account systematically over its useful economic life.

(ii) Ensure that any existing purchased goodwill is being amortised. Purchased goodwill should not be carried as a permanent item in the balance sheet, and should normally be written off immediately. The amount of purchased goodwill arising on each acquisition during the period should be separately disclosed where material. Purchased goodwill should be reconciled to goodwill recognised on acquisitions. More detailed disclosure is likewise required in respect of the underlying assets. (You should be aware that the proposals of a new exposure draft on accounting for goodwill require purchased goodwill to be amortised through the profit and loss account on a straightforward basis over a period of up to 40 years.)

(iii) Ensure that no amount has been attributed to non-purchased goodwill in the balance sheet.

(d) *Amortisation*

(i) Review amortisation rates used and determine by enquiry that they are reasonable in the circumstances. Check computation of amortisation charge for the year and trace to profit and loss account. Determine the effect of and reason for any change in rates compared to prior year.

(ii) Ascertain that the unamortised balances on intangible asset accounts represent continuing value, which are proper charges to future operations (including, if applicable, goodwill).

(e) *Income from intangibles*

(i) Review sales returns and statistics to verify the reasonableness of income derived from patents, trademarks, licences and so forth.

(ii) Where applicable, examine audited statements of third party sales covered by a patent, licence or trademark owned by the company.

Development costs

2.3 The Companies Act 1985 states that development costs may be included in the balance sheet (that is to say, capitalised) only in 'special circumstances' (Sch 4 Paragraph 20). This term is not defined in the Act. Where development costs are capitalised they must be amortised; the reasons for capitalisation and the period over which they are being written off, or are to be written off, must be disclosed in a note to the accounts.

2.4 To interpret 'special circumstances' we can turn to the guidance of SSAP 13 *Accounting for research and development.* The provisions of SSAP 13 are considered to be compatible with those of the Act.

2.5 SSAP 13 defines two categories of expenditure on research.

(a) *Pure (or basic) research:* experimental or theoretical work undertaken primarily to acquire new scientific or technical knowledge for its own sake rather than directed towards any specific aim or application.

(b) *Applied research:* original or critical investigation undertaken in order to gain new scientific or technical knowledge and directed towards a specific practical aim or objective.

2.6 'Development' is defined as:

> 'the use of scientific or technical knowledge in order to produce new or substantially improved materials, devices, products or services, to install new processes or systems prior to the commencement of commercial production or commercial applications, or to improving substantially those already produced or installed.'

2.7 Expenditure on pure and applied research (other than on fixed assets) is required to be written off in the year of expenditure.

2.8 The special circumstances which must be satisfied to justify deferral of development expenditure are:

(a) there is a clearly defined project; and

(b) the related expenditure is separately identifiable; and

(c) the outcome of such a project has been assessed with reasonable certainty as to:

(i) its technical feasibility; and

(ii) its ultimate commercial viability considered in the light of factors such as likely market conditions (including competing products), public opinion, consumer and environmental legislation; and

(d) the aggregate of the deferred development costs, any further development costs, and related production, selling and administration costs is reasonably expected to be exceeded by related future sales or other revenues; and

(e) adequate resources exist, or are reasonably expected to be available, to enable the project to be completed and to provide any consequential increases in working capital.

2.9 From the audit viewpoint, criteria (a) and (b) in Paragraph 2.8 should be relatively easy to establish. In examining criterion (c) the auditor will need to examine feasibility studies, market research reports and other documents, which may give an indication of each project's technical and commercial viability. He will also need to consult with technical experts employed by the client (this is another example of reliance on specialists). In testing the fourth criterion the auditor should examine, or if necessary perform, calculations of all future cash flows of the project and assess its overall economic viability. The last criterion is best tested by examining the overall cash flow forecasts for the company, which should anyway be part of his going concern review, together with the cash flow requirements of the project.

2.10 Once the auditor is satisfied that certain expenditure should justifiably be deferred he should, in subsequent years, review the deferred expenditure to ensure that the justifying criteria are still satisfied. If they are not the expenditure should be written off.

2.11 Finally, the auditor should ensure that the amortisation of deferred expenditure commences with the commercial production of the product or process and he should check that amortisation is charged on a systematic basis by reference either to the sale or use of the product or process or the period over which the product or process is expected to be sold or used.

2.12 The good news for the auditor in this audit area is that many companies adopt a prudent approach and write off research and development expenditure in the year it is incurred. The auditor's concern in these circumstances is whether the profit and loss account charge for research and development is complete, accurate and valid.

Exercise 2

Newstead Electronics plc manufactures and sells microprocessors, and it undertakes research and development to ensure that its products remain competitive.

During the year under review it has commenced the following products and incurred the following costs to date.

(a) Construction of a new facility for the research, development and manufacture of microprocessors at a cost of £50 million. This facility includes a building, air cleaning machinery and air-conditioning, and the plant required to manufacture the microprocessors.

(b) The design and development of a new microprocessor at a cost of £30 million. The company plans to start selling this microprocessor nine months after the balance sheet date.

(c) Research into new materials to construct microprocessors and into the feasibility of optical microprocessors. The costs incurred are £15 million. It is not expected that this research will lead to the manufacture and sale of microprocessors in the near future.

Required

For each of the projects (a) to (c) above, list and describe the audit work you will perform and the matters you will consider:

(i) to verify the value of research and development expenditure;

(ii) to decide whether the research and development expenditure can be included as an asset in Newstead Electronics' balance sheet. Also, you should state how the research and development expenditure should be disclosed in the profit and loss account and balance sheet.

Note. The accounting treatment should comply with SSAP 13 *Accounting for research and development*.

Solution

There will be similarities in the way in which I will check the expenditure incurred on each of the three projects listed. Before mentioning matters which are specific to each of the particular projects, the following common points can be made.

(a) I will arrange a visit to the research facility in each case, and discuss the project with senior staff involved in order to develop an understanding of it which is sufficient to enable me to conduct a review of the expenditure. A sample of fixed assets should be inspected at this stage.

(b) The costs for each project should be recorded in their own nominal ledger account. This will be the starting point for the tests I will perform, which will concentrate on higher value items.

(c) From the nominal ledger I will trace a sample of significant or unusual purchases to purchase invoices. I will review the invoices in order to check that the expenditure appears to relate to the particular project.

(d) Any internal charges included should be reviewed for reasonableness, checking that any overheads included do not incorporate a profit element.

(e) I will ensure that any items bought on hire purchase or finance lease terms are treated correctly (capitalised) in the company's accounts in accordance with SSAP 21. Operating leases should not be capitalised.

(f) I will carry out tests to ensure that cut-off at the year end is correct. Accrual should be made for invoices received after the year end relating to expenditure incurred before the year end so that such purchases are included in the cost of the project charged to the accounts in the year.

Particular procedures relating to individual projects, together with consideration of the accounting treatment of the research and development expenditure incurred in each project in the light of SSAP 13, are considered in the paragraphs that follow.

(a) (i) I would carry out work on the expenditure for this new facility in the ways set out above, checking significant items of expenditure from the nominal ledger to the appropriate supporting documentation.

(ii) The cost of fixed assets acquired or constructed to provide facilities for research and development activities should be capitalised and written off over their useful life in accordance with Paragraph 23 of SSAP 13. Expenditure on this facility should accordingly be capitalised and shown within tangible fixed assets under the categories of land and buildings, and plant and machinery.

I will assess the reasonableness of the rate of depreciation of the fixed assets. Land will not normally be depreciated. Plant will not normally be depreciated until it is brought into use. The likely life of the plant should be assessed in the light of the relatively rapid obsolescence of products which is typical in the industry.

(b) (i) Expenditure on the development for this project will be checked in a similar way to that outlined above, starting from the expenditure as recorded in the nominal ledger. Much of this expenditure may be made up of internal charges. I will check for a sample of employees that they have been working on the project for the periods for which their pay has been charged to the project. Any overheads charged should be reasonable and should be expenditure which can be linked with reasonable accuracy to the work done by the employees concerned.

Similarly any computer time charged internally should be checked to ensure that the time charged relates to the project involved. The charge rate for the computer charged should be checked for reasonableness. No profit element should be included.

Any other significant expenses should be checked from the nominal ledger to either purchase invoices or to details of internal charges made.

(ii) As development expenditure, the expenditure may be capitalised and charged to the profit and loss account over future periods beginning when the first sales of the product commence, subject to the expenditure meeting the criteria set out in SSAP 13.

I shall check that these criteria are satisfied. The criteria are as follows.

(1) There must be a clearly defined project.

(2) Related expenditure on the project should be separately identifiable. The work outlined above should confirm this.

(3) The outcome of the project should be assessed for its technical feasibility. I will discuss the project with senior technical personnel involved (for example the development engineer and the production engineer) in order to form a view on this. I would expect that a working prototype would be available at the time of the audit and I would enquire into the results of tests performed on this.

(4) Revenues from sale of the product should cover the deferred development costs incurred together with anticipated future costs on the project. I will review sales forecasts in order to consider whether they appear to be realistic. Manufacturing cost estimates and profit will need to be estimated in order to come to a view on whether anticipated revenue exceeds development costs incurred and anticipated. My knowledge of the accuracy of company forecasts, based on my prior experience with the client, will help me decide on the reliability of the forecasts relating to this particular project. I will also seek information on current conditions in the market for products of this sort. It is important to bear in mind that products in the electronics industry are prone to relatively rapid obsolescence.

Capitalised development costs will be included in the balance sheet as deferred development expenditure within the category of intangible fixed assets.

(c) (i) Research costs relating to the new materials will be checked in a similar way to that already set out above. Again, a substantial part of the expenditure may consist of internal charges such as wages and overheads, including computer time. I will check these in a similar manner to that already described above.

(ii) This expenditure cannot be capitalised under the rules set out in SSAP 13 since the research expenditure does not relate to a specific project. The expenditure must therefore be written off during the year through the profit and loss account. Paragraph 31 of SSAP 13 requires the research and development expenditure charged in the year to be disclosed in the accounts.

3 INVESTMENTS

3.1 This section applies to companies where dealing in investments is secondary to the main objectives of the company. Under the general heading of 'investments' four distinct items are considered:

(a) investment properties (not on your syllabus);
(b) investments in companies, whether listed or unlisted, fixed interest or equity;
(c) income arising from the investments in (b); and
(d) investment in subsidiary and associated companies (not on your syllabus).

Investments in companies

(*Note*. The following comments apply equally to investments treated as fixed or current.)

Internal control considerations

3.2 As with all other material assets, the person responsible for recording the purchase and sale of investments should not also have custody of the assets themselves. In practice, it is common for a bank to have custody of the title documents in which case the person with authority to deposit or withdraw securities should be independent of the person responsible for recording investment transactions. As an investment may be misappropriated by being pledged as collateral, it is also important that those responsible, directly or indirectly, for the custody of assets should not have access to cash.

3.3 Authority for controlling investment dealing should be at a high level, usually the board, but this may be delegated to an investment manager or company secretary provided all transactions are later sanctioned by the board.

Existence and ownership.

3.4 Stockbrokers should not normally be entrusted with the safe custody of share certificates on a continuing basis since they have ready access to the Stock Exchange. It is not, therefore, acceptable to rely on a certificate from a broker stating that he holds the company's securities; if securities are being transferred over the year-end the auditor should obtain a broker's certificate but the transaction should be further verified by examining contract notes, and in the case of purchases, examination of the title documents after the year-end.

Profit or loss on disposal of investments

3.5 In computing the profit or loss on sale of investments the auditor should consider the following specific aspects.

(a) Bonus issues of shares.

(b) Consistent basis of identifying cost of investment sold (for example FIFO, LIFO, or average cost).

(c) Eights issues.

(d) Accrued interest.

(e) Taxation.

Valuation

3.6 The auditor should establish that the company's policy on valuing investments has been correctly applied and is consistent with previous years, for example cost or market value.

3.7 A permanent diminution in value should be reflected in the accounts. Stock market fluctuations are normally temporary, but the value of unlisted investments should be reviewed by reference to:

(a) net asset value and income dividend yield according to the latest accounts (audited accounts provide better quality evidence);

(b) any restrictions on realisation or on the remittance of income (particularly for foreign investments);

(c) audit qualifications (if any) in respect of the accounts.

3.8 Investments should be valued individually, not on a portfolio basis, the latter treatment being discouraged by the Companies Act 1985. If the value of an individual investment is difficult to determine because it is not included on the Stock Exchange Daily Official List, a stockbroker may be contacted.

Substantive procedures: investments

3.9 The following tests are suggested.

(a) Obtain or prepare a statement to be placed on the current file reconciling the book value of listed and unlisted investments at the last balance sheet date and the current balance sheet date. The schedule or supporting list should include the title and particulars of the holding, cost and the market value or valuation at the balance sheet date.

(b) Examine certificates of title to investments listed in investment records, at year-end or certificates from any bank authorised to hold the documents in safe custody, ensuring that they are held for the company free from any charges or lien. Inspect blank transfers and declarations of trust where the investment is registered in the name of a nominee. Certificates of shares held for safe custody must not be accepted from stockbrokers.

(c) Verify purchases and sales recorded in the investment records by examining agreements, contract notes, correspondence and the minute book.

(d) Check with Stubbs, Extel cards or appropriate financial statements that all bonus and rights issues are properly accounted for.

(e) Ensure that the investments are properly categorised in the financial statements into listed and unlisted.

(f) Review for evidence of charges and pledging in minutes and other statutory books.

(g) Consider whether there are likely to be any restrictions on realisation of the investment or remittance of any income due (especially for investments abroad) and ensure these are properly disclosed in the financial statements.

(h) In the case of listed investments, confirm the value by reference to the Stock Exchange Daily Lists or the quotations published in the Financial Times or Times. The middle market value should be used.

(i) In the case of unlisted investments, obtain a copy of the accounts of the company or companies concerned and:

    (i) calculate the net assets value of the shares and value the investment on a yield basis;

    (ii) ensure that the value at which the investment is stated in the accounts or valued by the directors is reasonable in the light of the net assets value and yield value.

    (iii) see directors' minutes expressing the board's opinion as to the value of such investments, or obtain management representations.

(j) Ascertain that no substantial fall in the value of the investments has taken place since the balance sheet date.

Investment income

3.10 The basis of recognising investment income may vary from company to company particularly for dividends, for example:

(a) credit taken only when received (cash basis);

(b) credit taken when declared; or

(c) credit taken only after ratification of the dividend by the investee's shareholders in general meeting.

A consistent basis must be applied from year to year.

3.11 Suggested substantive procedures are as follows.

(a) Check that all income due has been received, by reference to Stubbs or Extel cards for listed investments, and appropriate (audited) financial statements for unlisted investments.

(b) Review investment income account for irregular or unusual entries, or those not apparently pertaining to investments held (particular attention should be paid to investments bought and sold during the year).

(c) Ensure that the basis of recognising income is consistent with previous years.

(d) Compare investment income with prior years and explain any significant fluctuations.

Exercise 3

For many companies investments in stocks and shares represent a substantial portion of total assets, for others investments are only temporary assets, or merely reflect incidental aspects of company operations.

Required

(a) Describe the audit procedures which would verify the existence and ownership of investments in stocks and shares.

(b) Describe how the auditor would determine that all investment income from stocks and shares had been properly recorded in the accounting records.

Solution

(a) The existence and ownership of investments in stocks and shares would be verified using the following audit procedures.

(i) Inspection of share certificates and contract notes would be carried out. All documents should be inspected together at the same time, and should be in the name of the client.

(ii) Documentary evidence would be examined to verify all purchases and sales during the year, including authorisation minutes. Purchase cost and sales income would be vouched and traced to the bank.

(iii) Third parties holding share certificates pending delivery, whether for safe custody or as collateral, would be asked by the auditor to confirm directly to them their holding on behalf of the client. Verification is unsatisfactory in the following cases and the matter would be referred for action to the audit manager.

(1) Where stock is being held by brokers for safe custody and not merely pending delivery (since brokers are not considered to be appropriate as custodians except in the event of purchase or sale of investment).

(2) Where stock is held in the name of a third party other than a bank nominee, for example, a director.

(iv) Agreements, board minutes and supporting correspondence will be examined in respect of unquoted shares and the equity valuation of shares in associated companies.

(v) Investment income received would be closely scrutinised, as it is prima facie evidence of the existence and beneficial ownership of the securities that it arises from.

(b) To determine that all investment income had been properly recorded the auditor would do the following work.

(i) Verify a proportion of equity holdings as to income received, especially in respect of those purchased and sold during the period. Check to Extel or stock exchange lists, or company accounts in respect of unquoted companies, to determine the dividends that should have been received in the period.

(ii) Obtain information on all bonus and rights issues during the year and investigate action taken and issues received.

(iii) Where interest is fixed, examine to ensure that the amount due is received on the due date and that it relates correctly to the nominal value of the security.

(iv) Verify the correctness of calculation and recording of capital gains and losses, and their treatment in the financial statements.

(v) Review the reasonableness of investment income accounts, taking into consideration the amounts budgeted for and the amounts received in previous years. Material variation would need to be explained, taking into account purchases, bonus issues and sales in the period.

4 DEBTORS AND PREPAYMENTS

4.1 For most commercial and industrial enterprises trading on credit terms, debtors will be a material figure in the balance sheet. The auditor must hence give due weight to this important audit area when designing and conducting his balance sheet tests. Returning to our key objectives of completeness, existence, ownership and valuation, the auditor should normally have obtained valuable audit assurance on the completeness of debtors from his earlier sales cycle work. It is convenient to redefine existence, ownership and valuation in terms of rather more specific objectives for trade debtors.

(a) Do debtors represent *bona fide* amounts due to the company? (Existence and ownership)

(b) Is there a satisfactory cut-off between goods despatched and goods invoiced, so that sales and debtors are recognised in the correct year? (Ownership)

(c) Has adequate provision been made for bad debts, discounts and returns? (Valuation)

The auditor will also be concerned with other debtors, such as inter company current and loan account balances and prepayments (where material).

Debtors' listing and aged analysis

4.2 Much of the auditor's detailed work will be based on a selection of debtors' balances chosen from the sales ledger at the balance sheet date. To assist the auditor, a listing is normally prepared by the client. If this is not the case, the auditor will have to extract the list of balances himself. Assuming that the client has prepared the list, the following substantive procedures are necessary.

(a) Check the balances from the individual sales ledger accounts to the list of balances and vice versa.

(b) Check the total of the list to the sales ledger control account.

(c) Cast the list of balances and the sales ledger control account.

4.3 The determination of whether the company has made reasonable provision for bad and doubtful debts, objective (c) in Paragraph 4.1, will be facilitated if the company produces a breakdown of the debtors' listing, indicating the age of each debt. This 'aged analysis' is sometimes used as the basis for any general doubtful debt provision by applying a specific formula (for example X% of debts over three months, Y% of debts over two months). Where the sales ledger function is computerised, production of an aged analysis as a regular routine is clearly a simple and desirable procedure, enhancing credit control.

The debtors' circularisation

Strength of circularisation: relevance and reliability

4.4 The verification of trade debtors by direct communication is the normal means of providing audit evidence to satisfy objective (a) in Paragraph 4.1: 'Do debtors represent *bona fide* amounts due to the company?' The circularisation of debtors is best considered as a standard procedure which will only be omitted in special circumstances. Such circumstances might be where overall objectives can, or, occasionally, have to be achieved cost effectively by other means or where the debtors are immaterial. The circularisation will produce for the current audit file a written statement from each respondent debtor that the amount owed at the date of the circularisation is correct. This is, *prima facie*, reliable audit evidence, being from an independent source and in 'documentary' form.

Timing

4.5 Ideally the circularisation should take place immediately after the year-end and hence cover the year-end balances to be included in the balance sheet. However, time constraints may make it impossible to achieve this ideal. In these circumstances it may be acceptable to carry out the circularisation prior to the year-end provided that:

(a) the balances circularised are not more than, say, two to three months prior to the year-end; and

(b) the internal control system is such that the circularisation plus an investigation and reconciliation of the movements in the sales ledger balances in the intervening period between the circularisation date and the balance sheet date will provide the auditor with reasonable assurance. (Paragraph 4.17 below outlines the further work that may be necessary in respect of the intervening period.)

Client's mandate

4.6 Circularisation is essentially an act of the client, who alone can authorise third parties to divulge information to the auditors. If a suitable approach is made, the client's agreement will generally be forthcoming. Should the client refuse this will inevitably lead the auditors to consider whether they should qualify their report, as they may not be able to satisfy themselves, by means of other audit checks, as to the validity and accuracy of the debtor balances. In general, the weaker the internal control the more important it is to obtain external confirmation of debtor balances. The circularising of debtors on a test basis should not be regarded as replacing other normal audit checks, such as the testing in depth of sales transactions, but the results may influence the scope of such tests.

Positive v negative circularisation

4.7 When circularisation is undertaken the method of requesting information from the debtor may be either 'positive' or 'negative'. Under the positive method the debtor is requested to confirm the accuracy of the balance shown or state in what respect he is in disagreement. Under the negative method the debtor is requested to reply if the amount stated is disputed. In either case, the debtor is requested to reply direct to the auditor. Both methods may be used in conjunction.

4.8 Weak internal control, the suspicion of irregularities or that amounts may be in dispute, or the existence of numerous book-keeping errors are circumstances which indicate that the positive method is preferable as it is designed to encourage definite replies from those circularised. However, it will almost certainly be found in practice that certain classes of debtors, for example overseas customers and government departments (see Paragraph 4.16) either cannot or will not respond. Nevertheless, it is desirable, where the auditors judge it appropriate, to attempt verification, preferably by the positive method, but this should always be carried out in conjunction with such other audit tests as may be appropriate.

4.9 Good internal control, with a large number of small accounts, would suggest the negative method as likely to be appropriate. However, in some circumstances, say where there is a small number of large accounts and a large number of small accounts, a combination of both methods, as noted above, may be appropriate.

4.10 The following is a specimen 'positive' confirmation letter.

MANUFACTURING CO LIMITED
15 South Street
London

Date

Messrs (debtor)

In accordance with the request of our auditors, Messrs Arthur Daley & Co, we ask that you kindly confirm to them directly your indebtedness to us at (insert date) which, according to our records, amounted to £.......... as shown by the enclosed statement.

If the above amount is in agreement with your records, please sign in the space provided below and return this letter direct to our auditors in the enclosed stamped addressed envelope.

If the amount is not in agreement with your records, please notify our auditors directly of the amount shown by your records, and if possible detail on the reverse of this letter full particulars of the difference.

Yours faithfully,

For Manufacturing Co Limited

Reference No: ....

....

(Tear off slip)

The amount shown above is in agreement with our records as at

Account No	....	Signature	....
Date	....	Title or position	....

4.11 The statements will normally be prepared by the client's staff, from which point the auditors, as a safeguard against the possibility of fraudulent manipulation, must maintain strict control over the checking and despatch of the statements. Precautions must also be taken to ensure that undelivered items are returned, not to the client, but to the auditors' own office for follow-up by them.

Sample selection

4.12 It is seldom desirable to circularise all debtors and it is therefore necessary to establish an adequate sample, but if this sample is to yield a meaningful result it must be based upon a complete list of all debtor accounts. In addition, when constructing the sample, the following classes of account should receive special attention:

(a) old unpaid accounts;
(b) accounts written off during the period under review; and
(c) accounts with credit balances.

Similarly, the following should not be overlooked:

(d) accounts with nil balances; and
(e) accounts which have been paid by the date of the examination.

4.13 It may be convenient to apply stratification techniques to reflect the primarily substantive objective of a circularisation. This could be applied as follows to the main population (the selection of items within categories (a) to (e) above will be biased).

(a) The list of balances would be scrutinised to establish the size of the largest balances and the size and approximate frequency of the smallest balances and then four or five class intervals selected, ranges within which the balances will fall on the following basis:

   (i) the highest interval (say over £100,000) which will embrace a limited number of exceptionally large balances;

   (ii) the lowest interval (say under £1,000) which will embrace individually immaterial accounts;

   (iii) two or three intervals of equal size between these two extremes (say £1,001) to £35,000; £35,001 to £65,000; £65,001 to £100,000) which will collectively cover the substantial number of balances of an average size.

   The number of balances falling within each class interval should not be counted.

(b) A selection at random from each class would be made, probably three or four accounts would suffice. Further accounts may be selected from higher value classes in order to bring the selection up to the pre-determined monetary target if necessary.

Follow up procedures

4.14 When the positive request method is used the auditors must follow up by all practicable means those debtors who fail to respond. Second requests should be sent out in the event of no reply being received within two or three weeks (except in the case of overseas customers to allow for longer delivery periods) and if necessary this may be followed by telephoning the customer, with the client's permission. After two, or even three, attempts to obtain confirmation, a list of the outstanding items will normally be passed to a responsible company official, preferably independent of the sales accounting department, who will arrange for them to be investigated. This does not, of course, absolve the auditors from satisfying themselves that the clearance procedure is properly carried out and from examining the results. Where there is any limitation in the follow-up procedure it is all the more important to apply other auditing tests to establish that there existed a valid debt from a genuine customer at the date of the verification.

4.15 If it proves impossible to get confirmations from individual debtors, alternative procedures include the following.

(a) Check receipt of cash after date.

(b) Verify valid purchase orders if any.

(c) Examine the account to see if the balance outstanding represents specific invoices.

(d) Obtain explanations for invoices remaining unpaid after subsequent ones have been paid.

(e) See if the balance on the account is growing, and if so, why.

(f) Test company's control over the issue of credit notes and the write-off of bad debts.

Non purchase ledger accounting

4.16 Certain companies, government departments and local authorities operate systems, often computerised, which make it impossible for them to confirm the balance on their account. Typically in these circumstances their 'purchase ledger' is merely a list of unpaid invoices in date order. However, given sufficient information the debtor will be able to confirm that any given invoice is outstanding. Hence the auditor can circularise such enterprises, but he will need to break down the total on the account into its constituent outstanding invoices. It is good practice for such confirmation letters nevertheless to state the full balance so that the debtor has the option of confirming the balance and also has the opportunity to object if he thinks the total appears incorrect.

Additional procedures where circularisation is carried out before year-end

4.17 The auditor will need to carry out the following procedures where his circularisation is carried out before the year-end (see Paragraph 4.5).

(a) Review and reconcile entries on the sales ledger control account for the intervening period.

(b) Select sales entries from the control account and verify by checking sales day book entries, copy sales invoices and despatch notes.

(c) Select goods returned notes and other evidence of returns/allowances and check that appropriate credit entries have been posted to the sales ledger control account.

(d) Select a sample from the cash received records and ensure that receipts have been credited to the control account.

(e) Review the list of balances at the circularisation date and year end and investigate any unexpected movements or lack of them (it may be prudent to send further confirmation requests at the year end to material debtors where review results are unsatisfactory).

(f) Carry out analytical review procedures, comparing debtors' ratios at the confirmation date and year-end.

(g) Carry out year end cut-off tests, in addition to any performed at the date of the confirmation (see Paragraphs 4.19 and 4.20).

Evaluation and conclusions

4.18 All circularisations, regardless of timing, must be properly recorded and evaluated. All balance-disagreements and non-replies must be followed up and their effect on total debtors evaluated. Differences arising that merely represent invoices or cash in transit (normal timing differences) generally do not require adjustment, but disputed amounts, and errors by the client, may indicate that further substantive work is necessary to determine whether material adjustments are required.

Sales cut-off

4.19 We can now turn to objective (b) identified in Paragraph 4.1, the requirement to confirm that sales cut-off is satisfactory. During the stocktake the auditor will have obtained details of the last serial numbers of goods outward notes issued before the commencement of the stocktaking.

4.20 The following suggested substantive procedures are designed to test that goods taken into stock are not also treated as sales in the year under review and, conversely, goods despatched are treated as sales in the year under review and not also treated as stock.

(a) Check goods outwards and returns inwards notes around year-end to ensure:

- (i) invoices and credit notes are dated in the correct period; and
- (ii) invoices and credit notes are posted to the sales ledger and nominal ledger in the correct period.

(b) Reconcile entries in the sales ledger control around the year-end to daily batch invoice totals ensuring batches are posted in correct year.

(c) Review sales ledger control account around year-end for unusual items.

(d) Review material after-date invoices and ensure that they are properly treated as following year sales.

Provision for bad and doubtful debts, discounts and returns

4.21 Objective (c) in Paragraph 4.1 is concerned with the familiar concept of reducing the carrying value of an asset to net realisable value where prudence so demands. The following procedures are suggested.

(a) Debts against which specific provision has been made (and debts written off) should be examined in conjunction with correspondence, solicitors'/debt collection agencies' letters, liquidators' statements etc, and their necessity or adequacy confirmed. A general review of relevant correspondence may reveal debts where a provision is warranted, but has not been made.

(b) Where specific and/or general provisions have been determined using an aged analysis, the auditor should ensure that the analysis has been properly prepared. He should check the reasonableness and consistency of any formulae used to calculate general provisions.

(c) Additional tests that should be carried out on individual balances will include the ascertainment of the subsequent receipt of cash, paying particular attention to, and noting, round sum payments on account, examination of specific invoices and, where appropriate, goods received notes, and enquiry into any invoices which have been omitted from payments.

(d) Excessive discounts should be examined, as should journal entries transferring balances from one account to another and journal entries that clear debtor balances after the year end.

(e) Credit notes issued after the year end should be reviewed and provisions checked where they refer to current period sales.

(f) The collectibility of material debtor balances other than those contained in the sales ledger must also be confirmed and similar considerations to those set out above will apply. Certificates of loan balances at the end of the year should be requested from employees and others to whom loans have been extended, and where considered necessary, the authority should be seen.

Goods on sale or return/goods sold subject to reservation of title

4.22 Care should be exercised to ensure that goods on sale or return are properly treated in the accounts. Except where the client has been notified of the sale of the goods they should be reflected in the accounts as stock at cost and not as debtors, otherwise profits may be incorrectly anticipated.

4.23 Enquiries should be made concerning the supply of goods subject to reservation of title. If the client trades on terms whereby such a reservation of title exists the auditor must determine whether the accounting treatment is satisfactory. In reaching this decision it is considered that the commercial substance of the relevant transactions should take precedence over the legal form where they conflict. In most circumstances it is likely that sales of such goods should be construed as a normal commercial transaction and hence be treated as purchases in the accounts of the customer and a sale in the books of the client.

Inter-company indebtedness

4.24 Where significant trading occurs between group companies the auditor should have ascertained as a result of his transactions audit work whether trading has been at arm's length. As regards the balances at the year end, the following substantive procedures are suggested.

(a) Confirm balances owing from group and associated companies (current and loan accounts) with the other companies' records. This can be achieved directly where the auditor also audits the other companies; in other cases direct confirmation will be obtained from the companies' auditor.

(b) Ensure that cut-off procedures have operated properly regarding inter company transfers.

(c) Determine realisability of amounts owing.

(d) Ascertain the nature of the entries comprised in the balances at the year end. Ensure that any management charges contained therein have been calculated on a reasonable and consistent basis and have been acknowledged by the debtor companies.

Prepayments

4.25 The extent of audit testing will be consistent with the materiality of the amounts involved. Suggested procedures are as follows.

(a) Obtain or prepare a schedule of items paid in advance, including prior year's comparative figures.

(b) Verify the detailed items by reference to the cash book, expense invoices, correspondence and so on.

(c) Review the detailed profit and loss account to ensure that all likely prepayments have been provided for.

(d) Review the prepayments for reasonableness by comparing with prior years and using analytical review techniques where applicable.

Exercise 4

Sherwood Textiles plc manufactures knitted clothes and dyes these clothes and other textiles. You are carrying out the audit of the accounts of the company for the year ended 30 September 19X6 which show a turnover of about £10 million, and a profit before tax of about £800,000.

You are attending the final audit in December 19X6 and are commencing the audit of trade debtors, which are shown in the draft accounts at £2,060,000.

The interim audit (compliance tests) was carried out in July 19X6 and it showed that there was a good system of internal control in the sales system and no serious errors were found in the audit tests. The company's sales ledger is maintained on a computer, which produces at the end of each month:

(i) a list of transactions for the month;

(ii) an aged list of balances; and

(iii) open item statements which are sent to customers. (*Note.* Open item statements show all items which are outstanding on each account, irrespective of their age.)

Required

(a) List and briefly describe the audit tests you would carry out to verify trade debtors at the year end. You are not required to describe how you would carry out a debtors' circularisation.

(b) Describe the audit work you would carry out on the following replies to a debtors' circularisation:

(i) balance agreed by debtor;

(ii) balance not agreed by debtor;

(iii) debtor is unable to confirm the balance because of the form of records kept by the debtor;

(iv) debtor does not reply to the circularisation.

Solution

(a) For most commercial and industrial enterprises trading on credit terms, debtors will be a material figure in the balance sheet. The auditor must hence give due weight to this important audit area when designing and conducting his balance tests. It is convenient to define the specific objectives of audit tests for trade debtors as follows.

(i) Do debtors represent bona fide amounts due to the company? (Existence and ownership)

(ii) Is there a satisfactory cut-off between goods despatched and invoiced, so that sales and debtors are recognised in the correct year? (Ownership)

(iii) Has adequate provision been made for bad debts, discounts and returns? (Valuation)

Much of the auditor's detailed work will be based on a selection of debtors' balances chosen from the sales ledger at the balance sheet date. To assist the auditor, a listing is normally prepared by the client. If this is not the case, the auditor will have to extract the list of balances himself. Assuming that the client has prepared the list, the following substantive procedures are necessary.

(i) Check the balances from the individual sales ledger accounts to the list of balances and vice versa.

(ii) Check the total of the list to the sales ledger control account.

(iii) Cast the list of balances and the sales ledger control account.

The determination of whether the company has made reasonable provision for bad and doubtful debts, objective (iii) above, will be facilitated as the company produces an aged listing of balances. This objective is concerned with the familiar concept of reducing the carrying value of an asset to net realisable value where prudence so demands. The following procedures are suggested.

(i) Debts against which specific provision has been made (and debts written off) should be examined in conjunction with correspondence, solicitors'/debt collection agencies' letters, liquidators' statements and so on, and their necessity or adequacy confirmed. A general review of relevant correspondence may reveal debts where a provision is warranted, but has not been made.

(ii) Where specific and/or general provisions have been determined using the aged analysis, the auditor should ensure that the analysis has been properly prepared. He should check the reasonableness and consistency of any formula used to calculate general provisions.

(iii) Additional tests that should be carried out on individual balances will include the ascertainment of the subsequent receipt of cash, paying particular attention to, and noting, round sum payments on account, examination of specific invoices and, where appropriate, goods received notes, and enquiry into any invoices which have been omitted from payments.

(iv) Excessive discounts should be examined, as should journal entries transferring balances from one account to another and journal entries that clear debtor balances after the year end.

(v) Credit notes issued after the year end should be reviewed and provisions checked where they refer to current period sales;

The verification of trade debtors by direct communication is the normal means of providing audit evidence to satisfy objective (i) above. The circularisation of debtors is best considered as a standard procedure which will only be omitted in special circumstances. The circularisation will produce for the current audit file a written statement from each respondent debtor that the amount owed at the date of the circularisation is correct - this is *prima facie,* reliable audit evidence, being from an independent source and in 'documentary' form.

Turning to objective (ii) above, the auditor should, during the stocktake, have obtained details of the last serial numbers of goods outwards issued before the commencement of stocktaking. The following substantive tests are designed to test that goods taken into stock are not also treated as sales in the year under review and, conversely, goods despatched are treated as sales in the year under review and not also treated as stock.

(i) Check goods outwards and returns inwards notes around year end to ensure that:

(1) invoices and credit notes are dated in the correct period; and

(2) invoices and credit notes are posted to the sales ledger and nominal ledger in the correct period.

(ii) Reconcile entries in the sales ledger control around the year end to daily batch invoice totals ensuring batches are posted in correct year.

(iii) Review sales ledger control account around year end for unusual items.

(iv) Review material after date invoices and ensure that they are properly treated as following year sales.

(b) The audit work required on the various replies to a debtors' circularisation would be as follows.

(i) *Balances agreed by debtor*

Where the balance has been agreed by the debtor all that is required would be to ensure that the debt does appear to be collectable. This would be achieved by reviewing cash received after date or considering the adequacy of any provision made for a long outstanding debt.

(ii) *Balances not agreed by debtor*

All balance disagreements must be followed up and their effect on total debtors evaluated. Differences arising that merely represent invoices or cash in transit (which are normal timing differences) generally do not require adjustment, but disputed amounts, and errors by the client, may indicate that further substantive work is necessary to determine whether material adjustments are required.

(iii) *Debtor is unable to confirm the balance because of the form of records he maintains*

Certain companies, often computerised, operate systems which make it impossible for them to confirm the balance on their account. Typically in these circumstances their purchase ledger is merely a list of unpaid invoices. However, given sufficient information the debtor will be able to confirm that any given invoice is outstanding. Hence the auditor can circularise such enterprises successfully, but he will need to break down the total on the account into its constituent outstanding invoices.

(iv) *Debtor does not reply to circularisation*

When the positive request method is used the auditor must follow up by all practicable means those debtors who fail to respond. Second requests should be sent out in the event of no reply being received within two or three weeks and if necessary this may be followed by telephoning the customer with the client's permission. After two, or even three attempts to obtain confirmation, a list of the outstanding items will normally be passed to a responsible company official, preferably independent of the sales department, who will arrange for them to be investigated. This does not, of course, absolve the auditors from satisfying themselves that the clearance procedure is properly carried out and from examining the results. Where there is any limitation in the follow-up procedure it is all the more important to apply other auditing tests to establish that there existed a valid debt from a genuine customer at the date of the verification. Alternative procedures might include the following.

(1) Check receipt of cash after date.

(2) Verify valid purchase orders, if any.

(3) Examine the account to see if the balance represents specific outstanding invoices.

(4) Obtain explanations for invoices remaining unpaid after subsequent ones have been paid.

(5) See if the balance on the account is growing, and if so, why.

(6) Test company's control over the issue of credit notes and the write-off of bad debts.

5 BANK AND CASH

5.1 The objectives of the balance sheet audit work will be confined to determining whether:

(a) the amounts stated for bank balances, cash in transit and cash in hand are complete and properly described; and

(b) proper cut-off has been applied in the recording of cash transactions demonstrated by adequate reconciliations.

The day-to-day recording of cash book transactions is an integral part of the sales, purchases and wages/salaries cycles. Other receipts and payments relating to, for instance, purchase and sale of fixed assets are considered in this chapter under their appropriate headings.

Bank balances

5.2 The audit of bank balances will need to cover completeness, existence, ownership and valuation. All of these elements can be audited directly through the device of obtaining third party confirmations from the client's banks and reconciling these with the accounting records, having regard to cut-off.

The bank letter

5.3 The technique of the bank confirmation letter is the subject of a detailed operational guideline *Bank reports for audit purposes*. This is a somewhat more prescriptive guideline than most, for, as a result of consultation with the committees of the English and Scottish clearing banks, a standard audit request letter has been approved and prepared. On the following pages a specimen letter is reproduced.

AB & Co
Accountants
29 High Street
London N10

The Manager
Clearing Bank Ltd City Branch

Dear Sir/Madam,

....(Name of customer)
STANDARD REQUEST FOR BANK REPORT
FOR AUDIT PURPOSES FOR THE YEAR ENDED ....

In accordance with your above-named customer's instruction given

(1) hereon)
(2) in the attached authority) Delete as appropriate
(3) in the authority date .... already held by you)

please send to us, as auditors of your customer for the purpose of our business, without entering into any contractual relationship with us, the following information relating to their affairs at your branch as at the close of business on .... and, in the case of items 2, 4 and 10 during the period since .... For each item, please state any factors which may limit the completeness of your reply; if there is nothing to report, state 'none'.

We enclose an additional copy of this letter, and it would be particularly helpful if your reply could be given on the copy letter in the space provided (supported by an additional schedule stamped and signed by the bank where space is insufficient). If you find it necessary to provide the information in another form, please return the copy letter with your reply.

It is understood that any replies given are in strict confidence.

Information requested *Reply*

Bank accounts

(1) Please give full titles of all accounts whether in sterling or in any other currency together with the account numbers and balances thereon, including NIL balances:

(a) where your customer's name is the sole name in the title;

(b) where your customer's name is joined with that of other parties;

(c) where the account is in a trade name.

NOTES

(i) Where the account is subject to any restriction (eg a garnishee order or arrestment), this information should be stated.

(ii) Where the authority upon which you are providing this information does not cover any accounts held jointly with other parties, please refer to your customer in order to obtain the requisite authority of the other parties. If this authority is not forthcoming please indicate.

(2) Full titles and dates of closure of all accounts closed during the period.

(3) The separate amounts accrued but not charged or credited at the above date, of:

(a) provisional charges (including commitment fees); and

(b) interest.

(4) The amount of interest charged during the period if not specified separately in the bank statement.

(5) Particulars (ie date, type of document and accounts covered) of any written acknowledgement of set-off, either by specific letter of set-off, or incorporated in some other document or security.

(6) Details of:

(a) overdrafts and loans repayable on demand, specifying dates of review and agreed facilities;

(b) other loans specifying dates of review and repayment;

(c) other facilities.

Customer's assets held as security

(7) Please give details of any such assets whether or not formally charge to the bank.

If formally charged, give details of the security including the dates and type of charge. If a security is limited in amount or to a specific borrowing, or if there is to your knowledge a prior, equal or subordinate charge, please indicate.

If informally charged, indicate nature of security interest therein claimed by the bank.

Whether or not a formal charge has been taken, give particulars of any undertaking given to the bank relating to any assets.

Customer's other assets held

(8) Please give full details of the customer's other assets held, including share certificates, documents of title, deed boxes and any other items in your Registers maintained for the purpose of recording assets held.

Contingent liabilities

(9) All contingent liabilities, viz:

(a) total of bills discounted for your customer, with recourse;

(b) date, name of beneficiary, amount and brief description of any guarantees, bonds or indemnities given to you by the customer for the benefit of third parties;

(c) date, name of beneficiary, amount and brief description of any guarantees, bonds or indemnities given by you, on your customer's behalf, stating where there is recourse to your customer and/or to its parent or any other company within the group;

(d) total of acceptances;

(e) total sterling equivalent of outstanding forward foreign exchange contracts;

(f) total of outstanding liabilities under documentary credits;

(g) others - please give details.

Other information

(10) A list of other banks, or branches of your bank, or associated companies where you are aware that a relationship has been established during the period.

Yours faithfully,

....
(Official stamp of bank)

....
(Authorised signatory)

....
(Position)

5.4 The procedure is simple but important.

(a) The banks will require explicit written authority from their client to disclose the information requested.

(b) The auditor's request must refer to the client's letter of authority and the date thereof. Alternatively it may be countersigned by the client or it may be accompanied by a specific letter of authority.

(c) In the case of joint accounts, letters of authority signed by all parties will be necessary.

(d) Such letters of authority may either give permission to the Banks to disclose information for a specific request or grant permission for an indeterminate length of time.

(e) The request should reach the branch manager at least two weeks in advance of the client's year-end and should state both that year-end date and the previous year-end date.

(f) The auditor should himself check that the bank answers all the questions and, where the reply is not received direct from the bank, be responsible for establishing the authenticity of the reply.

(g) The standard letter should always be used in its complete form. Where further information is required a separate letter specifying the additional information should be sent. Note that the letter should only be used for audit purposes and not for the routine preparation of accounts.

(h) Note from the principal headings of the letter that the confirmations sought cover more than just the bank accounts, information is also requested concerning:

(i) customer's assets held as security;

(ii) customer's other assets held (as custodian);

(iii) contingent liabilities; and

(iv) other banks and branches that the respondent bank is aware have a relationship with the client.

5.5 It is, of course, essential that all points disclosed in the bank's reply should be followed up. For example, if question 10 in the specimen letter elicits a positive response, then unless the auditor has already sent a request for a report to the other banks concerned he should now do so.

Exercise 5

List the contents of a standard bank letter for audit purposes.

Solution

See Paragraph 5.3.

Reconciliation procedures

5.6 Bank reconciliations should be prepared by a person independent of those who handle receipts and payments. The reconciliation's should be checked by the auditor to the cash book and bank statements and cross-checked to the bank confirmation letter(s).

5.7 Care must be taken to ensure that there is no *window dressing*, by checking cut-off carefully. Window dressing in this context is usually manifested as an attempt to overstate the liquidity of the company by:

(a) keeping the cash book open to take credit for remittances actually received after the year end, thus enhancing the balance at bank and reducing debtors; and/or

(b) recording cheques paid in the period under review which are not actually despatched until after the year end, thus decreasing the balance at bank and reducing creditors.

A combination of (a) and (b) can contrive to present an artificially healthy looking current ratio.

5.8 With the possibility of (a) above in mind, where lodgements have not been cleared by the bank until the new period the auditor should examine the paying-in slip to ensure that the amounts were actually paid into the bank on or before the balance sheet date. As regards (b) above, where there appears to be a particularly large number of outstanding cheques at the year-end, the auditor should check whether these were cleared within a reasonable time in the new period. If not, this may indicate that despatch occurred after the year-end.

Cash balances

5.9 Cash balances/floats are often individually immaterial but they may require some audit emphasis because of the opportunities for irregularities that could exist where internal control is weak and because in total they may be material. In enterprises such as hotels, the amount of cash in hand at the balance sheet date could be considerable; the same goes for retail organisations.

5.10 Where the auditor determines that cash balances are potentially material he may conduct a cash count, ideally at the balance sheet date. Rather like attendance at stocktaking, the conduct of the count falls into three phases: planning, the count itself and follow up procedures. Planning is an essential element, for it is an important principle that all cash balances are counted at the same time as far as possible. Cash in this context may include *inter alia*, unbanked cheques received, IOUs and credit card slips, in addition to notes and coins. Physical verification of any securities should also take place at the same time. As part of his planning procedures the auditor will hence need to determine the locations where cash is held and which of these locations warrant a count. Planning decisions will need to be recorded on the current audit file including:

(a) the precise time of the count(s) and location(s);
(b) the names of the audit staff conducting the counts; and
(c) the names of the client staff intending to be present at each location.

Where a location is not visited it may be expedient to obtain a letter from the client confirming the balance.

5.11 The following matters apply to the count itself.

(a) All cash/petty cash books should be written up to date in ink (or other permanent form at the time of the count.

(b) All balances must be counted at the same time.

(c) All negotiable securities must be available and counted at the time the cash balances are counted.

(d) At no time should the auditor be left alone with the cash and negotiable securities.

(e) All cash and securities counted must be recorded on working papers subsequently filed on the current audit file. Reconciliations should be prepared where applicable (for example imprest petty cash float).

5.12 Follow up procedures should ensure that:

(a) unbanked cheques/cash receipts have subsequently been paid in and agree to the bank reconciliation;

(b) IOUs and cheques cashed for employees have been reimbursed; and

(c) the balances as counted are reflected in the accounts (subject to any agreed amendments because of shortages and so on).

Summary of cash and bank procedures

5.13 The following suggested substantive balance sheet tests summarise the principal audit procedures discussed above relevant to cash and bank balances.

(a) Obtain standard bank confirmations from each bank with which the client conducted business during the audit period;

(b) In respect of each bank account:

(i) obtain a reconciliation of the year end balance and check its arithmetical accuracy;

(ii) trace items outstanding from the bank reconciliation to the after date bank statements and record details of any items not cleared at the time of the audit;

(iii) verify by reference to pay-in slips that uncleared bankings are paid in prior to the year end;

(iv) verify the bank balances with reply to standard bank letter;

(v) scrutinise the cash book and bank statements before and after the balance sheet date for exceptional entries or transfers which have a material effect on the balance shown to be in hand.

Note. As regards (ii) above, ensure that all cheques are despatched immediately after signature and entry in the cash book. Examine the interval between dates of certain of the larger cheques in the cash book and payment by the bank since this may indicate that cheques were despatched after the year-end (window dressing).

(c) Identify whether any accounts are secured on the assets of the company.

(d) Consider whether there is a legal right of set-off of overdrafts against positive bank balances.

(e) Determine whether the bank accounts are subject to any restrictions.

(f) In respect of cash in hand:

(i) count cash balances held and agree to petty cash book or other record:

(1) count all balances simultaneously;

(2) all counting to be done in the presence of the individuals responsible;

(3) enquire into any IOUs or cashed cheques outstanding for unreasonable periods of time; or

(ii) obtain certificates of cash in hand from responsible officials.

(g) Confirm that bank and cash balances as reconciled above are correctly stated in the accounts.

Chapter roundup

- The disclosure and valuation requirements for all fixed assets under CA 1985 are relevant here.
- Third party confirmation and expert advice might be required to test the ownership and valuation of tangible fixed assets.
- Depreciation must be charged and disclosed according to SSAP 12 *Accounting for depreciation*.
- Intangible fixed assets, including goodwill, must be amortised. This may be a contentious area.
- Investments (if quoted) should be valued at mid-market price at the balance sheet date.
- The debtors figure can be one of the largest in a company's accounts. It is therefore very important from an audit point of view.
- A circularisation of trade debtors is a major procedure. The method of choosing a sample and performing the circularisation must be carefully thought out.
- The recoverability of debts can be tested by a combination of methods. The provision for bad debts can have a significant impact on profits.
- Bank balances are usually confirmed directly with the bank in question. The bank letter can be used to ask a variety of questions, including queries about outstanding interests, contingent liabilities and guarantees.
- Cash balances should be checked in case of irregularities.

Test your knowledge

1 What information should the auditor look out for when inspecting deeds to verify ownership of property? (see para 1.4)

2 What audit procedures might the auditor perform in respect of depreciation applied to tangible fixed assets? (1.13(d))

3 In what special circumstances may development expenditure be deferred? (2.8)

4 What audit work might the auditor perform in respect of investment income? (3.11)

5 In what circumstances might it be acceptable to carry out a debtors' circularisation prior to the year end to provide audit assurance as regards the balance sheet debtor figure? (4.5)

6 When might a 'positive' debtors' circularisation be undertaken? (4.8)

7 What classes of account require special attention when selecting a sample for a debtors' circularisation? (4.12)

8 What additional procedures should the auditor carry out when his circularisation is conducted prior to the year end? (4.17)

9 What procedures might the auditor carry out to determine whether the provision for bad and doubtful debts is reasonable? (4.21)

10 How might management seek to use the cash book at the year-end to 'window dress'? (5.7)

Chapter 14

SHARE CAPITAL, RESERVES AND LIABILITIES

This chapter covers the following topics.

1 Share capital, reserves and statutory books

2 Current liabilities

3 Long-term liabilities

Introduction

Some of the liability components of the balance sheet are technically quite difficult in that they are regulated by company law. This mainly applies to share capital and reserves. In this chapter we will try to avoid the more complex legalistic aspects of these items and concentrate on the fundamental auditing procedures involved.

In the case of other liabilities, circularisation for verification purposes is quite rare and other procedures are normally used. This can be one of the most sensitive areas of the audit as it affects the company's liquidity and gearing ratios and these may be closely related to bank borrowing covenants or debenture agreements.

1 SHARE CAPITAL, RESERVES AND STATUTORY BOOKS

1.1 This section discusses three areas which, although only tenuously related, are often bracketed together for audit purposes. The audit objectives are to ascertain that:

(a) share capital has been properly classified and disclosed in the financial statements and changes properly authorised;

(b) movements on reserves have been properly authorised and, in the case of statutory reserves, only used for permitted purposes;

(c) statutory records have been properly maintained and returns properly and expeditiously dealt with.

Share capital, reserves and distributions

1.2 The issued share capital as stated in the accounts must be agreed in total with the share register. Although the auditor does not usually carry out complete 'share transfer audits', an examination of transfers on a test basis should be made in those cases where a company handles its own registration work. Where the registration work is dealt with by independent registrars it is normally sufficient to examine the reports submitted by them to the company during the year and to obtain from them at the year-end a certificate of the share capital in issue.

1.3 Dividend payments should be checked on a sample basis to ascertain whether there are any outstanding dividends and unclaimed dividends unrecorded.

1.4 If shares have been issued at a premium it will be necessary to ensure that the share premium account has been properly credited. Special care will need to be taken if the company has purchased or redeemed any of its own shares (in the case of a private company such a purchase or redemption may be out of capital). Where such purchase or redemption is wholly or partly out of profits then a transfer must be made to capital redemption reserve equal to the nominal value of the shares purchased or redeemed less the proceeds of any fresh issue.

1.5 The following suggested substantive procedures are relevant.

(a) Agree the authorised share capital with the memorandum and articles of association. Agree any changes with properly authorised resolutions. File copy of certificate from the Registrar on the permanent file.

(b) Verify any issue of share capital or other changes during the year with the minutes and ensure issue or change is within the terms of the memorandum and articles of association.

(c) Verify transfers of shares by reference to:

(i) correspondence;
(ii) completed and stamped transfer forms;
(iii) cancelled share certificates; and
(iv) minutes of directors' meeting.

(d) Check the balances on shareholders' accounts in the register of members and the total list with the amount of issued share capital in the nominal ledger.

(e) Agree dividends paid and proposed to authority in minute books and check calculation with total share capital issued. (*Note*. It will also be necessary to check that the dividends do not contravene the distribution provisions of the Companies Act 1985.)

(f) Check dividend payments with documentary evidence (say, the returned dividend warrants).

(g) Check that advance corporation tax has been accounted for to the Inland Revenue and correctly treated in the accounts.

(h) Check movements on reserves to supporting authority. Scrutinise the minutes book for relevant resolutions. Ensure that movements are sanctioned by the Companies Act 1985 and the memorandum and articles of association. Confirm that the company can distinguish those reserves at the balance sheet date that are distributable from those that are non-distributable.

Statutory books

1.6 This heading includes eight items.

(a) The register of directors and secretaries
(b) The register of directors' interests in shares and debentures
(c) The minute books of general and directors' meetings
(d) The register of interests in shares (public companies only)
(e) The register of charges
(f) The accounting records
(g) Directors' service contracts
(h) The register of members (reviewed during the audit work on share capital)

1.7 In addition to the statutory books above, the auditor should also concern himself with the various regulatory returns to ensure that they have been filed promptly. With regard to accounting records, the auditor will need to be mindful of the requirements of the Act throughout his audit; nevertheless it is at the balance sheet stage that he must form an opinion as to whether proper accounting records have been kept. The auditor should also consider, at the same time, whether the nominal ledger and journal have been satisfactorily maintained.

1.8 Suggested substantive procedures are as follows.

(a) *Register of directors and secretaries*

(i) Update permanent file giving details of directors and secretary.

(ii) Verify any changes with the minutes and ensure that the necessary details have been filed at Companies House.

(iii) Verify that the number of directors complies with the regulations (if any) in the Articles.

(b) *Register of directors' interests in shares and debentures*

(i) Ensure that directors' interests are noted on the permanent file for cross-referencing to directors' reports.

(ii) Ensure that directors' shareholdings are in accordance with any requirements of the Articles.

(c) *Minute books*

(i) Obtain photocopies or prepare extracts from the minute books of meetings concerning financial matters, cross-referencing them to appropriate working papers. Ensure that extracts of agreements referred to in the minutes are prepared for the permanent file.

(ii) Check agreements with the company's seal book where one is kept.

(iii) Note the date of the last minute reviewed.

(iv) Check that meetings have been properly convened and that quorums attended them.

(d) *Register of interests in shares (if applicable)*

Scrutinise register and verify that *prima facie* it appears to be in order.

(e) *Register of charges*

(i) Update permanent file schedule from the register. Ensure that details of any assets which are charged as security for loans from third parties are disclosed in the accounts.

(ii) If no entries appear in the register, obtain verbal confirmation that there are no charges to be recorded.

(iii) Consider carrying out company search at Companies House to verify the accuracy of the register.

(f) *Accounting records*

Consider whether the accounting records are adequate:

(i) to show and explain the company's transactions;

(ii) to disclose with reasonable accuracy, at any time, the financial position of the company;

(iii) to comply with the Act by recording money received and expended, assets and liabilities, year-end stock and stock-taking, sales and purchases; and

(iv) to enable the directors to ensure that the accounts give a true and fair view.

(g) *Nominal ledger and journal*

(i) Check opening balances in nominal ledger to previous year's audited accounts.

(ii) Check additions of nominal ledger accounts.

(iii) Review nominal ledger accounts and ensure significant transfers and unusual items are *bona fide*.

(iv) Review the journal and ensure that significant entries are authorised and properly recorded.

(v) Check extraction and addition of trial balance (if prepared by the client).

(h) *Returns*

Check that the following returns have been filed properly:

(i) annual return and previous year's accounts;
(ii) notices of change in directors or secretary;
(iii) memoranda of charges or mortgages created during the period;
(iv) VAT returns; and
(v) other tax returns.

(i) *Directors' service contracts*

(i) Inspect copies of directors' service contracts or memoranda.

(ii) Ensure that they are kept at either:

(1) the registered office;

(2) the principal place of business; or

(3) the place where the register of members is kept, if not the registered office.

(iii) Verify that long-term service contracts (lasting more than five years) have been approved in general meeting.

Exercise 1

List the rules relating to the disclosure of reserves and provisions contained in the CA 1985.

Solution

Disclosures required by the Companies Act 1985 are as follows.

(a) *Profit retained for the financial year*. Any amount to be transferred to and from reserves must be disclosed separately on the face of the profit and loss account (Sch 4 paragraph 3(7)(a)).

(b) *Share premium account*. Disclose the opening and closing balances and movements (Sch 4 paragraph 46).

(c) *Revaluation reserve*. Disclose movements in all reserves and the opening and closing balances (Sch 4 paragraph 46).

(d) In group accounts disclose the cumulative amount of *goodwill* written off in relation to acquisitions in current and prior years, net of goodwill relating to disposals prior to the balance sheet date (Sch 4A paragraph 14).

(e) Disclose the amount of each of the *provisions* at the beginning and end of the year (Sch 4 paragraph 46).

(f) The *deferred tax provision* should be stated separately from any other tax provision (Sch 4 paragraph 47).

(g) Treatment for tax purposes of amounts credited or debited to the *revaluation reserve* should be disclosed (Sch 4 paragraph 34(4)).

2 CURRENT LIABILITIES

2.1 As with debtors, creditors are likely to be a material figure in the balance sheet of most enterprises. The purchases cycle transactions audit work will have provided the auditor with some assurance as to the completeness of liabilities but he should be particularly aware, when conducting his balance sheet work, of the possibility of understatement of liabilities. The primary objective of his balance sheet work will be to ascertain whether liabilities existing at the year-end have been completely and accurately recorded.

2.2 As regards *trade creditors*, this primary objective can be subdivided into two detailed objectives.

(a) Is there a satisfactory cut-off between goods received and invoices received, so that purchases and trade creditors are recognised in the correct year?

(b) Do trade creditors represent the *bona fide* amounts due by the company?

2.3 Before we ascertain how the auditor designs and conducts his tests with these objectives in mind, we need to establish the importance, as with trade debtors, of the list of balances.

Trade creditors listing and accruals listing

2.4 The list of balances will be the principal source from which the auditor will select his samples for testing. The listing should be extracted from the purchase ledger by the client. The auditor will carry out the following substantive tests to verify that the extraction has been properly performed:

(a) check from the purchase ledger accounts to the list of balances and *vice versa*;
(b) check the total of the list with the purchase ledger control account; and
(c) cast the list of balances and the purchase ledger control account.

The client should also prepare a detailed schedule of trade and sundry accrued expenses.

Purchases cut-off

2.5 The procedures applied by the auditor will be designed to ascertain whether:

(a) goods received for which no invoice has been received are accrued;

(b) goods received which have been invoiced but not yet posted are accrued; and

(c) goods returned to suppliers prior to the year-end are excluded from stock and trade creditors.

2.6 At the year-end stocktaking the auditor will have made a note of the last serial numbers of goods received notes. Suggested substantive procedures are as follows.

(a) Check from goods received notes with serial numbers before the year-end to ensure that invoices are either:

(i) posted to purchase ledger prior to the year-end; or
(ii) included on the schedule of accruals.

(b) Review the schedule of accruals to ensure that goods received after the year-end are not accrued.

(c) Check from goods returned notes prior to year-end to ensure that credit notes have been posted to the purchase ledger prior to the year-end or accrued.

(d) Review large invoices and credit notes included after the year-end to ensure that they refer to the following year.

(e) Reconcile daily batch invoice totals around the year-end to purchase ledger control ensuring batches are posted in the correct year.

(f) Review the control account around the year-end for any unusual items.

The creditors' circularisation

2.7 Verification of trade debtors by direct communication is virtually a standard procedure. Is it therefore also standard procedure to carry out a creditors' circularisation? The answer is a qualified 'No'. The principal reason for this lies in the nature of the purchases cycle: third party evidence in the form of suppliers' invoices and even more significantly, suppliers' statements, are part of the standard documentation of the cycle. The auditor will hence concentrate on these documents when designing and conducting his tests to gain assurance in respect of objective (b) in Paragraph 2.2: 'Do trade creditors represent *bona fide* amounts due by the company?'.

2.8 In the following circumstances the auditor may, however, determine that a circularisation is necessary.

(a) Where suppliers' statements are, for whatever reason, unavailable or incomplete.

(b) Where weaknesses in internal control or the nature of the client's business make possible a material misstatement of liabilities that would not otherwise be picked up.

(c) Where it is thought that the client is deliberately trying to understate creditors.

(d) Where the accounts appear to be irregular or if the nature or size of balances or transactions is abnormal.

In these cases confirmation requests should be sent out and processed in a similar way to debtors' confirmation requests. 'Positive' requests will be the order of the day in these circumstances.

2.9 In normal circumstances the following substantive procedures, based on the accounting records and documentation maintained and retained by the company, will be performed.

(a) Select from the trade creditors listing and check to supporting documentation (invoices, goods received notes, purchase orders, and so on) that the purchase was for the purpose of the business.

(b) Reconcile a sample of purchase ledger balances with suppliers' statements.

(c) Review balances for unusually low balances with major suppliers.

(d) Compare ratio of trade creditors to purchases with previous year's figures.

(e) Compare ratio of trade creditors to stock with previous year's figures.

(f) Verify reasonableness of deductions from liability figures (such as discounts) by reference to subsequent events.

(g) Ascertain reasons for significant debit balances.

Purchase of goods subject to reservation of title clauses

2.10 We have already mentioned briefly the existence of transactions where the seller may retain legal ownership of goods passed to a 'purchaser' in the context of the audit of debtors. The main burden is, however, on the auditor of the purchaser not the seller. We now look at the audit implications of such 'reservation of title clauses' in more detail.

2.11 It would seem, following *Borden (UK) Limited v Scottish Timber Products, Re Bond Worth* and the earlier *Romalpa* case, that a reservation of title clause will only be upheld if it states that:

(a) the legal ownership of the goods remains with the vendor while they stay in their original state;

(b) the 'purchaser' holds the goods as bailee and, where he is permitted to dispose of them to his customers, he acts as agents for the vendor;

(c) where the goods are to be incorporated by the 'purchaser' into his products, the vendor has a charge over the products for the money owed to him (this charge will need to be registered under the Companies Act 1985);

(d) the goods, any products made from them and any sale proceeds are kept separately and are readily identifiable.

The practical consequences of (c) and (d) are likely to reduce the popularity of reservation clauses.

2.12 The existence of this type of transaction will place an additional burden on the auditor of the purchaser. One point of special importance is the relevance of the going concern concept to the accounting treatment adopted.

2.13 Generally, the auditor's approach should be as follows.

(a) Ascertain what steps the client takes to identify suppliers selling on terms which reserve title by enquiry of those responsible for purchasing and of the board.

(b) Ascertain what steps are taken to quantify the liability to such suppliers for balance sheet purposes, including liabilities not yet reflected in the creditors ledger.

(c) Where there are material liabilities to such suppliers:

(i) if the liabilities are quantified in the accounts, review and test the procedures by which the amounts disclosed have been computed;

(ii) if the directors consider that quantification is impracticable, but have either estimated the liabilities or indicated their existence, review and test the information upon which their disclosure is based;

(iii) consider the adequacy of the information disclosed in the accounts;

(iv) ensure that the basis on which the charge for taxation is computed takes account of the accounting treatment adopted and, where necessary, is adequately disclosed.

(d) Where liabilities to such suppliers are said not to exist or to be immaterial, review the terms of sale of major suppliers to confirm that this is so.

(e) Obtain formal written representation from the directors either that there are no material liabilities of this nature to be disclosed or that the information disclosed is, in their view, as accurate as it is reasonably possible to achieve.

2.14 It will be appreciated that the above procedures should, where applicable, be carried out as an integral part of the balance sheet audit of trade creditors, though the existence of suppliers selling on terms which reserve title (procedure (a)) should be clarified as early as possible in the audit to assist the balance sheet work.

Verification of sundry accruals: creditors and provisions

2.15 Sundry accruals is an area that lends itself to analytical review and reconciliation techniques, although care must be taken with statutory liabilities such as PAYE and VAT where there is, arguably, an expectation that the auditor verifies these liabilities regardless of materiality.

2.16 The following substantive procedures are suggested.

(a) From the client's sundry accruals listing check that accruals are fairly calculated and verify by reference to subsequent payments.

Note. For PAYE and VAT the following approach should be adopted.

(i) PAYE. Normally this should represent one month's deductions. Check amount paid to Revenue by inspecting receipted annual declaration of tax paid over, or returned cheque.

(ii) VAT. Check reasonableness to next VAT return. Verify paid cheque for last amount paid in year.

(b) Review the profit and loss account and prior years' figures and consider liabilities inherent in the trade to ensure that all likely accruals have been provided.

(c) Scrutinise payments made after year-end to ascertain whether any payments made should be accrued.

(d) Consider and document basis for round sum accruals and ensure it is consistent with prior years.

(e) Ascertain why any payments on account are being made and ensure that the full liability is provided.

(f) Review list of sundry accruals against previous year's figures and liabilities expected.

(g) **For provisions (other than provisions for depreciation, tax and bad debts):**

(i) **prepare a schedule of any provisions indicating their purpose and basis, showing details of movement during the period;**

(ii) **decide whether any of the provisions are sufficiently material to be separately disclosed in the accounts.**

Inter-company indebtedness

2.17 The same procedures apply as discussed in the section on inter-company indebtedness in the last chapter.

Exercise 2

In January 19X1 you carried out an interim audit of Bradley Headstone Ltd, a medium sized manufacturing company. This audit revealed no significant areas of weakness.

Required

Draft a final audit programme to cover purchases and trade creditors.

Solution

FINAL AUDIT PROGRAMME: PURCHASES AND TRADE CREDITORS

Trade creditors listing and accruals listing

(a) Check the balances from the purchase ledger accounts to the list of balances and *vice versa*.

(b) Check the total of the list of balances to the purchase ledger control account.

(c) Cast the list of balances and the purchase ledger control account.

Purchases cut-off

(a) Check from goods received notes with serial numbers before the year-end to ensure that invoices are either:

(i) posted to purchase ledger prior to the year-end; or
(ii) included on the schedule of accruals.

(b) Review the schedule of accruals to ensure that goods received after the year-end are not accrued.

(c) Check from goods returned notes before the year-end to ensure that credit notes have been posted to the purchase ledger prior to the year-end or accrued.

(d) Review large invoices and credit notes included after the year-end to ensure that they refer to the following year.

(e) For the period around the year-end, reconcile daily batch invoice totals to purchase ledger control to confirm that batches are posted in the correct year.

(f) Review the control account around the year-end for any unusual items.

Completeness, existence and ownership

(a) Consider the effectiveness of a creditors' circularisation and perform if necessary.

(b) Select from the trade creditors listing and check to supporting documentation (invoices, goods received notes, purchase orders, and so on) that the purchase was for the purpose of the business.

(c) Reconcile a sample of purchase ledger balances with suppliers' statements.

(d) Review balances for unusually low balances with major suppliers.

(e) Compare ratio of trade creditors to purchases with previous year's figures.

(f) Compare ratio of trade creditors to stock with previous year's figures.

(g) Verify reasonableness of deductions from liability figures (such as discounts) by reference to subsequent events.

(h) Ascertain reasons for significant debit balances.

General

(a) Check whether any goods have been purchased subject to reservation of title ('Romalpa') clauses.

(b) Follow up any queries or work left unfinished after the interim audit.

3 LONG-TERM LIABILITIES

3.1 We are concerned here with long-term liabilities comprising debentures, loan stock and other loans repayable at a date more than one year after the year-end.

3.2 The auditor's objective will be to determine whether long-term liabilities are properly classified and disclosed in the accounts and that the associated interest has been charged to the profit and loss account correctly and consistently.

3.3 The major complication for the auditor is that debenture and loan agreements frequently contain conditions with which the company must comply, including restrictions on the company's total borrowings and adherence to specific borrowing ratios. Furthermore, the auditor is sometimes specifically engaged to monitor and report to the debenture/loan stock trustees on the company's adherence to these conditions.

Substantive procedures applicable to all audits

3.4 The following suggested substantive procedures are relevant.

(a) Obtain/prepare schedule of loans outstanding at the balance sheet date showing, for each loan: name of lender, date of loan, maturity date, interest date, interest rate, balance at the end of the period and security.

(i) Compare opening balances to previous year's papers.

(ii) Test the clerical accuracy of the analysis.

(iii) Compare balances to the nominal ledger.

(iv) Check name of lender etc, to register of debenture holders or equivalent (if kept).

(v) Trace additions and repayments to entries in the cash book.

(vi) Examine cancelled cheques and memoranda of satisfaction for loans repaid.

(vii) Verify that borrowing limits imposed either by Articles or by other agreements are not exceeded.

(viii) Examine signed Board minutes relating to new borrowings/repayments.

(b) Obtain direct confirmation from lenders of the amounts outstanding and what security they hold.

(c) Verify interest charged for the period and the adequacy of accrued interest.

(d) Review the permanent files to ensure that appropriate extracts from current loan agreements and other relevant information are included and that changes made during the year are appropriately noted.

(e) Review restrictive covenants and provisions relating to default:

(i) review any correspondence relating to the loan;
(ii) review confirmation replies for non-compliance;
(iii) if a default appears to exist, determine its effect, and schedule findings.

Note. The above review should be conducted regardless of whether the auditor has a specific responsibility to report to the trustees under the terms of the loan agreement(s).

Reports to debenture and loan stock trustees

3.5 A company which issues debentures or loan stock will usually enter into an agreement with the trustees for the stockholders. This trust deed will usually impose certain restrictions on the company's activities (for example by placing a limit on its borrowings). It is also common for the deed to contain a provision for an annual report from the company's auditors as to the company's compliance or non-compliance with the trust deed. The form of the report may be specified by the trustees.

Exercise 3

You are the audit senior at Blacklock plc, a large steel-producing company. The company has suffered in the recession and it is heavily geared. A recent restructuring of the company's debt is expected to aid recovery. While reviewing the new loan agreements you read the following.

'The following covenants will apply and any breach will lead to immediate foreclosure on the debt herein.

1 The audited accounts shall show interest cover (profit before interest and tax compared to interest charged) greater than or equal to two times.

2 The audited accounts shall show a gearing ratio of the company (*total* debt, including overdraft, compared to total capital) less than or equal to 80%.'

Required

State the audit procedures you would carry out to check that the restrictive covenants have not been breached.

Solution

Our first problem is that the accounts have not yet been audited. We can however carry out various procedures on the draft accounts.

(a) Calculate interest cover and gearing according to the method listed in the agreement.

(b) Compare the interest cover and gearing according to the method listed in the agreement.

Where the calculated figures are within the limits set, it will be necessary to determine the risk that the figures in the draft accounts are not accurate. If any numbers are changed during the audit then the results of the calculations performed in (a) may also change. This risk can be calculated and expressed in terms of a percentage rise or fall which would pass the danger point. For example, 'the interest cover covenant will be broken if the interest charge is increased by 20%'. These calculations can be made for all the component figures.

These results should be recorded for review by the partner and cross-referenced to those sections of the audit which might impinge on the loan covenants.

(a) The audit of the interest expense.

(b) The audit of creditors, both long and short term.

(c) The audit of bank and cash, particularly the overdraft and any undisclosed liabilities highlighted by the bank confirmation letter.

(d) The overall analytical review of the draft results.

Where the covenants appear to have been breached the partner should be informed immediately and a meeting should be arranged with the client to discuss the matter. It may be necessary to institute a going concern review, to estimate the value of the company on a break up basis, rather than as a going concern.

All correspondence relating to the loan should be reviewed.

Chapter roundup

- Share capital, reserves and statutory books will usually be examined together in an audit.
- The main concern with share capital and reserves (including distributions) will be that all transactions comply with CA 1985.
- The largest figure in current liabilities will normally be trade creditors.
- A creditors' circularisation might be appropriate, although they are relatively rare in practice compared to the frequency of debtors' circularisations.
- Accruals can be significant in total. Expense accruals will tend to repeat from one year to the next.
- Long term liabilities are usually authorised by the board and should be well documented.

Test your knowledge

1 What statutory books are required by the Companies Act 1985? (see para 1.6)

2 How would you check that a list of purchase ledger balances has been correctly extracted? (2.4)

3 In what circumstances might the auditor decide that a creditors' circularisation is necessary? (2.8)

4 What procedures might the auditor adopt to establish whether his client purchases goods sold subject to reservation of title and to assess the impact on the accounts, if any? (2.13)

5 What substantive procedures should the auditor undertake in relation to restrictive covenants on long term loans? (3.4(e))

Chapter 15

AUDITING IN A COMPUTER ENVIRONMENT

This chapter covers the following topics.

Introduction

Auditing in a computer environment requires special knowledge and skills. It is true to say, however, that the principles of auditing and internal controls, discussed in earlier chapters, still apply. You should bear this in mind as you work through this chapter.

Those students who have direct experience of working with computers (not just in an audit context) will obviously have an advantage in this area. Make sure you can relate the 'theory' of this chapter to the practical situations you meet at work.

Those of you who do not have hands on computer experience should not worry too much as far as this Tutorial Text is concerned. Learn the technical terms and particularly the controls necessary in a computer system and then apply auditing principles as normal. A computer system performs the same functions as a manual system, but it is more sophisticated and therefore requires more sophisticated auditing techniques. Remember, though, that you may be asked to show experience of auditing in an IT environment.

1 COMPUTERS IN AUDITING

1.1 The use of computers has increased dramatically over the last ten years. It is unusual to find a business, whatever its size, without a computer of some sort. We will consider how the computerisation of client records affects the auditor in the rest of the chapter. To begin with, however, we will consider how auditors use computers themselves, as an audit tool.

1.2 Until recently, auditing firms used computers for very basic administrative functions, such as time records, word processing and basic mathematical tasks. Programs have now been developed which allow more sophisticated use of computers in the audit.

Working papers

1.3 Automated working paper packages have now been developed which can make the documenting of audit work much easier. Such programs will aid preparation of working papers, lead schedules, trial balance and the financial statements themselves. These are automatically cross referenced and balanced by the computer.

1.4 There are obviously great advantages to automated working papers. Whenever an adjustment is made, the computer will automatically update all the necessary schedules, including the trial balance, rather than the auditor having to do so manually (a laborious task!). The risk of errors is reduced and the working papers produced will be neater and easier to review. The time saved is substantial, as adjustments can be added, changed or reversed and all working papers will automatically updated.

1.5 Another advantage is the way the ratios and statistics which the auditor relies on to make informed judgements will also be changed each time an adjustment is made. The auditor can use the updated ratios throughout the audit to make decisions.

1.6 The development of a system of electronic audit working 'papers' to replace the paper-based files of completed standard audit working paper forms which still characterise so much auditing work is as the heart of automating the audit. Eventually, standard forms will no longer have to be carried to audit locations. It will not be necessary for an audit manager to visit auditors 'in the field' in order to review completed audit working paper files: these can now be transmitted to the audit manager at audit HQ or at home for review. This can be done from the auditor's laptop via a modem to the audit firm's or department's equivalent computer. Alternatively the fax facility can be used, with no need for hard copy to be produced if both the sending and receiving computers have fax boards and fax software.

1.7 Standard word processing software is all that is needed to develop and use a reasonably satisfactory system of electronic audit working papers. Standard audit working paper forms can be designed to be called up and completed on the computer screen. Of course the same word processing software will have other audit uses, notably for drafting the audit report, preferably towards the end of the audit field work. Tailor-made audit working paper software may have special advantages as it can be designed to allow logical steps to be automated, as follows.

(a) *Automated checking of electronic working papers for completeness*

   (i) Is there evidence of supervision and review on each schedule?
   (ii) Is there an audit conclusion on each lead schedule?
   (iii) Have all points raised by the auditors on 'audit point sheets' been answered?

(b) *Automated checking of electronic working papers for accuracy*

   (i) Are all the totals of numeric data consistent?
   (ii) Do numeric totals carry forward accurately to lead schedule?

(c) *Automated processing*

   (i) Footing and crossfooting (standard word processing software can also do this).
   (ii) Carry forward of numeric data to lead schedules.
   (iii) Highlight proposed audit recommendations for audit management review.
   (iv) Consolidate and reformat material contained within the audit working papers in order to prepare the draft audit report.

1.8 More generally, the audit can be assisted or facilitated by software dealing with graphics production image processing and desk-top publishing. Auditors may also benefit from on-line accessing and real-time file updating.

Statistical sampling and analytical review

1.9 Auditors can now use microcomputer packages to perform analytical review procedures. These packages are most useful when information can be input directly from the client's computer system. This information can be added to year after year, building up cumulative data.

1.10 Such information can also be used for statistical sampling. The package can then perform such tasks as determining sample sizes, computing standard ratios, generating random numbers from a given sequence and evaluating results from tests based on samples.

Decision support systems

1.11 These systems are, on the whole, still in the development stage. They involve judgemental processes which would normally only be carried out by a 'human' auditor. The main developments in this area include the automation of checklists, such as those used for internal control evaluation, statutory requirements and materiality estimations. These checklists are formulates so as to follow different logic paths in response to answers given at various stages of the checklist, including omitting questions.

Controls over audit computers

1.12 As with all computers (as we will see in later sections of this chapter), controls must be exercised over the input, processing and output of computers used on an audit. The main areas where controls should operate are:

(a) security;
(b) completeness (of input); and
(c) accuracy (of input, processing and output).

Exercise 1

(a) List two types of software which the auditor could use with a microcomputer as an aid to audit work.

(b) List five ways in which the auditor could use a microcomputer as an audit aid.

(c) What controls must be in place over a microcomputer used in an audit?

Solution

(a) Examples of software which the auditor might use on a microcomputer in order to aid his audit work are as follows.

(i) Standard software for word processing and spreadsheets which can be used to carry out the tasks listed in (b) below.

(ii) 'Expert' systems (often developed in house by the large audit firms) which will determine sample sizes based on specified risk criteria.

(b) A microcomputer may be used by the auditor in order to assist his audit work as follows.

(i) The production of time budgets and budgetary control. The time budget by area for the audit can be produced on the microcomputer and actual hours worked can be input to obtain a variance. The variance which arises on the interim audit can be used as a basis for updating the final audit time budget.

(ii) The production of working papers, in particular lead schedules, trial balances and schedules of errors.

(iii) Analytical review procedures can be more efficiently carried out on a microcomputer as the necessary calculations can be carried out at much greater speed and year-on-year information built up.

(iv) The production and retention of audit programmes. These can then be reviewed and updated from year to year.

(v) The maintenance of permanent file information (for example systems) which can be updated from one year to the next.

Note. Other uses might include the evaluation of internal controls, the selection of audit samples.

(c) Controls which must be exercised when microcomputers are used by the auditor in his work are as follows.

(i) Access controls for users by means of passwords.

(ii) Back-up of data contained on files, regular production of hard copy; back-up disks held off the premises.

(iii) Viral protection for programmes.

(iv) Training for users.

(v) Evaluation and testing of programs before use.

(vi) Proper recording of input data, to ensure reasonableness of output.

2 CONTROLS IN A COMPUTER ENVIRONMENT

2.1 The use of computers for accounting purposes has dramatically increased in recent years. This expansion will certainly continue and the auditor must hence be able to cope with the special problems that arise when auditing in a computer environment and keep abreast of technical innovation.

2.2 First we look in a rather general way at the nature of controls in a computer environment and the auditor's operational approach. Broad guidance is provided for the auditor in the form of the operational guideline *Auditing in a computer environment*. The introduction to this guideline sets the scene.

> 'The auditor's operational standard and the guidelines on planning, controlling and recording, accounting systems, audit evidence, internal controls and review of financial statements apply irrespective of the system of recording and processing transactions. However, computer systems do record and process transactions in a manner which is significantly different from manual systems, giving rise to such possibilities as a lack of visible evidence and systematic errors. As a result, when auditing in a computer environment, the auditor will need to take into account additional considerations relating to the techniques available to him, the timing of his work, the form in which the accounting records are maintained, the internal controls which exist, the availability of the data and the length of time it is retained in readily usable form, as further described below.'

2.3 Internal controls over computer based accounting systems may conveniently be considered under the following two main headings.

(a) *Application controls*. These relate to the transactions and standing data appertaining to each computer-based accounting system and are therefore specific to each such application. The objectives of application controls, which may be manual or programmed, are to ensure the completeness and accuracy of the accounting records and the validity of the entries made in these records resulting from both manual and programmed processing.

(b) *General controls*. These are controls, other than application controls, which relate to the environment within which computer based accounting systems are developed, maintained and operated, and which are therefore applicable to all the applications. The objectives of general controls are to ensure the proper development and implementation of applications and the integrity of program and data files and of computer operations. Like application controls, general controls may be either manual or programmed.

2.4 Application controls and general controls are inter-related. Strong general controls contribute to the assurance which may be obtained by an auditor in relation to application controls. On the other hand, unsatisfactory general controls may undermine strong application controls or exacerbate unsatisfactory application controls.

2.5 The draft version of the auditing guideline *Auditing in a computer environment* contained useful appendices identifying typical, and desirable, application and general controls. The authorised guideline did not retain these appendices; nevertheless, a relatively detailed knowledge of controls is useful, so the appendices are reproduced below.

Examples of application controls

2.6 To achieve the overall objectives of application controls identified above, the specific requirements are:

(a) controls over the completeness, accuracy and authorisation of input;

(b) controls over the completeness and accuracy of processing;

(c) controls over the maintenance of master files and the standing data contained therein.

Controls over input

2.7 Control techniques for ensuring the completeness of input in a timely fashion include:

(a) manual or programmed agreement of control totals;

(b) one for one checking of processed output to source documents;

(c) manual or programmed sequence checking;

(d) programmed matching of input to a control file, containing details of expected input;

(e) procedures over resubmission of rejected controls.

2.8 Controls over the accuracy of input are concerned with the data fields on input transactions. Control should be exercised not only over value fields, such as invoice amounts, but also important reference fields, such as account number or date of payment. Some of the completeness control techniques, such as a batch total, will also control accuracy but others, such as sequence checks, will not. Additional techniques to ensure accuracy include:

(a) programmed check digit verification (a check digit included in a reference number is arithmetically checked to ensure that it bears the required relationship to the rest of the number);

(b) programmed reasonableness checks, including checking the logical relationship between two or more files;

(c) programmed existence checks against valid codes;

(d) manual scrutiny of output.

2.9 Controls over authorisation involve checking that all transactions are authorised and that the individual who authorised each transaction was so empowered. This will generally involve a clerical review of input transactions, although a programmed check to detect transactions that exceed authorisation limits may be possible. The clerical review should be done either after a control total has been established or after processing, to ensure that unauthorised transactions cannot be introduced after the review.

Controls over processing

2.10 Controls are required to ensure that:

(a) all input data is processed;

(b) the correct master files and standing data files are used;

(c) the processing of each transaction is accurate;

(d) the updating of data, and any new data generated during processing, is accurate and authorised;

(e) output reports are complete and accurate.

2.11 The control techniques used to ensure the completeness and accuracy of input may also be used to ensure the completeness and accuracy of processing provided the techniques are applied to the results of processing, such as a batch reconciliation produced after the update and not the one produced after the initial edit. Another technique for ensuring the completeness and accuracy of processing is summary processing.

Controls over master files and the standing data contained therein

2.12 Techniques for ensuring the completeness, accuracy and authorisation of amendments to master files and standing data files and for ensuring the completeness and accuracy of the processing of these amendments are similar to the techniques for transaction input. However, in view of the greater importance of master files and standing data, there is often sufficient justification for using the more costly control techniques such as one for one checking. It may also be appropriate to users to check all master files and standing data, perhaps on a cyclical basis.

Controls are also required to ensure the continuing correctness of master files and the standing data contained therein. Frequently control techniques such as record counts or hash totals for the file, are established and checked by the user each time the file is used.

Examples of general controls

2.13 To achieve the overall objectives of general controls identified in Paragraph 2.3(b) above, controls are required:

(a) over application development;
(b) to prevent or detect unauthorised changes to programs;
(c) to ensure that all program changes are adequately tested and documented;
(d) to prevent or detect errors during program execution;
(e) to prevent unauthorised amendments to data files;
(f) to ensure that systems software is properly installed and maintained;
(g) to ensure that proper documentation is kept; and
(h) to ensure continuity of operations.

Controls over application development

2.14 The auditor might consider the adequacy of such matters as: system design standards, programming standards, documentation controls and standards, testing procedures, approval of development stages by users and computer management, internal audit involvement, segregation of duties for system design, programming and operations, training and supervision.

Controls to prevent or detect unauthorised changes to programs

2.15 This covers both accidental and fraudulent corruption of program logic during program maintenance or program execution. In addition to such matters as the segregation of duties and the training and supervision of staff for program maintenance, the auditor would consider such matters as: authorisation of jobs prior to processing, the record of program changes and its review to detect unauthorised changes, password protection of programs, emergency modification procedures, integrity of back up copies of programs, physical protection of production programs and programs stored off-line, and comparison of production programs to controlled copies. For program execution, the auditor would consider: the operations manual procedures to prevent access to programs during execution, controls over use of utility programs, restricted access to the computer and remote terminals, review of job accounting reports and investigation of unusual delays, and rotation of duties.

Controls to ensure that all program changes are adequately tested and documented

2.16 As program changes may range from a small alteration of an output report to a major redesign, most installations will have more than one set of standards for testing and documenting changes. The auditor would consider the adequacy of such matters as: testing procedures, documentation controls and standards, approval of changes by users and computer management, internal audit involvement, and segregation of duties, training and supervision of the staff involved.

Controls to prevent or detect errors during program execution

2.17 The auditor might consider the adequacy of operations controls included in the systems software, use of job control procedure libraries, an operations manual detailing set up and execution procedures, job scheduling, emergency back up procedures and training and supervision. These procedures should provide protection against errors such as incorrect data files, wrong versions of production programs, running programs in the wrong sequence, incorrect response to a program request and job control errors.

Controls to prevent unauthorised amendment to data files

2.18 Controls to prevent unauthorised amendments to data files are dependent upon the application controls over the file, the manner in which the file is maintained and the file management software used. The auditor might consider the adequacy of such general control procedures as: authorisation of jobs prior to processing, procedures to detect unauthorised amendments, password protection and procedures for recording and investigating unauthorised access attempts, emergency modification procedures, integrity of back up files, physical protection of data files, restricted use of utility programs and the segregation of duties.

Controls to ensure that systems software is properly installed and maintained

2.19 Systems software includes the operating system, teleprocessing monitors, data base management systems, spooling systems and other software used to increase the efficiency of processing and to control processing. The auditor should consider not only the controls exercised by the software but also the controls over the software, such as: frequency of amendments, amendment procedures, access controls and the segregation of duties.

Controls to ensure that proper documentation is kept

2.20 Proper documentation aids efficient and accurate operations by users and computer personnel, setting up and amendments to applications, and recovery from disaster. The auditor would consider such matters as: quality of documentation, quality of standards used, enforcement of standards, internal audit involvement and updating procedures.

Controls to ensure continuity of operation

2.21 As part of his overall assessment of the enterprise the auditor might consider the back up procedures, testing of back up facilities and procedures, protection of equipment against fire and other hazards, emergency and disaster recovery procedures, maintenance agreements and insurance.

3 THE AUDITOR'S OPERATIONAL APPROACH

3.1 Audits are performed in a computer environment wherever computer-based accounting systems, large or small, are operated by an enterprise, or by a third party on behalf of the enterprise, for the purpose of processing information supporting the amounts included in the financial statements.

3.2 The nature of computer-based accounting systems is such that the auditor is afforded opportunities to use either the enterprise's or another computer to assist him in the performance of his audit work. Techniques performed with computers in this way are known as Computer Assisted Audit Techniques (CAATs) of which the following are the major categories.

(a) *Use of audit software:* computer programs used for audit purposes to examine the contents of the enterprise's computer files.

(b) *Use of test data:* data used by the auditor for computer processing to test the operation of the enterprise's computer programs.

Audit software and test data are considered in detail later in the chapter.

3.3 Where there is a computer-based accounting system, many of the auditor's procedures may still be carried out manually. For instance, the ascertainment of the accounting system and the assessment of its adequacy will normally be performed manually, and in appropriate circumstances the auditor may also decide to select manual audit techniques.

Knowledge and skills

3.4 When auditing in a computer environment, the auditor should obtain a basic understanding of the fundamentals of data processing and a level of technical computer knowledge and skills which, depending on the circumstances, may need to be extensive. This is because the auditor's knowledge and skills need to be appropriate to the environment in which he is auditing, and because ethical statements indicate that he should not undertake or continue professional work which he is not himself competent to perform unless he obtains such advice and assistance as will enable him competently to carry out his task. The impact of the computer environment on the conduct of the audit is now considered by looking at each paragraph of the operational standard in turn.

Planning, controlling and recording

3.5 'The auditor should adequately plan, control and record his work.' The principles relating to planning, controlling and recording are the same in a computer environment as in other circumstances, but there are additional considerations that need to be taken into account.

Planning

3.6 In order to plan and carry out an audit in a computer environment, the auditor will need an appropriate level of technical knowledge and skill. As part of his additional planning considerations, he should decide at an early stage what effect the system itself and the way it is operated, will have on the timing of and the manner in which he will need to perform and record his work. In this respect he may have had the opportunity to consider these matters during the development and implementation of the system.

3.7 The auditor should also consider the use of CAATs, as this may have a significant effect on the nature, extent and timing of his audit tests. As indicated in Paragraph 3.8 below, in certain circumstances the auditor will need to use CAATs in order to obtain the evidence he requires, whereas in other circumstances he may use CAATs to improve the efficiency or effectiveness of his audit. For example, the availability of audit software may mean that substantive tests can be performed more economically or quickly than substantive tests performed manually, which may persuade him to place less reliance on internal controls and to reduce his compliance testing accordingly.

3.8 In choosing the appropriate combination of CAATs and manual procedures, the auditor will need to take the following points into account.

(a) Computer programs often perform functions of which no visible evidence is available. In these circumstances it will frequently not be practicable for the auditor to perform tests manually.

(b) In many audit situations the auditor will have the choice of performing a test either manually or with the assistance of a CAAT. In making this choice, he will be influenced by the respective efficiency of the alternatives, taking into account:

(i) the extent of compliance or substantive testing achieved by both alternatives;

(ii) the pattern of cost associated with the CAAT;

(iii) the ability to incorporate within the use of the CAAT a number of different audit tests.

(c) In some cases, the auditor will need to report within a comparatively short time-scale. In such cases it may be more efficient to use CAATs because they are quicker to apply, even though manual methods are practicable and may cost less.

(d) There is a need before using a CAAT to ensure that the required computer facilities, computer files and programs are available. Furthermore, given that enterprises do not retain copies of computer files and programs for an indefinite period, the auditor should plan the use of any CAAT in good time so that these copies are retained for his use.

(e) The operation of some CAATs requires frequent attendance or access by the auditor. The auditor may be able to reduce the level of his tests by taking account of CAATs performed by the internal auditors, but the extent to which he can do this in any given situation will depend, amongst other things, on his assessment of the effectiveness and relevance of the internal audit function.

(f) Where the enterprise's accounting records include computer data, the auditor will need to have access to that data. Further, where the auditor wishes to perform a CAAT, it is often necessary for the enterprise to make computer facilities available to the auditor to enable him to discharge his responsibilities.

Controlling

3.9 Whether or not the audit is being carried out in a computer environment, audit procedures should always be controlled to ensure that the work has been performed in a competent manner. Where CAATs are used, however, particular attention should be paid to:

(a) the need to co-ordinate the work of staff with specialist computer skills with the work of others engaged on the audit;

(b) the approval and review of the technical work by someone with the necessary computer expertise.

It is acceptable for an auditor to use a CAAT on copies of computer records or programs, provided he has taken steps to gain reasonable assurance that the copies are identical to the originals.

Recording

3.10 The standard of the audit working papers relating to computer-based accounting systems, and the retention procedures in respect of them, should be the same as those adopted in relation to other aspects of the audit.

3.11 Where a CAAT is used, it is appropriate that the working papers indicate the work performed by the CAAT, the results of the CAAT, the auditor's conclusions, the manner in which any technical problems were resolved and may include any recommendations about the modification of the CAAT for future audits.

Accounting systems

3.12 'The auditor should ascertain the enterprise's system of recording and processing transactions and assess its adequacy as a basis for the preparation of financial statements.' The principles relating to this are the same in a computer environment, but it should be borne in mind that many computer-based accounting systems are specified in far greater detail than non-computer-based accounting systems.

Audit evidence

3.13 'The auditor should obtain relevant and reliable audit evidence sufficient to enable him to draw reasonable conclusions therefrom.' The principles relating to the obtaining of audit evidence do not change because the audit is being carried out in a computer environment.

3.14 However, the availability of computer facilities results in opportunities for auditors to use computers. CAATs may be used at various stages of an audit to obtain audit evidence. For instance where the auditor chooses to place reliance on internal controls, he may use a CAAT to assist in the performance of compliance tests. Furthermore, he may also use CAATs to perform substantive tests, including analytical review procedures.

Internal controls

3.15 'If the auditor wishes to place reliance on any internal controls, he should ascertain and evaluate those controls, and perform compliance tests on their operation.' The principles relating to internal controls are the same in a computer environment as in any other environment, but there are additional considerations which are discussed in the following paragraphs.

3.16 As with controls in other circumstances, the evaluation of application controls and general controls will be assisted by the use of documentation designed to help identify the controls on which the auditor may wish to place reliance. Such documentation can take a variety of forms but might consist of questions asking whether there are controls in a system which meet specified overall control objectives (ICQs), or which prevent or detect the occurrence of specified errors or omissions (ICEQs). For application controls, an integrated set of internal control questions may be used covering controls over both the manual part and the programmed part of the application, and the impact of relevant general controls.

3.17 Where preliminary evaluation of the application controls and general controls discloses the absence of, or uncompensated weaknesses in, controls, and therefore the auditor cannot rely on the controls, he should move directly to substantive tests which may be assisted by the use of CAATs.

3.18 However, where preliminary evaluation reveals application controls or general controls which may meet the auditor's objectives, he should design and carry out compliance tests if he wishes to rely on those controls. In determining whether he wishes to place reliance on application controls or general controls, the auditor will be influenced by the cost effectiveness and ease of testing and by the following matters.

(a) Where application controls are entirely manual the auditor may decide to perform compliance tests in respect of the application controls only, rather than to place any reliance on general controls. However, before he can place reliance on application controls which involve computer programs, the auditor needs to obtain reasonable assurance that the programs have operated properly, by evaluating and testing the effect of relevant general controls or by other tests on specific parts of the programs.

(b) Sometimes a programmed accounting procedure may not be subject to effective application controls. In such circumstances, in order to put himself in a position to limit the extent of his substantive testing, the auditor may choose to perform his compliance tests by testing the relevant general controls either manually or by using CAATs, to gain assurance of the continued and proper operation of the programmed accounting procedure. Where as a result of his compliance tests the auditor decides he cannot place reliance on the controls, he should move directly to substantive tests.

(c) As indicated earlier, in a computer environment there is the possibility of systematic errors. This may take place because of program faults or hardware malfunction in computer operations. However, many such potential recurrent errors should be prevented or detected by general controls over the development and implementation of applications, the integrity of the program and data files, and of computer operations. As a result, the controls which the auditor may evaluate and test may include general controls.

(d) On the other hand, the extent to which the auditor can rely on general controls may be limited because many of these controls might not be evidenced, or because they could have been performed inconsistently. In such circumstances, which are particularly common where small computers are involved, if he wishes to limit his substantive tests, the auditor may obtain assurance from compliance tests on manual application controls or by tests on specific parts of the programs.

3.19 In performing compliance tests on application or general controls, the auditor should obtain evidence which is relevant to the control being tested. Procedures the auditor may consider include observing the control in operation, examining documentary evidence of its operation, or performing it again himself. In the case of programmed application controls, the auditor may test specific parts of the programs, or re-perform them, by taking advantage of CAATs. He may also obtain evidence by testing relevant general controls.

Review of financial statements

3.20 'The auditor should carry out such a review of the financial statements as is sufficient, in conjunction with the conclusions drawn from the other audit evidence obtained, to give him a reasonable basis for his opinion on the financial statements.' CAATs (particularly audit software) may be of assistance to auditors in carrying out certain aspects of this work.

The auditor's use of CAATs

3.21 Traditionally, the ways in which an auditor could approach the audit of computer based systems fell into the following two categories:

(a) 'round the computer' approach;
(b) 'through the computer' approach.

A few years ago it was widely considered that an accountant could discharge his duties as auditor of a company with computer-based systems without having any detailed knowledge of such systems. The auditor would commonly audit 'round the computer' by ignoring the procedures which take place within the computer programs and concentrating solely on the input and corresponding output. Audit procedures would include checking authorisation, coding and control totals of input and checking the output with source documents and clerical control totals.

3.22 This view is now frowned upon and it is recognised that one of the principal problems facing the auditor is that of acquiring an understanding of the workings of the EDP department and of the computer itself. It is now customary for auditors to audit 'through the computer'. This involves an examination of the detailed processing routines of the computer to determine whether the controls in the system are adequate to ensure complete and correct processing of all data. With the advent of 'embedded audit facilities' (discussed in Section 4) we are increasingly seeing the introduction of auditing from 'within the computer'.

3.23 One of the major reasons why the 'round the computer' audit approach is no longer considered adequate is that as the complexity of computer systems has increased there has been a corresponding loss of audit trail. An audit trail is the means by which an individual transaction can be traced sequentially through the system from source to completion, and its loss will mean that normal audit techniques will break down.

Audit trail

3.24 The original concept of an audit trail was to print out data at all stages of processing so that an auditor could follow transactions stage-by-stage through a system to ensure that they had been processed correctly. Computer auditing methods have now cut out much of this laborious, time-consuming stage-by-stage working, and make use of:

(a) a more limited audit trail;
(b) efficient control totals;
(c) use of enquiry facilities;
(d) audit packages;
(e) file dumps.

3.25 An audit trail should ideally be provided so that every transaction on a file contains a unique reference back to the original source of the input (a sales system transaction record should hold a reference to the customer order, delivery note and invoice). Where master file records are updated several times, or from several sources, the provision of a satisfactory audit trail is more difficult, but some attempt should nevertheless be made to provide one.

3.26 Typical audit problems that arise as audit trails move further away from the hard copy trail include:

(a) testing computer generated totals when no detailed analysis is available;
(b) testing the completeness of output in the absence of control totals.

In these situations it will often be necessary to employ computer assisted audit techniques.

4 COMPUTER ASSISTED AUDIT TECHNIQUES (CAATs)

4.1 As indicated earlier there are two principal categories of computer assisted audit technique (CAAT), test data and audit software. As test data has a primarily compliance objective we shall look at this technique first. Audit software is particularly appropriate to substantive testing of balances and hence will often be of greater impact during the final stages of the audit.

Test data

4.2 Audit test data consists of data submitted by the auditor for processing by the enterprise's computer based accounting system. It may be processed during a normal production run ('live' test data) or during a special run at a point in time outside the normal cycle ('dead' test data).

Audit objectives

4.3 The primary use of test data is in compliance testing of application controls. For example, an application control to ensure the completeness of input may consist of programmed agreement of batch totals. The auditor may choose to compliance test his control by submitting test data with correct and incorrect batch totals. Rather more advanced CAATs with compliance objectives are referred to as 'embedded audit facilities'.

Planning

4.4 The level of expertise necessary for use of audit test data and other compliance CAATs varies greatly depending on the complexity of the testing procedures. The user of test data will need at least a basic understanding of data processing and a good understanding of the accounting system and the operating environment which will process the test data. Extensive technical expertise in the areas of systems analysis, programming languages and operating systems may not be needed in a straightforward application of audit test data but may well be necessary when using an embedded audit facility.

4.5 In planning the use of test data the auditor should consider whether he intends to submit data during a normal production run or during a special processing run. If live test data is submitted the auditor will need to ensure that any resulting corruption of the data files is corrected. Where dead test data is submitted the auditor will need to gain reasonable assurance that the programs processing this test data are those in use during normal processing. Where the auditor is using test data for compliance testing purposes he must also obtain reasonable assurance that the programs processing his test data were used throughout the audit period, whether by testing relevant general controls or by repeating the test at other times during the period.

4.6 The use of test data requires the same operational disciplines as those expected during the running of normal production data. However, as some uses of test data involve the submission of data over several processing cycles the auditor will need to control the sequence of submission with great care. In more complex circumstances it may be appropriate for the auditor to perform trials containing small amounts of test data before submitting his main audit test data. Other important points to note are as follows.

(a) Provided that there is adequate evidence to demonstrate that the test data was run against the correct versions of the programs it is not necessary for the auditor to be present during processing. In considering the adequacy of this evidence the auditor will consider the effectiveness of the general controls at the installation.

(b) The auditor will need to predict the results of the test data separately from the test data output. He should predict the results anticipated from each transaction and not merely check off the results on the output.

Recording

4.7 As the use of test data does not always provide any visible evidence of the audit work performed, both direct and indirect evidence should also be recorded. Working papers will normally include details of the controls to be tested and an explanation of how they are to be tested, details of the transactions and master files used, details of the predicted results, the actual results and evidence of the predicted and actual results having been compared.

Embedded audit facilities

4.8 The use of test data provides compliance comfort to the auditor in respect of the *whole* period only if he obtains reasonable assurance that the programs processing his test data were used throughout the period under review. To allow a *continuous* review of the data recorded and the manner in which it is treated by the system, it may be possible to use CAATs referred to as 'embedded audit facilities'. An embedded facility consists of program code or additional data provided by the auditor and incorporated into the computer element of the enterprise's accounting system. Two frequently encountered examples are: Integrated Test Facility (ITF); and Systems Control and Review File (SCARF).

4.9 ITF is the more complex of the two techniques. It involves the creation of a fictitious entity (for example department or customer) within the framework of the regular application. Transactions are then posted to the fictitious entity along with the regular transactions, and the results produced by the normal processing cycle are compared with those predetermined. It is important to ensure that the fictitious entities do not become part of the financial reporting of the organisation and several methods can be adopted to prevent this. The simplest and most secure method is to make reversing journal entries at appropriate cut-off dates. ITF enables management and auditors to keep a constant check on the internal processing functions applied to all types of valid and invalid transactions.

4.10 SCARF is a relatively simple technique to build into an application. It is best described by illustrating an example, in this case, a general (nominal) ledger application.

4.11 Each general ledger account has two fields. These are a Yes/No field indicating whether or not SCARF applies to this account; and a monetary value which is a threshold amount set by the auditor.

4.12 If SCARF does not apply to the account then all transactions posted to the account which have a value in excess of the threshold amount are also written to a SCARF file. The contents of that file can be read by the user, but usually can only be altered or deleted by the organisation's external auditors. The same restriction applies to the Yes/No and threshold fields associated with each account. When a new account is opened, it is automatically assigned as a SCARF account (Yes) and with a threshold of £zero. Only the external auditor can change these fields.

4.13 Sometimes the organisation is permitted to change the threshold, by reducing but not increasing it. To protect the auditor's exclusive access, the programs to alter threshold and clear SCARF files can be initiated by applying a formula, held only by the auditor, to a set of random numbers generated by the machine, the answer being similar to a password. SCARF thus enables the organisation and its auditor to monitor material transactions or sensitive accounts with ease and provides an assurance that all such transactions are under scrutiny.

Audit software

4.14 Audit software comprises computer programs used by the auditor to examine an enterprise's computer files. It may consist of package programs or utility programs which are usually run independently of the enterprise's computer-based accounting system. It includes interrogation facilities available at the enterprise. The features of the main types of audit software are as follows.

(a) *Package programs*: consist of prepared generalised programs for which the auditor will specify his detailed requirements by means of parameters, and sometimes by supplementary program code.

(b) *Purpose written programs*: involve the auditor satisfying his detailed requirements by means of program code specifically written for the purpose.

(c) *Utility programs*: consist of programs available for performing simple functions, such as sorting and printing data files.

Audit objectives

4.15 Although audit software may be used during many compliance and substantive procedures, its use is particularly appropriate during substantive testing of transactions and especially balances. By using audit software, the auditor may scrutinise large volumes of data and concentrate skilled manual resources on the investigation of results, rather than on the extraction of information.

4.16 During substantive testing the auditor may, for example, use audit software to reperform calculations, by adding individual transactions, to verify aged account balances, to select individual transactions for subsequent manual substantive tests, or to obtain information relevant to his analytical review.

4.17 When performing compliance tests of application controls, the auditor may use audit software to assist in various ways. For example, when testing the controls that ensure that completeness of input, audit software may be used to simulate programmed controls such as those used to identify any missing items from a sequence.

Planning

4.18 The level of expertise necessary for the use of audit software and its related techniques varies considerably. As a minimum, where the auditor is using generalised audit software to achieve straightforward audit objectives with simple detailed specifications, he will require a basic understanding of data processing and the enterprise's computer application together with a detailed knowledge of the audit software and the computer files to be used. Depending on the complexity of the application, the auditor may need to have a sound appreciation of systems analysis, operating systems, and where program code is used, experience of the programming language to be utilised.

4.19 During his planning of the use of audit software, the auditor will need to ensure that the required versions of the computer files are created and retained for his use. Similarly, he will need to ensure that appropriate computer facilities are available at a convenient time.

Controlling

4.20 In common with other computer programs, audit software requires design, compilation and testing. Although audit software normally checks the format of parameters, it cannot check to ensure that the logic and the values specified meet the auditor's detailed specifications. The auditor should, therefore, check his parameters and logic. Where program code is used, this detailed check may consume a considerable amount of time. Important points to note are as follows.

(a) It will normally be desirable for the auditor to request computer staff from the installation where the audit software is to be run to review the operating system instruction to ensure that the software will run in that installation.

(b) It is usually appropriate for the auditor to test his software on small test files before running on the main data files to avoid excessive consumption of computer time.

(c) Once the audit software has been run, the auditor should check the identity and version of the data files used, whether supplied by the client or additional data supplied by himself. This will normally involve checking with external evidence, such as control totals maintained by the user.

(d) Given that there is evidence to provide reasonable assurance that the audit software functioned as planned, it is not necessary for the auditor to be present during its use, although there are frequently practical advantages from doing so. In considering the adequacy of this evidence, the auditor will consider the results of his compliance tests of general controls at the installation.

Recording

4.21 As the use of audit software does not usually provide any visible evidence of the audit work performed, additional evidence should be recorded. This will normally include detailed specifications (including file layouts), parameters listing, source listings, results of testing, and other evidence to provide reasonable assurance that the software functioned as planned.

Exercise 2

When auditing a computer based accounting system, it is possible for most of the audit to be completed using conventional audit techniques. In some computer based systems however, it is necessary for the auditor to employ computer assisted audit techniques (CAATs).

Required

(a) Outline the major types of CAATs and describe the potential benefits that might be derived from using them.

(b) Explain what is meant by a 'test pack'.

(c) Briefly explain the use that an auditor could make of such a test pack when examining a sales ledger system maintained on a computer system.

(d) Briefly outline the main practical problems encountered when using a test pack.

Solution

(a) Audit techniques that involve, directly or indirectly, the use of a client's computer are referred to as Computer Assisted Audit Techniques (CAATs), of which the following are two principal categories.

(i) *Audit software*: computer programs used for audit purposes to examine the contents of the client's computer files.

(ii) *Test data*: data used by the auditor for computer processing to test the operation of the enterprise's computer programs.

The benefits of using CAATs are as follows.

(i) By using computer audit programs, the auditor can scrutinise large volumes of data and concentrate skilled manual resources on the investigation of results, rather than on the extraction of information.

(ii) Once the programs have been written and tested, the costs of operation are relatively low, indeed the auditor does not necessarily have to be present during its use (though there are frequently practical advantages in the auditor attending).

(b) A 'test pack' consists of input data submitted by the auditor for processing by the enterprise's computer based accounting system. It may be processed during a normal production run ('live') or during a special run at a point in time outside the normal cycle ('dead').

The primary use of the test pack is in compliance testing of application controls. The data used in the test pack will often contain items which should appear in exception reports produced by the system. The results of the processed test pack will be compared with the expected results.

(c) The auditor could use a test pack to test the sales ledger system by including data in the pack which would normally be processed through the system, such as:

(i) sales;
(ii) credits allowed;
(iii) cash receipts;
(iv) discounts allowed.

The processing of the input would involve:

(i) production of sales invoices (with correct discounts);

(ii) production of credit notes;

(iii) posting of cash received, invoices and credit notes to individual debtor's accounts to appear on statements;

(iv) posting all transactions to the sales ledger control account and producing balances.

The result produced would be compared with those predicted in the test pack. Errors should appear on exception reports produced by the computer, for example, a customer credit limit being breached.

(d) The practical problems involved in using a test pack are as follows.

(i) In using 'live' processing there will be problems removing or reversing the test data, which might corrupt master file information.

(ii) In using 'dead' processing the auditor does not test the system actually used by the client.

(iii) The system will be checked by the test pack, but not the year end balances, which will still require sufficient audit work. Costs may therefore be high.

(iv) Any auditor who wishes to design a test pack must have sufficient skill in computing, and also a thorough knowledge of the client's system.

(v) Any changes in the client's system will mean that the test pack will have to be rewritten which will be costly and time-consuming.

5 CONTROLS IN ON-LINE AND REAL-TIME SYSTEMS

Nature of on-line and real-time systems

5.1 Whilst traditional batch processing is still a common method of using a computer to process accounting data there is a rapid increase in the use of an on-line system, including those in real-time. On-line systems provide the facilities for data to be passed to and from the central computer via remote terminals. Real-time systems are a further development of on-line systems and permit immediate updating of computer held files. The data input and file update phases are therefore merged and the system accepts individual transactions rather than batches of data.

5.2 Real-time systems, which are often referred to as one-write systems, are the computerised equivalent of bookkeeping systems like Kalamazoo or Twinlock. In those systems, several accounting records are prepared simultaneously by the use of carbon paper between specially aligned sheets of paper, the bottom sheet being, say, a sales day book, followed by the customer's account, then the customer's statement.

5.3 Most minis and micros can operate in real time. We shall consider the problems associated with such systems later. The following paragraphs are concerned primarily with larger, multi-terminal, on-line systems.

Control problems and strengths

5.4 On-line systems vary considerably, but as implied above, a broad distinction can be drawn between those with remote input devices which collect data for subsequent processing in batches and those operating in real time. There are, however, certain control problems and advantages associated with most on-line systems. The main points to remember are as follows.

(a) *Segregation of duties*. When remote terminals are located at the point at which data is originated, it may be found that the same person is responsible for producing and processing the same information. To compensate for the reduction in internal check, supervisory controls should be strengthened.

(b) *Data file security*. The ability of a person using a remote terminal to gain access to the computer at will results in the need for special controls to ensure that files are neither read nor written to (nor destroyed), either accidentally or deliberately, without proper authority.

(i) The controls may be partly physical. For example:

(1) access to terminals is restricted to authorised personnel;

(2) the terminals and the rooms in which they are kept are locked when not in use.

(ii) They may be partly-operated by the operating system, including the following.

(1) The use of passwords (or lockwords), or special badges or keys, sometimes linked to a user's personal identification code which must be used before the terminal operator can gain access to the computer/particular files. In some systems it is found that one password or other identification is required before it is possible to read a file, a second before it is possible to write new data and yet a third if both operations are permitted. Obviously, the code given to a particular individual will depend on his job function and status within the organisation.

(2) Restriction, by the operating system, of certain terminals to certain files. For example, the terminal in the wages department may only be given access to the wages files.

(3) Logging of all attempted violations of the above controls possibly accompanied by the automatic shut down of the terminal used. Obviously all violations should be speedily and thoroughly investigated.

(c) *Program security.* The points discussed above apply equally to the use of programs.

(d) *File reconstructions.* Dumping, the method of allowing for the reconstructing of direct access files in batch processing systems, is of limited use in on-line systems as the contents of the file are being continually changed. Although the complete file will be dumped periodically, it is also necessary to maintain a file giving details of all transactions processed since the last dump.

(e) One of the greatest advantages of on-line systems is the ability to make editing more effective. This is partly because the immediate access to a master file and pipeline files allows more sophisticated checks to be performed (for example more extensive use of computer matching where the information input may be checked for accuracy against that held on file) and partly because the terminal operator will be able to correct certain types of error immediately. It should be noted, however, that it is essential that strict control is kept over rejections particularly in systems using a database. It may otherwise be found that subsequent processing is performed in ignorance of the fact that master files, which should have been updated, have not been.

5.5 In a batch processing system, the establishment of batch totals provides a strong control over the completeness and accuracy of processing. In an on-line system, this facility will, to a greater or lesser extent, be absent. Occasionally it is found that input documents are batched retrospectively, the totals obtained then being reconciled to those generated by the computer. The fact that this technique is not popular is because it is time consuming (and therefore expensive) and because, in many systems, it may prove difficult, if not impossible, to identify the cause of any discrepancies after the processing for a selected period has been completed. In most on-line systems it is, therefore, essential that there are strong controls, particularly supervisory controls, over data capture and input. These may be backed up, for example, by programming the computer to check whether all serial numbered documents up to a given number have been processed. After input, the computer can accumulate totals for different classes of transactions which can then be used to control subsequent processing.

Database management systems (DBMS)

5.6 DBMS are normally designed for use in real-time environments and enable elements of data to be accessed by different programs. This avoids the duplication of data which inevitably occurs in a traditional system. As data is normally only stored once, and may be accessible to all users that require it, the principal control problems raised concern the authorisation of data amendments and restriction of access to data. Any data amendments must take into account the requirements of all the users. It is good practice to set up an administration function specifically to run and control the day to day operation of the database, thereby enhancing segregation of duties (this function will be independent of the systems development personnel and programmers and data processing manager).

5.7 The following controls, some of which are common to all real-time systems, might be incorporated into DBMS.

(a) *Controls to prevent or detect unauthorised changes to programs*

(i) No access to live program files by any personnel except for the operations personnel at the central computer.

(ii) Password protection of programs.

(iii) Restricted access to the central computer and terminal.

(iv) Maintenance of a console log and scrutiny by the data processing manager and by an independent party such as the internal auditors.

(v) Periodic comparison of live production programs to control copies and supporting documentation.

(b) *Controls to prevent or detect errors during operation*

(i) Restriction of access to terminals by use of passwords and restrictions of programs themselves to certain fields.

(ii) Satisfactory application controls over input, processing and master files and their contents, including retrospective batching (see Paragraph 5.5).

(iii) Use of operations manuals and training of all users.

(iv) Maintenance of logs showing unauthorised attempts to access and regular scrutiny by the data processing manager and internal auditors.

(v) Physical protection of data files.

(vi) Training in emergency procedures.

(c) *Controls to ensure integrity of the database system*

(i) Restriction of access to the data dictionary (this contains standard descriptions, including definitions, characteristics and inter-relationship of data. This codification and cross referencing is important as the various user departments may apply inconsistent terminology).

(ii) Segregation of duties between the data processing manager, the database administration function (including its manager) and systems development personnel.

(iii) Liaison between the database administration function and systems development personnel to ensure integrity of systems specifications.

(iv) Preparation and update as necessary of user manuals in conjunction with the data dictionary in (i) above.

5.8 The audit of DBMS creates particular problems as the two principal CAATs, test data and audit software, tend to work unsatisfactorily on the programs and files contained within such systems. The auditor may, however, be able to use embedded audit facilities such as described in Paragraphs 4.8 to 4.13. Close liaison with the internal auditors may also provide audit comfort depending on the nature and continuity of their DBMS review functions. The auditor *must* realistically be involved at the evaluation, design and development stages so that he is able to determine his audit requirements and identify control problems *before* implementation.

Exercise 3

You are the auditor of Oilco plc, a major petroleum refiner, and you are about to commence the interim audit. The company utilises an on-line computerised accounting system operated by a central mainframe computer with terminals located in several departments. The audit senior has asked you to take charge of the interim audit of sales and debtors, and has arranged a meeting between yourself and the accountant responsible for the debtors section.

The audit senior further informs you that he wishes you to review the controls in existence not only as regards the accounting for sales and debtors but also the database facility as far as it concerns your audit assignment.

Required

(a) List ten questions you would ask the accountant responsible for the debtors section in order to provide an initial evaluation of the effectiveness of the computer controls over sales and debtors.

(b) Explain the controls which ought to be in existence in order to maintain the integrity of the database.

(c) Explain the reasons why it is important for the auditor to constantly keep up to date with the developments in computerised systems.

Solution

(a) The questions to be asked in order to review the computer controls in existence over sales and debtors must cover controls over input, processing, access, files and output. The following questions could be asked of the accountant responsible for the debtors section.

(i) What systematic action is taken to ensure the completeness, accuracy and authorisation of input of sales invoices, credit notes, journal entries, cash and so on? For example, batch totalling, sequence checking, programmed matching of input to control files containing details of expected input, and authorisation limits and reasonableness checks.

(ii) Are source documents checked one-for-one to processed output and output control totals matched to predetermined manually prepared control totals in the debtors section?

(iii) By what methods is it established that all input is fully and accurately processed? Examples are batch reconciliation after records update, summary totals, programmed validity checks.

(iv) What controls are in place to prevent or detect unauthorised amendments to programs and data files (for example, restrictions of access to programmers and to users of the on-line terminals)?

(v) What controls exist over the work done by computer operators (for example, division of duties, job scheduling, computer logs, cross-checks to input control, authorisation of file issue)?

(vi) What procedures are in operation to ensure the continuing correctness of master files and the standing data they contain? For example, record counts or hash totals for the files, produced and checked each time they are used, regular checks of all contents, run-to-run control totals.

(vii) Are there procedures for the review and despatch of output by the computer control section? Examples are: comparison of output with prelist totals of input, checking all queries have been properly dealt with, distribution list for all output and close control over exception reports, audit totals and so on.

(viii) Is the reasonableness of output tested? For example, is output tested against file totals after update, and compared with manually prepared totals and balances on individual debtors accounts?

(ix) Is there an adequate management (audit) trail of generated data and regular listing of ledger balances and debtor analysis?

(x) Is there an accounting manual in existence, detailing all procedures and clerical processes relating to the sales and debtors system, and is it up to date?

(b) A database is a collection of interrelated data, stored together in order to minimise redundant data and to serve multiple applications. The controls which ought to be in existence are as follows.

(i) Proper authorisation of input prior to submission of data to the system. Validation tests on input and on its authorisation should be built into the system. As the company uses on-line terminals, it may only be practical to authorise input after submission. In this case, the input will need to be prevented from being amended or used to produce output until it is cleared.

(ii) Access must be restricted to authorised personnel and should be logged. Passwords should be used to identify and permit different levels of access.

(iii) Permissible activity should be defined to ensure that operator access to terminals, terminal access to programs and program access to data are restricted and controlled and that evidence is available to demonstrate this.

(iv) The database manager should have overall responsibility for the integrity of the database, and should approve all program modifications and new types of input data and reports to be generated. The database manager must control all aspects of the database, but his work should be segregated for control purposes from applications development, systems analysis, programming operators, librarians and the control section staff.

(v) Controls should be incorporated to help the auditor to use the database control programme to generate analysis, totals and reports. To compensate for the lack of audit trail, the auditors may require the building in of resident audit monitoring systems and the use of test data and enquiry programs. The centralisation of so much data with access possible in several departments increases audit risk and calls for tighter and more sophisticated control than stand-alone applications with their own set of master files.

(c) Auditors must keep up to date with developments in computer systems, hardware and software in order to carry out their statutory duties efficiently and effectively. They need to appreciate fully the scope and areas of audit risk to be found in modern computerised systems. Specialist training will be necessary to keep their expertise up to the standard required by clients and by the needs of their own audit firm. An up to date understanding of computer systems will also help the auditor in the following ways.

   (i) To advise clients at the development stage on audit aids and controls to be built into, or provided for, in the system.

   (ii) To understand what totals and print out are needed at different program stages and how to test controls.

   (iii) To highlight key features and help assess audit risk and sensitivity to error.

   (iv) To obtain stratified files to aid testing and random samples, as a basis for statistical testing.

   (v) To obtain computer print outs for direct use on the audit, for example for the circularisation of debtors and creditors.

   (vi) To appreciate the need to revise audit software to use on new operational systems. In modern computer systems, the auditor may do some of his audit work at the time the data is being processed by the operating system, by tagging audit flags on to user accounts.

6 BUREAUX AND SOFTWARE HOUSES

6.1 Computer service bureaux are third party service organisations who provide EDP facilities to their clients. Most bureaux are members of COSBA (Computer Services and Bureaux Association) which provides a code of practice for its members.

6.2 The main types of bureaux are:

(a) independent companies formed to provide specialist computing services;

(b) computer manufacturers with bureaux;

(c) computer users (for example universities) with spare capacity who hire out computer time when it is not required for their own purposes. This type of bureau is now much less common than it was some years ago.

Why use a bureau?

6.3 The following are the most common reasons for using a bureau.

(a) *New user*: a company that is considering acquiring a computer may find it extremely beneficial to use a bureau because:

   (i) it can evaluate the type of computer it is interested in;

   (ii) it can test and develop its programs prior to the delivery of its own computer;

   (iii) its staff will become familiar with the requirements of a computer system.

   In some cases a new system may be initially implemented using a bureau. This will involve file conversion and pilot or parallel running.

(b) *Cost:* many companies cannot justify the installation of an in-house computer on cost-benefit grounds. With the enormous increase in the number of VRCs and mini-computers available this basis is becoming less common.

(c) *Peak loads:* some computer users find it convenient to employ a bureau to cope with peak loads arising for example from seasonal variations in sales; bureaux may be used for data preparation work for file conversion, prior to the implementation of a new computer system.

(d) *Stand by:* a bureau's computer may be used in the event of breakdown of an in-house machine.

(e) *Specialised skills:* management feel that the job of data processing should be left to the experts.

(f) *Consultancy:* bureaux can provide advice and assistance in connection with feasibility studies, system design, equipment evaluation, staff training and so on.

(g) *For one-off use.*

Advantages and disadvantages to the user

6.4 The reasons for using a bureau effectively constitute a list of their *advantages*. It should be emphasised, however, that very few users can afford to pay for the services of systems analysts and programmers of the quality that will be found working for the large bureaux; a company using a bureau will probably not need them. Other advantages include:

(a) use of a bureau should enable a customer to obtain the use of up-to-date computer technology in the bureau;

(b) unloading responsibility on to the bureau (for example payroll);

(c) use of a bureau does not require a high capital outlay.

6.5 The principal *disadvantages* of using a bureau are as follows.

(a) Loss of control over time taken to process data and in particular the inability to reschedule work should input delays occur.

(b) Problems may be encountered in the transfer of data to and from the bureau.

(c) The bureau may close down leaving the customer without any DP facilities.

(d) Many potential users will not employ a bureau's services because they feel that they will lose control over an important area of their business and furthermore that it is bad security to allow confidential information to be under the control of an outsider. Their fears are normally ungrounded; the bureau will certainly not try to run the business and its security may well be considerably better than that of its customers.

(e) Its employees will be uninterested in and often unaware of the type of data they are processing.

(f) Standards of service and the provision of adequate documentation control and any audit trail are also important considerations.

Planning and control exercised by the user

6.6 When a system using a bureau is set up it is essential that a full feasibility study and system design should be carried out. In practice the bureau may provide assistance in performing these tasks.

6.7 A *small* DP department should be set up to liaise with the bureau and to ensure that adequate systems controls are maintained. The controls kept by the client should cover:

(a) physical movement of data to and from the bureau;
(b) accuracy and completeness of processing;
(c) resubmission of rejected data;
(d) correct distribution of output;
(e) system testing involving all clerical procedures at the user company;
(f) control over the maintenance of data on master files;
(g) adequate back-up facilities both for processing and for file reconstruction;
(h) security of data.

The audit approach where controls are in the hands of third parties

6.8 To set the scene we can briefly return to the guideline *Auditing in a computer environment*. Under the heading 'Third party service organisations' it states:

> 'Where enterprises use a third party service organisation such as a computer service bureau or a software house for the purpose of maintaining part or all of their accounting records and procedures, the auditor still has a responsibility to follow *The auditor's operational standard*. However, the auditor may encounter practical obstacles, as the enterprise may be placing some reliance on the proper operation of internal control exercised by the third party. Consequently, where the auditor finds it impracticable to obtain all the information and explanations that he requires from the enterprise itself (because the enterprise may not be maintaining sufficient controls to minimise that reliance) he should perform other procedures. These may include taking the steps he considers necessary to enable him to rely on the work performed by other auditors or carrying out procedures at the premises of the third party.'

6.9 The above statement implies that, wherever possible, the auditor would opt to obtain assurance by testing his client's controls, provided they are adequate, rather than by seeking to rely on controls operated by the bureau. This may be feasible, and cost effective, where, for instance, batch processing is involved. Visible data is generally abundant and loss of audit trail is normally not encountered. Reliance will be sought from the user controls at the input and output stages which should provide evidence of the proper functioning of programmed procedures performed by the bureau. However, the auditor will also be concerned with the operation of general controls at the bureau, in particular (f) (g) and (h) in Paragraph 6.7:

(a) security over the client's data (sensitive information such as names of customers and employees should be coded if necessary);

(b) adequate facilities for reconstruction; and

(c) control over master file data (all master file amendments should be printed out and checked to ensure that they have all been authorised by the user).

6.10 Where the auditor wishes to evaluate and test the controls at the bureau (whether general and/or application), and permission is obtained, there appear to be two courses of action available:

(a) a separate examination of controls by the auditors of each of the bureau's clients (unlikely to be feasible);

(b) an examination of controls by a third party reviewer (probably another firm of auditors, perhaps even the bureau's own auditors) and issue of a report which can be made available to auditors of each of the bureau's clients.

6.11 The second option also has some problems.

(a) A particular auditor may be unwilling to place reliance on an examination of controls commissioned by the computer bureau.

(b) The interaction between the general controls exercised by the bureau and the application controls exercised by the client may be unclear.

(c) It is often the case that different users place varying degrees of reliance on certain controls and auditors need to gain different levels of knowledge about these controls.

6.12 The auditor may conclude that he can rely on an examination by a third party review if he is satisfied that all the procedures which he himself would have wished to perform have indeed been carried out and with the same level of expertise as he would have applied. This is likely to involve consultations with the third party reviewer, where the evidence provided by him is, in the auditor's opinion, insufficient for his particular purposes. Remember that the bureau is the client of the third party reviewer and as such must give permission before a consultation can take place.

6.13 Finally, it is important in all cases for the auditor to consider the circumstances of the use of the computer bureau's services and the extent to which the control procedures within the computer bureau and at the client are comprehensive. Where the auditor is unable to rely on an examination by a third party reviewer and is not granted permission to perform his own examination of the controls at the bureau, he may have to resort to extensive substantive testing (unless he can obtain sufficient assurance from the user controls). There is no reason why the auditor should not employ CAATs such as test data and audit software to assist him where his client uses a bureau. In the case of audit software, permission of the client *and* bureau would normally be necessary.

7 CONTROL PROBLEMS IN SMALL COMPUTER SYSTEMS

7.1 The design of modern mini-computers is well-adapted to these systems; the one-write concept has been developed to the point where an order clerk can enter details of an order using a VDU terminal and the system will immediately proceed to update the inventory, sales ledger, customer account, and general ledger and print the picking list, delivery notes, and invoice in respect of that transaction.

7.2 A big advantage of these systems, apart from the degree of automation, is that the organisation's accounting records are always up to date. However, if the system is not fully and properly controlled, serious problems can arise for management and auditor alike.

7.3 In this section we look at the control and audit problems peculiar to minis and micros. It is, incidentally, rather difficult to specify which machines fall into the category of mini as distinct from micro. One categorisation is to define the 'mini' as capable of supporting multiple keyboards and VDUs whereas the 'micro' is desk size, comprising a processor with single keyboard and VDU, a printer and, probably, magnetic (floppy) disc storage. From the audit viewpoint the distinction is not significant: all the machines have the common features of relatively compact size and ability to operate in a normal office environment (as distinct from the protected environment necessary with mainframes). For consistency's sake, the term 'mini' is used throughout this section.

Summary of the control problems

7.4 The majority of the potential problems arise due to the departure from the formal structure of the traditional data processing department, where a controlled environment was provided over the acquisition, maintenance and distribution of computer information. In the world of the mini-computer this controlled structure does not exist and the environment is more informal.

7.5 These problem areas surrounding mini computers can be grouped under three headings:

(a) lack of planning over the acquisition and use of minis:
(b) lack of documentary evidence; and
(c) lack of security and confidentiality.

7.6 All these areas could produce problems for the auditor, giving him difficulties when attempting to assess the documentation, the adequacy of design processes and testing, the completeness, accuracy and authority of data and, of course, audit trails. Each of the three problem areas is now considered in more detail.

Lack of planning over the acquisition and use of mini-computers

7.7 When an organisation sets out to acquire a computer system, a series of steps should be undertaken before making the decision to purchase.

Authorisation

7.8 A feasibility study should be carried out, examining the requirements, the costs and the benefits, to ensure that the expense is justified. Suppliers should be invited to tender, and responses from the suppliers should be evaluated and compared. Contracts should be negotiated with the final choice of supplier and only then should the equipment be installed. All interested parties within the organisation should be identified and involved throughout the whole procedure, irrespective of the size of the system which is being purchased.

Suitability

7.9 There is a risk when purchase of a mini-computer is under consideration that the client will not have the expertise to evaluate the relative merits of systems. This could give rise to compatibility and/or capacity problems thereby restricting future developments, unless in the last resort, the entire system is replaced. Many first time users tend to purchase standard software packages which creates an even greater risk as regards suitability, for such systems may not fit precisely the company's trading methods. Moreover, the first time user is unlikely to have the expertise required to tailor such packages.

Support facilities

7.10 The support facilities offered by the supplier and/or software house should be ascertained to ensure that:

(a) in the event of machine breakdown, prompt service and, if necessary, backup facilities are available;

(b) any bugs in the programme can be sorted out;

(c) minor modifications to the program can be carried out;

(d) adequate systems documentation and operator manuals have been provided, such documentation falling into three generally accepted categories:

   (i) program documentation: which states in detail how each program within each part of the system operates, what files are being opened and accessed, and what functions are being performed;

   (ii) operator instructions: which are designed to be 'desk-top' instructions enabling the micro user to access and use the system as required;

   (iii) user manual: which is the 'layman's guide' to the operation of the whole system and would usually include the operator instructions; and

(e) operators have received adequate instruction.

Standards

7.11 In a formal data processing environment there will normally be standards to which all procedures regarding hardware and software should conform. All programs, whether written by the user or brought in from outside, should meet specified criteria and satisfy minimum standards, covering aspects such as controls and accounting principles. With minis, where the time taken from ordering, through installation to operation, may be a matter of weeks only, there is great danger that standards are not set.

7.12 Strict disciplines must be imposed to ensure that recognised systems development controls are applied and sufficient administration procedures are implemented.

Lack of documentary evidence

7.13 We have identified that many mini-computers operate in real time via VDUs, which allows users to have direct access to the computer thus enabling them to input data, update files and make one-off enquiries on data held on files. The necessity for edit programs and hard copy is avoided. Although this may be conceived as an 'advantage' from the viewpoint of computer operators/users, management and the auditor will recognise the inherent control problems. Control can be enhanced by ensuring that edit programs are in-built at the design stage and by incorporating into the system a user-usage file which logs details of the user's identification, the application involved, the records accessed or updated and so on. Such a file can be reviewed periodically by a responsible official and the auditor.

Lack of audit trail

7.14 Frequently in mini computer systems there is no trail to follow since all the processing is done inside the computer and no intermediate printouts are produced. The quality of audit evidence can be questionable if there is a lack of primary records (for example telephone sales orders entered straight into the computer via the VDU to take our previous example). It may be prudent to implement manual controls to ensure that transactions can only be processed when supported by an appropriate initiating document. Similarly, manual batching can be imposed.

Lack of security and confidentiality

Lack of segregation of duties

7.15 Poor segregation of duties all too easily occurs since frequently the same person prepares the data, feeds it into the computer, supervises the processing and acts as end user. This lack of division of duties leads to enhanced opportunities for fraud, the user having access to assets and the recording and disposal of assets. The auditor may well have to perform extensive substantive verification work to compensate for this serious lack of control.

Lack of control over users

7.16 Because mini-computers do not require a protected environment the terminals are readily available to any user. In order to safeguard the records, controls to prevent unauthorised users from using the computer are necessary (use of locks, passwords and so on).

Lack of control over alterations to programs

7.17 We have emphasised in Paragraph 7.9 that a lack of expertise, particularly in the case of first time users, may lead to imprudent purchase in terms of capacity and compatibility. Conversely, there are dangers arising because of the relative ease with which expertise may be acquired once a machine is installed and operational. Mini-computers employ high level languages and a working knowledge can be grasped within a short time. In the wrong hands there is a danger that programs might be altered without detection or that programs are written at the time data is being processed without adequate testing.

7.18 Stringent supervisory arrangements are required to prevent unauthorised personnel from having access to the programs together with programmed controls preventing unauthorised running. A degree of security will be guaranteed to the extent that the programs are permanently etched onto silicon chips and are hence an integral part of the hardware ('ROMs'). Such programs can only be altered by specialist electronics engineers.

Exercise 4

Microcomputers have been marketed for small and medium sized businesses that have previously been using manual or mechanical systems for bookkeeping and accounting functions. In reviewing computer controls in this environment, the auditor is likely to find general control weaknesses which would not be anticipated in larger computer installations using for example an on-line, real-time system.

Required

(a) Explain why the auditor is likely to find weaknesses in the controls over a microcomputer accounting system in a small company.

(b) Describe the impact that this lack of internal control will have upon the approach to the audit of a business using a microcomputer system.

(c) Describe the controls which the auditor would expect to be operating within an on-line, real-time system in order to ensure the accurate processing of accounting data.

Solution

(a) Reasons for weaknesses in small company microcomputer systems include the following.

(i) Small companies generally have few accounting staff, so that it will often be difficult to create good conditions for segregation of duties. The accountant, for instance, may be the only person in the company fully conversant with the accounting system. This weakens security and problems may arise if the computer 'expert' is ill or away on holiday. If one person has specialised programming knowledge not shared by others, s/he may be able to put through unauthorised programme changes undetected.

(ii) Controls over access to the system may be poor or non-existent. In a small office, it will probably be difficult to create physical security by putting the computer in a secure area. Controls over programmes and discs may also be poor.

(iii) Clerical staff in a small company may be required to use the computer for routine processing without an understanding of the system or of its possible risks and pitfalls. If a malfunction occurs or if and error is made, untrained staff may not be able to take proper corrective action, and there is a risk that files may be corrupted or data lost as a result.

(iv) Poor access controls, combined with real-time processing, may result in poor control over input; there is a risk that data may be input twice or not at all.

(v) Small companies with few resources may not have made adequate provision for maintenance or stand-by equipment in case of breakdown or damage.

(b) The auditor needs to obtain an understanding of the client's system and identify the extent to which it contains controls upon which reliance can be placed. These may be of two kinds: user controls and program controls. User controls will include control accounts and management review. If these appear to be in operation, the auditor may choose to rely on them and test the system accordingly. Program procedures may be in operation which monitor, for instance, reasonableness or completeness of certain types of data. Having conducted a review and evaluation of the software in use, the auditor may identify such controls. If the auditor does not find adequate controls of either kind, it will be necessary to carry out substantive testing to give proper audit assurance.

(c) Online real-time processing has two distinctive features. Transactions will often be recorded as they occur, for instance a sale may be recorded by the system at the same time as it is entered on the cash register. Audit trail will be reduced because there will not be a separate hard copy of the data entered, as is the case in batch processing systems. As a result, the most important feature of such a system will be the control over access, to ensure that only authorised users input data.

The main safeguard is the use of passwords. These should be confidential and subject to frequent change. The more sensitive the application, the more passwords should be required, operated in a so-called hierarchical system. Passwords should be supplemented by physical controls over access to terminals, and may where appropriate be supplemented by such techniques as voice or thumbprint recognition.

Terminals should log off automatically if left unattended for more than a short period. They should also close down if a number of unsuccessful attempts at access are made, as these may be the work of an unauthorised person attempting to access the system. All unauthorised access attempts should be logged.

Input data should be logged to provide an audit trail, for instance by means of a regular print-out at the terminal or a record at the point of input. Programs should be regularly checked to ensure they have not been altered. Back-up files should be used to prevent corruption of data by unauthorised input.

8 SYSTEMS DEVELOPMENT

8.1 When an audit client computerises the business, the implications for the auditor are great. The whole nature of the audit will change and the auditor must obtain the requisite knowledge to audit the system. The auditor may also be involved in the process of installing a computer system by giving advice and help. In any case, the auditor will want to audit the implementation of a new system as well as its continued use and maintenance.

8.2 The procedure for implementing a new system will be as shown in the network diagram on the next page.

8.3 The auditor reviewing the development process will want to satisfy himself that each of these stages is being completed in a controlled manner. The influence of the user on the development should be pervasive and the auditor must ensure that this has been the case.

8.4 The company should have a set procedure for the development of new systems. The *feasibility study* would usually be conducted by a *systems analyst* and the authorisation to proceed should be based on that study. The auditor should ensure that the matters which ought to be covered in the feasibility report are in fact included. The auditor should review the report for reasonableness.

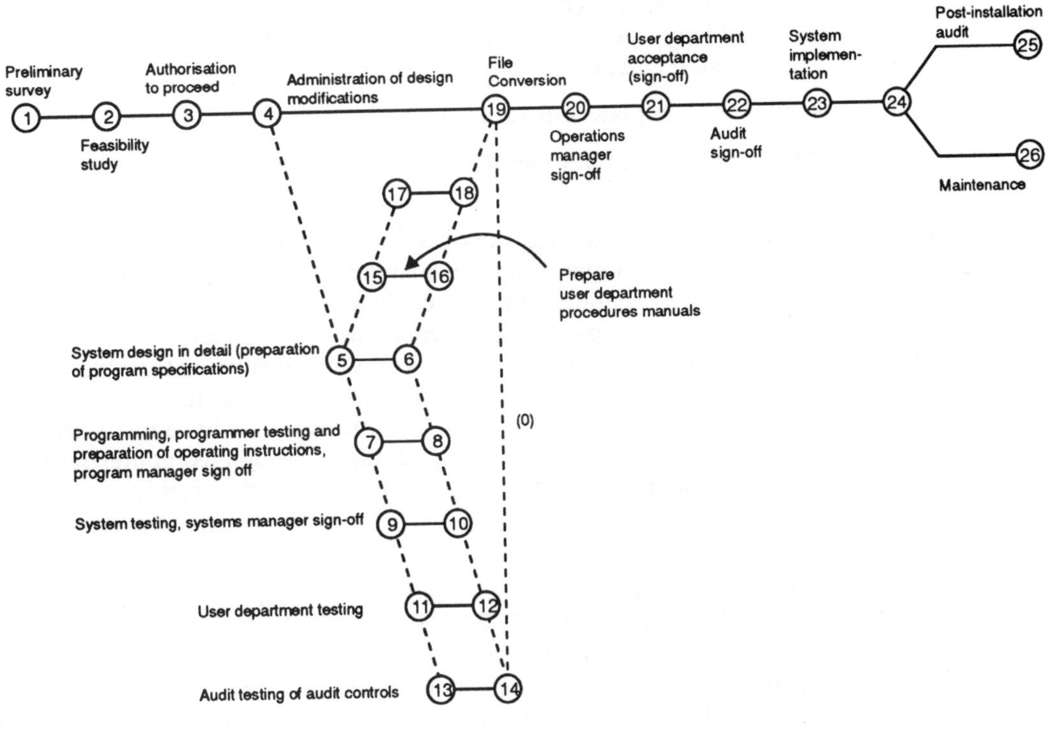

8.5 The auditor will be involved at the systems design stage to check that various rules are clearly established, for example specific rules relating to access to different types of data.

8.6 The auditor should review the *program specifications* and ensure that they are formally accepted by the programmer. The auditor should also review the issuing of amendments to program specifications and satisfy himself that they are being processed in a formal manner. If there are a large number of amendments, this may be an indication that something more fundamental has gone wrong. The auditor will depend at this stage on the program specifications to indicate whether adequate programmed controls are being built into the system. The main purpose of these controls will be to ensure the completeness and accuracy of data processing as well as its security.

8.7 The auditor will review the programming work to satisfy himself that standards laid down have been complied with. It is unlikely that he will review the program code itself for this purpose, but he will confirm that all programming work has been test-checked by other programmers.

8.8 The programmer will *test the program* against test data. The auditor will review the *program file* which contains information on how each program works. The system should be tested in detail using the test data, not only by the programmer, but also (separately) by the user.

8.9 Audit can be invaluable in ensuring that no system goes live with inadequately *trained staff* or without a *full procedures manual*. Training can only be completed with hands on experience once the system is up and running.

8.10 Good *file conversion procedures* are crucial and the auditor must satisfy himself that the size and nature of the task has been allowed for. The auditor should enquire about the file conversion procedures very early in the system development.

8.11 Where he is required to formally sign-off the system he would only do so if he were satisfied that:

(a) the system meets user requirements; and the programs, which function satisfactorily and have been tested thoroughly, have been developed with adequate controls incorporated and are auditable;

(b) the master files are complete and accurate;

(c) a satisfactory implementation program has been devised.

8.12 *Implementation* is often done in phases, possibly linked to a phased construction of the master files. Initially a pilot implementation may be followed section by section until implementation is complete. Parallel running of the old and new systems should occur, at least for the first sections to be implemented until confidence is built up. The decision must be made as to whether to use the computer results or the manual results, if parallel running is taking place. Parallel running doubles the task of the user department at a time when they are ill-placed to cope and may have lost staff due to a premature run-down in anticipation of staff savings through computerisation. The auditor should be vigilant for impending problems in the staffing of the user department.

8.13 After implementation, a *post-installation audit* should take place. It is not the responsibility of the internal auditor to conduct this audit but he should conduct a review to ensure that it is done by the project team. The user department should be involved in this and approve the findings. The objective of this audit is to check that design objectives have been met. The audit is made much easier if data were collected about the performance of the old system before it was superseded.

8.14 The ongoing *maintenance* task of a computer system is facilitated if the initial development of the system was well controlled. Good documentation, proper authorisation of all program modifications and the continued analysis of performance data of the system are the hallmarks of sound maintenance which the auditor will look for. In some cases the auditor will feature in the program change control process, even though in theory this is unsound.

8.15 A summary of the main control procedures over the in-house development of a system is as follows.

(a) Adopt a recognised and documented system analysis and design method.

(b) Full ongoing documentation must be completed throughout the development stage.

(c) Review and approval should be carried out throughout the development stages.

(d) Test data must be designed to impact on all system areas with pre-determined results.

(e) Full testing should be carried out prior to implementation.

(f) Approval of system documentation with external auditors.

(g) Full training schemes should be set up.

(h) User documentation should be reviewed prior to implementation.

(i) Controlled file conversion from old to new system.

(j) Review of ability of development staff.

The new system and the external auditor

8.16 The external auditor might not be involved in a client's systems development because the client company is large enough to have its own control procedures. The 'auditor' referred to in the above sections might be an internal auditor. The effect on the external audit will still be significant. Even if he was not involved with the development of the system the external auditor will follow the development, checking the controls in the process, in his review of the system.

Small companies

8.17 In the case of a small business, the system will probably be bought in as a package. A summary of the control procedures in this situation is as follows.

(a) Define the objectives of the system and ensure those needs are met.

(b) Purchase from a reputable supplier.

(c) Review the available documentation.

(d) Assess the on-going financial viability of the supplier to ensure future support and development will be available.

(e) Enter a maintenance contract.

(f) Identify other users of that system and ask for their opinion of that system.

(g) Control the conversion of files from the old to the new system.

9 IT AND THE AUDIT

9.1 In this section we will examine, very briefly, the developments in information technology (IT) which will be most likely to affect auditing in the future (or at least in the 1990s). These new developments will not change either management objectives or audit processes and techniques. The technical knowledge required of the auditor, however, will be increased and detailed audit procedures and techniques will be different.

Developments in hardware

9.2 The major trend in hardware development is the increased use of personal computers (PCs) and workstations. It is now possible to purchase a PC at a very low price with the same power and capacity as a mini-computer. Such computers are capable of exploiting the most sophisticated software. The movement has been towards *graphical user interfaces* to connect the user to the machine. Graphical user interfaces involve using pull down menus, windows, a mouse and icons and applications windowing, first adopted by Apple.

9.3 This is a rapidly expanding market and competition is increasingly fierce, with the aim of producing the fastest machine for the lowest price. In future, one of the techniques used with this aim in mind is *reduced instruction set computing* (risc). This is based on a long-known principle that simple instructions occur 80% of the time, whereas complex instructions (which take the computer some time to process) are used only 20% of the time. 'Risc' will involve a small number of simple instructions which can be processes very quickly. Complex instructions are built up in the software from a set of simple instructions using 'optimising compilers'.

9.4 In contrast to the rapid growth in the PC market, the mainframe market is growing much more slowly. These systems are often seen as outdated, unable to compete with the flexibility of PCs. A new role for mainframes, the 'distributed computing' model, may change this. The mainframe is no longer a processor, it merely holds large quantities of data which is then processed on PCs. This will lead to an integrated system combining mainframes, PCs and any other necessary components.

9.5 Supercomputer research is still in progress, aiming to produce computers a thousand times faster than those presently available.

9.6 Smart cards are being developed as an alternative to PINs and signatures. Biometric data from the customer is stored on the card and read by a terminal. These cards store information on micro-processors rather than magnetic stripes and therefore have a memory and intelligence. The main advantage of smart cards is their increased resistance to fraud.

9.7 Other current developments include image processing (photographs etc) and rewritable optical disks.

9.8 The main effect on the auditor of developments in hardware is the increased volume of information which computers will be able to store, leading to greater reporting output on that data. Access is now much easier for the non-specialist, who may not be able to discriminate between important and non-important information. This increased flow of information has a direct impact on the auditor, who must analyse and collate it and consider its relevance.

9.9 The increased speed of computers will obviously increase the speed of reporting. This means that the organisation can report far more frequently than yearly: monthly, weekly or even continuously. This is unlikely to lead to more frequent statutory reporting, but such reporting might be made to the market and the auditor would be involved in assessing the information provided.

Knowledge-based systems

9.10 We mentioned *expert systems* in Section 1. The development of expert systems is important to the auditor in relation to the client's system, as well as in the development of audit software. Expert systems are being developed for use in areas which the auditor or accountant has controlled, either historically or legally.

9.11 The recent developments in expert systems will produce a system which responds only to one user, and only responds in a specific way. This will provide additional security within a system.

9.12 Expert systems will eventually respond using voice recognition and image processing and it will provide a direct link between the user, the system and any resulting automated processes. Auditors will have to be equipped with better technical skills to assess the system.

9.13 The use of expert systems (and robotics) will often lead to the combination of the manufacturing and financial systems of an organisation. The auditor must advise on the implementation of controls in such a system, to ensure that information produced can be used for decision making by the management.

9.14 Expert systems are likely to save the auditor's time and money as they can increase the efficiency of the audit procedures used, and the maintenance of audit records. Other cost savings include the reduction in the number of staff required, and the fact that routine tasks can be assigned to technicians, who are helped by the expert system.

9.15 As 'decision support systems', expert systems will be used as a check, to corroborate the auditor's own judgement and decisions. Such information would reduce the risk of liability in litigation.

Electronic data interchange (EDI)

9.16 EDI indicates a system where data is transferred between several bodies in an agreed format, using predetermined standards of control and authentication, for example the SWIFT world-wide inter-bank system. The use of EDI is expanding at present, in conjunction with the deregulation of and attempt to harmonise the telecommunications system. The problems in the expansion of EDI have been the lack of a cohesive standard and unfamiliarity with the technology.

9.17 Control of networking and interactive systems is of the utmost importance. The auditor must be able to analyse the risks of unauthorised access such as line tapping or interception and to evaluate preventative measures. Authentication programmes and encryption are used for security and the auditor must understand such matters and he should be able to recommend on implementation. Password security is also extremely important, and the auditor may be called upon to recommend complex password procedures for sophisticated systems.

9.18 Networked systems will reduce the need for paper records be a minimum so the auditor will need to have the technical ability to find the audit trail in a sophisticated system. The controls in the system will be of vital importance. Once again, the technical skills of the auditor must be adequate to the task of assessing such controls, to ensure that they will guarantee accurate and valid output.

9.19 One other general point worth mentioning is legislation surrounding computers and the information they carry. Although we have some legislation in the UK in the form of the Data Protection Act 1984, the increasing complexity and internationalisation of computing and communication may require further legislation.

Chapter roundup

- The continuing development of more and more advanced mini/micro systems, particularly in terms of capacity, means that the control problems currently confronting the auditor are likely, at best, merely to continue, and at worst to increase. The auditor must carefully evaluate such systems, but the almost inevitable conclusion is going to be that an extensive amount of substantive testing is necessary. The main hope for the future is that CAATs, which have been developed principally to operate on large mainframe applications, can be scaled down to be effective on minis and micros.
- You must recognise the practical impact of computerisation in recent years and the fact that every auditor will encounter computer-based systems in his professional work.
- There are two principal categories of Computer Assisted Audit Techniques (CAATs), test data and audit software. Make sure that you can describe them, their function and their usefulness.
- The increased use of real-time and on-line systems create control problems.
- Bureaux and software houses can offer help in certain areas, and there are various reasons for using such organisations. Make sure that you can discuss the advantages and disadvantages to the user.
- Controls over systems development and maintenance are extremely important. Although the external auditor may not be directly involved with the system development he will need to monitor it carefully.
- Information technology is making constant advances. The effect on the auditing profession will surely be great. Remember to keep up to date with your reading - look out for relevant articles on this topic.

Test your knowledge

1 What are the main advantages in using an automated working papers package? (see para 1.4)

2 What are the definitions of application controls and general controls? (2.3)

3 What application controls might ensure completeness of input? (2.7)

4 In which eight areas should general controls operate? (2.13)

5 What are the two principal categories of CAAT? (3.2)

6 What factors will determine whether the auditor performs a test manually or by using a CAAT? (3.7)

7 In what circumstances may the reliance that the auditor wishes to place on general controls be limited? (3.18(d))

8 What is meant by 'audit trail'? (3.24)

9 What planning points arise when the auditor wishes to use test data? (4.5)

10 What is the advantage of an embedded audit facility? (4.8)

11 What is an 'integrated test facility'? (4.9)

12 What special control points should be considered when the auditor uses audit software? (4.20)

13 What control problems and strengths can be identified in on-line computer systems? (5.4)

14 Suggest three categories of controls which might be incorporated into a database management system. (5.7)

15 List four disadvantages of using the services of a computer bureau. (6.5)

16 What support facilities should be offered by a mini-computer supplier? (7.10)

17 What security and confidentiality problems are likely to be encountered in a small computer environment? (7.15 - 7.17)

18 Sketch the network diagram showing the procedures for systems development. (8.2)

Part C

Preparation of draft reports

Chapter 16

FORMING AN AUDIT JUDGEMENT

This chapter covers the following topics.

Introduction

At the end of an audit, after the bulk of the audit work has been completed but before the auditor can give an opinion, there are various procedures which the auditor must undertake.

Although each of these procedures are separated here for studying purposes, they are linked by their common aim of giving assurance as to the company's stability and the validity of the financial statements. The results of analytical review testing will be applied when considering the going concern situation and so on; in other words, these procedures are inter-connected.

These procedures are extremely important; failure to carry them out can lead to the gravest consequences for an auditor. Given this fact, they tend to be fairly standard in most audit approaches. A useful summary of these procedures is given in the checklist on Pages 296 and 297 and you should refer to the checklist throughout this chapter.

1 REVIEW OF THE FINANCIAL STATEMENTS

1.1 So far we have concentrated on the evaluation and testing of the accounting and control systems and substantive work on items or groups of items in the balance sheet. We now focus on the review of the financial statements as a whole. Clearly, one objective of this review must be to assess whether the financial statements conform with statutory and other regulatory requirements, including relevant SSAPs and FRSs, but the review is also concerned more imaginatively with interpretation of the figures in the accounts to assess whether the accounts as a whole make sense. Are they consistent within themselves? Do they form part of a logical pattern over a period of years?

The objectives of the review of the financial statements

1.2 Paragraph 6 of *The operational standard* states:

> 'The auditor should carry out such a review of the financial statements as is sufficient, in conjunction with the conclusions drawn from the other audit evidence obtained, to give him a reasonable basis for his opinion on the financial statements.'

1.3 It is important to note the term 'in conjunction with': reviewing the accounts is further audit evidence, it is not an exercise in isolation. Thus the results of the review must be considered in the light of all the other audit evidence, compliance and substantive, obtained to date through Stages 1 to 9 of the audit process identified in our diagrammatic approach.

1.4 To identify how we can achieve compliance with the standard we should turn initially to the auditing guideline *Review of financial statements*. First, the guideline states that the objectives of the review are to determine whether:

(a) the financial statements have been prepared using acceptable accounting policies which have been consistently applied and are appropriate to the enterprise's business;

(b) the results of operations, state of affairs and all other information included in the financial statements are compatible with each other and with the auditor's knowledge of the enterprise;

(c) there is adequate disclosure of all appropriate matters and the information contained in the financial statements is suitably classified and presented;

(d) the financial statements comply with all statutory requirements and other regulations relevant to the constitution and activities of that enterprise; and ultimately whether:

(e) the conclusions drawn from the other tests which he has carried out, together with those drawn from his overall review of the financial statements, enable him to form an opinion on the financial statements.

1.5 The following points should be borne in mind when determining the procedures necessary to achieve the above.

(a) Throughout the review the auditor needs to take account of the materiality of the matters under review and the confidence which his other audit work has already given him in the accuracy and completeness of the information contained in the financial statements.

(b) Skill and imagination are required to recognise the matters to be examined in carrying out an overall review and sound judgement is needed to interpret the information obtained. Accordingly, the review should not be delegated to someone lacking the necessary experience and skill. (The task will typically fall to the senior in charge in the first instance, but the manager and subsequently the reporting partner will need to be involved in the review process.)

(c) An overall review of the financial statements based on the auditor's knowledge of the business of the enterprise is not of itself a sufficient basis for the expression of an audit opinion on those statements. However, it provides valuable support for the conclusions arrived at as a result of his other audit work. In addition apparent inconsistencies could indicate areas in which material errors, omissions or irregularities may have occurred which have not been disclosed by other auditing procedures.

Review procedures

1.6 The guideline considers that the review procedures should include the following.

'*Accounting policies*

The auditor should review the accounting policies adopted by the enterprise to determine whether such policies:

(a) comply with statements of standard accounting practice or, in the absence thereof, are otherwise acceptable;

(b) are consistent with those of the previous period;

(c) are consistently applied throughout the enterprise;

(d) are disclosed in accordance with the requirements of statement of standard accounting practice No 2 Disclosure of accounting policies.'

1.7 When considering whether the policies adopted by management are acceptable the auditor should have regard *inter alia*, to the policies commonly adopted in particular industries and to policies for which there is substantial authoritative support.

'General review

The auditor should consider whether the results of operations and the state of affairs of the enterprise as reported in the financial statements are consistent with his knowledge of the underlying circumstances of the business.

In addition to any analytical review procedures carried out during the course of the audit, the auditor should carry out an overall review of the information in the financial statements themselves and compare it with other available data. For such a review to be effective the auditor needs to have sufficient knowledge of the activities of the enterprise and of the business which it operates to be able to determine whether particular items are abnormal. This background information should be available in the auditor's working papers as a result of his planning and earlier audit procedures.

Presentation and disclosure

The auditor should consider the information in the financial statements in order to ensure that the conclusions which a reader might draw from it would be justified and consistent with the circumstances of the enterprise's business. In particular, he should bear in mind the need for the financial statements to reflect the substance of the underlying transactions and balances and not merely their form. He should consider also whether the presentation adopted in the financial statements may have been unduly influenced by management's desire to present facts in a favourable or unfavourable light.

The auditor should also consider whether the financial statements adequately reflect the information and explanations obtained and conclusions reached on particular aspects of the audit.

The auditor should consider whether his review has disclosed any new factors which affect the presentation or accounting policies adopted. For example, it may become apparent as a result of his review of the financial statements as a whole, that the enterprise has liquidity problems and the auditor should consider whether or not the financial statements should have been prepared on a going concern basis.'

1.8 The presentation and disclosure requirements for limited companies are now so onerous that many firms utilise a checklist, commonly referred to as an 'Accounting requirements checklist', to ensure that the financial statements contain *prima facie*, all the disclosures required by the Companies Act 1985, SSAPs and, where applicable, The Stock Exchange. Mere completion of such a checklist, is of course, not an end in itself: further objective review will be necessary to determine whether the accounts present a true and fair view in the underlying circumstances. (It is beyond the scope of this text to provide such an accounting requirements checklist: reference should be made to an appropriate Financial Accounting source.)

1.9 When performing the general review identified above, it is the technique of analytical review that will provide the principal audit comfort and it is now time to identify how this technique can be applied to the review of financial statements.

2 ANALYTICAL REVIEW

2.1 Analytical review is a substantive technique that can be used at the initial planning stage of the audit, during the course of the audit and at or near the completion of the audit when reviewing the financial statements. Our analytical review procedures in respect of the financial statements will serve as an overall test of the reasonableness of the figures contained therein and are intended to corroborate conclusions formed during the previous stages of the audit in respect of transactions and balances and hence may highlight areas requiring further investigation where unusual matters or inconsistencies with earlier audit evidence are disclosed.

The techniques

2.2 It is meaningless to attempt a standardised approach to analytical review. Every industry is different and each company within that industry differs in certain respects.

What can be stated for all audits is that the reviewer must have an in-depth knowledge of the company, its history and the industry within which it operates.

2.3 To assist in analysing trends it is useful to make use of ratio analysis. The choice of accounting ratios is a matter of judgement, based on knowledge of the client, the industry, and the general state of the economy. In any event, ratios mean very little when used in isolation. Ratios should be calculated for previous periods and for comparable companies. This may involve a certain amount of initial research, but subsequently it is just a matter of adding new statistics to the existing information each year. The permanent file should contain a section with summarised accounts and the chosen ratios for prior years.

2.4 Important accounting ratios that could be examined include:

(a) gross profit margins, in total and by product;
(b) debtors ratio (average collection period);
(c) stock turnover ratio (stock divided into cost of sales);
(d) current ratio (current assets to current liabilities);
(e) quick or acid test ratio (liquid assets to current liabilities);
(f) gearing ratio (debt capital to equity capital);
(g) return on capital employed.

2.5 In addition to looking at the more usual ratios the auditor should consider examining other ratios that may be relevant to the particular clients' business, such as revenue per passenger mile for an airline operator client, or fees per partner for a professional office.

2.6 One further important technique is to examine important related accounts in conjunction with each other. It is often the case that revenue and expense accounts are related to balance sheet accounts and comparisons should be made to ensure that the relationships are reasonable. Examples of such related accounts are:

(a) creditors and purchases;
(b) stocks and cost of sales;
(c) fixed assets and depreciation, repairs and maintenance expense;
(d) intangible assets and amortisation;
(e) loans and interest expense;
(f) investments and investment income;
(g) debtors and bad debt expense;
(h) debtors and sales.

2.7 Other areas that might be investigated in the analytical review include the following.

(a) In terms of sales, examine changes in products, customers and levels of returns, looking for any noticeable trends.

(b) Assess the effect of price changes on the cost of sales.

(c) Consider the effect of inflation, industrial disputes, changes in production methods, and so on the charge for wages.

(d) Where appropriate obtain explanations for all major variances analysed using a standard costing system. Particular attention should be paid to those relating to the over or under absorption of overheads since these may, inter alia, affect stock valuations.

(e) Compare trends in production and sales and assess the effect on any provisions for obsolete stocks.

(f) Ensure that changes in the percentage labour or overhead content of production costs are also reflected in the stock valuation.

(g) Other profit and loss expenditure comparing:

(i) rent with annual rent per rental agreement;

(ii) rates with previous year and known rates increases;

(iii) interest payable on loans with outstanding balance and interest rate per loan agreement;

(iv) hire or leasing charges with annual rate per agreements;

(v) other items related to activity level with general price increase and change in relevant level of activity (for example telephone expenditure will increase disproportionately if export or import business increases);

(vi) other items not related to activity level with general price increases (or specific increases if known).

(h) Review profit and loss account for items which may have been omitted (eg scrap sales, training levy, special contributions to pension fund, provisions for dilapidations etc).

(i) Generally ensure expected variations arising from the following have occurred:

(i) review of minutes;

(ii) discussions with client officials;

(iii) industry or local trends;

(iv) known disturbances of the trading pattern (for example strikes, depot closures, failure of suppliers).

2.8 Certain of the comparisons and ratios measuring liquidity and longer-term capital structure will assist in evaluating whether the company is a going concern, in addition to contributing to the overall view of the accounts. We shall see in the next section, however, that there are factors other than declining ratios that may indicate going concern problems.

2.9 The working papers must contain the completed results of the analytical review. These might comprise:

(a) the outline programme of the review work;

(b) the summary of significant figures and relationships for the period;

(c) a summary of comparisons made with budgets and with previous years;

(d) details of all significant variations considered;

(e) details of the results of investigations into such variations;

(f) the audit conclusions reached;

(g) information considered necessary for assisting in the planning of subsequent audits.

Exercise 1

You are the audit senior in charge of the audit of Tetterby Tools plc, a large manufacturing company. The following information has been provided to you in advance of the finalisation of the audit for the year to 30 April 19X2.

PROFIT AND LOSS ACCOUNT	*19X2*	*19X1*
	£'000	£'000
Turnover	48,000	38,250
Cost of sales	36,000	27,050
	12,000	11,200
Distribution costs*	4,950	4,800
Administration expenses*	3,300	3,150
	8,250	7,950
Trading profit	3,750	3,250
Interest paid	1,200	620
Profit before taxation	2,550	2,630
**Note*. Depreciation included as part of these figures	3,200	2,950

BALANCE SHEET

Fixed assets	33,525	33,260
Current assets		
Stock	8,375	6,428
Debtors	8,166	4,922
	16,541	11,350
Current liabilities		
Trade creditors	4,500	4,200
Other creditors	1,000	500
Bank overdraft	2,850	1,400
	8,350	6,100
Net current assets	8,191	5,250
Total assets less current liabilities	41,716	38,510
Long term loan (repayable 19X9)	10,000	8,000
	31,716	30,510
Share capital	3,000	3,000
Reserves	28,716	27,510
	31,716	30,150

Required

(a) Identify six matters which you consider require special attention when auditing the accounts of Tetterby Tools plc.

(b) For each of these state why you consider them to be of importance.

(c) Briefly explain the purpose of analytical review and the stages at which such a review should be carried out.

Solution

(a) The matters which require special attention include (any six of) the following.

(i) The reason for an increase in turnover by 25%.

(ii) Gross profit percentage, which has fallen from 29.3% to 25.0%.

(iii) Trading profit, which has increased by 15%, although it has fallen when calculated as a percentage of sales.

(iv) Profit before taxation, which has fallen in spite of increased turnover.

(v) Fixed assets, to which there have been additions or revaluation of at least £3,465,000.

(vi) Stock, which has increased by 30%.

(vii) Debtor days, which have increased from 49 to 62.

(viii) Bank overdraft, which has increased by 104%.

(ix) Long term loan, which has increased by £2,000,000.

(b) Each of the matters is important for the following reasons.

(i) Turnover might be overstated as the result of including post year end sales. The same error could have understated stocks. Analysing sales on a monthly basis might reveal inconsistencies, for example unusually high sales in April 19X0 and unusually low sales in May 19X0.

(ii) It may be that the gross profit percentage has fallen due to changed trading conditions such as increased supplier prices, or a change in the company's pricing policy to boost turnover. There may have been errors which have mis-stated purchases or stock.

(iii) The increase in trading profits suggests that distribution costs or administrative expenses may be incorrect. Distribution costs have only increased by 3% while turnover has increased by 25%. Normally, distribution costs would be expected to increase in line with turnover.

(iv) Profit before taxation is affected by the further figure of interest paid. Interest paid could be over- or under-stated. Understatement could result from failing to accrue for all interest payable up to the year end.

(v) All additions should be checked to ensure that cost has been correctly recorded, and that the additions have been authorised. If revaluations of fixed assets have taken place, it is important to check that the revaluations are reasonable.

(vi) A misstatement in the stock valuation has a direct effect on profit. The large increase in stock could indicate overvaluation of stocks held. Increased stock levels alternatively suggest that there may be significant quantities of stock which cannot be sold (for example obsolete stock). Such stocks should be recorded at net realisable value where this is below cost.

(vii) The risk in debtor days could indicate possible bad debts for which provision should be made. However, it will be more useful if debtor days were calculated using monthly sales figures: it may be that much of the increased turnover for 19X0 occurred in the final months of the year, in which case the debtors' collection position may not be as bad as our figures suggest.

(viii) The bank overdraft should be checked with bank statements, and the terms and conditions of the overdraft should be reviewed.

(ix) The reason for the increase in long term loan should be ascertained, and the amount and terms of the loan should be checked to original documentation.

(c) Analytical review is a set of techniques which the auditor may use and which uses various sources of information to ascertain whether the figures in the financial statements 'make sense' in the light of that information. The techniques include the examination and comparison of financial accounting ratios and the investigation of unexpected variations in figures. Analytical review may be carried out at various stages of the audit. Two stages at which analytical review is particularly valuable are the planning stage of the audit, when analytical review can indicate areas to which audit work should be directed, and at the stage of the final review of the financial statements.

3 PRECEDING YEAR AMOUNTS

3.1 In the case of ongoing audit clients, preceding year amounts present few difficulties. The auditor must ensure that comparatives in the financial statements are correctly stated according to the previous year's financial statements. any other disclosures required by accounting standards or the Companies Act must also be checked.

3.2 Any prior year adjustments will affect the figures for the previous year. The auditor must ensure that the prior year adjustment is correctly stated and disclosed according to FRS 3 *Reporting financial performance.*

3.3 In expressing an opinion on the accounts of a new client the auditor accepts responsibility not only for the accounts of the year being reported on, but also:

(a) the consistency of the application of accounting policies;

(b) the reliability of the opening balances (which have an effect on the profit or loss for the current year);

(c) the appropriateness of the comparative figures included in the accounts, in as much as they may render the current year's figures misleading.

3.4 Clarification of the auditor's responsibility for amounts taken from the preceding period's financial statements is provided in the detailed operational guideline *Amounts derived from the preceding financial statements.*

3.5 Financial statements of companies incorporated under the provisions of the Companies Act 1985 are required to disclose corresponding amounts for all items in a company's balance sheet and profit and loss account. In other cases, financial statements usually contain corresponding amounts as a matter of law, regulation or good practice. Their purpose, unless stated otherwise, is to complement the amounts relating to the current period and not to re-present the complete financial statements for the preceding period. The auditor is *not* required to express an opinion on the corresponding amounts as such. His responsibility is to ensure that they are the amounts which appeared in the preceding period's financial statements or, where appropriate, have either been properly

Audit completion checklist

Client:
Period ended:
Instructions:
1 All questions must be answered by ticking one of the columns as appropriate.
2 Any 'No' answer must be referenced to the 'points for partner' schedule.

Section I - To be completed by the manager	*Yes*	*No*	*N/A*	*Reference to points for partner schedule*
Permanent audit file 1 Have the following been updated in the course of the audit: (a) Flowcharts and related documentation for: (i) computer systems? (ii) non-computer systems? (b) Internal /key control evaluation questionnaire conclusions? (c) Details of the client organisation? (d) Financial history?				
2 Is a current letter of engagement in force?				
Transaction (interim) audit file 3 Were walk-through tests performed to confirm our record of the accounting systems?				
4 Was the audit programme tailored?				
5 Was adequate audit attention given to internal control weaknesses?				
6 Were levels of audit testing (compliance and substantive) appropriate?				
7 Have audit programmes been signed off as complete?				
8 Are there adequate explanations of work done and are conclusions drawn?				
9 Is there evidence of the review of work?				
10 Have weaknesses arising on the interim audit been reported to management in a formal letter				
11 Has the client replied to the weaknesses already notified in respect of matters arising from the previous year's audit?				
12 Have major internal control weaknesses previously notified been rectified?				
Final (balance sheet) audit file 13 Have lead schedules been prepared for each audit area and cross-referenced and agreed with the financial statements?				
14 Have all the working papers been initialled and dated by the members of staff who prepared them?				

	Yes	*No*	*N/A*	*Reference to points for partner schedule*
15 Have all the working papers been cross-referenced?				
16 Do the working papers show comparative figures where appropriate?				
17 Have audit conclusions been drawn for each balance sheet audit area as appropriate?				
18 Has the balance sheet audit programme been completed, initialled and cross-referenced to the working papers?				
19 Have the necessary profit and loss account schedules been prepared and do they agree with the detailed accounts?				
20 Current assets: (a) Were debtors circularised and were the results satisfactory? (b) Was the client's stocktaking attended and were the results satisfactory? (c) Is the basis of stock and work in progress valuation satisfactory and correctly disclosed in the accounts?				
21 Liabilities: (a) Were creditors circularised and were the results satisfactory? (b) Have all liabilities, contingent liabilities, and capital commitments been fully accounted for or noted in the accounts?				
Audit completion 22 Have formal representations been obtained or has a draft letter been set up (including representations in respect of each director regarding transactions involving himself and his connected persons required to be disclosed by the Companies Act 1985)?				
23 Have all audit queries been satisfactorily answered?				
24 Post balance sheet event review: (a) Has a comprehensive review been performed and evidenced? (b) Has the review been carried out at the most recent date possible with regard to the anticipated date of the audit report?				
25 Have all audit queries been satisfactorily answered?				
26 Have all closing adjustments been agreed with the client?				
27 Are you satisfied that all material instances where we have not received the information and explanations we require have been referred to in the points for partner schedule?				

	Yes	No	N/A	Reference to points for partner schedule
28 Review of working papers? (a) Have you reviewed all the working papers? (If not, briefly describe review procedure adopted) (b) Have arrangements been made for the financial statements to be reviews by: (i) a second partner (a brief review or special review)? and/or (ii) the audit review panel? (c) Has the planning memorandum and, where applicable, client risk evaluation questionnaire been completed?				
Subsidiary and associated companies 29 Where secondary auditors have been involved in the audit of subsidiary and associated companies, have we: (a) Sent our group accounts audit questionnaire? (b) Received satisfactory answers? or (c) Reviewed and approved the working papers of secondary auditors?				
30 Have all accounts of subsidiary and associated companies been approved by the directors and audited?				
31 If any of the audit reports have been qualified has the fact and nature of the qualification been referred to in the points for partner schedule?				
Financial statements and directors' report 32 Is the financial statements layout in accordance with the firm's standard accounts pack?				
33 Has the analytical review memorandum been properly completed and are the review conclusions consistent with the conclusions drawn in respect of our other audit work?				
34 Is the reliance placed on analytical review reasonable in the circumstances?				
35 Is any proposed dividend covered by the distributable profits as disclosed in the financial statements?				
36 Has the firm's accounting disclosure checklist been completed to ensure that the financial statements and directors' report comply with: (a) the Companies Act 1985? (b) Statements of Standard Accounting Practice and Financial Reporting Standards? (c) Stock Exchange requirements? (d) Other reporting requirements?				
37 Has the directors' report been reviewed for consistency with the financial statements?				
38 Has other financial information to be issued with the audited financial statements (eg contained in the Chairman's Statement or Employee Accounts) been reviewed for consistency with the financial statements?				

....
Audit Manager

....
Date

Section II - To be completed by the reporting partner	Yes	No	Comments
1 Has Section I of the checklist been satisfactorily completed?			
2 Have all the points on the 'points for partner' schedule been satisfactorily resolved or are there any material matters outstanding which should be referred to the audit panel?			
3 Has your review of the current and permanent file indicated that the working paper evidence is sufficient to enable you to form an opinion on the financial statements, having regard to the firm's audit manual procedures?			
4 Are the conclusions you have drawn from your overall review of the financial statements based on your knowledge of the client, consideration of the analytical review memorandum, review of post balance sheet events and where appropriate, client risk evaluation questionnaire, consistent with those contained in the detailed working papers?			
5 Have all improvements which you consider could be made in the conduct of future audits been noted on 'points forward' (for consideration at the audit debriefing)?			
6 (a) Are there any specialist areas in which the client could benefit from our expertise, for example tax planning? (b) Has the provision of such services been drawn to his attention?			

I confirm that the report of the auditors will be unqualified*/unqualified with an explanatory paragraph */qualified* as set out in the attached draft financial statements.

....
Reporting Partner

....
Date

*Delete as appropriate

restated to achieve consistency and comparability with the current period's amounts, or have been restated due to a change of accounting policy or a correction of a fundamental error as required by FRS 3.

3.6 In these special circumstances the new auditor will have to satisfy himself as to the matters identified in Paragraph 3.3, but his lack of prior knowledge of the preceding period's financial statement will require him to apply additional procedures in order to obtain the necessary assurance.

3.7 The additional procedures that should be performed by the auditor may include any of the following:

(a) consultations with the client's management;

(b) review of the client's records, working papers and accounting and control procedures for the preceding period, particularly in so far as they affect the opening position;

(c) audit work on the current period, which will usually provide some evidence regarding opening balances; and

(d) in exceptional circumstances, substantive testing of the opening balances, if he does not consider the results of procedures (a) to (c) to be satisfactory.

3.8 In addition, the auditor may be able to hold consultations with the previous auditor. Whilst outgoing auditors can normally be expected to afford reasonable co-operation to their successors, neither ethical statements nor the law place them under a specific obligation to make working papers or other information available to their successors. Consultations would normally be limited to seeking information concerning the previous auditor's examination of particular areas which are important to his successor, and to obtaining clarification of any significant accounting matters which are not adequately dealt with in the client's records. If, however, such consultations are not possible or alternatively, if the preceding period's financial statements were unaudited, the only evidence about the opening position available to the auditor will be that generated by procedures such as those set out in Paragraph 3.7 above.

3.9 Under normal circumstances the auditor will be able to satisfy himself as to the opening position by performing the work set out in Paragraphs 3.7 and 3.8. If he is not able to satisfy himself in any material respect he will need to qualify his report for the possible effect on the financial statements.

4 UNAUDITED PUBLISHED INFORMATION

4.1 S 235 Companies Act 1985 states that:

> 'the auditors shall consider whether the information given in the directors' report for the financial year for which the accounts are prepared is consistent with those accounts; and if they are of opinion that it is not they shall state that fact in their report.'

4.2 The Act does not provide any interpretative assistance as to what is meant by an 'inconsistency' or indeed what matters may give rise to an inconsistency in this context. What is in no doubt, however, is that this requirement is not equivalent to forming an opinion on the directors' report itself.

4.3 This statutory provision prompted the APC to develop guidance for the auditor. This is in the form of a detailed operational guideline entitled *Financial information issued with audited financial statements.*

4.4 It should also be noted, however, that this guideline clarifies the auditor's responsibilities in relation to other financial information which may be published with audited financial statements (for example five year summary, employee report) and that it will be relevant to the audit of enterprises other than those incorporated under the Companies Acts.

The directors' report: statutory responsibilities

4.5 As already noted, the Companies Act 1985 does not require the auditor to form an opinion on the directors' report itself and, for this reason, the page references given in the first paragraph of an audit report on the annual financial statements of an enterprise should not extend to those pages containing the directors' report. The auditor should therefore, under normal circumstances, confine his work to satisfying himself that the directors' report does not contain any matters which are inconsistent with the financial statements.

4.6 Matters which may give rise to inconsistencies would include the following.

(a) An inconsistency between actual figures or narrative appearing in, respectively, the audited financial statements and the directors' report.

(b) An inconsistency between the bases of preparation of related items appearing in the financial statements and the directors' report, where the figures themselves are not directly comparable and the different bases are not disclosed.

(c) An inconsistency between figures contained in the audited financial statements and a narrative interpretation of the effect of those figures in the directors' report.

4.7 Where the auditor considers that some inconsistency exists, he should consider carefully its implications and hold discussions with the client's management in order to try and achieve its elimination.

4.8 If management are not prepared to put through the adjustments considered necessary by the auditor, then the further action to be taken by the auditor will depend on where he believes that the adjustment is required.

4.9 If, in the auditor's opinion, the adjustment is required in the directors' report, he should, in a separate paragraph in his report on the financial statements, refer to the inconsistency.

4.10 If, in the auditor's opinion, the adjustment is required in the *audited financial statements* then he should consider qualifying his report. The auditor will also have to make reference in his report to the inconsistency between the financial statements and the directors' report as it will still exist. Since the identification of such inconsistencies will normally occur only when the audit has been largely completed, it would be exceptional if it was the financial statements which required amendment.

Non-statutory responsibilities

4.11 The auditor has no statutory responsibilities in respect of items in the directors' report which in his opinion are *misleading but not inconsistent with the financial statements*, (for example there may be a statement given in the directors' report for which there is no corresponding financial information in the financial statements but which is nevertheless misleading), or in respect of other financial information contained elsewhere in the annual report (say the chairman's statement).

4.12 However, where information of this kind is published as part of, or in conjunction with, the annual report, the auditor should review that information. The auditor does this as part of his overall professional responsibility to ensure that the credibility of the financial statements is not undermined, and in so doing meets the expectations of those to whom the information is directed.

4.13 Where the auditor considers that there is a material inconsistency between the financial statements and other financial information or that an item is misleading in some other respect, he should consider its implications and hold discussions with directors, or other senior members of management, and may also make his views known in writing to all the directors in order to achieve its elimination. Where communication with directors and their representatives does not result in elimination of the problem, he should consider whether an amendment is required to the financial statements, the directors' report or the other financial information.

4.14 If, in the auditor's opinion, it is the financial statements which require amendment he should follow the guidance given earlier and consider qualifying his report.

4.15 Assuming it is not the financial statements which require amendment, there is no statutory requirement for the auditor to comment in his report. However, there may be occasions when a matter is potentially so misleading to a reader of the financial statements that it would be inappropriate for the auditor to remain silent. In these circumstances the auditor should seek legal and other professional advice on what action may be appropriate.

4.16 If the auditor decides that he should refer to the matter in his report, he should be aware that Counsel has advised that the qualified privilege (the defence to an action for defamation) which an audit report normally enjoys may not extend to comments on:

(a) an item in the directors' report which, while not inconsistent with the financial statements, is misleading in some other respect; or

(b) financial information contained elsewhere in an annual report which is inconsistent with the financial statements or otherwise misleading.

4.17 The auditor may make use of his right under s 390 of the Companies Act 1985 to be heard at any general meeting of the members on any business of the meeting which concerns him as auditor. This includes the right to draw attention to those matters described above.

4.18 The auditor should urge the company not to publish its annual report until after he has completed his review of the other financial information and he should make arrangements to see, prior to publication, any documents in which the financial statements are to be included. The auditor should deal with these procedures in the audit engagement letter. Where, notwithstanding this, the auditor is not given an opportunity to complete his review before the date of issue, he should complete it before the general meeting at which the financial statements are laid before the members. In the event that there is something with which he disagrees, the auditor should take legal and other professional advice and consider drawing the attention of members in accordance with s 390, taking the course of action set out in Paragraph 4.18.

4.19 It should be appreciated that only very rarely will the auditor encounter problems of inconsistencies or misleading information, either in the directors' report or in the other financial information, where the directors are unwilling to amend as necessary. The review of such information is usually relatively straightforward.

5 POST BALANCE SHEET EVENTS AND GOING CONCERN EVALUATION

The audit of post balance sheet events

5.1 The auditing guideline *Events after the balance sheet date* has clarified the responsibilities of the auditor regarding examining and reporting upon post balance sheet events, including the significance of the date of the audit report. The following is a summary of the principal matters, written in the context of the audit of a limited company, affecting the dating of the audit report.

(a) The auditor should always date his audit report. The date used should, generally, be that on which he signs his report on the financial statements. If, for administrative reasons, final copies of the financial statements are not available at the date at which the auditor declares himself willing to sign his report, he may use that date, provided the delay in the preparation of final copies is only of short duration.

(b) The auditor's responsibility is to report on the financial statements as presented by the directors, These statements do not exist in law until approved by the directors and, indeed, SSAP 17 requires disclosure of the date of approval in the financial statements. It follows that the auditor cannot date his report earlier than the date of approval by the directors. Before signing he should obtain evidence that the financial statements have been approved by the directors; this might typically be a board minute.

(c) At the date on which the financial statements are approved by the directors, they do not have to be in the final typed form, but the auditor should satisfy himself that the approved financial statements are materially complete. Hence they should not leave unresolved any matters requiring exercise of judgement or discretion.

(d) The auditor should plan his work so that, wherever practicable, his report is dated as close as possible to the date of approval of the financial statements. In practice, the auditor's report date and directors' approval date will be the same, assuming the auditor has completed all his post balance sheet work to his satisfaction.

Action up to the date of the audit report

5.2 As the auditor's responsibility extends to the date on which he signs his report it follows that he must obtain reasonable assurance up to that date in respect of all significant events. The procedures necessary to achieve this assurance are described later in this chapter. The auditor should ensure that any such significant events are, where appropriate, accounted for or disclosed in the financial statements: if not, a qualification of his report may be necessary.

Action after the date of the audit report

5.3 This is a tricky area, for the auditor's responsibilities are not clear cut as they are in the period prior to the date of his report. The following is a summary of his responsibilities and practical problems that could arise.

(a) After the date of the audit report the auditor does not have a duty to search for evidence of post balance sheet events. However, if he becomes aware of information before the general meeting at which the financial statements are laid before the members (normally, of course, the AGM) of information, from sources either within or outside the company, which might have led him to give a different audit opinion had he possessed the information at the date of his report he should act as follows.

(i) Discuss the matter with the directors and then consider whether the financial statements should be amended by the directors (the auditor does not have powers to amend accounts).

(ii) If the directors are unwilling to take action which the auditor considers necessary to inform the members of the changed situation, the auditor should consider exercising his statutory rights to make a statement at the general meeting. He should also consider taking legal advice on his position. The auditor does not have a statutory right to communicate directly in writing with the members except where he wishes to resign or where it is proposed to remove him.

(iii) If the directors wish to amend after the auditor has signed his report but before the accounts have been sent to the members, the auditor will need to consider whether the proposed amendments affect his report. His report should not be dated before the date on which the amended financial statements are approved by the directors.

(iv) Where, after the financial statements have been sent to the members, the directors wish to prepare and approve an amended set of financial statements to lay before the members, further post balance sheet audit work as in (iii) above will be necessary to cover events up to the revised date of his audit report. In this latter report he should refer to the original financial statements and his report thereon.

(b) If after the general meeting the auditor becomes aware of information which suggests that the financial statements which were laid before that meeting are wrong, he should inform the directors. He should ascertain how the directors intend to deal with the situation. In particular he should ascertain whether they intend to communicate with the members. If the auditor considers that the directors are not dealing correctly with the situation he may, exceptionally, wish to take legal advice.

5.4 The audit responsibilities can be summarised in the form of a diagram.

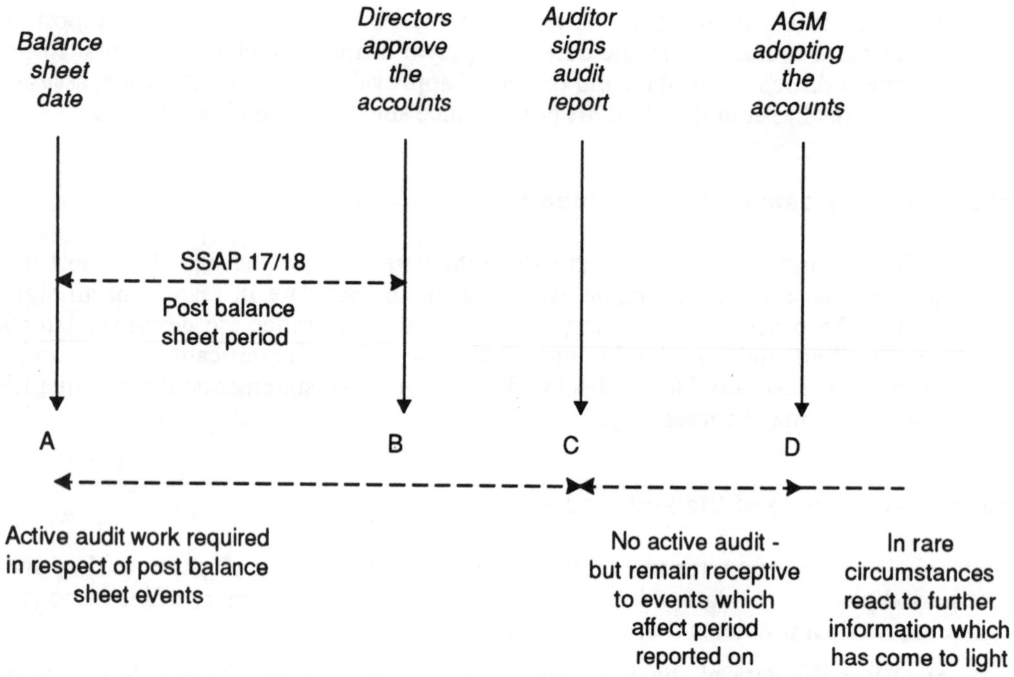

The period between B and C should be kept as short as possible. Ideally, assuming the auditor has performed the underlying post balance sheet work satisfactorily, these events will occur on the same day. C can never precede B, as the financial statements do not legally exist until approved by the directors.

5.5 Before describing the steps taken by the auditor to obtain reasonable assurance in respect of post balance sheet events it is prudent to revise the accounting requirements of the relevant accounting standards SSAP 17 *Accounting for post balance sheet events* and SSAP 18 *Accounting for contingencies.*

SSAP 17

5.6 SSAP 17 *Accounting for post balance sheet events* defines post balance sheet events in the following terms.

> 'Post balance sheet events are those events, both favourable and unfavourable, which occur between the balance sheet date and the date on which the financial statements are approved by the board of directors.

Adjusting events are post balance sheet events which provide additional evidence of conditions existing at the balance sheet date. They include events which because of statutory conventional requirements are reflected in financial statements.

Non-adjusting events are post balance sheet events which concern conditions which did not exist at the balance sheet date.

The date on which the financial statements are approved by the board of directors is the date the board of directors formally approves a set of documents as the financial statements. In respect of unincorporated enterprises the date of approval is the corresponding date. In respect of group accounts, the date of approval is the date when the group accounts are formally approved by the board of directors of the holding company.'

5.7 Standard practice in respect of the disclosure of post balance sheet events is as follows.

'Financial statements should be prepared on the basis of conditions existing at the balance sheet date.

A material post balance sheet event requires changes in the amounts to be included in financial statements where:

(a) it is an adjusting event; or

(b) it indicates that application of the going concern concept to the whole or a material part of the company is not appropriate.

A material post balance sheet event should be disclosed where:

(a) it is a non-adjusting event of such materiality that its non-disclosure would affect the ability of the users of financial statements to reach a proper understanding of the financial position; or

(b) it is the reversal or maturity after the year end of a transaction entered into before the year end, the substance of which was primarily to alter the appearance of the company's balance sheet.'

5.8 In respect of each post balance sheet event which is required to be disclosed under the sub-paragraph immediately above, the following information should be stated by way of note in the financial statements:

(a) the nature of the event; and

(b) an estimate of the financial effect, or a statement that it is not practicable to make such an estimate.

The date on which the financial statements were approved by the board should be disclosed.

5.9 There is an important overriding consideration that should be applied to non-adjusting events. In order to accord with the prudence concept, an adverse event which would normally be classified as non-adjusting may need to be reclassified as adjusting: in such circumstances, full disclosure of the adjustment would be required.

5.10 By way of illustration, if a company suffered serious damage to property and/or trading stocks in the post balance sheet period this would normally be classified as a non-adjusting event requiring disclosure in the notes to the financial statements. If, however, the resulting loss was under-insured, or uninsured, prudence may indicate that the event should be reclassified as adjusting, hence requiring amendment to the financial statements and disclosure as an exceptional or extraordinary item.

5.11 It is important to stress the two categories of material post balance event requiring changes in the amounts to be included in the financial statements:

(a) the adjusting event described above; and

(b) the event indicating that application of the going concern concept to the whole or a material part of the company is not appropriate.

5.12 The auditor's post balance sheet review must clearly concern itself with both categories of event and, as we shall see, many of the procedures that the auditor adopts are specifically designed to appraise whether the company is a going concern.

SSAP 18

5.13 SSAP 18 *Accounting for contingencies* defines contingencies in the following terms.

> 'Contingency is a condition which exists at the balance sheet date, where the outcome will be confirmed only on the occurrence or non-occurrence of one or more uncertain future events. A contingent gain or loss is a gain or loss dependent on a contingency.'

5.14 Standard practice in relation to contingencies is as follows.

> 'In addition to amounts accrued under the fundamental concept of prudence in SSAP 2 *Disclosure of accounting policies,* a material contingent loss should be accrued in financial statements where it is probable that a future event will confirm a loss which can be estimated with reasonable accuracy at the date on which the financial statements are approved by the board of directors.
>
> A material contingent loss not accrued above should be disclosed except where the possibility of loss is remote.
>
> Contingent gains should not be accrued in financial statements. A material contingent gain should be disclosed in financial statements only if it is probable that the gain will be realised.'

5.15 In respect of each contingency required to be disclosed the following information should be stated by way of note in the financial statements:

(a) the nature of the contingency;

(b) the uncertainties which are expected to affect the ultimate outcome; and

(c) a prudent estimate of the financial effect, made at the date on which the financial statements are approved by the board of directors; or a statement that it is not practicable to make such an estimate.

5.16 Where there is disclosure of an estimate of the financial effect of a contingency, the amount disclosed should be the potential financial effect. In the case of a contingent loss, this should be reduced by:

(a) any amounts accrued; and
(b) the amounts of any components where the possibility of loss is remote.

The net amount only need be disclosed.

5.17 This accounting standard is by no means easy to interpret and apply as it is in the nature of a contingency that the outcome is uncertain. It is helpful, therefore, first to identify some examples of contingencies and then interpret the tests of 'probability' and 'remoteness' required by the standard. Examples of contingencies are as follows.

(a) *Contingent gains*

(i) An insurance recovery expected in respect of a loss previously provided for.

(ii) Legal claims initiated by the client, where damages are expected to be awarded.

(iii) Compensation payable by a foreign government for assets nationalised and written off.

(b) *Contingent liabilities*

(i) Legal claims against the client in respect of faulty goods or other alleged breaches of contract.

(ii) Product warranties or guarantees.

(iii) Bills discounted with recourse.

(iv) Pension liabilities, if unfunded and not provided.

(v) Guarantees on behalf of subsidiary companies.

5.18 The standard does not require disclosure of 'remote' contingencies, whether assets or liabilities. Remoteness is best interpreted in terms of probability rather than of time scale.

5.19 The table below sets out the different degrees of probability (although no attempt is made to place a figure upon them) and the resulting treatment in the financial statements, based on the standard.

Probability	*Contingent asset*	*Contingent liability*
Remote	No disclosure	No disclosure
Possible/probable	No disclosure	Disclosure
Highly probable	Disclosure	Provision
Virtually certain	Accrual	Provision

Procedures for the audit of events after the balance sheet date

5.20 The auditing guideline *Events after the balance sheet date* identifies that certain events falling within the scope of SSAP 17 are examined by the auditor as part of his normal verification work on the balance sheet. Examples include the checking of cash received from certain debtors after the balance sheet date or the amounts realised from the sale of stock after the year-end to assess net realisable value. There are, however, additional procedures described as a 'review of events after the balance sheet date', also commonly referred to as a 'subsequent event review', that the auditor should carry out.

5.21 The guideline states that the review should consist of discussions with management relating to such events, and may also include consideration of:

(a) procedures taken by management to ensure that all events after the balance sheet date have been identified, considered and properly evaluated as to their effect on the financial statements;

(b) any management accounts and relevant accounting records;

(c) profit forecasts and cash flow projections for the new period;

(d) known 'risk' areas and contingencies, whether inherent in the nature of the business or revealed by previous audit experience;

(e) minutes of shareholders', directors' and management meetings and correspondence and memoranda relating to items included in the minutes;

(f) relevant information which has come to attention, from sources outside the enterprise including public knowledge of competitors, suppliers and customers.

5.22 This review should be updated to a date as near as practicable to that of the audit report by making enquiries of management and considering the need to carry out further tests.

5.23 The review above is necessarily broad-brush in approach to cater for all circumstances, but it should be appreciated that it contains procedures to investigate the three critical post balance sheet areas:

(a) adjusting events;
(b) evaluation of the company as a going concern; and
(c) contingencies.

5.24 To develop a more practical approach it is useful to look at procedures relevant to going concern evaluation and the audit of contingencies in greater detail.

Going concern evaluation

5.25 The auditor's responsibility to form an opinion as to whether a company is a going concern at the date of his report is beyond dispute, but it is only recently that formal guidance has been issued by the APC identifying procedures that the auditor should carry out to discharge his duties. The guidance is in the form of an auditing guideline entitled *The auditor's considerations in respect of going concern.*

5.26 It is an important theme of the guideline that it is very rare for an enterprise to cease to carry on business without any prior indications and hence any procedures that provide early identification that the enterprise may be unable to continue in business will be of assistance to management as well as the auditor. Nevertheless, going concern considerations cannot be confined to the early stages of the audit and hence the procedures need to be continued to the date of the audit report. Of particular practical assistance in the guideline are the paragraphs identifying possible symptoms of going concern problems. These paragraphs are reproduced here as a listing to make them more palatable:

(a) *Symptoms indicating an inability to meet debts as they fall due*

(i) Adverse financial figures or ratios:

(1) recurring operating losses;

(2) financing to a considerable extent out of overdue suppliers and other creditors (for example, VAT, PAYE, National Insurance);

(3) heavy dependence on short-term finance for long-term needs;

(4) working capital deficiencies;

(5) low liquidity rates;

(6) over-gearing, in the form of high or increasing debt to equity ratios;

(7) under-capitalisation, particularly if there is a deficiency of share capital and reserves.

(ii) Borrowings in excess of limits imposed by debenture trust deeds.

(iii) Default on loans or similar agreements.

(iv) Dividends in arrears.

(v) Restrictions placed on usual trade terms.

(vi) Excessive or obsolete stock.

(vii) Long overdue debtors.

(viii) Non-compliance with statutory capital requirements.

(ix) Deterioration of relationship with bankers.

(x) Necessity of seeking new sources or methods of obtaining finance.

(xi) The continuing use of old fixed assets because there are no funds available to replace them.

(xii) The size and content of the order book.

(xiii) Potential losses on long-term contracts.

(b) *Other factors not necessarily suggesting inability to meet debts*

(i) Internal matters:

(1) loss of key management or staff;

(2) significantly increasing stock levels;

(3) work stoppages or other labour difficulties;

(4) substantial dependence on the success of a particular project or particular asset;

(5) excessive reliance on the success of a new product;

(6) uneconomic long-term commitments.

(ii) External matters:

(1) legal proceedings or similar matters that may jeopardise a company's ability to continue in business;

(2) loss of a key franchise or patent;

(3) loss of a principal supplier or customer;

(4) the undue influence of a market dominant competitor;

(5) political risks;

(6) technical developments which render a key product obsolete;

(7) frequent financial failures of enterprises in the same industry.

5.27 The indications above vary in importance and some may only have significance as audit evidence when viewed in conjunction with others. Many audit firms incorporate symptoms such as those itemised above in formal checklists, often referred to as 'Going concern review checklists', to provide documentary evidence of their review. The significance of the indications above may diminish because they are matched by audit evidence indicating that there are mitigating factors. Indications that the enterprise, for instance, is unable to meet its debts may be mitigated by factors relating to alternative means for maintaining adequate cash flows; for example, the ability to dispose of assets or postpone replacement of assets without adversely affecting operations, to obtain new sources of finance or to renew or extend loans and to restructure debts.

5.28 The auditor should carry out procedures as early as possible in the audit in order to determine whether any of the indications described above are present and to give management more time to consider its response if symptoms are discovered.

5.29 In the post balance sheet period the auditor will tend to concentrate on the review of forecasts and budgets as indicated above, but such information may well be lacking in necessary detail in the case of small enterprises. Where the auditor considers that an enterprise is facing difficulties based on his ongoing review he may well have to insist that forecast and budgetary information will need to be developed, regardless of the size of the enterprise; although small companies need not be expected to provide the same amount and quality of evidence as large companies.

5.30 When forming his opinion at the conclusion of the post balance sheet period the auditor should have regard to the term 'foreseeable future' identified in SSAP 2 in the context of going concern. While the foreseeable future must be judged in relation to specific circumstances, the auditor should normally consider information which relates to a minimum of 6 months following the date of the audit report or 1 year after the balance sheet date, whichever is the later. It will also be necessary to take account of events which will or are likely to occur later, for example, where the enterprise is due to repay significant indebtedness. Where there is doubt about the enterprise's ability to continue in business then the auditor may have to consider qualifying his audit report. The auditor should not refrain from qualifying his report on the grounds that it may lead to the appointment of a receiver or liquidator.

5.31 As a point of interest you should note that in May 1992 the APB produced an exposure draft *Going concern*. This will be come a Statement of Auditing Standards (SAS) in due course. The main provisions are as follows.

(a) The auditor should obtain a written statement from the directors confirming the directors' view that the company is a going concern.

(b) The auditor should plan and perform procedures specifically designed to identify material matters which might cast doubt on the directors' view in (a) above.

The rest of the exposure draft is concerned with the procedures the auditors should undertake, evaluation of the results and the effect on the audit report. You should read the *Accounting Technician* in case the SAS comes into force and comes on to the syllabus during your studies.

Contingencies: obtaining audit evidence

5.32 The importance of the auditor considering the existence and treatment of contingencies as part of his subsequent event review has been stressed above. He will have to pay particular regard to the different treatment required by SSAP 18 on grounds of prudence for contingent gains on the one hand and contingent losses on the other. He will also need to use his judgement in determining 'remoteness' and 'probability' in individual cases. The audit of contingencies is the subject of an early guidance statement (U16) published by the ICAEW in 1970. Although this statement predates the accounting standard, SSAP 18, its recommendations are still broadly relevant to contingencies such as legal claims.

5.33 The following audit procedures are suggested for the verification of the existence of such contingencies as pending lawsuits or other actions against the company, though they will not necessarily provide the auditor with adequate information of the likely amounts for which the company may ultimately be responsible.

(a) Review the client's system of recording claims and the procedure for bringing these to the attention of the management or board.

(b) Discuss the arrangements for instructing solicitors with the official responsible for legal matters.

(c) Examine the minutes of the Board of Directors and/or executive or other relevant committee for references to, or indications of, possible claims.

(d) Examine bills rendered by solicitors and correspondence with them, in which connection the solicitors should be requested to furnish bills or estimates of charges to date, or to confirm that they have no unbilled charges.

(e) Obtain a list of matters referred to solicitors from the appropriate director or official with estimates of the possible ultimate liabilities.

(f) Obtain a written assurance from the appropriate director or official that he is not aware of any matters referred to solicitors other than those disclosed.

5.34 In appropriate circumstances, the auditor may decide to obtain written representations in respect of legal actions from the company's legal advisers. Requests for such confirmation should be kept within the solicitor-client relationship and should thus be issued by the client with a request that a copy of the reply be sent direct to the auditors. As with a debtors' circularisation it should be appreciated that the auditor does not have a right to communicate with third parties directly.

5.35 In order to ascertain whether the information provided by the directors is complete an auditor may, especially in certain overseas countries, decide to arrange for solicitors to be requested to advise whether they have matters in hand which are not listed in the letter of request, and to provide information as to the likely amounts involved. When considering such a non-specific inquiry, the auditor should note that the Council of the Law Society has advised solicitors that it is unable to recommend them to comply with requests for information which are more widely drawn than the specimen form of wording set out below.

> In connection with the preparation and audit of our accounts for the year ended .... the directors have made estimates of the amounts of the ultimate liabilities (including costs) which might be incurred and are regarded as material in relation to the following matters on which you have been consulted. We should be obliged if you would confirm that in your opinion these estimates are reasonable.
>
> *Matter* — *Estimated liability, including costs*
>
> .... — ....

5.36 Despite the above views of the Council of the Law Society regarding non-specific enquiries, there may be circumstances in which it is necessary as an audit procedure for an enquiry of a general nature to be addressed to the solicitors in order to confirm that the information provided by the directors is complete in all material particulars.

5.37 If the outcome of his enquiries appears satisfactory, the auditor would not normally regard the absence of a corroboration of the completeness of a list of legal matters as a reason in itself for qualifying his report. If the enquiries lead to the discovery of significant matters not previously identified, the auditor will wish to extend his enquiries and to request his client to address further enquiries to, and arrange a meeting with, the solicitors, at which the auditor will wish to be present. If, having regard to all the circumstances, the auditor is unable to satisfy himself that he has received all the information he requires for the purpose of his audit, he must qualify his report.

5.38 It is not uncommon for the auditor, notwithstanding the procedures considered above, to conclude that he has not been able to obtain adequate evidence to support estimates and use his experience to reach an opinion as to their reasonableness in the case of major litigation. In these circumstances he may consider it necessary to qualify his report.

Evidence of review of post balance sheet events

5.39 The audit working papers must contain a record of the work carried out to identify events after the balance sheet date. In practice, many firms use a checklist, often referred to as a 'subsequent events review programme', to ensure that the identification of adjusting events and contingencies and their treatment is adequately documented. Where discussions have taken place with management regarding matters arising from the subsequent events review, a record should be retained by the auditor. The auditor may wish to obtain formal representations from management concerning events after the balance sheet date or the fact that there have not been any. If such representations are obtained, they should be dated as close as possible to the date of the audit report. This is just one example of a management representation, a concept further developed in the following section.

Exercise 2

You are auditing the financial statements of Hope Engineering Ltd for the year ending 31 March 19X8. The partner in charge of the audit instructs you to carry out a review of the company's activities since the financial year end. Mr Smith, the managing director of Hope Engineering Ltd, overhears the conversation with the partner and is surprised that you are examining accounting information which relates to the next accounting period.

Mr Smith had been appointed on 1 March 19X8 as a result of which the contract of the previous managing director, Mr Jones, was terminated. Compensation of £500,000 had been paid to Mr Jones on 2 March 19X8.

As a result of your investigations you find that the company is going to bring an action against Mr Jones for the recovery of the compensation paid to him, as it had come to light that two months prior to his dismissal, he had contractually agreed to join the board of directors of a rival company. The company's solicitor had informed Hope Engineering Ltd that Mr Jones' actions constituted a breach of his contract with them, and that an action could be brought against the former managing director for the recovery of the moneys paid to him.

Required

(a) Explain the nature and purpose of a review of the post balance sheet period.

(b) List the audit procedures which would be carried out in order to identify any material post balance sheet events.

(c) Discuss the audit implications of the company's decision to sue Mr Jones for the recovery of the compensation paid to him.

Solution

(a) The auditor's responsibility extends to the date on which he signs his audit report. As this date is inevitably after the year end, it follows that in order to discharge his responsibilities, the auditor must extend his audit work to cover the post balance sheet period.

The objective of the audit of the post balance sheet period is to ascertain whether the directors have dealt correctly with any events, both favourable and unfavourable, which occurred after the year end and which need to be reflected in the financial statements, if those statements are to show a true and fair view and comply with the Companies Act.

The general rule is that in the preparation of year end financial statements, no account should be taken of post balance sheet events unless to do so is required by statute or to give effect to retrospective legislation, or to take account of an adjusting event. In accordance with SSAP 17, a material subsequent event may be an *adjusting event* where it provides information about a condition existing at the balance sheet date, for example realisable values of stock, or indicates that the going concern concept is no longer applicable. Additionally, *non-adjusting events* may have such a material effect on the company's financial condition, for example a merger, that disclosure is essential to give a true and fair view.

(b) The audit procedures which should be carried out in order to identify any material post balance sheet events consist of discussions with management, and may also include consideration of the following.

(i) Procedures should be implemented by management to ensure that all events after the balance sheet date have been identified, considered and properly evaluated as to their effect on the financial statements.

(ii) Relevant accounting records should be reviewed, specifically to identify subsequent cash received from debtors, to check items uncleared at the year end on the bank reconciliation, to check NRV of stocks from sales invoices, and so on. However, window dressing also may be identified.

(iii) Budgets, profit forecasts, cash flow projections and management accounts for the new period should be reviewed to assess the company's trading position.

(iv) Known 'risk' areas and contingencies, whether inherent in the nature of the business or revealed by previous audit experience, or by solicitors' letters, should be considered.

(v) Minutes of shareholders', directors' and management meetings and correspondence and memoranda relating to items included in the minutes should be reviewed.

(vi) Relevant information which has come to the auditor's attention from sources outside the enterprise, including public knowledge of competitors, suppliers and customers, should be taken into account.

The post balance sheet review should be carried out to a date as near as practicable to that of the audit report by making enquiries of management and considering the need to carry out further tests. It should be fully documented and, where appropriate, a letter of representation should be obtained from management.

(c) The compensation paid to Mr Smith would be disclosed as part of directors' emoluments for the year ended 31 March 19X8. However, the question then arises as to whether or not the financial statements need to take any account of the possible recovery of the compensation payment.

The auditor should first ascertain from the board minutes that the directors intend to proceed with the lawsuit and should then attempt to assess the outcome by consulting the directors, the company's legal advisors and perhaps by taking counsel's opinion. Only if it seems probable that the compensation will be recovered should a contingent gain be disclosed in the notes to the accounts (SSAP 18), along with a summary of the facts of the case. A prudent estimate of legal costs should be deducted.

It could be argued that Mr Smith's breach of contract existed at the balance sheet date and that the compensation should therefore be treated as a current asset, net of recovery costs. However, this would not be prudent, given the uncertainties over the court case.

6 COMPLETION OF THE AUDIT

6.1 Most of the audit evidence contributing to the auditor's judgement of sufficiency has been obtained from tests of transactions and balances, analytical review, reliance on internal controls (where applicable) and review of financial statements, but there are, nevertheless, some small but significant pieces still to be fitted into the audit evidence jigsaw. It is an important general principle that the auditor's responsibility extends to the date on which he signs his audit report and indeed, as we shall see a little later, he may retain some responsibility after that date. Certain audit procedures, therefore, are timed to take place as close as possible to the date of signing the audit report. The two principal procedures are:

(a) review of post balance sheet events (see Section 5); and

(b) the obtaining of audit evidence in the form of written representations from the directors confirming oral representations made to the auditor during the course of the audit.

6.2 There are, furthermore, important control and review considerations in this period at the latter end of the post balance sheet period before the audit report is signed. It cannot be emphasised too strongly that it is the reporting partner who is responsible for the audit opinion, so now is the time for a final review to be performed so that he can be satisfied that all members of the audit team have performed their duties to the required standard and to confirm that the results support the audit conclusions reached.

The final management letter

6.3 The final management letter can cover:

(a) additional matters under the same headings as the interim letter, if sent;

(b) details of inefficiencies or delays in the agreed timetable for preparation of the accounts or of workings schedules which delayed the completion of the audit and may have resulted in increased costs;

(c) any significant differences between the accounts and any management accounts or budgets which not only caused audit problems but also detract from the value of management information;

(d) any results of the auditor's analytical procedures of which management may not be aware and may be of benefit to them.

Summarising errors

6.4 During the course of the final audit, where substantive procedures are being undertaken by the auditor, errors will be discovered which may be material or immaterial to the financial statements. It is very likely that the client will adjust the financial statements to take account of such errors during the course of the audit. This will frequently apply to both material and immaterial items, for the sake of accuracy. At the end of the audit, however, some errors will still be outstanding and the auditor will summarise these unadjusted errors.

6.5 The summary of errors will not only list errors from the current year, but also those in the previous year(s). This will allow errors to be highlighted which are reversals of errors in the previous year, such as in the valuation of closing/opening stock. Cumulative errors may also be shown, which have increased from year to year. It is normal to show both the balance sheet and the profit and loss effect, as in the example given here.

SCHEDULE OF UNADJUSTED ERRORS

		19X2				*19X1*			
		P & L account		*Balance sheet*		*P & L account*		*Balance sheet*	
		Dr	*Cr*	*Dr*	*Cr*	*Dr*	*Cr*	*Dr*	*Cr*
		£	£	£	£	£	£	£	£
(a)	ABC Ltd debt unprovided	10,470			10,470	4,523			4,523
(b)	Opening/ closing stock under-valued*	21,540			21,540		21,540	21,540	
(c)	Closing stock undervalued		34,105	34,105					
(d)	Opening unaccrued expenses								
	Telephone*		453	453		453			453
	Electricity*		905	905		905			905
(e)	Closing unaccrued expenses								
	Telephone	427			427				
	Electricity	1,128			1,128				
(f)	Obsolete stock write off	2,528			2,528	3,211			3,211
Total		36,093	35,463	35,463	36,093	9,092	21,540	21,540	9,092
	*Cancelling items	21,540			21,540				
			453	453					
			905	905					
		14,553	34,105	34,105	14,553				

6.6 The schedule will be used by the audit manager and partner to decide whether the client should be requested to make adjustments to the financial statements to correct the errors. The following factors will be considered.

Representations by management

6.7 Representations by management are a source of audit evidence. The auditing guideline *Representations by management* provides the auditor with useful guidance as to the nature and scope of such representations, and the following comments are derived from the guideline.

6.8 Oral representations are made throughout an audit in response to specific enquiries. Whilst representations by management constitute audit evidence, the auditor should not rely solely on the unsupported oral representations of management as being sufficient reliable evidence when they relate to matters which are material to the financial statements. In most cases, oral representations can be corroborated by checking with sources independent of the enterprise or by checking with other evidence obtained by the auditor, and therefore do not need to be confirmed in writing.

6.9 However, in certain cases, such as:

(a) where knowledge of the facts is confined to management; or
(b) where the matter is principally one of judgement and opinion;

the auditor may not be able to obtain independent corroborative evidence and could not reasonably expect it to be available. In such cases, the auditor should ensure that there is no other evidence which conflicts with the representations made by management and he should obtain written confirmation of the representations.

6.10 Where written representations are obtained, the auditor will still need to decide whether in the circumstances these representations, together with such other audit evidence as he has obtained, are sufficient to enable him to form an opinion on the financial statements.

Procedures

6.11 Where oral representations by management are uncorroborated by sufficient other audit evidence and where they relate to matters which are material to the financial statements, they should be summarised in the audit working papers. The auditor should ensure that these representations are either:

(a) formally minuted as being approved by the board of directors; or

(b) included in a signed letter, addressed to the auditor, and known as a 'letter of representation'.

It is the latter alternative, the letter of representation, that is favoured in practice.

6.12 Because the representations are those of management, standard letters may not be appropriate. In any event, management should be encouraged to participate in drafting any letter of representation or, after review and discussion, to make appropriate amendments to the auditor's draft, provided that the value of the audit evidence obtained is not thereby diminished.

6.13 A letter of representation should be signed by persons whose level of authority is appropriate to the significance of the representations made, normally by one or more of the executive directors on behalf of the whole board. The signatories of the letter should be fully conversant with the matters contained in it. The auditor should request that the consideration of the letter, and its approval by the board for signature, be minuted. He may request that he be allowed to attend the meeting at which the board is due to approve the letter. Such attendance may also be desirable where the representations are to be formally minuted rather than included in a letter.

6.14 Procedures regarding written representations should be agreed at an early stage in order to reduce the possibility of the auditor being faced with a refusal by management to co-operate in providing such representations. In the case of a new engagement it is good practice to draw the directors' attention to the fact that the auditor will seek representations as part of his normal audit procedures in a paragraph in the letter of engagement.

6.15 In the past one of the reasons why management refused to co-operate was that they considered the representation letter to be an attempt by the auditor to shift responsibility for the audit opinion: an attitude with some justification, as the auditor frequently sought representations in respect of virtually all the material figures in the balance sheet involving any degree of judgement and opinion. Now that representations are to be confined to material matters that are principally areas of judgement and opinion and matters where knowledge of the facts is confined to management, there should be relatively few representations to be sought and this approach should hence lessen the reluctance of management to co-operate.

6.16 However, management may at the outset indicate that they are not willing to sign letters of representation or to pass minutes requested by the auditor. If they do so indicate, the auditor should inform management that he will himself prepare a statement in writing setting out his understanding of the principal representations that have been made to him during the course of the audit, and he should send this statement to management with a request for confirmation that his understanding of the representations is correct.

6.17 If management disagrees with the auditor's statement of representations, discussions should be held to clarify the matters in doubt and, if necessary, a revised statement prepared and agreed. Should management fail to reply, the auditor should follow the matter up to try to ensure that his understanding of the position, as set out in his statement, is correct.

6.18 In rare circumstances the auditor may be unable to obtain the written representations which he requires. This may be, for instance, because of a refusal by management to co-operate, or because management properly declines to give the representations required on the grounds of its own uncertainty regarding the particular matter. In either case, if the auditor is unable to satisfy himself, he may have to conclude that he has not received all the information and explanations that he requires, and consequently may need to consider qualifying his audit report.

Dating of formal record of representations

6.19 The formal record of representations by management should be approved on a date as close as possible to the date of the audit report and after all other work, including the review of events after the balance sheet date, has been completed. It should never be approved after the audit report since it is part of the evidence on which the auditor's opinion, expressed in his report, is based.

6.20 If there is a substantial delay between the approval of the formal record of representations by management and the date of the audit report, the auditor should consider whether to obtain further representations in respect of the intervening period and also whether any additional post balance sheet audit procedures need to be carried out.

Contents and wording of the letter of representation

6.21 Set out on the next page is an example letter of representation relating to matters which are material to financial statements prepared by an auditor for the company, and to circumstances where the auditor cannot obtain independent corroborative evidence and could not reasonably expect it to be available. You should note its relative brevity: there are only five representations, one of which, relating to transactions with directors, is a good example of a situation 'where knowledge of the facts is confined to management'. The others are principally matters of judgement and opinion.

6.22 The paragraphs included in the example letter relate to a specific set of circumstances. Set out below are some examples of additional paragraphs which, depending on the circumstances, may be appropriate for inclusion in a letter of representation or board minutes. It is most unlikely that the auditor will need to obtain all these representations as a matter of routine.

(a) There have been no breaches of the income tax regulations regarding payments to subcontractors in the construction industry which may directly or indirectly affect the view given by the financial statements.

(b) Having regard to the terms and conditions of sale imposed by major suppliers of goods, trade creditors include no amounts resulting from the purchase of goods on terms which include reservation of title by suppliers, other than £...... due to ABC plc.

(c) With the exception of the penalties described in note 17, we are not aware of any circumstances which could produce losses on long-term contracts.

(d) DEF Ltd, an associated company, is about to launch a new product which has received excellent test results. As a result, the amount of £....... outstanding since 6 January 19.. is expected to be fully recoverable.

(e) The company has guaranteed the bank overdraft of its subsidiary A Limited but has not entered into guarantees, warranties or other financial commitments relating to its other subsidiary or associated companies.

(f) The transaction shown in the profit and loss account as extraordinary is outside the course of the company's normal business and is not expected to recur frequently or regularly.

(g) Since the balance sheet date, the company has negotiated a continuation of its bank overdraft facilities with a limit of £...... There have been no other events which are likely to affect the adequacy of working capital to meet foreseeable requirements in the year following the adoption of the financial statements.

Dear Sirs,

We appreciate that there are matters which are material to the financial statements where you cannot obtain independent corroborative evidence and could not reasonably expect it to be available, and hence require written representations from us.

We confirm to the best of our knowledge and belief, and having made appropriate enquiries of other directors and officials of the company, the following representations given to you in connection with your audit of the company's financial statements for the year ended.............

General
We acknowledge as directors our responsibility for the financial statements (which you have prepared for the company). All the accounting records have been made available to you for the purpose of your audit and all the transactions undertaken by the company have been properly reflected and recorded in the accounting records. All other records and related information, including minutes of all management and shareholders' meetings, have been made available to you.

Legal claim
The legal claim by Mr........... has been settled out of court by the company paying him £.......... No further amounts are expected to be paid and no similar claims by employees or former employees have been received or are expected to be received.

Deferred tax
Deferred tax has been provided to the extent that liabilities will crystallise and at the rates at which they are expected to crystallise.

In connection with deferred tax not provided, the following assumptions reflect the intentions and expectations of the company:

(a) Capital investment of £....... is planned over the next ...... years.

(b) There are no plans to sell revalued properties.

(c) We are not aware of any indications that the situation is likely to change so as to necessitate the inclusion of a provision for tax payable in the financial statements in respect of the unprovided element.

Transactions with directors
The company has had at no time during the year any arrangement, transaction or agreement to provide credit facilities (including loans, quasi-loans or credit transactions) for directors nor to guarantee or provide security for such matters, except as disclosed in note ... to the financial statements.

Post balance sheet events
Other than the fire damage and related insurance claims described in note ... to the financial statements, there have been no events since the balance sheet date which necessitate revision of the figures included in the financial statements or inclusion of a note thereto. Should further material events occur, which may necessitate revision of the figures included in the financial statements or inclusion of a note thereto, we will advise you accordingly.

Yours faithfully,

(Signed on behalf of the Board of Directors)

____________________ Financial Director

Exercise 3

Management representations are an important source of audit evidence. These representations may be oral or written, and may be obtained either on an informal or formal basis. The auditor will include information obtained in this manner in his audit working papers where it forms part of his total audit evidence.

Required

(a) Explain the nature and role of the letter of representation.

(b) Explain why it is important for the auditor to discuss the contents of the letter of representation at an early stage of the audit.

(c) Explain why standard letters of representation are becoming less frequently used by the auditing profession.

Solution

(a) The letter of representation is a letter normally signed by appropriate directors normally on behalf of the whole board. Such a letter contains representations relating to matters which are material to the financial statements but concerning which knowledge of the facts is confined to management, or where the directors have used judgement or opinion in the preparation of the financial statements.

The precise scope and content of the letter of representation should be appropriate to the particular audit. As stated in the auditing guideline on the topic, an example of a typical situation in which representations may be required would be a case in which an employee's legal claim is settled out of court and the directors are asked to set out in writing their view that no further similar claims are expected to be paid. An absence of independent corroborative evidence and the fact that judgement on the part of directors is involved indicates the need for written evidence of the judgement in the letter of representation.

Representations are not a substitute for other necessary audit work, and they do not relieve the auditor of any of his responsibilities. Even where written representations are obtained, the auditor needs to decide whether in the circumstances these representations, together with other audit evidence obtained, are sufficient to justify an unqualified opinion on the financial statements.

However, written representations by the directors do form part of the total audit evidence, and forms part of the auditor's working papers. Their status as evidence is given weight by the fact that s 389 of the Companies Act 1985 makes it a criminal offence for directors knowingly or recklessly to make false statements to the auditor in the course of his duty.

One function which the letter of representation may also serve, although it is subsidiary to its central purposes, is that such a letter may act as a reminder to the directors of their responsibilities. For example, the letter will remind them of their responsibilities with regard to the truth and fairness of the accounts, and of their responsibility for statements made orally to the auditors but only recorded in writing in the letter of representation.

(b) The letter of representation should not be seen as an afterthought in the audit process, even though the letter should be finally approved and signed on a date as close as possible to the date of the audit report and after all other audit work has been completed.

Discussion of the contents of the letter early in the audit is an important part of the audit planning process. It makes the auditor aware at an early stage of the areas in which representations may be required. It also acts as prior warning to management of such errors. This may usefully give management a chance to think carefully about the nature of any representations which are likely to be required in writing, and may encourage directors to become more fully aware of their responsibilities in relation to such written responsibilities.

If discussion of the contents of the representation letter are left until the last stages of the audit, senior management may justifiably object that the matters covered by the content ought to have been raised earlier by the auditor. Management might object that if this had been done there would have been an opportunity to assemble appropriate corroborative evidence and thus avoid the need for written representations by the directors. Such objections may be made especially where audit deadlines are tight, which is often the case for companies which are part of a group. Lengthy discussions of judgemental matters on which representations are being sought may, if left until the end of the audit process, detract from a good working relationship between the auditor and client management, and in extreme cases management may become reluctant to comply with the auditor's requests.

(c) Some audit firms make uses of a standard form of letter of representation. The principal merit of using a standard letter is that by using a standard for all audit work in the firm, the firm has more assurance that staff on each audit will have considered all of the typical kinds of matter on which written representations are normally sought from clients. Audit staff may benefit from using such a standard letter as a checklist of possible matters to include in a draft letter to discuss with management. However, in all cases there will be a need to `tailor' the standard letter to suit the needs of the particular audit engagement. This may involve adapting paragraphs of a standard letter, or adding new paragraphs to cover matters special to the assignment. Instead of using a full standardised letter, some firms make use of `specimen paragraphs' to be included in draft letters of representation. Such specimen paragraphs offer the advantage of suggesting appropriate wording dealing with common matters on which representations are required. Given the judgmental nature of many such matters, such careful wording is important.

As with all standardised audit documentation, there remains the danger that standardisation may encourage a 'mechanical' approach to audit work and this probably explains why many firms are becoming reluctant to use standard forms of letter. Where audit staff fail to use their initiative and imagination, the standard letter may be followed too closely, and important matters may be missed. However, it could be argued that the problem in such cases lies more with a lack of adequate training of audit staff than with the fact that standardised documentation is available.

In presenting a letter of representation to the directors, it is important that the letter is not treated as merely a standard formality. Even if the letter for a particular assignment contains only similar material to that included generally in such letters, and is little different from last year's letter for the same client, each point should be discussed with management in order to encourage the signatories to consider its contents fully.

Chapter roundup

- The auditor must perform and document an overall review of the financial statements before he can reach an opinion.
- As it has been during the rest of the audit, analytical review is a very useful tool when attempting to form an opinion of the final accounts.
- Analytical review procedures should be used carefully. It is not appropriate to calculate a few ratios, decide that they are 'normal' and provide no further analysis. Analytical review can only be a useful tool if the auditor uses his judgement in analysing the results.
- The auditor's responsibilities for preceding year amounts and unaudited published information relate mainly to consistency, although preceding year amounts can have an impact on current results.
- The auditor has a duty to consider the effect of events after the balance sheet date on the accounts. For each such significant event he must decide whether it is an adjusting or no-adjusting item in the accounts.
- The going concern evaluation is most important, particularly in the current climate. Analytical review provides some help in this area, but the auditor should bear the going concern question in mind when examining *all* audit evidence *throughout* the audit.
- Completion procedures will include production of a final management letter, summarising unadjusted errors; obtaining representations from management; checking all work is complete (using an audit completion checklist).
- Representations from management should be restricted to items which *cannot* be verified by other audit procedures.

Test your knowledge

1 What is the ultimate objective of reviewing the financial statements? (see para 1.2)

2 What factors should the auditor have regard to when determining his review procedure? (1.5)

3 When reviewing accounting policies, what matters should concern the auditor? (1.6, 1.7)

4 Identify six key ratios that could be incorporated into an analytical review programme. (2.4)

5 What additional procedures might the auditor perform to check preceding year balances? (3.7)

6 What matters might give rise to an inconsistency between information in the directors' report and the financial statements? (4.6)

7 What action might the auditor take if he identifies items that are *misleading* in the directors' report? (4.13, 4.17)

8 When should the auditor date his report? (5.1)

9 What action need an auditor take after he has signed and dated his audit report? (5.3)

10 Distinguish between 'adjusting' and 'non-adjusting' events. (5.6)

11 What does the auditor understand by the term 'foreseeable future'? (5.30)

12 What procedures should the auditor carry out to verify the existence of contingencies? (5.33)

13 In what circumstances may the auditor seek to obtain written representations from the directors of a company? (6.9)

14 When should the letter of representation be dated? (6.19)

Chapter 17

THE STANDARD EXTERNAL AUDIT REPORT

This chapter covers the following topics.

1 Statutory requirements

2 SAS 600 *Auditors' report on financial statements*

3 True and fair

4 Qualifications in audit reports

5 Reporting inherent uncertainty

Introduction

The importance of the audit report is reflected in the fact that it is governed not only by an auditing standard (the new SAS 600), but also by statute, in the form of the Companies Act 1985. These statutory requirements are discussed in Section 1.

The audit report is the means by which the auditor expresses his opinion on the truth and fairness of a company's financial statements for the benefit principally of the shareholders, but also for other users. Statute has consistently recognised its importance by requiring that certain mandatory statements appear in the report. The ASC auditing standard *The audit report* has been superseded by a new Statement of Auditing Standards produced by the APB. This SAS is a step the APB is taking towards closing the 'expectations gap' which was defined in an earlier consultative paper as: 'the difference between the apparent public perceptions of the responsibilities of auditors on the one hand (hence the assurance that their involvement provides) and the legal and professional reality on the other'.

1 STATUTORY REQUIREMENTS

1.1 The audit report is the means by which the auditor expresses his opinion on the truth and fairness of a company's financial statements for the benefit principally of the shareholders, but also for other users. Statute has consistently recognised its importance by requiring that certain mandatory statements appear in the report.

1.2 The 1967 Companies Act introduced exception reporting to the audit report, whereby in an unqualified audit report, the auditors must state certain things specifically and their silence will imply satisfaction with various other matters. Hence the auditor was still required to establish that the matters indicated above had been complied with, but only had to mention them in his report, or 'qualify', to the extent that any of the requirements had not been met.

Requirements of the 1985 Act

1.3 The statutory approach since the 1967 Act through to the 1985 Act has been to retain the exception reporting approach. The following are matters with which the auditor *implies* satisfaction in an unqualified report under s 237 of the Companies Act 1985.

(a) Proper accounting records have been kept and proper returns adequate for the audit received from branches not visited.

(b) The accounts are in agreement with the accounting records and returns.

(c) All information and explanations have been received as the auditor thinks necessary and he has had access at all times to the company's books, accounts and vouchers.

(d) Details of directors' emoluments and other benefits, and particulars of higher paid employees have been correctly disclosed in the financial statements.

(e) Particulars of loans and other transactions in favour of directors and others in have been correctly disclosed in the financial statements.

(f) The information given in the director's report is consistent with the accounts.

1.4 The Act requires the auditor to state *explicitly* (s 235) whether in the auditor's opinion the annual accounts have been properly prepared in accordance with the Act and in particular whether a true and fair view is given:

(a) in the balance sheet, of the state of the company's affairs at the end of the financial year;

(b) in the profit and loss account, of the company's profit or loss for the financial year; and

(c) in the case of group accounts, of the state of affairs at the end of the financial year and the profit or loss for the year of the undertakings included in the consolidation, so far as concerns members of the company.

1.5 The legislation does not require any comments as to the nature and scope of the audit conducted although, as we shall see in the following section, this is a requirement of the auditing standard.

2 SAS 600 AUDITORS' REPORT ON FINANCIAL STATEMENTS

2.1 This is the APB's first statement based on a previous exposure draft. It is in the form of a series of 'auditing standards', each numbered SAS 600.1, SAS 600.2 and so on. Interspersed with these are explanatory paragraphs and paragraphs on matters of lesser importance. All the auditing standards are reproduced here and explained as necessary. The effective date for the SAS to be adopted by auditors is for financial statements with periods ending on or after 30 September 1993. Compliance with this SAS will ensure compliance with the proposed international standard on the same topic.

SAS 600.1 Introduction

2.2 SA6 600.1 states:

> 'Auditors' reports on financial statements should contain a clear expression of opinion, based on review and assessment of the conclusions drawn from evidence obtained in the course of the audit.'

2.3 The auditors' report should be placed before the financial statements. The directors' responsibilities statement (explained later) should be placed before the auditors' report.

2.4 The SAS makes an important statement about the nature of the assurance provided by the audit report.

> 'The view given in financial statements is derived from a combination of fact and judgement, and consequently cannot be characterised as either "absolute" or "correct". When reporting on financial statements, therefore, auditors provide a level of assurance which is reasonable in that context but, equally, cannot be absolute. Consequently it is important that the reader of financial statements is made aware of the context in which the auditors' report is given.'

Definitions

2.5 The following definitions are given by the SAS.

(a) '*Financial statements*. The balance sheet, profit and loss account (or other form of income statement), statements of cash flows and total recognised gains and losses, notes and other statements and explanatory material, all of which are identified in the auditors' report as being the financial statements.'

(b) '*Directors*. The directors of a company, the partners, proprietors or trustees of other forms of enterprise or equivalent persons responsible for the reporting entity's affairs, including the preparation of its financial statements.'

(c) '*Material*. A matter is material if its omission of mis-statement would reasonably influence the decisions of a user of the financial statements. Materiality may be considered in the context of the financial statements as a whole, any individual primary statement within the financial statements or individual items included in them.'

(d) '*Inherent uncertainty*. An uncertainty whose resolution is dependent upon uncertain future events outside the control of the reporting entity's directors at the date the financial statements are approved.'

(e) '*Fundamental uncertainty*. An inherent uncertainty is fundamental when the magnitude of its potential impact is so great that, without clear disclosure of the nature and implications of the uncertainty, the view given by the financial statements would be seriously misleading. The magnitude of an inherent uncertainty's potential impact is judged by reference to:

    (i) the risk that the estimate included in financial statements may be subject to change;

    (ii) the range of possible outcomes; and

    (iii) the consequence of those outcomes on the view shown in the financial statements.'

SAS 600.2 Basic elements of the auditors' report

2.6 'Auditors' reports on financial statements should include the following matters:

(a) a title identifying the person or persons to whom the report is addressed;
(b) an introductory paragraph identifying the financial statements audited;
(c) separate sections, appropriately headed, dealing with:

    (i) respective responsibilities of directors (or equivalent persons) and auditors;
    (ii) the basis of the auditors' opinion;
    (iii) the auditors' opinion on the financial statements;

(d) the manuscript or printed signature of the auditors' and
(e) the date of the auditors' report.'

Unqualified audit report

2.7 The following is given as an example of an unqualified audit report in an appendix to the SAS.

Example 1. Unqualified opinion: company incorporated in Great Britain

AUDITORS' REPORT TO THE SHAREHOLDERS OF XYZ PLC

We have audited the financial statements on pages ... to ... which have been prepared under the historical cost convention (as modified by the revaluation of certain fixed assets) and the accounting policies set out on page ....

Respective responsibilities of directors and auditors
As described on page ... the company's directors are responsible for the preparation of financial statements. It is our responsibility to form an independent opinion, based on our audit, on those statements and to report our opinion to you.

Basis of opinion
We conducted our audit in accordance with Auditing Standards issued by the Auditing Practices Board. An audit includes examination, on a test basis, of evidence relevant to the amounts and disclosures in the financial statements. It also includes an assessment of the significant estimates and judgements made by the directors in the preparation of the financial statements, and of whether the accounting policies are appropriate to the company's circumstances, consistently applied and adequately disclosed.

We planned and performed our audit so as to obtain all the information and explanations which we considered necessary in order to provide us with sufficient evidence to give reasonable assurance that the financial statements are free from material misstatement, whether caused by fraud or other irregularity or error. In forming our opinion we also evaluated the overall adequacy of the presentation of information in the financial statements.

Opinion
In our opinion the financial statements give a true and fair view of the state of the company's affairs as at 31 December 19.. and of its profit (loss) for the year then ended and have been properly prepared in accordance with the Companies Act 1985.

Registered auditors *Address*

Date

* A reference to the convention draws attention to the fact that the values reflected in the financial statements are not current but historical and, where appropriate, to the fact that there is a mixture of past and recent values.

2.8 The report recommends the use of standard format as an aid to the reader, including headings for each section, for example 'Qualified opinion'. The title and addressee and the introductory paragraph are fairly self explanatory. You may have noticed that the new audit report, unlike the old one, does not refer to the company's cash flows in the opinion paragraph. This is discussed in the next section.

SAS 600.3 Statements of responsibility and basic opinion

2.9 '(a) Auditors should distinguish between their responsibilities and those of the directors by including in their report:

(i) a statement that the financial statements are the responsibility of the reporting entity's directors;

(ii) a reference to a description of those responsibilities when set out elsewhere in the financial statements or accompanying information; and

(iii) a statement that the auditors' responsibility is to express an opinion on the financial statements.

(b) Where the financial statements or accompanying information (for example the directors' report) do not include an adequate description of directors' relevant responsibilities, the auditors' report should include a description of those responsibilities.'

2.10 A description of the directors' responsibilities is given in an example in an appendix. It can be produced by the directors or included by the auditors.

Example wording of a description of the directors' responsibilities for inclusion in a company's financial statements

2.11 'Company law requires the directors to prepare financial statements for each financial year which give a true and fair view of the state of affairs of the company and of the profit or loss of the company for that period. In preparing those financial statements, the directors are required to:

(a) select suitable accounting policies and then apply them consistently;

(b) make judgements and estimates that are reasonable and prudent;

(c) state whether applicable accounting standards have been followed, subject to any material departures disclosed and explained in the financial statements (large companies only);

(d) prepare the financial statements on the going concern basis unless it is inappropriate to presume that the company will continue in business (if not separate statement on going concern is made by the directors).

The directors are responsible for keeping proper accounting records which disclose with reasonable accuracy at any time the financial position of the company and to enable them to ensure that the financial statements comply with the Companies Act 1982. They are also responsible for safeguarding the assets of the company and hence for taking reasonable steps for the prevention and detection of fraud and other irregularities.'

This wording can be adapted to suit the specific situation.

SAS 600.4 Explanation of auditors' opinion

2.12 'Auditors should explain the basis of their opinion by including in their report:

(a) a statement as to their compliance or otherwise with Auditing Standards, together with the reasons for any departure therefrom;

(b) a statement that the audit process includes:

(i) examining, on a test basis, evidence relevant to the amounts and disclosures in the financial statements;

(ii) assessing the significant estimates and judgements made by the reporting entity's directors in preparing the financial statements;

(iii) considering whether the accounting policies are appropriate to the reporting entity's circumstances, consistently applied and adequately disclosed;

(c) a statement that they planned and performed the audit so as to obtain reasonable assurance that the financial statements are free from material misstatement, whether caused by fraud or other irregularity or error, and that they have evaluated the overall presentation of the financial statements.'

2.13 In some exceptional circumstances, a departure from auditing standards may be appropriate to fulfil the objectives of a specific audit more effectively. If this is the case, the auditors should explain the reasons for that departure in their report. Other than in such exceptional and justifiable circumstances, a departure from an auditing standard is a limitation on the scope of work undertaken by the auditors (see later).

SAS 600.5 Expression of opinion

2.14 'An auditors' report should contain a clear expression of opinion on the financial statements and on any further matters required by statute or other requirements applicable to the particular engagement.'

2.15 An unqualified opinion on financial statements is expressed when in the auditors' judgement they give a true and fair view (where relevant) and have been prepared in accordance with relevant accounting or other requirements. This judgement entails concluding whether *inter alia*:

(a) the financial statements have been prepared using appropriate accounting policies, which have been consistently applied;

(b) the financial statements have been prepared in accordance with relevant legislation, regulations or applicable accounting standards (and that any departures are justified and adequately explained in the financial statements); and

(c) there is adequate disclosure of all information relevant to the proper understanding of the financial statements.

SAS 600.9 Date and signature of the auditors' report

2.16 '(a) Auditors should not express an opinion on financial statement until those statements and all other financial information contained in a report of which the audited financial statements form a part have been approved by the directors, and the auditors have considered all necessary available evidence.

(b) The date of an auditors' report on a reporting entity's financial statements is the date on which the auditors signed their report expressing an opinion on those statements.'

2.17 The date of the auditors' report is, therefore, the date on which, following:

(a) receipt of the financial statements and accompanying documents in the form approved by the directors for release;

(b) review of all documents which they are required to consider in addition to the financial statements (for example the directors' report, chairman's statement or other review of an entity's affairs which will accompany the financial statements); and

(c) completion of all procedure necessary to form an opinion on the financial statements (and any other opinions required by law or regulation) including a review of post balance sheet events;

the auditors sign their report expressing an opinion on the financial statements for distribution with those statements.

2.18 If the date on which the auditors sign the report is later than that on which the directors approve the financial statements, then the auditors must check that the post balance sheet event review has been carried out up to the date they sign their report and that the directors would also have approved the financial statements on that date.

Forming an opinion on financial statements

2.19 Appendix 1 of the SAS considers the process of forming an audit opinion using the flowchart shown opposite. The flowchart is drawn up on the basis that the directors make no further amendments to the financial statements following the audit.

2.20 The principal matters which auditors consider in forming an opinion may be expressed in three questions.

(a) Have they completed all procedures necessary to meet auditing standards and to obtain all the information and explanations necessary for their audit?

(b) Have the financial statements been prepared in accordance with the applicable accounting requirements?

Note. These requirements are referred to in terms of generally accepted accounting principles.

(c) Do the financial statements, as prepared by the directors, give a true and fair view?

FORMING AN OPINION ON FINANCIAL STATEMENTS

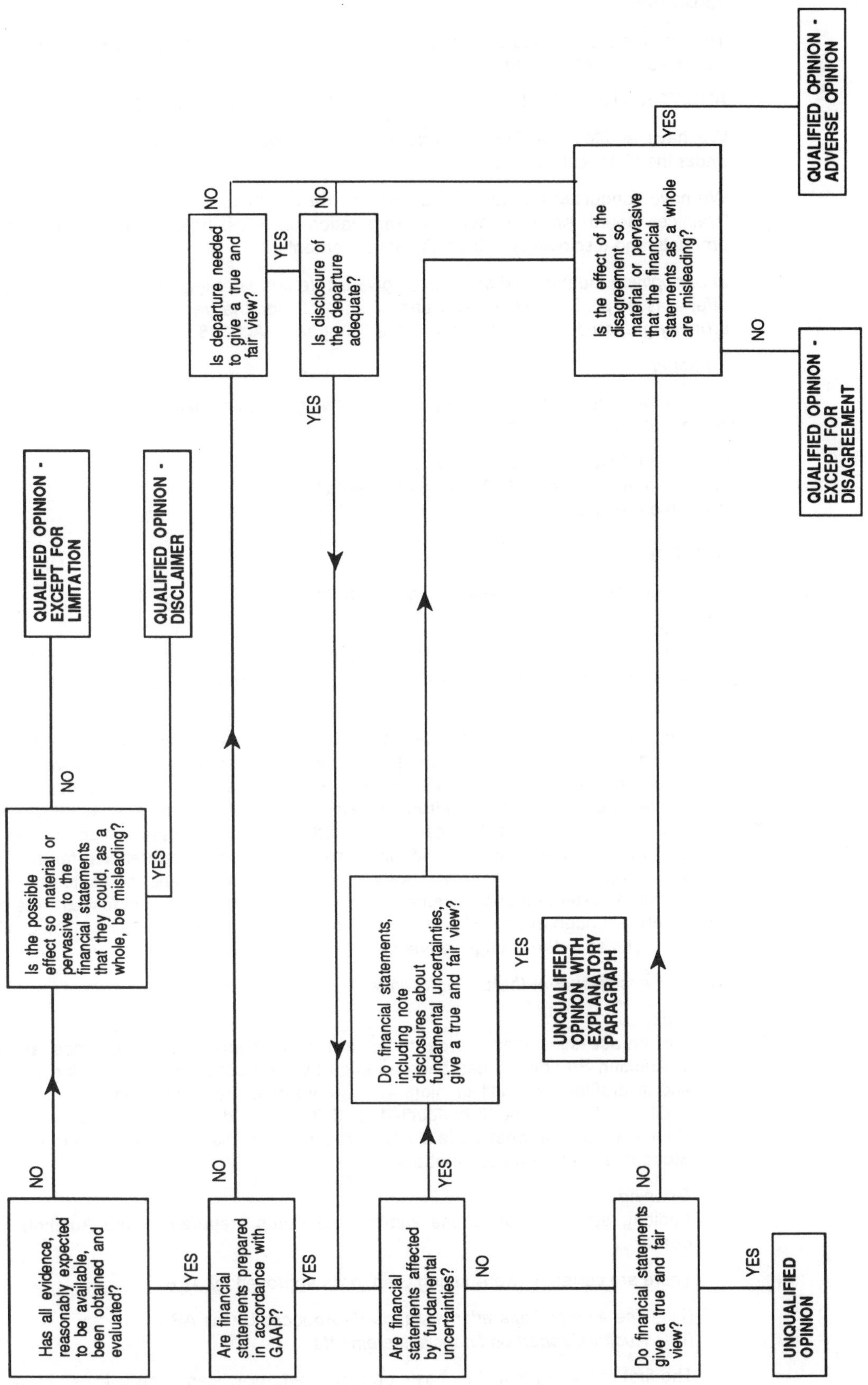

Exercise 1

The following is a series of extracts from an unqualified audit report which has been signed by the auditors of Kiln Ltd.

AUDITOR'S REPORT TO THE SHAREHOLDERS OF KILN LIMITED

We have audited *the financial statements on pages .... to ....* which have been prepared under the historical cost convention.

We have conducted our audit *in accordance with Auditing Standards* issued by the Auditing Practices Board. An audit includes examination on a test basis of evidence relevant to the amounts and disclosures in the financial statements.

In our opinion the financial statements give a true and fair view of the state of the company's affairs as at 31 December 1993 and of its profit for the year then ended and have been properly prepared in accordance with the Companies Act 1985.

Required

Explain the purpose and meaning of the following phrases taken from the above extracts of an unqualified audit report.

(a) '... the financial statements on pages .... to ....'
(b) '... in accordance with Auditing Standards.'
(c) 'In our opinion ...'

Solution

(a) *'...the financial statements on pages 8 to 20...'*

Purpose
The purpose of this phrase is to make it clear to the reader of an audit report the part of a company's annual report upon which the auditor is reporting his opinion.

Meaning
An annual report may include documents such as a chairman's report, employee report, five year summary and other voluntary information. However, under the Companies Act, only the profit and loss account, balance sheet and associated notes are required to be audited in true and fair terms. FRS 1 requires a cash flow and FRS 3 requires a statement of total recognised gains and losses which, under auditing standards, is audited in true and fair terms. Thus the page references (for instance, 8 to 20) cover only the profit and loss account, balance sheet, notes to the accounts, cashflow statement and statement of total recognised gains and losses. The directors' report, although examined and reported on by exception if it contains inconsistencies, is not included in these page references.

(b) *'...in accordance with Auditing Standards...'*

Purpose
This phrase is included in order to confirm to the reader that best practice, as laid down in Auditing Standards, has been adopted by the auditor in both carrying out his audit and in drafting his audit opinion. This means that the reader can be assured that the audit has been properly conducted, and that should he wish to discover what such standards are, or what certain key phrases mean, he can have recourse to Auditing Standards to explain such matters.

Meaning
Auditing Standards are those auditing standards prepared by the Auditing Practices Board.

There are currently two Auditing Standards approved by APB.

(i) *The auditors' operational standard* (produced by the ASC)
(ii) *Auditors' report on financial statements*

The first of these prescribes basic principles and practices to be followed by auditors in the planning, designing and carrying out of audit work. The second governs the content of audit reports, both qualified and unqualified. Members are expected to follow both of these standards.

(c) *'In our opinion ...'*

Purpose

Under the Companies Act, an auditor is required to report on every balance sheet, profit and loss account or group accounts laid before members. In reporting, he is required to state his or her *opinion* on those accounts. Thus, the purpose of this phrase is to comply with the statutory requirement to report an opinion.

Meaning

An audit report is an expression of opinion by a suitably qualified auditor as to whether the financial statements give a true and fair view, and have been properly prepared in accordance with the Companies Act. *It is not a certificate*; rather it is a statement of whether or not, in the professional judgement of the auditor, the financial statements give a true and fair view.

3 TRUE AND FAIR

3.1 The accounts of a limited company are required by s 226(2) of the Companies Act 1985 to show a true and fair view of the company's financial position as at the balance sheet date and of its profit or loss for the year ending on that date. The auditor is required to state in his report whether, in his opinion, the accounts satisfy that requirement.

3.2 Although the Companies Act 1985 contains many detailed requirements as to the form and content of company accounts, it does not attempt to define what is meant by the term 'true and fair view'. This may seem surprising, particularly since the requirement to present a true and fair view is stated in the Act to override any other requirement with which it might conflict. The expression was first used in the Companies Act 1947 and has therefore been a part of company law for over 40 years. The meaning of 'true and fair' can best be understood by considering a written Counsel's Opinion prepared for the Accounting Standards Committee (ASC), the precursor to the Accounting Standards Board (ASB).

3.3 In part, the following paragraphs summarise the rather lengthy opinion.

> 'A SSAP is a declaration by the ASC, on behalf of its constituent professional bodies, that save in exceptional circumstances accounts which do not comply with the standard will not give a true and fair view.'

3.4 'True and fair view' is also a legal concept and the question of whether company accounts comply with s 226(2) Companies Act 1985 can be authoritatively decided only by a court. The nature of the 'true and fair view' as used in the Companies Act is discussed, particularly the subjective nature of the concept. The opinion then reaches an important conclusion.

> 'In the end, as we have said, the question of whether accounts give a true and fair view in compliance with the Companies Acts must be decided by a judge. But the courts look for guidance on this question to the ordinary practices of professional accountants. This is not merely because accounts are expressed in a language which judges find difficult to understand. This may sometimes be true but it is a minor reason for the importance which the courts attach to evidence of accountancy practice. The important reason is inherent in the nature of the "true and fair" concept. Accounts will not be true and fair unless the information they contain is sufficient in quantity and quality to satisfy the reasonable expectations of the readers to whom they are addressed. On this question, accountants can express an informed professional opinion on what, in current circumstances, it is thought that accounts should reasonably contain. But they can do more than that. The readership of accounts will consist of businessmen, investors, bankers and so forth, as well as professional accountants. But the expectations of the readers will have been moulded by the practices of accountants because by and large they will expect to get what they ordinarily get and that in turn will depend upon the normal practices of accountants.
>
> For these reasons, the courts will treat compliance with accepted accounting principles as *prima facie* evidence that the accounts are true and fair. Equally, the deviation from accepted principles will be *prima facie* evidence that they are not.'

3.5 With regards to the relationship between generally accepted accounting principles and the legal concept of 'true and fair', counsel made the following points.

'The function of the ASC is to formulate what it considers should be generally accepted accounting principles. Thus the value of a SSAP to a court which has to decide whether accounts are true and fair is two-fold. First, it represents an important statement of professional opinion about the standards which readers may reasonably expect in accounts which are intended to be true and fair. The SSAP is intended to crystallise professional opinion and reduce penumbra areas in which divergent practices exist and can each have a claim to being "true and fair". Secondly, because accountants are professionally obliged to comply with a SSAP, it creates in the readers an expectation that the accounts will be in conformity with the prescribed standards. This is in itself a reason why accounts which depart from the standard without adequate justification or explanation may be held not to be true and fair. The importance of expectations was emphasised by the Court of Appeal in what may be regarded as a converse case, *Re Press Caps 1949*. An ordinary historic cost balance sheet was said to be "true and fair" notwithstanding that it gave no information about the current value of freehold properties because, it was said, no one familiar with accounting conventions would expect it to include such information.'

'A SSAP therefore has no direct legal effect. It is simply a rule of professional conduct for accountants. But in our opinion it is likely to have an indirect effect on the content which the courts will give to the "true and fair" concept.'

3.6 In an appendix to the ASB's *Foreword to accounting standards*, a new legal opinion has been obtained on the 'true and fair requirement'. The opinion is given by the Honourable Mrs Justice Arden. The following extracts are relevant in showing how CA 1989 and other recent developments have changed the previous opinion on 'true and fair'.

'The changes brought about by the Companies Act 1989 will in my view affect the way in which the Court approaches the question whether compliance with an accounting standard is necessary to satisfy the true and fair view requirement. The Court will infer from Section 256 that statutory policy favours both the issue of accounting standards (by a body prescribed by regulation) and compliance with them: indeed Section 256(3)(c) additionally contemplates the investigation of departures from them and confers power to provide public funding for such purpose. The Court will also in my view infer from paragraph 36A of Schedule 4 that (since the requirement is to disclose particulars of non-compliance rather than of compliance) accounts which meet the true and fair requirement will in general follow rather than depart from standards and that departure is sufficiently abnormal to require to be justified. These factors increase the likelihood, to which the earlier joint Opinions referred, that the Courts will hold that in general compliance with accounting standards is necessary to meet the true and fair requirement.'

'The status of accounting standards in legal proceedings has also in my view been enhanced by the changes in the standard-setting process since 1989.'

'In my view, the Court is likely to treat UITF abstracts as of considerable standing even though they are not envisaged by the Companies Acts. This will lead to a readiness on the part of the Court to accept that compliance with the abstracts of the UITF is also necessary to meet the true and fair requirement.'

'As regards the concept of true and fair, I would emphasise the point made in the joint Opinions that the true and fair view is a dynamic concept. Thus what is required to show a true and fair view is subject to continuous rebirth and in determining whether the true and fair requirement is satisfied the Court will not in my view seek to find synonyms for the words "true" and "fair" but will seek to apply the concepts which those words imply.'

3.7 You should particularly note that the main thrust of recent developments in company law and standard setting have considerably strengthened the previous opinion that compliance with accounting standards indicates that a true and fair view is being shown. The implication is that companies which do *not* follow accounting standards are presumed 'guilty', ie their accounts do not show a true and fair view. Note also that UITF pronouncements are included as well.

Exercise 2

Why are the directors, rather than the auditor, responsible for the detection of fraud? You should consider the practical, rather than the legal aspects of this question.

Solution

The following factors are relevant.

(a) Any fraud which, although causing loss to the company is not material to the company accounts, will be of no interest to the auditor as it does not prevent the accounts showing a true and fair view.

(b) The directors are much more familiar with the day to day procedures, staff and transactions of the company and should therefore have more chance of spotting any fraud.

(c) The directors are the people responsible for running the company well for the members. This is known as their fiduciary duty, which includes safeguarding the assets of the company. The auditor is a reporter, not a manager.

(d) Auditors are under a duty of confidentiality and they therefore cannot report to any authority regarding any suspicions they may have. This is not the case in the financial service services sector where auditors have a duty to report suspected fraud to the regulating authorities. (*Note*. The Cadbury report suggests that a statutory protection for auditors for reporting suspicions of fraud should be extended to all company audits.)

4 QUALIFICATIONS IN AUDIT REPORTS

4.1 Prior to the introduction of auditing standards, qualified audit reports were often criticised as failing to convey the meaning intended.

The standard on audit reports aimed:

(a) to outlaw the use of ambiguous ways of qualifying;
(b) to categories the circumstances giving rise to qualification;
(c) to prescribe suggested wording and format for different categories of qualification;
(d) to introduce a distinction between material and fundamental problems;
(e) to promote better drafting by using non-technical language and clear presentation.

The qualification 'matrix'

4.2 SAS 600 gives the circumstances in which each sort of qualification would be appropriate. Where the auditor is unable to report affirmatively on the matters contained in the paragraphs about which he has reservations, a full explanation of the reasons for the qualification should be given, together with, whenever possible, a quantification of its effect on the financial statements. Where appropriate, reference should be made to non-compliance with relevant legislation and other requirements.

4.3 It has long been accepted that it is not sufficient that a qualified audit report should merely 'prompt further inquiry'. The standard re-affirms this view and stresses the fact that *a qualified audit report should leave the reader in no doubt as to its meaning and its implications for an understanding of the financial statements*. In order to promote a more consistent understanding of qualified audit reports, the APB recommends that the forms of qualification described in the standard should be used unless, in the auditor's opinion, to do so would fail to convey clearly the intended meaning.

4.4 The APB takes the view that the nature of the circumstances giving rise to a qualification of the auditor's opinion will generally fall into one of two categories:

(a) where there is a limitation in the scope of work which prevents the auditor from forming an opinion on a matter (uncertainty - see SAS 600.7); or

(b) where the auditor is able to form an opinion on a matter but this conflicts with the view given by the financial statements (disagreement - see SAS 600.8).

4.5 Either case, uncertainty or disagreement, may give rise to alternative forms of qualification. This is because the uncertainty or disagreement can be:

(a) of fundamental importance to the overall true and fair view; or
(b) material but not fundamental.

The standard requires that the following forms of qualification should be used in the different circumstances outlined below.

QUALIFICATION MATRIX

Nature of circumstances	*Material but not fundamental*	*Fundamental*
Uncertainty	Except for .. might	Disclaimer of opinion
Disagreement	Except for ...	Adverse opinion

4.6 The meaning of the above forms can be summarised as follows.

(a) A disclaimer of opinion is one where the auditor states that he is unable to form an opinion as to whether the accounts give a true and fair view;

(b) An adverse opinion is one where the auditor states that in his opinion the accounts do not give a true and fair view.

(c) An 'except for ... might' opinion is one where the auditor disclaims an opinion on a particular aspect of the accounts which is not considered fundamental.

(d) An 'except for ...' opinion is one where the auditor expresses an adverse opinion on a particular aspect of the accounts which is not considered fundamental.

Circumstances giving rise to uncertainties

4.7 In the explanatory notes to the standard the APB suggests that circumstances giving rise to uncertainties include *limitations in the scope of the audit*. Scope limitations will arise where the auditor is unable for any reason to obtain all the information and explanations which he considers necessary for the purpose of his audit. Limitations in the scope of the audit would result from the absence of proper accounting records or an inability to carry out audit procedures considered necessary as, for example, where the auditor is unable to obtain satisfactory evidence of the existence or ownership of material assets, or of the amounts at which they have been stated on the basis adopted. SAS 600 gives the following examples.

Example 8. Qualified opinion: limitation on the auditors' work

(Basis of opinion: excerpt)

.... or error. However, the evidence available to us was limited because £... of the company's recorded turnover comprises cash sales, over which there was no system of control on which we could rely for the purposes of our audit. There were no other satisfactory audit procedures that we could adopt to confirm that cash sales were properly recorded.

In forming our opinion we also evaluated the overall adequacy of the presentation of information in the financial statements.

Qualified opinion arising from limitation in audit scope

Except for any adjustments that might have been found to be necessary had we been able to obtain sufficient evidence concerning cash sales, in our opinion the financial statements give a true and fair view of the state of the company's affairs as at 31 December 19.. and of its profit (loss) for the year then ended and have been properly prepared in accordance with the Companies Act 1985.

In respect alone of the limitation on our work relating to cash sales:

(a) we have not obtained all the information and explanations that we considered necessary for the purpose of our audit; and

(b) we were unable to determine whether proper accounting records had been maintained.

Example 9. Disclaimer of opinion

(Basis of opinion: excerpt)

.... or error. However, the evidence available to us was limited because we were appointed auditors on (date) and in consequence we were unable to carry out auditing procedures necessary to obtain adequate assurance regarding the quantities and condition of stock and work in progress, appearing in the balance sheet at £... . Any adjustment to this figure would have a consequential significant effect on the profit for the year.

In forming our opinion we also evaluated the overall adequacy of the presentation of information in the financial statements.

Opinion: disclaimer on view given by financial statements

Because of the possible effect of the limitation in evidence available to us, we are unable to form an opinion as to whether the financial statements give a true and fair view of the state of the company's affairs as at 31 December 19.. or of its profit (loss) for the year then ended. In all other respects, in our opinion the financial statements have been properly prepared in accordance with the Companies act 1985.

In respect of the limitation on our work relating to stock and work-in-progress:

(a) we have not obtained all the information and explanations that we considered necessary for the purpose of our audit; and

(b) we were unable to determine whether proper accounting records had been maintained.

Note. Because of the length of the audit report, we have only shown those parts of each qualified report which differ from the unqualified report shown in Section 1.

Circumstances giving rise to disagreements

4.8 The explanatory notes suggest that circumstances giving rise to disagreement include the following.

(a) Inappropriate accounting policies; (for a limited company this could mean failure to comply with the accounting requirements of the Companies Act 1985, and/or SSAPs or FRSs or additional Stock Exchange disclosures).

(b) Disagreement as to the facts or amounts included in the financial statements.

(c) Disagreement as to the manner or extent of disclosure of facts or amounts in the financial statements.

(d) Failure to comply with relevant legislation or other requirements.

4.9 'Where the auditors disagree with the accounting treatment or disclosure of a matter in the financial statements, and in the auditors' opinion the effect of that disagreement is material to the financial statements:

(a) the auditors should include in the opinion section of their report:

(i) a description of all substantive factors giving rise to the disagreement;

(ii) their implications for the financial statements;

(iii) whenever practicable, a quantification of the effect on the financial statements;

(b) when the auditors conclude that the effect of the matter giving rise to disagreement is so material or pervasive that the financial statements are seriously misleading, they should issue an adverse opinion;

(c) in the case of other material disagreements, the auditors should issue a qualified opinion indicating that it is expressed except for the effects of the matter giving rise to the disagreement.'

SAS 600.8

Example 7. Qualified opinion: disagreement

Qualified opinion arising from disagreement about accounting treatment

Included in the debtors shown on the balance sheet is an amount of £Y due from a company which has ceased trading. XYZ plc has no security for this debt. In our opinion the company is unlikely to receive any payment and full provision of £Y should have been made, reducing profit before tax and net assets by that amount.

Except for the absence of this provision, in our opinion the financial statements give a true and fair view of the state of the company's affairs as at 31 December 19.. and of its profit (loss) for the year then ended and have been properly prepared in accordance with the Companies Act 1985.

Example 10. Adverse opinion

Adverse opinion

As more fully explained in note ... no provision has been made for losses expected to arise on certain long-term contracts currently in progress, as the directors consider that such losses should be off-set against amounts recoverable on other long-term contracts. In our opinion, provision should be made for foreseeable losses on individual contracts as required by Statement of Standard Accounting Practice 9. If losses had been so recognised the effect would have been to reduce the profit before and after tax for the year and the contract work in progress at 31 December 19.. by £.. .

In view of the effect of the failure to provide for the losses referred to above, in our opinion the financial statements do not give a true and fair view of the state of the company's affairs as at 31 December 19.. and of its profit (loss) for the year then ended. In all other respects, in our opinion the financial statements have been properly prepared in accordance with the Companies Act 1985.

5 REPORTING INHERENT UNCERTAINTY

Fundamental uncertainty

5.1 SAS 600 states the following.

> '(a) In forming their opinion on financial statements, auditors should consider whether the view given by the financial statements could be affected by inherent uncertainties which, in their opinion, are fundamental.
>
> (b) When an inherent uncertainty exists which:
>
> (i) in the auditors' opinion is fundamental; and
>
> (ii) is adequately accounted for and disclosed in the financial statements;
>
> the auditors should include an explanatory paragraph referring to the fundamental uncertainty in the section of their report setting out the basis of their opinion.
>
> (c) When adding an explanatory paragraph, auditors should use words which clearly indicate that their opinion on the financial statements is not qualified in respect of its concepts.'
>
> (SAS 600.6)

Example 11. Qualified opinion and fundamental uncertainty

Fundamental uncertainty

In forming our opinion we have considered the adequacy of the disclosure made in the financial statements concerning the possible outcome of negotiations for additional finance being made available to replace an existing loan of £... which is repayable on 30 April 19.. . The financial statements have been prepared on a going concern basis, the validity of which depends upon future funding being available. The financial statements do not include any adjustments that would result from a failure to obtain funding. Details of the circumstances relating to this fundamental uncertainty are described in note.... . Our opinion is not qualified in this respect.

Qualified opinion arising from disagreement about accounting treatment

The company leases plant and equipment which have been accounted for in the financial statements as operating leases. In our opinion, these leases should be accounted for as finance leases as required by Statement of Standard Accounting Practice 21. If this accounting treatment were followed, the finance leases would be reflected in the company's balance sheet at £X and the profit for the year would have been reduced by £Y. The financial statements do not include an explanation for this departure from an applicable accounting standard as required by the Companies Act 1982.

Except for the failure to account for the leases referred to above as required by SSAP 21, in our opinion the financial statements give a true and fair view of the state of the company's affairs as at 31 December 19.. and of its profit (loss) for the year then ended and have been properly prepared in accordance with the Companies Act 1985.

Inherent uncertainties

5.2 The following points are relevant.

(a) Inherent uncertainties about the outcome of future events frequently affect, to some degree, a wide range of components of the financial statements at the date they are approved.

(b) In forming an opinion, auditors take into account the adequacy of the accounting treatment, estimates and disclosures of inherent uncertainties in the light of evidence available at the date they express their opinion.

(c) Inherent uncertainties are regarded as fundamental when they involve a significant level of concern about the validity of the going concern basis or other matters whose potential effect on the fundamental statements is unusually great. A common example of a fundamental uncertainty is the outcome of major litigation.

Example 4. Unqualified opinion with explanatory paragraph describing a fundamental uncertainty.

Fundamental uncertainty (insert just before opinion paragraph)

In forming our opinion, we have considered the adequacy of the disclosures made in the financial statements concerning the possible outcome to litigation against B Limited, a subsidiary undertaking of the company, for an alleged breach of environmental regulations. The future settlement of this litigation could result in additional liabilities and the closure of B Limited's business, whose net assets included in the consolidated balance sheet total £... and whose profit before tax for the year is £... . Details of the circumstances relating to this fundamental uncertainty are described in note .... . Our opinion is not qualified in this respect.

Exercise 2

During the course of your audit of the fixed assets of Eastern Engineering plc at 31 March 19X4 two problems have arisen.

(i) The calculations of the cost of direct labour incurred on assets in course of construction by the company's employees have been accidentally destroyed for the early part of the year. The direct labour cost involved is £10,000.

(ii) The company has received a government grant of £25,000 towards the cost of plant and equipment acquired during the year and expected to last for ten years. The grant has been credited in full to the profit and loss account as exceptional income.

(iii) Other relevant financial information is as follows.

	£
Profit before tax	100,000
Fixed asset additions	133,000
Assets constructed by company	34,000
Fixed asset at net book value	666,667

Required

(a) List the general forms of qualification available to auditors in drafting their report and state the circumstances in which each is appropriate.

(b) State whether you feel that a qualified audit report would be necessary for each of the two circumstances outlined above, giving reasons in each case.

(c) On the assumption that you decide that a qualified audit report is necessary with respect to the treatment of the government grant, draft the section of the report describing the matter (the whole report is not required).

(d) Outline the auditor's general responsibility with regard to the statement in the directors' report concerning the valuation of land and buildings.

Solution

(a) Statement of Auditing Standards 600 *Auditors' report on financial statements* suggests that the auditor may need to qualify his audit opinion under one of two main circumstances:

(i) limitation in scope of the auditors' examination; and

(ii) disagreement with the treatment or disclosure of a matter in the financial statements (including inherent uncertainties).

For both circumstances there can be two 'levels' of qualified opinion:

(i) *material but not fundamental* - where the circumstances prompting the uncertainty or disagreement is material but confined to one particular aspect of the financial statements, so that it does not affect their overall value to any potential user;

(ii) the more serious qualification where the extent of the uncertainty or disagreement is such that it will be *fundamental* to the overall view shown by the financial statements, ie the financial statements are or could be misleading.

The general form of qualification appropriate to each potential situation may be seen by the following table.

Circumstance	*Material but not fundamental*	*Fundamental*
Uncertainty	Except for ... might	Disclaimer of opinion
Disagreement	Except for ...	Adverse opinion

(b) Whether a qualification of the audit opinion would be required in relation to either of the two circumstances described in the question would depend on whether or not the auditor considered either of them to be material. An item is likely to be considered as material in the context of a company's financial statements if its omission, misstatement or non-disclosure would prevent a proper understanding of those statements on the part of a potential user. Whilst for some audit purposes materiality will be considered in absolute terms, more often than not it will be considered as a relative term.

(i) *Loss of records relating to direct labour costs for assets in the course of construction*

The loss of records supporting one of the asset figures in the balance sheet would cause a limitation in scope of the auditor's work. The £10,000, which is the value covered by the lost records, represents 29.4% of the expenditure incurred during the year on assets in course of construction but only 6% of total additions to fixed assets during the year and 1.5% of the year end net book value for fixed assets. The total amount of £10,000 represents 10% of pre-tax profit but, as in relation to asset values, the real consideration by the auditor should be the materiality of any over- or under-statement of assets resulting from error in arriving at the £10,000 rather than the total figure itself.

Provided there are no suspicious circumstances surrounding the loss of these records and the total figure for additions to assets in the course of construction seems reasonable in the light of other audit evidence obtained, then it is unlikely that this matter would be seen as sufficiently material to merit any qualification of the audit opinion. If other records have been lost as well, however, it may be necessary for the auditor to comment on the directors' failure to maintain proper books and records.

(ii) *Government grant credited in total to profit and loss account*

The situation here is one of disagreement, since best accounting practice, as laid down by SSAP 4, requires that capital-based grants should be credited to the profit and loss account over the useful life of the asset to which they relate.

This departure from SSAP 4 does not seem to be justifiable and would be material to the reported pre-tax profits for the year, representing as it does 22.5% of that figure.

Whilst this overstatement of profit (and corresponding understatement of undistributable reserves) would be material to the financial statements, it is not likely to be seen as fundamental and therefore an 'except for' qualified opinion would be appropriate.

(c) *Qualified audit report extract*

'As explained in note ... government grants in respect of new plant and equipment have been credited in full to profits instead of being spread over the lives of the relevant assets as required by Statement of Standard Accounting Practice 4; the effect of so doing has been to increase profits before and after tax for the year by £22,500.

Except for ...'

(d) The auditor's general responsibility with regard to the statement in the directors' report concerning the valuation of land and buildings is to satisfy himself that this is consistent with the treatment and disclosure of this item in the audited financial statements. If the auditor is not satisfied on the question of consistency then an appropriate opinion will be required following his audit report.

Chapter roundup

- The statutory requirements surrounding the audit report are important: remember that the auditor reports *by exception*.
- The new Statement of Auditing Standards *Auditors' report on financial statements* has radically altered the form of both unqualified and qualified audit reports.
- You must be able to define a 'true and fair view', although this is not easy given the lack of definition in company legislation.
- You must be able to draft unqualified and qualified audit reports, explain the terms used in the SAS and, at this stage, discuss what impact you think this SAS will have on financial reporting.
- The examples of qualification are given only as an indication of what is required. Each case will be different and will require different disclosure.
- The new SAS is seen as a step in closing the 'expectation gap' and the improvement of the audit report as a means of communications.

Test your knowledge

1 What are the matters with which the auditor of a limited company implies satisfaction in an unqualified report? (see para 1.3)

2 What are the express references in an audit report required by CA 1985? (1.4)

3 What are the basic elements of the new auditors' report? (2.6)

4 Write down a description of the directors' responsibilities which should be included in the financial statements. (2.11)

5 What will the judgement of whether the financial statements show a true and fair view entail? (2.15)

6 CA 1985 defines 'true and fair'. True or false? (3.2)

7 What conclusion did Counsel reach about the relationship between SSAPs and the true and fair concept? (3.6)

8 When will a qualified opinion be issued? (4.2)

9 Sketch the qualification matrix. (4.5)

10 What is the effect of a limitation of scope on the audit report? (4.7)

11 What should the auditor consider when determining whether an uncertainty is fundamental? (5.2)

Chapter 18

AUDITORS' RESPONSIBILITIES AND LEGAL LIABILITIES

This chapter covers the following topics.

1 Background
2 Liability under statute
3 Liability under contract law
4 Actions for negligence against auditors
5 Liability to third parties
6 Fraud, irregularities and errors: the auditor's responsibilities
7 Quality control

Introduction

The question of the liability of the auditor, to third parties in particular, is extremely vexed and is still in the courts.

Concentrate on the important aspects of these topics *and* the important cases. You should be able to describe the main facts and decision of the *Caparo* case, at a *minimum*.

Auditor liability may be raised in any oral questions you are asked about your final portfolio, so you *must* know what you are talking about.

1 BACKGROUND

1.1 The main topic that concerns us in this chapter is liability of the statutory auditor for professional negligence but we also consider more generally the relationship between an accountant and his client and between an accountant and third parties.

1.2 In the USA litigation against accountants (and especially auditors) has long been a common event. The trend has more recently been spreading to the UK. Newspaper reports of legal actions, involving huge sums claimed in compensation for negligence, have become commonplace.

1.3 In theory, partners of firms which are sued have all their assets on the line. It is arguable that the combination of unlimited liability and substantial insurance cover makes accountants an easy target. In practice, accountants take out professional indemnity insurance to provide cover against claims of negligence, although the level of insurance cover obtained will not be unlimited.

1.4 By no means all the major actions against auditors arise because of alleged failure to detect fraud. Nevertheless, the auditor's responsibility to detect fraud is an important debating point. This issue is discussed in detail in connection with the April 1990 auditing guideline *The auditor's responsibility in relation to fraud, other irregularities and errors.*

1.5 Auditor's liability can be categorised under the following headings:

(a) liability under statute, civil and criminal;

(b) negligence under the common law:

(i) to clients under contract law (and possibly law of tort);
(ii) to third parties under law of tort.

1.6 Each of these specific headings will be considered separately in the following sections, but first a few comments concerning the nature of negligence and the auditor/accountant's duty of care summarised from an ethical guidance statement entitled *Professional liability of accountants and auditors* issued in November 1983.

1.7 Negligence means some act or omission which occurs because the person concerned has failed to exercise that degree of professional care and skill, appropriate to the circumstances of the case, which is expected of accountants and auditors. It would be a defence to an action for negligence to show:

(a) that there has been no negligence; or
(b) that no duty of care was owed to the plaintiff in the circumstances; or
(c) in the case of actions in tort that no financial loss has been suffered by the plaintiff.

The third defence would not be available to a claim in contract, but only nominal damages would be recoverable and in those circumstances it is unlikely that such an action would be brought.

1.8 In recent years there have been a number of cases where substantial sums have been claimed as damages for negligence against accountants and auditors. In a number of cases it appears that the claims may have arisen as a result of some misunderstanding as to the degree of responsibility which the accountant was expected to assume in giving advice or expressing an opinion. It is therefore important to distinguish between (i) disputes arising from misunderstandings regarding the duties assumed and (ii) negligence in carrying out agreed terms.

2 LIABILITY UNDER STATUTE

Civil liability

2.1 S 212 Insolvency Act 1986 (IA 1986) provides that officers of the company may be liable for financial damages in respect of the civil offences of 'misfeasance' and 'breach of trust'. The decisions in both the Kingston Cotton Mill and London and General Bank cases imply that, for the purposes of this section, the auditor may be regarded as an officer of the company. This section, which relates only to a winding up, refers to the situation where officers have mis-used their positions of authority for personal gain.

2.2 There is, however, a relieving provision under s 727 of the Companies Act 1985 such that in any proceedings for negligence, default, breach of duty or breach of trust against an officer or an auditor of a company, the court may relieve him wholly or in part from his liability on such terms as it thinks fit, if it appears to the court that:

(a) he is or may be liable; but

(b) he acted honestly and reasonably; and

(c) having regard to all the circumstances of the case, including those connected with his appointment, he ought fairly to be excused for the negligence or default.

This section applies to both civil and criminal actions.

Criminal liability

2.3 The principal statutory provisions under which it is possible for an auditor to be held criminally liable are:

(a) ss 206-211 Insolvency Act 1986;
(b) ss 17, 18 and 19 Theft Act 1968;
(c) s 47(1) Financial Services Act 1986.

Insolvency Act 1986

2.4 Ss 206-211 Insolvency Act 1986 relate to criminal offences involving officers in a winding-up. These provisions are hence not of general application, but it should be noted that, as in s 212 discussed above, the term officer may again include the auditor for the purpose of these sections (even though for eligibility purposes an auditor of a company cannot be an officer of that company s 389(6) CA 1985).

Theft Act 1986

2.5 S 17 Theft Act 1968 states that a person commits an offence who dishonestly, with a view to gain for himself or another or with intent to cause loss to another:

(a) destroys, defaces, conceals or falsifies any account or any record or document made or required for any accounting purpose; or

(b) in furnishing information for any purpose produces or makes use of any account, or any such record or document as aforesaid, which to his knowledge is or may be misleading, false or deceptive in a material particular.

S 18 states that where an offence is committed by a body corporate under s 17 with the consent or connivance of any officer of the body corporate then he as well as the body corporate shall be guilty of that offence.

2.6 Under s 19 an officer of a company will be guilty of an offence if he publishes or concurs in the publication of a written statement or account which to his knowledge is or may be misleading, false or deceptive in a material particular with intent to deceive members or creditors of the company about its affairs. A written statement may be considered false within the meaning of this section not only by what it actually states, but also by virtue of any significant matter which it may have concealed, omitted or implied. An officer found guilty may be imprisoned for up to 7 years. Again, the term 'officer' may include an auditor for the purposes of ss 17, 18 and 19. It can be assumed that any auditor found guilty under this Act would also be expelled from membership of his professional body under the application of the disciplinary code.

Financial Services Act 1986

2.7 Under s 47(1) Financial Services Act 1986 any person who:

(a) makes a statement, promise or forecast which he knows to be misleading, false or deceptive or dishonestly conceals any material facts; or

(b) recklessly makes (dishonestly or otherwise) a statement, promise or forecast which is misleading, false or deceptive,

is guilty of an offence if he makes the statement, promise or forecast or conceals the facts for the purpose of inducing, or is reckless as to whether it may induce, another person (whether or not the person to whom the statement, promise or forecast is made or from whom the facts are concealed) to enter or offer to enter into, or to refrain from entering or offering to enter into, an investment agreement or to exercise, or refrain from exercising, any rights conferred by an investment.

2.8 Guilty parties are liable to imprisonment 'for a term not exceeding seven years'. Note that mere recklessness is sufficient for a criminal prosecution: fraud does not have to be proven. This somewhat harsh looking measure reflects the long history of situations where prospectuses, inviting the public to subscribe for shares, have contained positively dishonest or wildly optimistic statements.

3 LIABILITY UNDER CONTRACT LAW

3.1 The guidance statement *Professional liability of accountants and auditors 1983* makes the following observations regarding the accountant's duty of care.

> 'There is a contractual relationship between an accountant and his client. Unless an express agreement is made between them to the contrary, the standard of work required of an accountant is defined by s 13, Supply of Goods and Services Act 1982: in a contract for the supply of a service where the supplier is acting in the course of a business, there is an implied term that the supplier will carry out the service with reasonable skill and care. The degree of skill and care required will depend principally on the nature of the work undertaken. An accountant who undertakes work of an unusually specialised nature, or work of a kind whose negligent performance is particularly liable to cause substantial loss, will usually be taken to have assumed a duty to exercise a higher degree of skill and care than would be appropriate for less demanding work. This will, especially, be the case if he holds himself out as being experienced in the kind of work in question. In no case, however, is the duty likely to be absolute. Opinions expressed or advice given will not give rise to claims merely because in the light of later events they prove to have been wrong.'

3.2 As regards the auditor, his duties and thus his potential liabilities will clearly be determined by the nature and terms of his appointment, hence the engagement letter is crucial in at least clarifying the 'express terms' of his appointment.

3.3 The auditor must remember that he has a duty to be aware of relevant statutory or constitutional provisions in relation to a client company. This fact was clearly established by Astbury J in the case of *Republic of Bolivia Exploration Syndicate Ltd 1914* where he said:

> '... I think that the auditors of a limited company are bound to know or make themselves acquainted with their duties under the articles of the company, whose accounts they are appointed to audit, and under the Companies Acts for the time being in force ....'

This need for the auditor to fully acquaint himself with the articles of a client company was also stressed by Lindley L J in *Re Kingston Cotton Mill (No 2) 1896*.

3.4 Although the articles of a company may extend the auditor's responsibilities beyond those envisaged by the Companies Act, they cannot be used so as to restrict the auditor's statutory duties, neither may they place any restriction upon the auditor's statutory rights which are designed to assist him in the discharge of those duties. This point was well made by Buckley J in the case of *Newton v BSA Co Ltd 1906* where he said:

> '... any regulations which preclude the auditors from availing themselves of all the information to which under the Act they are entitled as material for the report which under the Act they are to make as to the true and correct state of the company's affairs are, I think, inconsistent with the Act.'

3.5 If the auditor is involved in a non-statutory audit then the only 'express terms' will be those which are contained in any specific contract which may exist with the client. An auditor is always likely to be judged on the content of any report which he has issued, and so he should always ensure that his report clearly states the effect of any limitations that there have been upon the extent and scope of his audit work where such limitations exist. The auditor must take special care to ensure that his report does not in any way imply that he has in fact done more work than that required by the terms of his contract. Great care must be taken in the first instance to establish that the client really does require an audit, not an accounting exercise.

3.6 As well as 'express terms' of an auditor's appointment, we must also consider the question of the 'implied terms' of any such appointment. 'Implied terms' are those which the parties to a contract may have left unstated because they consider them too obvious to express, but which, nevertheless, the law will impart into a contract.

3.7 The 'implied terms' which the law will impart into a contract of the type with which we are currently concerned are as follows:

(a) the auditor has a duty to exercise reasonable care;
(b) the auditor has a duty to carry out the work required with reasonable expediency;
(c) the auditor has a right to reasonable remuneration.

The most important of these generally implied terms is the auditor's duty to exercise reasonable care which we shall consider in the light of decided cases in the following paragraphs.

The auditor's duty of care

3.8 As explained above the standard of work of an accountant is generally as defined by the Supply of Goods and Services Act 1982. As regards the auditor of a limited company there are a number of celebrated judgements that give us a flavour of how his duty of care has been gauged at various points in time.

3.9 Nowhere in the Companies Act does it clearly state the manner in which the auditor should discharge his duty of care; neither is it likely that this would be clearly spelt out in any contract setting out the terms of an auditor's appointment. As Warrington L J said in *Re City Equitable Fire Assurance Co Ltd 1925:*

> '... the Act (Companies Act 1908) does not lay down any rule at all as to the amount of care, or skill, or investigation which is to be brought to bear by the auditors in performing the duties which are imposed upon them. ... That is left to be determined by the general rules which, in point of law, are held to govern the duties of the auditors, whether these rules are to be derived from the ordinary law, or from the terms under which the auditors are to be employed.'

3.10 To identify the 'general rules' to which Warrington L J refers, it is perhaps necessary to consider what the court regard as being the purpose of an audit. To do this we can refer to the opinion of Lindley L J in *Re London and General Bank (No 2) 1895* where he said:

> '... it evidently is to secure to the shareholders independent and reliable information respecting the true financial position of the company at the time of the audit.'

3.11 When Lopes L J considered the degree of skill and care required of an auditor in *Re Kingston Cotton Mill* he declared:

> '... it is the duty of an auditor to bring to bear on the work he has to perform that skill, care and caution which a reasonably competent, careful and cautious auditor would use. What is reasonable skill, care and caution, must depend on the particular circumstances of each case.'

3.12 Both Lindley and Lopes were careful to point out that what constitutes reasonable care depends very much upon the facts of a particular case. One should also note that another criteria by which the courts will determine the adequacy of the auditor's work is by assessing it in relation to the generally accepted auditing standards of the day. The fact that the courts will be very much concerned with accepted advances in auditing techniques was clearly evidenced by Pennycuick J in *Re Thomas Gerrard & Son Ltd 1967* where he observed:

> '... the real ground on which *Re Kingston Cotton Mill* ... is, I think, capable of being distinguished is that the standards of reasonable care and skill are, upon the expert evidence, more exacting today than those which prevailed in 1896.'

3.13 Lord Denning in the case of *Fomento (Sterling Area) Ltd v Selsdon Fountain Pen Co Ltd 1958* sought to define the auditor's proper approach to his work by saying:

> '... he must come to it with an inquiring mind - not suspicious of dishonesty .... - but suspecting that someone may have made a mistake somewhere and that a check must be made to ensure that there has been none.'

3.14 As regards the auditor's responsibility to keep himself abreast of professional developments, it is perhaps worth noting again what the APC say in the *Explanatory foreword* in relation to the matter of 'Auditing Standards and the Guidelines and the Law'.

> 'Members are advised that a court of law may, when considering the adequacy of the work of an auditor, take into account any pronouncements or publications which it thinks may be indicative of good practice. Auditing Standards and Guidelines are likely to be so regarded.'

3.15 When the auditor is exercising judgement he must act both honestly and carefully. Lord Morris of Borth-y-Gest in the case of *Sutcliffe v Thackrah 1974* made the following comment in relation to valuers (although it would be equally relevant in relation to auditors):

> '... (a valuer's) carefully and honestly formed opinion would not make him liable to action merely because in the opinion of some other honest and careful valuer it was thought to be wrong. But suppose it was proved that he had been clearly negligent and so given a wrong figure I see no reason why there should not then be liability.'

3.16 Obviously, if an auditor is to be 'careful' in forming an opinion, he must give due consideration to all relevant matters. Provided he does this and can be seen to have done so, then his opinion should be above criticism. But if the opinion reached by an auditor is one that no reasonably competent auditor would have been likely to reach then he would still possibly be held negligent. This is because however carefully an auditor may appear to have approached his work, it clearly could not have been careful enough, if it enabled him to reach a conclusion which would be generally regarded as unacceptable.

3.17 In order to give his report the auditor must examine each of the items which go to make up the financial statements to which his report relates. In the course of such examination the auditor must reasonably satisfy himself that each item is fairly stated and in doing this he should bear in mind that, as per Lindley L J in *Re London and General Bank*, his:

> 'duty is to examine the books, not merely for the purpose of ascertaining what they do show, but also for the purpose of satisfying himself that they show the true financial position of the company.'

The auditor's duty when put upon enquiry

3.18 If an auditor's suspicions are aroused, he must conduct further investigations until such suspicions are either confirmed or allayed. Over the years, there have been many occasions where the courts have had to consider cases in which it has been held, on the facts of those cases, that the auditors ought to have been put upon inquiry.

3.19 Some of the more common situations in which an auditor should be put upon inquiry, because of the strong possibility of the existence of errors, either clerical or fraudulent, are detailed below.

(a) Knowledge of dishonesty in an employee of the company:

Todd Motor Co v Gray 1928
Nelson Guarantee Corporation Ltd v Hodgson 1958

(b) Entries made in the books after a relevant date:

Irish Wool Co Ltd v Tyson & Others 1900

(c) Alterations or erasures in the records:

Re Thomas Gerrard & Son Ltd 1967
Ross & Co v Wright, Fitzsimmons & Mays 1896
Armitage v Brewer and Knott 1936

(d) The existence or possibility of deficiencies:

Brown and Wright v Thomson, Plucknett & Co 1939

(e) Existence of increasing or unusually large cash balances:

The London Oil Storage Co Ltd v Seear, Hasluck & Co 1904

(f) Acceptability of explanations of directors or other officers after having been put upon inquiry:

Re Thomas Gerrard & Son Ltd 1967
Pacific Acceptance Corp Ltd v Forsyth 1970

(g) Need to report suspicious circumstances to directors:

Tenant's Corporation v Max Rothenburg & Co 1970.

3.20 By way of summary we can say that it is the duty of the auditor to employ reasonable care in all he does. He must employ generally accepted auditing techniques when seeking to satisfy himself that the matters upon which he reports accurately reflect the true financial state of his client's business. If during the course of his work the auditor comes across any matter which puts him upon inquiry then he has a duty to investigate such matter until he is able to resolve it to his own reasonable satisfaction. It will never be prudent for the auditor to accept any explanation unless he has first carried out such investigations as will enable him properly to assess whether the explanation offered is in fact a reasonable one.

The auditor's responsibility in relation to specific aspects of his work

3.21 Frequently the courts may have to consider the auditor's responsibility in relation to certain specific aspects of his work. The examples cited here will not of course cover every conceivable aspect of an auditor's work, however, the cases referred to will help to establish some of the more important principles applied by the courts in reaching their judgement.

Securities

3.22 One of the problems which may arise here is whether or not the auditor should insist upon the personal inspection of all the relevant documentation or whether he is entitled to rely upon a certificate obtained from some third party who is perhaps holding such securities on behalf of the client. As a result of the case of *Re City Equitable Fire Insurance Co Ltd 1925*, it would appear that the auditor's duty is always to insist on personal inspection of securities held by a third party unless he is satisfied, and can show that he has reasonable grounds for being so satisfied, that it is proper for such securities to be held by that third party. It follows that such third party must be trustworthy in the opinion of the auditor and that any suggestion that the third party was 'connected' with the client would reduce the reliability of their testimony and necessitate further investigations on the part of the auditor.

Stock and WIP

3.23 There have perhaps been more cases revolving around problems in relation to stock and WIP than any other single item typically appearing in the accounts of a company. Undoubtedly, this is because stock is one of the easiest figures to manipulate in the accounts, and has a direct result upon the profit or loss made by a company. Lindley L J held in the *Re Kingston Cotton Mill (No 2)* case that:

> 'It is no part of an auditor's duty to take stock. No one contends that it is. He must rely on other people for details of the stock in trade on hand.'

3.24 Whilst accepting this judgement, we will see when we go on to study the balance sheet audit that the auditor does have a duty to satisfy himself as to the accuracy and completeness of the client's assessment of the quantity and type of stocks held and the reasonableness of the subsequent valuation of such stocks.

3.25 As regards the auditor's need to confirm the physical existence of stocks, the case of *Henry Squire Cash Chemist Ltd v Ball Baker & Co 1911* held that there was, by the accepted standards of the day, no need for an auditor to gain contact with the client's stocks. However, as a better indication of the likely attitude of the courts today we could perhaps refer to a report of the American Securities and Exchange Commission, following the famous case of *McKesson and Robins 1939*, which stated:

> '... auditors should gain physical contact with the inventory either by test counts, by observation of the inventory taking, or by a combination of these methods.'

3.26 The auditing guideline *Attendance at stocktaking* states that 'Where stocks are material in the enterprise's financial statements, and the auditor is placing reliance upon management's stocktake in order to provide evidence of existence, then the auditor should attend the stocktaking.'

3.27 In relation to the valuation of stocks, the auditor is entitled to rely upon the valuation arrived at by a competent person provided that he has satisfied himself that such valuation has been reasonably given. The auditor cannot of course simply rely upon the certificate of a competent person without carrying out any audit work at all in that area, this principle was established in the case of *Fomento (Sterling Area) Ltd v Selsdon Fountain Pen Co Ltd 1958*.

Debtors

3.28 The auditor must consider the debtors from a critical viewpoint so as to ensure that they are not stated in the accounts at a figure in excess of their realisable value; such was the implication in the judgement of Romer L J in the case of *Scarborough Harbour Commissioners v Robinson, Couslon Kirby & Co 1934*. In the case of *Arthur E Green & Co v The Central Advance and Discount Corporation Ltd 1920*, it was held by Shearman J that the auditors may be held negligent for accepting schedules of bad debts supplied to them by the client where there were reasonable grounds for doubting the realisability of debts against which no provision had been made. As regards circularisation of debtors, the practice is now so widespread in this country that it is likely that the courts would hold it negligent not to follow it where trade debtors are material.

Cash

3.29 It is likely that the attitude of the courts will be to say that the auditor should always hold a cash count, unless the auditor is satisfied as to the effectiveness of the internal control in respect of cash and has assured himself that the system is operating satisfactorily. Even where controls are deemed to be effective the auditor should consider holding a cash count occasionally, if not every year. As regards cash at bank recognised best practice dictates that as well as examining the underlying records, the auditor should obtain a certificate from the bank.

3.30 The courts have accepted the basic principle that the auditor may use the technique of random test checking. As always, the amount and nature of test checking required, and considered necessary by the courts, must vary with each audit assignment, the aim always being to ensure that whatever the test relates to appears to be in order. Referring once again to the judgement of Lindley L J in the case of *Re London and General Bank*:

> '... Where there is nothing to excite suspicion, very little inquiry will be reasonably sufficient, and in practice I believe businessmen select a few cases at random, see that they are right, and assume that others like them are correct also. Where suspicion is aroused, more care is obviously necessary; but, still, an auditor is not bound to exercise more than reasonable care and skill, even in a case of suspicion ...'

3.31 Above we have looked at just some of the cases arising in relation to specific aspects of the auditor's work. The list has not been exhaustive, but is perhaps sufficient for us to see that the general principle applied by the courts has been to see whether the duty to exercise reasonable care has been properly discharged. As always, it is important to remember that each case must be judged on its own merit.

4 ACTIONS FOR NEGLIGENCE AGAINST AUDITORS

4.1 There are two methods by which civil proceedings may be taken against auditors for damages occasioned by negligent or unskilful discharge of the duties imposed upon them:

(a) by way of action for negligence;
(b) by way of misfeasance summons as discussed earlier.

4.2 A client who brings a civil claim does so in order to fasten on the auditor the financial responsibility for loss occasioned to them through the failure of the auditor to perform his duty or through his negligence in the manner of performing it.

4.3 If a client is to bring a successful action against an auditor then they, as the plaintiff, must satisfy the court in relation to three matters, all of which must be established.

(a) *Duty of care*: that there existed a duty of care enforceable at law. Such duty could be found to exist, under:

  (i) common law;
  (ii) contract;
  (iii) statute.

(b) *Negligence*: that in a situation where a duty of care existed, the auditor was negligent in the performance of that duty, judged by the accepted professional standards of the day.

(c) *Damages*: that the client has suffered some pecuniary loss as a direct consequence of the negligence on the part of the auditor.

4.4 A good early example of a client action for negligence is that of *Wilde & Others v Cape & Dalgleish 1897*. In this case the auditors were held to have been negligent in failing to detect defalcations, the primary reason for this being that they did not examine the bank pass books contrary to generally accepted best practice. An interesting point which arises from this case is that despite any disclaimers concerning the discovery of frauds that may appear in a letter of engagement, where the auditors do not carry out the audit with the due professional diligence expected of auditors they will be liable for losses arising out of their negligence.

4.5 We have already seen that it is the auditor's duty to take reasonable care. This duty to a client is a contractual one in almost every instance and failure to fulfil that duty can give rise to an action for negligence. However, it is perhaps worth noting that in recent years it has been held that a professional man, such as an auditor, may owe a duty of care to his clients in tort as well as in contract. Lord Denning in the case of *Esso Petroleum v Marden 1976* said:

> '... in the case of a professional man, the duty to use reasonable care arises not only in contract, but is also imposed by the law apart from contract, and is therefore actionable in tort.'

4.6 There has been an increase in civil actions against auditors for negligence in the recent past. Some of these are actions by third parties under the law of tort which we will consider in the next section, but many have arisen where there is a contractual duty to the client. It is pertinent therefore to consider whether there are any circumstances in which the accountant or auditor might be able to restrict liability to a client. The following comments are derived from the guidance statement *Professional liability of accountants and auditors*.

Excluding or restricting liability to a client

4.7 An agreement with a client designed to exclude or restrict an accountant's liability may not always be effective in law. The following are the main relevant considerations.

4.8 S 310 Companies Act 1985 makes void any provision in a company's articles or any contractual arrangement purporting to exempt the auditor from or to indemnity him against any liability for negligence, default, breach of duty or breach of trust. Although the courts have power in certain circumstances to grant relief either wholly or in part from any of such liabilities, it appears that these powers have seldom been exercised and it would be prudent to assume that an auditor might not be relieved of liability.

4.9 The Unfair Contract Terms Act 1977 (UCTA 1977) introduces extensive restrictions upon the enforceability of exclusions of liability for negligence and breaches of contract. S 2 of UCTA 1977, which applies in England, Wales and Northern Ireland, makes void any contractual exclusion or restriction of liability for negligence, even in a case where the client has agreed to it and where legal consideration exists, unless the person seeking to rely on that exclusion or restriction can show that it was reasonable. Part II of the Act contains somewhat similar provisions applying as part of the law of Scotland.

4.10 There is at present, little case law which affords guidance as to what exclusions or restrictions of liability for negligence will be regarded as reasonable. However, unless the work undertaken presents unusual difficulties or is required to be carried out in unusually difficult circumstances, it would be prudent to assume that an exclusion of liability for negligence may be treated by the courts as unreasonable. A limitation of liability for negligence to a particular sum will more readily be treated by the courts as reasonable, particularly if the accountant relying upon it can show that he would have difficulty in obtaining professional indemnity insurance for any greater sum.

4.11 An exclusion of restriction of an accountant's liability will not generally avail him against a third party. Avoidance of liability to third parties is dealt with separately in later paragraphs. In summary, we can conclude that the auditor of a limited company cannot limit or exclude liability and that in other circumstances it is probably prudent to assume that an exclusion of liability will be treated by the courts as unreasonable.

5 LIABILITY TO THIRD PARTIES

Relevant cases

5.1 An accountant may be liable for negligence not only in contract, but also in tort if a person to whom he owed a duty of care has suffered loss as a result of the accountant's negligence. An accountant, as we have seen, will almost always owe a duty of care to his own client, but that duty is likely to be co-extensive with his contractual duty. In practice, the possibility of liability in tort will be important mainly in the context of claims by third parties.

5.2 Certain relatively recent decisions of the courts appeared to expand the classes of case in which a person professing some special skill (as an accountant does) may be liable for negligence to someone other than his own client: *Hedley Byrne & Co Ltd v Heller & Partners 1963 AC 465* and *Anns v Merton London Borough Council 1978 AC 728*.

5.3 Before we ascertain the current view as to when a liability might arise, it is useful to review the situation before the decision in the first of the cases cited above, *Hedley Byrne*, and then progress to *Hedley Byrne* itself.

5.4 For many years, it was the widely held view of the accounting profession that the auditor could have no legally enforceable duty of care as regards third parties with whom he had no direct contractual or fiduciary relationship. Indeed there was a consensus of legal opinion which supported this view, one of the leading cases in this area being that of *Candler v Crane, Christmas & Co 1951*.

5.5 The facts of this case were that the managing director of a company had instructed the defendants, a firm of accountants and auditors, to prepare the company's accounts. It was known to the defendants that such accounts would be used to induce the plaintiff to invest money in the company. The draft accounts were shown to the plaintiff in the presence of the defendant's clerk. Relying on their accuracy, he duly subscribed for shares. However, the accounts were negligently prepared and did not give an accurate picture of the company's financial state. Within less than a year the company was wound up and the plaintiff lost the money which he had invested.

5.6 Candler now sued Crane, Christmas & Co in negligence. The Court of Appeal, in a majority verdict, Denning L J dissenting, held that, in the absence of a contractual or fiduciary relationship between the parties, the defendants owed no duty of care to the plaintiff in preparing the accounts. Lord Denning as he now is was of the opinion that the defendants might be liable because they did in fact know that the accounts were to be shown to the plaintiff, though he would not have found them liable to complete strangers. Lord Denning had the following to say when considering the question of to whom a duty of care was owed by accountants:

> '... take accountants ... They owe the duty, of course, to their employer or client, and also, I think, to any third person to whom they themselves show the accounts, or to whom they know their employer is going to show the accounts so as to induce him to invest money or take some other action on them. I do not think, however, the duty can be extended still further so as to include strangers of whom they have heard nothing and to whom their employer without their knowledge may choose to show their accounts. Once the accountants have handed their accounts to their employer, they are not, as a rule, responsible for what he does with them without their knowledge or consent.'

The Hedley Byrne decision

5.7 The situation with regard to third party liability was, however, changed quite significantly with the decision by the House of Lords in the case of *Hedley Byrne & Co Ltd v Heller & Partners Ltd 1963*. Here the earlier judgement of Lord Denning in the *Candler* case was confirmed.

5.8 Hedley Byrne & Co Ltd were advertising agents and the defendants were merchant bankers. They had a mutual client called Easipower Ltd. The agency had contracted to place orders for advertising the company's products with the media, and since this involved extending credit to the company, they asked the company's bankers for a reference as to its credit worthiness. The bank replied that the company was respectably constituted and considered good, though they said that the statement was made without responsibility on their part. The agency, relying on this reply, placed advertisements for the company and in so doing assumed personal responsibility for payment to the television and newspaper companies concerned. Shortly after this, Easipower Ltd went into liquidation and the agency lost over £17,000 on the advertising contracts. The agency then sued the bank for the amount of the loss, claiming that the bank had not informed themselves sufficiently about the company before writing the statement of credit worthiness and were therefore liable in negligence.

5.9 It was held, in this case, that the bank's disclaimer was sufficient to absolve them from liability, but that, in the absence of the disclaimer, the circumstances would have given rise to a duty of care in spite of the absence of a contractual or fiduciary relationship. Thus the dissenting judgement of Denning in the *Candler* case was approved.

5.10 The implications of the Hedley Byrne decision appeared at first to be very far reaching, particularly for auditors and accountants. The Institute of Chartered Accountants took legal advice on the effects of the case and issued the following statement.

'In Counsel's view third parties entitled to recover damages under the 'Hedley Byrne' principle will be limited to those who by reason of accountants' negligence in preparing reports, accounts or financial statements on which the third parties place reliance suffer financial loss in circumstances where the accountants knew or ought to have known that the reports, accounts or financial statements in question were being prepared for the specific purpose or transaction which gave rise to the loss and that they would be shown to and relied on by third parties in that particular connection. There is no general principle that accountants may be liable for damages if a report or statement which proves to have been prepared negligently by them is shown casually or in the course of business to third parties who suffer loss through reliance on the report or statement.'

5.11 The *Hedley Byrne* decision left as its legacy a test of liability which rested upon the 'special relationship' between the parties involved. As such it was unacceptable because it limited too closely the range of injured parties who were entitled to bring such an action. However, the alternative is a pure, unqualified test of an auditor's liability based upon reasonable foresight. This too is unacceptable since it could render the auditor vulnerable to indeterminate liability and to a multiplicity of legal actions.

5.12 Since 1963, there have been three cases which are important in considering the consequences of *Hedley Byrne.*

(a) *Jeb Fasteners Ltd v Marks Bloom & Co 1980*, where the decision seems to have been a compromise: broader than Hedley Byrne but narrower than the unrestricted view.

(b) *Twomax Ltd and Goode v Dickson McFarlane Robinson 1983*, where the decision in this Scottish case was that the auditor should have foreseen that the accounts might be relied upon by a potential investor.

(c) *Caparo Industries plc v Dickman & Others 1990*, where the Appeal Court judged that the auditors were found to owe a duty to shareholders as a body or class which should not extend to individual shareholders making investment decisions or to other potential investors. The House of Lords broadly upheld this judgement: the auditor owed no duty to the public at large.

Jeb Fasteners Ltd v Marks Bloom & Co 1980

5.13 In April 1975 the defendants, a firm of accountants, prepared an audited set of accounts for a manufacturing company for the year ended 31 October 1974. The company's stock, which had been purchased for some £11,000, was shown as being worth £23,080, that figure being based on the company's own valuation of the net realisable value of the stock. The defendants nevertheless described the stock in the accounts as being 'valued at lower of cost and net realisable value'. On the basis of the inflated stock figure the accounts showed a net profit of £11, whereas if the stock had been included at cost with a discount for possible errors the accounts would have shown a loss of over £13,000.

5.14 The defendants were aware when they prepared the accounts that the company faced liquidity problems and was seeking outside financial support from, *inter alia*, the plaintiffs, who manufactured similar products and were anxious to expand their business. The accounts prepared by the defendants were made available to the plaintiffs, who, although they had reservations about the stock valuation, decided to take over the company in June 1975 for a nominal amount, because they would thereby obtain the services of the company's two directors who had considerable experience in the type of manufacturing carried on by the plaintiffs. In discussions between the plaintiffs and the defendants during the takeover the defendants failed to inform the plaintiffs that the stock had been put in the accounts at an inflated value.

5.15 The plaintiffs takeover of the company proved to be less successful than they had anticipated and they brought an action for damages against the defendants alleging that the defendants had been negligent in preparing the company's accounts, that they had relied on the accounts when purchasing the company, and that they would not have purchased the company had they been aware of its true financial position. The plaintiffs contended that an auditor when preparing a set of accounts owed a duty of care to all persons whom he ought reasonably to have seen would rely on the accounts. The defendants contended that if a duty of care existed it was only owed to persons who made a specific request for information.

5.16 By a writ issued on 31 May 1978, the plaintiffs, Jeb Fasteners Ltd, claimed against the defendants, Marks, Bloom & Co, damage for loss suffered by the plaintiffs following the acquisition of the issued share capital of a company, BG Fasteners Ltd, which the plaintiffs claimed to have done in reliance on the accounts of the company negligently prepared by the defendants as accountants and auditors of the company. The judgement was as follows.

(a) Whether the defendants owed a duty of care to the plaintiffs in regard to their preparation of the accounts of the company depended on whether they knew or ought reasonably to have foreseen at the time the accounts were prepared that persons such as the plaintiffs might rely on the accounts for the purpose of deciding whether to take over the company and might suffer loss if the accounts were inaccurate. Since the defendants knew at the time the accounts were prepared that the company needed outside financial support and ought reasonably to have foreseen that a takeover was a possible means of obtaining finance and that a person effecting a takeover might rely on those accounts, it followed that the defendants owed the plaintiffs a duty of care in the preparation of the accounts. The defendants were in breach of that duty by negligently including in the accounts stock at a value of some £13,000 over the discounted cost without appending a note in the accounts to that effect.

(b) However, even though the plaintiffs had relied on the accounts, they would not have acted differently had they known the true position since they knew the company was in financial difficulties, their reason for taking over the company was to obtain the services of its directors and the consideration paid for the company was only nominal. Accordingly, the defendants' negligence in preparing the accounts was not a cause of any loss suffered by the plaintiffs as a result of taking over the company. The plaintiffs' action would therefore be dismissed.

The significance of the Jeb Fasteners decision

5.17 The most significant aspect of the Jeb Fasteners decision is, clearly, the finding of the existence of a legal duty of care owed by auditors to a stranger at the time of the audit, and half of the summing up is devoted to this one issue.

5.18 Mr Justice Woolf, in so finding, derived considerable support from a recent House of Lords authority (not concerning accountants and whose facts bore no relationship to the case in hand) in *Anns v Merton Borough Council 1978 AC 728*, where it had been held that:

(a) to establish that a duty of care arises in a particular situation, it is not necessary to bring the facts of that situation within those of already-decided cases in which a duty of care has been held to exist;

(b) *prima facie*, a duty of care arises if, as between defendant and plaintiff, there is a sufficient relationship of proximity or neighbourhood such that, in the reasonable contemplation of the former, carelessness on his part may be likely to cause damage to the plaintiff; and

(c) *prima facie*, this position will stand unless there are any policy considerations which ought to negative, reduce or limit the scope of the duty, or the class of person to whom it is owed, or the damages to which a breach of it may give rise.

5.19 After citation of a recent authority on solicitors' negligence in *Ross v Caunters 1979* and the dissenting judgement of Cooke J in the New Zealand Court of Appeal case of *Scott Group Ltd v McFarlane*, Mr Justice Woolf went on to consider the liability of auditors: the appropriate test for establishing whether a duty of care exists is whether the defendant auditors knew, or reasonably should have foreseen at the time the accounts were audited, that a person might rely on those accounts for the purpose of deciding whether or not to take over the company, and therefore could suffer loss if the accounts were inaccurate.

5.20 This approach was said to place a limit on those entitled to contend that there had been a breach of duty owed to them by auditors. First, they must have relied on the accounts; and second, they must have done so in circumstances where either the auditors knew that they would, or ought to have known, that they might so rely.

5.21 If the situation was one where it would not be reasonable for the accounts to be relied on, then, in the absence of the auditors' express knowledge, the auditor would be under no duty. In any event, there was a limit to the period for which audited accounts can be relied on. The longer the period which elapses prior to the accounts being relied on, from the date on which the auditor makes his report, the more difficult it will be to establish that the auditor ought to have foreseen that his report would, in the circumstances, be relied on.

5.22 That the decision might have been expected to cause some concern among the profession there can be no doubt, since it results in a significantly larger number of potential plaintiffs to whom the auditor could be liable in damages, if negligent, than hitherto. Indeed, the decision had an influence on the outcome of another case of alleged accountant's negligence.

Twomax Ltd and Goode v Dickson McFarlane & Robinson 1983

5.23 Twomax Ltd acquired a majority shareholding in a private company, Kintyre Knitwear Ltd. Goode was introduced into Kintyre by Twomax, and subsequently became chairman, whereupon he purchased shares in the company. Gordon also took shares in Kintyre and later became a director. The three plaintiffs argued that in making the acquisitions they had relied on the balance sheets and accounts prepared and audited by the defendants. In particular, the accounts for the year ending 31 March 1973 had much influenced the plaintiffs in that they disclosed a sizeable move from a loss of £12,318 to a profit of £20,346. In subsequent years, the trading position of the company deteriorated to a loss of £87,727 in 1975, whereupon the company went into liquidation and all three plaintiffs lost their entire investment.

5.24 It was found that the profit figure for 1973 was incorrect to the extent of an understatement of doubtful debts and an error in agents' commission, thus reducing the profit to £16,779. Lord Stewart also held that the enormous loss in 1975 could only be explained by the fact that two earlier years had been unprofitable, and despite the fact that the plaintiffs were unable to prove what the true figure of profit or loss for 1973 should have been, he concluded that the accounts produced a seriously distorted picture.

5.25 The judgement was that the auditors of Kintyre Knitwear Ltd, Dickson, McFarlane & Robinson were liable to pay damages to the plaintiffs, who had purchased shares on the strength of accounts which had been negligently audited. The level of damages was set at the full amounts paid for the shares on the basis that the shares would not have been purchased at any price had the accounts disclosed the current position.

5.26 On the question of whether the auditors owed a duty to the plaintiffs, Lord Stewart observed:

> 'The auditors of a company, public or private, must know that reliance is likely to be placed upon their work by a number of persons for a number of purposes. While their contractual and statutory duty may be to the shareholders, their work has repercussions in a wider field. The question is whether that duty extends to persons such as the plaintiffs in the present case, who relied upon the audited accounts, in coming to a decision to acquire shares.'

5.27 His Lordship was impressed by the decision of the New Zealand Court of Appeal in *Scott Group Ltd v McFarlane 1978* and by the *Jeb Fasteners* decision. In particular, he considered commendable Woolf J's approach for establishing whether a duty of care exists by reference to whether the defendant knew, or reasonably should have foreseen at the time the accounts were audited, that a person might rely on the accounts for the purpose of deciding whether or not to take-over the company. Such an approach combines:

> 'the simplicity of the proximity or neighbour principle with a limitation which has regard to the warning against exposing accountants to indeterminate liability.'

5.28 Lord Stewart held that although auditors did not know of the specific interest of the plaintiffs at the time of the audit they were, nevertheless, aware that Kintyre was short of capital, that the accounts were made available to lenders in that they were lodged with the company's bank, and that a director wanted to sell his shares. The auditors:

> 'knew that "clean" certificates were commonly relied on by shareholders, potential investors and potential lenders. In the whole circumstances, I consider that McFarlane (the auditor) should have foreseen before he certified the accounts that these accounts might be relied on by a potential investor. The situation was such that I would have thought it an inevitable inference that McFarlane should have realised by the time he came to grant his certificate that there would shortly be some dealings in the issued shares of Kintyre.'

Caparo Industries plc v Dickman & Others 1990

5.29 The facts as pleaded were that in 1984 Caparo Industries purchased 100,000 Fidelity shares in the open market. On June 12 1984, the date on which the accounts (audited by Touche Ross) were published, they purchased a further 50,000 shares. Relying on information in the accounts, further shares were acquired. On September 4, Caparo made a bid for the remainder and by October had acquired control of Fidelity. Caparo alleged that the accounts on which they had relied were misleading in that an apparent pre-tax profit of some £1.3 million should in fact have been shown as a loss of over £400,000. The plaintiffs argued that Touche owed a duty of care to investors and potential investors.

5.30 The conclusion of the House of Lords hearing of the case in February 1990 was that the auditors of a public company's accounts owed no duty of care to members of the public at large who relied upon the accounts in deciding to buy shares in the company. And as a purchaser of further shares, while relying upon the auditor's report, a shareholder stood in the same position as any other investing member of the public to whom the auditor owed no duty. The purpose of the audit was simply that of fulfilling the statutory requirements of the Companies Act 1985. There was nothing in the statutory duties of a company auditor to suggest that they were intended to protect the interests of investors in the market. And in particular, there was no reason why any special relationship should be held to arise simply from the fact that the affairs of the company rendered it susceptible to a takeover bid.

5.31 In its report *The financial aspects of corporate governance*, the Cadbury Committee gave an opinion on the current situation as reflected in the Caparo ruling. It felt that Caparo did not lessen auditors' duty to use skill and care because auditors are still fully liable in negligence to the companies they audit and their shareholders collectively. Given the number of different users of accounts, it was impossible for the House of Lords to have broadened the boundaries of the auditor's legal duty of care.

Concluding remarks

5.32 The conclusions must be that the decision in *Caparo v Dickman* has considerably narrowed the auditor's potential liability to third parties and that the case could have far-reaching implications for the idea of there being various classes of 'user groups' who may make use of audited accounts. The judgement would appear to imply that members of various such user groups, which could include creditors, potential investors or others, will not be able to sue the auditors for negligence by virtue of their placing reliance on audited annual accounts. A case which pre-dates *Caparo* upholds this view. In *Al Saudi*

Banque v Clarke Pixley 1989 it was held that the auditor did not owe a duty of care to a bank which lent on the basis of the accounts and audit report.

5.33 In *James McNaughton Paper Group Ltd v Hicks Anderson & Co 1990*, Lord Justice Neill set out the following position in the light of Caparo and earlier cases:

> '(a) that in England a restrictive approach was now adopted to any extension of the scope of the duty of care beyond the person directly intended by the maker of the statement to act upon it; and
>
> (b) that in deciding whether a duty of care existed in any particular case it was necessary to take all the circumstances into account; but
>
> (c) that, notwithstanding (b), it was possible to identify certain matters which were likely to be of importance in most cases in reaching a decision as to whether or not a duty existed.'

5.34 Although we have probably not yet heard the last on the matter, and further cases can be expected to shed further light on the issue, this provides a useful statement of the current position in law on the limits of the scope of duty of care. Certain terms should now be defined: the adviser is the maker of a statement (such as an audit report) or the giver of advice, while the advisee is the recipient who acts in reliance upon it. The matters to be identified (see (c) in the previous paragraph) could be subsumed under a number of headings.

(a) The purpose for which the statement was made.

(b) The purpose for which the statement was communicated. (Presumably, in the case of a company audit report, its statutory purpose would be considered to be of importance.)

(c) The relationship between the adviser, the advisee and any relevant third party. Where the statement had been prepared or made in the first instance to or for the benefit of someone other than the advisee it would be necessary to consider the relationship between the parties.

(d) The size of any class to which the advisee belonged.

(e) The state of the knowledge of the adviser. In this context, knowledge includes not only actual knowledge but also such knowledge as would be attributed to a reasonable person in the circumstances in which the adviser had been placed. Whether the adviser had known that the advisee would rely on the statement without obtaining independent advice would also need to be considered.

Avoiding or disclaiming liability to third parties

5.35 The cases above suggest that a duty of care to a third party may arise when an accountant does not know that his work will be relied upon by a third party, but only knows that it is work of a kind which is liable in the ordinary course of events to be relied upon by a third party. Conversely, an accountant may sometimes be informed, before he carries out certain work, that a third party will rely upon the results. An example likely to be encountered in practice is a report upon the business of a client which the accountant has been instructed to prepare for the purpose of being shown to a potential purchaser or potential creditor of that business. In such a case it would be prudent for an accountant to assume that he will be held to owe the same duty to the third party as to his client.

5.36 One way that the accountant may seek to avoid liability to third parties is to limit access to his work or reports. Another approach might be to include a disclaimer of liability in the relevant documents or reports. To obtain guidance on both these possibilities we can return to the ethical statement *Professional liability of accountants and auditors*. A brief summary of the statement may be useful.

(a) When publishing documents generally an accountant may find it advantageous to include in the document a clause disclaiming liability. For example:

'While every care has been taken in the preparation of this document, it may contain errors for which we cannot be held responsible.'

(b) When submitting unaudited accounts or other unaudited financial statements or reports to the client, an accountant should ensure that any special purpose for which the statements or reports have been prepared is recorded on their face, and in appropriate cases should introduce a clause recording that the report or statement is confidential and has been prepared solely for the private use of the client. For example:

'This report (statement) has been prepared for the private use of X (the client) only and on condition that it must not be disclosed to any other person without the written consent of Y (the accountant).'

(c) It should be recognised that there are areas of professional work (for example when acting as an auditor under the Companies Act), where it is not possible for liability to be limited or excluded, and that there are other areas of professional work (for example when preparing reports on a business for the purpose of being submitted to a potential purchaser) where although such a limitation or exclusion may be included, its effectiveness will depend on the view which a court may subsequently form of its reasonableness.

Exercise 1

Read the financial and accountancy press on a regular basis between now and your examination and note any new cases or developments in the question of auditor liability.

---

6 FRAUD, IRREGULARITIES AND ERRORS: THE AUDITOR'S RESPONSIBILITIES

6.1 The incidence of financial fraud, particularly in a computer environment, is increasing and has been a central feature in a number of financial scandals in recent years. This fact, together with the increasing sophistication of fraudsters, creates difficult problems for management and auditors. A few years ago the then Minister for Corporate and Consumer Affairs called on the profession to be 'the front line of the public's defences against fraud'.

There are some who would argue that the detection of fraud should be the auditor's principal function. This prevailing attitude clearly gives rise to a public expectation which is neither shared nor fulfilled by the profession.

6.2 It is against this background that the auditing guideline *The auditor's responsibility in relation to fraud, other irregularities and errors* was issued in 1990. Parts of what follows are extracted from that guideline.

The guideline

6.3 The purpose of the guideline is to provide auditors with guidance on:

(a) the extent of their responsibilities for the detection of fraud, other irregularities and errors; and

(b) the extent to which fraud, other irregularities and errors that have been detected should be reported to management, members and third parties.

'Fraud and other irregularities' includes:

(a) fraud, which involves the use of deception to obtain an unjust or illegal financial advantage;

(b) intentional misstatements in, or omissions of amounts or disclosures from, an entity's accounting records or financial statements;

(c) theft, whether or not accompanied by misstatements of accounting records or financial statements;

(d) 'error' is used to refer to unintentional misstatements in, or omissions of amounts or disclosures from, an entity's accounting records or financial statements.

Errors in financial statements are detected with relative frequency by auditors. It is significant that the guideline considers fraud and other irregularities along with errors: this suggests the approach that the auditor does not need to adopt special procedures designed specifically to detect intentional misstatements.

6.4 The responsibility within an entity for the prevention and detection of fraud, other irregularities and errors rests with management. As part of its business responsibilities, management has the fiduciary role of safeguarding assets since the directors of a company are regarded in law as acting in a stewardship capacity concerning the property under their control. The Cadbury Committee has suggested that the auditor should check that the board had established its legal requirements and that a working system for monitoring compliance was in place.

6.5 The following help management to fulfil these responsibilities:

(a) the installation of an effective accounting system;

(b) the institution and the operation of an appropriate system of internal control (including authorisation controls and controls covering segregation of duties);

(c) ensuring that employees understand relevant codes of conduct; and

(d) monitoring relevant legal requirements and ensuring that operating procedures and conditions meet these requirements.

In larger entities, these methods may be supplemented by:

(e) the establishment of an independent internal audit function; and
(f) the appointment of an audit committee.

6.6 The recurring annual audit may act as a deterrent to fraud. And reporting weaknesses to management in the management letter will draw management's attention to improvements which could be made to cut down on fraud, irregularities and errors. But the auditor is not responsible for preventing fraud, other irregularities or errors. Audit procedures should be designed to give the auditor a reasonable expectation of detecting any material misstatements, whether intentional or unintentional, in an entity's financial statements. Such misstatements may arise through fraud and other irregularities as well as error.

6.7 Auditors in the public sector generally have wider responsibilities than those set out above. Statutory requirements also sometimes impose wider responsibilities on auditors outside the State sector; for example, the auditor of a building society is required to report to the Building Societies Commission whether or not the control systems comply with the requirements of the Building Societies Act 1986.

6.8 The guideline is keen to justify the position of the auditor who is faced with the general public expectation that the auditor has failed if a fraud goes undetected. Indeed it argues that even a properly planned and executed audit may fail to detect a particular material misstatement arising from fraud or some other irregularity. It uses the following reasoning:

> 'Because of the characteristics of fraud and other irregularities, particularly those involving forgery and collusion, a properly designed and executed audit may not detect a material fraud or other irregularity. For example, current auditing practice does not normally involve the auditor in establishing the authenticity of original documents. Also, audit procedures that will usually be effective for detecting a misstatement that is unintentional may be ineffective for a misstatement that is intentional and is concealed through collusion between client personnel and third parties or among management or employees of the client. The auditor's opinion on the financial statements is based on the concept of reasonable assurance; his report does not constitute a guarantee that the financial statements are free of misstatement.'

You should bear this in mind when considering the current controversy over auditors and large-scale company crashes and/or frauds, such as BCCI and the Maxwell Corporation.

6.9 If the auditor discovers a possible fraud, other irregularity or error, the action he should take is as follows.

(a) Clarify whether the event has actually occurred.

(b) Consider taking copies of relevant original records.

(c) Inform senior management (unless senior management is suspected of fraud).

(d) Carry out tests to quantify the amounts involved.

(e) Consider the effect on the financial statements, agreeing any adjustments with management (or otherwise qualifying his report).

(f) Reconsider the reliability of other audit evidence (for example fraud by senior management casts doubt on their representations).

(g) Consider approaching the company's lawyers if they have advised, or seeking his own legal advice, on any further action necessary. (In the public sector, auditors have particular responsibilities regarding unlawful items of account and improper losses.)

6.10 Where an auditor concludes that, as a result of fraud or other irregularity, the financial statements do not give a true and fair view, he should qualify his opinion on the financial statements. There may, however, be other grounds for qualifying the audit report. For example, the following applies in the case of a company.

(a) The auditor must state in his report whether in his opinion the financial statements have been properly prepared in accordance with the Companies Act 1985.

(b) There is also a requirement for the auditor to qualify his report if he considers that proper accounting records have not been kept or if he considers that the financial statements are not in agreement with the accounting records. A qualification on either of these grounds may be appropriate where the auditor has evidence of fraud or other irregularities.

(c) The auditor must also state in his report if he has not obtained all the information and explanations he considered necessary for the purpose of his audit. (In such circumstances, it will also often be the case that the scope of his audit has been restricted and he should qualify his report accordingly.)

6.11 In the following extreme circumstances, the auditor should consider resigning.

(a) Where the entity refuses to issue its financial statements.

(b) Where he has considerable doubts about management's integrity and there is no immediate way of reporting to members.

6.12 Does the auditor's duty of confidence prevent him from disclosing findings of fraud and other irregularities? The guideline states:

> 'The duty of confidence is not absolute. In certain exceptional circumstances the auditor is not bound by his duty of confidence and can disclose matters to a proper authority in the public interest or for other specific reasons. The auditor needs to weigh the public interest in maintaining confidential client relationships against the public interest in disclosure to the proper authority. Determination of where the balance of public interest lies will require careful consideration.'

6.13 Matters which should be taken into account when considering whether disclosure is justified in the public interest may include the following.

(a) The extent to which the fraud or other irregularity is likely to result in a material gain or loss for any person or is likely to affect a large number of persons.

(b) The extent to which the non-disclosure of the fraud or other irregularity is likely to enable it to be repeated with impunity.

(c) The gravity of the matter.

(d) Whether there is a general management ethos within the entity of flouting the law and regulations.

(e) The weight of evidence and the auditor's assessment of the likelihood that a fraud or other irregularity has been committed.

6.14 Where it is in the public interest to disclose and where information is disclosed to an appropriate body or person, and there is no malice motivating the disclosure, the auditor is protected from the risk of breach of confidence or defamation.

The auditor retains this protection of qualified privilege only if he reports matters to one who has a proper interest to receive information (per Denning in *Initial Services v Putterill 1968*).

6.15 Which body or person is the proper authority in a particular instance will depend on the nature of the fraud or other irregularity. In cases of doubt, the auditor should consult the Investigation Division of the Department of Trade and Industry. Proper authorities could include the Serious Fraud Office, the Police, the International Stock Exchange, the Securities and Investments Board and the various Self-Regulating Organisations under the Financial Services Act 1986.

6.16 The auditor may have a legal obligation to disclose fraud or other irregularities for other specific reasons.

(a) The auditor may be obliged to make disclosure of the commission of a criminal offence, if ordered to do so by a court or a government officer empowered to request such information.

(b) He may be obliged to disclose certain information to the liquidator, administrative receiver or administrator of a client.

(c) He is obliged to disclose information to inspectors appointed under ss 431 and 432 of the Companies Act 1985, under the provisions of s 434 or under s 105(4) of the Financial Services Act 1986.

(d) In the public sector, the auditor may have an additional responsibility, where required by statute or other terms of engagement, to report certain matters arising from the audit, including significant fraud or other irregularities to a third party such as a sponsoring department or audit supervisory body.

6.17 The Cadbury Committee has said in its recent report that it would be pointless to place a duty on the auditor to detect material fraud because he will never be in a position to guarantee that no such fraud has taken place. The Committee does suggest, however, that legislation should be considered which would extend the statutory protection, already available to auditors in the financial sector, to the auditors of all companies, so that they can report any suspicions of fraud or other misdemeanour to the appropriate authorities, without breaching the confidence of the client.

Exercise 2

You have been the auditor of Dennis Trading Ltd for many years. During this period you have never had occasion to qualify your audit report, nor have your had any reason to doubt the honesty of the management or the employees of the company.

The following matters have come to your attention this year.

(a) Your audit manager informs you that she has heard from a member of the wages department that the head of the department has recently bought a villa in Barbados, a yacht, a four-seater aeroplane and a new Porsche motor car.

(b) A junior carrying out sequence checks on sales invoices from one of the branches has discovered that invoices are missing; it appears that this only happens on one day a week and they always relate to cash sales.

(c) During the whole of the period you have been auditor, the managing director has misappropriated substantial (and increasing) sums of money reported as 'construction costs'.

Required

Describe the steps that you might take to attempt to resolve the situations outlined above. Indicate also how they may affect you personally as auditor.

Solution

I would carry out the following work.

(a) (i) Discreetly enquire as to the possible truth of the reports. There may be legitimate reasons for the staff member's lavish lifestyle (such as inherited money).

(ii) If a fraud appears possible, review audit work already carried out in this and recent years to check that the results of the work are satisfactory.

(iii) Carry out any additional audit work which is considered necessary, for example analytical review and review of the internal controls over wages.

(iv) Discuss findings with the audit partner, and then with senior management, so that management can decide what action to take.

(v) Assess whether any fraud is material and consider whether a qualification of the audit report is necessary.

Provided that I meet the requirements of best practice as an auditor in my work on this matter, it should not present problems for me.

(b) (i) Carry out further sequence checks of sales invoices to corroborate the junior's findings.

(ii) Ascertain staffing arrangements and other procedures relating to cash sales to see whether the incidence of the missing invoices may be linked to these procedures.

(iii) Review audit evidence on stocks to see whether there appear to be significant losses.

(iv) Discuss my findings with the audit partner and with senior management, so that management can decide what action to take.

(v) Assess whether any fraud is material and consider the effect on the audit report.

Again, there should be no problems for me as auditor provided that I have met the requirements of best professional practice.

(c) (i) Review the audit files for all years in which I have been auditor and confirm that all audit work has been carried out in a satisfactory manner, particularly where the work could relate to the misappropriation of funds.

(ii) Ascertain whether any suspicions were raised in earlier years and if so whether these suspicions were properly investigated.

(iii) Satisfy myself that the audit opinions reached in previous years were reasonable in the light of the evidence, and that sufficient audit existence had been obtained to support the opinions.

(iv) In the absence of any independent senior management to whom the matter may be reported, consider taking legal advice on my position as auditor.

In this case, there is the possibility that a negligence claim will be brought against me. The elements of good professional practice would require me to design my work so as to have a reasonable expectation of detecting material fraud or other irregularity. If the steps above do not suggest any shortcoming in the standard of my audit work, I will have a defence against the claim.

7 QUALITY CONTROL

7.1 The review procedures discussed in the previous section are concerned with ensuring that work on an individual audit is properly controlled in the context of the operational guideline *Planning, controlling and recording* such that the reporting partner can form the audit opinion. Paragraph 17 of the guideline states that the auditor 'should also consider how the overall quality of the work carried out within the firm can best be monitored and maintained'. This is quality control in a broader sense and, indeed, is applicable not only to auditing but to the entire range of professional services provided by a firm. The APC published an operational guideline *Quality control* in January 1985. This guideline defines quality control as:

> 'the means by which a firm obtains reasonable assurance that its expression of audit opinions always reflects observance of approved auditing standards, any statutory or contractual requirements and any professional standards set by the firm itself. Quality control should also promote observance of the personal standards relevant to the work of an auditor, which are described in the ethical statements published by the Accountancy Bodies.'

Scope of quality control procedures

7.2 The guideline stresses that the objectives of quality control procedures are the same for all firms and proceeds to define six specific objectives which it considers to be universally applicable. The procedures that a firm may adopt to meet the objectives will depend on its size, the nature of its practice, the number of its offices and its organisation. The objectives are as follows.

(a) *Communication*. Each firm should establish procedures appropriate to its circumstances and communicate them to all partners and relevant staff, and to other professionals employed by the firm in the course of its audit practice.

(b) *Acceptance of appointment and reappointment as auditor*. Each firm should ensure that, in making a decision to accept appointment or reappointment as auditor, consideration is given to the firm's own independence and its ability to provide an adequate service to the client.

(c) *Professional ethics*. There should be procedures within the firm to ensure that all partners and professional staff adhere to the principles of independence, objectivity, integrity and confidentiality, set out in the ethical statements issued by the Accountancy Bodies.

(d) *Skills and competence*. The firm's partners and staff have attained the skills and competence required to fulfil their responsibilities.

(e) *Consultation*. There should be procedures for consultation.

(f) *Monitoring the firm's procedures*. The firm should monitor the effectiveness of its application of the quality control procedures outlined above.

7.3 The guideline provides a brief description of the procedures that firms may adopt to meet the above objectives, placing particular emphasis on the procedures appropriate to smaller firms. Worthy of detailed consideration are the procedures necessary to meet the objectives (d), (e) and (f) above.

Skills and competence

7.4 This involves procedures relating to:

(a) recruitment;
(b) technical training and updating;
(c) on-the-job training.

Staff should be informed of the firm's procedures for example by means of manuals and standardised documentation or programmes. The firm's procedures should be regularly updated.

7.5 (a) *Recruitment*. Effective recruitment of personnel with suitable qualifications including any necessary expertise in specialised areas and industries involves both planning for staffing needs and determining criteria for recruitment based on such needs. Such criteria should be designed to ensure that cost considerations do not deter the firm from recruitment of audit staff with the experience and ability to exercise the appropriate judgement.

(b) *Technical training and updating*. All partners and staff should be required to keep themselves technically up-to-date on matters that are relevant to their work. The firm should assist them to meet this requirement. Such assistance should include:

   (i) circulating digests or full texts, where appropriate, of professional publications and relevant legislation;

   (ii) maintaining a technical library;

   (iii) issuing technical circulars and memoranda on professional developments as they affect the firm;

   (iv) encouraging attendance at professional courses;

   (v) maintaining appropriate training arrangements.

   The methods of implementing the above procedures may vary according to the size of the firm. For example, a smaller firm can ensure that it has copies of essential reference books relevant to its practice where a fuller technical library would be impracticable. Also manuals do not need to be produced internally by the smaller firms but can be acquired from various professional bodies and commercial sources; and co-operative arrangements with other firms can help meet training needs.

(c) *On-the-job training*. The guideline *Planning, controlling and recording* relates staff assignment to the needs of the particular audit visit but, in the context of quality control generally, a further factor in staff assignment should be the opportunity for on-the-job training and professional development. This should provide staff with exposure to different types of audit and with the opportunity to work with more experienced members of the team who should be made responsible for the supervision and review of the work of junior staff. It is important that the performance of staff on audits is evaluated and that the results of these assessments are communicated to the staff concerned, giving the opportunity for staff to respond to comments made and for any action to be agreed.

Consultation

7.6 Procedures for consultation would include:

(a) a structured approach to audit file review (so that the review procedures recommended in the auditing guideline *Planning, controlling and recording* are effective for every audit);

(b) reference of technical problems to designated specialists within the firm; and

(c) resolution of matters of judgement.

7.7 For smaller firms, and particularly for sole practitioners, consultation at the appropriate professional level within the firm may not be possible. Consultation with another practitioner or with any relevant professional advisory service, may be a suitable alternative, provided that confidentiality of the client's affairs is maintained.

Monitoring the firm's procedures

7.8 The monitoring process should provide reasonable assurance that measures to maintain the professional standards of the firm are being properly and effectively carried out. This process should include periodic review of a sample of the firm's audit files by independent reviewers from within the firm.

7.9 The firm should:

(a) have procedures for selection of particular audits for review, and for the frequency, timing, nature and extent of reviews;

(b) set the levels of competence for the partners and staff who are to participate in review activities;

(c) establish procedures to resolve disagreements which may arise between the reviewers and audit staff.

7.10 The purpose of this independent review is to provide an assessment of the overall standards of the firm, and so it is quite separate from the purpose of the earlier review procedures concerned with control over the individual audit. Where, in the smaller firm, independent review within the firm is not possible, attendance at professional courses and communication with other practitioners can provide the opportunity of comparison with the standards of others, thereby identifying potential problem areas. Whatever action is taken by the firm to monitor the effectiveness of quality control procedures, the firm should ensure that recommendations that arise are implemented.

7.11 In terms of scope and objectives three types of review are commonly performed:

(a) the detailed review;
(b) the brief review;
(c) the special purpose review.

Each of the above in terms of timing may be performed 'hot' or 'cold'. The characteristic of a hot review is that it is carried out before the audit report is signed and dated, hence providing an opportunity to take remedial action resulting from the review findings before the completion of the audit. The cold (or post) audit review takes place after the audit report has been signed.

The detailed review

7.12 The objectives of a detailed review may be summarised as follows.

(a) To check the extent of compliance with the firm's standards and policies with regard to:

   (i) auditing procedures;
   (ii) accounting and reporting principles;
   (iii) working paper preparation and presentation.

(b) To determine whether the scope and results of the audit work (audit evidence) is adequate to support the audit opinion.

(c) To review the performance of the audit staff and to assist them in improving their future performance.

(d) To identify areas of weakness in the firm's procedures, or application thereof, and to establish new procedures and implement them.

(e) To ensure that unnecessary work is eliminated and efficiency thus improved.

7.13 The key objective above that distinguishes the detailed review from the brief review considered below is the determination of the adequacy of audit evidence to support the audit opinion. The review must hence be detailed enough for the reviewer to be able to form his own opinion as to the sufficiency, relevance and reliability of the audit evidence.

7.14 It is essential that the reviewer has access to all the audit files, including the permanent file, and it is recommended in practice that the reviewer commences his review with the permanent/interim files (if applicable) and then the final audit file and financial statements. He thus reviews each phase of the audit in the same order, as far as possible, as the work was carried out.

7.15 Clearly, this particular cold review technique is time-consuming as it is an in-depth investigation, but it is probably a more valuable quality control tool than the brief review technique considered below.

The brief review

7.16 It is clear that the commitment in time and effort demanded of a reviewing partner to carry out a detailed review is formidable. It is expedient, therefore, to supplement detailed reviews with a programme of brief reviews, which provide a realistic opportunity to review all, or at worst, the majority of audits in a practice on a regular basis.

7.17 The brief review is of necessity superficial and its limited objective is to ascertain from a relatively brief scrutiny of the audit files whether, *prima facie*, the firm's procedures and standards have been applied. It is not possible to draw valid conclusions regarding the sufficiency of audit evidence when applying this technique (except in a negative sense where it is apparent that there is a conspicuous lack of evidence).

7.18 The most effective way to carry out the review is to commence with the financial statements subject to the review and work 'backwards' through the current and permanent files. (*Note*. This directional approach is the opposite of that for detailed reviews above.)

The special purpose review

7.19 The special purpose review is a review of specific aspects of an audit designed to achieve a particular limited objective. Such reviews tend to be performed on an ad hoc basis and often concentrate on 'high risk' or contentious areas of an audit. The objectives of such reviews clearly vary widely and it is not possible to suggest a standardised approach but it is perhaps useful to give examples of the type of area that might be the subject of a special purpose review.

(a) A review to check compliance with a newly implemented firm procedure.

(b) A review of a number of specially selected audits to check consistency of audit approach and application of a particular statement of standard accounting practice.

(c) A review of a particular audit area which is consistently causing problems, as evidenced, perhaps, by brief and detailed reviews. This type of review may often be more effectively performed by a reviewer with the appropriate specialist knowledge, but he must, as always, be independent of the audit subject to the review.

Frequency of reviews and communication of results

7.20 The guideline does not give any indication as to how frequently reviews should be performed; it merely suggests that there must be a policy regarding selection. Many firms set up a selection policy that requires all audits of listed companies, major public and private companies and 'high risk' clients to be reviewed each year usually applying the rigorous detailed review technique. Certainly the selection process should ensure that at least one audit of each partner is reviewed each year.

7.21 A vital aspect of a post audit review is the communication of the findings. These must be fully discussed with the partner whose work has been subject to the review, but it must be made abundantly clear that the review is intended as a constructive process not a witch hunt.

7.22 It is important after the end of a series of reviews, to draw the results together in summary form, and it is then generally considered prudent to destroy the results of individual reviews as they are potentially self-incriminating.

7.23 The firm, perhaps via a technical committee, should then consider the areas of weakness highlighted in the summary and consider what appropriate action might be taken and finally devise an action programme.

Chapter roundup

- In order to learn the cases affecting auditors' liability, you may find it useful to list them under the headings given as topics right at the start of the chapter. You may wish to test yourself on what points each case illustrates.
- Remember that it is not part of the auditors' responsibilities to prevent fraud, other irregularities or errors. The auditor should design his work so as to have a reasonable expectation of detecting material misstatements, whether intentional or unintentional, in the financial statements. Such misstatements may result from fraud and other irregularities as well as from error.
- Quality control procedures should be implemented by every auditing firm.

Test your knowledge

1 On what grounds might an accountant defend an action for negligence? (see para 1.7)

2 When might an auditor be subject to a civil action under statute? (2.1)

3 Under what statutory provisions is it possible for an auditor to be criminally liable? (2.3)

4 What Act normally determines the standard of work required of an accountant? (3.1)

5 What was said about the auditor's skill and care in the *Re Kingston Cotton Mill* case? (3.11)

6 Which American case confirmed that normal best practice is for the auditor to 'gain physical contact with the inventory'? (3.25)

7 What is the relevance of the Unfair Contract Terms Act 1977 to the accountant when attempting to restrict liability to a client? (4.9)

8 What third parties may be entitled to recover damages under the *Hedley Byrne* judgement? (5.10)

9 What is the significance of the *Caparo* case? (5.29 - 5.31)

10 How can 'fraud' be defined? (6.3)

11 What should an auditor do when he discovers an impropriety or error? (6.9)

12 What are the objectives of the guideline on quality control? (7.2)

13 What are the objectives of a detailed review? (7.12)

Appendix:
Project skills

PROJECT SKILLS

This appendix covers the following topics.

1 The nature of research

2 Gathering data

3 Writing up your report

Introduction

The projects which you will need to complete for the AAT Technician stage (NVQ/SVQ level 4) will demand determination, application and resourcefulness on your part.

Each of the projects has its own requirements, but there is a range of general skills which you may need to draw upon in carrying out any project. Information must be gathered, assimilated and analysed. Critical issues may demand special investigation and may require you to consult and seek advice. The report of the project needs to be presented in a logical way, clearly and concisely.

Most of the project skills explained in the following pages are not complicated. Indeed many of the points may seem obvious to you. Yet it is surprising how many people neglect some of these basics, with the result that their work turns out to be less methodical and less effective than it might have been. The notes provided here are designed to help you produce effective and well presented work, whether for your Technician stage projects or for some other investigative or reporting task.

In the case of Unit 18 *Auditing* in particular, this appendix may be useful if you find it necessary to submit a description of the audit work you have done because of an inability to submit the work itself. You should also find the sections on interviewing useful.

1 THE NATURE OF RESEARCH

Basic steps in a project

1.1 The research process usually starts with a problem or a question. It is a decision-taking process, involving the following framework.

(a) Identify broad area of research
(b) Select research topic/Set up a hypothesis
(c) Decide research approach and develop a method
(d) Formulate project proposal
(e) Gather the data
(f) Draw conclusions
(g) Write up report

The purpose of research

1.2 At its grandest, research can be described as an organised and systematic effort to investigate critically, and then solve, a specific problem.

There are four key terms here.

(a) The effort has to be *organised* if it is to address the problem in an efficient manner, and make best use of the opportunities and resources available.

(b) It has to be *systematic* if it is going to provide a coherent and logical path to a reliable and useful outcome.

(c) It needs to be *critical* in its investigative methods in order to maintain a balanced and objective (as far as possible) perspective on the problem at hand.

(d) It needs a *specific problem* or issue to address in order that a definable objective is set, which directs the research activity.

1.3 The purposes of research can be, singly or combined:

(a) to review and synthesize existing knowledge;
(b) to investigate some existing situation or problem;
(c) to generate new knowledge;
(d) to construct something novel;
(e) to explain new phenomena.

Project feasibility

1.4 Your choice of topic for your project will require consultation with your tutor or trainer. The feasibility of successfully completing your project must be uppermost in your mind when selecting a topic.

1.5 How practical your project is depends on a number of important factors, including the following.

(a) *Data availability and access*

Before you are committed too far, spend some time deciding what sort of information you expect to find, where you are most likely to find it, and whether you have enough time to acquire it.

You might want to consider the following questions here.

(i) *Does the data you will need already exist, or will it need to be generated?* The former (secondary data) requires less time to compile, while the latter (primary data) has the benefit of originality.

(ii) *Will access to existing data be a problem?* For example, confidential corporate information may be difficult to obtain and use. You will need to obtain clearance from a manager or other appropriate person for the inclusion of any confidential or sensitive materials in your project.

(iii) *If you need to generate data, is this practical?* This is not just a question of the time required, but also whether it will be generated in the appropriate quality and quantity.

(b) *Opportunity*

While it may be that a number of possible topics are of interest to you, some areas are likely to be more accessible than others. Partly, this will be related to costs, resources and so on, but also it is dependent on the approval of superiors and the co-operation of others.

(c) *Time*

The availability of time, to collect data and compile a final report, is always a bugbear. It will be worthwhile to prepare a time schedule and action plan.

Points to consider include the following.

(i) Are some tasks dependent on others, whose time pressures may be even greater than your own?

(ii) It's desirable that two or more tasks are carried out concurrently. But is it possible?

(iii) As a rough guide, it is likely that

$^1/_3$ of the time will be spent investigating the project
$^1/_3$ collecting data
$^1/_3$ writing it up.

Stages in report preparation

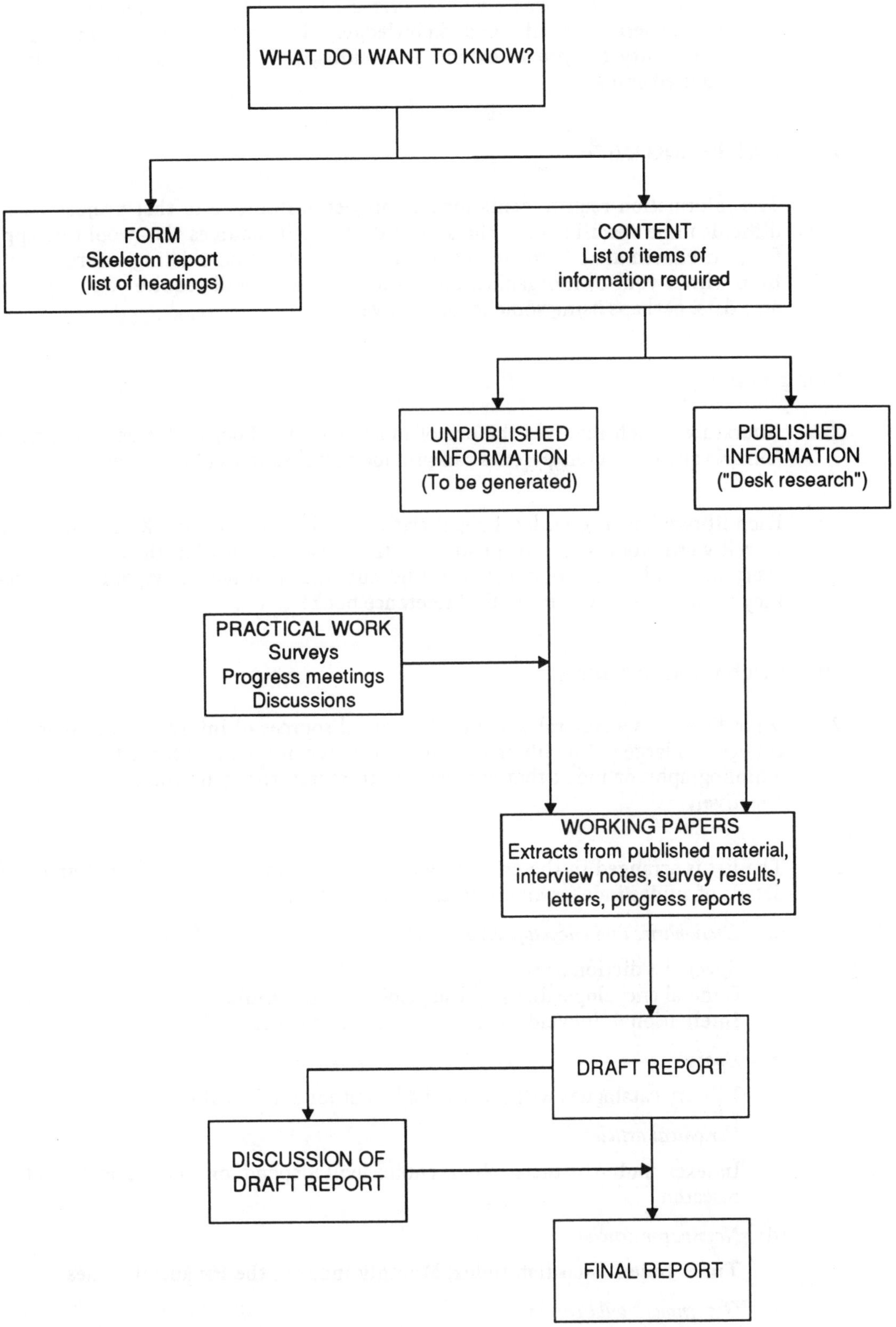

(iv) It is very important not to delay starting work on your project. Remember: a week lost during the project can sometimes be regained, but a week lost before getting started is lost forever.

(d) *Technical skills*

The success of a project will be increased if the topic selected makes use of your own expertise, skills and knowledge. However, a project may provide an opportunity for you to extend your skills, plus the challenge of applying newly acquired skills.

2 GATHERING DATA

2.1 The information requirements for any project are unique to that project, so it is very difficult to be specific about the sort of data and its sources that would be appropriate for your chosen area. Some topics will be more reliant on existing information perhaps from within your own organisation, while other areas will require you to generate your own data, perhaps using some form of survey.

Using a library

2.2 Literature search involves the use of more than just books - for example, newspapers, journals and computer searches can provide useful sources of information.

2.3 Each library has its own local peculiarities and its own system. When using a library it is well worth your while to spend some time discovering what the system is and where everything is located. For instance, find out what journals, newspapers and magazines they take, and where you can find reference books.

The search for information

2.4 What follows is a general guide to the typical sources of information available in many college and large public libraries. For each source or type of information there is usually a bibliography or index that enables you to search that particular type of source more effectively.

2.5 The list is arranged in the order in which a search might be conducted and gives some details of guides/indexes and sources of information.

(a) *Dictionaries and encyclopaedias*

Specialist dictionaries
General encyclopaedias - eg Encyclopaedia Britannica
International Encyclopaedia of the Social Sciences

(b) *Books*

Library catalogues will usually list by author and by subject

(c) *Periodical articles*

Indexes and Abstracts. Your choice will depend on the subject matter of the research

(d) *Newspaper articles*

Times Index, Guardian Index, Monthly Index to the Financial Times

(e) *Government publications*

Annual catalogue (HMSO) and the Catalogue of British Official Publications

(f) *Statistics*

Guide to Official Statistics
Sources of Unofficial Statistics

(g) *Directories*

For example, Current British Directories (CBD)

(h) *Annual reports*

These can be obtained directly from relevant companies

(i) *Computerised databases of research articles*

Abstracts and/or original articles can be viewed

Taking notes

2.6 Throughout your work on a project, keep good and careful notes and develop a system of note-keeping (eg card-index or indexed note-book entries). The notes that you have for particular areas should give some indication of the relative importance and how much of your project should be devoted to each particular area of research.

2.7 Also keep detailed records of research sources. If you do not discipline yourself to the habit of always writing down this information, you will lose endless hours in an irritating search for the exact reference, or if you need to check or to amend a note.

Data collection methods

2.8 The major problem with existing sources of data is that their relevance may be limited. Relying mainly on the techniques of sampling, interviewing and/or the questionnaire, surveying can provide useful information on many issues. A survey may not be a major undertaking: for example, it might involve asking three members of staff in a department about how a particular accounting procedure could be improved.

2.9 Surveys are based on the very simple procedure: if you wish to know what people think about certain things, you must ask them. Because of the great variety in data techniques, it would be impossible to introduce all such methods here. Data collection is one of the areas you should discuss with your tutor or trainer. Given below is a brief review of the main methods.

Sampling

2.10 Sampling is a technique used in various contexts.

Auditing is one example: when detailed tests of transactions are carried out as part of an audit, it is usually impractical to test all of the transactions occurring in a particular period or all of the individual items making up the balance on an account. Therefore, a sample of items is chosen for test, the results being used to draw conclusions about the population from which the sample was drawn.

A survey is another context in which sampling is used. Before respondents can be approached, it is necessary to decide who is to be approached. This decision involves taking a sample to represent the total population which is of interest. Whatever the context, the basic principles of sampling are the same.

2.11 The sampling process has a number of steps.

Step 1: Specify the sampling frame

A sampling frame is a list of all those in the population of interest.

Step 2: Specify the sampling unit

Select the particular unit that is most relevant to your area of research.

Step 3: Selection of sampling method

How are the specific sampling units to be identified? For instance taking every 10th or 20th or 100th name in a sampling frame is one method. The sampling method should avoid bias if at all possible. For example, picking names at random from a telephone directory means that those who have no telephone or who are ex-directory cannot be selected.

Step 4: Determine sample size

In practice the sample needs to be big enough to get a representative view. However, the time available is likely to be a major constraint.

Step 5: Implement the plan

Specify the process of turning the theory into practice.

Interviewing

2.12 There are a number of interviewing options each with advantages and disadvantages.

(a) *Personal interviewing*

Here, respondents are contacted and interviewed on a face-to-face basis. Many of the interviews carried out by an auditor are of this type.

An interview usually takes the form of a questionnaire (see below) with the interviewer recording the responses to prepared questions.

Advantages

(i) Usually a high percentage of acceptable returns are obtained.

(ii) There is a low refusal rate, so the sample is likely to be more representative.

(iii) A skilled interviewer can clear up contradictory statements, improving the accuracy of information.

(iv) Through observation, useful additional information can often be added.

(v) It is usually possible to hold the respondent's attention for a long time and thus get a lot of information.

Disadvantages

(i) It is time consuming.

(ii) Interviewer bias may occur, as in the case of 'leading questions'.

(iii) Respondents may give false responses in order to please or to try to impress the interviewer.

(b) *Telephone interviewing*

You might need to use this approach, especially if your organisation is spread over a wide geographical area.

Advantages

(i) Telephone interviewing is quick.
(ii) Otherwise inaccessible people can be reached by phone more conveniently.
(iii) People can be recontacted easily.

Disadvantages

(i) If a representative sample is needed, telephone subscribers may not be representative.

(ii) Attention span is shorter on the telephone, and so shorter questionnaires are necessary.

(iii) With no visual aids, questions must be easily understood.

(iv) There are limited times when people can be called.

(v) No additional information is gained through observation, as it is with face-to-face interviewing.

(c) *Interviewing by post*

Obviously, questionnaires have to be self-completed and it is easy to avoid a postal survey by throwing it away. Once again, however, a wide geographical area can be covered.

Advantages

(i) A widespread sample can be reached.
(ii) The method is relatively cheap.
(iii) There is no interviewer bias.
(iv) Everyone can be reached by post.
(v) Respondents can complete the questionnaire at leisure.

Disadvantages

(i) Respondents self-select: often those with strong interest in the issue are more likely to reply and the 'silent majority' do not, thus giving an unrepresentative view.

(ii) Typically, there are high refusal rates - often about 70% do not reply, again affecting representativeness.

(iii) Respondents may misinterpret questions and/or give misleading answers.

(iv) Questions need to be short - limiting information.

(v) We cannot check that the intended respondent has been the one to fill in the questionnaire.

(vi) The method is slow.

How to choose an appropriate interviewing method

2.13 The factors which need to be applied in choosing which method should be used for a particular survey include:

(a) cost factors (postal methods are cheapest);
(b) time taken (telephone methods are quicker);
(c) level of accuracy required (personal methods give better accuracy);
(d) geographic spread of sample (mail is cheaper for a widely dispersed sample);
(e) type of sampling unit: who is to be interviewed.

Questionnaires

2.14 A questionnaire may be defined as a series of questions designed to obtain information about a defined problem so that more effective analysis of the problem is achieved.

A questionnaire might include five questions or fifty. It might be distributed by post or provide the structure for a personal interview. Questionnaires are used widely, for example to guide the work of auditors.

How do you construct a questionnaire?

Designing a questionnaire is a tricky matter. The questions included need to be designed to give *valid* and *reliable* information with a minimum of bias.

Types of question

2.15 Questions which may be used in questionnaires fall into the following types.

(a) *Dichotomous*

The simplest type of questions are those that require YES or NO answers. These are known as dichotomous questions.

Advantages

(i) Quick and easy to ask.
(ii) Easy to understand.
(iii) Quick to record.

(iv) Easy to analyse.

Disadvantages

(i) No shades of meaning.

(ii) To get any amount of detail, a large number of yes/no questions are needed. Are you aged 18 or over? YES/NO.

(iii) If the question is misunderstood, the wrong answer is given.

(b) *Multiple choice questions (polychotomous)*

Here, a list of possible, mutually exclusive answers are given and the respondent ticks one only.

Advantages

(i) Gives more information than dichotomous questions.
(ii) Gives some shades of meaning.
(iii) More freedom of choice for respondent.
(iv) Easily recorded.
(v) Easily analysed.

Disadvantages

(i) It is hard to construct question so that all possible answers are given.

(ii) It can be difficult to phrase mutually exclusive answers. An example would be as follows:

Which age group are you in:

under 18
18 - 24
25 - 34
35 - 44
45 - 64
65 or over?

(iii) The list of possible answers can confuse if it is too long.

(c) *Open-ended questions*

This method is used when little knowledge exists on the topic and it is not possible to construct possible answers in advance.

Advantages

(i) An extensive amount of information is gained.
(ii) There is no interviewer bias
(iii) Many unexpected facets of behaviour and attitudes are shown in responses.

Disadvantages

(i) They can produce long responses, which are difficult to analyse.
(ii) Answers may not be meaningful.
(iii) Much irrelevant information is generated

(d) *Scales*

Scales can be used to measure feelings, attitudes and motivations in ways not possible by direct questions. A typical scale will ask people whether they:

Strongly agree
Agree
Neither agree nor disagree
Disagree, or
Strongly disagree

with a number of statements.

For example, 'Ford cars are more reliable than Vauxhalls'.

SA	A	NA ND	D	SD
☐	☐	☐	☐	☐

Advantages

(i) Easy to use.
(ii) Easy to record.
(iii) Easy to analyse.
(iv) Shades of meaning.
(v) Insight is gained into underlying influences such as attitudes, behaviour and motives.

Disadvantages

(i) Scale items difficult to construct.
(ii) Respondents may opt out and tick the middle box.
(iii) Some people avoid extreme views, and so responses can be misleading.

Guidelines

2.16 Here are some guidelines on questions.

(a) The theme of the survey must be clear and well understood. Questions should be formulated to obtain the information that is required. This information should be formulated in terms of the problem/opportunity being investigated.

(b) Questions should be clear and concise and capable of only one meaning.

(c) Language used should be easily understood by the intended audience.

(d) Questions should follow a logical sequence and only when one topic has been completed should another be started.

(e) A questionnaire which is to be used widely should first be tested on a few people of the type to be interviewed to iron out any unforeseen difficulties.

Final notes on data

2.17 Your AAT Technician stage projects should display adequate preparation and investigation. While no-one wants to do work in vain, it is common when researching a subject to end up with information that cannot be incorporated into the final draft. Do not include irrelevant information just because you have it.

2.18 Whatever information you do receive cannot be put to use until it is properly recorded. Facts should be recorded as soon as possible, with a note of their source and date. Once recorded, the facts should be *checked* and corrected if necessary.

3 WRITING UP YOUR REPORT

3.1 Your research turns up raw materials. Writing and rewriting turns them into finished, usable products.

3.2 For the writing to proceed efficiently, a logical structure for the report is needed. When you begin writing-up you might want to consider the following points.

(a) Is the purpose of the report clearly defined from the outset?

(b) Who or what is the target of your report? The intended target of the report can influence the way data is handled or the recommendations made.

(c) Is there a wider audience for the report? The likely audience could influence the style in which the report needs to be written (for example, use of technical jargon, diagrammatic presentation of information). Your Unit 18 report may well be a useful document for junior staff in your section, especially those new to the job.

(d) Are any recommendations made likely to be considered for action by the targeted audience? The answer to this is almost certainly 'yes', given that your manager at work, who will be expected to testify to the validity and usefulness of your project, is part of the targeted audience.

3.3 You may not be able to judge a book by its cover but the nature and presentation of the final document will significantly influence the manner in which it is received.

Report plan

3.4 The advantage of having a clear structure is that your ideas and material are forced into some sort of order. If there is a great deal you want to say then order is essential, and a good way of achieving it is to produce a *report plan* at an early stage.

3.5 The best approach is to jot down all the things you want to say as a series of headings, with perhaps a little expansion of some points. Then look at them together and, by experiment if necessary, put them into a logical order by putting numbers against each. Only if you are very certain that your thoughts are logical and coherent as they stand should you omit putting them on paper as a plan - apart from any other reason, you are likely to forget vital material if you do not have a plan.

You might try writing 'network' notes to present your headings visually (see the diagram).

A network note

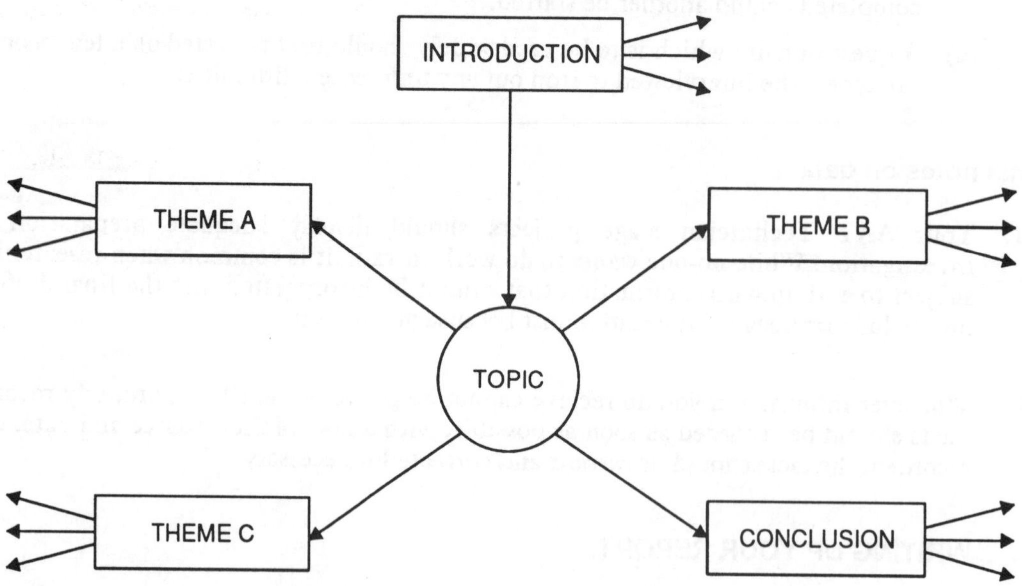

Draft version

3.6 Once you have assembled your material and established your plan, it is time to write the report itself along the lines of the plan. Many people suffer from 'writer's block' at this point and simply cannot get started, writing paragraph after paragraph of introduction and throwing each away. If you have this problem, try starting on the main body first, then go back to the introduction and end with the conclusion.

Final version

3.7 Work on your draft so as to produce a finished report. The draft will have given you confidence and shown you, perhaps, any flaws in your argument. The break will have allowed your brain to sort things out into a better order and more fluent style. All new ideas should be noted on the draft copy before you start afresh to write the final version.

Suggested structure

3.8 Any report should be arranged so that the basic message and the main topics of argument emerge progressively and so that the conclusions and recommendations follow logically from those arguments and analysis.

All documents to be presented in a report, including any appendices, need to state clearly their contents, the source of the information and the date.

3.9 No strict version of an AAT Technician stage report structure is, or could be, imposed. The topics of the project will, in part, determine the structure of the report. However, a generalised structure is suggested below, with appropriate guidelines as necessary.

(a) *Title page*

A succinct but precise title is desirable. It should immediately identify the subject matter.

(b) *Contents page*

Besides detailing the chapters/sections involved, this should also include a list of tables, diagrams etc

(c) *Acknowledgements*

It may be just a matter of courtesy to acknowledge those who have assisted in the preparation of your project, but reference to them may also lend weight to the report.

(d) *Summary*

A summary provides a brief review of the main report and should also create interest by whetting the reader's appetite.

A brief review should note the purpose of the research, how it addressed the particular issue or topic and what conclusions and recommendations have been made.

(e) *Introduction*

This will probably be where the following topics are addressed.

(i) Objectives, terms of references, hypotheses. What is the report about and why has it been written?

(ii) Background material.

(iii) Data collection and methods.

(f) *Findings*

Presentation, analysis and discussion of data and other research information. There should be a logical flow, with ideas being presented in sequence. In some cases, a chronological sequence may be appropriate.

If there is any sort of problem situation in the question, your structure should be on the following lines:

(i) analysing the facts of the situation;
(ii) stating the principles of the matter in hand and any exceptions to them;
(iii) applying those principles to the facts of the case;
(iv) identifying any ambiguities and problems thrown up by this process.

(g) *Conclusions*

The conclusions are directly drawn from the analysis and discussion.

(h) *Recommendations*

Strong, well-founded proposals for change will reflect a successful project and an impressive report. Avoid non-committal recommendations and try to present recommendations in a logical order, for example presenting recommendations for the short, medium and long term in sequence.

For each recommendation the following can be tabulated:

(i) *what* is recommended;

(ii) *who* needs to act on the recommendation;

(iii) *costs and benefits* of the recommendation, with figures if possible, indicating the time scale involved;

(iv) *cross-references* to the points in the report leading to the recommendation.

(i) *Appendices*

To be included here are a listing of any references, any other appropriate bibliography, glossaries of technical terms used, and copies of any important supporting documentation. It may be necessary to include in an appendix any body of material that is too large or detailed for the findings section (eg computer analyses).

Presentation

3.10 The key is organisation: into sentences, into paragraphs, into chapters, into parts. A poorly organised report will be hard to read and it will be difficult for the reader to extract the value of the research you have done.

(a) Use wide-lined A4 paper so as to give your writing a clear look.

(b) Write only on one side - this will allow your tutor or trainer to cross-refer more easily when reading your work.

(c) Number your pages so none gets lost or misplaced.

(d) Write *legibly* - this may mean having to write more *slowly* than usual. It usually helps if you write in black ink.

(e) If you have access to word-processing software and can use it effectively, by all means do so. Spreadsheet software might be used for presenting tabular information.

(f) Try to include graphs and charts where relevant. Be very neat when drawing them (they should be clearly labelled) and make sure you include all the visual material to which you refer.

Using quotations

3.11 If you use quotes from any source, clearly reference your work.

3.12 Short quotes which form part of the text should run on in single inverted commas. Any reference given should either be in a footnote or follow the quotation immediately in brackets. Longer quotations should be separated from the preceding and following text and should be indented.

Writing style

3.13 It may worry you that you do not feel you can express yourself clearly in writing. This is a common problem but one which can be overcome if the following points are heeded.

(a) Write clearly and simply. Long sentences are no 'better' than short ones and often serve to confuse: many people lose track of what they wanted to say by the end of one! We need to communicate information in a way which other people will understand.

(b) Use vocabulary with which you are familiar. Do not be tempted to adopt a 'fancy style' of words which you would not use in normal life and which you may not fully understand. You have met many new terms and ideas in this Tutorial Text but, as we said at the outset, you should only use what is relevant to you.

(c) Try to vary your vocabulary and sentence structure as much as possible whilst keeping your meaning clear. Your AAT Technician stage studies allow you a chance to *develop* your style, and one of the best ways to do this is to read fairly widely. You will find that, by reading books and newspapers, the use and meaning of words which you thought you had forgotten do return to you.

(d) Avoid the first person singular - eg 'I think that'. You will feel and sound more objective if you introduce an idea in another way - 'it could be said that...'

(e) Write in short paragraphs - *nothing* is more off-putting to an assessor than a dense area of intricately connected (or often totally unconnected) sentences.

 (i) Each paragraph should relate to a central idea, introduced as early in it as possible (and possibly 'flagged' in a header).

 (ii) Each paragraph should contain more than one sentence but the content of each should relate to and develop the central idea.

(f) Paragraphs should connect smoothly with each other. Connecting words are often used for this purpose, such as 'therefore', 'however' and 'thus'.

(g) As an antidote to the above, do not be so conscious of your writing style that you are actually inhibited from writing what you think. If there is only one way to say a thing, say it that way!

Accuracy and unity

3.14 *Accuracy* is probably the most important requirement of any research project - not just in terms of the honest presentation of data, but also in giving the correct emphasis to the main themes - in order that an objective and useful report results.

3.15 Keeping within the terms of reference and only addressing the central issue at hand will enhance the *unity* of the report. Leave out material that is not really relevant and avoid discussions of marginal issues.

Completing your project

3.16 A well-presented, professionally produced report attracts more positive attention than a scruffy set of papers.

3.17 Also remember that the finishing touches - typing up, proofing, copying, duplicating, collating and binding - nearly always take longer than you would expect.

Conclusion

- It is hoped that these notes will encourage you to start preparing for your Technician stage projects, and suggest ways in which you might handle the task that you set yourself.
- In applying some of the guidelines outlined here, you may find it worthwhile to go back to your study material for the Foundation and Intermediate stages. For example, skills in the extraction and presentation of information were covered at the AAT Foundation (NVQ/SVQ level 2) stage (see BPP's *Foundation Business Knowledge* Combined Text) and report writing is one of the skills required for *Unit 7: Preparing reports and returns* at the AAT Intermediate (NVQ/SVQ level 3) stage (see BPP's *Intermediate Management Accounting II* Tutorial Text and Workbook).

Test your knowledge

Statutory provisions

1 Which persons are ineligible to act as auditor to a company on ground of lack of independence?

2 What matters must be specifically referred to in the auditor's report?

3 What are the matters with which an auditor will imply satisfaction in an unqualified audit report?

4 What are the statutory disclosure provisions which must be detailed in the auditor's report if not given elsewhere in the financial statements?

5 What are the main statutory rights of the auditor?

6 Who may qualify to act as the auditor to a company in the UK?

7 Who may appoint the auditor to a UK company?

8 How is the auditor's remuneration fixed?

9 What type of resolution must be passed to remove an auditor from office, and what notice of such resolution must be given?

10 What rights does the existing auditor have if he feels that his proposed removal is unjustified?

11 What action may be taken by the company or any other person who claims to be aggrieved by the auditor's representations?

12 What additional rights are available to any auditor who has been removed from office?

13 What action must be taken by an auditor who wishes to resign part way through his term of office?

14 What additional statutory right may be exercised by an auditor as a consequence of his resignation?

15 When a private company seeks to re-register as a plc, the company's auditor is required to produce a special report.

(a) To whom is the special report addressed?
(b) On what must the auditor express an opinion?

16 Under what circumstances will the issue of shares by a plc possibly involve the company's auditor in the issuing of special report?

17 Define 'profits available for the purpose' of making a distribution.

18 List the undistributable reserves of a public limited company.

19 What must the auditor do if a client company wishes to take advantage of the provision whereby the company may seek to file abbreviated accounts (formerly 'modified accounts' under CA 1985)?

20 What is the auditor's duty in relation to the directors' report?

Auditing standards and guidelines

21 Define an audit.

22 Define internal control.

23 Define compliance tests.

24 Define substantive tests.

25 What are seen as the four main advantages to the auditor of adequate audit planning?

26 What are seen as the most important elements of control of an audit?

27 What may be seen as the main criteria by which one would judge the quality of audit working papers?

28 What are the four main reasons why the management of an enterprise requires complete and accurate accounting and other records?

29 What does The operational standard state in relation to audit evidence?

30 Name the main types of controls which the auditor may find in many enterprises and on some or a combination of which he may seek to place some degree of reliance.

31 Having accumulated audit evidence about individual items or groups of items, why is it necessary for the auditor to carry out an overall review of the financial statements?

32 According to the auditing standard *Auditors' report on financial statements*, to what must the auditor expressly refer in his report?

33 Give the main headings under which information should be requested in accordance with the standard form of bank letter recommended by the APC.

34 Certain events and transactions occurring after the balance sheet date are examined by the auditor as part of his normal verification work on the balance sheet. In addition, the auditor should carry out audit procedures which are described as a 'review of events after the balance sheet date'. What are the main procedures that should be included in such a review?

35 The APC have suggested that consideration of the financial statements of the preceding period is necessary in the audit of the current period's financial statements in relation to three main aspects. What are those three aspects?

36 Where a client operates a system of continuous stockchecking the auditor needs to gain assurance that the stock-checking system as a whole is effective in maintaining accurate stock records from which the amount of stocks in the financial statements can be derived. What are the main considerations of the auditor in the designing of tests to meet the above objective?

37 What should be the initial response of an auditor where management have, at the outset, indicated that they are not willing to sign letters of representation or to pass minutes requested by the auditor in relation to representations he has received during the course of his audit?

38 In relation to internal control in a computerised accounting system, you are required to indicate the main objectives of:

(a) application controls;
(b) general controls.

39 Name five important control techniques for ensuring the completeness of computer input in a timely fashion.

40 What are the seven main areas in which controls are likely to be required in order to achieve the main objective of 'general controls' as indicated in answer to Q 38 above?

41 To perform a CAAT, the auditor may use the same computer as that used by the enterprise, or he may choose to use alternative computer facilities. What are the main factors which will affect the auditor's choice?

42 What is the main purpose of an engagement letter?

43 Identify three matters which might typically be seen as giving rise to an inconsistency between the directors' report and the audited financial statements.

44 Give five examples of procedures which a firm of accountants might consider adopting to assist all partners and audit staff in keeping themselves technically up-to-date on matters that are relevant to their work.

45 What are the five main matters to be considered by the external auditor in determining the extent of the reliance that he can place on internal audit?

46 Define 'going concern'.

47 What are the three main matters the auditor should consider when determining the need for specialist evidence?

48 When planning the audit the auditor should consider the likelihood of irregularities in relation to three main stages. What are those three stages?

49 Give five examples of circumstances which could be indicative of the presence of irregularities.

50 What is the principal purpose of an auditor's report to management?

Multiple choice questions

51 According to the auditing guideline Accounting systems the auditor will need to ascertain and record a client's accounting system

A only when they are complex
B only when he plans to rely on internal controls
C only when he plans to dispense with compliance tests
D always, regardless of any other work he may plan

52 The auditor should carry out tests to obtain reasonable assurance that internal controls on which he wishes to rely were functioning properly throughout the period under review. This kind of test is described as

A a compliance test
B a walk through test
C a depth test
D a substantive test

53 Having recorded a client's accounting systems an auditor may wish to check that they operate in the manner recorded. To do this he would use

A walk through tests
B compliance tests
C substantive tests
D internal control questionnaires

54 An internal control evaluation questionnaire for the sales/revenue cycle includes the question 'Is there reasonable assurance that all goods despatched are invoiced?' Which one of the following controls might validly be listed in support of a favourable answer to the question?

A Sequentially numbered invoices are attached to the related despatch notes and gaps in the invoice sequence are investigated

B Goods can only leave the premises if accompanied by a despatch note, which is the second copy of a three-part invoice

C Sales invoices are matched with the related customer orders and unmatched invoices are investigated

D All despatch notes are initialled by the stock controller as evidence that the goods listed have left the premises

55 According to the auditing guideline Accounting systems, the management of an enterprise require complete and accurate accounting and other records to assist in controlling the business, preparing financial statements and complying with legislation. One other objective is identified by the guideline. What is it?

A Complying with professional pronouncements
B Safeguarding the enterprise's assets
C Satisfying the information needs of accounts users
D Establishing the enterprise's profitability

56 Which of the following is implied, *but not stated*, by a limited company's unqualified audit report?

A The company's internal controls are adequate for its size and the nature of its business
B There have been no material changes in the company's accounting policies during the period
C The auditors have not discovered any instances of fraud during the period
D The directors' report is not inconsistent with the financial statements

57 Which of the following aspects of a computerised accounting system is an application control?

A Review of computer operators' daily logs
B One-for-one checking of information held on standing data files
C Testing of the company's back-up security
D Use of passwords

58 Which of the following would not normally be included in the letter of engagement?

A Recommendations for improving internal controls
B Outline of scope of an audit
C Details of the basis on which fees are to be charged
D Request for agreement to terms of the letter

59 The audit report on the financial statements of K Ltd for the year ended 31 December 19X5 is to be signed on 12 July 19X6. Normally, the minimum period which should be considered in assessing whether the accounts should be prepared on a going concern basis is the period up to

A 12 January 19X6
B 31 December 19X6
C 12 January 19X7
D 12 July 19X7

60 Which of the following control techniques is designed to help ensure the completeness of data input to a computer system via a VDU?

A Review of data prior to input
B Passwords
C Check digits
D Hash totals

Statutory provisions

1 (a) An officer or employee of the company.

(b) A partner or employee of such a person, or a partnership of which such a person is a partner.

(c) Someone ineligible by virtue of (a) or (b) for appointment as auditor of any parent or subsidiary undertaking of any parent undertaking of the company.

(d) There exists between the person and any associate of his and the company or any associated undertaking a connection of such description as may be specified by regulations laid down by the Secretary of State.

2 Whether in the auditor's opinion the financial statements:

(a) show a true and fair view of the state of the company's affairs at the balance sheet date and of the results for the period then ended, and

(b) have been properly prepared in accordance with the Companies Act 1985.

3 (a) Proper accounting records have been maintained.
(b) Adequate returns have been received in respect of any branches not visited.
(c) The financial statements are in agreement with the underlying records.
(d) All information and explanations considered necessary have been received.
(e) The directors' report is consistent with the financial statements.

4 (a) Details of directors' emoluments.
(b) Details of directors' emoluments waived.
(c) Details of loans to officers.
(d) Details of directors' interests in material transactions with the company.
(e) Details of higher paid employees.

5 (a) Right of access to all books, accounts and vouchers of the company.

(b) Right to all such information and explanations as he considers necessary for the performance of his duties.

(c) Right to attend any general meeting and to receive all notices and communications relating thereto which any member of the company is entitled to receive.

(d) Right to speak at general meetings on any part of the business which concerns him as auditor.

6 Under CA 1985 (as amended by CA 1989), a company auditor must be a member of a Recognised Supervisory Body (RSB).

7 (a) The members.
(b) The directors (first appointment or to fill a casual vacancy).
(c) The Secretary of State for the Department of Trade and Industry.

8 Either by the person(s) making the appointment or in such manner as the company in general meeting may determine.

9 (a) An ordinary resolution is required.
(b) Special notice (28 days) is required.

10 (a) He may make representations and provided these are not received too late and are of reasonable length, require the company:

(i) to state in any notice of resolution given to members that representations have been made; and

(ii) to send a copy of the representations to the members.

(b) If the representations are not sent out, he can require them to be read at the meeting.

11 They may make application to the court for an injunction to prevent any publicity being given to the auditor's representations.

12 (a) He is entitled to receive all notices relating to:

(i) the general meeting at which his term of office would have expired;

(ii) any general meeting at which it is proposed to fill the casual vacancy caused by his removal.

(b) He is entitled to attend any such meetings and to be heard on any part of the business which concerns him as the former auditor.

13 (a) Deposit formal written notice of his resignation at the registered office of the company.

(b) Accompany such notice with a statement as to whether there are any surrounding circumstances connected with his resignation which require communication to the members or creditors of the company.

14 He may requisition the directors to convene an extraordinary general meeting where he feels that the surrounding circumstances warrant such action.

15 (a) To the registrar of companies.

(b) (i) Whether any qualification in his audit report on the relevant balance sheet is material for the present purposes.

(ii) Whether by reference to the relevant balance sheet, the amount of the company's net assets is not less than the aggregate of its called up share capital plus undistributable reserves.

16 Where a plc issues shares for other than cash consideration, apart from in a takeover or merger situation, then an independent accountant's report will be required on the value of the assets to be received by the company; the independent accountant must be somebody who is qualified to act as auditor to the company, and it may well be the auditor himself.

17 '....accumulated realised profits, so far as not previously utilised by distribution or capitalisation, less accumulated realised losses, so far as not previously written off in a reduction or re-organisation of capital duly made.'

18 (a) Share premium account.

(b) Capital redemption reserve.

(c) Any excess of accumulated unrealised profits over accumulated unrealised losses.

(d) Any other reserve which the company is prohibited from distributing by its memorandum and articles or any other enactment.

19 He should produce a special report addressed to the directors, in which he:

(a) gives an opinion on whether the company satisfies the requirements for exemption as a small/medium size company; and

(b) on whether the abbreviated accounts have been properly prepared; and

(c) in which he reproduces in full his audit report on the full financial statements as presented to the members of the company.

20 To consider whether the information relating to the financial year given in the directors' report is consistent with the accounts. Inconsistencies must be reported in the auditor's report but no comment is necessary if there is nothing to report.

Auditing standards and guidelines

21 The independent examination of, and expression of opinion on, the financial statements of an enterprise.

22 The whole system of controls, financial and otherwise, established by the management in order to carry on the business of the enterprise in an orderly and efficient manner, ensure adherence to management policies, safeguard the assets and secure as far as possible the completeness and accuracy of the accounting records.

23 Those tests which seek to provide audit evidence that internal control procedures are being applied as subscribed.

24 Those tests of transactions and balances, and other procedures such as analytical review, which seek to provide audit evidence as to the completeness, accuracy and validity of the information contained in the accounting records or in the financial statements.

25 (a) It establishes the intended means of achieving the objectives of the audit.
(b) It assists in the direction and control of audit work.
(c) It helps to ensure that attention is devoted to critical aspects of the audit.
(d) It helps to ensure that the work is completed expeditiously.

26 Direction and supervision of audit staff and review of the work that they have done.

27 Whether they are sufficiently complete and detailed to enable an experienced auditor with no previous connection with the audit subsequently to ascertain from them what work was performed and to support the conclusions reached.

28 To assist it in:

(a) controlling the business;
(b) safeguarding the assets;
(c) preparing financial statements;
(d) complying with legislation.

29 The auditor should obtain relevant and reliable audit evidence sufficient to enable him to draw reasonable conclusions therefrom.

30 (a) Organisation.
(b) Segregation of duties.
(c) Physical.
(d) Authorisation and approval.
(e) Arithmetical and accounting.
(f) Personnel.
(g) Management supervision.

31 To determine whether in his opinion:

(a) the financial statements have been prepared using acceptable accounting policies which have been consistently applied and are appropriate to the enterprise's business;

(b) the results of operations, state of affairs and all other information included in the financial statements are compatible with each other and with the auditor's knowledge of the enterprise;

(c) there is adequate disclosure of all appropriate matters and the information contained in the financial statements is suitably classified and presented;

(d) the financial statements comply with all statutory requirements and other regulations relevant to the constitution and activities of that enterprise;

(e) ultimately, whether the conclusions drawn from the other tests which he has carried out, together with those drawn from his overall review of the financial statements, enable him to form an opinion on the financial statements.

32 (a) Whether the financial statements have been audited in accordance with auditing standards.

(b) Whether in the auditor's opinion the financial statements give a true and fair view of the state of affairs, profit or loss and, where applicable, source and application of funds.

(c) Any matters prescribed by relevant legislation or other requirements.

33 (a) Bank accounts.
(b) Customer's assets held as security.
(c) Customer's other assets.
(d) Contingent liabilities.
(e) Other information.

34 The review should consist of discussions with management relating to post balance sheet events and may also include consideration of:

(a) procedures taken by management to ensure that all events after the balance sheet date have been identified, considered and properly evaluated as to their effect on the financial statements;

(b) any management accounts and relevant accounting records;

(c) profit forecasts and cash flow projections for the new period;

(d) known 'risk' areas and contingencies, whether inherent in the nature of the business or revealed by previous audit experience;

(e) minutes of shareholders', directors and management meetings, and correspondence and memoranda relating to items included in the minutes;

(f) relevant information which has come to his attention, from sources outside the enterprise including public knowledge, of competitors, suppliers and customers.

35 (a) The opening position: obtaining satisfaction that those amounts which have a direct effect on the current period's results or closing position have been properly brought forward.

(b) Accounting policies: determining whether the accounting policies adopted for the current period are consistent with those of the previous period.

(c) Corresponding amounts: determining that the corresponding amounts, which are commonly known as comparative figures, are properly shown in the current period's financial statements.

36 The auditor should perform tests designed to confirm that management:

(a) maintains adequate stock records that are kept up-to-date;

(b) has satisfactory procedures for stock-taking and test-counting, so that in normal circumstances the programme of counts will cover all stocks at least once during the year; and

(c) investigates and corrects all material differences between the book stock records and the physical counts.

37 The auditor should inform management that he will himself prepare a statement in writing setting out his understanding of the principal representations that have been made to him during the course of the audit, and he should send this statement to management with a request for confirmation that his understanding of the representations is correct.

38 (a) The objective of application controls is to ensure the completeness and accuracy of the accounting records and the validity of the entries therein resulting from both computer and manual processing.

(b) The objective of general controls is to ensure the integrity of application development and implementation, program and data files, and computer operations.

39 (a) Manual or programmed agreement of control totals.
(b) One-for-one checking of processed output to source documents.
(c) Manual or programmed sequence checking.
(d) Programmed matching of input to a control file, containing details of expected input.
(e) Procedures over re-submission of rejected data.

40 (a) Over application development.
(b) To prevent or detect unauthorised changes to programs.
(c) To ensure that all program changes are adequately tested and documented.
(d) To prevent or detect errors during program execution.
(e) To prevent unauthorised amendment to data files.
(f) To ensure that proper documentation is kept.
(g) To ensure continuity of operation.

41 The choice is affected by the following:

(a) some CAATs, such as live test data, must use the same computer as that operating the enterprise's computer based accounting system;

(b) many CAATs will often be found to be more cost effective when used on the enterprise's computer;

(c) the auditor may not have access to audit package programs that will run on the enterprise's computer. In such cases he may convert the files to run on another computer.

42 To define clearly the extent of the auditor's responsibilities and so minimise the possibility of any misunderstanding between the management of the enterprise and the auditor.

43 (a) An inconsistency between actual figures appearing in, respectively, the audited financial statements and the directors' report.

(b) An inconsistency between the bases of preparation of related items appearing in the audited financial statements and the directors' report, where the figures themselves are not directly comparable.

(c) An inconsistency between figures contained in the audited financial statements and a narrative interpretation of the effect of those figures in the directors' report.

44 (a) Circulating digests or full texts, where appropriate, of professional publications and relevant legislation.

(b) Maintaining a technical library.

(c) Issuing technical circulars and memoranda on professional developments as they effect the firm.

(d) Encouraging attendance at professional courses.

(e) Maintaining appropriate training arrangements.

45 (a) The materiality of the areas of the items to be tested or of the information to be obtained.

(b) The level of audit risk inherent in the areas or items to be tested or in the information to be obtained.

(c) The level of judgement required.

(d) The sufficiency of complementary audit evidence.

(e) Specialist skills possessed by internal audit staff.

46 The going concern assumption is the assumption that the enterprise will continue in operational existence for the foreseeable future. This means in particular that the profit and loss account and the balance sheet assume no intention or necessity to liquidate or curtail significantly the scale of operation.

47 (a) The materiality of, and the risk of significant error in, the information being examined.

(b) The complexity of the information, together with his knowledge and understanding of it and any specialism relating to it.

(c) Other sources of audit evidence available.

48 (a) Business environment.
(b) Control environment.
(c) Account areas.

49 Any five of:

(a) missing vouchers or documents;
(b) evidence of falsified documents;
(c) unsatisfactory explanations;
(d) figures, trends or results which do not accord with expectations;
(e) unexplained items on reconciliation or suspense accounts;
(f) evidence of disputes;

(g) evidence of unduly lavish life styles by officers or employees;
(h) unusual investment of funds held in a fiduciary capacity;
(i) evidence that the system of internal control is not operating as it was believed or intended to.

50 It is to enable the auditor to give his comments on the accounting records, systems and controls that he has examined during the course of his audit. Significant areas of weakness in systems and controls that might lead to material errors should be highlighted and brought to management's attention.

Multiple choice

51 D

52 A

53 A

54 B

55 B

56 D

57 B

58 A

59 C

60 D

Glossary and Index

The following glossary, which is in *draft form* has been produced by the Auditing Practices Board and it is reproduced here with the kind permission of the APB.

As part of the revisions project, a glossary of terms used in the proposed SASs and in SAS 600 *Auditors' report on financial statements* has been compiled. A similar glossary is being prepared by the IAPC as part of their codification project.

It is intended that the glossary should help auditors and others to find definitions of terms used in SASs. It will be revised to take account of any comments on the definitions in these and other proposed SASs which comprise the revisions project, and will be updated to include terms defined in subsequent SASs.

Accounting estimate An approximation of the amount of an item in the absence of a precise means of measurement.

Accounting system The series of tasks and records of an entity by which transactions are processed as a means of maintaining financial records. Such systems identify, assemble, analyse, calculate, classify, record, summarise and report transactions and other events.

Analytical procedures The analysis of significant ratios and trends including the resulting investigation of fluctuations and relationships that are inconsistent with other relevant information or which deviate from predictable patterns.

Annual report A document which an entity usually issues on an annual basis which includes its financial statements together with the audit report thereon.

Assistants Personnel involved in an audit other than the audit engagement partner.

Audit engagement partner The person who assumes ultimate responsibility for the conduct of the audit and for issuing an opinion on the financial statements.

Audit evidence The information auditors obtain in arriving at the conclusions on which the audit is based. Audit evidence comprises source documents and accounting records underlying the financial statement assertions and corroborative information from other sources.

Audit program A set of instructions to assistants involved in the audit and a means of control and record the proper execution of the work.

Audit risk The risk that auditors may give an inappropriate audit opinion on financial statements. Audit risk has three components: inherent risk, control risk and detection risk.

Audit sampling The application of audit procedures to less than 100% of the items within an account balance or class of transactions to enable auditors to obtain and evaluate evidence about some characteristic of the items selected in order to form or assist in forming a conclusion concerning the population which makes up that account balance or class of transaction.

Comparatives The corresponding amounts and other related disclosures from the preceding period which are part of the current period's financial statements as required by relevant legislation and applicable Accounting Standards. Such comparatives are intended to be read in relation to the amounts and other disclosures related to the current period. Except where there has been a prior year adjustment or change in accounting policy, the opening balances are the same as the balance sheet comparatives.

Component A division, branch, subsidiary, joint venture, associated company or other entity whose financial information is included in financial statements audited by the principal auditors.

Computation Checking the arithmetical accuracy of source documents and accounting records or performing independent calculations.

Confirmation The response to an enquiry to corroborate information contained in the accounting records.

Continuing auditors The auditors who audited and reported on the preceding period's financial statements and continue as the auditors for the current period.

Control environment The overall attitude, awareness and actions of directors and management regarding internal controls and their importance in the entity.

Control procedures Those policies and procedures in addition to the control environment which are established to provide management with evidence that specific entity objectives are achieved.

Control risk The risk that material misstatement could occur in an account balance or class of transactions either individually or when aggregated with misstatements in other balances or classes, and not be prevented, or detected on a timely basis, by the accounting and internal control systems.

Detection risk The risk that the auditors' substantive procedures do not detect a material misstatement that exists in an account balance or class of transactions, individually or when aggregated with misstatements in other balances or classes.

Directors The directors of a company or other body, the partners, proprietors, committee of management or trustees of other forms of entity, or equivalent persons responsible for directing the entity's operations and preparing its financial statements.

Engagement letter A letter which provides written confirmation of the terms of the engagement as agreed by both the auditors and their client.

Enquiry The seeking of information of knowledgeable persons inside or outside the entity.

Error An unintentional mistake in financial statements.

Expert A person or firm possessing special skill, knowledge and experience in a particular field other than accounting and auditing.

Financial statements The balance sheet, profit and loss account (or other form of income statement), statements of cash flows and total recognised gains and losses, notes and other statements and explanatory material, all of which are identified in the auditor's report as being part of the financial statements.

Financial statement assertions The representations by management, explicit or implicit, that are embodied in the financial statements. There are seven classifications of financial statement assertions: existence; rights and obligations; occurrence; completeness; valuation; measurement; and presentation and disclosure.

Existence	An asset or liability exists at a given date
Rights and obligations	An asset or liability pertains to the entity, at a given date
Occurrence	A transaction or event took place which pertains to the entity during the relevant period
Completeness	There are no unrecorded assets, liabilities, transactions or events, or undisclosed items
Valuation	An asset or liability is recorded at an appropriate carrying value
Measurement	A transactions or event is recorded in the proper amount and revenue or expense is allocated to the proper period
Presentation and disclosure	An item is disclosed, classified and described in accordance with the applicable reporting framework (eg relevant legislation and applicable accounting standards).

Fraud The use of deception to obtain an unjust or illegal financial advantage, or intentional misrepresentations, by one or more individuals among management, employees or third parties.

Fundamental uncertainty An inherent uncertainty is fundamental when the magnitude of its potential impact is so great that, without clear disclosure of the nature and implications of the uncertainty, the view given by the financial statements would be seriously misleading.

Incoming auditors The auditors who are auditing and reporting on the current period's financial statements having not audited and reported on those for the preceding period.

Inherent risk The susceptibility of an account balance or class of transactions to material misstatement, either individually or when aggregated with misstatements in other balances or classes, while assuming no related internal controls.

Inherent uncertainty An uncertainty whose resolution is dependent upon uncertain future events outside the control of the reporting entity's directors at the date the financial statements are approved.

Inspection The examining of records, documents or tangible assets.

Internal audit An appraisal activity established by management for the review of the accounting and control systems as a service to the entity. It functions by, amongst other things, examining, evaluating and reporting to management on the adequacy and effectiveness of components of the accounting and internal control systems.

Internal control systems This comprises the control environment and control procedures. It includes all the policies and procedures (internal controls) adopted by the management of an entity to assist in achieving management's objective of ensuring, as far as practicable, the orderly and efficient conduct of its business, including adherence to management policies, the safeguarding of assets, the prevention and detection of fraud and error, the accuracy and completeness of the accounting records, and the timely preparation of reliable financial information. Internal controls may be incorporated within computerised accounting systems. However, the internal control system extends beyond those matters which relate directly to the functions of the accounting system.

Management Those persons who have executive responsibility for the conduct of the entity's operations and the preparation of its financial statements.

Material weakness A condition in accounting and internal control systems which may result in a material misstatement in the financial statements.

Materiality An expression of the relevant significance or importance of a particular matter in the context of financial statements as a whole. A matter is material if its omission or misstatement would reasonably influence the decisions of a user of the financial statements. Materiality may also be considered in the context of any individual primary statement within the financial statements or of individual items included in them. Materiality is not capable of general mathematical definition as it has both qualitative and quantitative aspects.

Non-sampling risk The risk that the auditors might use inappropriate procedures or might misinterpret evidence and thus fail to recognise an error.

Observation Looking at a process or procedure being performed by others.

Opening balances Those account balances which exist at the beginning of the period. Opening balances are based upon the closing balances of the preceding period and reflect the effect of transactions of preceding periods and accounting policies applied in the preceding period.

Other auditors Auditors, other than the principal auditors, with responsibility for reporting on the financial information of a component which is included in the financial statements audited by the principal auditors. Other auditors include affiliated firms, whether using the same name or not, and correspondent firms as well as unrelated auditors.

Planning Developing a general strategy and a detailed approach for the expected nature, timing and extent of the audit.

Population The entire set of data which the auditors wish to sample in order to reach a conclusion.

Predecessor auditors The auditors who previously audited and reported on the financial statements of an entity and who have been replaced by the incoming auditors.

Principal auditors The auditors with responsibility for reporting on the financial statements of an entity when those financial statements include financial information of one or more components audited by other auditors.

Sampling risk The risk that the auditors' conclusion, based on a sample, may be different from the conclusion that would be reached if the entire population were subjected to the same audit procedure.

Sampling units The individual items that make up the population.

Stratification The process of dividing a population into subpopulations, each of which is a group of sampling units, which have similar characteristics (often monetary value).

Subsequent events Those relevant events (favourable or unfavourable) which occur and those facts which are discovered between the period end and the laying of the financial statements before the members, or equivalent.

Substantive procedures Tests to obtain audit evidence to detect material misstatements in the financial statements. They are of two types: (a) tests of details of transactions and balances; and (b) analytical procedures.

Tests of control Tests to obtain audit evidence about the suitability of design and effective operation of the accounting and internal control systems.

Tolerable error The maximum error in the population that the auditors are willing to accept and still conclude that the audit objective has been achieved.

Working papers The material the auditors prepare or obtain, and retain in connection with the performance of the audit. Working papers may be in the form of data stored on paper, film, electronic media or other media. Working papers are a record of the planning and performance of the audit, the supervision and review of the audit work, and the evidence resulting from the audit work performed to support the auditors' opinion.

FURTHER READING

BPP publishes a companion Workbook for Unit 18 *Auditing* (July 1994). This contains practice case studies and guidance on the final portfolio for the unit. Full solutions are given.

To order your Workbook, ring our credit card hotline on 081-740 6808. Alternatively, send this page to our Freepost address or fax it to us on 081-740 1184.

To: BPP Publishing Ltd, FREEPOST, London W12 8BR

Tel: 081-740 6808
Fax: 081-740 1184

Forenames (Mr / Ms): ____________________

Surname: ____________________

Address: ____________________

____

Post code: __________ Date of assessment (month/year): __________

Please send me the following books:	Quantity	Price	Total
AAT *Auditing* Workbook	....	£7.95	....

Please include postage:

UK: £2.00 for first plus £1.00 for each extra book. ....

Europe (inc ROI): £3.00 for first plus £2.00 for each extra book. ....

Rest of the World: £5.00 for first plus £3.00 for each extra book. ....

I enclose a cheque for £ __________ **or charge to Access/Visa**

Card number | | | | | | | | | | | | | | | | |

Expiry date __________ Signature ____________________

To order any further titles in the AAT range, please use the form overleaf.

ORDER FORM

Any books from our AAT range can be ordered by ringing our credit card hotline on 081-740 6808. Alternatively, send this page to our Freepost address or fax it to us on 081-740 1184.

To: BPP Publishing Ltd, FREEPOST, London W12 8BR **Tel: 081-740 6808** **Fax: 081-740 1184**

Forenames (Mr / Ms): ____________________

Surname: ____________________

Address: ____________________

____

Post code: ____________________

Please send me the following books:

		Price		Quantity		Total
		Tutorial Text	*Workbook*	*Tutorial Text*	*Workbook*	
Foundation		£	£			£
Unit 1	Cash Transactions	8.95	8.95	....	....	....
Unit 2	Credit Transactions	8.95	8.95	....	....	....
Unit 3	Payroll Transactions	10.95	10.95	....	....	....
Unit 20	Data processing	11.95*		....		....
Units 24-28	Business knowledge	9.95*		....		....
Intermediate						
Units 4&5	Financial Accounting	11.95	11.95	....	....	....
Unit 6	Cost Accounting I	10.95	10.95	....	....	....
Units 7&8	Cost Accounting II	10.95	10.95	....	....	....
Units 21&22	Information Technology	11.95*		....		....
Technician						
Unit 9	Cash Management & Credit Control	8.95	7.95	....	....	....
Unit 10	Managing Accounting Systems	10.95	7.95	....	....	....
Units 11&12	Management Accounting I	9.95	7.95	....	....	....
Unit 13	Management Accounting II	8.95	7.95	....	....	....
Unit 14	Financial Statements	10.95	7.95	....	....	....
Unit 18	Auditing	8.95	7.95	....	....	....
Unit 19	Taxation	10.95	7.95	....	....	....
Unit 23	Information Management Systems	10.95	7.95	....	....	....
Unit 25	Health and Safety	2.00		....		....

(Price includes postage; this booklet is an extract from units 24-28 Business Knowledge combined text)

* Combined text

Please include postage:

UK: £2.00 for first plus £1.00 for each extra book.	....	....	....
Europe (inc ROI): £3.00 for first plus £2.00 for each extra book.	....	....	....
Rest of the World: £5.00 for first plus £3.00 for each extra book.	....	....	....
		Total	

I enclose a cheque for £ __________ or charge to Access/Visa

Card number | | | | | | | | | | | | | | | | |

Expiry date ____________________ Signature ____________________

REVIEW FORM

Name: ______________________________

How have you used this Tutorial Text?

Home study (book only)	☐	With 'correspondence' package	☐
On a course: college__________	☐	Other__________	

How did you obtain this Tutorial Text?

From us by mail order	☐	From us by phone	☐
From a bookshop	☐	From your college	☐

Where did you hear about BPP Tutorial Texts?

At bookshop	☐	Recommended by lecturer	☐
Recommended by friend	☐	Mailshot from BPP	☐
Advertisement in __________	☐	Other __________	

Have you used the companion Workbook for this subject? **Yes/No**

Your comments and suggestions would be appreciated on the following areas

Coverage of elements of competence

Errors (please specify, and refer to a page number)

Structure and presentation

Other

Please return to: BPP Publishing Ltd, FREEPOST, London W12 8BR

6/94